ORDNANCE SURVEY

# STREET ATLAS
# Nottinghamshire

## Contents

IV *Key to maps*

VI *Administrative boundaries*

1 *Street maps*

222 *Index explanation and abbreviations*

223 *Index of towns, villages and rural localities*

224 *Index of street names*

PHILIP'S

First edition published 1994 by

Ordnance Survey and Philip's
Romsey Road
Maybush
Southampton SO9 4DH

Philip's
an imprint of Reed Consumer Books Limited
Michelin House, 81 Fulham Road, London, SW3 6RB
and Auckland, Melbourne, Singapore and Toronto

ISBN 0-540-05858-0 (Philip's, hardback)
ISBN 0-540-05859-9 (Philip's, softback)
ISBN 0-319-00377-9 (Ordnance Survey, hardback)
ISBN 0-319-00378-7 (Ordnance Survey, softback)



To the best of the Publishers' knowledge, the information in this atlas was correct at the time of going to press. No responsibility can be accepted for any errors or their consequences.

The representation in this atlas of a road, track or path is no evidence of the existence of a right of way.

Printed and bound in Great Britain by
Butler & Tanner Ltd, Frome and London

# Key to map symbols

British Rail station

London transport station

Private railway station

Bus or coach station

Heliport

**Police station** (may not be open 24 hours)

**Hospital with casualty facilities** (may not be open 24 hours)

Post office

Place of worship

Important building

P Parking

174 Adjoining page indicator

No adjoining page

Motorway or dual carriageway

A27(T) **Main or through road** (with Department of Transport number)

**Gate or obstruction to traffic** (restrictions may not apply at all times or to all vehicles)

Footpath

Bridleway

Path

Track

The representation in this atlas of a road, track or path is no evidence of the existence of a right of way

| | | | |
|---|---|---|---|
| Amb Sta | **Ambulance station** | LC | **Level crossing** |
| Coll | **College** | Liby | **Library** |
| FB | **Footbridge** | Mus | **Museum** |
| F Sta | **Fire station** | Sch | **School** |
| Hospl | **Hospital** | TH | **Town hall** |

| 0 | | ¼ | | ½ | | ¾ | | 1 mile |
|---|---|---|---|---|---|---|---|---|
| 0 | 250m | | 500m | | 250m | | 1 Kilometre | |

**The scale of the maps is 3½ inches to 1 mile (1:18103)**

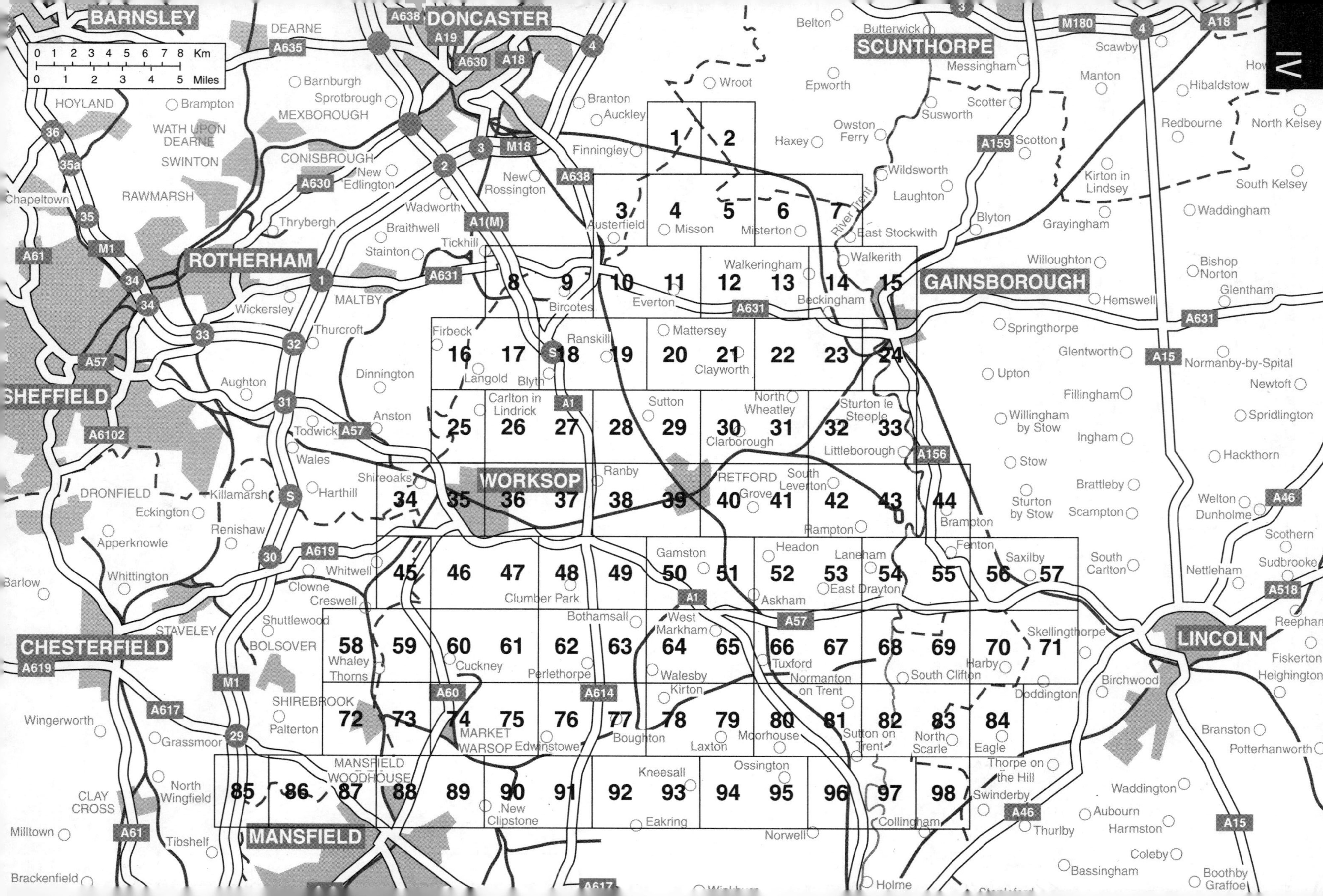
BARNSLEY
DONCASTER
SCUNTHORPE
ROTHERHAM
GAINSBOROUGH
SHEFFIELD
WORKSOP
RETFORD
CHESTERFIELD
LINCOLN
MANSFIELD
0 1 2 3 4 5 6 7 8 Km
0 1 2 3 4 5 Miles
DEARNE
HOYLAND
WATH UPON DEARNE
SWINTON
RAWMARSH
MEXBOROUGH
CONISBROUGH
MALTBY
DRONFIELD
STAVELEY
BOLSOVER
SHIREBROOK
MARKET WARSOP
MANSFIELD WOODHOUSE
CLAY CROSS
Barnburgh
Sprotbrough
Brampton
Chapeltown
Thrybergh
New Edlington
Wadworth
Braithwell
Stainton
Tickhill
Wickersley
Thurcroft
Aughton
Dinnington
Anston
Todwick
Wales
Shireoaks
Harthill
Killamarsh
Eckington
Renishaw
Apperknowle
Whittington
Barlow
Whitwell
Clowne
Creswell
Shuttlewood
Wingerworth
Grassmoor
Palterton
North Wingfield
Milltown
Tibshelf
Brackenfield
Branton
Auckley
Finningley
New Rossington
Austerfield
Misson
Misterton
East Stockwith
River Trent
Wroot
Belton
Epworth
Haxey
Owston Ferry
Butterwick
Messingham
Scotter
Susworth
Scotton
Wildsworth
Laughton
Blyton
Walkerith
Walkeringham
Beckingham
Everton
Bircotes
Firbeck
Langold
Blyth
Ranskill
Mattersey
Clayworth
Carlton in Lindrick
Sutton
North Wheatley
Clarborough
Sturton le Steeple
Littleborough
Ranby
Grove
South Leverton
Rampton
Brampton
Fenton
Gamston
Headon
Laneham
East Drayton
Askham
Clumber Park
Bothamsall
West Markham
Walesby
Tuxford
Normanton on Trent
South Clifton
Saxilby
Skellingthorpe
Harby
Doddington
Whaley Thorns
Cuckney
Perlethorpe
Kirton
Edwinstowe
Boughton
Laxton
Moorhouse
Sutton on Trent
North Scarle
Eagle
Thorpe on the Hill
Swinderby
Kneesall
Ossington
Eakring
New Clipstone
Norwell
Collingham
Holme
Scawby
Manton
Hibaldstow
Redbourne
North Kelsey
South Kelsey
Kirton in Lindsey
Waddingham
Grayingham
Willoughton
Bishop Norton
Glentham
Hemswell
Springthorpe
Glentworth
Normanby-by-Spital
Newtoft
Upton
Fillingham
Spridlington
Willingham by Stow
Ingham
Hackthorn
Stow
Brattleby
Sturton by Stow
Scampton
Welton
Dunholme
Scothern
Sudbrooke
South Carlton
Nettleham
Reepham
Fiskerton
Heighington
Birchwood
Branston
Potterhanworth
Waddington
Aubourn
Harmston
Thurlby
Coleby
Bassingham
Boothby Graffoe
M1
M18
M180
A1
A1(M)
A15
A18
A19
A46
A57
A60
A61
A156
A159
A518
A614
A617
A619
A630
A631
A635
A638
A6102
1 2 3 4 5 6 7 8 9 10 11 12 13 14 15
16 17 18 19 20 21 22 23 24
25 26 27 28 29 30 31 32 33
34 35 36 37 38 39 40 41 42 43 44
45 46 47 48 49 50 51 52 53 54 55 56 57
58 59 60 61 62 63 64 65 66 67 68 69 70 71
72 73 74 75 76 77 78 79 80 81 82 83 84
85 86 87 88 89 90 91 92 93 94 95 96 97 98

# Key to map pages

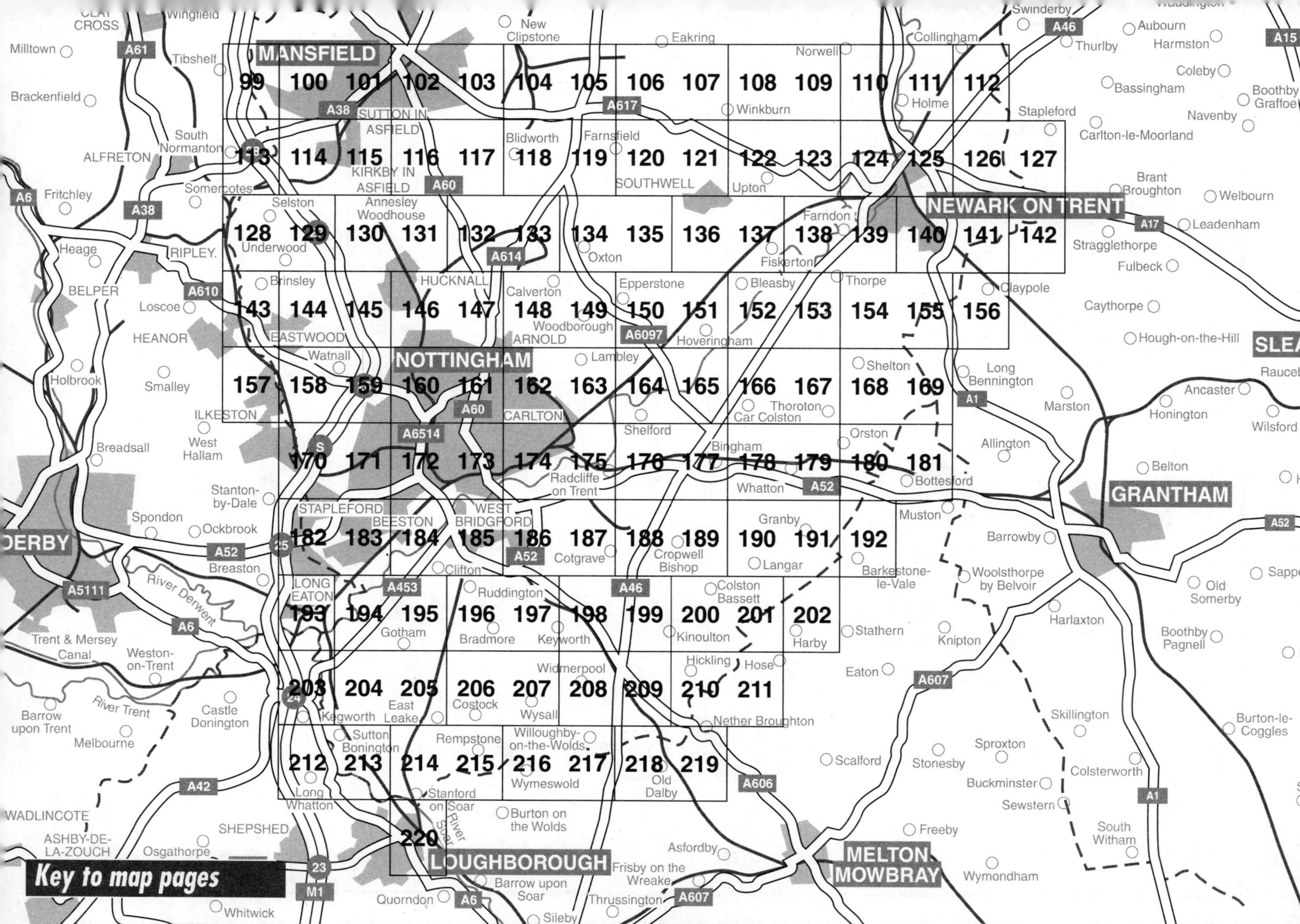

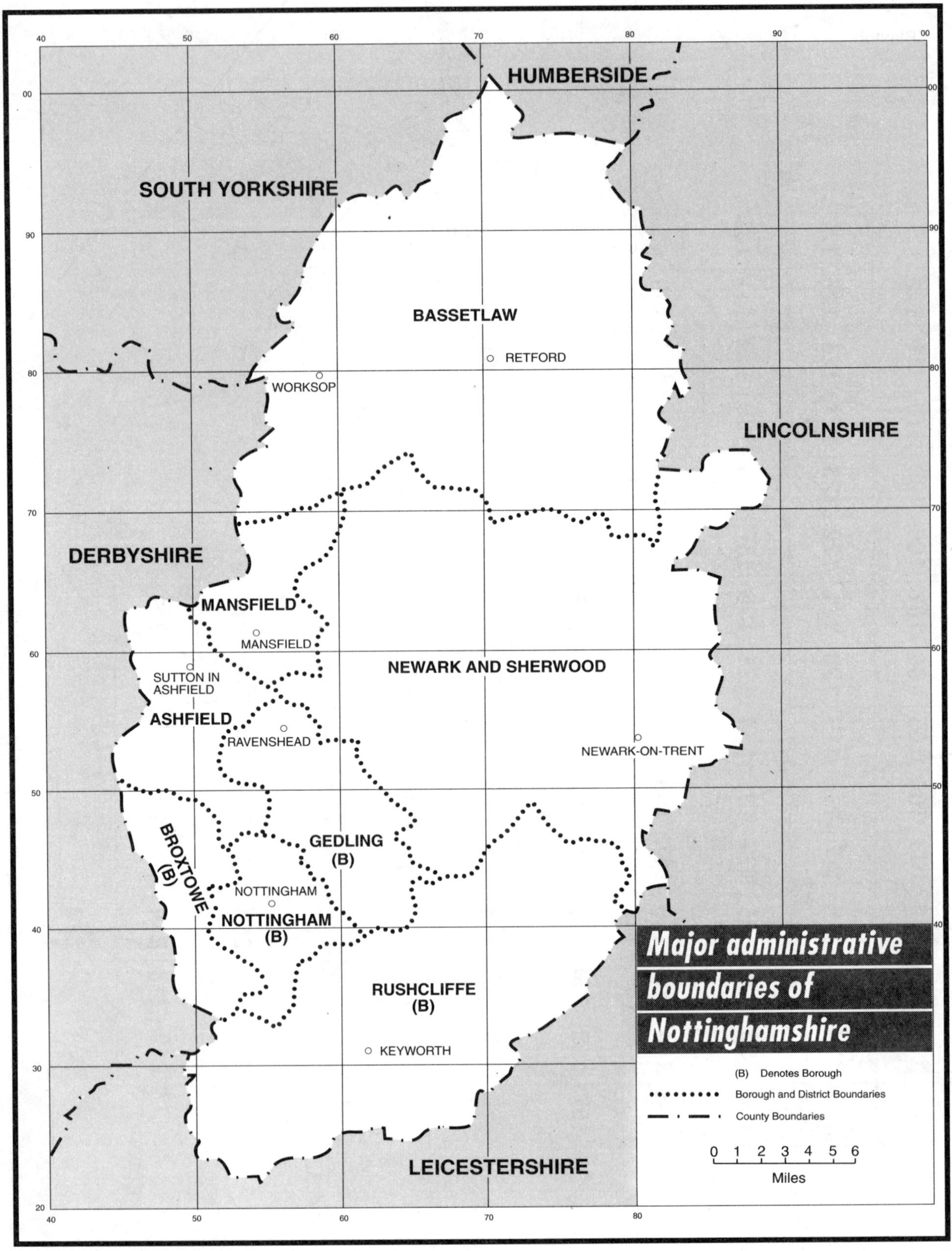
HUMBERSIDE
SOUTH YORKSHIRE
BASSETLAW
RETFORD
WORKSOP
LINCOLNSHIRE
DERBYSHIRE
MANSFIELD
MANSFIELD
SUTTON IN ASHFIELD
ASHFIELD
NEWARK AND SHERWOOD
RAVENSHEAD
NEWARK-ON-TRENT
BROXTOWE (B)
GEDLING (B)
NOTTINGHAM
NOTTINGHAM (B)
RUSHCLIFFE (B)
KEYWORTH
LEICESTERSHIRE
Major administrative boundaries of Nottinghamshire
(B) Denotes Borough
Borough and District Boundaries
County Boundaries
0 1 2 3 4 5 6
Miles

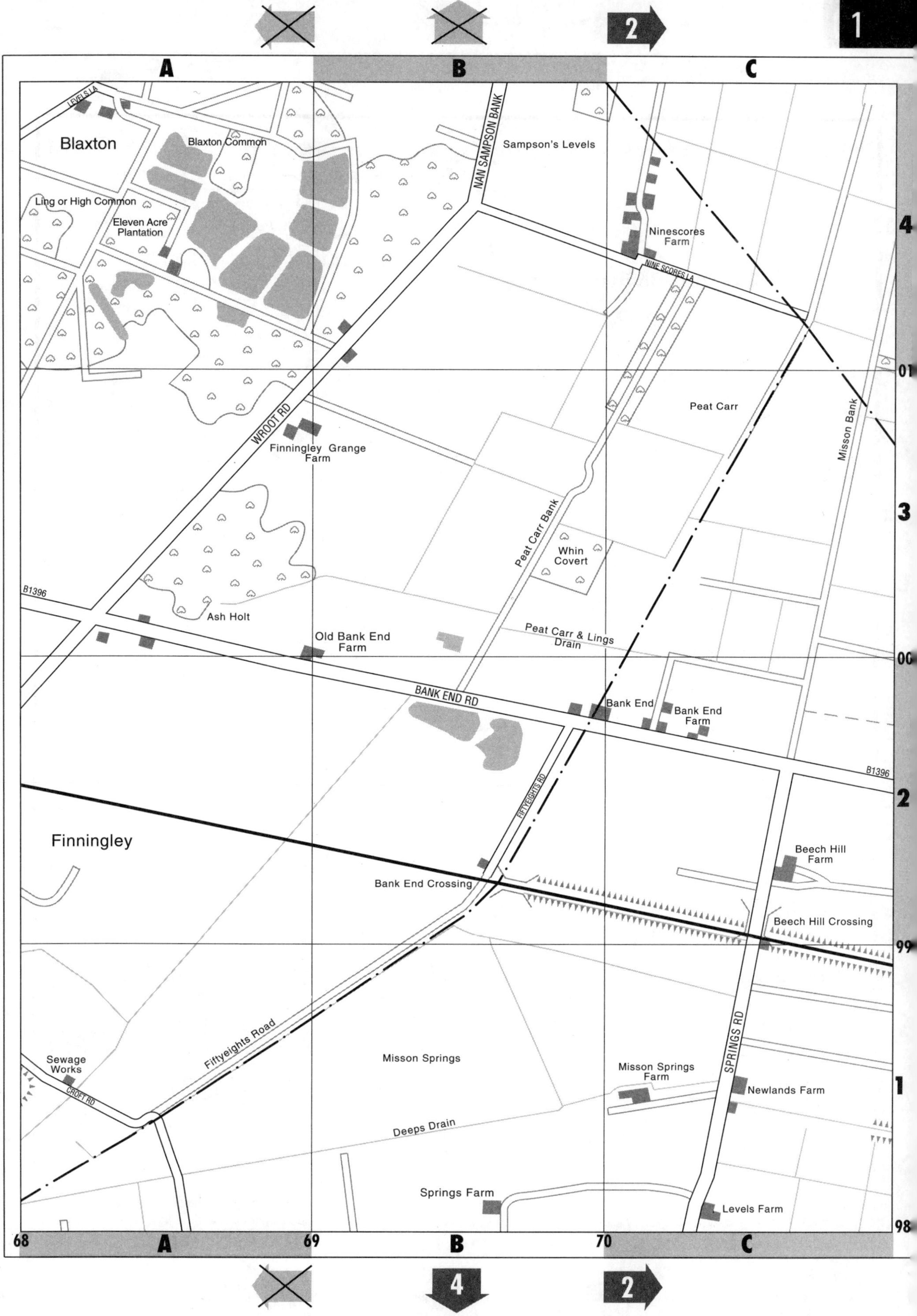
2
A
B
C
Blaxton
Blaxton Common
LEVELS LA
Ling or High Common
Eleven Acre Plantation
NAN SAMPSON BANK
Sampson's Levels
Ninescores Farm
NINE SCORES LA
WROOT RD
Finningley Grange Farm
Peat Carr
Misson Bank
Peat Carr Bank
Whin Covert
Ash Holt
B1396
Old Bank End Farm
Peat Carr & Lings Drain
BANK END RD
Bank End
Bank End Farm
FIFTYEIGHTS RD
Finningley
Beech Hill Farm
Bank End Crossing
Beech Hill Crossing
SPRINGS RD
Fiftyeights Road
Sewage Works
CROFT RD
Misson Springs
Misson Springs Farm
Newlands Farm
Deeps Drain
Springs Farm
Levels Farm
4
01
3
00
2
99
1
98
68
69
70
4
2

1

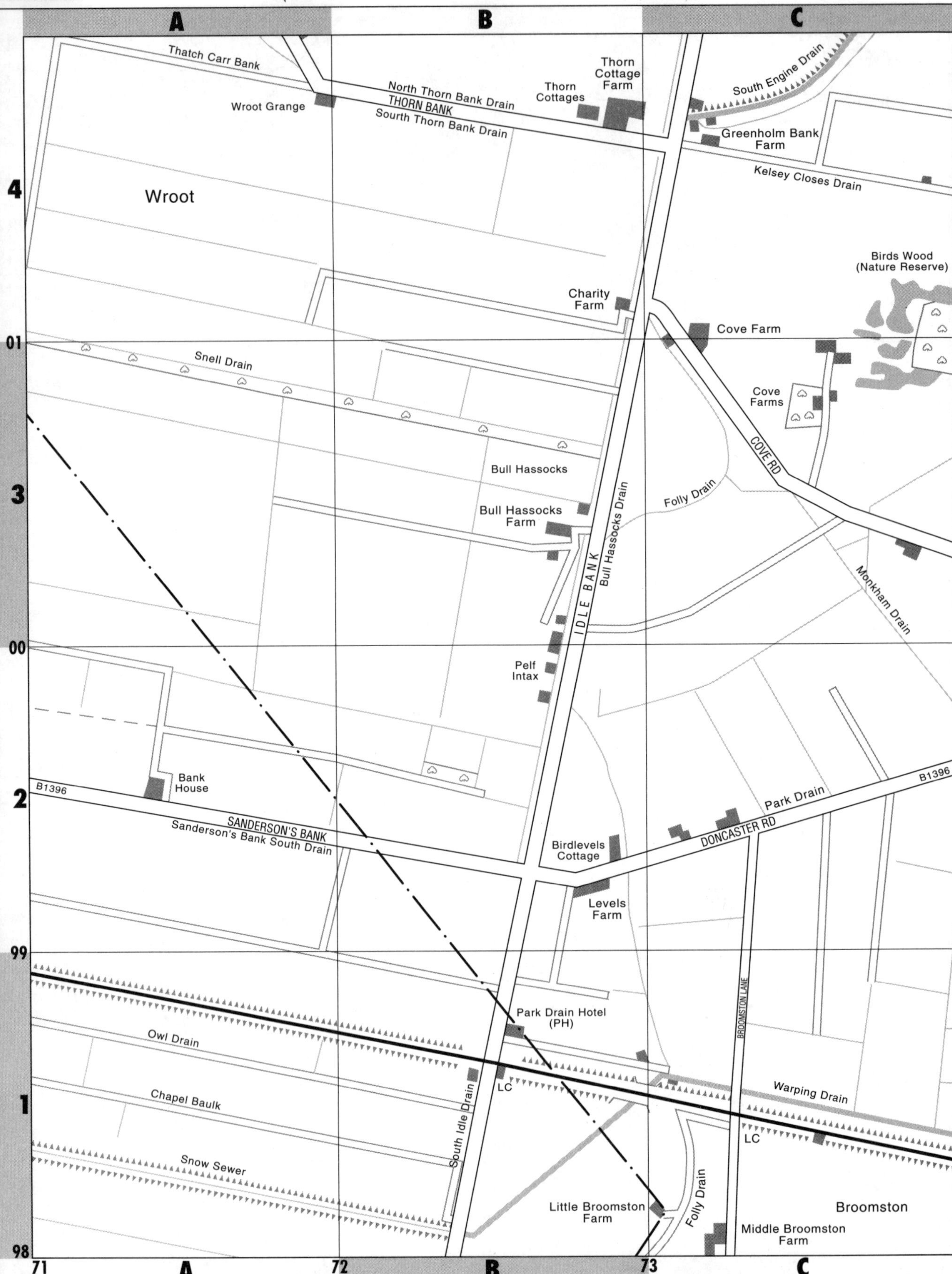
A
B
C
Thatch Carr Bank
Wroot Grange
North Thorn Bank Drain
THORN BANK
Sourth Thorn Bank Drain
Thorn Cottages
Thorn Cottage Farm
South Engine Drain
Greenholm Bank Farm
Kelsey Closes Drain
Wroot
Birds Wood (Nature Reserve)
Charity Farm
Cove Farm
Snell Drain
Cove Farms
COVE RD
Bull Hassocks
Bull Hassocks Farm
Bull Hassocks Drain
Folly Drain
IDLE BANK
Monkham Drain
Pelf Intax
Bank House
B1396
SANDERSON'S BANK
Sanderson's Bank South Drain
Park Drain
B1396
DONCASTER RD
Birdlevels Cottage
Levels Farm
BROOMSTON LANE
Park Drain Hotel (PH)
Owl Drain
LC
South Idle Drain
Warping Drain
Chapel Baulk
LC
Snow Sewer
Folly Drain
Little Broomston Farm
Broomston
Middle Broomston Farm
4
01
3
00
2
99
1
98
71
72
73
A
B
C

1
5

4

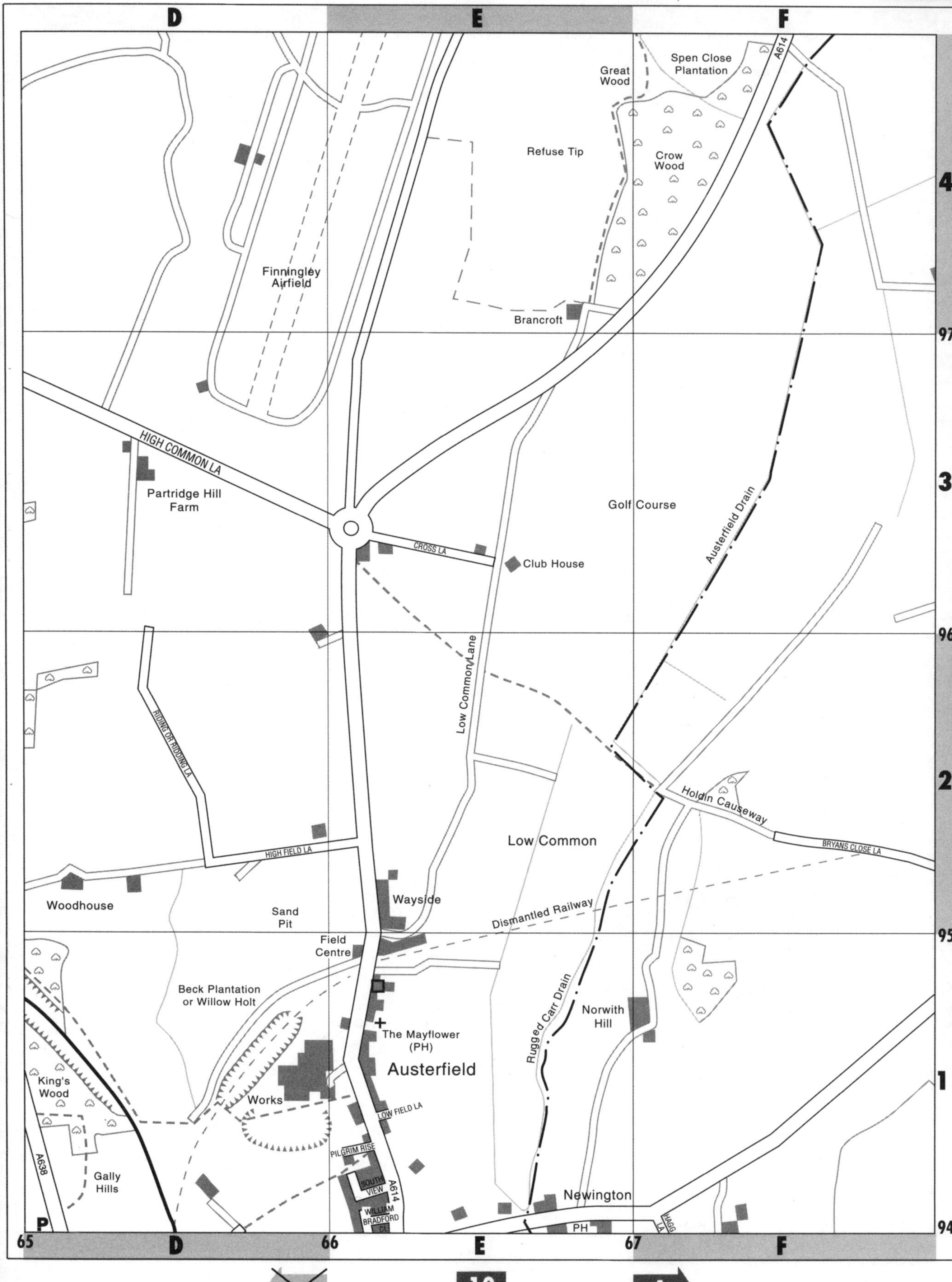
D
E
F
Spen Close
Plantation
Great
Wood
A614
Refuse Tip
Crow
Wood
Finningley
Airfield
Brancroft
HIGH COMMON LA
Partridge Hill
Farm
Golf Course
Austerfield Drain
CROSS LA
Club House
Low Common Lane
RIDING OR RIDDING LA
Holdin Causeway
BRYANS CLOSE LA
Low Common
HIGH FIELD LA
Wayside
Woodhouse
Sand
Pit
Dismantled Railway
Field
Centre
Beck Plantation
or Willow Holt
Norwith
Hill
Rugged Carr Drain
The Mayflower
(PH)
Austerfield
King's
Wood
Works
LOW FIELD LA
PILGRIM RISE
A638
Gally
Hills
SOUTH
VIEW
A614
WILLIAM
BRADFORD
CL
Newington
PH
HAGG
LA
P
4
3
2
1
97
96
95
94
65
66
67
D
E
F

10

4

3
1

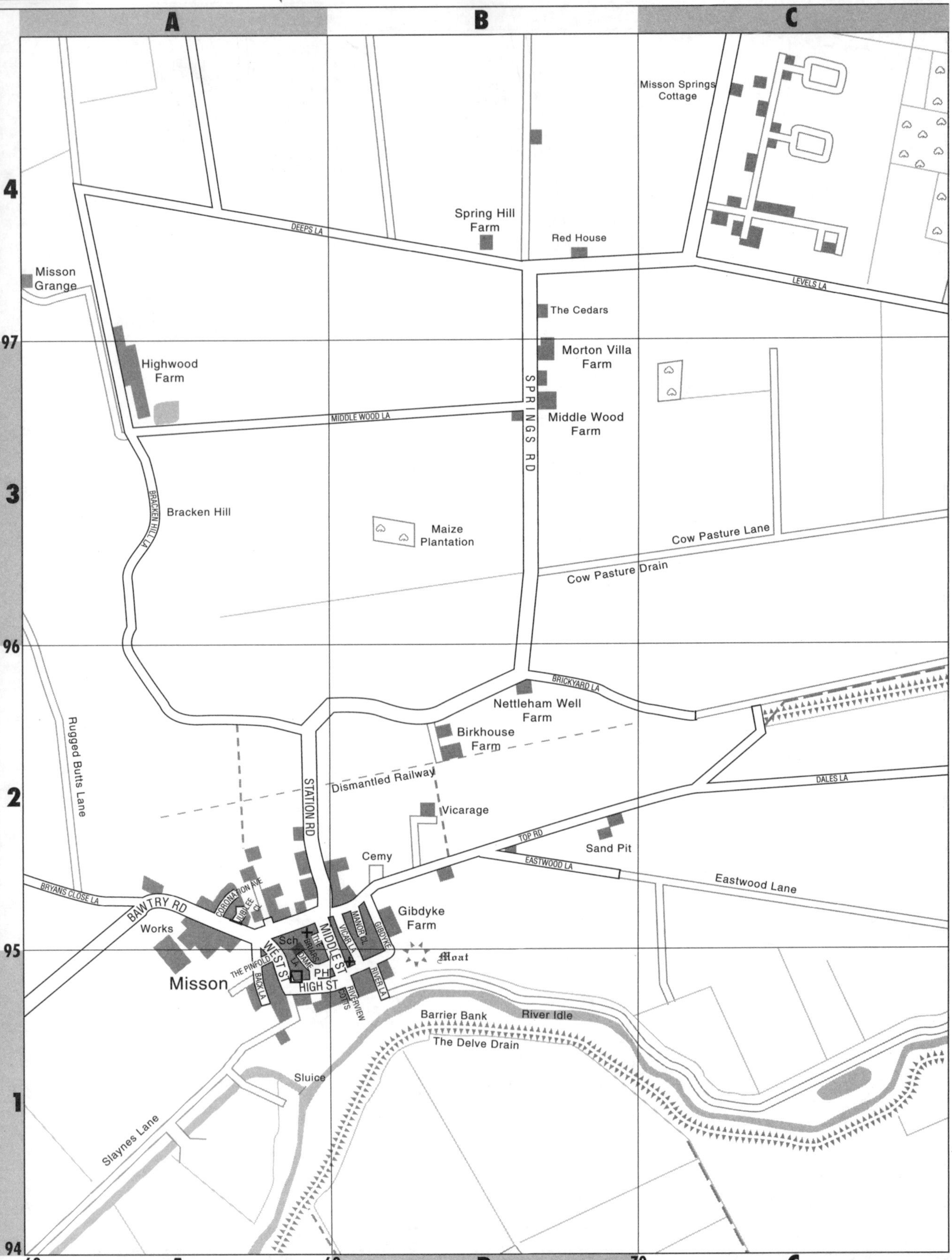
A
B
C
Misson Springs Cottage
Spring Hill Farm
Red House
DEEPS LA
LEVELS LA
Misson Grange
The Cedars
Morton Villa Farm
Highwood Farm
SPRINGS RD
Middle Wood Farm
MIDDLE WOOD LA
Bracken Hill
BRACKEN HILL LA
Maize Plantation
Cow Pasture Lane
Cow Pasture Drain
BRICKYARD LA
Nettleham Well Farm
Birkhouse Farm
Rugged Butts Lane
STATION RD
Dismantled Railway
DALES LA
Vicarage
TOP RD
Sand Pit
Cemy
EASTWOOD LA
Eastwood Lane
BRYANS CLOSE LA
CORONATION AVE
JUBILEE CL
BAWTRY RD
Gibdyke Farm
Works
Sch
MIDDLE ST
VICAR LA
MANOR CL
GIBDYKE
WEST ST
THE BRIARS
DAME LA
Moat
THE PINFOLD
PH
RIVER LA
Misson
BACK LA
HIGH ST
RIVERVIEW
Barrier Bank
River Idle
The Delve Drain
Sluice
Slaynes Lane
4
97
3
96
2
95
1
94
68
69
70

3
11

2
6

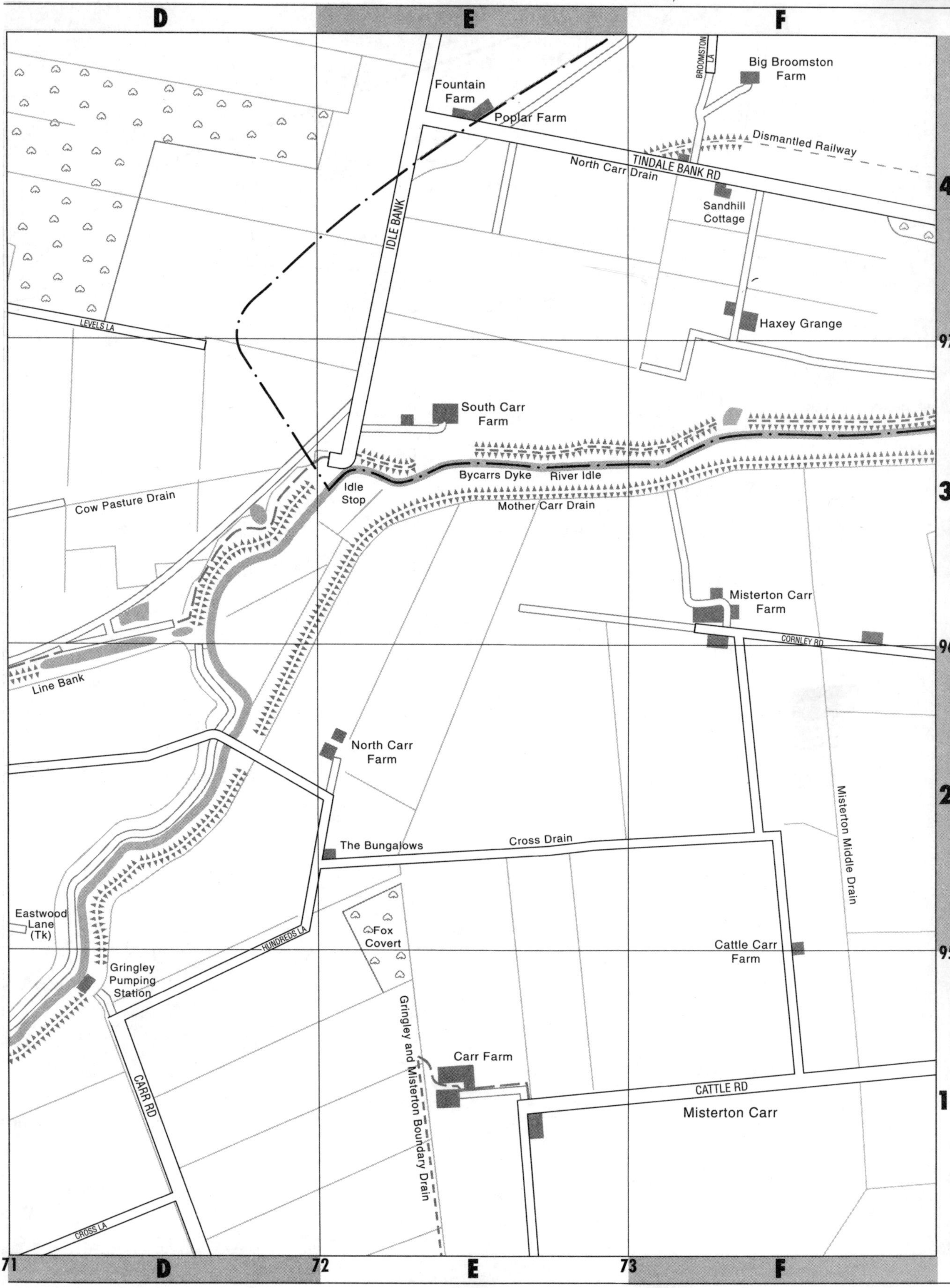
D
E
F
Fountain Farm
Poplar Farm
BROOMSTON LA
Big Broomston Farm
Dismantled Railway
TINDALE BANK RD
North Carr Drain
Sandhill Cottage
IDLE BANK
LEVELS LA
Haxey Grange
South Carr Farm
Bycarrs Dyke
River Idle
Idle Stop
Mother Carr Drain
Cow Pasture Drain
Misterton Carr Farm
CORNLEY RD
Line Bank
North Carr Farm
Misterton Middle Drain
The Bungalows
Cross Drain
Eastwood Lane (Tk)
HUNDREDS LA
Fox Covert
Cattle Carr Farm
Gringley Pumping Station
Gringley and Misterton Boundary Drain
Carr Farm
CARR RD
CATTLE RD
Misterton Carr
CROSS LA
4
97
3
96
2
95
1
71
72
73

12
6

5

A
B
C
4
97
3
96
2
95
1
94
74
75
76
Langholme
Langholme Wood
Haxey
Warping Drain
Langholme Farm
Dismantled Railway
Langholme
A161
STATION RD
Cornley Farm
TINDALE BANK RD
Langholme Manor
LC
Cornley Lane
Hunter's Hill
Richmond Farm
North Carr
North Carr Farm
HAXEY GATE RD
River Idle
Mother Drain
Haxey Gate Bridge
Haxey Gate Inn (PH)
NORTH CARR RD
Debdhill Farm
Mother Drain Bridge
Cornley Farm
Cornley Carr Farm
Debd Hill
Cornley
Debdhill Road
HAXEY RD
New Cemy
CORNLEY RD
Red House
White House Farm
LAUREL AVE
PARK AVE
ROOK'S LA
DEBDHILL RD
COLTON ST
CHURCH ST
CARR LA
Sandholes Lane
Cattle Farm
CHURCH LA
HIGH ST
ASHLEA
WILLOW AVE
OLD FORGE RD
CHURCH DR
MEADOW DR
CHAPEL CL
A161
STATION ST
HILLSYDE AVE
DEANS CL
ASHDOWN WAY
MINSTER RD
Liby
Misterton
WHARF RD
CATTLE RD
Cooper's Bridge
GRINGLEY RD
Wharf Bridge
Chesterfield Canal
GROVE WOOD TERR
GROVE WOOD RD
GROVE PARK
Green's Yard
GRAVELHOLES LA


5
13

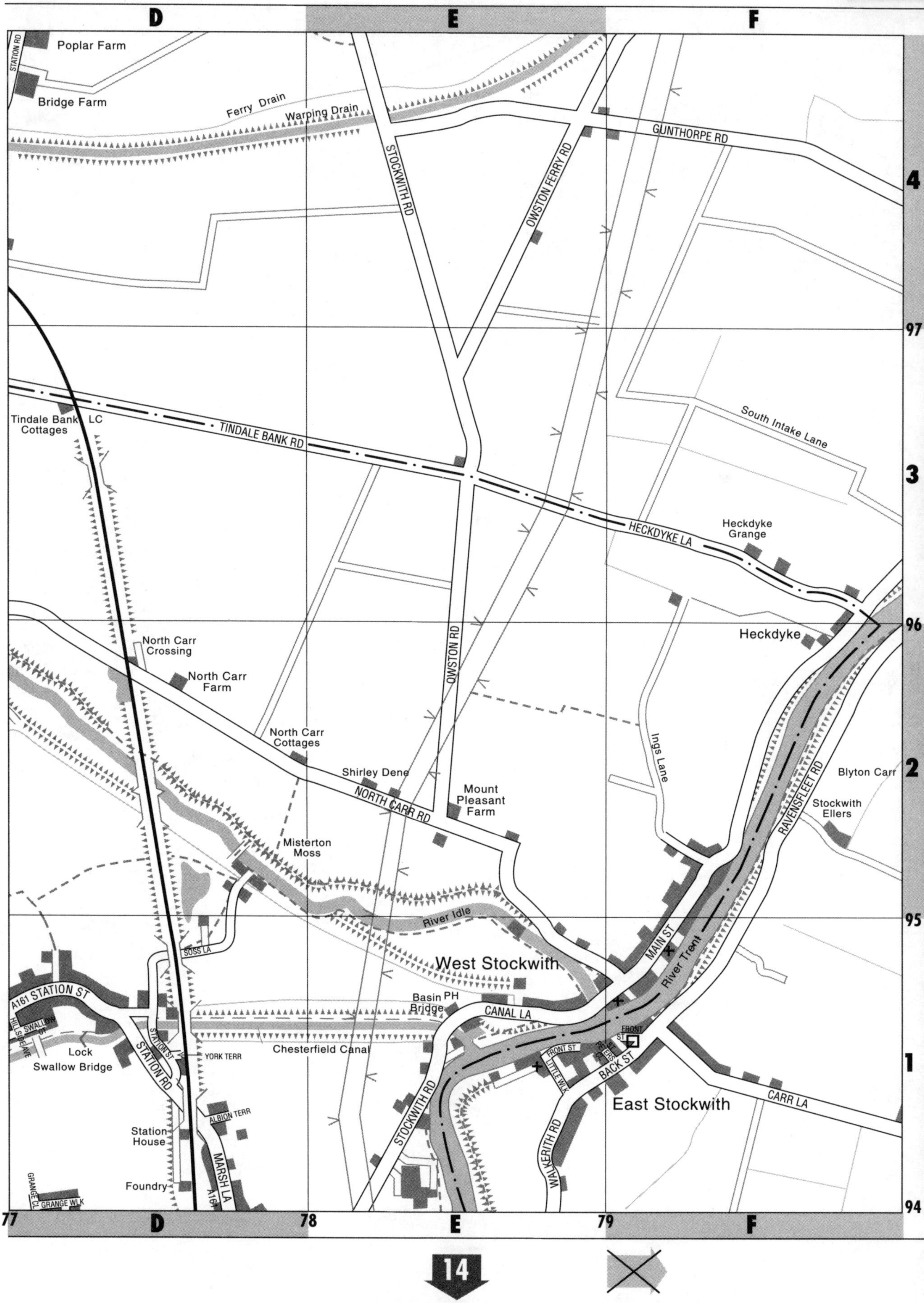
D
E
F
Poplar Farm
Bridge Farm
STATION RD
Ferry Drain
Warping Drain
GUNTHORPE RD
STOCKWITH RD
OWSTON FERRY RD
4
97
Tindale Bank LC Cottages
TINDALE BANK RD
South Intake Lane
3
HECKDYKE LA
Heckdyke Grange
96
Heckdyke
North Carr Crossing
North Carr Farm
OWSTON RD
North Carr Cottages
Ings Lane
Shirley Dene
Mount Pleasant Farm
NORTH CARR RD
2
Blyton Carr
RAVENSFLEET RD
Stockwith Ellers
Misterton Moss
River Idle
95
SOSS LA
West Stockwith
MAIN ST
River Trent
A161 STATION ST
SWALLOW CT
HILLSIDE LANE
Basin Bridge
PH
CANAL LA
FRONT ST
Lock
Swallow Bridge
STATION ST
YORK TERR
Chesterfield Canal
FRONT ST
PETERS CL
BACK ST
1
STATION RD
LITTLE WLK
CARR LA
STOCKWITH RD
ALBION TERR
East Stockwith
Station House
WALKERITH RD
MARSH LA
Foundry
A161
GRANGE CL
GRANGE WLK
94
77
78
79
D
E
F

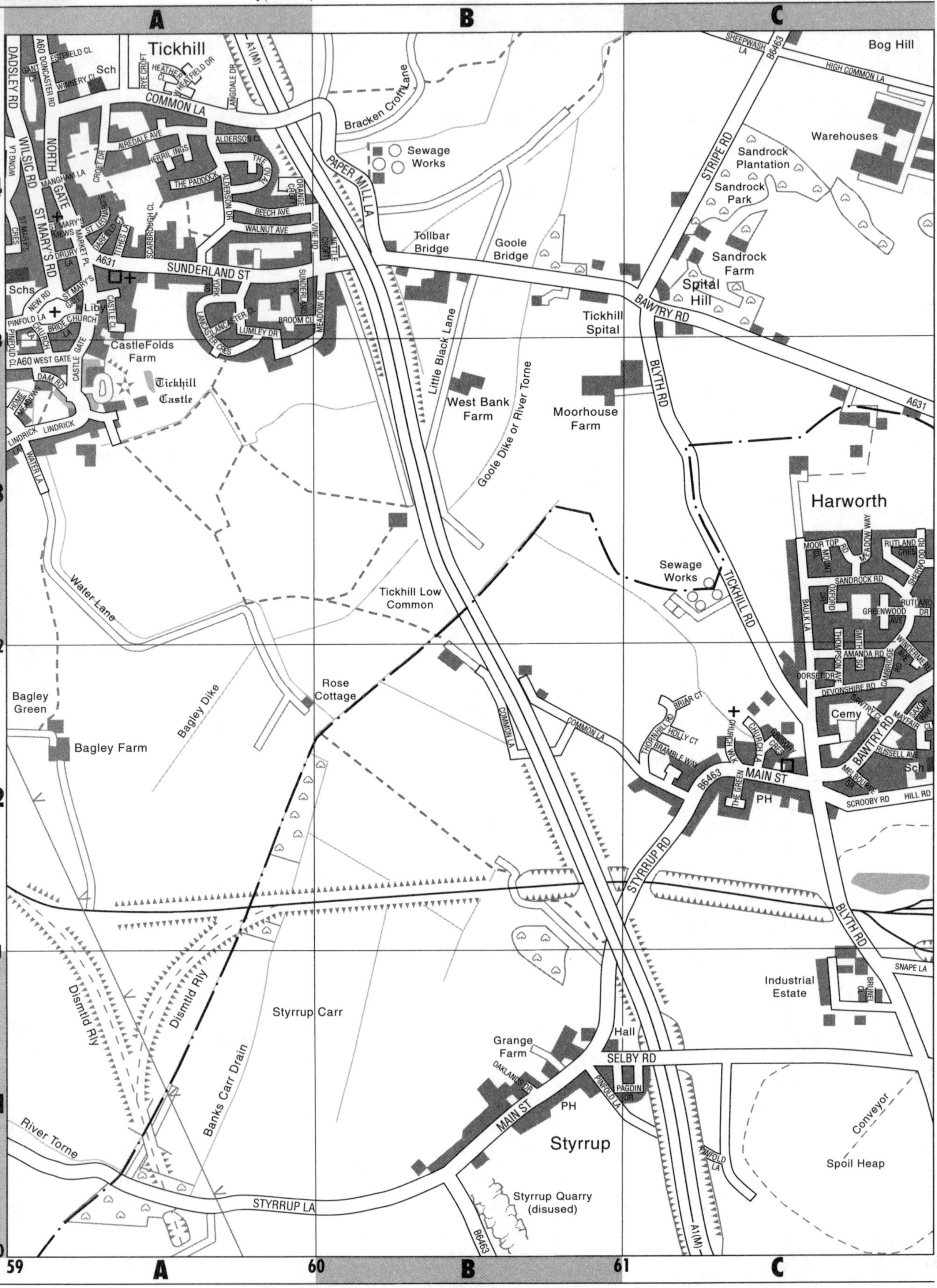
A
B
C
Tickhill
Sch
COMMON LA
DADSLEY RD
A60 DONCASTER RD
ESTFIELD CL
WINNERY CL
RYE CROFT
HEATHER CL
WHEATFIELD DR
LANGDALE DR
A1(M)
Bracken Croft Lane
Sewage Works
SHEEPWASH LA
B6463
Bog Hill
HIGH COMMON LA
Warehouses
STRIPE RD
Sandrock Plantation
Sandrock Park
Sandrock Farm
Spital Hill
NORTH GATE
ST MARY'S RD
WILSIC RD
MANGHAM LA
AIREDALE AVE
HERRIL INGS
THE PADDOCK
ALDERSON CL
ALDERSON DR
THE OVAL
ORANGE CROFT
BEECH AVE
WALNUT AVE
VINE RD
NETTLE CROFT
PAPER MILL LA
Tollbar Bridge
Goole Bridge
SUNDERLAND ST
A631
SCARBROUGH CL
TITHES LA
DARFIELD CL
ST LEONARDS
MARKET PL
DRURY LA
ST MARY'S MEWS
ST MARY'S CRES
Schs
NEW RD
ST MARY'S GATE
PINFOLD LA
PINFOLD CL
CHURCH LA
BRIDE CHURCH
CASTLE CL
Liby
YORK RD
LANCASTER CL
LANCASTER CRES
LUMLEY DR
SUNDERLAND PL
BROOM CL
MEADOW DR
BAWTRY RD
Tickhill Spital
A60 WEST GATE
CASTLE GATE
DAM RD
CastleFolds Farm
Tickhill Castle
HOME MEADOWS
LINDRICK
WATER LA
Little Black Lane
West Bank Farm
Goole Dike or River Torne
Moorhouse Farm
BLYTH RD
A631
Harworth
MOOR TOP RD
MOUNT CL
MEADOW WAY
RUTLAND CRES
SHERWOOD RD
SANDROCK RD
OXFORD DR
BAULK LA
GREENWOOD AVE
RUTLAND DR
THOMPSON AVE
SMITH SQ
AMANDA RD
CAMBRIDGE AVE
WINDERMERE RD
DORSET DR
DEVONSHIRE RD
Water Lane
Tickhill Low Common
Sewage Works
TICKHILL RD
Bagley Green
Bagley Farm
Bagley Dike
Rose Cottage
COMMON LA
BRIAR CT
THORNHILL RD
HOLLY CT
BRAMBLE WAY
CHURCH WALK
CHURCH LA
GREGORY CRES
Cemy
BAWTRY CL
MAYFAIR CL
SAXON WAY
BAWTRY RD
RUSSELL AVE
MELBOURNE GR
Sch
MAIN ST
B6463
THE GREEN
PH
SCROOBY RD
HILL RD
STYRRUP RD
Dismtld Rly
Dismtld Rly
Styrrup Carr
Banks Carr Drain
BLYTH RD
SNAPE LA
Industrial Estate
BRUNEL CL
Grange Farm
Hall
SELBY RD
OAKLANDS DR
PINFOLD LA
PAGDIN DR
MAIN ST
PH
Styrrup
River Torne
PINFOLD LA
Conveyor
Spoil Heap
Styrrup Quarry (disused)
STYRRUP LA
B6463
A1(M)
4
93
3
92
2
91
1
90
59
60
61

17

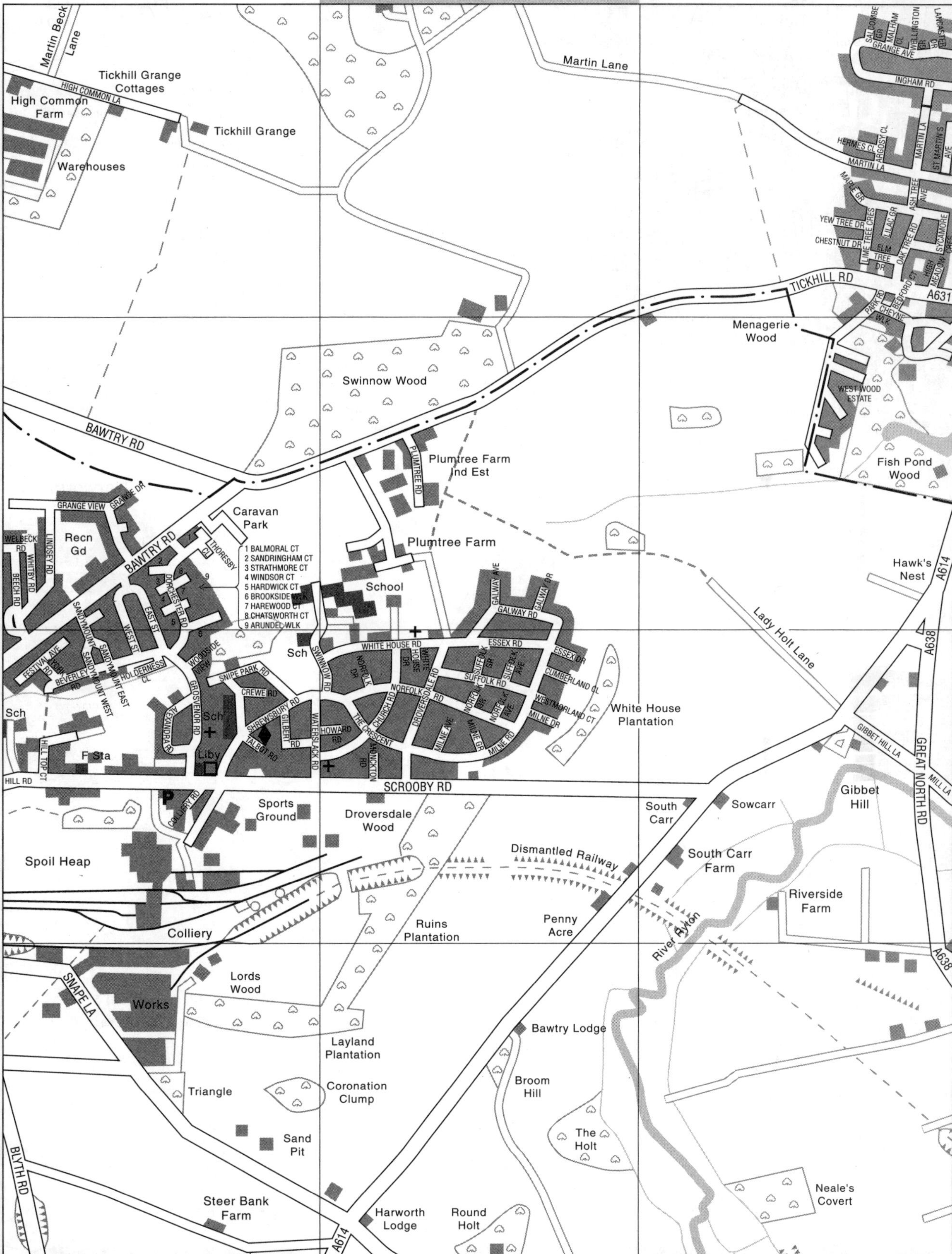
D
E
F
Martin Beck Lane
Tickhill Grange Cottages
High Common Farm
HIGH COMMON LA
Tickhill Grange
Warehouses
Martin Lane
INGHAM RD
GRANGE AVE
HERMES CL
ARGOSY CL
MARTIN LA
ST MARTIN'S AVE
YEW TREE DR
CHESTNUT DR
TICKHILL RD
A631
Menagerie Wood
WEST WOOD ESTATE
Swinnow Wood
BAWTRY RD
Plumtree Farm Ind Est
PLUMTREE RD
Fish Pond Wood
Caravan Park
Recn Gd
GRANGE VIEW
Plumtree Farm
School
1 BALMORAL CT
2 SANDRINGHAM CT
3 STRATHMORE CT
4 WINDSOR CT
5 HARDWICK CT
6 BROOKSIDE WLK
7 HAREWOOD CT
8 CHATSWORTH CT
9 ARUNDEL WLK
Hawk's Nest
A614
Lady Holt Lane
GALWAY AVE
GALWAY RD
ESSEX RD
WHITE HOUSE RD
Sch
NORFOLK RD
SUFFOLK RD
CUMBERLAND CL
WESTMORLAND CT
MILNE DR
White House Plantation
A638
SWIPE PARK RD
CREWE RD
SHREWSBURY RD
HOWARD RD
THE CRESCENT
MONCKTON RD
DROVERSDALE RD
MILNE AVE
MILNE GR
MILNE RD
Sch
F Sta
Liby
HILL RD
HILL TOP CT
SCROOBY RD
GIBBET HILL LA
GREAT NORTH RD
MILL LA
Gibbet Hill
Sports Ground
Droversdale Wood
South Carr
Sowcarr
Spoil Heap
Dismantled Railway
South Carr Farm
Riverside Farm
Colliery
Ruins Plantation
Penny Acre
River Ryton
SNAPE LA
Lords Wood
Works
Bawtry Lodge
Layland Plantation
Triangle
Coronation Clump
Broom Hill
The Holt
Sand Pit
BLYTH RD
Steer Bank Farm
Harworth Lodge
Round Holt
Neale's Covert
4
93
3
92
2
91
1
90
62
63
64

9
3

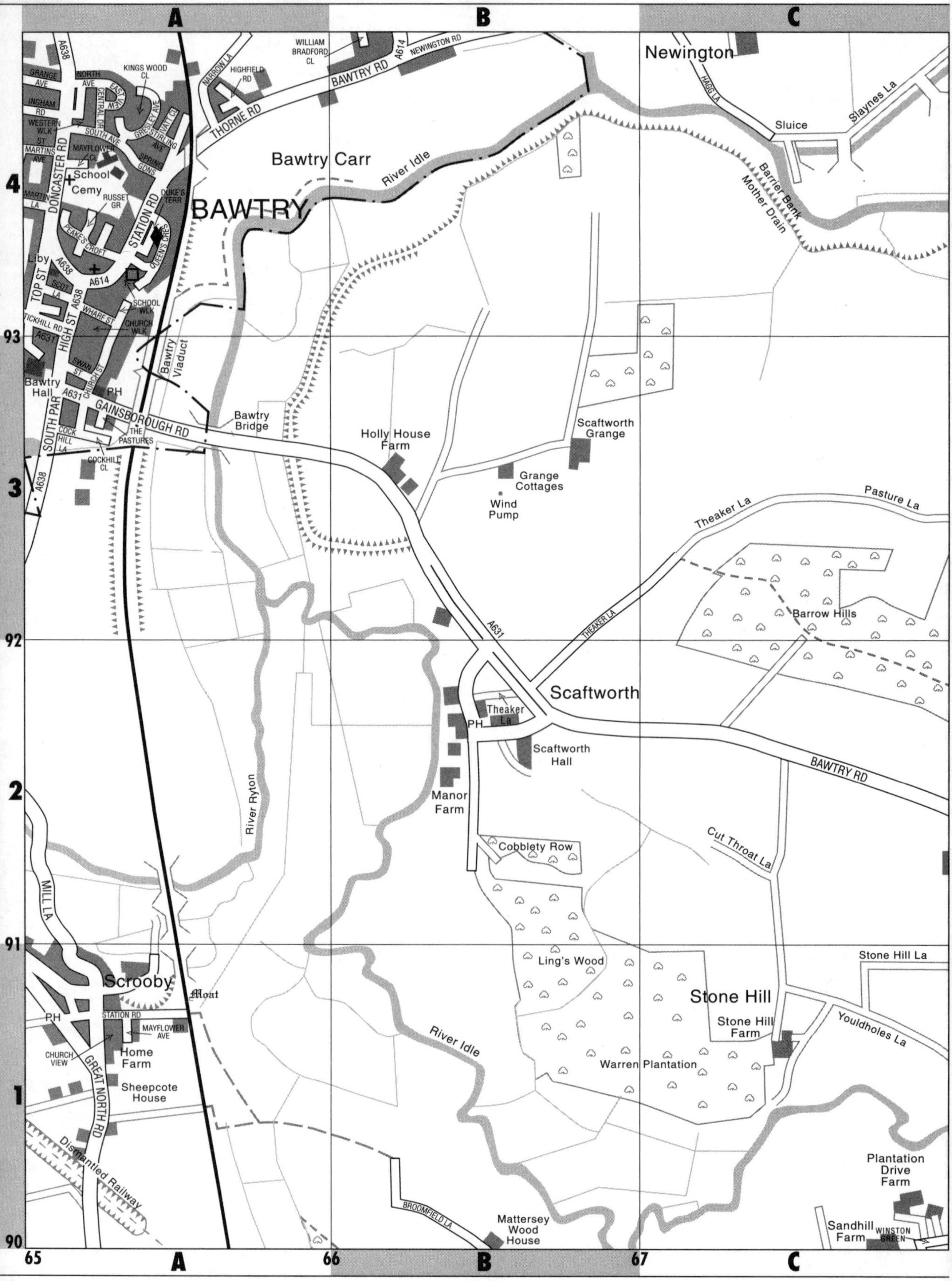
A
B
C
Newington
Hagg La
Slaynes La
Sluice
Barrier Bank
Mother Drain
Bawtry Carr
River Idle
BAWTRY
Bawtry Rd
Newington Rd
A614
Thorne Rd
Narrow La
Highfield Rd
William Bradford Cl
Kings Wood Cl
Grange Ave
North Ave
Ingham Rd
Western Wlk
St Martins Ave
Martins La
Doncaster Rd
Central Dr
East View
South Ave
Gresley Ave
Stirling Ave
Spring Gdns
Mayflower Cl
School
Cemy
Russet Gr
Station Rd
Duke's Terr
Queen's Cres
Peake's Croft
Liby
A638
Top St
Scot La
A614
School Wlk
Wharf St
Church Wlk
Tickhill Rd
High St
A631
Swan St
Church St
Bawtry Hall
PH
South Par
Cock Hill La
Cockhill Cl
The Pastures
Gainsborough Rd
Bawtry Viaduct
Bawtry Bridge
Holly House Farm
Scaftworth Grange
Grange Cottages
Wind Pump
Theaker La
Pasture La
Barrow Hills
A631
Scaftworth
Theaker La
PH
Scaftworth Hall
Bawtry Rd
Manor Farm
River Ryton
Cobblety Row
Cut Throat La
Mill La
Ling's Wood
Stone Hill La
Stone Hill
Stone Hill Farm
Youldholes La
Warren Plantation
River Idle
Scrooby
Moat
PH
Station Rd
Mayflower Ave
Church View
Home Farm
Great North Rd
Sheepcote House
Dismantled Railway
Broomfield La
Mattersey Wood House
Plantation Drive Farm
Sandhill Farm
Winston Green
4
93
3
92
2
91
1
90
65
66
67

9
19

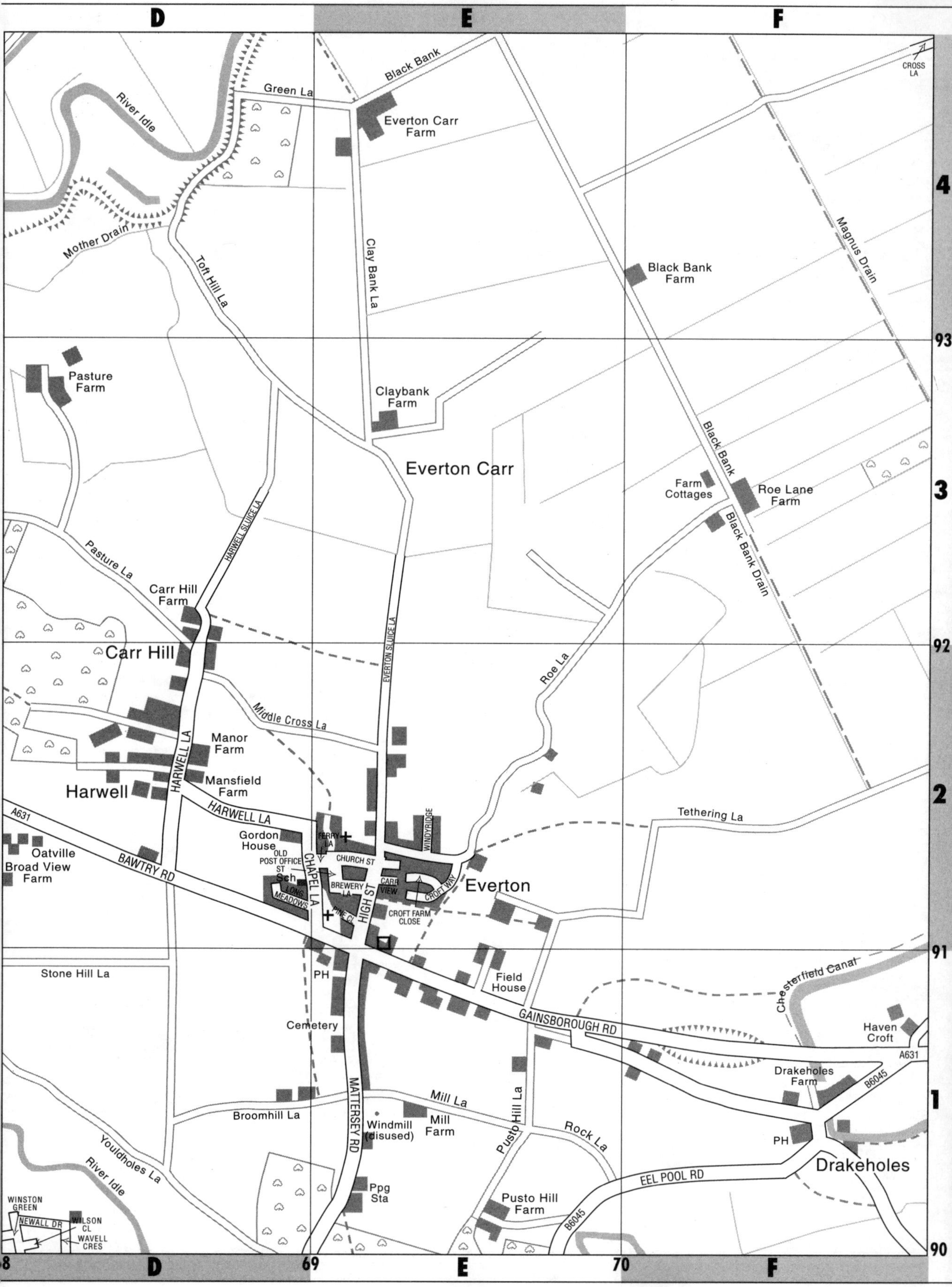
D
E
F
4
3
2
1
93
92
91
90
69
70
Green La
Black Bank
CROSS LA
River Idle
Everton Carr Farm
Mother Drain
Clay Bank La
Toft Hill La
Black Bank Farm
Magnus Drain
Pasture Farm
Claybank Farm
Everton Carr
Black Bank
Farm Cottages
Roe Lane Farm
Black Bank Drain
HARWELL SLUICE LA
Pasture La
Carr Hill Farm
EVERTON SLUICE LA
Carr Hill
Roe La
Middle Cross La
Manor Farm
HARWELL LA
Mansfield Farm
Harwell
A631
HARWELL LA
WINDYRIDGE
Tethering La
Gordon House
FERRY LA
Oatville
Broad View Farm
BAWTRY RD
OLD POST OFFICE ST
CHURCH ST
Sch
CHAPEL LA
BREWERY LA
CARR VIEW
CROFT WAY
Everton
LONG MEADOWS
HIGH ST
PINE CL
CROFT FARM CLOSE
Stone Hill La
PH
Field House
Chesterfield Canal
Cemetery
GAINSBOROUGH RD
Haven Croft
A631
Drakeholes Farm
B6045
MATTERSEY RD
Mill La
Pusto Hill La
Broomhill La
Windmill (disused)
Mill Farm
Rock La
PH
Youldholes La
Drakeholes
River Idle
EEL POOL RD
Ppg Sta
Pusto Hill Farm
WINSTON GREEN
NEWALL DR
WILSON CL
WAVELL CRES
B6045

11
5

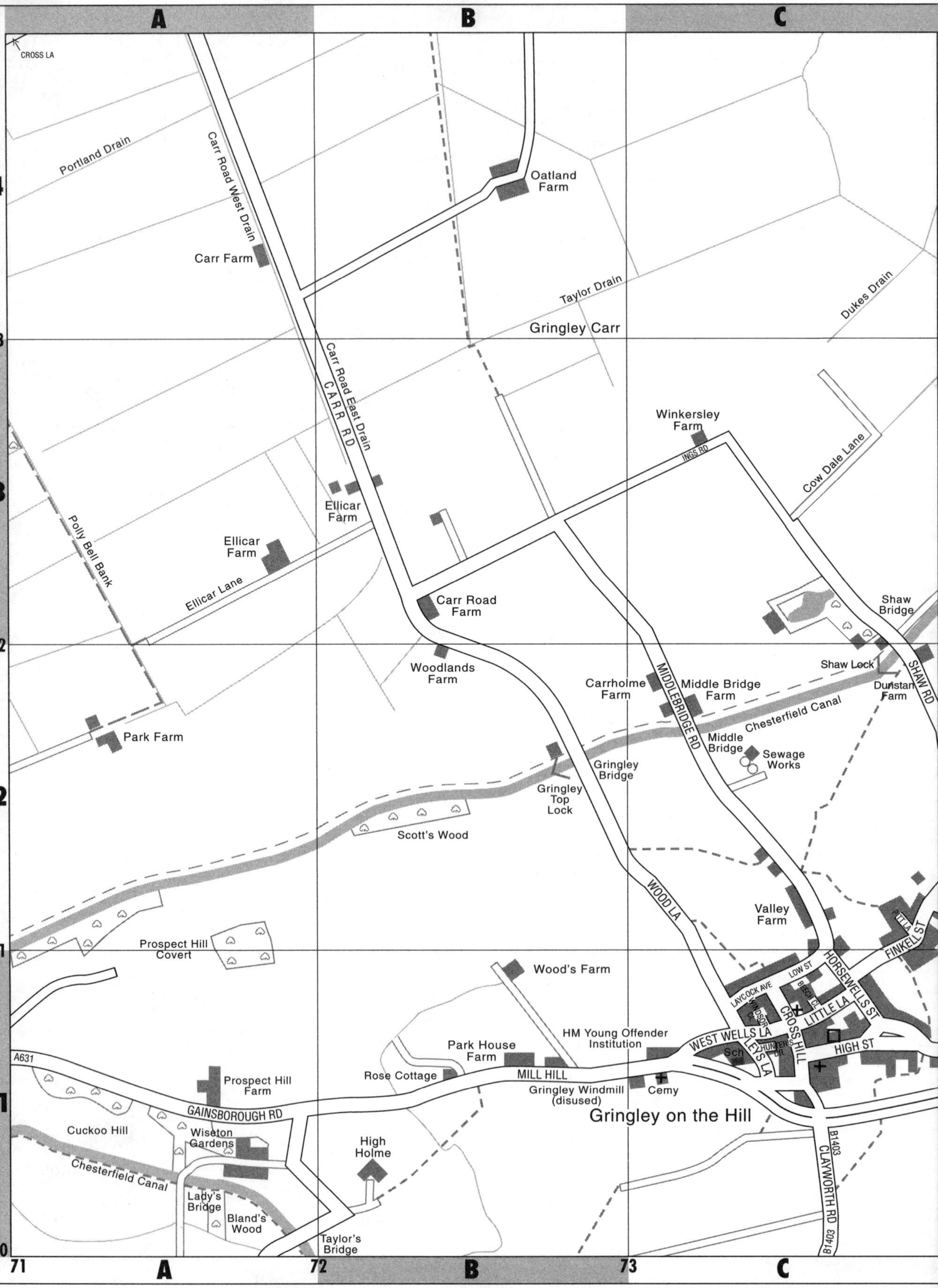
A
B
C
CROSS LA
Portland Drain
Carr Road West Drain
Oatland Farm
Carr Farm
Taylor Drain
Dukes Drain
Gringley Carr
Carr Road East Drain
CARR RD
Winkersley Farm
INGS RD
Cow Dale Lane
Polly Bell Bank
Ellicar Farm
Ellicar Farm
Ellicar Lane
Carr Road Farm
Shaw Bridge
Woodlands Farm
Shaw Lock
SHAW RD
Carrholme Farm
MIDDLEBRIDGE RD
Middle Bridge Farm
Dunstan Farm
Chesterfield Canal
Park Farm
Middle Bridge
Sewage Works
Gringley Bridge
Gringley Top Lock
Scott's Wood
WOOD LA
Valley Farm
Prospect Hill Covert
Wood's Farm
LOW ST
HORSEWELLS ST
FINKELL ST
LAYCOCK AVE
BEECH CL
LITTLE LA
WINDSOR CL
CROSS HILL
HM Young Offender Institution
WEST WELLS LA
LEYS LA
HUNTERS DR
HIGH ST
Park House Farm
Sch
A631
Rose Cottage
MILL HILL
Prospect Hill Farm
Gringley Windmill (disused)
Cemy
GAINSBOROUGH RD
Gringley on the Hill
Cuckoo Hill
Wiseton Gardens
High Holme
B1403
CLAYWORTH RD
Chesterfield Canal
Lady's Bridge
Bland's Wood
Taylor's Bridge
4
93
3
92
2
91
1
90
71
72
73

11
21

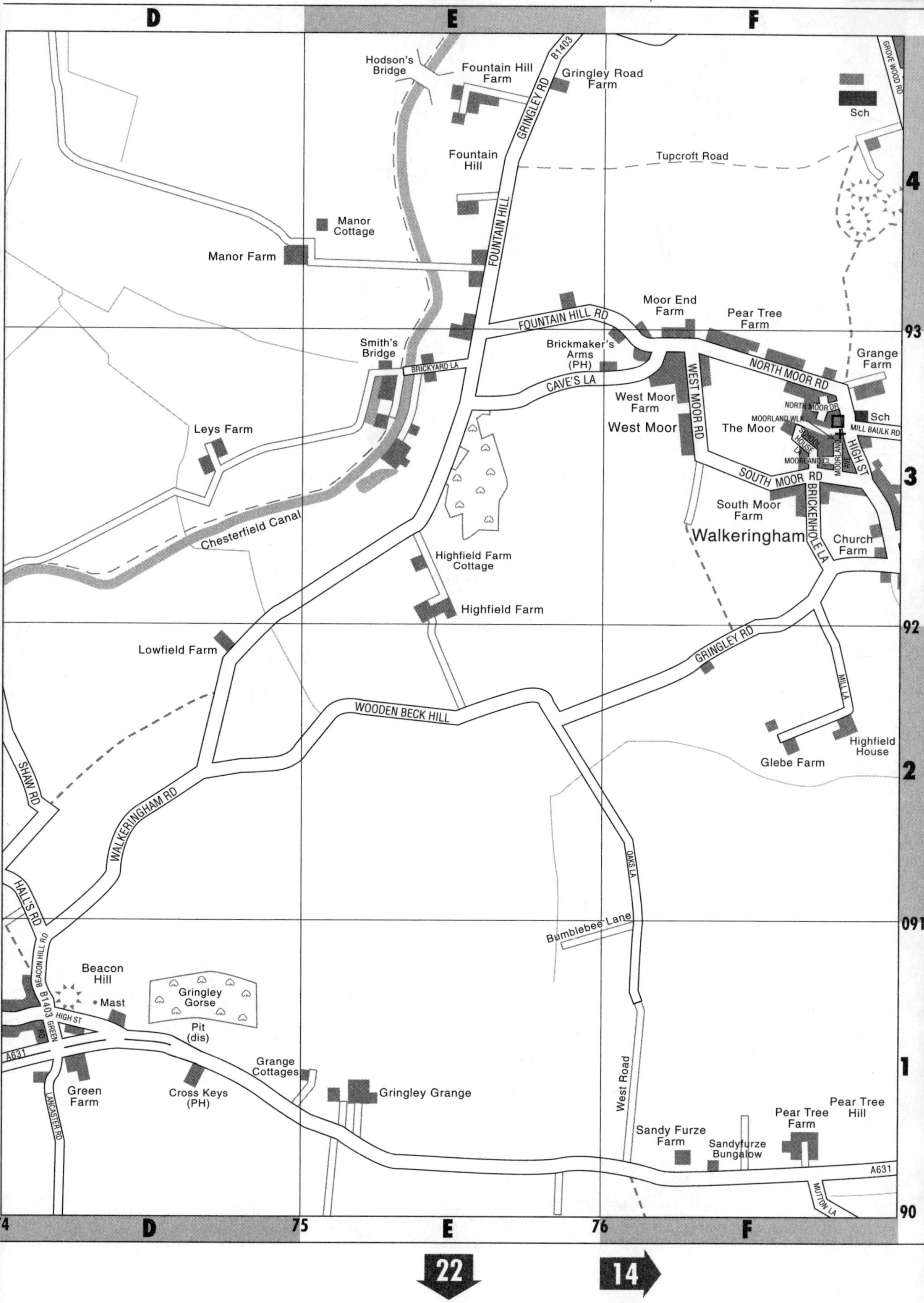
6
14
D
E
F
Hodson's Bridge
Fountain Hill Farm
Gringley Road Farm
GRINGLEY RD
B1403
Sch
Fountain Hill
Tupcroft Road
Manor Cottage
Manor Farm
FOUNTAIN HILL
Moor End Farm
Pear Tree Farm
FOUNTAIN HILL RD
Smith's Bridge
BRICKYARD LA
Brickmaker's Arms (PH)
CAVE'S LA
Grange Farm
NORTH MOOR RD
WEST MOOR RD
West Moor Farm
West Moor
The Moor
NORTH MOOR DR
MOORLAND WLK
SCHOOL HOUSE LA
MOORLAND CL
MOORLAND AVE
HIGH ST
MILL BAULK RD
Leys Farm
SOUTH MOOR RD
South Moor Farm
BRICKENHOLE LA
Walkeringham
Church Farm
Chesterfield Canal
Highfield Farm Cottage
Highfield Farm
Lowfield Farm
GRINGLEY RD
MILL LA
WOODEN BECK HILL
Highfield House
Glebe Farm
SHAW RD
WALKERINGHAM RD
OAKS LA
HALL'S RD
Bumblebee Lane
BEACON HILL RD
Beacon Hill
Mast
Gringley Gorse
B1403
HIGH ST
GREEN
RD
Pit (dis)
A631
Grange Cottages
Green Farm
Cross Keys (PH)
Gringley Grange
West Road
Pear Tree Hill
Pear Tree Farm
Sandy Furze Farm
Sandyfurze Bungalow
LANCASTER RD
A631
MUTTON LA
GROVE WOOD RD
4
93
3
92
2
091
1
90
74
75
76
22
14

13
7

A
B
C
4
93
3
92
2
91
1
90
77
78
79
GRANGE CL
GRANGE DR
GRANGE AVE
AMCOTT AVE
FOX COVERT LA
A161
STOCKWITH RD
F Sta
Newells Terrace
STOCKWITH RD
Line Croft Farm
Marsh Drain
Lyne House Farm
LINECROFT LA
WALKERITH RD
STOCKWITH RD
Willow Bank Farm
Blyton Carr
Willow Bank Lane
Walkerith Drain
Wood Close Drain
North Carr Farm
Brooklyn
Jubilee Farm
The Poplars
WALKERITH RD
Walkerith
Ings lane
Wood Close Drain
Field Lane
Sewage Works
MILL BAULK RD
Point Farm
River Trent
Station House
MARSH RD
STATION RD
HIGH ST
BIRDCROFT LA
GRINGLEY RD
Church End
LC
Holmes Villa
Marsh Drain
Holmes Road
BECKINGHAM RD
Pinewood
Bar Bank
Greenfields Farm
WALKERINGHAM RD
Tetheringrass Lane
LC
VICARAGE LA
Badgers Dell
Mill Farm
A161
BECHER LA
Hall Farm
Beckingham
New Drain
Depot
CHURCH ST
CHURCH VIEW
LOW ST
A631
THE GROVE
THE PADDOCKS
HIGH ST
WILDMAN VILLAS
RECTORY GDNS
RAVENCROFT LA
THE CRESCENT
THE LIMES
Sch
Fretwell Farm
Back House
OLD TRENT RD

13
23

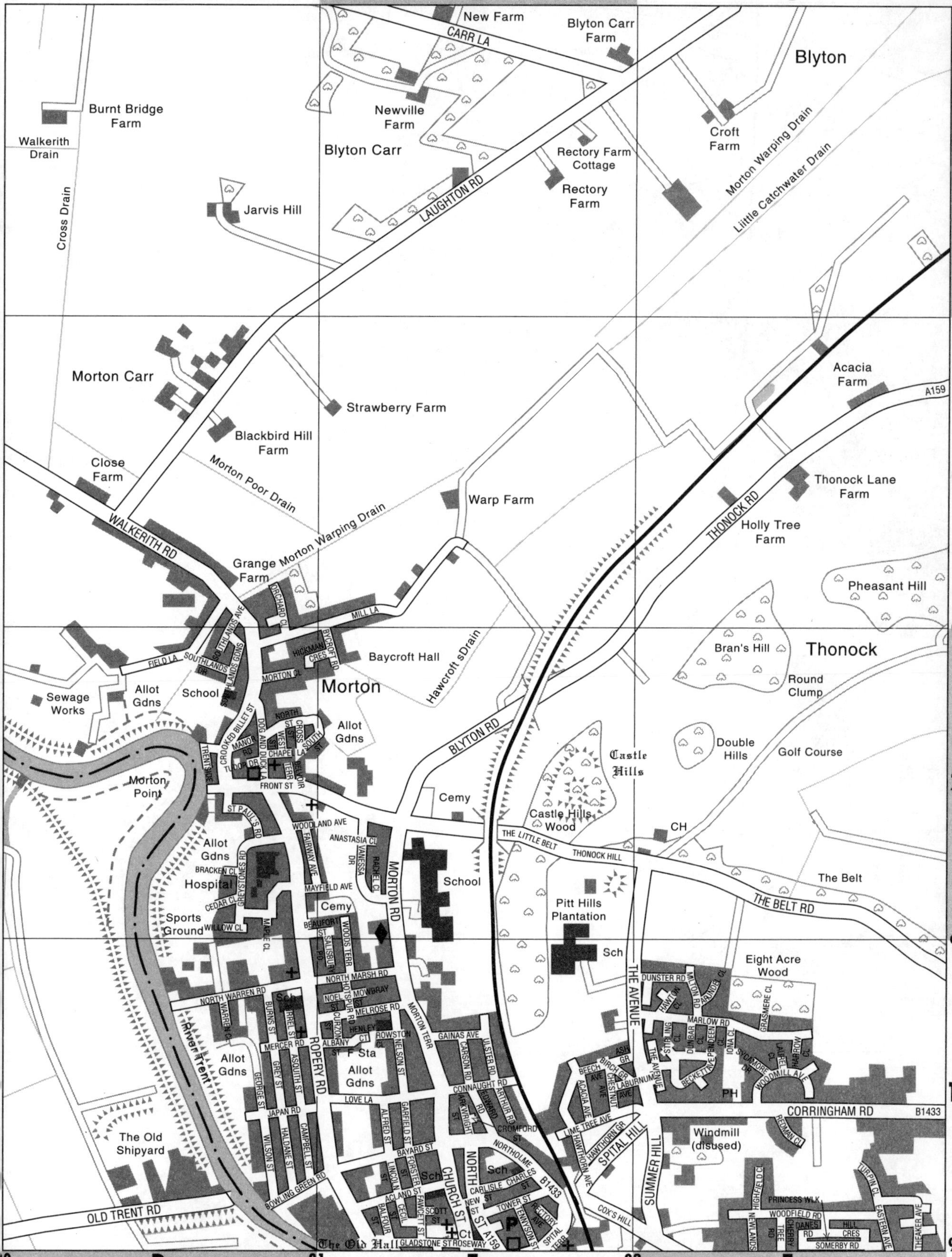
D
E
F
New Farm
CARR LA
Blyton Carr Farm
Blyton
Burnt Bridge Farm
Walkerith Drain
Newville Farm
Blyton Carr
Croft Farm
Morton Warping Drain
Rectory Farm Cottage
Little Catchwater Drain
Rectory Farm
LAUGHTON RD
Cross Drain
Jarvis Hill
Morton Carr
Acacia Farm
A159
Strawberry Farm
Blackbird Hill Farm
Close Farm
Morton Poor Drain
Warp Farm
Thonock Lane Farm
THONOCK RD
Holly Tree Farm
WALKERITH RD
Morton Warping Drain
Grange Farm
Pheasant Hill
MILL LA
Baycroft Hall
Hawcroft sDrain
Bran's Hill
Thonock
Morton
Round Clump
Sewage Works
Allot Gdns
School
Allot Gdns
Double Hills
Golf Course
Castle Hills
BLYTON RD
Morton Point
FRONT ST
Cemy
Castle Hills Wood
CH
THE LITTLE BELT
THONOCK HILL
Allot Gdns
Hospital
School
The Belt
THE BELT RD
Pitt Hills Plantation
Sports Ground
Cemy
MORTON RD
Sch
Eight Acre Wood
THE AVENUE
NORTH WARREN RD
River Trent
ROPERY RD
F Sta
Allot Gdns
Allot Gdns
PH
CORRINGHAM RD
B1433
Windmill (disused)
The Old Shipyard
SPITAL HILL
SUMMER HILL
Sch
Sch
CHURCH ST
NORTH ST
OLD TRENT RD
The Old Hall
Ct
P
90
91
92
93
3
4
2
1
80
81
82

24

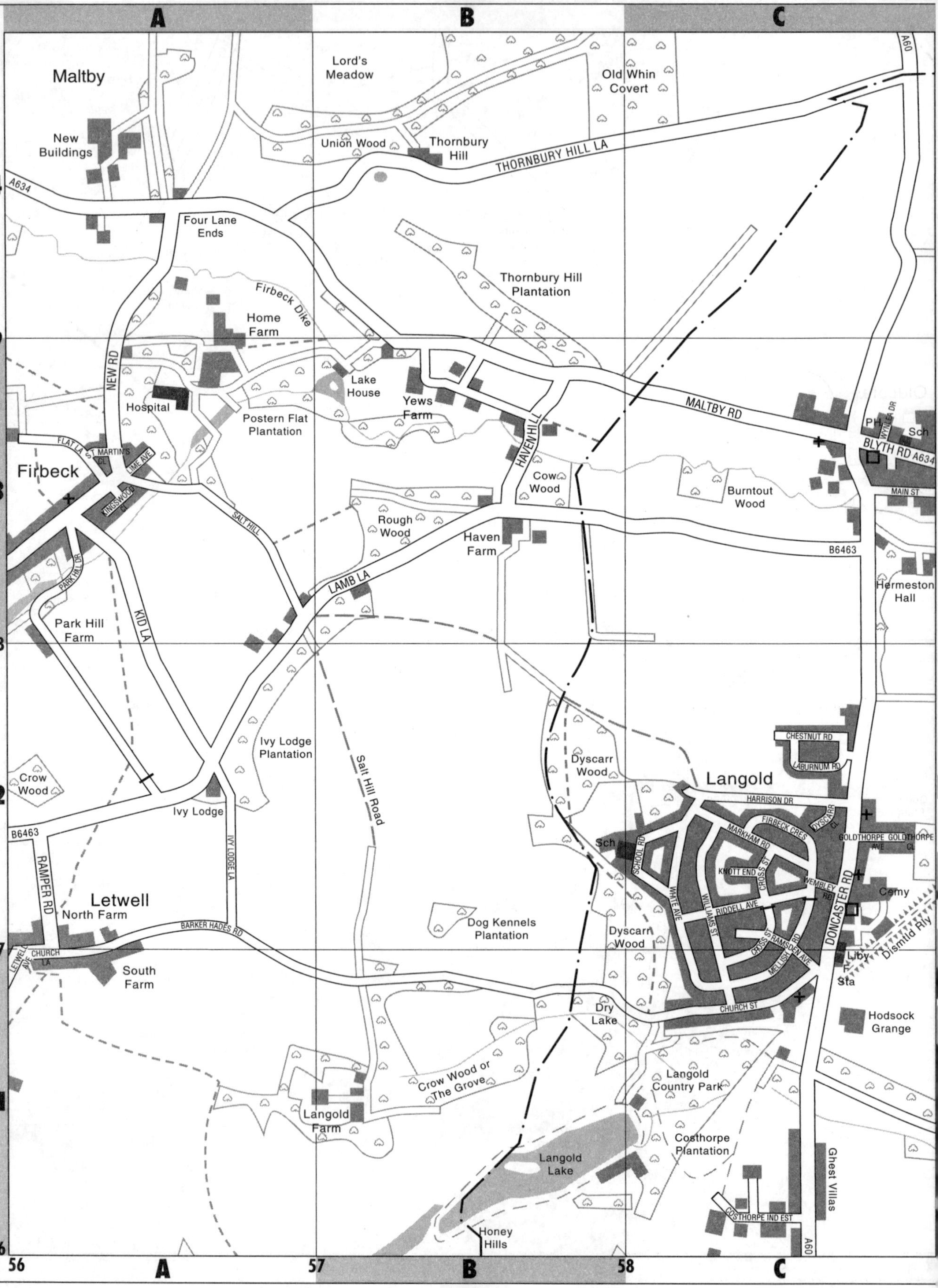
A
B
C
Maltby
New Buildings
Lord's Meadow
Union Wood
Thornbury Hill
Old Whin Covert
THORNBURY HILL LA
A634
A60
4
Four Lane Ends
Firbeck Dike
Home Farm
Thornbury Hill Plantation
89
NEW RD
Hospital
Lake House
Yews Farm
Postern Flat Plantation
MALTBY RD
HAVEN HILL
PH
Sch
WYLIA DR
BLYTH RD A634
FLAT LA
ST MARTIN'S CL
LIME AVE
Firbeck
KINGSWOOD CL
3
Cow Wood
Burntout Wood
MAIN ST
SALT HILL
Rough Wood
Haven Farm
B6463
PARK HILL DR
LAMB LA
KID LA
Hermeston Hall
Park Hill Farm
88
Ivy Lodge Plantation
Salt Hill Road
CHESTNUT RD
LABURNUM RD
Crow Wood
Dyscarr Wood
Langold
2
Ivy Lodge
HARRISON DR
FIRBECK CRES
DYSCARR CL
MARKHAM RD
B6463
IVY LODGE LA
Sch
SCHOOL RD
GOLDTHORPE AVE
GOLDTHORPE CL
RAMPER RD
KNOTT END
CROSS ST
WEMBLEY RD
Letwell
WHITE AVE
WILLIAMS ST
RIDDELL AVE
DONCASTER RD
Cemy
North Farm
Dog Kennels Plantation
BARKER HADES RD
Dyscarr Wood
CROSS ST
RAMSDEN RD
Dismtld Rly
87
LETWELL AVE
CHURCH LA
MELLISH AVE
Liby
South Farm
F Sta
Dry Lake
CHURCH ST
Hodsock Grange
Crow Wood or The Grove
Langold Country Park
1
Langold Farm
Costhorpe Plantation
Langold Lake
Ghest Villas
COSTHORPE IND EST
Honey Hills
A60
86
56
57
58

8
18

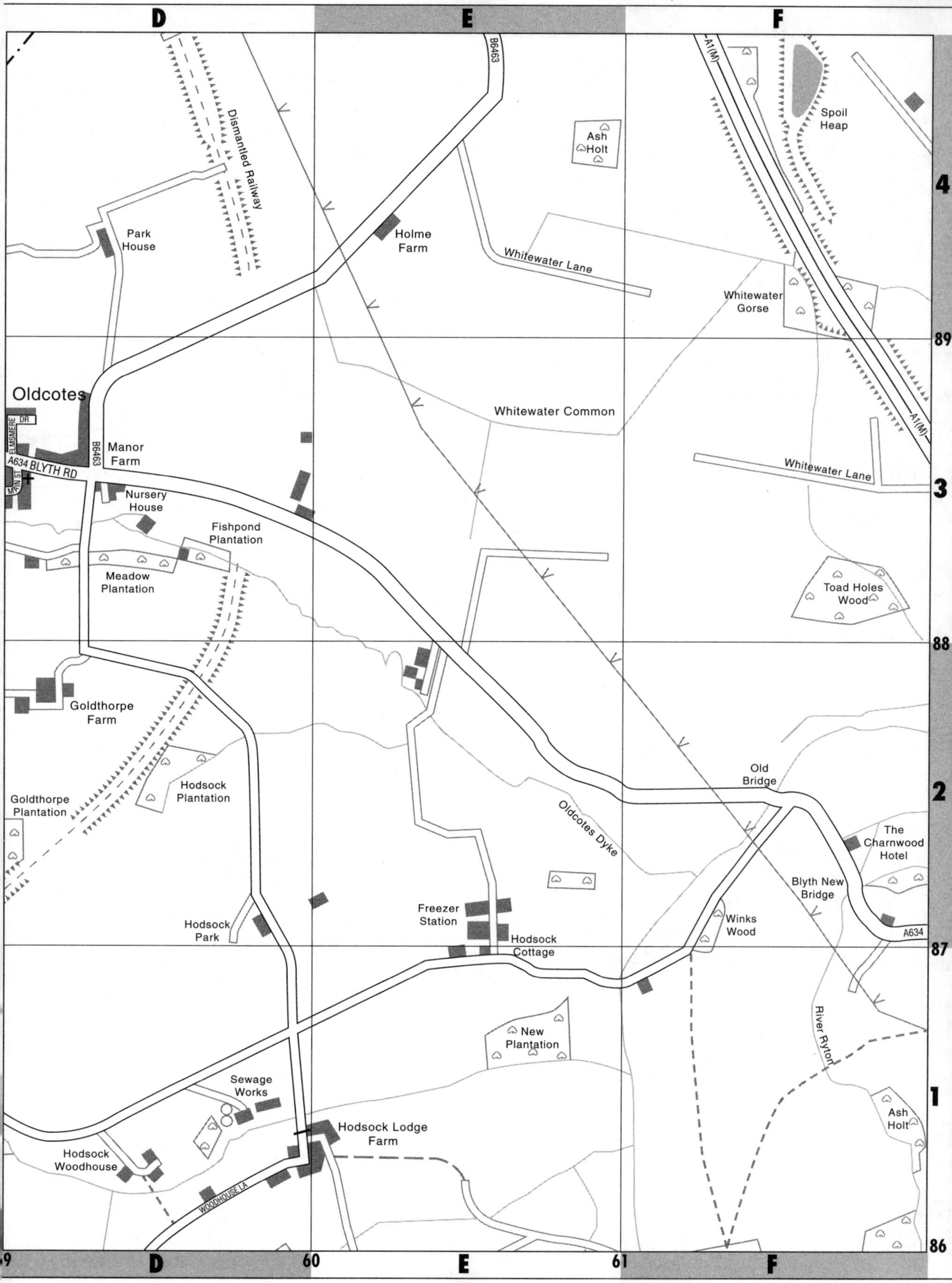
D
E
F
B6463
Dismantled Railway
A1(M)
Spoil Heap
Ash Holt
Park House
Holme Farm
Whitewater Lane
Whitewater Gorse
4
89
Oldcotes
Whitewater Common
ELMSMERE DR
Manor Farm
A634 BLYTH RD
MAIN ST
Nursery House
Fishpond Plantation
Meadow Plantation
Whitewater Lane
3
Toad Holes Wood
88
Goldthorpe Farm
Hodsock Plantation
Goldthorpe Plantation
Old Bridge
2
Oldcotes Dyke
The Charnwood Hotel
Blyth New Bridge
Freezer Station
Hodsock Park
Hodsock Cottage
Winks Wood
A634
87
New Plantation
River Ryton
Sewage Works
Hodsock Lodge Farm
Hodsock Woodhouse
WOODHOUSE LA
Ash Holt
1
86
60
61

26
18

17
9

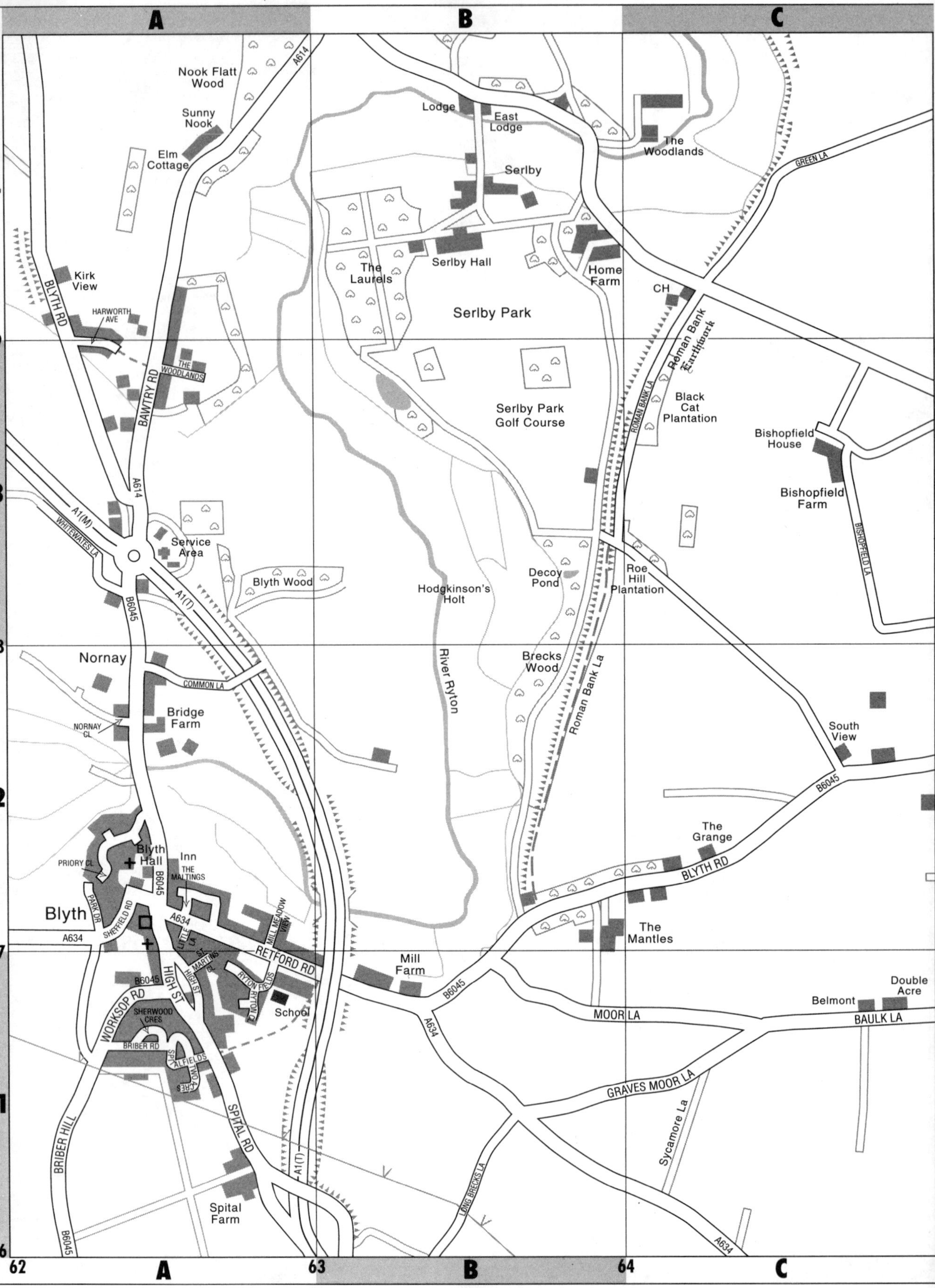
A
B
C
4
3
2
1
89
88
87
86
62
63
64
Nook Flatt Wood
A614
Sunny Nook
Elm Cottage
Lodge
East Lodge
The Woodlands
GREEN LA
Serlby
Serlby Hall
The Laurels
Home Farm
Kirk View
BLYTH RD
HARWORTH AVE
THE WOODLANDS
BAWTRY RD
CH
Serlby Park
Roman Bank Earthwork
ROMAN BANK LA
Black Cat Plantation
Serlby Park Golf Course
Bishopfield House
Bishopfield Farm
BISHOPFIELD LA
A1(M)
WHITEWATES LA
Service Area
Blyth Wood
A1(T)
B6045
Decoy Pond
Roe Hill Plantation
Hodgkinson's Holt
Nornay
COMMON LA
River Ryton
Brecks Wood
Roman Bank La
Bridge Farm
NORNAY CL
South View
B6045
The Grange
PRIORY CL
Blyth Hall
Inn
THE MALTINGS
BLYTH RD
Blyth
PARK DR
SHEFFIELD RD
A634
LITTLE LA
MILL MEADOW VIEW
The Mantles
A634
ST MARTINS CL
RETFORD RD
Mill Farm
HIGH ST
RYTON FIELDS
RYTON CL
School
B6045
WORKSOP RD
SHERWOOD CRES
BRIBER RD
ALFIELDS
MOOR LA
Belmont
Double Acre
BAULK LA
GRAVES MOOR LA
SPITAL RD
BRIBER HILL
Sycamore La
LONG BRECKS LA
Spital Farm
A1(T)
A634

17
27

10
20

D
E
F
4
89
3
88
2
87
1
86
65
66
67
Mattersey Wood
Main Drain
Mattersey Grange
BROOMFIELD LA
WINSTON GREEN
CUNNINGHAM CL
KEYES CL
KEYES RISE
KEYES CT
GREEN LA
A638
Hollins Holt
Lodge Farm
Lodge Court
Scrooby Top House
LC
BRECK LA
B6045
RANSKILL RD
MATTERSEY RD
FOLLY NOOK LA
ARUNDEL DR
OAKS CL
STONEHILL CL
SOUTHFALL CL
SPINNEYMEAD
School
CHERRY TREE WALK
Bridge House
STATION AVE
BISHOPFIELD LA
WHITTON CL
RAVENSHILL CL
PH
High House Farm
B6045
STATION RD
COMMON LA
Sewage Works
BLYTH RD
BACK LA
Ranskill
Headlands La
GREAT NORTH RD
Antcliff Plantation
Cemy
HUNTSMAN PL
UNDERWOOD AVE
HOLDS LA
BLACKSMITH LA
The Poplars
BAULK LA
LOW ST
Moat Farm
Torworth
Daneshill Lakes (Nature Reserve)
Works
DANESHILL RD
Torworth Crossing
Daneshill Piggery
Daneshill Lakes (Nature Reserve)
Works
Torworth Grange

28
20

19
11

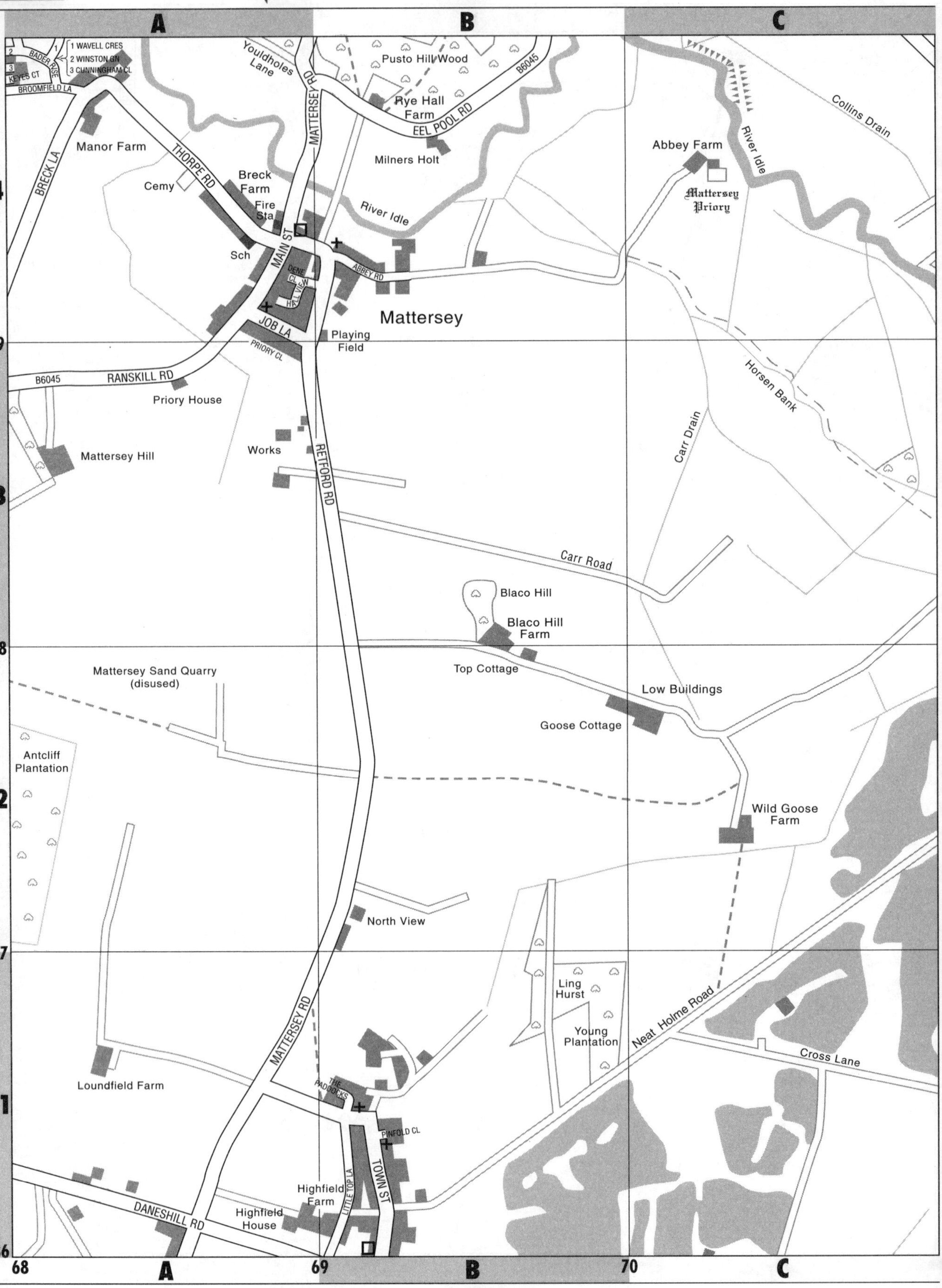
A
B
C
1 WAVELL CRES
2 WINSTON GN
3 CUNNINGHAM CL
BADER RISE
KEYES CT
BROOMFIELD LA
Youldholes Lane
MATTERSEY RD
Pusto Hill Wood
Rye Hall Farm
EEL POOL RD
B6045
Milners Holt
Manor Farm
THORPE RD
BRECK LA
Cemy
Breck Farm
Fire Sta
River Idle
MAIN ST
Sch
DENE CL
HILL VIEW
ABBEY RD
JOB LA
PRIORY CL
Mattersey
Playing Field
Abbey Farm
Mattersey Priory
Collins Drain
River Idle
B6045
RANSKILL RD
Priory House
Horsen Bank
Carr Drain
Mattersey Hill
Works
RETFORD RD
Carr Road
Blaco Hill
Blaco Hill Farm
Top Cottage
Low Buildings
Goose Cottage
Mattersey Sand Quarry (disused)
Antcliff Plantation
Wild Goose Farm
North View
Ling Hurst
Young Plantation
Neat Holme Road
Cross Lane
MATTERSEY RD
Loundfield Farm
THE PADDOCKS
PINFOLD CL
TOWN ST
LITTLE TOP LA
Highfield Farm
Highfield House
DANESHILL RD
4
89
3
88
2
87
1
86
68
69
70

19
29

12
22

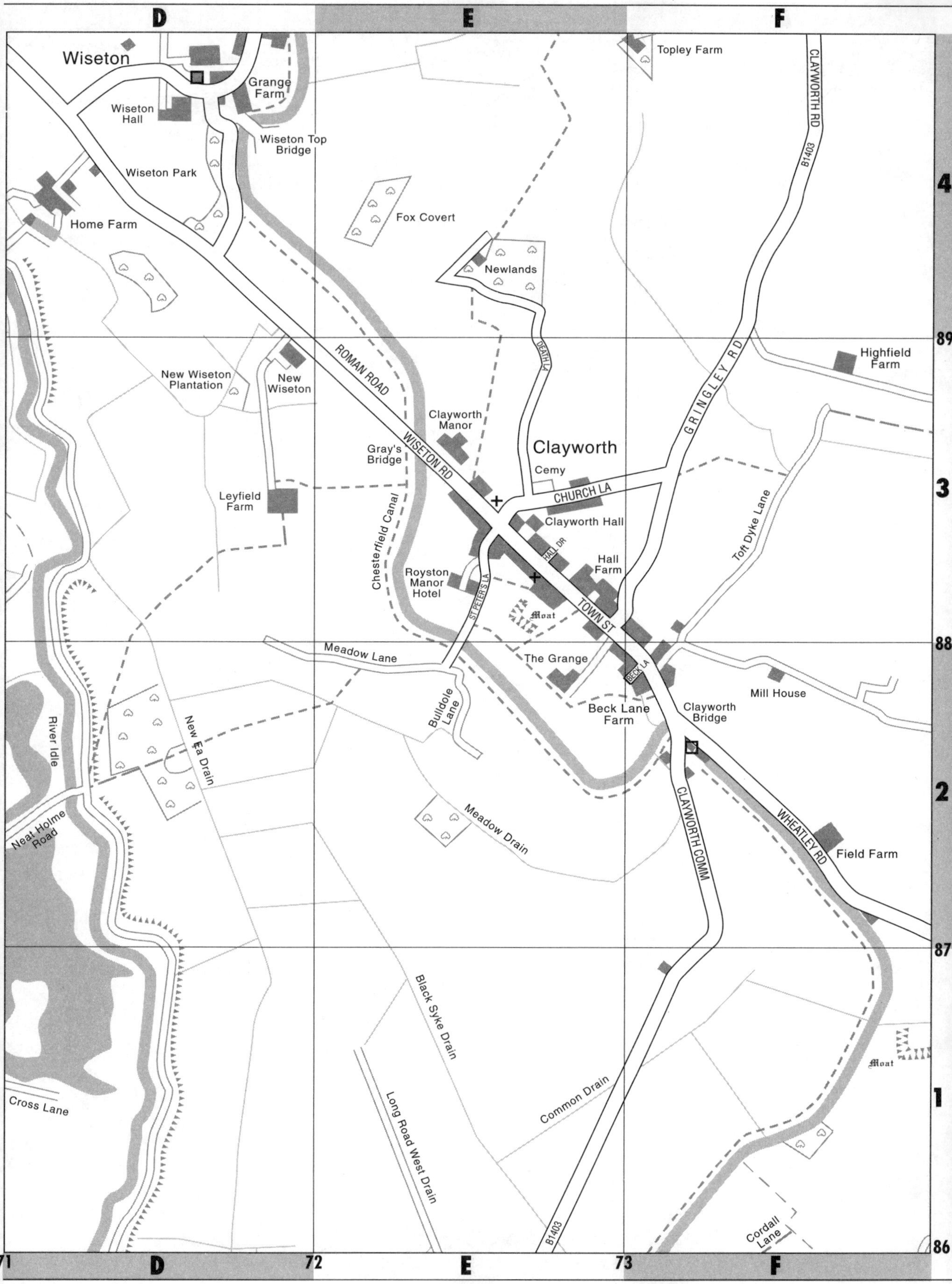
D
E
F
Wiseton
Grange Farm
Wiseton Hall
Wiseton Top Bridge
Wiseton Park
Home Farm
Topley Farm
CLAYWORTH RD
B1403
Fox Covert
Newlands
DEATH LA
ROMAN ROAD
New Wiseton Plantation
New Wiseton
Highfield Farm
GRINGLEY RD
Clayworth Manor
Clayworth
Gray's Bridge
WISETON RD
Cemy
CHURCH LA
Leyfield Farm
Chesterfield Canal
Clayworth Hall
HALL DR
Toft Dyke Lane
Hall Farm
Royston Manor Hotel
ST PETER'S LA
Moat
TOWN ST
Meadow Lane
The Grange
BECK LA
Mill House
Bulldole Lane
Beck Lane Farm
Clayworth Bridge
New Ea Drain
River Idle
Meadow Drain
CLAYWORTH COMM
WHEATLEY RD
Field Farm
Neat Holme Road
Black Syke Drain
Moat
Cross Lane
Long Road West Drain
Common Drain
B1403
Cordall Lane
4
89
3
88
2
87
1
86
71
72
73

21
13

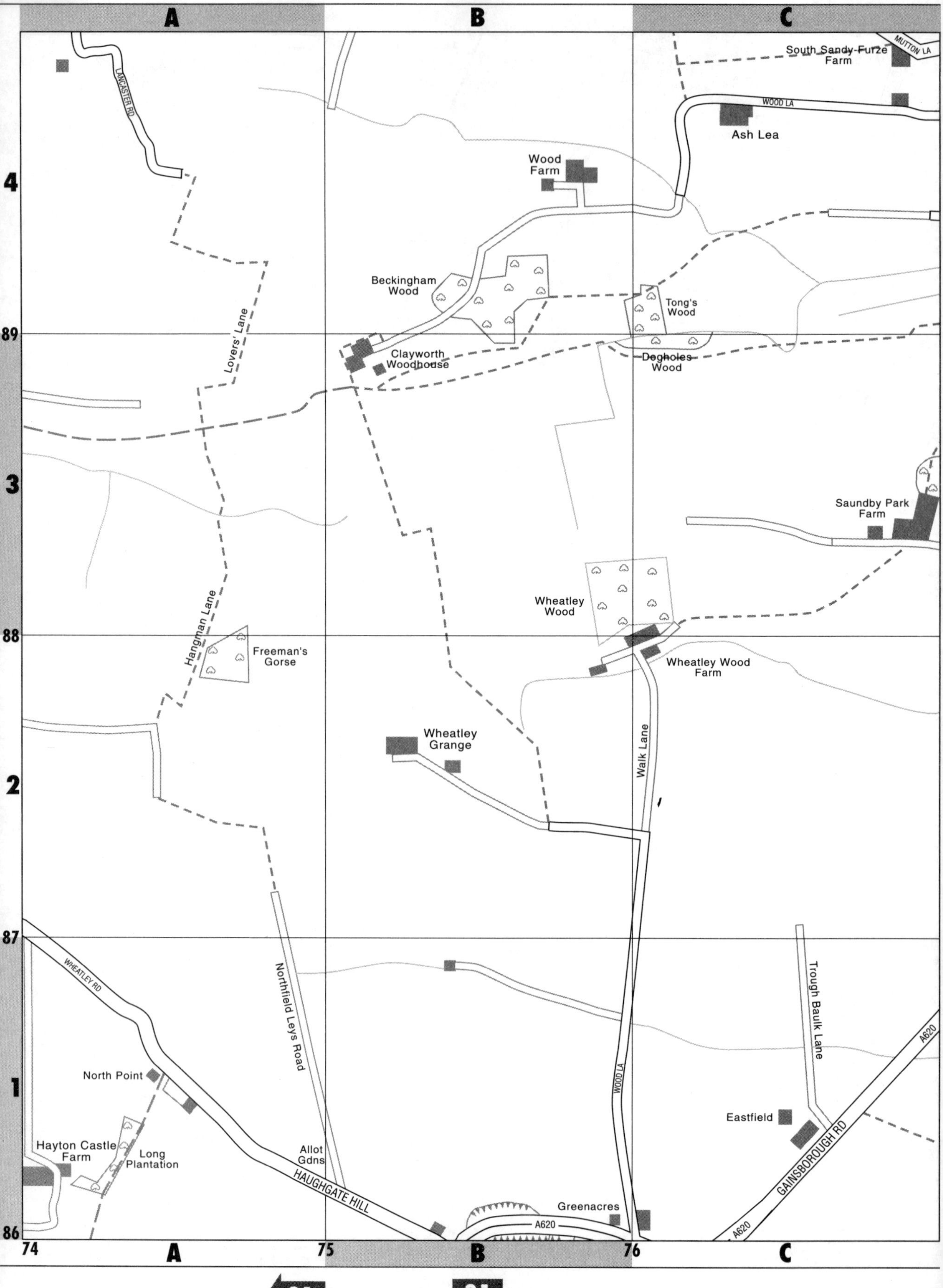
A
B
C
MUTTON LA
South Sandy-Furze Farm
WOOD LA
Ash Lea
LANCASTER RD
Wood Farm
4
Beckingham Wood
Tong's Wood
89
Lovers' Lane
Clayworth Woodhouse
Degholes Wood
3
Saundby Park Farm
Hangman Lane
Wheatley Wood
88
Freeman's Gorse
Wheatley Wood Farm
Wheatley Grange
Walk Lane
2
87
WHEATLEY RD
Northfield Leys Road
Trough Baulk Lane
A620
1
North Point
WOOD LA
Eastfield
GAINSBOROUGH RD
Hayton Castle Farm
Long Plantation
Allot Gdns
HAUGHGATE HILL
Greenacres
A620
A620
86
74
75
76

21
31

14
24

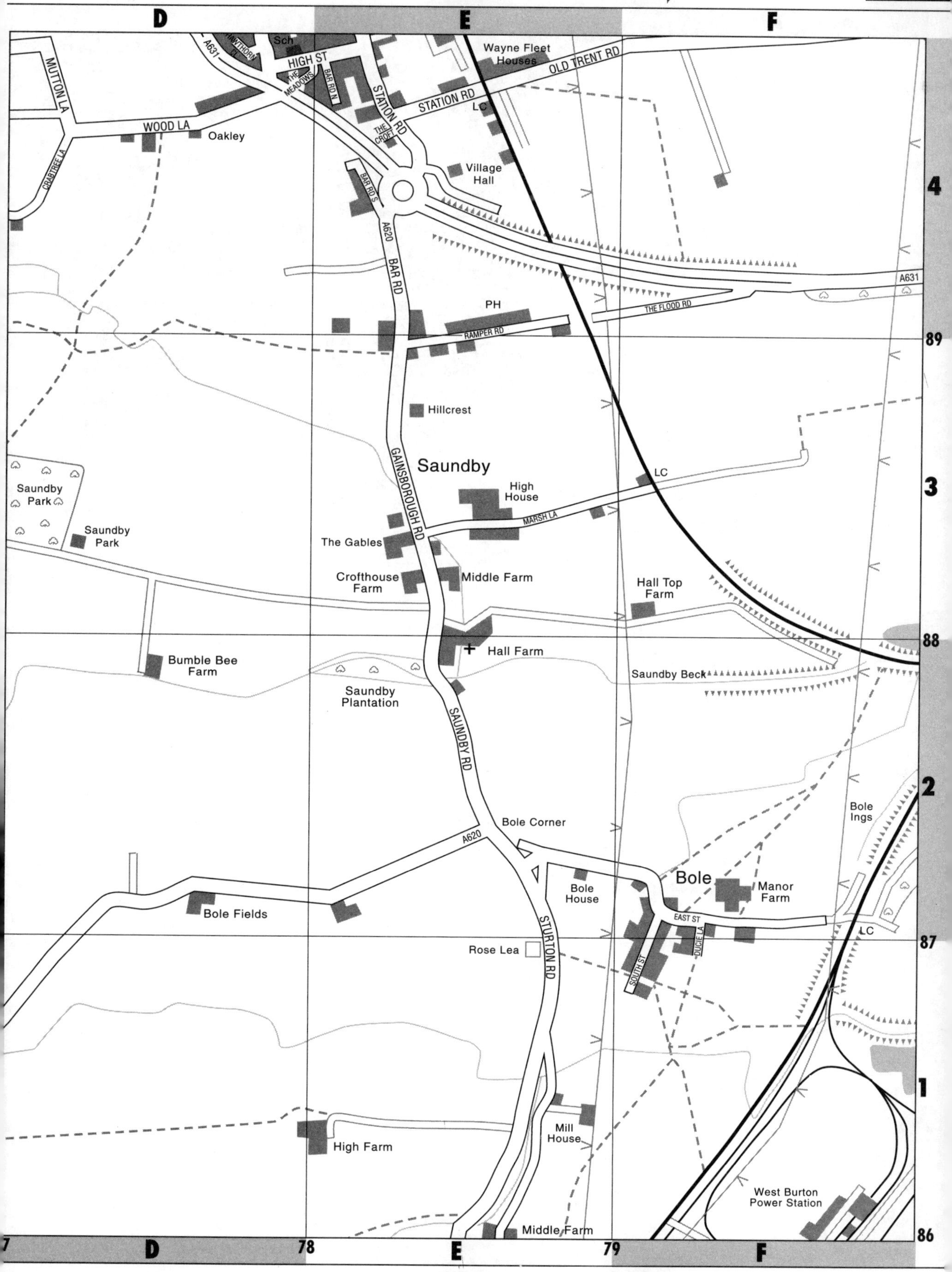
D
E
F
Sch
HIGH ST
A631
MUTTON LA
WOOD LA
Oakley
CRABTREE LA
THE MEADOWS
BAR RD N
STATION RD
THE CROFT
BAR RD S
Wayne Fleet Houses
OLD TRENT RD
LC
Village Hall
A620
BAR RD
PH
RAMPER RD
THE FLOOD RD
A631
Hillcrest
Saundby
GAINSBOROUGH RD
High House
MARSH LA
Saundby Park
Saundby Park
The Gables
Crofthouse Farm
Middle Farm
Hall Top Farm
Hall Farm
Bumble Bee Farm
Saundby Beck
Saundby Plantation
SAUNDBY RD
Bole Corner
Bole Ings
A620
Bole
Bole House
Manor Farm
EAST ST
Bole Fields
Rose Lea
STURTON RD
SOUTH ST
DUCIE LA
Mill House
High Farm
Middle Farm
West Burton Power Station
4
89
3
88
2
87
1
86
77
78
79
D
E
F

32
24

23 15

A
B
C
4
89
3
88
2
87
1
86
80
81
82
GAINSBOROUGH
Gainsborough Central Station
Lea Road Station
River Trent
Gainsborough Bridge
THE FLOOD RD
A631
Flood Arches
Beckingham Main Drain
Moat
Dog Island
PH
Cemy
Offices
Wks
Guildhall
Liby
Sta Hill
BRIDGE ST
TRINITY ST
THORNDIKE WAY
MIDDLEFIELD LA
FOXBY LA
FOXBY HILL
LEA RD
Factory
Mill
LC
CARR LA
East Trent Junction
West Trent Junction
Long Bank
Saundby Beck
Humble Carr Lane
Humble Carr Drain
SUMMERGANGS LA
Brickyard Plantation
Warren Wood
Lea Wood Farm
MAYFLOWER CL
CAUSEWAY
Sewage Works
Bole Ings Drain
Bole Ings
Lea Marsh
Lea Marsh Drain
GREEN LA
GAINSBOROUGH RD
Lea
B1241
Lea Park
Sherriff's Walk
A156
River Road
Sch
1 PROSPECT TERR
2 WHEELDON ST
3 DICKENSON TERR
4 BRITANNIA TERR
5 HIGH ST
6 CLEVELAND ST
1 RUSKIN ST
2 DARWIN ST
3 WASHINGTON ST
MORLEY ST 1
BRIGHT ST 2
PARNELL ST 3

23 33

16
26

D
E
F
Miller Lands
Acorn Piece
Langold Holt
Woodland Farm
Buckwood Farm
ROTHERHAM BAULK
CHILTERN WAY 1
PENTLAND DR 2
HAMBLETON CT 3
LOWTHER SQ 4
CLEVELAND CL 5
BEVERLEY WLK 6
CHICHESTER WLK 7
CHEVIOT CT 8
MENDIP CT 9
CANTERBURY WLK 10
LICHFIELD WLK 11
COTSWOLD CT 12
A60
WEST VIEW
Costhorpe
Ingham Bungalows
LAWN RD
Trading Estate
NORTHUMBERLAND AVE
SUTHERLAND CL
HIGHFIELD VILLAS
WESTMORLAND DR
CUMBERLAND CL
DONCASTER RD
PH
LILAC GR
WILLOW AVE
LIME TREE AVE
SYCAMORE RD
HAWTHORN WAY
BEECH GR
KNATON RD
STEWART CL
STEWART RD
KINGSTON RD
LE BRUN SQ
BECKETT AVE
RAMSDEN CRES
QUEENS RD
DADLEY RD
NORTH WAY
MULBERRY CRES
LINDRICK CL
OXFORD RD
AMANDA AVE
Liby
LONG LA
WINDSOR GDNS
Schs
CARISBROOK RD
CRATHIE RD
CRAIGSTON RD
STIRLING DR
GLAMIS RD
PEMBROKE DR
RICHMOND RD
CONWAY DR
BALMORAL CL
STRATHAVON RD
STRATHMORE DR
KENILWORTH DR
WARWICK AVE
WINDSOR RD
ARUNDEL DR
Green Lane
WALLINGWELLS LA
Castle Garden
Wallingwells Wood
Carlton in Lindrick
Carlton Wood
Wallingwells
Wallingwells Hall
Owlands Wood
Wallingwells Park
Hollin Hills
CARLTON HALL LA
The Lawns
Mus
CHURCH LA
Carlton Lake
Corn Mill Farm
The Ashes
Holme Wood
South Carlton
Field House Farm
The Bottoms
Wks
Owlands Wood Dyke
Holme House Farm
Hardwick Ashes
OWDAY LA
Broom Farm
Woodsetts
Owday Wood
WORKSOP RD
The Homestead
Owday Plantation
Nab's Ashes Wood
Little Broom Wood
Rough Piece
Whipman Wood
Sand Hill Plantation
Cocked Hat Wood
CARLTON RD
WORKSOP RD
A57(T)
GATEFORD RD
Fox Covert
WOODSETTS LA
Ashes Wood
Dog Kennel Plantation
4
85
3
84
2
83
1
82
57
58

35
26

25
17

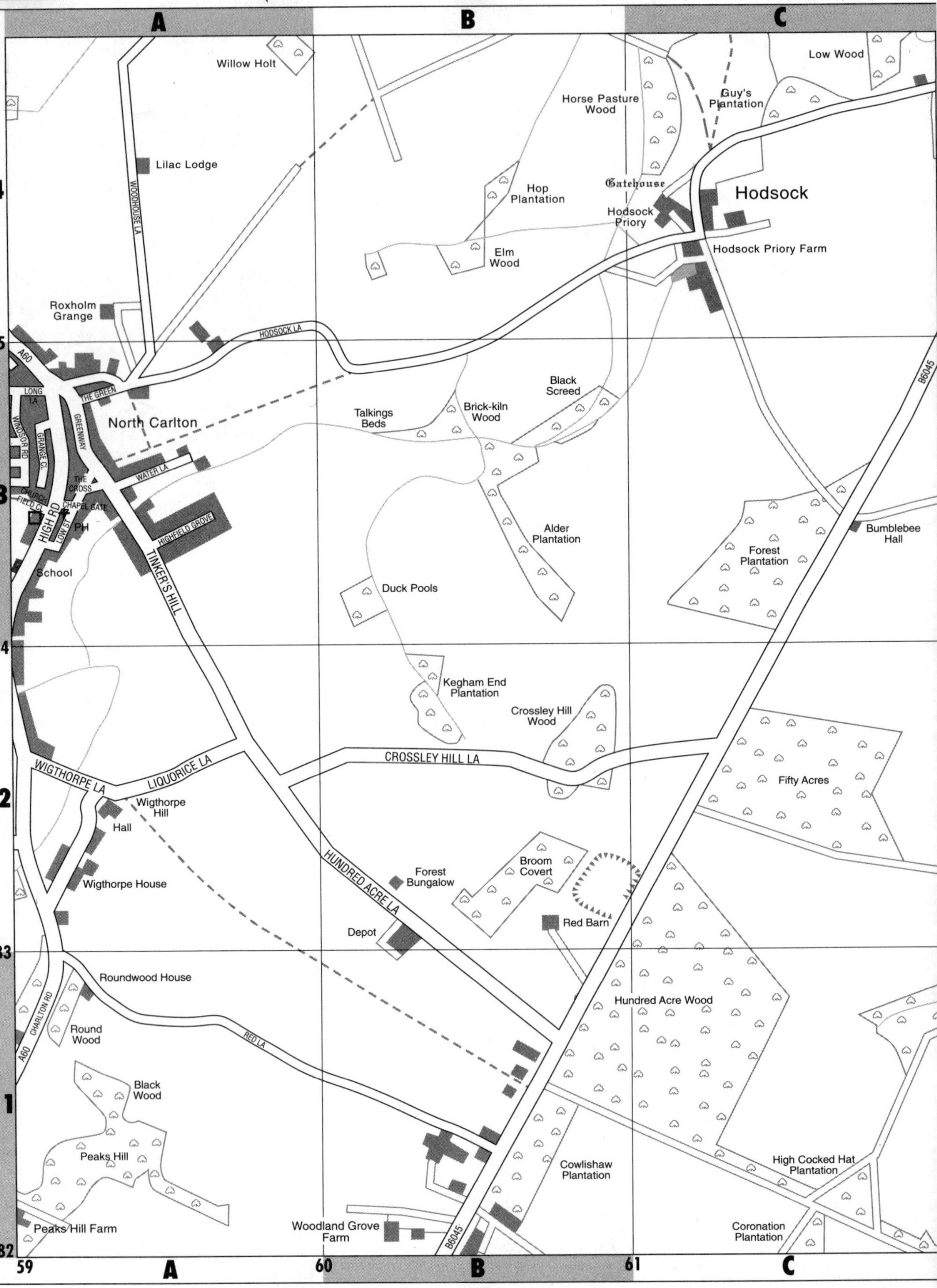
A
B
C
Willow Holt
Low Wood
Horse Pasture Wood
Guy's Plantation
Lilac Lodge
Hop Plantation
Gatehouse
Hodsock
Hodsock Priory
Hodsock Priory Farm
Elm Wood
WOODHOUSE LA
Roxholm Grange
HODSOCK LA
A60
LONG LA
THE GREEN
North Carlton
WINDSOR RD
GRANGE CL
GREENWAY
WATER LA
THE CROSS
CHURCH FIELD CL
HIGH RD
CHAPEL GATE
LOW ST
PH
HIGHFIELD GROVE
School
TINKER'S HILL
Talkings Beds
Brick-kiln Wood
Black Screed
B6045
Alder Plantation
Duck Pools
Forest Plantation
Bumblebee Hall
Kegham End Plantation
Crossley Hill Wood
CROSSLEY HILL LA
Fifty Acres
WIGTHORPE LA
LIQUORICE LA
Wigthorpe Hill
Hall
Wigthorpe House
HUNDRED ACRE LA
Forest Bungalow
Broom Covert
Red Barn
Depot
Roundwood House
Hundred Acre Wood
CHARLTON RD
Round Wood
RED LA
Black Wood
Peaks Hill
Cowlishaw Plantation
High Cocked Hat Plantation
Peaks Hill Farm
Woodland Grove Farm
Coronation Plantation
4
85
3
84
2
83
1
82
59
60
61

25
36

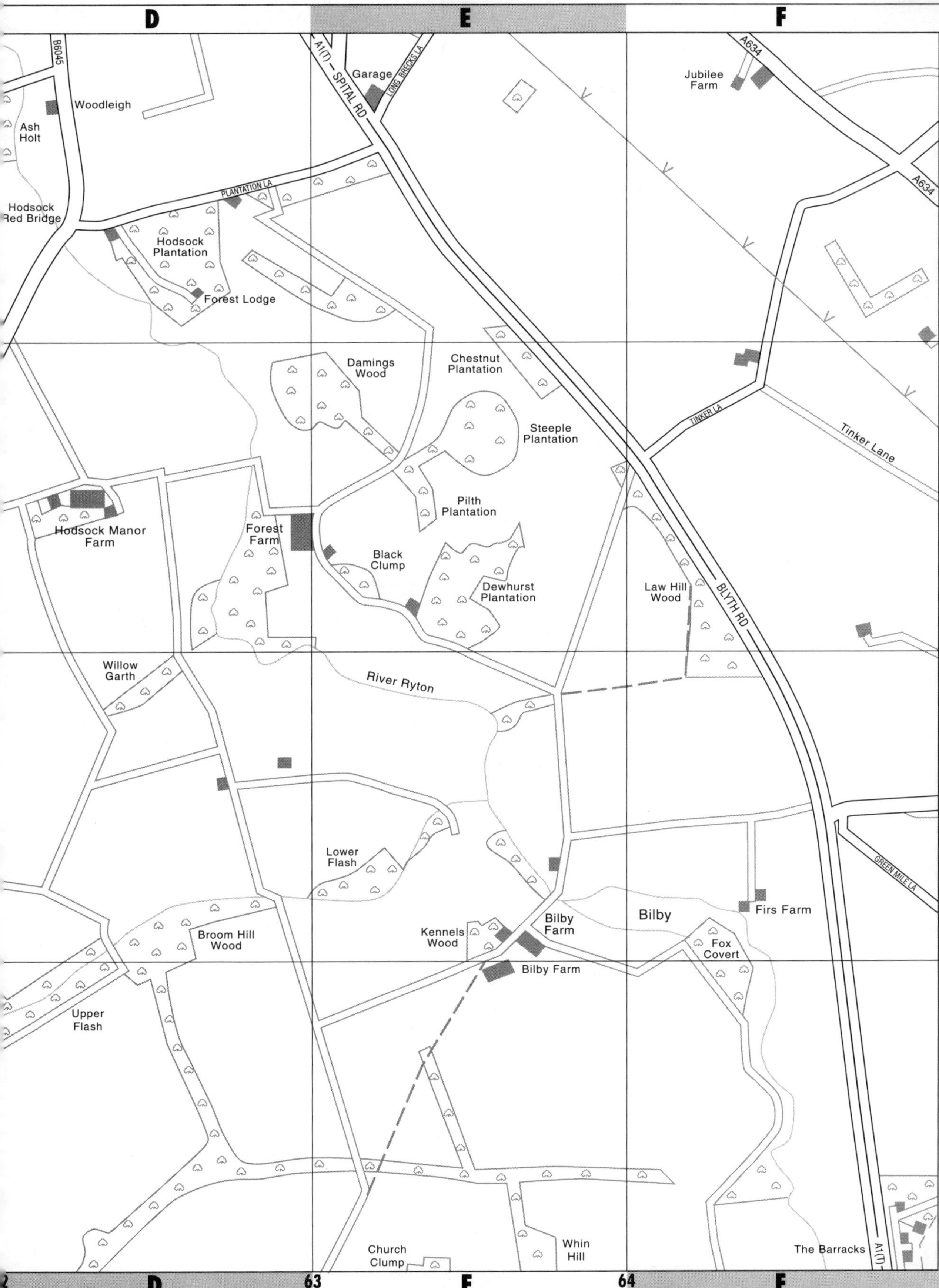
D
E
F
B6045
Woodleigh
Ash Holt
Hodsock Red Bridge
A1(T) – SPITAL RD
Garage
LONG BRECKS LA
A634
Jubilee Farm
A634
4
PLANTATION LA
Hodsock Plantation
Forest Lodge
85
Damings Wood
Chestnut Plantation
Steeple Plantation
TINKER LA
Tinker Lane
3
Hodsock Manor Farm
Forest Farm
Pilth Plantation
Black Clump
Dewhurst Plantation
Law Hill Wood
BLYTH RD
84
Willow Garth
River Ryton
2
GREEN MILE LA
Lower Flash
Bilby
Firs Farm
Broom Hill Wood
Kennels Wood
Bilby Farm
Fox Covert
Bilby Farm
83
Upper Flash
1
Church Clump
Whin Hill
The Barracks
A1(T)
82
D
63
E
64
F

27
19

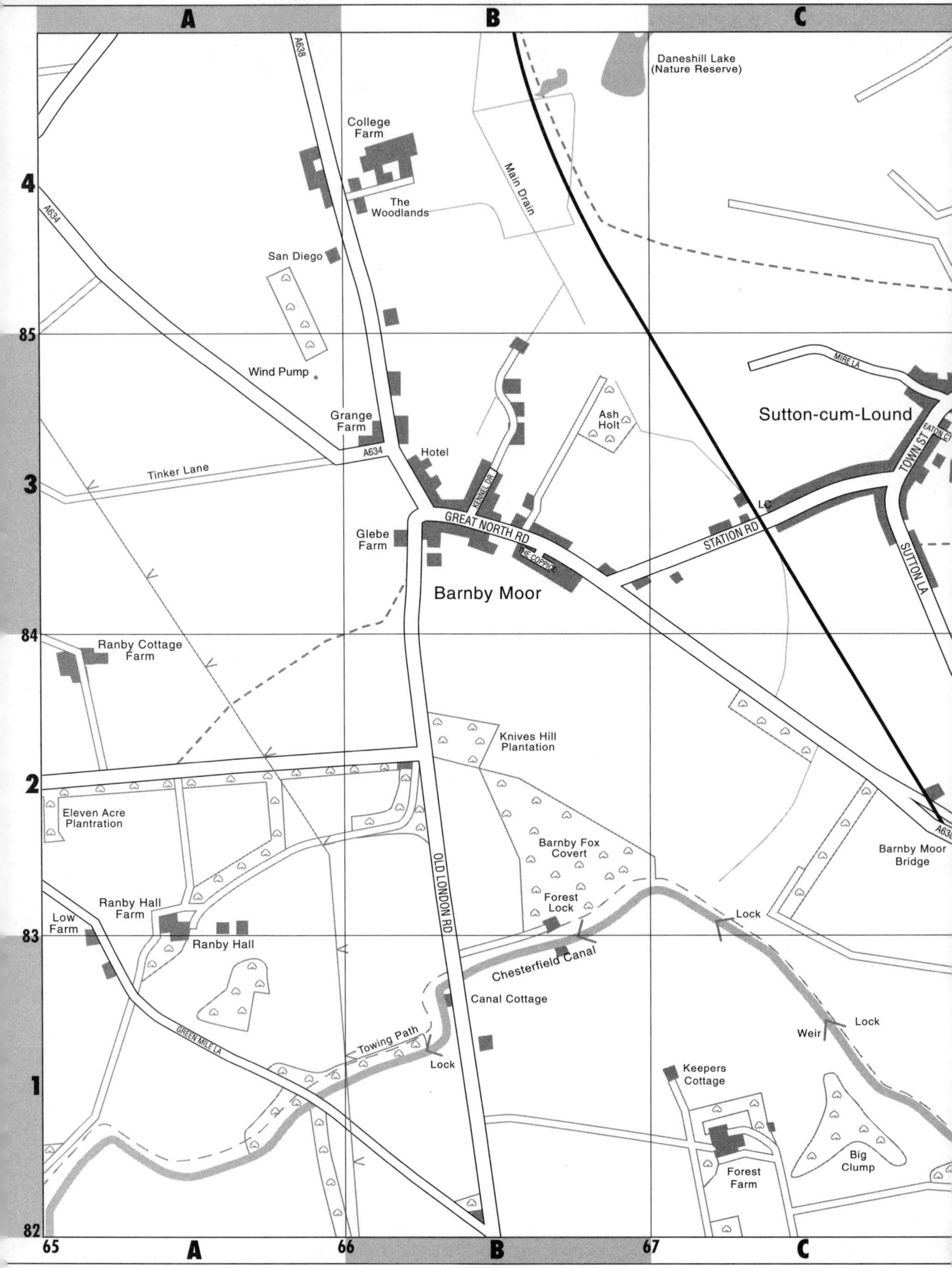
A
B
C
A638
A634
Daneshill Lake
(Nature Reserve)
College
Farm
The
Woodlands
Main Drain
San Diego
4
85
Wind Pump
Grange
Farm
A634
Hotel
Tinker Lane
Ash
Holt
Sutton-cum-Lound
MIRE LA
TOWN ST
EATON CT
3
KENNEL DR
GREAT NORTH RD
LC
STATION RD
Glebe
Farm
THE COPPICE
SUTTON LA
Barnby Moor
84
Ranby Cottage
Farm
Knives Hill
Plantation
2
Eleven Acre
Plantration
Barnby Fox
Covert
Barnby Moor
Bridge
A638
OLD LONDON RD
Ranby Hall
Farm
Forest
Lock
Low
Farm
Lock
Ranby Hall
83
Chesterfield Canal
Canal Cottage
Lock
Weir
GREEN MILE LA
Towing Path
Lock
Keepers
Cottage
1
Forest
Farm
Big
Clump
82
65
A
66
B
67
C

27
38

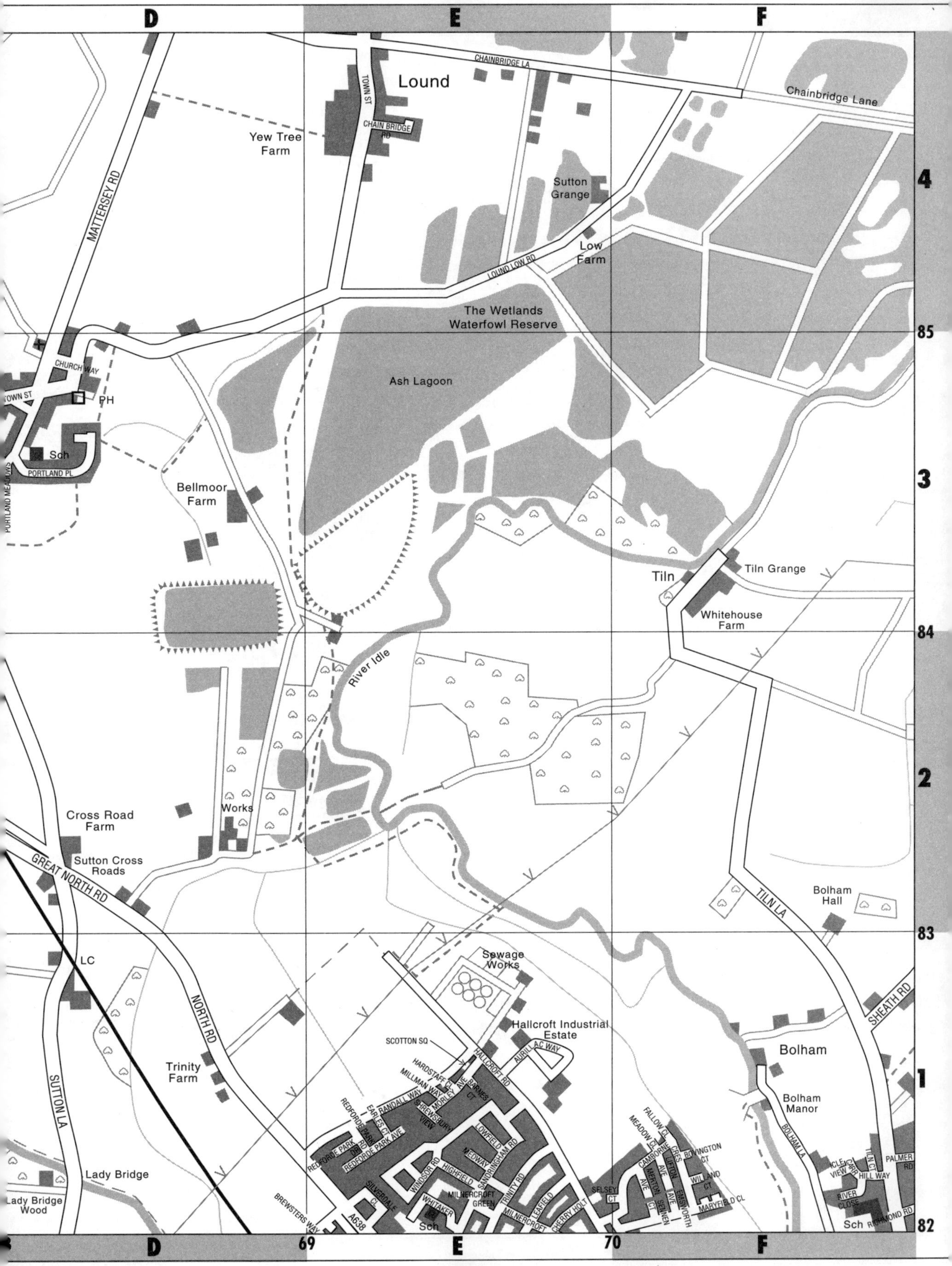
D
E
F
Lound
Chainbridge Lane
CHAINBRIDGE LA
TOWN ST
CHAIN BRIDGE RD
Yew Tree Farm
MATTERSEY RD
Sutton Grange
Low Farm
LOUND LOW RD
The Wetlands Waterfowl Reserve
Ash Lagoon
CHURCH WAY
TOWN ST
PH
Sch
PORTLAND PL
PORTLAND MEADOWS
Bellmoor Farm
Tiln
Tiln Grange
Whitehouse Farm
River Idle
Cross Road Farm
Works
Sutton Cross Roads
GREAT NORTH RD
Bolham Hall
TILN LA
LC
Sewage Works
NORTH RD
Hallcroft Industrial Estate
SHEATH RD
Bolham
Bolham Manor
Trinity Farm
SUTTON LA
Lady Bridge
Lady Bridge Wood
BOLHAM LA
A638
Sch
4
85
3
84
2
83
1
82
69
70

29 21

A B C
4 3 2 1
85 84 83 82
71 72 73
Chainbridge Lane
River Idle
Folly Dyke
Old Ea Drain
Tiln Holt
Guns Beck
Meadow Lane
Scotter Lane
Church Lane
Church Bridge
Hayton
Townend Bridge
B1403
BURNTLEYS RD
Bridge Farm
PH
MAIN ST
TCB
Lovers' Walk
TOPYARD LA
CHURCH LA
VICARAGE DR
Cordall Lane
Hollinhill Lane
Goit Lane
Hangingside Lane
A620
Hill Top Farm
CLARBOROUGH HILL
Clarborough
PH
SMEATH LA
BROAD GORES
PEAR TREE CL
GILL GREEN WLK
HILLVIEW CRES
Sch
HOWBECK LA
ST JOHN'S DR
SOUTH VIEW DR
BIG LA
Markfield Farm
Chesterfield Canal
SMEATH RD
Barcroft Lane
CHURCH LA
Sch
Works
Church Farm
WHINLEYS RD
Bolham Farm
Bolham Cottage Farm
Clarborough Hall
BONEMILL LA
Bonemill Farm
Meadow Farm
The Baulk
Moorgate Farm
Longholme Farm
Welham
Pinfolds Farm
Market Hill
Whitsunday Pie Lock
A620
WELHAM RD
DURHAM GR
PALMER RD
CORNWALL RD
WINSTON GR
BIGSBY RD
THE DRIVE
PARK LA
LONGHOLME RD
RICHMOND RD
ELMWOOD CL
PARK LA

29 40

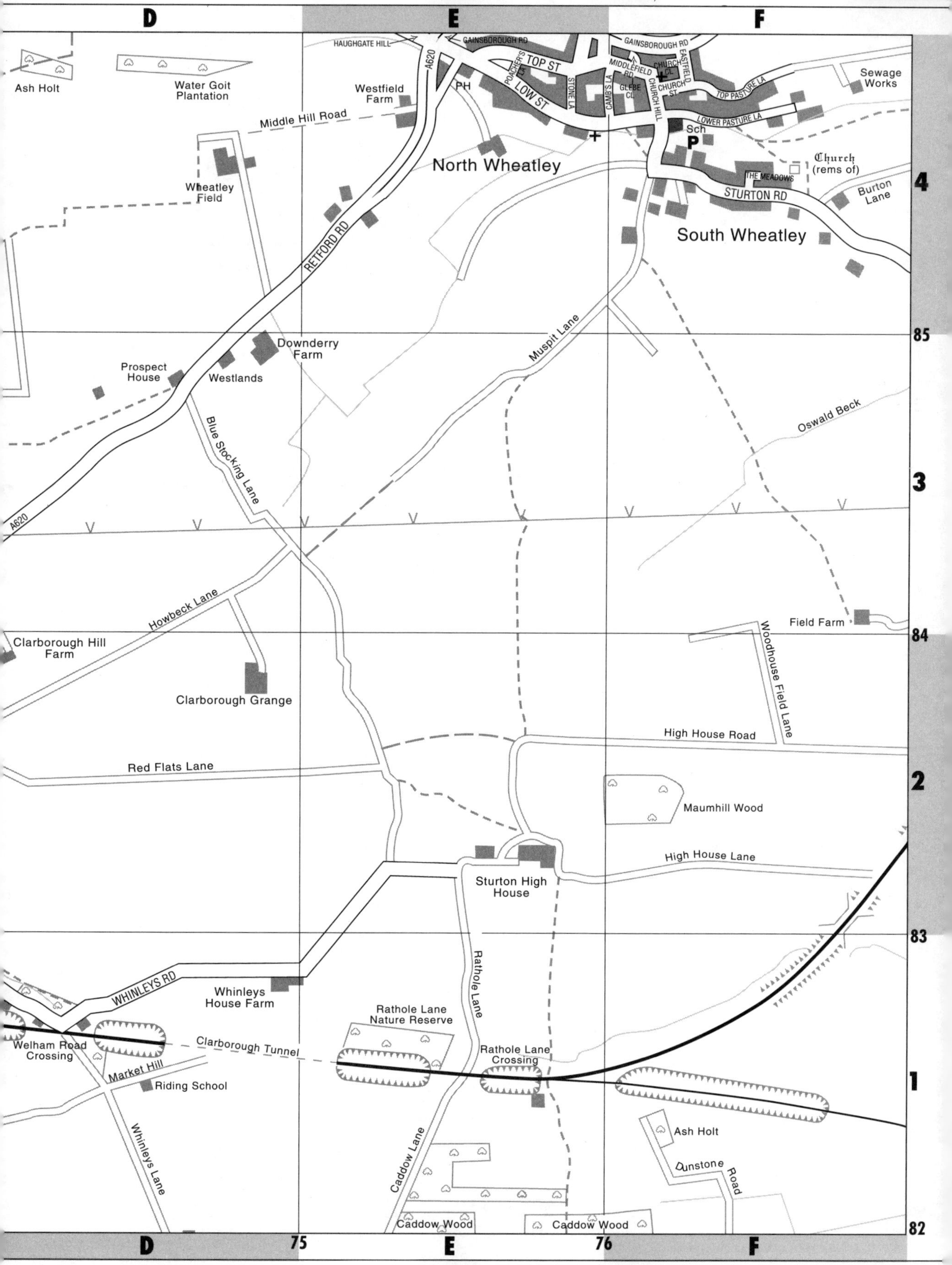
D
E
F
Ash Holt
Water Goit Plantation
Westfield Farm
Middle Hill Road
Wheatley Field
North Wheatley
South Wheatley
Sewage Works
Church (rems of)
Burton Lane
HAUGHGATE HILL
GAINSBOROUGH RD
TOP ST
LOW ST
STONE LA
CAMB'S LA
MIDDLEFIELD RD
GLEBE CL
CHURCH HILL
CHURCH CL
CHURCH ST
EASTFIELD
TOP PASTURE LA
LOWER PASTURE LA
THE MEADOWS
STURTON RD
Sch
PH
A620
RETFORD RD
Downderry Farm
Prospect House
Westlands
Muspit Lane
Oswald Beck
Blue Stocking Lane
Howbeck Lane
Clarborough Hill Farm
Clarborough Grange
Field Farm
Woodhouse Field Lane
High House Road
Red Flats Lane
Maumhill Wood
High House Lane
Sturton High House
Rathole Lane
WHINLEYS RD
Whinleys House Farm
Rathole Lane Nature Reserve
Welham Road Crossing
Clarborough Tunnel
Rathole Lane Crossing
Market Hill
Riding School
Whinleys Lane
Caddow Lane
Ash Holt
Dunstone Road
Caddow Wood
Caddow Wood
85
84
83
82
4
3
2
1
75
76

31
23

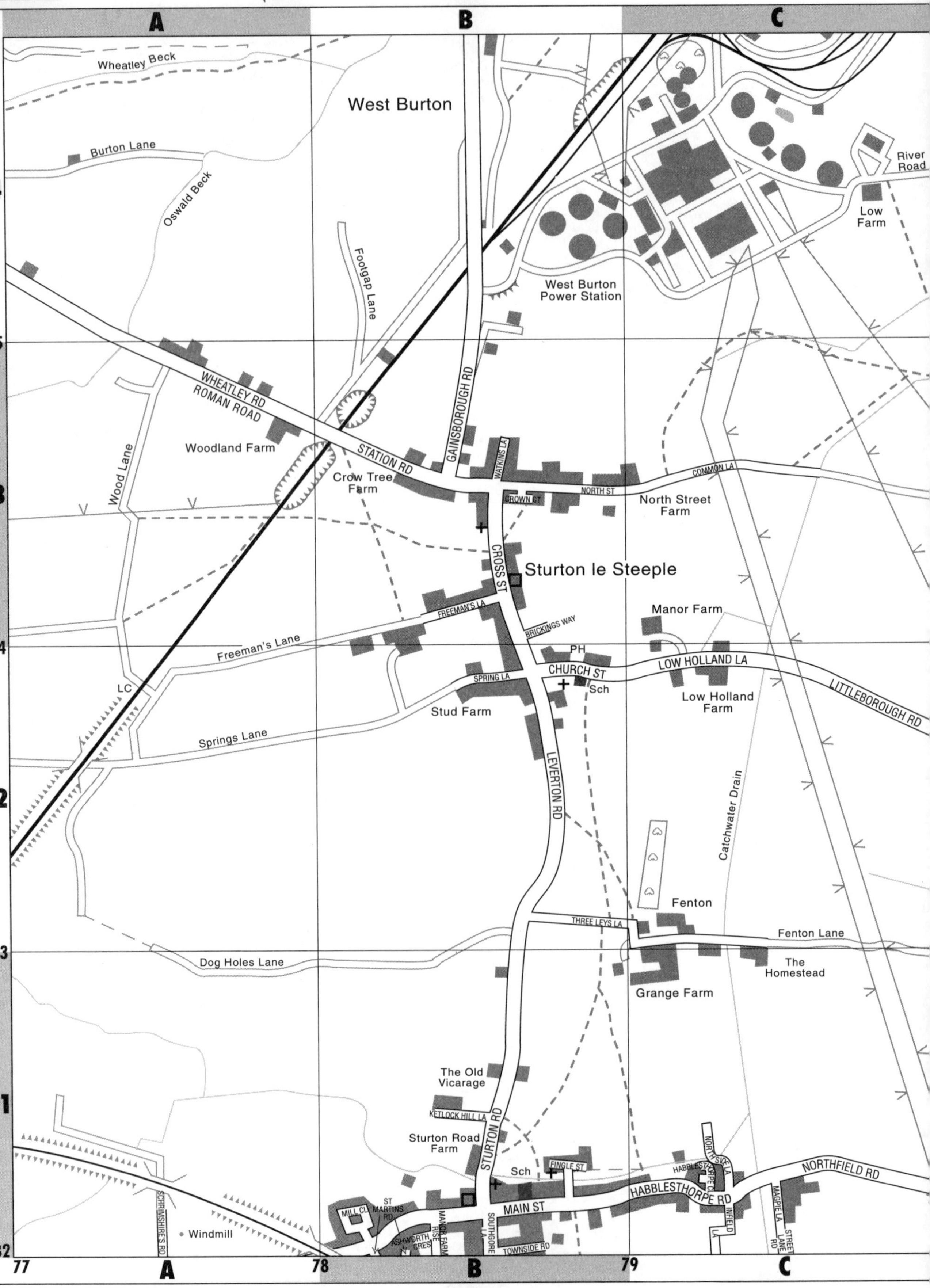
West Burton
Wheatley Beck
Burton Lane
Oswald Beck
Footgap Lane
West Burton Power Station
River Road
Low Farm
WHEATLEY RD
ROMAN ROAD
Woodland Farm
Wood Lane
STATION RD
Crow Tree Farm
GAINSBOROUGH RD
WATKINS LA
NORTH ST
COMMON LA
CROWN CT
North Street Farm
CROSS ST
Sturton le Steeple
Manor Farm
FREEMAN'S LA
Freeman's Lane
BRICKINGS WAY
PH
CHURCH ST
LOW HOLLAND LA
Sch
LITTLEBOROUGH RD
Low Holland Farm
SPRING LA
Stud Farm
LC
Springs Lane
LEVERTON RD
Catchwater Drain
Fenton
THREE LEYS LA
Fenton Lane
Dog Holes Lane
The Homestead
Grange Farm
The Old Vicarage
KETLOCK HILL LA
STURTON RD
Sturton Road Farm
Sch
FINGLE ST
NORTHSIDE LA
HABBLESTHORPE CL
NORTHFIELD RD
HABBLESTHORPE RD
MAIN ST
MILL CL
ST MARTINS RD
ASHWORTH CRES
MANOR FARM RISE
SOUTHGORE LA
TOWNSIDE RD
INFIELD LA
MAGPIE LA
STREET LANE RD
SCHRIMSHIRE'S RD
Windmill
A
B
C
4
85
3
84
2
83
1
82
77
78
79

31
42

D
E
F
4
3
2
1
85
84
83
82
81
River Road
Catchwater Drain
The Ferries
Burton Round
Ppg Sta
Knaith Reach
Lea Marshes Main Drain
GAINSBOROUGH RD A156
New Ings Drain
New Ings Lane
North End Lane
Out Ings
Ferry Lane
Cowpasture Lane
Mother Drain
Middle Lane
Knaith Hall
Remains of Priory
(Cistercian Nuns)
A156
Old Upper Ings Lane
Knaith Hall Lane
South End Lane
River Trent
Upper Ings
Upper Ings Lane
Long Farm Lane
Red Hill
LITTLEBOROUGH RD
Fenton Gorse
Littleborough
Cottage
Fenton Lane
THORNHILL LA
White Bridge
Littleborough
SEGELOCVM
ROMAN
SETTLEMENT
Trent Bank
Farm
Ferry Farm
MARSH LA
NORTHFIELD RD
Smythe
Lane
NORTH LEYS
RD

A
B
C
4
81
3
80
2
79
1
78
53
54
55
Fan Field
Dismtd Rly
Fan Field Farm
Quarry (dis)
Brancliffe Grange
Canal Feeder
Low Spring Wood
Potters Nook Bridge
Sch
Turnerwood Bridge
Broad Wood
Towing Path
Old Spring Wood
Chesterfield Canal (disused)
Turnerwood
Shireoaks Station
SHIREOAKS COMM
BRANCLIFFE LA
CARTWRIGHT ST
GLENTHORN CL
LEEDS RD
CORNWALL RD
WOODSIDE RD
WALNUT AVE
CHERRY TREE AVE
PEMBROKE RD
YORK PL
LC
BACK LA
BETHEL TERR
SHIREOAKS ROW
Allot Gdns
Hatfield Farm
Colliery
Shireoaks
LITTLE LA
Bondhay Dyke
Bottom Farm
THORPE LA
SHIREOAKS RD
Thorpe Salvin
Moat
Shireoaks Park
Ford
Netherthorpe
Lob Wells Wood
Top Farm
The Hall
Netherthorpe Airfield
Oak Wood
Top Hall
COMMON RD
Shireoaks Park Wood
SPRING LA
NETHER THORPE RD
Holme Carr Wood
WHITWELL RD
Thorpe Common
Holme Carr
DUMB HALL LA
Scratts Wood
Whitwell Road
Silver Birches
STEETLEY LA
Works
SCRATTA LA
Dumb Hall
Armstrong Quarry
Steetley Farm Cottages
Firbeck Farm
Firbeck House
Steetley House
Firbeck Common
FEATHERBED LA
Darfoulds
Firbeck Lane
A619
Harness Grove
Arrow Farm

25
36

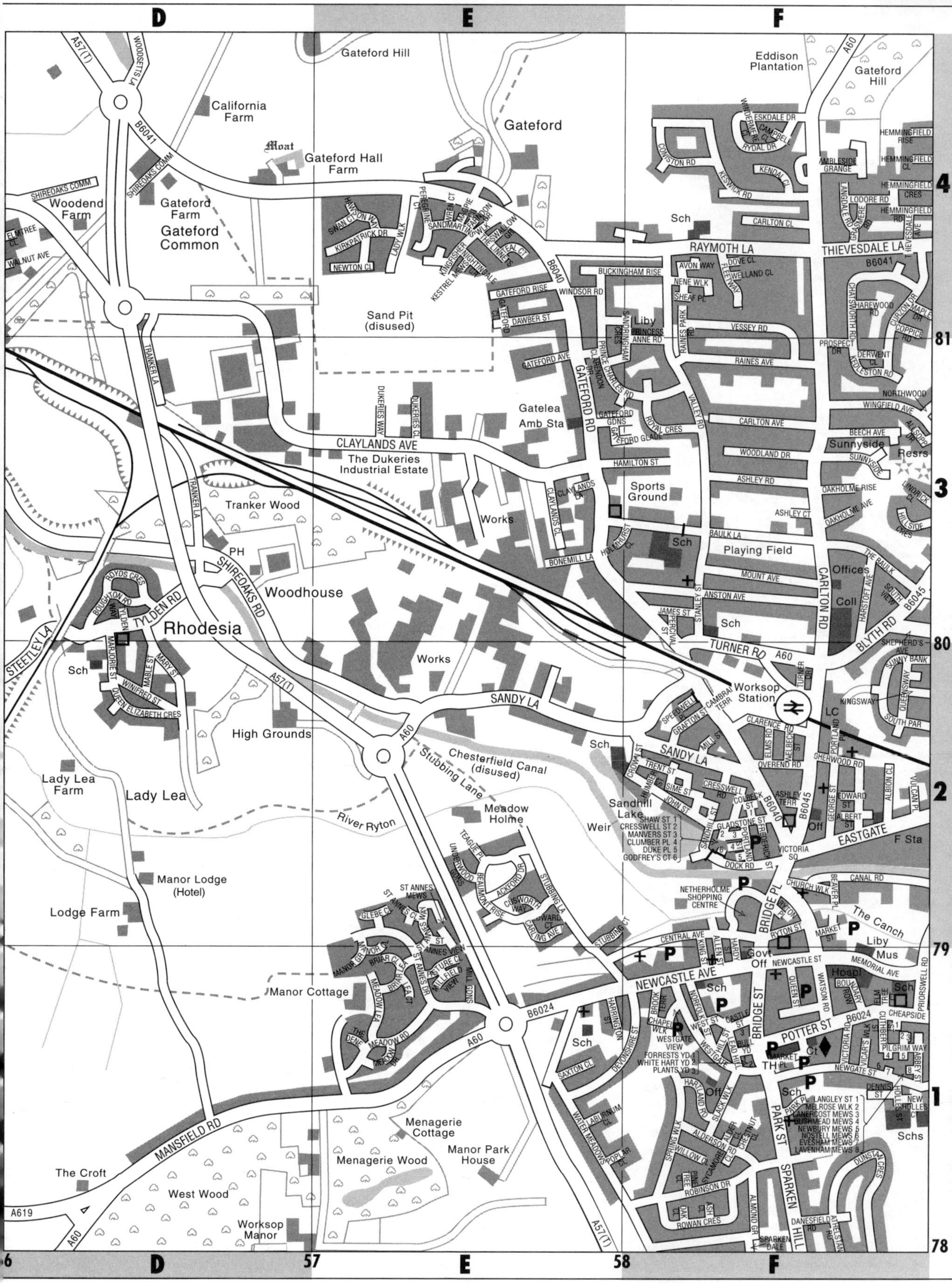
D
E
F
4
81
3
80
2
79
1
78
57
58
Gateford Hill
Eddison Plantation
Gateford Hill
California Farm
Gateford
Moat
Gateford Hall Farm
Woodend Farm
Gateford Farm
Gateford Common
Sand Pit (disused)
Liby
Gatelea
Amb Sta
Sports Ground
The Dukeries Industrial Estate
Tranker Wood
Works
PH
Woodhouse
Playing Field
Offices
Coll
Sch
Rhodesia
Works
Worksop Station
High Grounds
Chesterfield Canal (disused)
Stubbing Lane
Lady Lea Farm
Lady Lea
Meadow Holme
Sandhill Lake
Weir
River Ryton
F Sta
Manor Lodge (Hotel)
Lodge Farm
NETHERHOLME SHOPPING CENTRE
The Canch
Liby
Mus
Govt Off
Hospl
Manor Cottage
Menagerie Cottage
Menagerie Wood
Manor Park House
The Croft
West Wood
Worksop Manor
Schs
MANSFIELD RD
A619
A60
A57(T)
B6041
B6040
B6024
B6045
CLAYLANDS AVE
SANDY LA
SHIREOAKS RD
TYLDEN RD
RAYMOTH LA
THIEVESDALE LA
CARLTON RD
GATEFORD RD
TURNER RD
BLYTH RD
EASTGATE
NEWCASTLE AVE
POTTER ST
BRIDGE ST
PARK ST
SPARKEN HILL
SHAW ST 1
CRESSWELL ST 2
MANVERS ST 3
CLUMBER PL 4
DUKE PL 5
GODFREY'S CT 6
FORRESTS YD 1
WHITE HART YD 2
PLANTS YD 3
LANGLEY ST 1
MELROSE WLK 2
LANERCOST MEWS 3
BUSHMEAD MEWS 4
NEWBURY MEWS 5
NOSTELL MEWS 6
EVESHAM MEWS 7
LAVENHAM MEWS 8

46
36

35
26

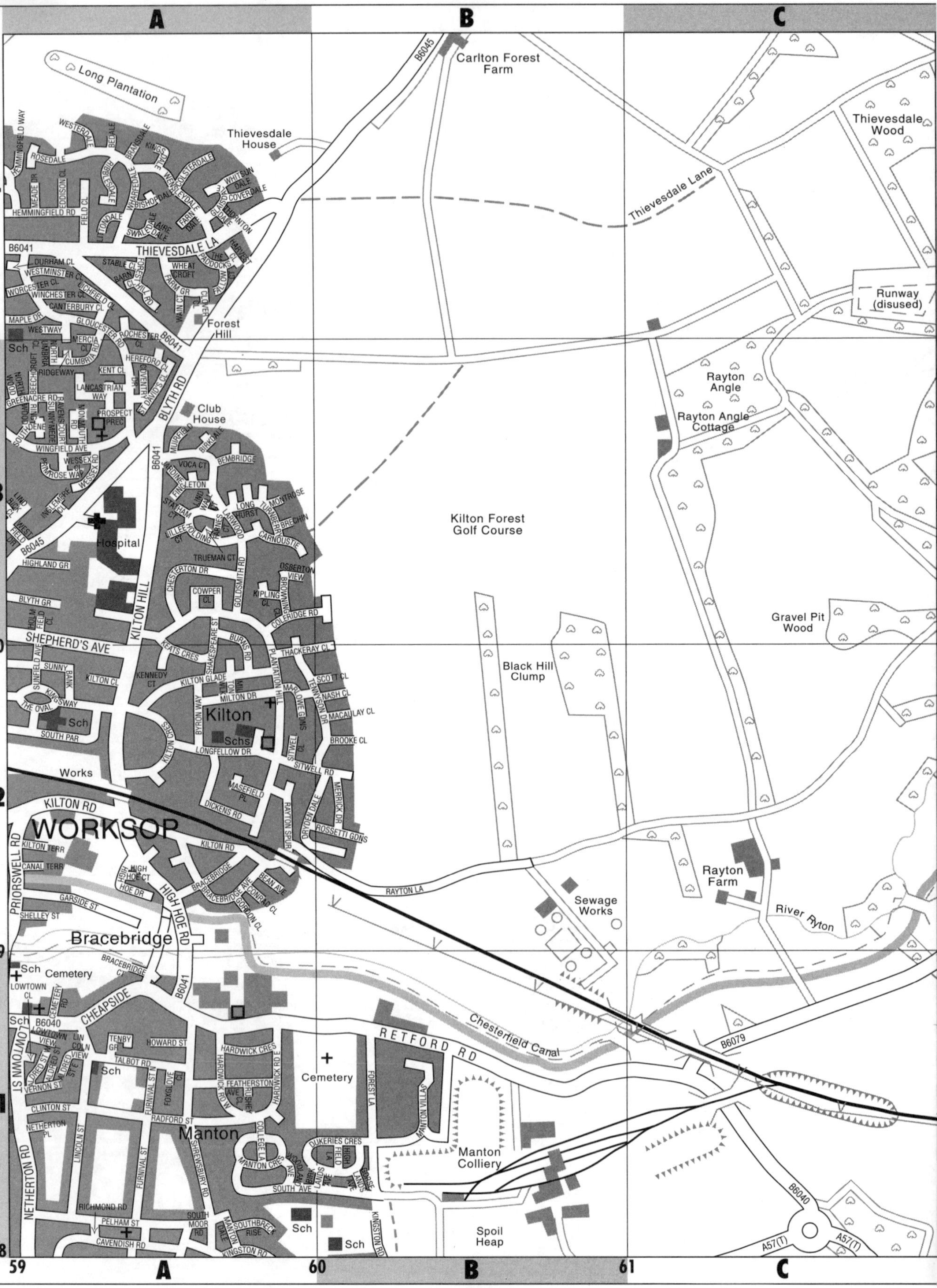
A
B
C
Long Plantation
Carlton Forest Farm
Thievesdale House
Thievesdale Wood
Thievesdale Lane
Runway (disused)
THIEVESDALE LA
Forest Hill
B6041
B6045
BLYTH RD
Club House
Rayton Angle
Rayton Angle Cottage
Hospital
Kilton Forest Golf Course
Gravel Pit Wood
KILTON HILL
SHEPHERD'S AVE
Black Hill Clump
Kilton
Schs
Sch
Works
KILTON RD
WORKSOP
RAYTON LA
Rayton Farm
Sewage Works
River Ryton
HIGH HOE RD
Bracebridge
Cemetery
CHEAPSIDE
B6040
RETFORD RD
Chesterfield Canal
B6079
Manton
Manton Colliery
Spoil Heap
B6040
A57(T)
4
81
3
80
2
79
1
78
59
60
61

35
47

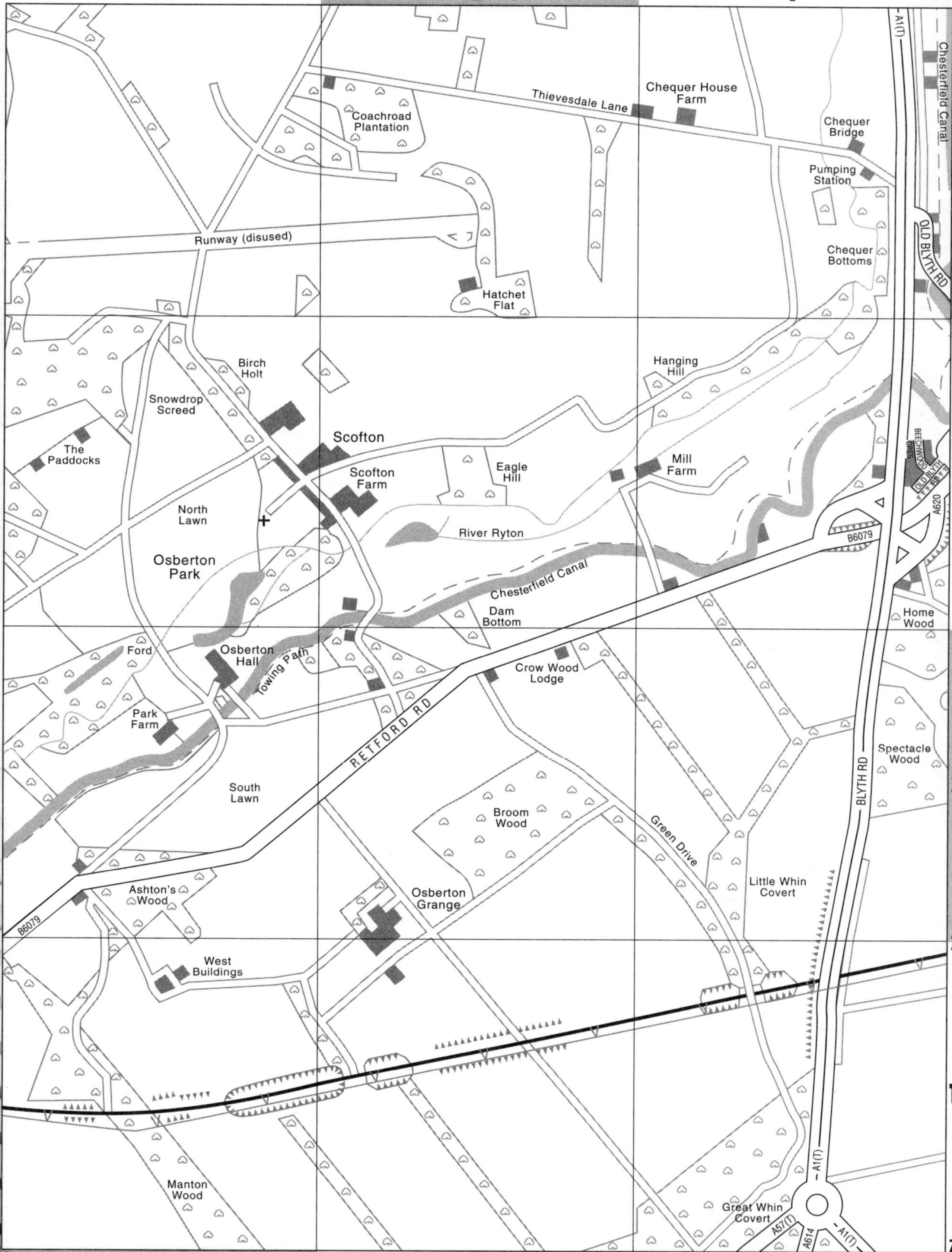
D
E
F
Thievesdale Lane
Chequer House Farm
Coachroad Plantation
Chequer Bridge
Chesterfield Canal
Pumping Station
Runway (disused)
OLD BLYTH RD
Chequer Bottoms
Hatchet Flat
81
Birch Holt
Hanging Hill
Snowdrop Screed
Scofton
The Paddocks
Scofton Farm
Eagle Hill
Mill Farm
BEECHWOOD GRES
OLD BLYTH RD
North Lawn
River Ryton
A620
B6079
Osberton Park
Chesterfield Canal
Dam Bottom
Home Wood
80
Ford
Osberton Hall
Towing Path
Crow Wood Lodge
Park Farm
RETFORD RD
Spectacle Wood
South Lawn
Broom Wood
Green Drive
BLYTH RD
Ashton's Wood
Osberton Grange
Little Whin Covert
B6079
West Buildings
79
Manton Wood
Great Whin Covert
A1(T)
A57(T)
A614
78
4
3
2
1
62
63
64

37
28

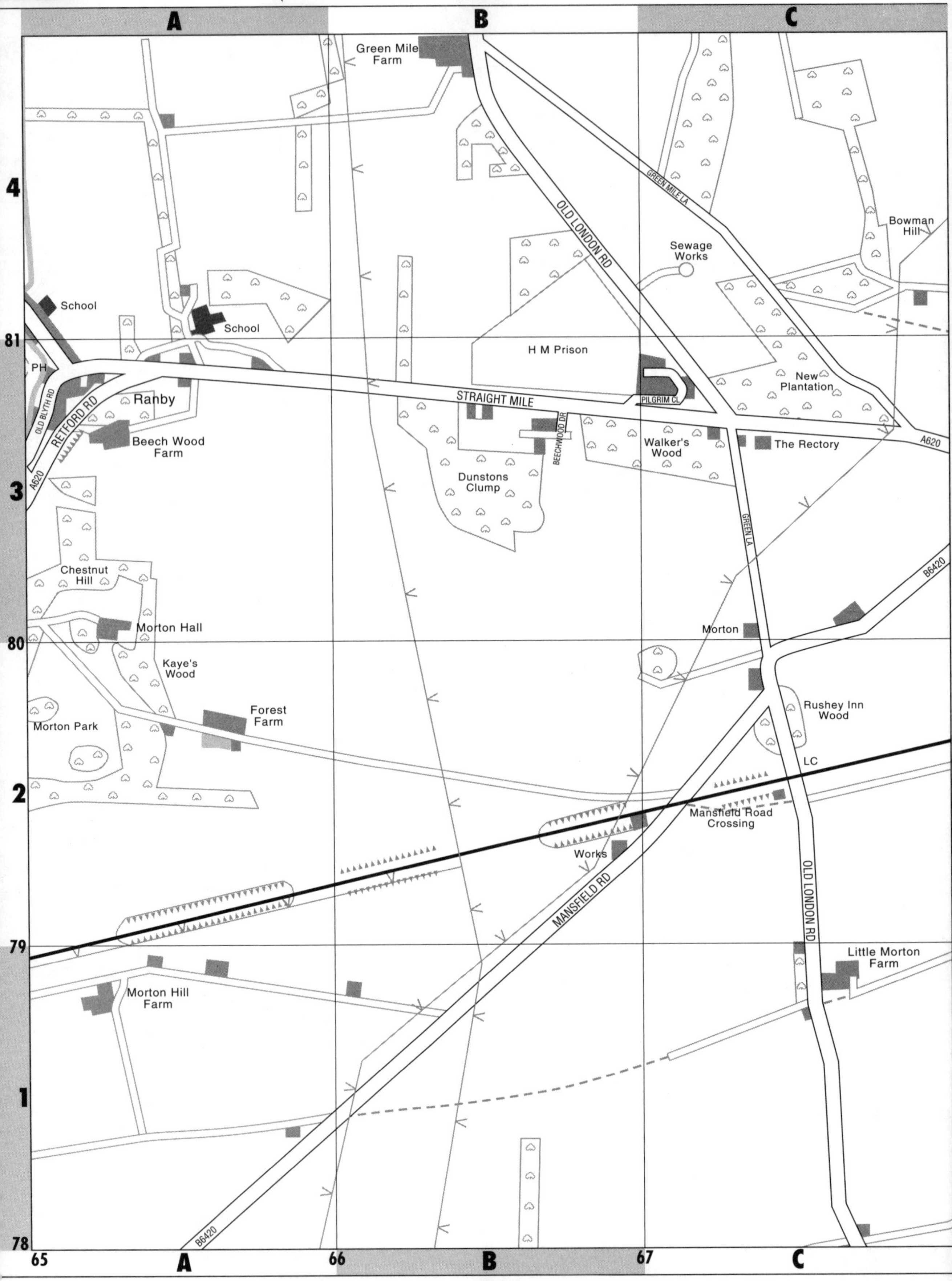
A
B
C
4
3
2
1
81
80
79
78
65
66
67
Green Mile Farm
School
School
PH
Ranby
OLD BLYTH RD
RETFORD RD
A620
Beech Wood Farm
STRAIGHT MILE
OLD LONDON RD
GREEN MILE LA
Sewage Works
Bowman Hill
H M Prison
PILGRIM CL
BEECHWOOD DR
New Plantation
Walker's Wood
The Rectory
A620
Dunstons Clump
GREEN LA
B6420
Chestnut Hill
Morton Hall
Morton
Kaye's Wood
Forest Farm
Morton Park
Rushey Inn Wood
LC
Mansfield Road Crossing
Works
MANSFIELD RD
OLD LONDON RD
Little Morton Farm
Morton Hill Farm
B6420

37
49

29 40

RETFORD
West Retford
South Retford
Ordsall
Thrumpton
Babworth
Babworth Home Farm
Babworth Park
Babworth Hall
Haygarth House
West Town Wood
Ordsall Hall
Water Works
Ash Holt
Great Morton
Whisker Hill
Retford Golf Course
Morton Grange
Breck Plantation
Fox Covert
Gate Inn (PH)
River Idle
Chesterfield Canal
NORTH RD
HOSPITAL RD
BABWORTH RD
ORDSALL RD
WEST CARR RD
OLLERTON RD
WEST HILL RD
HIGH ST
ALL HALLOWS ST
GOOSEMOOR LA
LONDON RD
ARLINGTON WAY
BRIDGEGATE
AMCOTT WAY
ALBERT RD
QUEEN ST
SUTTON LA
MANSFIELD RD
STRAIGHT MILE
Brecks Road


50 40

39 30

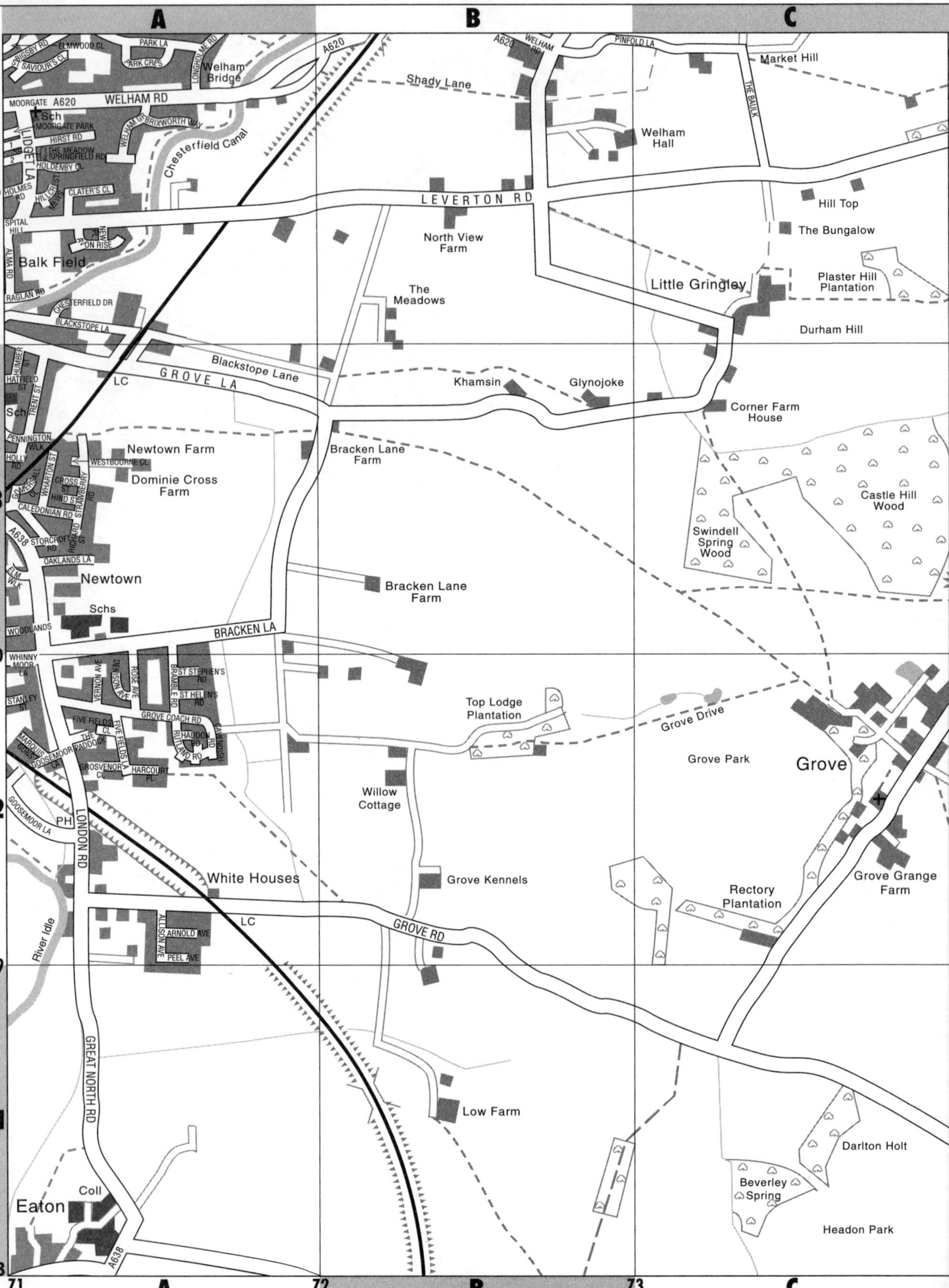

A
B
C
Welham Bridge
WELHAM RD
A620
Shady Lane
Chesterfield Canal
Welham Hall
Market Hill
PINFOLD LA
THE BAULK
LEVERTON RD
North View Farm
Hill Top
The Bungalow
Balk Field
The Meadows
Little Gringley
Plaster Hill Plantation
Durham Hill
BLACKSTOPE LA
Blackstope Lane
GROVE LA
LC
Khamsin
Glynojoke
Corner Farm House
Newtown Farm
Dominie Cross Farm
Bracken Lane Farm
Castle Hill Wood
Swindell Spring Wood
Newtown
Schs
Bracken Lane Farm
BRACKEN LA
Top Lodge Plantation
Grove Drive
Grove Park
Grove
Willow Cottage
White Houses
Grove Kennels
Rectory Plantation
Grove Grange Farm
GROVE RD
River Idle
LONDON RD
GREAT NORTH RD
Low Farm
Darlton Holt
Beverley Spring
Headon Park
Eaton
Coll
A638
4
81
3
80
2
79
1
78
71
72
73


39 51

31 42

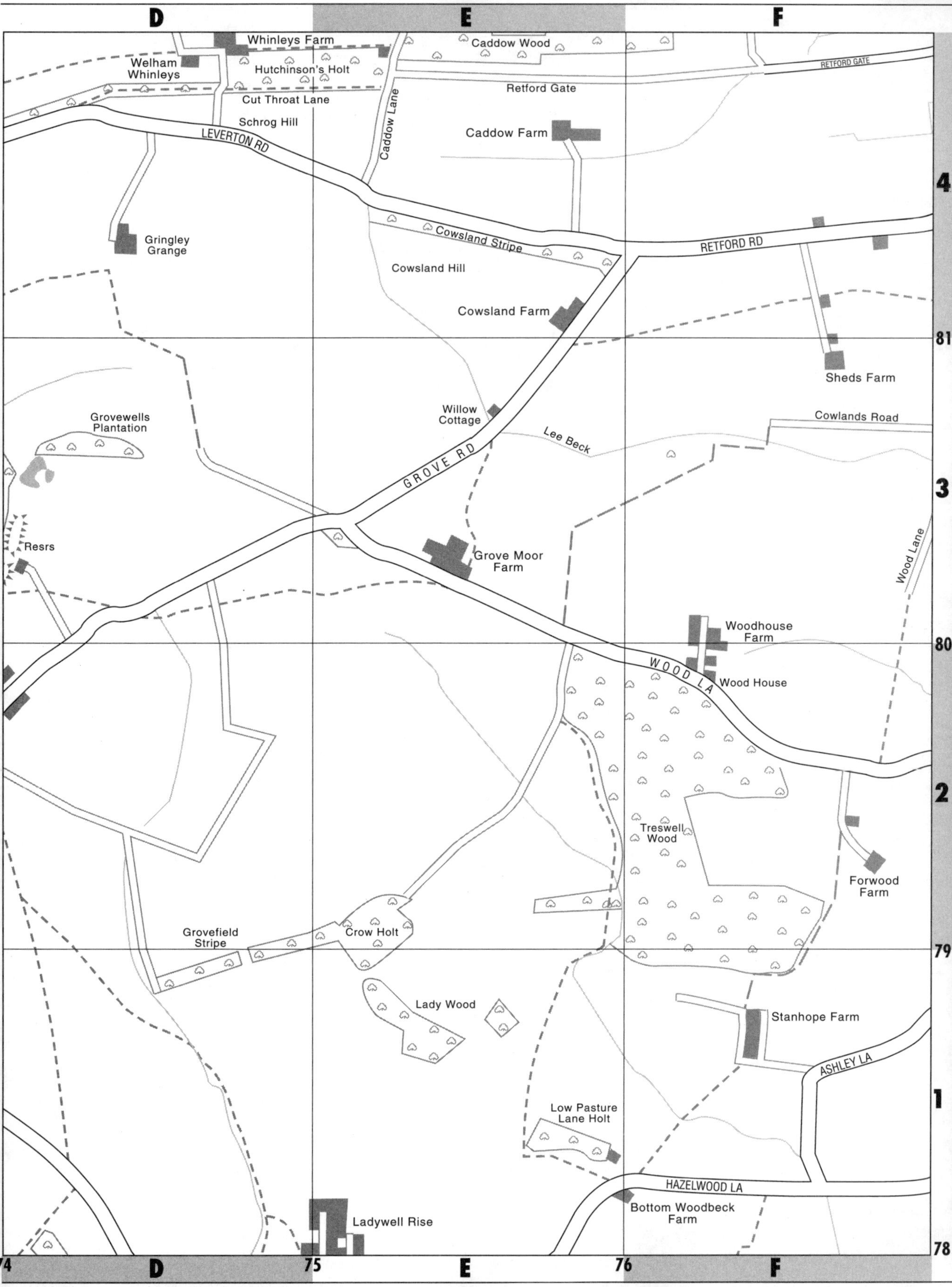
D
E
F
Whinleys Farm
Caddow Wood
Welham Whinleys
Hutchinson's Holt
RETFORD GATE
Retford Gate
Cut Throat Lane
Schrog Hill
Caddow Lane
Caddow Farm
LEVERTON RD
4
Gringley Grange
Cowsland Stripe
RETFORD RD
Cowsland Hill
Cowsland Farm
81
Sheds Farm
Willow Cottage
Cowlands Road
Grovewells Plantation
Lee Beck
GROVE RD
3
Resrs
Grove Moor Farm
Wood Lane
Woodhouse Farm
80
WOOD LA
Wood House
2
Treswell Wood
Forwood Farm
Grovefield Stripe
Crow Holt
79
Lady Wood
Stanhope Farm
ASHLEY LA
1
Low Pasture Lane Holt
HAZELWOOD LA
Bottom Woodbeck Farm
Ladywell Rise
78
74
75
76

52 42

41
32

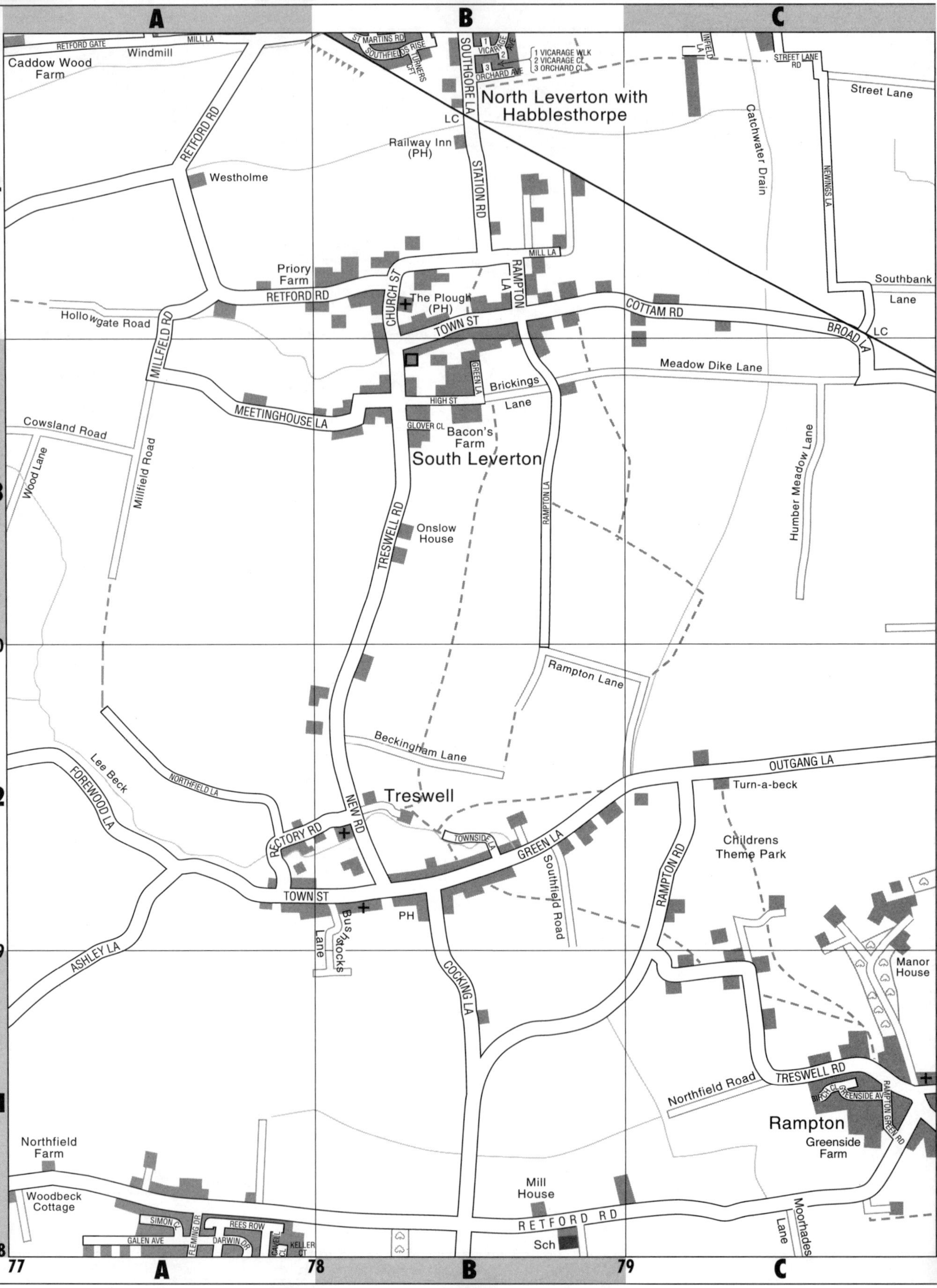
A
B
C
RETFORD GATE
MILL LA
Windmill
Caddow Wood Farm
ST MARTINS RD
SOUTHFIELDS RISE
TURNERS CFT
SOUTHGORE LA
VICARAGE AVE
1 VICARAGE WLK
2 VICARAGE CL
3 ORCHARD CL
ORCHARD AVE
INFIELD LA
STREET LANE RD
Street Lane
North Leverton with Habblesthorpe
LC
Railway Inn (PH)
Catchwater Drain
RETFORD RD
Westholme
STATION RD
NEWINGS LA
4
MILL LA
Priory Farm
RETFORD RD
CHURCH ST
RAMPTON LA
The Plough (PH)
COTTAM RD
Southbank Lane
Hollowgate Road
TOWN ST
BROAD LA
LC
81
MILLFIELD RD
GREEN LA
Meadow Dike Lane
Brickings Lane
HIGH ST
MEETINGHOUSE LA
Cowsland Road
GLOVER CL
Bacon's Farm
South Leverton
Humber Meadow Lane
Wood Lane
Millfield Road
3
RAMPTON LA
TRESWELL RD
Onslow House
80
Rampton Lane
Beckingham Lane
OUTGANG LA
Lee Beck
FOREWOOD LA
NORTHFIELD LA
2
NEW RD
Treswell
Turn-a-beck
RECTORY RD
TOWNSIDE LA
GREEN LA
Childrens Theme Park
RAMPTON RD
Southfield Road
TOWN ST
PH
Bush Stocks
Lane
ASHLEY LA
79
COCKING LA
Manor House
TRESWELL RD
Northfield Road
BIRCH CL
GREENSIDE AVE
RAMPTON GREEN RD
1
Rampton
Greenside Farm
Northfield Farm
Mill House
Woodbeck Cottage
Moorhades Lane
SIMON CL
REES ROW
FLEMING DR
DARWIN DR
GALEN AVE
CAVELL CL
KELLER CT
RETFORD RD
Sch
78
77
78
79

41
53

33
44

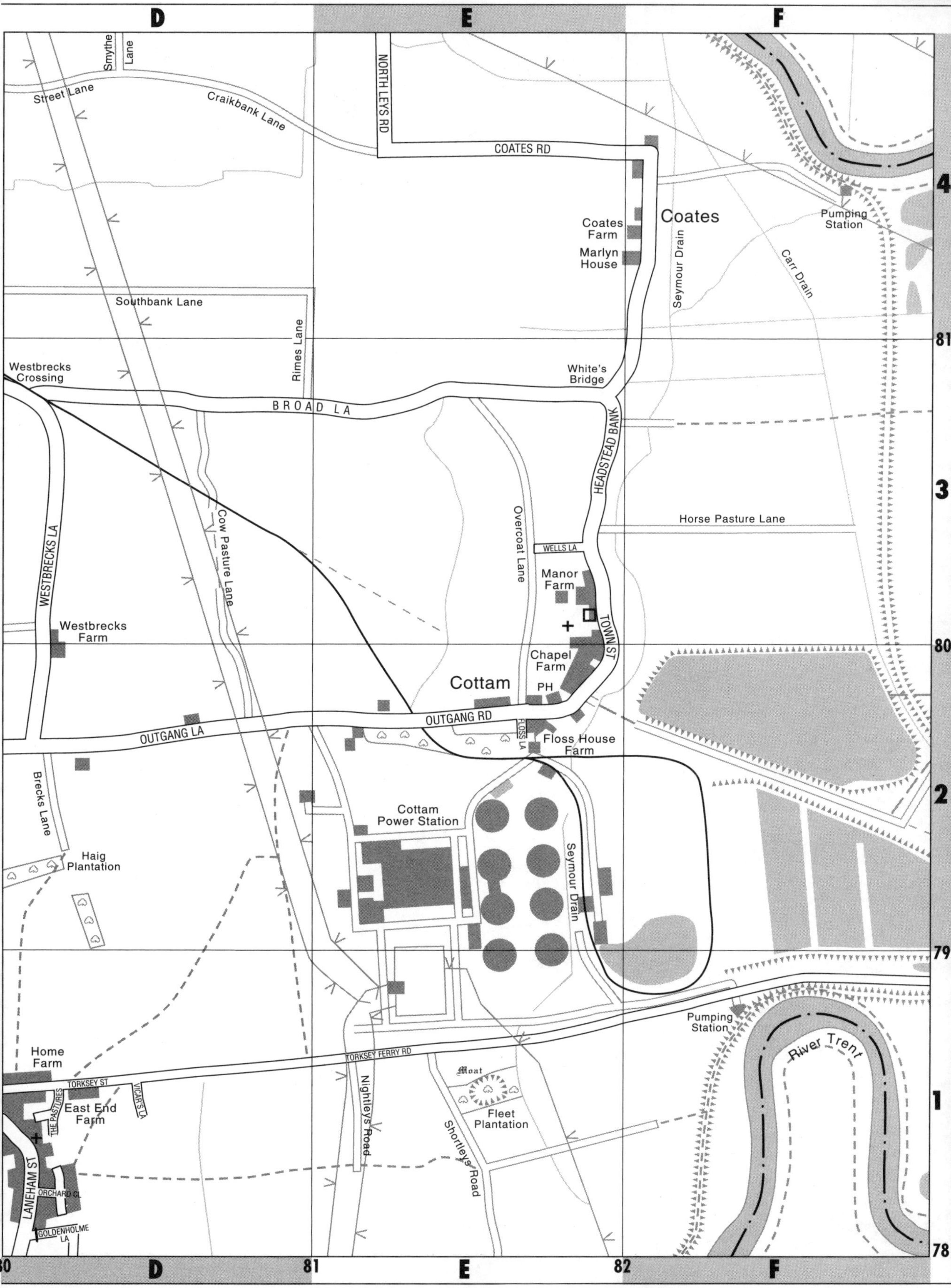
D
E
F
Smythe Lane
Street Lane
Craikbank Lane
NORTH LEYS RD
COATES RD
Coates
Coates Farm
Marlyn House
Pumping Station
Seymour Drain
Carr Drain
Southbank Lane
Rimes Lane
Westbrecks Crossing
White's Bridge
BROAD LA
HEADSTEAD BANK
WESTBRECKS LA
Cow Pasture Lane
Overcoat Lane
Horse Pasture Lane
WELLS LA
Manor Farm
TOWN ST
Westbrecks Farm
Chapel Farm
Cottam
PH
OUTGANG RD
OUTGANG LA
FLOSS LA
Floss House Farm
Brecks Lane
Cottam Power Station
Seymour Drain
Haig Plantation
Pumping Station
River Trent
Home Farm
TORKSEY FERRY RD
TORKSEY ST
Moat
THE PASTURES
VICAR'S LA
East End Farm
Nightleys Road
Fleet Plantation
Shortleys Road
LANEHAM ST
ORCHARD CL
GOLDENHOLME LA
4
81
3
80
2
79
1
78
80
81
82

54
44

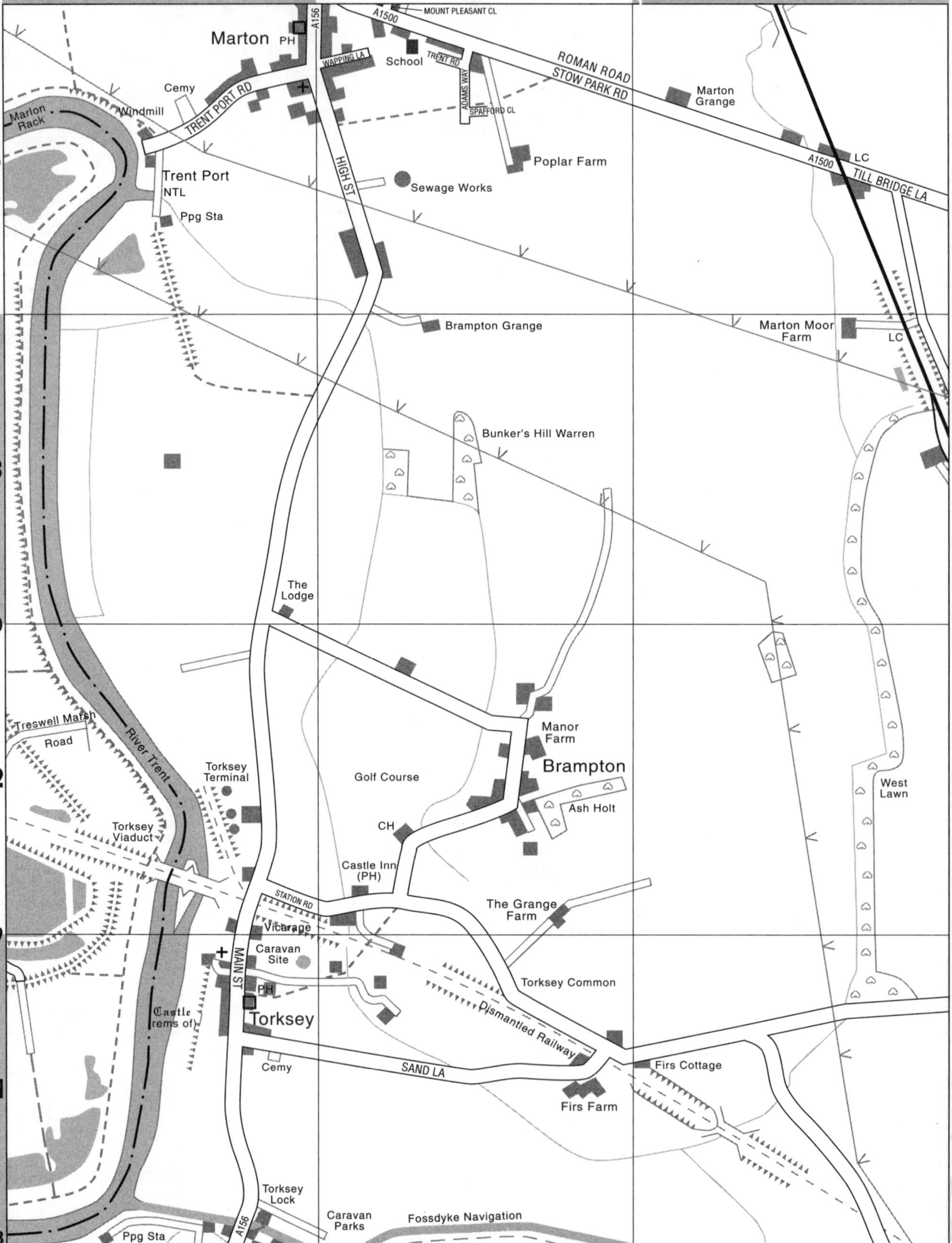
Marton
PH
A156
A1500
MOUNT PLEASANT CL
WAPPING LA
School
TRENT RD
ROMAN ROAD
STOW PARK RD
ADAMS WAY
SPAFFORD CL
TRENT PORT RD
Cemy
Windmill
Marton Rack
Marton Grange
Poplar Farm
Trent Port
NTL
Ppg Sta
HIGH ST
Sewage Works
LC
TILL BRIDGE LA
Brampton Grange
Marton Moor Farm
Bunker's Hill Warren
The Lodge
Treswell Marsh Road
River Trent
Manor Farm
Brampton
Torksey Terminal
Golf Course
Ash Holt
West Lawn
Torksey Viaduct
CH
Castle Inn (PH)
STATION RD
The Grange Farm
Vicarage
Caravan Site
MAIN ST
Torksey Common
Castle (rems of)
Torksey
Dismantled Railway
Cemy
SAND LA
Firs Cottage
Firs Farm
Torksey Lock
Caravan Parks
Fossdyke Navigation
Ppg Sta

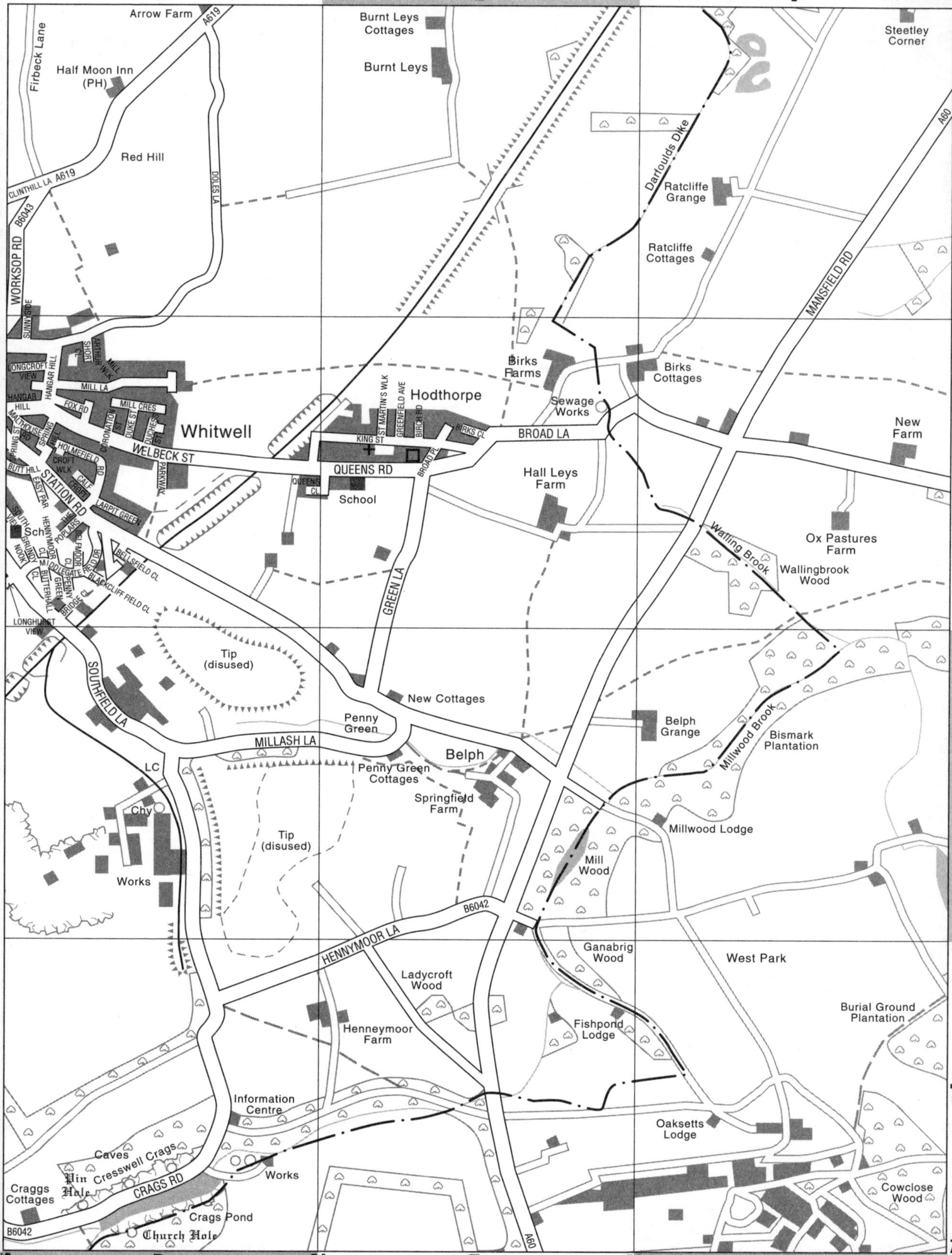
D
E
F
Arrow Farm
Firbeck Lane
Half Moon Inn (PH)
Red Hill
Burnt Leys Cottages
Burnt Leys
Steetley Corner
Darfoulds Dike
Ratcliffe Grange
Ratcliffe Cottages
MANSFIELD RD
A60
A619
CLINTHILL LA
B6043
WORKSOP RD
DOLES LA
Birks Farms
Birks Cottages
Sewage Works
Hodthorpe
Whitwell
WELBECK ST
QUEENS RD
BROAD LA
KING ST
School
Hall Leys Farm
New Farm
Ox Pastures Farm
Walling Brook
Wallingbrook Wood
GREEN LA
STATION RD
Sch
Tip (disused)
SOUTHFIELD LA
New Cottages
Penny Green
MILLASH LA
Belph
Belph Grange
Millwood Brook
Bismark Plantation
Penny Green Cottages
Springfield Farm
LC
Chy
Works
Mill Wood
Millwood Lodge
B6042
HENNYMOOR LA
Ganabrig Wood
West Park
Ladycroft Wood
Henneymoor Farm
Fishpond Lodge
Burial Ground Plantation
Information Centre
Oaksetts Lodge
Caves
Cresswell Crags
Pin Hole
CRAGS RD
Craggs Cottages
Works
Crags Pond
Church Hole
Cowclose Wood
4
77
3
76
2
75
1
74
53
54
55

45
35

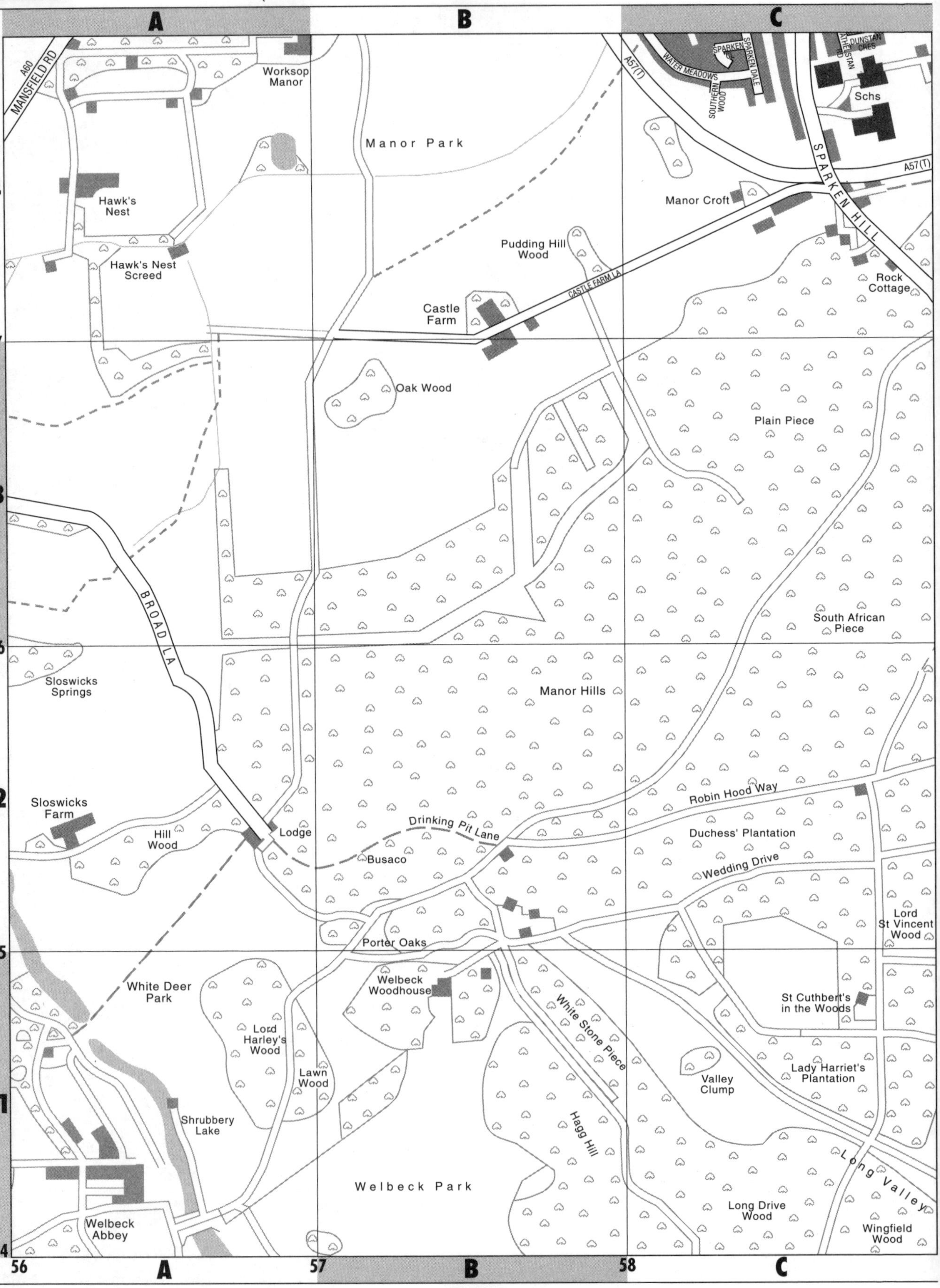

A
B
C
A60
MANSFIELD RD
Worksop Manor
Manor Park
A57(T)
WATER MEADOWS
SPARKEN RD
SPARKEN DALE
SOUTHERN WOOD
ATHELSTAN RD
DUNSTAN CRES
Schs
SPARKEN HILL
Hawk's Nest
Manor Croft
Pudding Hill Wood
Hawk's Nest Screed
CASTLE FARM LA
Rock Cottage
Castle Farm
Oak Wood
Plain Piece
BROAD LA
South African Piece
Sloswicks Springs
Manor Hills
Sloswicks Farm
Robin Hood Way
Hill Wood
Lodge
Drinking Pit Lane
Duchess' Plantation
Busaco
Wedding Drive
Lord St Vincent Wood
Porter Oaks
White Deer Park
Welbeck Woodhouse
White Stone Piece
St Cuthbert's in the Woods
Lord Harley's Wood
Lawn Wood
Valley Clump
Lady Harriet's Plantation
Shrubbery Lake
Hagg Hill
Long Valley
Welbeck Park
Long Drive Wood
Welbeck Abbey
Wingfield Wood
4
77
3
76
2
75
1
74
56
57
58


45
60

36
48

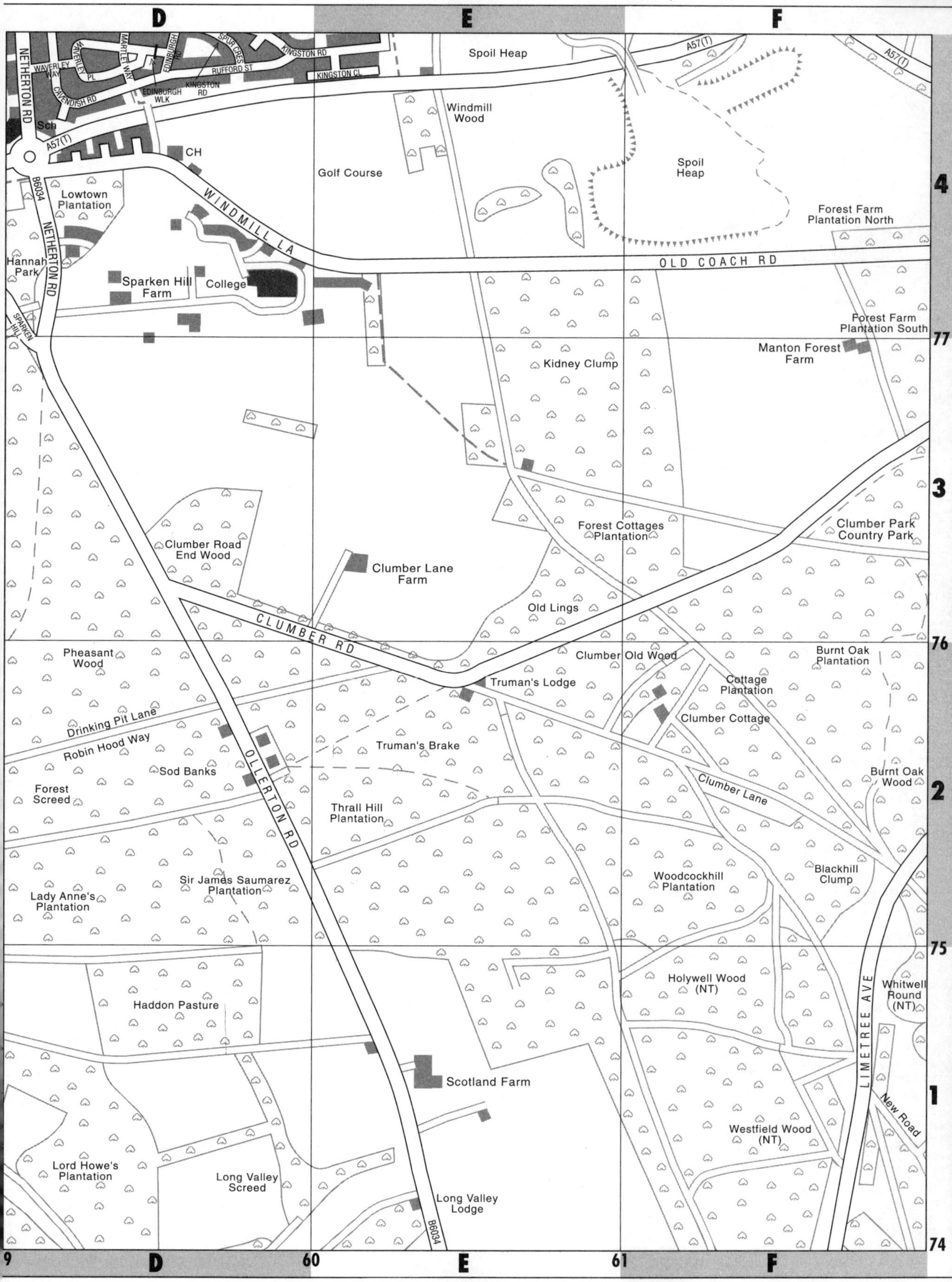
D
E
F
NETHERTON RD
WAVERLEY WAY
WAVERLEY PL
MARTLEY WAY
EDINBURGH RD
SPUR CRES
KINGSTON RD
RUFFORD ST
KINGSTON CL
CAVENDISH RD
EDINBURGH WLK
KINGSTON RD
Sch
A57(T)
CH
Spoil Heap
Windmill Wood
Golf Course
Spoil Heap
A57(T)
Lowtown Plantation
B6034
WINDMILL LA
Forest Farm Plantation North
OLD COACH RD
Hannah Park
Sparken Hill Farm
College
SPARKEN HILL
Forest Farm Plantation South
Manton Forest Farm
Kidney Clump
77
4
3
Forest Cottages Plantation
Clumber Park Country Park
Clumber Road End Wood
Clumber Lane Farm
Old Lings
CLUMBER RD
76
Pheasant Wood
Clumber Old Wood
Burnt Oak Plantation
Truman's Lodge
Cottage Plantation
Drinking Pit Lane
Clumber Cottage
Robin Hood Way
Truman's Brake
Sod Banks
OLLERTON RD
Forest Screed
Burnt Oak Wood
Clumber Lane
2
Thrall Hill Plantation
Blackhill Clump
Woodcockhill Plantation
Sir James Saumarez Plantation
Lady Anne's Plantation
75
Holywell Wood (NT)
Whitwell Round (NT)
Haddon Pasture
LIMETREE AVE
Scotland Farm
1
New Road
Westfield Wood (NT)
Lord Howe's Plantation
Long Valley Screed
Long Valley Lodge
B6034
74
9
D
60
E
61
F

61
48

47
37

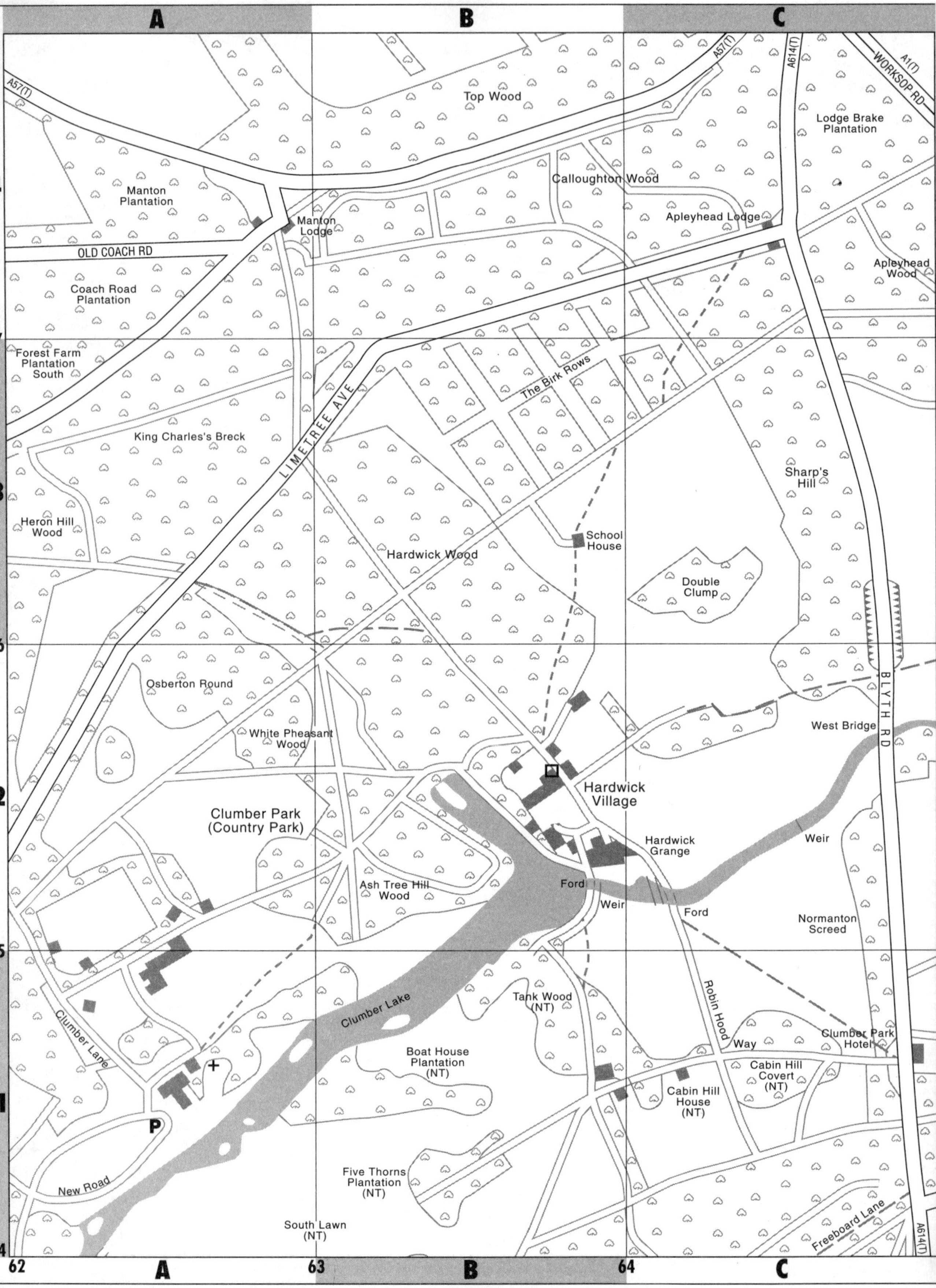
A
B
C
A57(T)
A57(T)
A614(T)
A1(T)
WORKSOP RD
Top Wood
Lodge Brake Plantation
4
Manton Plantation
Calloughton Wood
Apleyhead Lodge
Manton Lodge
OLD COACH RD
Apleyhead Wood
Coach Road Plantation
77
Forest Farm Plantation South
The Birk Rows
LIMETREE AVE
King Charles's Breck
Sharp's Hill
3
Heron Hill Wood
School House
Hardwick Wood
Double Clump
76
Osberton Round
BLYTH RD
West Bridge
White Pheasant Wood
2
Hardwick Village
Clumber Park (Country Park)
Hardwick Grange
Weir
Ash Tree Hill Wood
Ford
Weir
Ford
Normanton Screed
75
Robin Hood Way
Tank Wood (NT)
Clumber Lake
Clumber Lane
Boat House Plantation (NT)
Clumber Park Hotel
Cabin Hill Covert (NT)
1
Cabin Hill House (NT)
P
Five Thorns Plantation (NT)
New Road
Freeboard Lane
South Lawn (NT)
A614(T)
74
62
A
63
B
64
C

47
62

38
50

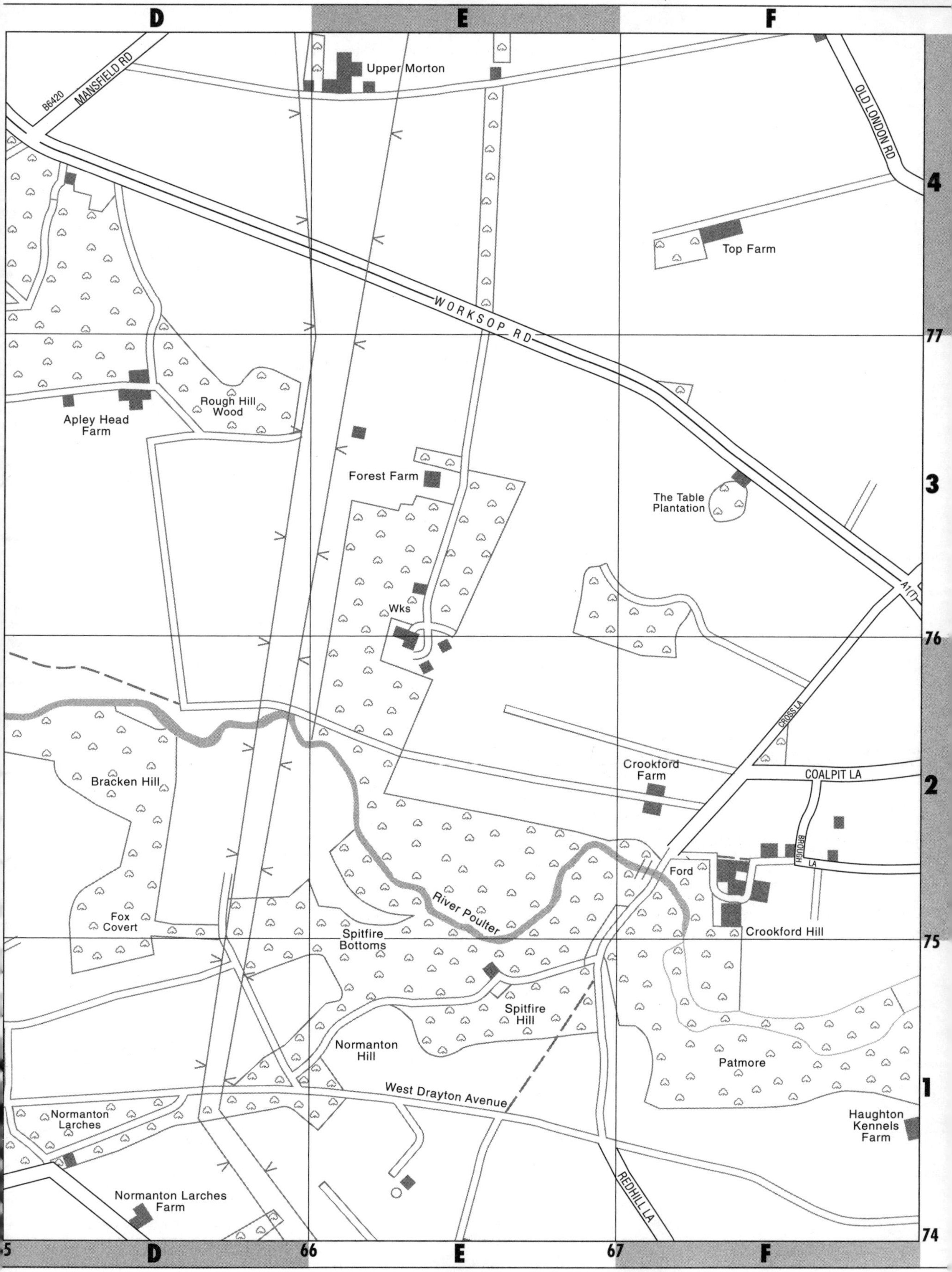
D
E
F
Upper Morton
B6420
MANSFIELD RD
OLD LONDON RD
WORKSOP RD
Top Farm
Apley Head Farm
Rough Hill Wood
Forest Farm
The Table Plantation
Wks
A1(T)
CROSS LA
COALPIT LA
Crookford Farm
BROUGH LA
Bracken Hill
Ford
River Poulter
Crookford Hill
Fox Covert
Spitfire Bottoms
Spitfire Hill
Normanton Hill
Patmore
West Drayton Avenue
Normanton Larches
Haughton Kennels Farm
REDHILL LA
Normanton Larches Farm
4
77
3
76
2
75
1
74
5
66
67

63
50

49
39

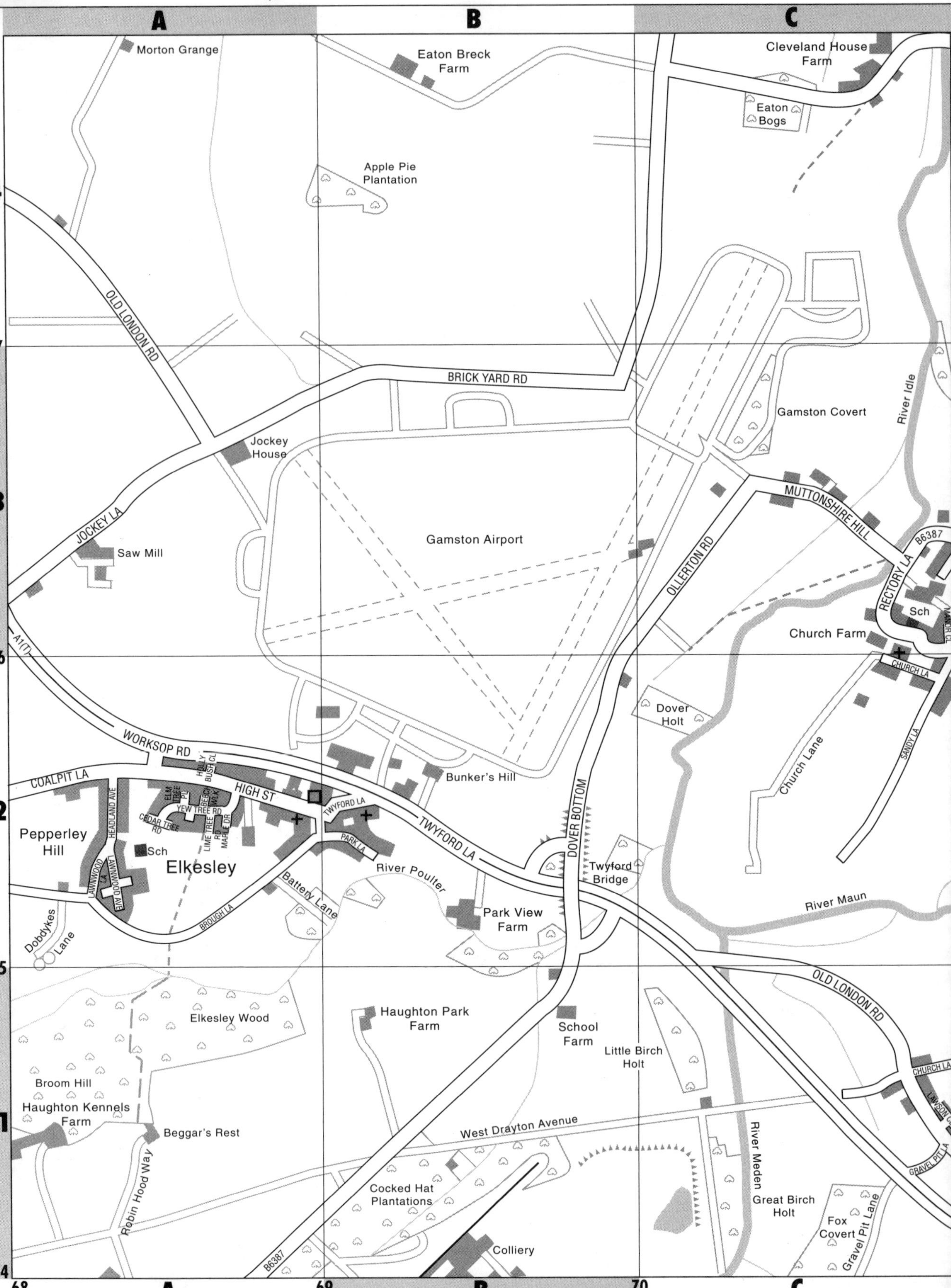
A
B
C
4
3
2
1
77
76
75
74
68
69
70
Morton Grange
Eaton Breck Farm
Cleveland House Farm
Eaton Bogs
Apple Pie Plantation
OLD LONDON RD
BRICK YARD RD
Gamston Covert
River Idle
Jockey House
JOCKEY LA
Saw Mill
Gamston Airport
MUTTONSHIRE HILL
OLLERTON RD
B6387
RECTORY LA
Sch
MANOR CL
Church Farm
CHURCH LA
A1(T)
Dover Holt
Church Lane
SANDY LA
WORKSOP RD
COALPIT LA
HOLLY BUSH CL
HIGH ST
ELM TREE PL
BEECH WLK
YEW TREE RD
CEDAR TREE RD
LIME TREE RD
MAPLE DR
HEADLAND AVE
TWYFORD LA
PARK LA
Bunker's Hill
DOVER BOTTOM
Pepperley Hill
Sch
Elkesley
LAWNWOOD LA
LAWNWOOD AVE
River Poulter
Battery Lane
Twyford Bridge
River Maun
Park View Farm
BROUGH LA
Dobdykes Lane
OLD LONDON RD
Elkesley Wood
Haughton Park Farm
School Farm
Little Birch Holt
CHURCH LA
LAWSON CL
Broom Hill
Haughton Kennels Farm
Beggar's Rest
West Drayton Avenue
River Meden
GRAVEL PIT LA
Robin Hood Way
Cocked Hat Plantations
Great Birch Holt
Fox Covert
Gravel Pit Lane
Colliery
B6387

49
64

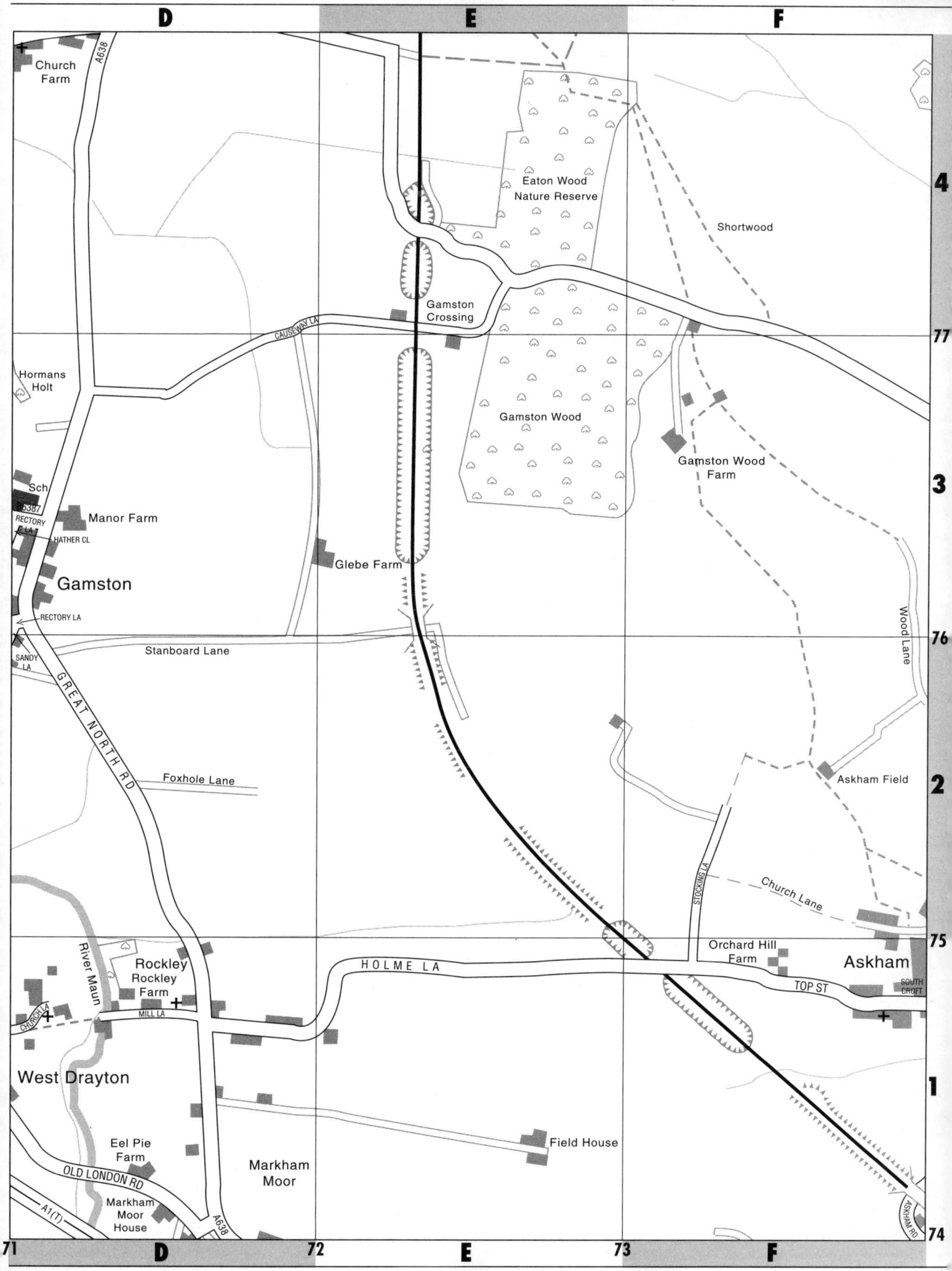
D
E
F
Church Farm
A638
Eaton Wood Nature Reserve
Shortwood
Gamston Crossing
CAUSEWAY LA
Hormans Holt
Gamston Wood
Gamston Wood Farm
Sch
B6387
RECTORY LA
HATHER CL
Manor Farm
Glebe Farm
Gamston
RECTORY LA
Wood Lane
Stanboard Lane
SANDY LA
GREAT NORTH RD
Foxhole Lane
Askham Field
STOCKING LA
Church Lane
River Maun
Rockley
Rockley Farm
HOLME LA
Orchard Hill Farm
Askham
TOP ST
SOUTH CROFT
CHURCH LA
MILL LA
West Drayton
Eel Pie Farm
OLD LONDON RD
Markham Moor
Field House
A1(T)
Markham Moor House
A638
ASKHAM RD
4
77
3
76
2
75
1
74
71
72
73
D
E
F

51
41

A B C

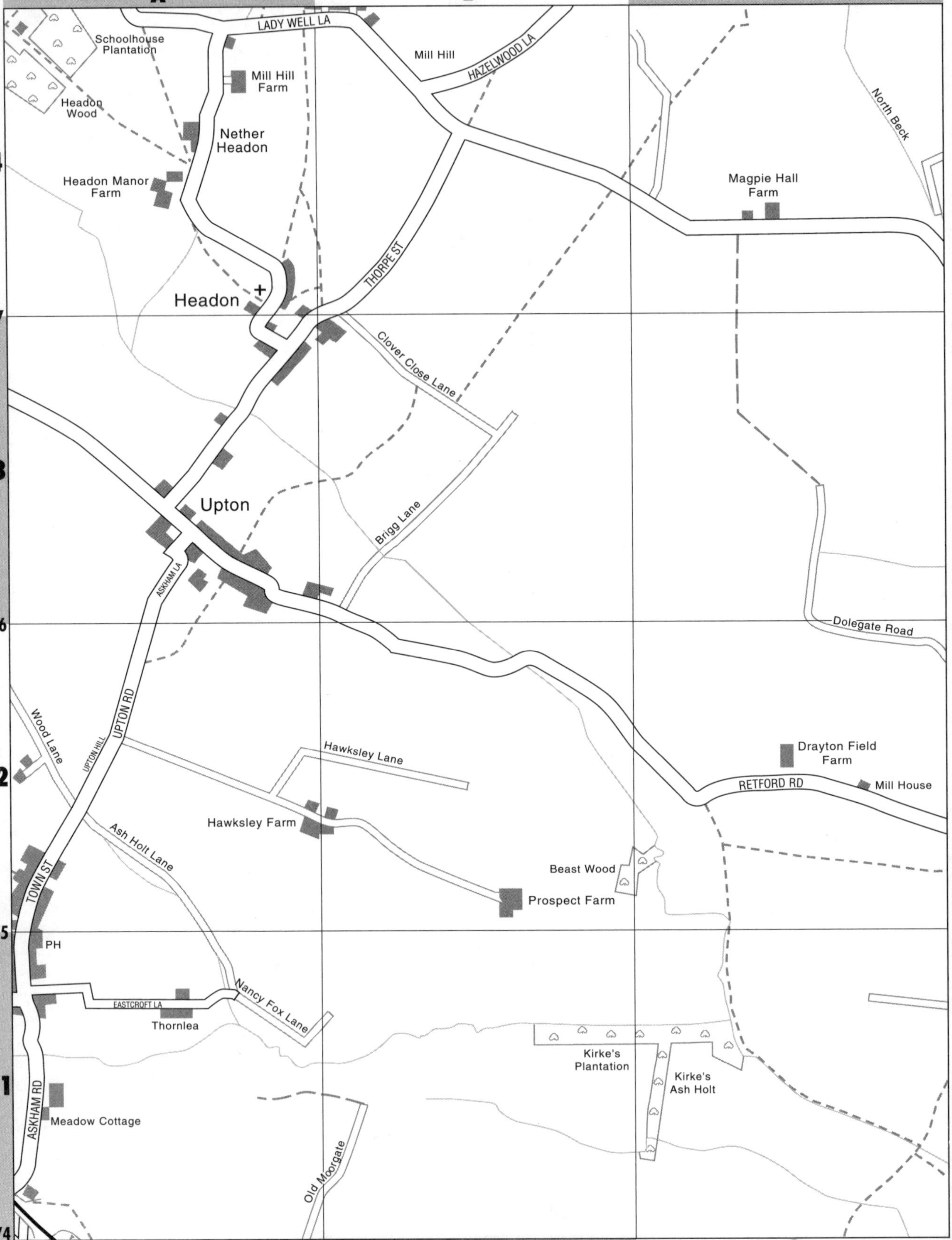


4 77 3 76 2 75 1 74

74 75 76

A B C

51
66

42
54

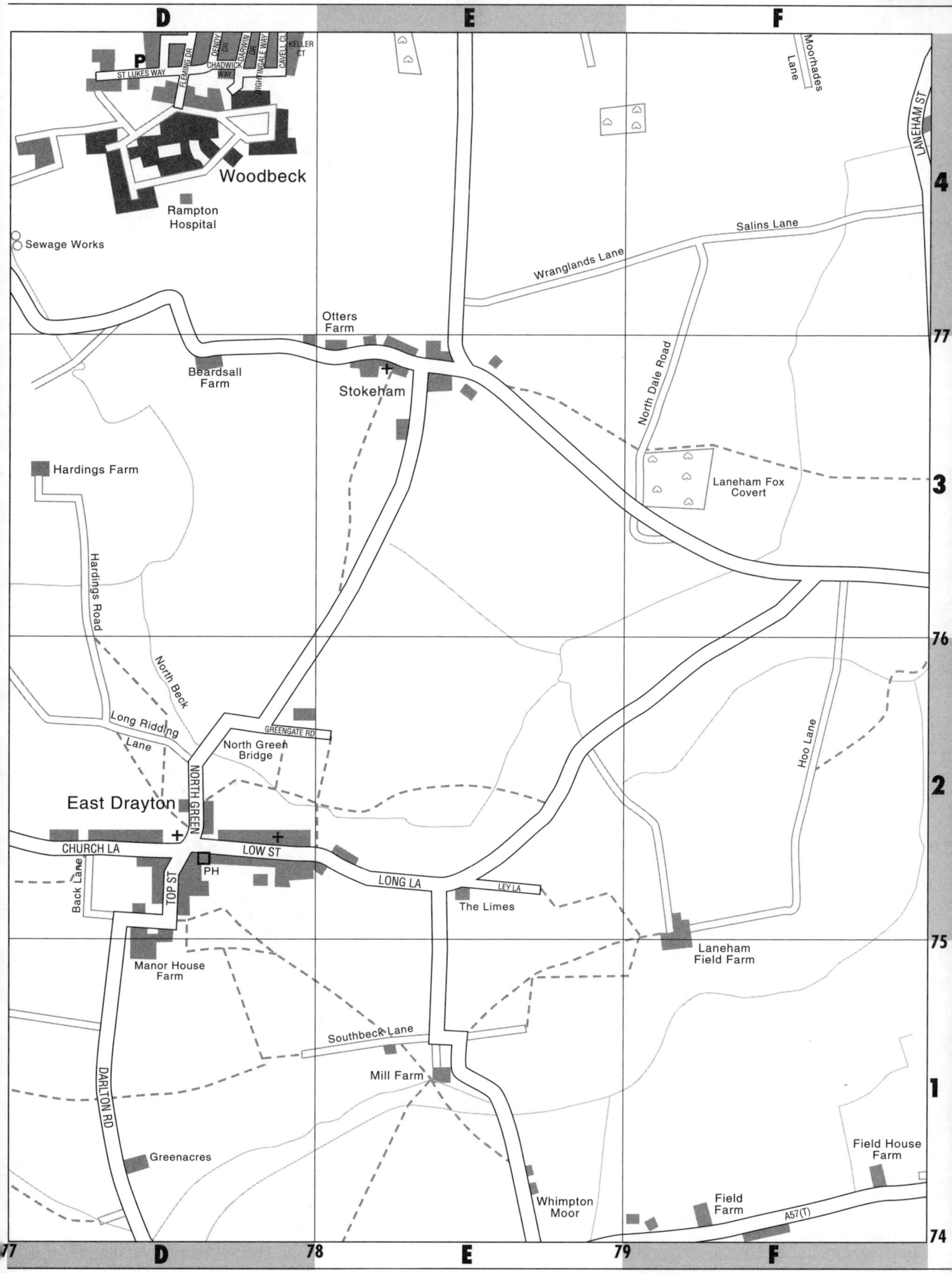
D
E
F
ST LUKES WAY
FLEMING DR
DENDY DR
CHADWICK WAY
DARWIN DR
NIGHTINGALE WAY
CAVELL CL
KELLER CT
P
Woodbeck
Rampton Hospital
Sewage Works
Moorhades Lane
LANEHAM ST
Salins Lane
Wranglands Lane
Otters Farm
Beardsall Farm
Stokeham
North Dale Road
Hardings Farm
Laneham Fox Covert
Hardings Road
North Beck
Long Ridding Lane
GREENGATE RD
North Green Bridge
Hoo Lane
East Drayton
NORTH GREEN
CHURCH LA
LOW ST
PH
Back Lane
TOP ST
LONG LA
LEY LA
The Limes
Laneham Field Farm
Manor House Farm
Southbeck Lane
Mill Farm
DARLTON RD
Greenacres
Whimpton Moor
Field Farm
Field House Farm
A57(T)
4
77
3
76
2
75
1
74
77
78
79

67
54

53
43

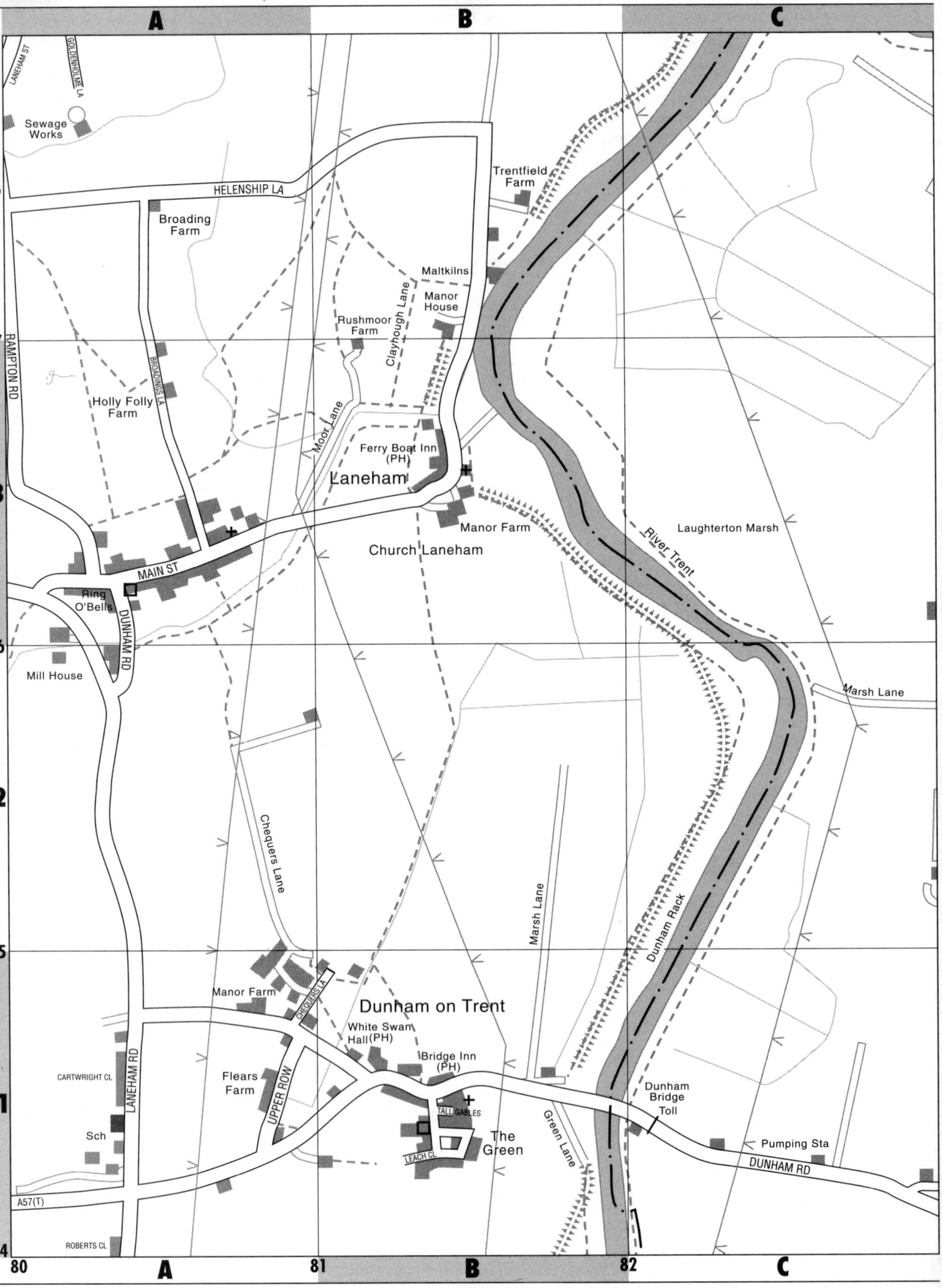
A
B
C
4
77
3
76
2
75
1
74
80
81
82
LANEHAM ST
GOLDENHOLME LA
Sewage Works
HELENSHIP LA
Broading Farm
Trentfield Farm
Maltkilns
Manor House
Rushmoor Farm
Clayhough Lane
RAMPTON RD
BROADINGS LA
Holly Folly Farm
Moor Lane
Ferry Boat Inn (PH)
Laneham
Manor Farm
Church Laneham
Laughterton Marsh
River Trent
MAIN ST
Ring O'Bells
DUNHAM RD
Mill House
Marsh Lane
Chequers Lane
Marsh Lane
Dunham Rack
Manor Farm
CHEQUERS LA
Dunham on Trent
White Swan Hall (PH)
Bridge Inn (PH)
CARTWRIGHT CL
LANEHAM RD
Flears Farm
UPPER ROW
TALL GABLES
The Green
LEACH CL
Green Lane
Dunham Bridge Toll
Pumping Sta
DUNHAM RD
Sch
A57(T)
ROBERTS CL

53
68

44
56

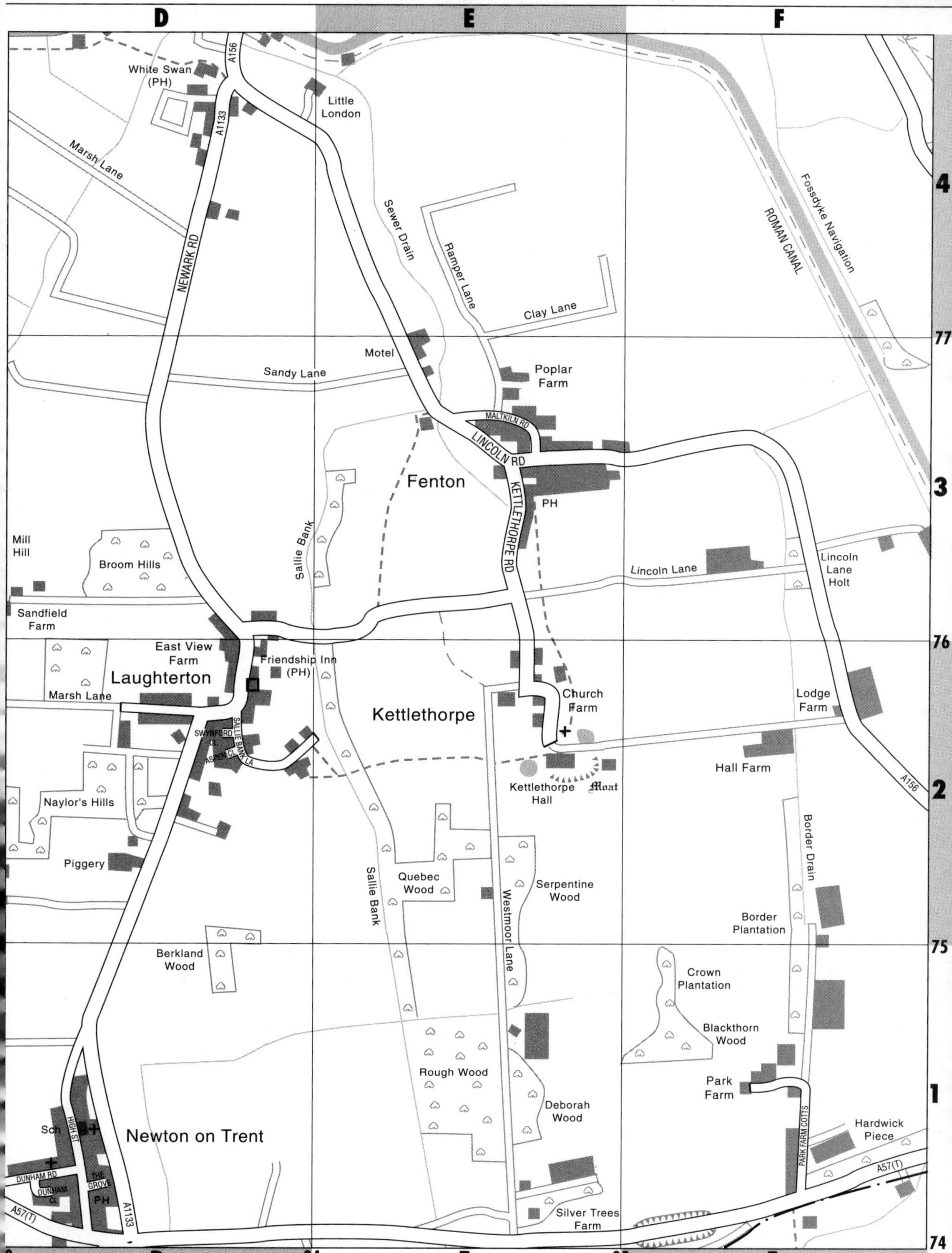
D
E
F
White Swan (PH)
Little London
Marsh Lane
A156
A1133
NEWARK RD
Sewer Drain
Ramper Lane
Clay Lane
ROMAN CANAL
Fossdyke Navigation
Motel
Sandy Lane
Poplar Farm
MALTKILN RD
LINCOLN RD
Fenton
KETTLETHORPE RD
PH
Mill Hill
Broom Hills
Sallie Bank
Lincoln Lane
Lincoln Lane Holt
Sandfield Farm
East View Farm
Friendship Inn (PH)
Laughterton
Marsh Lane
Kettlethorpe
Church Farm
Lodge Farm
SWYNFORD CL
SALLIE BANK LA
ASPEN CL
Hall Farm
Kettlethorpe Hall
Moat
A156
Naylor's Hills
Piggery
Quebec Wood
Sallie Bank
Westmoor Lane
Serpentine Wood
Border Drain
Border Plantation
Berkland Wood
Crown Plantation
Blackthorn Wood
Rough Wood
Park Farm
Deborah Wood
Sch
HIGH ST
Newton on Trent
PARK FARM COTTS
Hardwick Piece
DUNHAM RD
DUNHAM CL
THE GROVE
PH
A57(T)
A1133
Silver Trees Farm
A57(T)
4
77
3
76
2
75
1
74
83
84
85

69
56

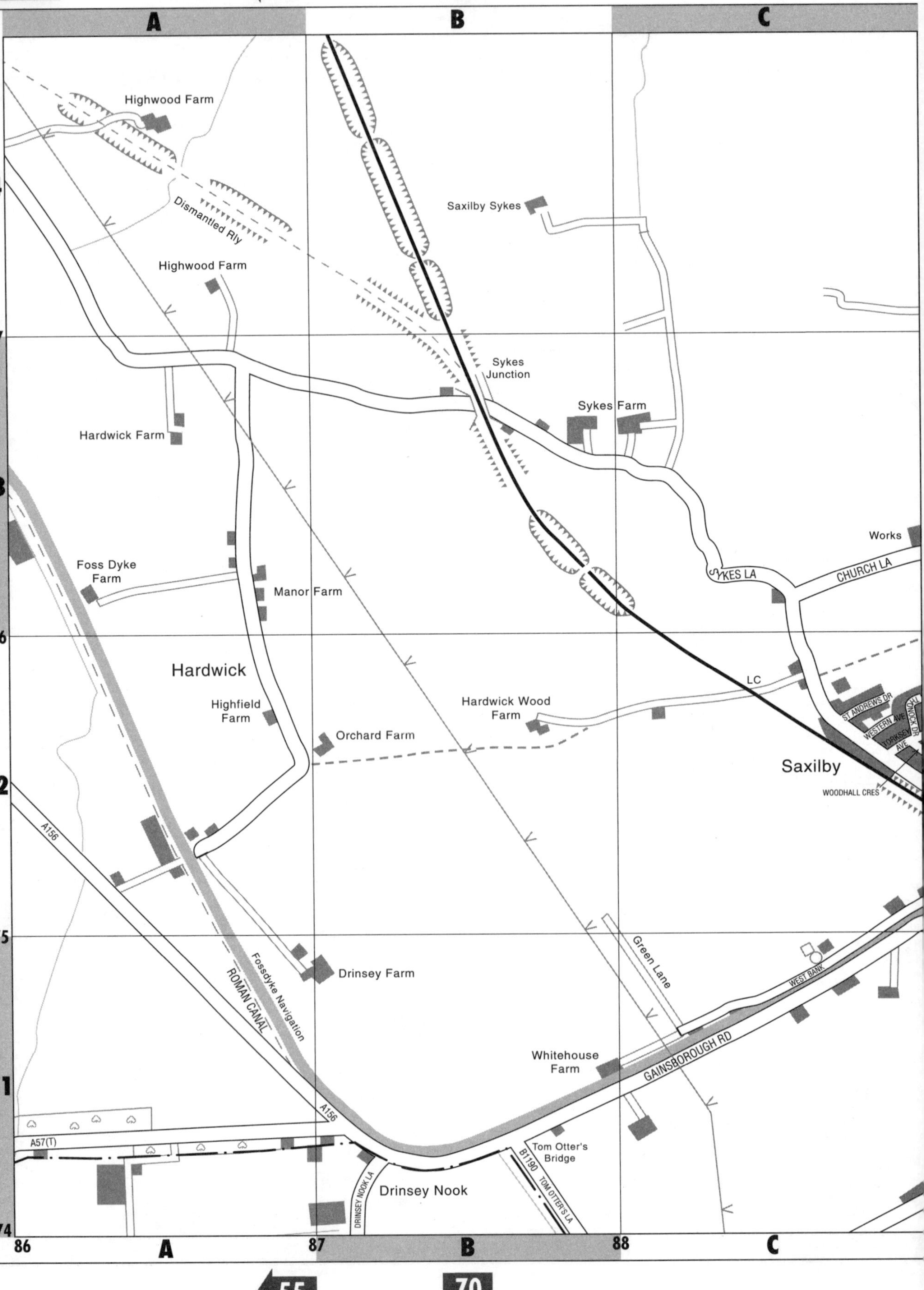
A
B
C
4
77
3
76
2
75
1
74
86
87
88
Highwood Farm
Dismantled Rly
Highwood Farm
Saxilby Sykes
Sykes Junction
Sykes Farm
Hardwick Farm
Foss Dyke Farm
Manor Farm
Works
SYKES LA
CHURCH LA
Hardwick
Highfield Farm
Orchard Farm
Hardwick Wood Farm
LC
ST ANDREWS DR
WESTERN AVE
TORKSEY AVE
Saxilby
WOODHALL CRES
A156
Fossdyke Navigation
ROMAN CANAL
Drinsey Farm
Green Lane
WEST BANK
GAINSBOROUGH RD
Whitehouse Farm
A156
A57(T)
Tom Otter's Bridge
B1190
TOM OTTER'S LA
DRINSEY NOOK LA
Drinsey Nook

D
E
F
B1241
Ingleby Hall
Ingleby Hall Farm
Manor Farm
Moat
Ingleby Grange
STURTON RD
CARLTON LA
Cornhills Farm
Broxholme
BROXHOLME LA
River Till
BROXHOLME LA
Wheelgate Farm
CHURCH LA
ST BOTOLPHS CL
WEST CROFT DR
CHURCH RD
MEADOW RISE
SOUTH PARADE
MANOR RD
ALMOND CL
BLANKNEY CL
TORKSEY AVE
OTTER AVE
NURSERY CL
MILLFIELD AVE
ELM CL
MILL LA
WOODHALL CRES
ORCHARD LA
HIGHFIELD RD
HIGH ST
Sch
SYKES LA
SKIRBECK DR
OAKFIELD
WILLOW CL
FOSSDYKE GDNS
Eastfield House Farm
MAYS LA
WILLIAM ST
FOSSE GR
Saxilby Sta
Fire Sta
THE SIDINGS
BRIDGE PL
QUEENSWAY
B1241
LC
BRIDGE ST
QUEENSWAY
WEST BANK
PH
A57(T)
GAINSBOROUGH RD
LINCOLN RD
ROMAN CANAL
Odda Farm
Odder
Odder Farm
The Old Mill
Fossdyke Navigation
A57(T)
Moor House Farm
Crossing Cottage
LC
River Bank Farm
BROADHOLME RD
Broadholme
Bartons Farm
Birchwood Farm
Whitehouse Farm
Highland Farm
MANOR LA
Ouseness Farm
4
77
3
76
2
75
1
74
90
91


71

A
B
C
Markland Farm
MARKLAND LA
Archaeological Trail
WOOD LA
ELMTON RD
Camp Hill
MODEL VILLAGE
Fox Green
DUCHESS ST
A616
MORVEN ST
WELBECK ST
HAZELBY RD
The Oaks
Dismantled Railway
OXCROFT LA
Grange Farm
Elmton
SPRING LA
PH
Elm Tree Farm
Green Farm
FRITHWOOD LA
Colliery
Spoil Heap
Frithwood Farm
Frith Wood
The Old Hag
OXPASTURE LA
Whaley Moor
LC
Norwood Farm
MAG LA
Whaley Hall
WHALEY COMMON
Whaley Common
Whaley
PH
MOORFIELD LA
Bolsover Moor Quarry
Grave Wood
Whaley Farm
Mill Pond
Mill Farm
P
Country Park
Scarcliffe Park
Owl Sick
WHALEY RD
Owl Spring
Apsley Grange
P
P
Dismtd Rly
River Poulter
Archaeological Trail
Scarcliffe Grange
A632
MAIN RD
LANGWITH MALTINGS
DEVONSHIRE DR
PH
4
73
3
72
2
71
1
70
50
51
52

72

45
60

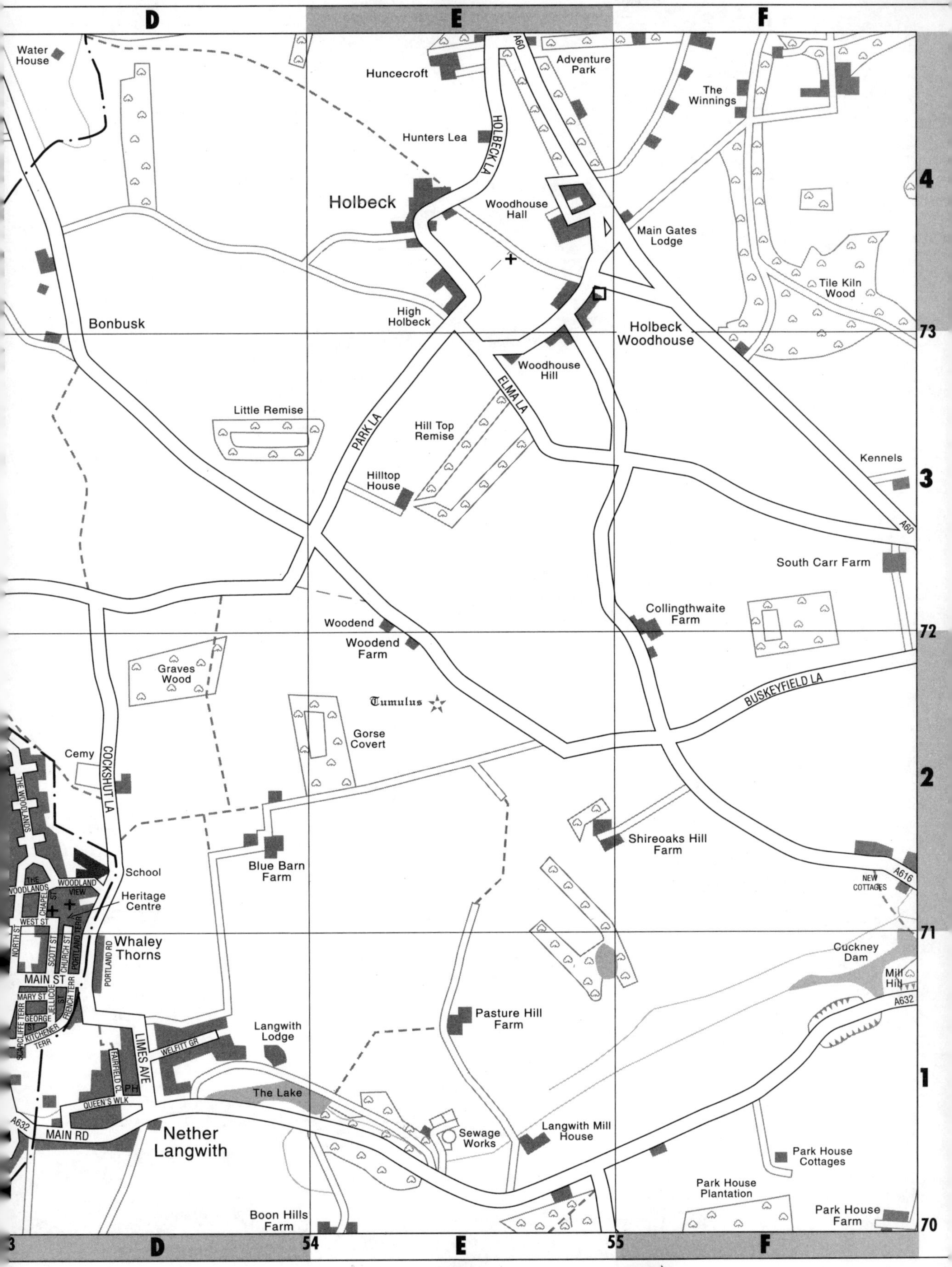
D
E
F
Water House
Huncecroft
Adventure Park
The Winnings
Hunters Lea
HOLBECK LA
A60
Holbeck
Woodhouse Hall
Main Gates Lodge
Tile Kiln Wood
High Holbeck
Bonbusk
Holbeck Woodhouse
Woodhouse Hill
ELMA LA
Little Remise
PARK LA
Hill Top Remise
Hilltop House
Kennels
South Carr Farm
Collingthwaite Farm
Woodend
Woodend Farm
Graves Wood
Tumulus
BUSKEYFIELD LA
Gorse Covert
Cemy
COCKSHUT LA
THE WOODLANDS
Shireoaks Hill Farm
Blue Barn Farm
School
Heritage Centre
NEW COTTAGES
A616
WOODLAND VIEW
CHAPEL ST
WEST ST
NORTH ST
SCOTT ST
CHURCH ST
PORTLAND TERR
PORTLAND RD
Whaley Thorns
MAIN ST
MARY ST
GEORGE ST
JELLICOE ST
FRENCH TERR
SCARCLIFFE TERR
KITCHENER TERR
Cuckney Dam
Mill Hill
A632
Pasture Hill Farm
Langwith Lodge
LIMES AVE
WELFITT GR
FAIRFIELD CL
PH
The Lake
QUEEN'S WLK
MAIN RD
Nether Langwith
Sewage Works
Langwith Mill House
Park House Cottages
Park House Plantation
Park House Farm
Boon Hills Farm
4
73
3
72
2
71
1
70
53
54
55

73
60

59
46

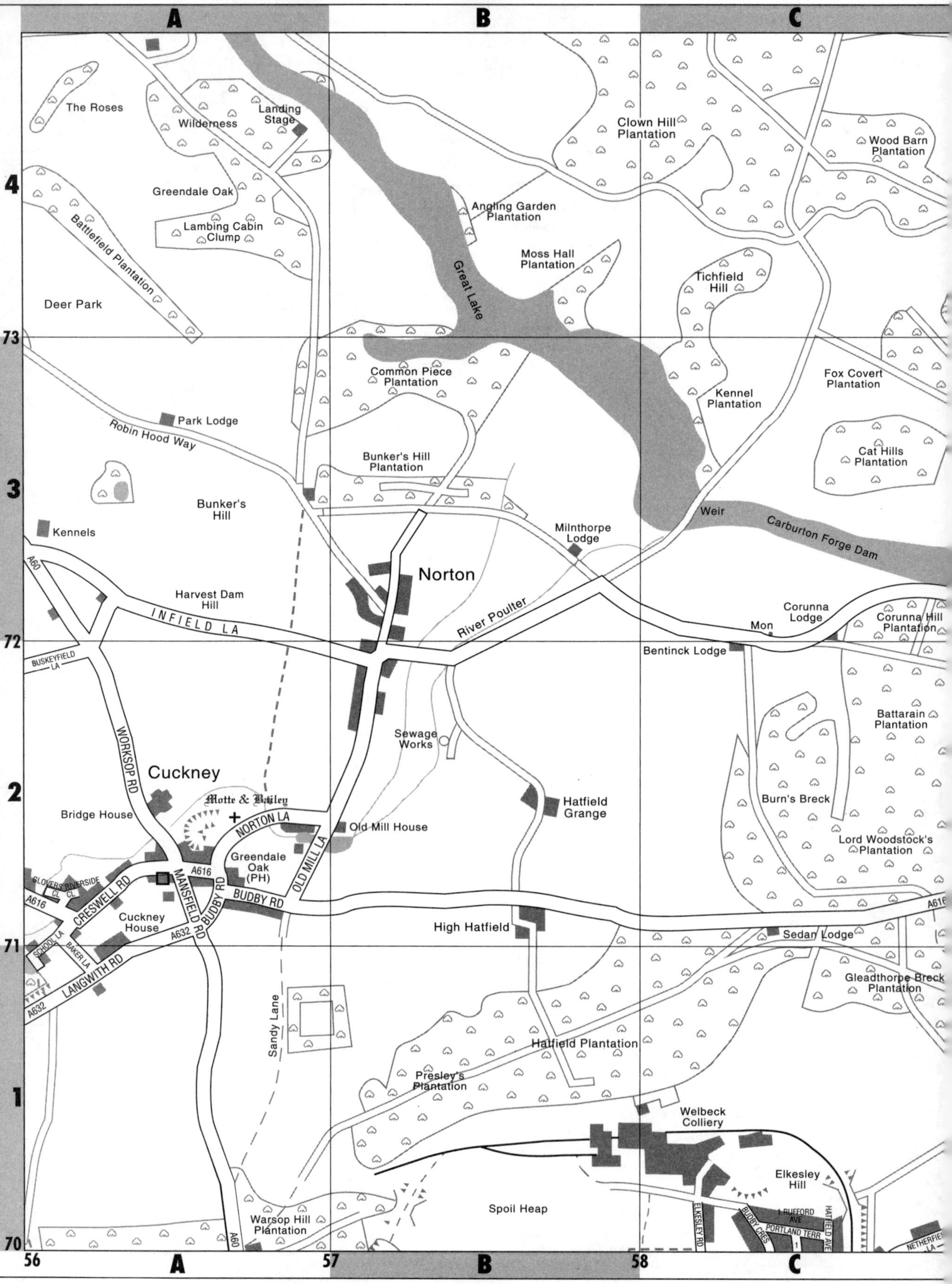
A
B
C
4
73
3
72
2
71
1
70
56
57
58
The Roses
Wilderness
Landing Stage
Greendale Oak
Lambing Cabin Clump
Battlefield Plantation
Deer Park
Great Lake
Angling Garden Plantation
Moss Hall Plantation
Clown Hill Plantation
Wood Barn Plantation
Tichfield Hill
Kennel Plantation
Fox Covert Plantation
Cat Hills Plantation
Common Piece Plantation
Park Lodge
Robin Hood Way
Bunker's Hill Plantation
Bunker's Hill
Kennels
Weir
Carburton Forge Dam
Milnthorpe Lodge
Norton
River Poulter
Harvest Dam Hill
A60
INFIELD LA
Corunna Lodge
Mon
Corunna Hill Plantation
Bentinck Lodge
BUSKEYFIELD LA
WORKSOP RD
Sewage Works
Battarain Plantation
Cuckney
Motte & Bailey
NORTON LA
Hatfield Grange
Burn's Breck
Bridge House
Old Mill House
Lord Woodstock's Plantation
Greendale Oak (PH)
OLD MILL LA
A616
GLOVERS CL
RIVERSIDE CL
CRESWELL RD
MANSFIELD RD
BUDBY RD
Cuckney House
High Hatfield
Sedan Lodge
SCHOOL LA
BAKER LA
A632
LANGWITH RD
Gleadthorpe Breck Plantation
Sandy Lane
Hatfield Plantation
Presley's Plantation
Welbeck Colliery
Elkesley Hill
Spoil Heap
Warsop Hill Plantation
ELKESLEY RD
BUDBY CRES
RUFFORD AVE
PORTLAND TERR
HATFIELD AVE
NETHERFIELD LA

59
74

47
62

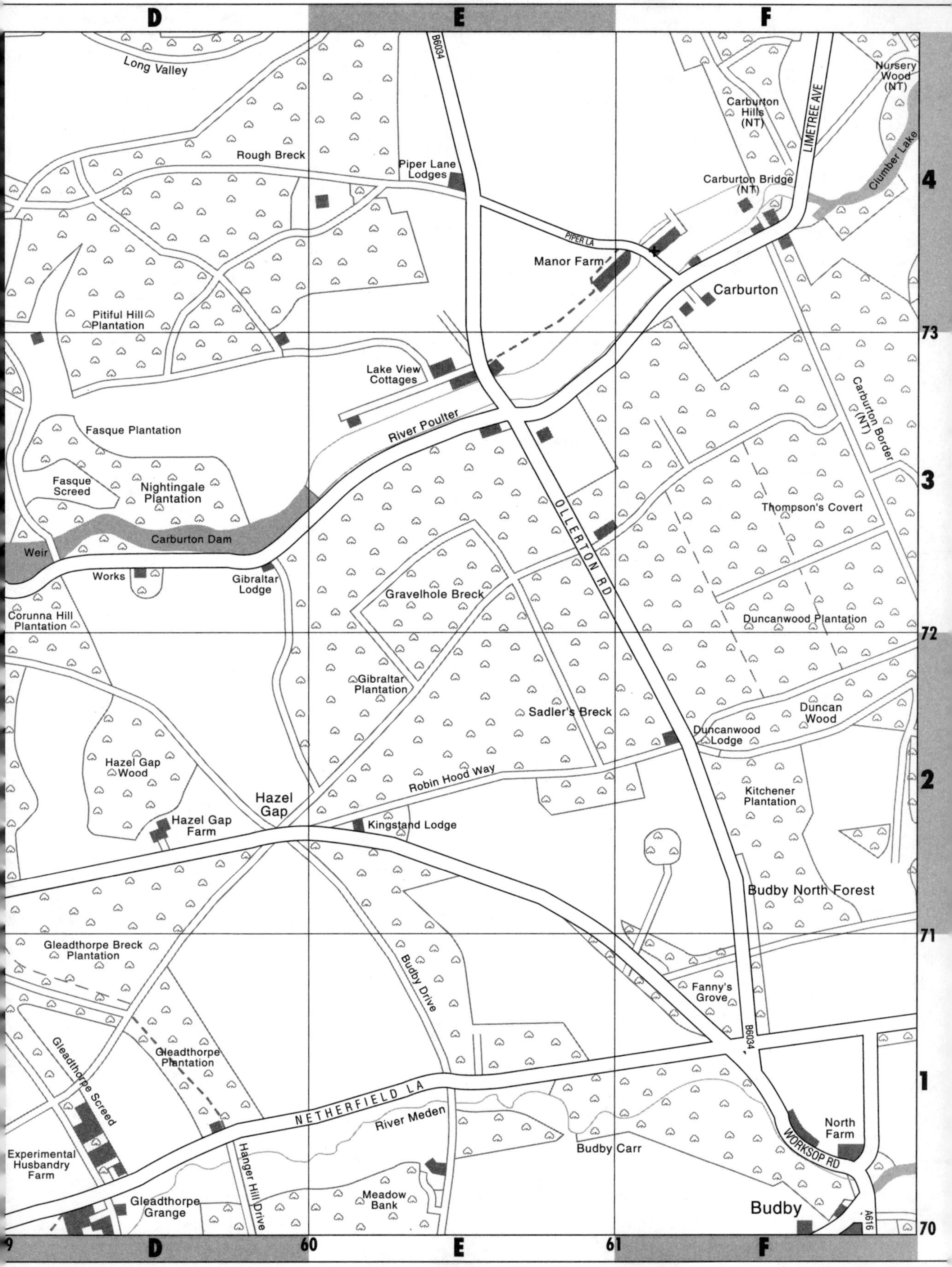
D
E
F
Long Valley
Rough Breck
Piper Lane Lodges
B6034
Carburton Hills (NT)
LIMETREE AVE
Nursery Wood (NT)
Clumber Lake
Carburton Bridge (NT)
PIPER LA
Manor Farm
Carburton
Pitiful Hill Plantation
Lake View Cottages
River Poulter
Fasque Plantation
Carburton Border (NT)
Fasque Screed
Nightingale Plantation
OLLERTON RD
Thompson's Covert
Weir
Carburton Dam
Works
Gibraltar Lodge
Gravelhole Breck
Corunna Hill Plantation
Duncanwood Plantation
Gibraltar Plantation
Sadler's Breck
Duncan Wood
Duncanwood Lodge
Hazel Gap Wood
Robin Hood Way
Kitchener Plantation
Hazel Gap
Hazel Gap Farm
Kingstand Lodge
Budby North Forest
Gleadthorpe Breck Plantation
Budby Drive
Fanny's Grove
B6034
Gleadthorpe Screed
Gleadthorpe Plantation
NETHERFIELD LA
River Meden
North Farm
WORKSOP RD
Experimental Husbandry Farm
Hanger Hill Drive
Budby Carr
Gleadthorpe Grange
Meadow Bank
Budby
A616
4
73
3
72
2
71
1
70
9
60
61

75
62

61
48

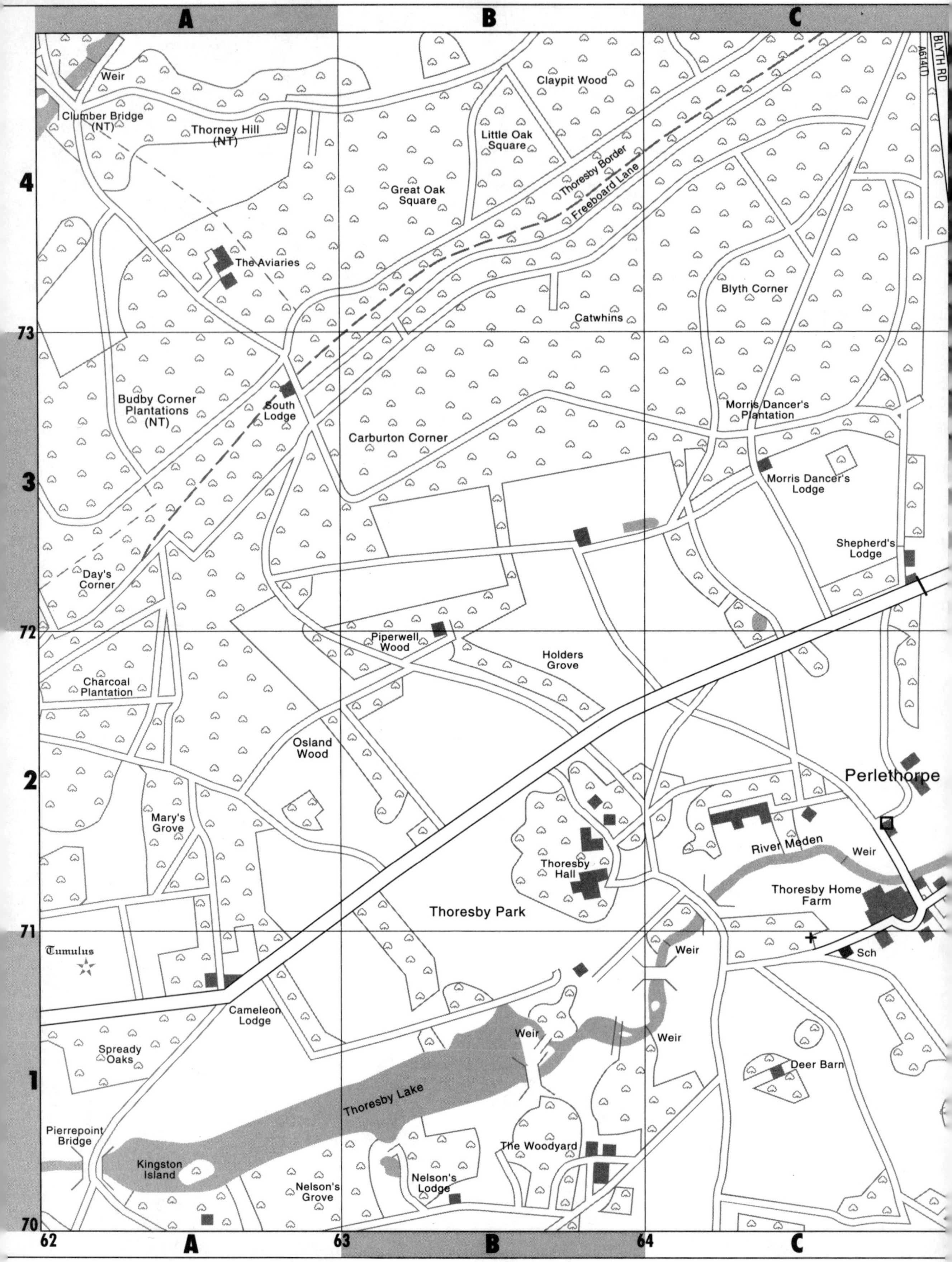
A
B
C
BLYTH RD
A614(T)
Weir
Clumber Bridge (NT)
Thorney Hill (NT)
Claypit Wood
Little Oak Square
Great Oak Square
Thoresby Border
Freeboard Lane
The Aviaries
Catwhins
Blyth Corner
Budby Corner Plantations (NT)
South Lodge
Carburton Corner
Morris Dancer's Plantation
Morris Dancer's Lodge
Shepherd's Lodge
Day's Corner
Piperwell Wood
Holders Grove
Charcoal Plantation
Osland Wood
Perlethorpe
Mary's Grove
River Meden
Weir
Thoresby Hall
Thoresby Home Farm
Thoresby Park
Tumulus
Weir
Sch
Cameleon Lodge
Weir
Weir
Spready Oaks
Deer Barn
Thoresby Lake
Pierrepoint Bridge
The Woodyard
Kingston Island
Nelson's Grove
Nelson's Lodge
4
73
3
72
2
71
1
70
62
63
64

61
76

49
64
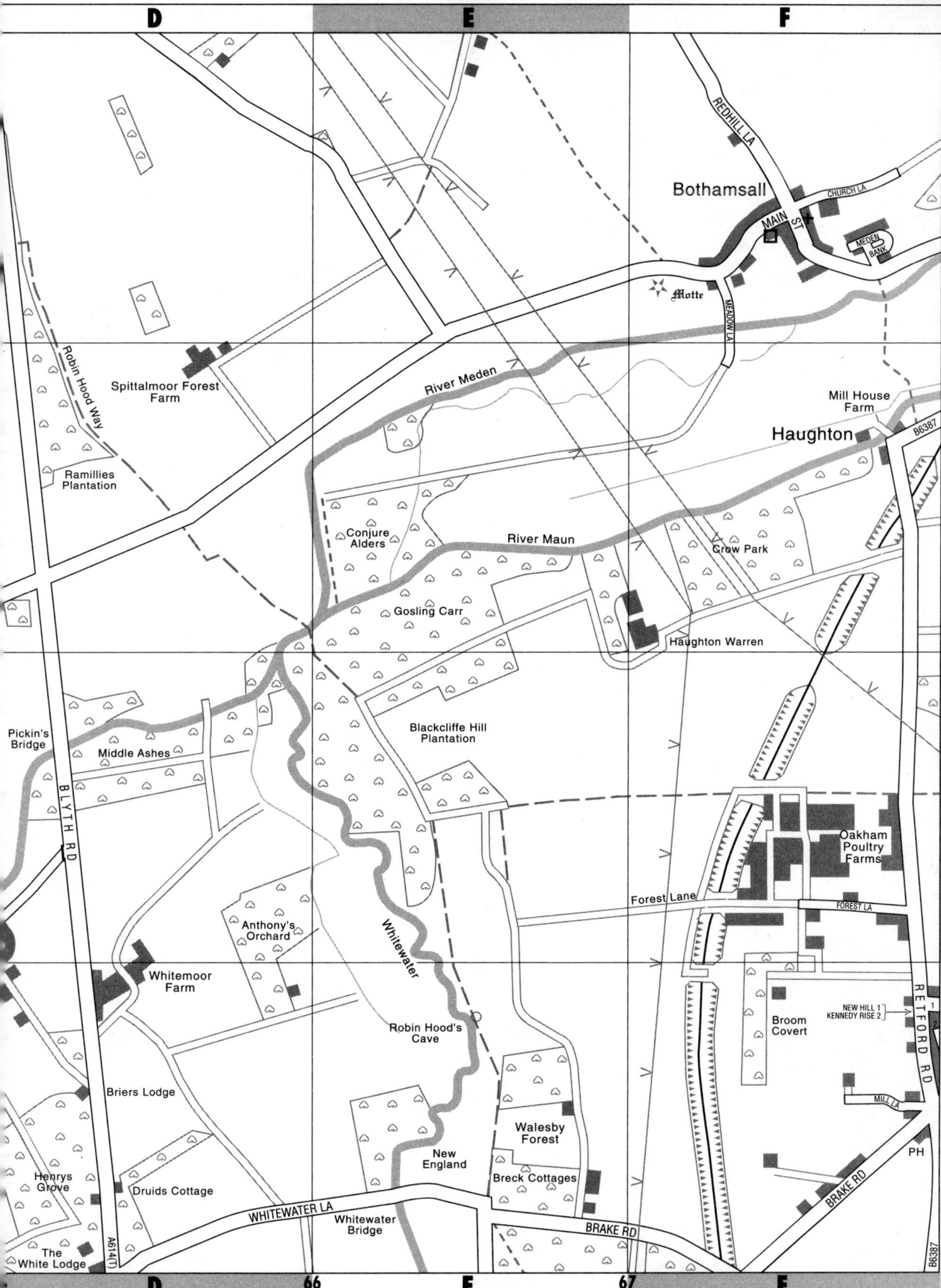
D
E
F
Bothamsall
REDHILL LA
CHURCH LA
MAIN ST
MEDEN BANK
Motte
MEADOW LA
Robin Hood Way
Spittalmoor Forest Farm
River Meden
Mill House Farm
Haughton
B6387
Ramillies Plantation
Conjure Alders
River Maun
Crow Park
Gosling Carr
Haughton Warren
Pickin's Bridge
Middle Ashes
Blackcliffe Hill Plantation
BLYTH RD
Oakham Poultry Farms
Forest Lane
FOREST LA
Anthony's Orchard
Whitewater
Whitemoor Farm
NEW HILL 1
KENNEDY RISE 2
RETFORD RD
Broom Covert
Robin Hood's Cave
Briers Lodge
MILL LA
Walesby Forest
New England
PH
Henrys Grove
Breck Cottages
BRAKE RD
Druids Cottage
WHITEWATER LA
Whitewater Bridge
A614(T)
The White Lodge
4
73
3
72
2
71
1
70
66
67
77
64

63
50

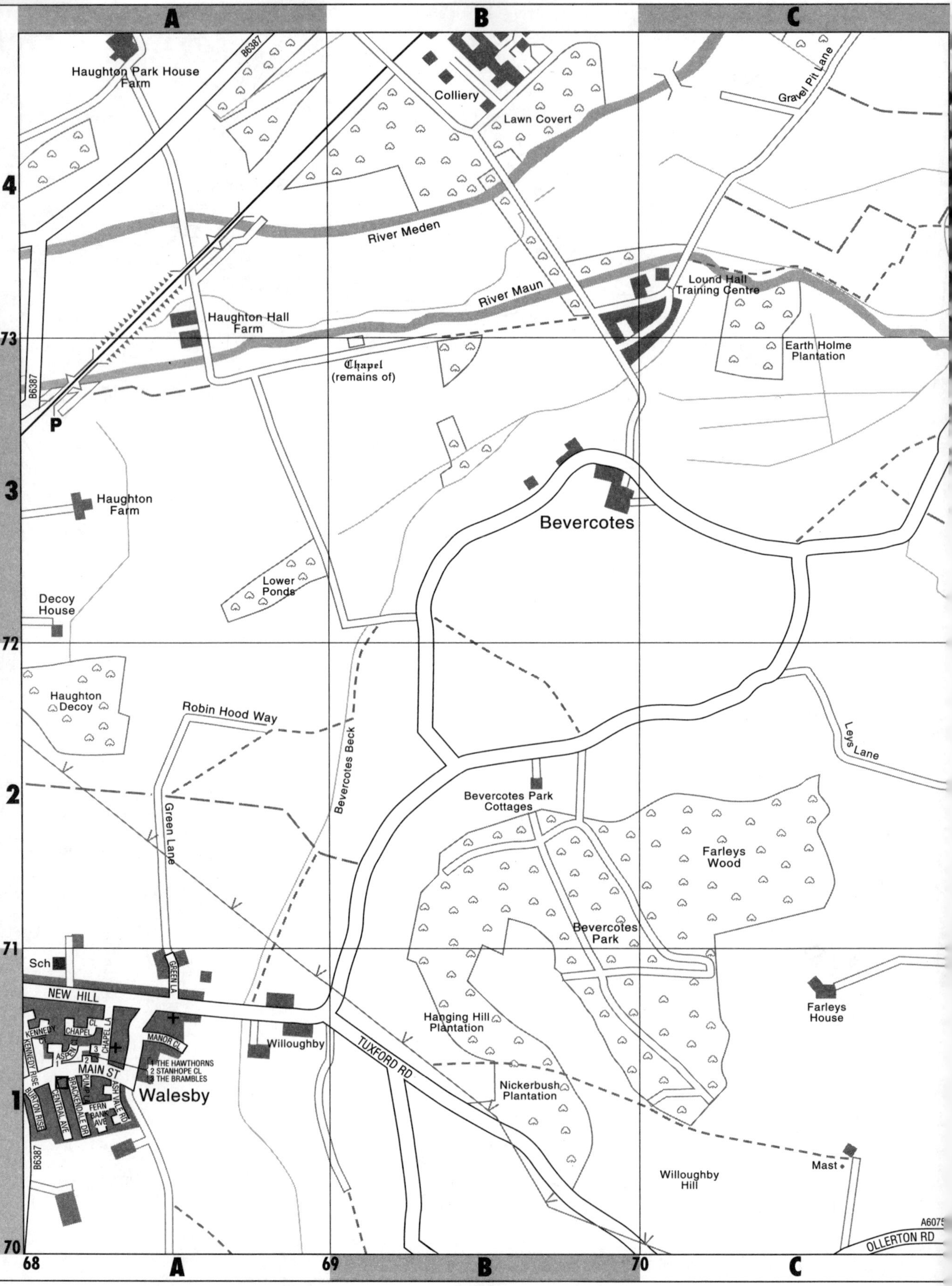
A
B
C
Haughton Park House Farm
B6387
Colliery
Lawn Covert
Gravel Pit Lane
River Meden
River Maun
Lound Hall Training Centre
Haughton Hall Farm
Earth Holme Plantation
Chapel (remains of)
P
Haughton Farm
Bevercotes
Lower Ponds
Decoy House
Haughton Decoy
Robin Hood Way
Bevercotes Beck
Leys Lane
Green Lane
Bevercotes Park Cottages
Farleys Wood
Bevercotes Park
Sch
GREEN LA
NEW HILL
Farleys House
Hanging Hill Plantation
KENNEDY CL
CHAPEL CL
CHAPEL LA
MANOR CL
ASPEN CL
Willoughby
TUXFORD RD
KENNEDY RISE
MAIN ST
1 THE HAWTHORNS
2 STANHOPE CL
3 THE BRAMBLES
Walesby
BURTON RISE
CENTRAL AVE
BRACKENDALE DR
FERN BANK AVE
ASH VALE RD
Nickerbush Plantation
Mast
Willoughby Hill
A6075
OLLERTON RD
4
73
3
72
2
71
1
70
68
69
70

63
78

D
E
F
A1(T)
A638
GREAT NORTH RD
Markham Moor Inn
Service Area
Service Area
A57(T)
Service Area
CLIFF GATE
Finney Lane
A57(T)
B1164
Beacon Hill
Sibthorpe
River Maun
Milton
Royal Oak (PH)
Cleveland Hill Farm
MILTON RD
GREAT NORTH RD
Folley House
West Markham
Water Works
Cleveland Farm
Windmill
Harold Lane
HIGH ST
Sch
ASKHAM RD
GREAT LA
FARM LA
OLD HALL LA
YORK ST
LOW ST
East Markham
BECKLAND HILL
PRIESTGATE
Northolme
MARK LA
EAST VIEW
TUXFORD RD
Broomhill
Mill Mount
High Croft
MARKHAM RD
Green Lane
South Hills Farm
Back Lane
BEVERCOTES RD
ELDON ST
B1164
LINCOLN RD
A6075
ASH VALE RD
CHANTRY WLK
Works
BRITISH FIELDS
A6075
GRANDOS CT
MARKET PL
Liby
BLUE BELL YD
THE PASTURES
PH
NEWARK RD
NEWCASTLE ST
Sch
ORCH CRES
PEEL AVE
THE BEECHES
BIRCH CT
A1(T)
F
Sta
ORCHARD CRES
CLARK LA
CLINTON GDN LA
LEXINGTON GDNS
LEXINGTON CT
Cemetery
Long Lane
Westwood
OLLERTON RD
Westwood Farm
A6075
EGMANTON RD
HOPYARD LA
4
73
3
72
2
71
1
70
72
73

65 52

A
B
C
High Brecks Farm
High Brecks Plantation
Brecks Plantation
Low Brecks Farm
Old Moorgate
A57(T)
BROAD GATE
A6075
Earthworks
Kingshaugh Farm
PH
HIGH ST
LINCOLN RD
COLLEGE LA
HALL LA
LOW ST
Markham Hall
MARK LA
CHURCH ST
PLANTATION RD
Back Lane
NOOKIN
QUAKEFIELD RD
ASKHAM RD
Darlton Field
Highfields Farm
Lodge Farm
Darlton Gaps
DARLTON RD
Goodhouses Farm
Eastfield House
PH
LINCOLN RD
HILLSIDE
A6075
WELBECK PL
FLEMING AVE
Sch
Tuxford
Merryfields Farm
MARNHAM RD
Park Cottage
ASHVALE RD
B1164
A1(T)
LODGE LA
Dismtd Rly
Ashvale
GREAT NORTH RD
Goosemoor Dyke
Lodge Farm
Ruddingwood
Peter Barn
4
73
3
72
2
71
1
70
74
75
76

65 80

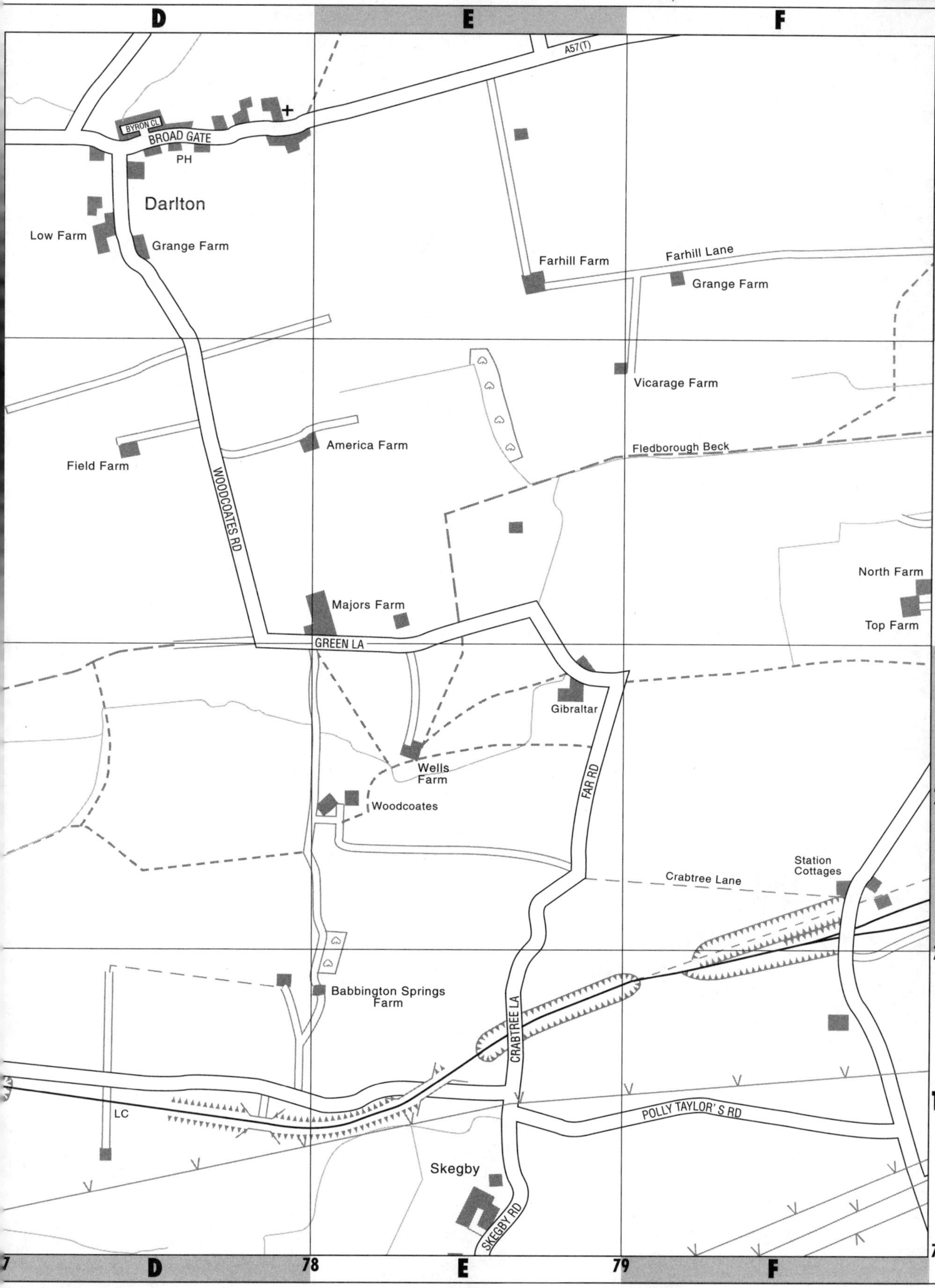
D
E
F
A57(T)
BYRON CL
BROAD GATE
PH
Darlton
Low Farm
Grange Farm
Farhill Farm
Farhill Lane
Grange Farm
4
73
Vicarage Farm
America Farm
Field Farm
Fledborough Beck
WOODCOATES RD
3
North Farm
Top Farm
Majors Farm
GREEN LA
72
Gibraltar
Wells Farm
FAR RD
Woodcoates
2
Station Cottages
Crabtree Lane
71
Babbington Springs Farm
CRABTREE LA
1
LC
POLLY TAYLOR'S RD
Skegby
SKEGBY RD
70
7
D
78
E
79
F

67
54

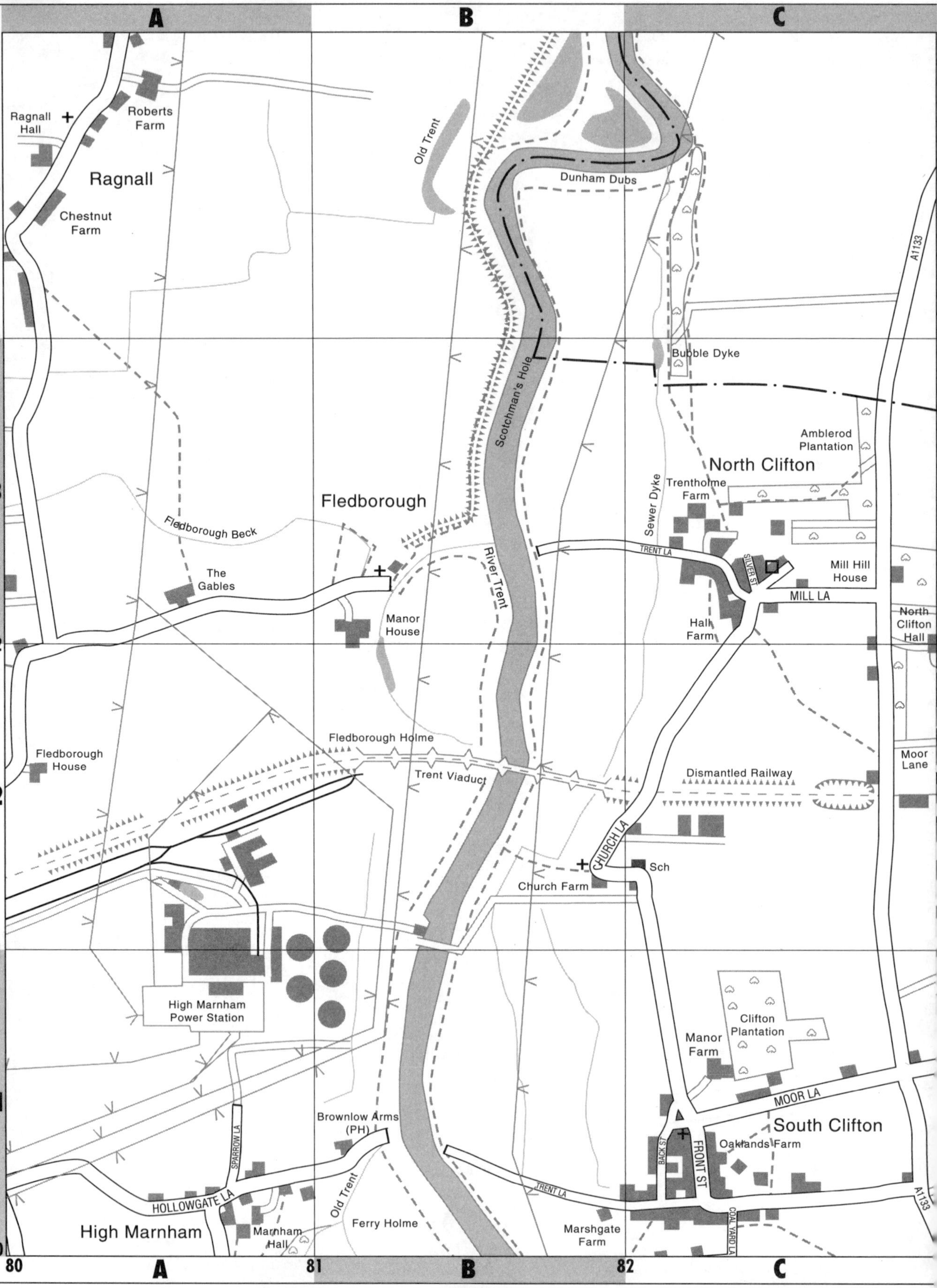
A
B
C
Ragnall Hall
Roberts Farm
Ragnall
Chestnut Farm
Old Trent
Dunham Dubs
Bubble Dyke
Scotchman's Hole
Amblerod Plantation
North Clifton
Trentholme Farm
Sewer Dyke
Fledborough
Fledborough Beck
The Gables
Manor House
River Trent
TRENT LA
SILVER ST
Mill Hill House
MILL LA
Hall Farm
North Clifton Hall
A1133
Fledborough House
Fledborough Holme
Trent Viaduct
Dismantled Railway
Moor Lane
CHURCH LA
Sch
Church Farm
High Marnham Power Station
Clifton Plantation
Manor Farm
MOOR LA
Brownlow Arms (PH)
South Clifton
Oaklands Farm
SPARROW LA
HOLLOWGATE LA
BACK ST
FRONT ST
TRENT LA
Old Trent
Ferry Holme
High Marnham
Marnham Hall
Marshgate Farm
COAL YARD LA
4
73
3
72
2
71
1
70
80
81
82

67
82

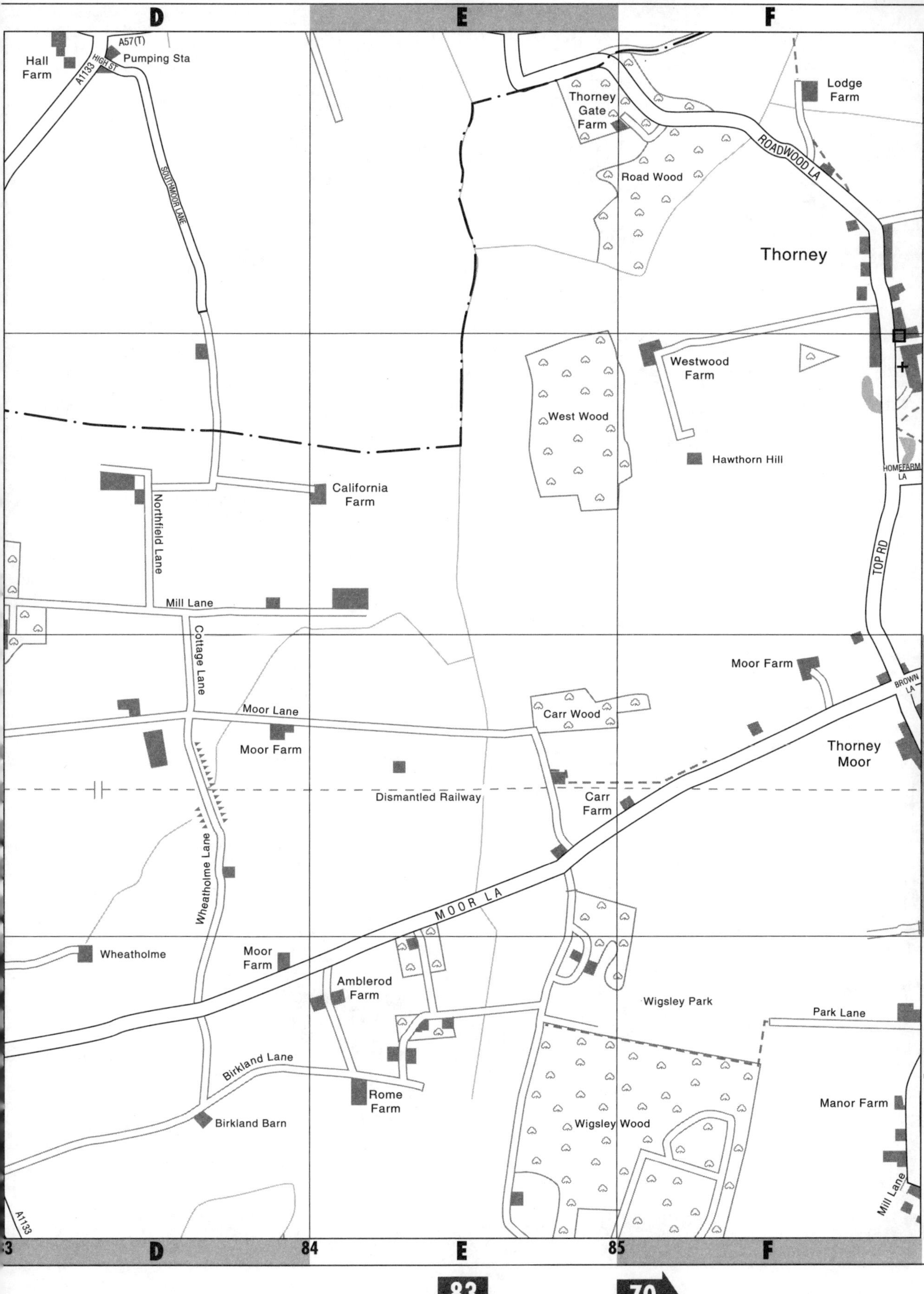
D
E
F
Hall Farm
A57(T)
Pumping Sta
A1133
HIGH ST
SOUTHMOOR LANE
Thorney Gate Farm
Lodge Farm
ROADWOOD LA
Road Wood
Thorney
4
73
Westwood Farm
West Wood
Hawthorn Hill
HOMEFARM LA
3
California Farm
Northfield Lane
TOP RD
Mill Lane
Cottage Lane
72
Moor Farm
BROWN LA
Moor Lane
Carr Wood
Moor Farm
Thorney Moor
Dismantled Railway
Carr Farm
2
Wheatholme Lane
MOOR LA
71
Wheatholme
Moor Farm
Amblerod Farm
Wigsley Park
Park Lane
Birkland Lane
Rome Farm
1
Manor Farm
Birkland Barn
Wigsley Wood
Mill Lane
A1133
70
83
84
85

69
56

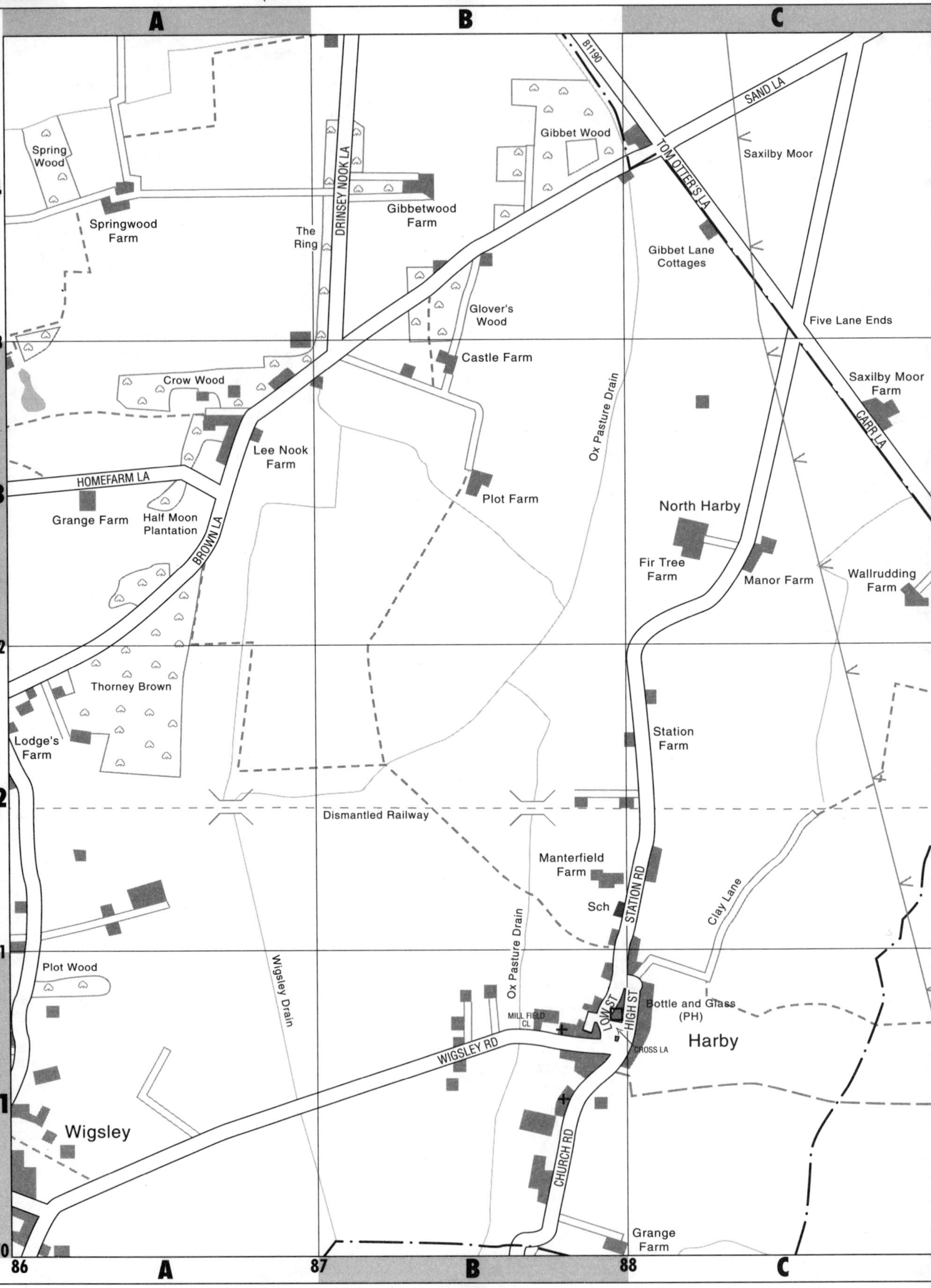
A
B
C
4
3
2
1
73
72
71
70
86
87
88
Spring Wood
Springwood Farm
The Ring
DRINSEY NOOK LA
Gibbetwood Farm
Gibbet Wood
B1190
SAND LA
TOM OTTER'S LA
Saxilby Moor
Gibbet Lane Cottages
Glover's Wood
Five Lane Ends
Castle Farm
Saxilby Moor Farm
CARR LA
Crow Wood
Lee Nook Farm
Ox Pasture Drain
HOMEFARM LA
Plot Farm
North Harby
Grange Farm
Half Moon Plantation
BROWN LA
Fir Tree Farm
Manor Farm
Wallrudding Farm
Thorney Brown
Lodge's Farm
Station Farm
Dismantled Railway
Manterfield Farm
Sch
STATION RD
Clay Lane
Plot Wood
Wigsley Drain
Ox Pasture Drain
MILL FIELD CL
LOW ST
HIGH ST
Bottle and Glass (PH)
CROSS LA
Harby
WIGSLEY RD
Wigsley
CHURCH RD
Grange Farm

69
84

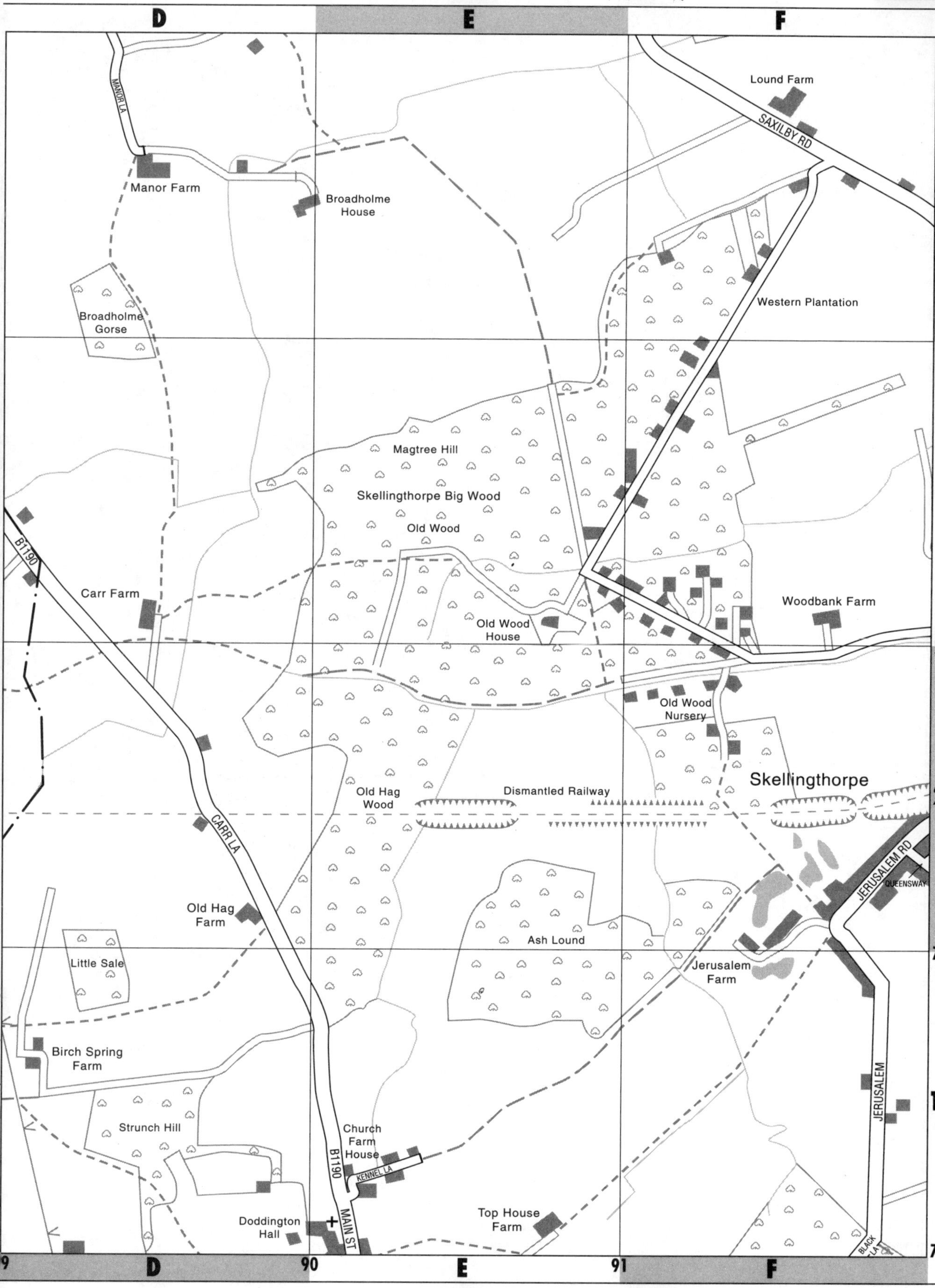
D
E
F
Lound Farm
SAXILBY RD
MANOR LA
Manor Farm
Broadholme
House
4
Western Plantation
Broadholme
Gorse
73
Magtree Hill
Skellingthorpe Big Wood
3
Old Wood
B1190
Carr Farm
Woodbank Farm
Old Wood
House
72
Old Wood
Nursery
Skellingthorpe
Old Hag
Wood
Dismantled Railway
2
CARR LA
JERUSALEM RD
QUEENSWAY
Old Hag
Farm
Ash Lound
Little Sale
71
Jerusalem
Farm
Birch Spring
Farm
JERUSALEM
1
Strunch Hill
Church
Farm
House
B1190
KENNEL LA
MAIN ST
Doddington
Hall
Top House
Farm
BLACK
LA
70
9
D
90
E
91
F

58

A
B
C
4
3
2
1
69
68
67
66
50
51
52
A632
MOOR LA
Cross Hills
SCARCLIFFE LA
Upper Langwith
Old Hall
Cave
River Poulter
Scarcliffe Lanes
The Jays
Dismantled Railway
School
A632
DALE CL
LANGWITH MALTINGS
HARDWICK ST
COMPTON ST
HARTINGTON ST
DEVONSHIRE DR
CAVENDISH ST
MALTHOUSE COTTAGES
Langwith
Gildwells Farm
PH
Bradshaw Wood
New Plantation
Scarcliffe
Archaeological Trail
Langwith Junction
HADDON PL
THE BASSETT
VAUGHAN PL
ALBINE RD
STATION RD
CHATSWORTH AVE
THE CRESCENT
BURLINGTON AVE
EAST VIEW
RECREATION RD
RECREATION VIEW
CHERRY CL
ORANGE CL
BOUNDARY CL
OLIVE AVE
PINE CL
BRAMBLE CL
WILLOW AVE
ALMOND AVE
ROWAN DR
STUBBINS WOOD
STUBBINS WOOD LA
Schools
Offices
LANGWITH RD
Deans Plantation
Langwith Wood
School
ALDER CL
ASH GR
WOODSIDE RD
LILAC GR
LABURNUM AVENUE
VALLEY RD
BROOKFIELD CRES
SPRINGFIELD AVE
ORCHARD CL
PARK RD
ARCADIA DR
Sch
ALANDALE AVE
THE CLOSE
ELAND RD
Wks
Sch
YEW TREE DR
LIMES CRES
ACORN RIDGE
BIRCH GR
ALDER WAY
LINDEN GR
AUSTIN ST
THICKLEY CL
Roseland Wood
SLANT LA
CHESTNUT DR
OAK AVE
LARCH AVE
ELM TREE AVE
HAWTHORNE AVE
HAZEL CRES
CARTER LA W
GARDEN AVE
THORESBY AVE
SHERWOOD AVE
HARDWICK AVE
PARK AVE
CARTER LA
Lby
VICTORIA ST
MAIN ST
DIVISION RD
MARKET ST
STATION RD
HEREWOOD CL
PORTLAND RD
B6407
F Sta
Roseland Farm
Roseland Lane
COMMON LA
THE ROCKLANDS
MAYFLOWER CT
ROCKLEY WAY
BYRON ST
KING EDWARD ST
HILL TOP AVE
SUMMIT DR
HIGHCLIFFE AVE
LITTLE LA
HILL CREST
MAIN ST
STATION VIEW
LONG LA
NICHOLSON'S ROW
SOOKHOLME RD
SOOKHOLME
B6407
MALLARD CL
VICARAGE
YORK RD
CENTRAL CL
Sch
Sch
THE SPINNEY
THE LEAWAY
THE KNOLL
HILLSWAY
THE COPPICE
LEEN VALLEY DR
THE PEAK
TEAL CL
EIDER CL
Shirebrook
CENTRAL DR
CHURCH DR
SHERWOOD DR
SWANWICK AVE
BRUNNER AVE
SOUTH AVE
LONG LA
PROSPECT DR
RECREATION DR
VALE DR
ACREAGE LA
CORONATION DR
FIELD DR
BRIAR CL
Works
Cemy
STINTING LA
NEWBARN CL
Balkham Lane
Archaeological Trail
Forge La
Green Lane
Dismantled Railway
Hodhill Farm
WOOD LA
Woodland Farm
B6407
Pleasleypark Farm

87

59 74

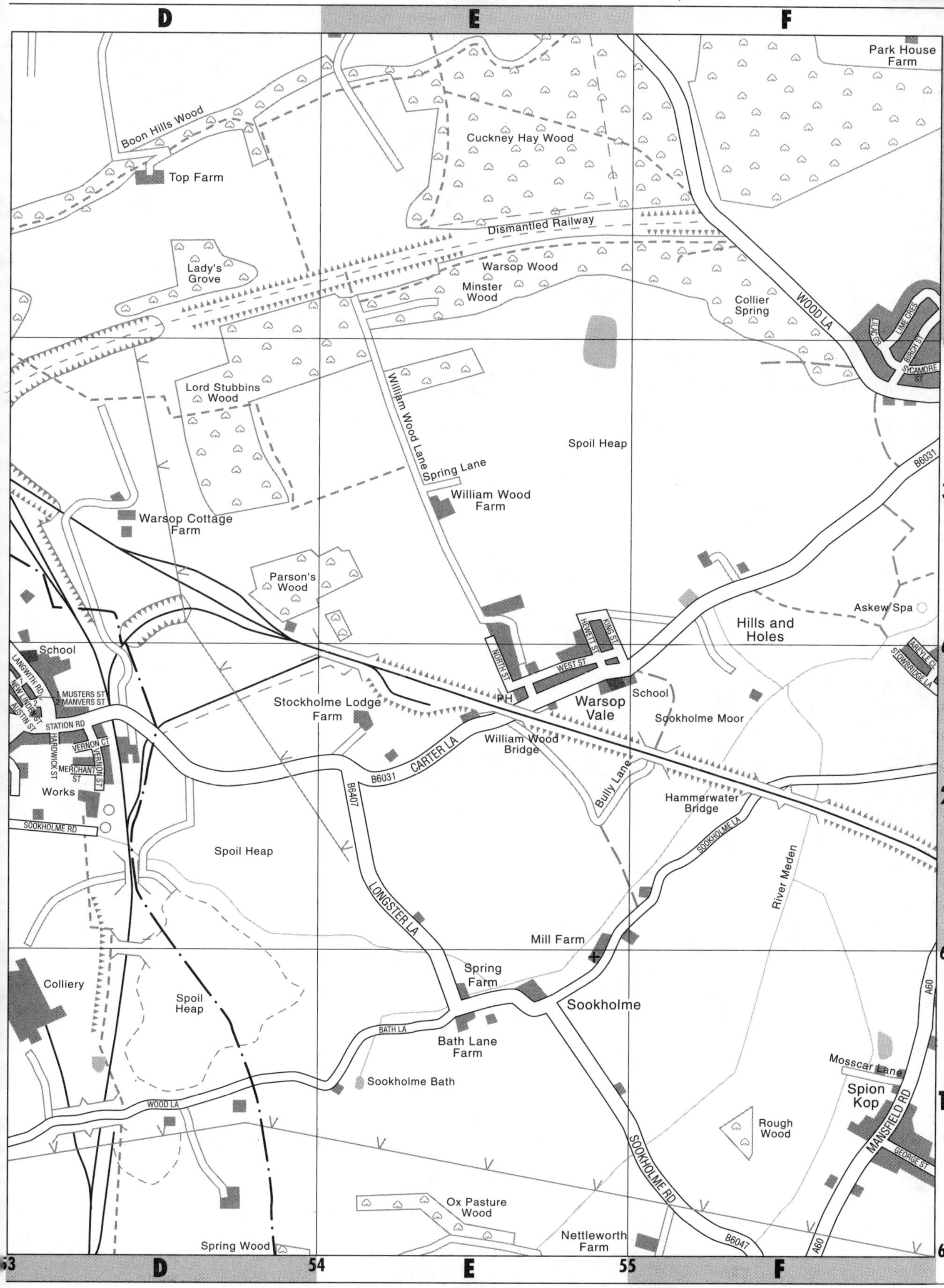
D
E
F
Park House Farm
Boon Hills Wood
Cuckney Hay Wood
Top Farm
Dismantled Railway
Lady's Grove
Warsop Wood
Minster Wood
Collier Spring
WOOD LA
LILAC GR
LIME CRES
BIRCH ST
SYCAMORE ST
Lord Stubbins Wood
William Wood Lane
Spoil Heap
Spring Lane
B6031
William Wood Farm
Warsop Cottage Farm
Parson's Wood
Askew Spa
Hills and Holes
School
HEWETT ST
KING ST
NORTH ST
WEST ST
ARGYLE CL
STOWBRIDGE LA
LANGWITH RD
NEW UNION ST
AUSTIN ST
1 MUSTERS ST
2 MANVERS ST
PH
Stockholme Lodge Farm
Warsop Vale
School
Sookholme Moor
STATION RD
HARDWICK ST
VERNON CT
VERNON ST
MERCHANT ST
William Wood Bridge
CARTER LA
B6031
Works
SOOKHOLME RD
B6407
Bully Lane
Hammerwater Bridge
SOOKHOLME LA
Spoil Heap
River Meden
LONGSTER LA
Mill Farm
Spring Farm
Colliery
Spoil Heap
Sookholme
A60
BATH LA
Bath Lane Farm
Mosscar Lane
Sookholme Bath
Spion Kop
WOOD LA
Rough Wood
MANSFIELD RD
GEORGE ST
SOOKHOLME RD
Ox Pasture Wood
Nettleworth Farm
B6047
Spring Wood
A60
4
69
3
68
2
67
1
66
53
54
55

88 74

73
60

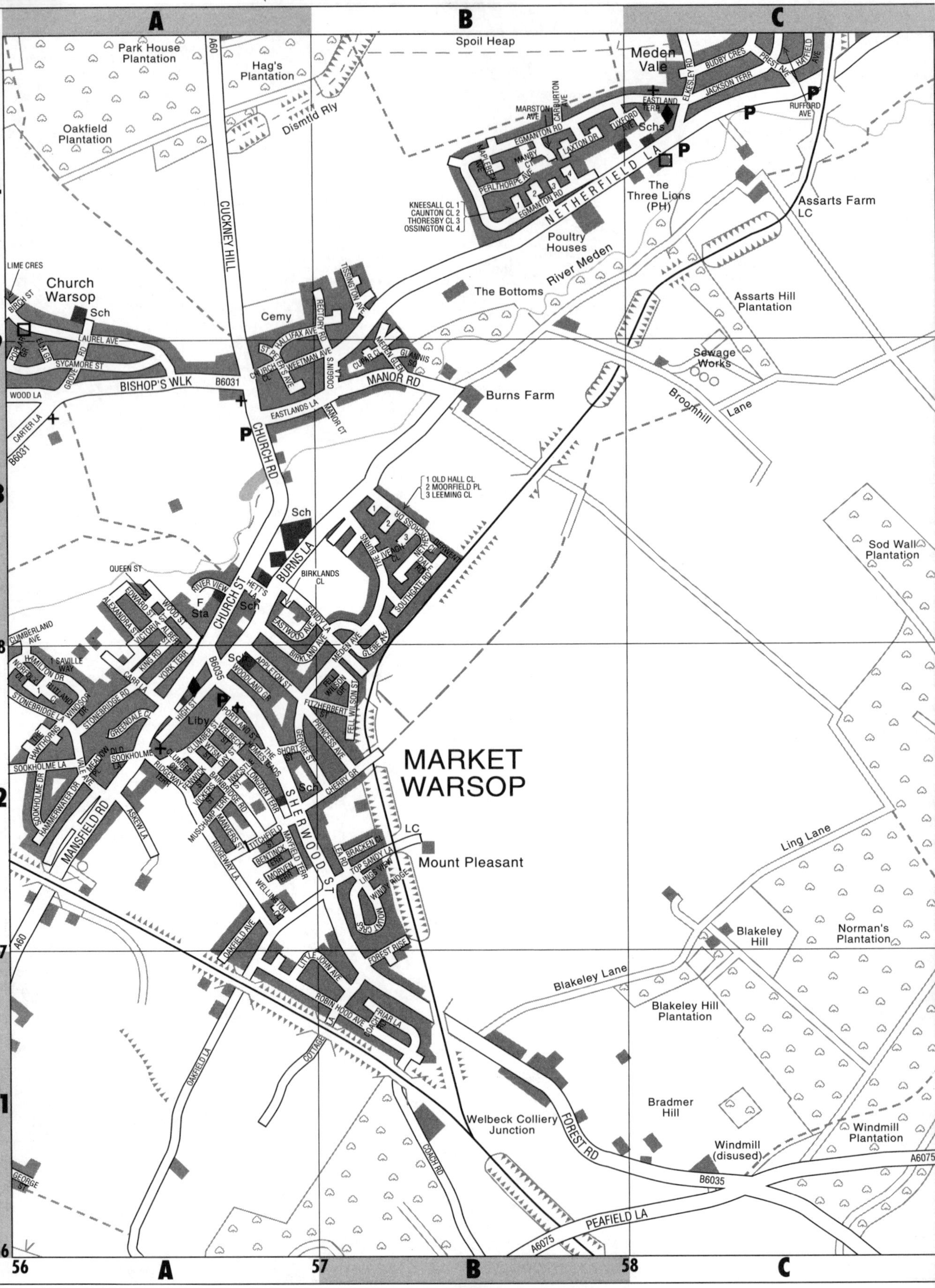
A
B
C
Spoil Heap
Park House Plantation
Hag's Plantation
Dismtld Rly
Oakfield Plantation
Meden Vale
Schs
The Three Lions (PH)
Poultry Houses
Assarts Farm
LC
Netherfield La
Kneesall Cl 1
Caunton Cl 2
Thoresby Cl 3
Ossington Cl 4
Church Warsop
Sch
Cemy
Cuckney Hill
The Bottoms
River Meden
Assarts Hill Plantation
Sewage Works
Burns Farm
Broomhill Lane
Bishop's Wlk
B6031
Manor Rd
Eastlands La
Church Rd
Wood La
Carter La
1 Old Hall Cl
2 Moorfield Pl
3 Leeming Cl
Sod Wall Plantation
Queen St
Birklands Cl
Church St
Burns La
Southgate Rd
F Sta
Liby
MARKET WARSOP
Sherwood St
Mansfield Rd
Sookholme La
Mount Pleasant
Ling Lane
Norman's Plantation
Blakeley Hill
Blakeley Lane
Blakeley Hill Plantation
Bradmer Hill
Windmill (disused)
Windmill Plantation
Welbeck Colliery Junction
Forest Rd
Oakfield La
Coach Rd
Peafield La
A6075
B6035
A60
4
69
3
68
2
67
1
66
56
57
58

73
89

61
76

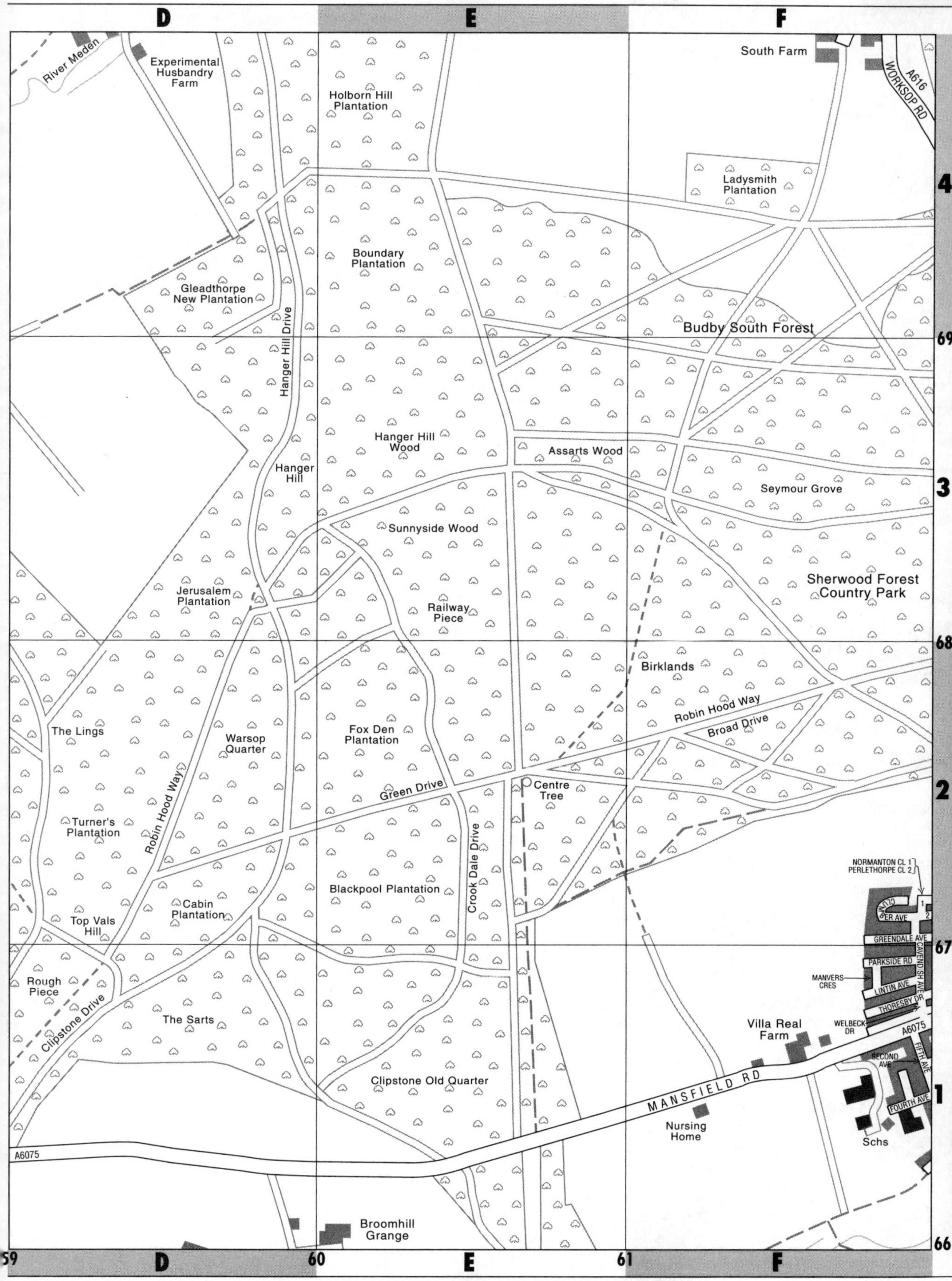
D
E
F
River Meden
Experimental Husbandry Farm
Holborn Hill Plantation
South Farm
A616
WORKSOP RD
Ladysmith Plantation
4
Boundary Plantation
Gleadthorpe New Plantation
Budby South Forest
69
Hanger Hill Drive
Hanger Hill Wood
Assarts Wood
Hanger Hill
Seymour Grove
3
Sunnyside Wood
Sherwood Forest Country Park
Jerusalem Plantation
Railway Piece
68
Birklands
Robin Hood Way
Broad Drive
The Lings
Warsop Quarter
Fox Den Plantation
Green Drive
Centre Tree
2
Robin Hood Way
Turner's Plantation
Crook Dale Drive
NORMANTON CL 1
PERLETHORPE CL 2
Blackpool Plantation
Cabin Plantation
Top Vals Hill
GREENDALE AVE
67
PARKSIDE RD
CAVENDISH AVE
MANVERS CRES
LINTIN AVE
THORESBY DR
Rough Piece
Clipstone Drive
The Sarts
Villa Real Farm
WELBECK DR
A6075
SECOND AVE
FIFTH AVE
Clipstone Old Quarter
MANSFIELD RD
1
FOURTH AVE
Nursing Home
Schs
A6075
Broomhill Grange
66
59
60
61

90
76

75
62

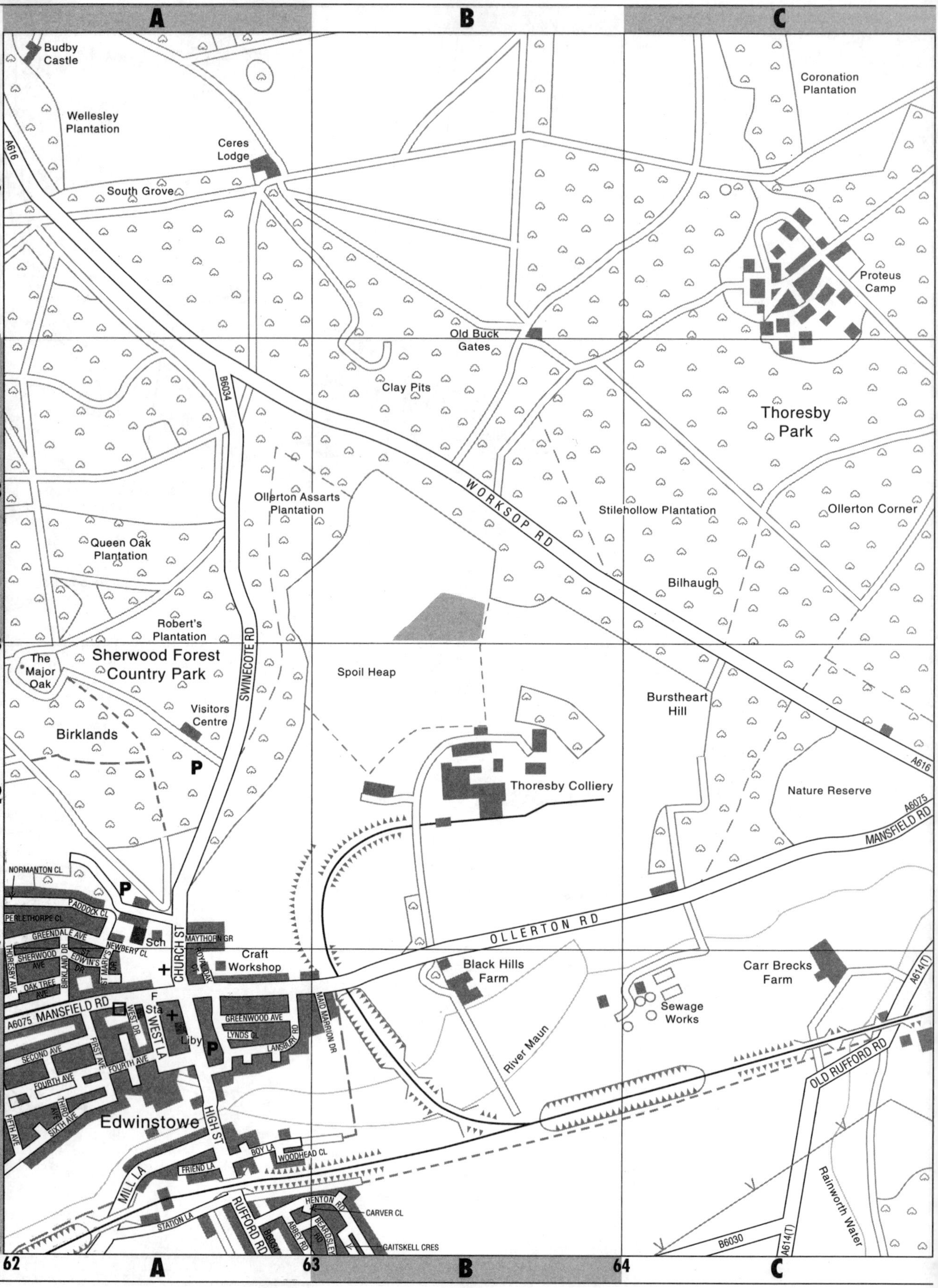
A
B
C
Budby Castle
Wellesley Plantation
Coronation Plantation
Ceres Lodge
South Grove
A616
Proteus Camp
Old Buck Gates
Clay Pits
Thoresby Park
B6034
Ollerton Assarts Plantation
WORKSOP RD
Stilehollow Plantation
Ollerton Corner
Queen Oak Plantation
Bilhaugh
Robert's Plantation
The Major Oak
Sherwood Forest Country Park
Spoil Heap
Visitors Centre
Burstheart Hill
Birklands
SWINECOTE RD
Thoresby Colliery
Nature Reserve
A6075
MANSFIELD RD
NORMANTON CL
PADDOCK CL
PERLETHORPE CL
GREENDALE AVE
NEWBERY CL
Sch
CHURCH ST
MAYTHORN GR
OLLERTON RD
SHERWOOD AVE
THORESBY AVE
OAK TREE AVE
BIRKLAND DR
EDWIN'S DR
ST MARY'S GR
ROYAL OAK CT
Craft Workshop
Black Hills Farm
Carr Brecks Farm
A614(T)
A6075 MANSFIELD RD
WEST DR
WEST LA
F Sta
Liby
GREENWOOD AVE
LYNDS CL
LANSBURY RD
MAID MARRION DR
Sewage Works
River Maun
SECOND AVE
FIRST AVE
FOURTH AVE
THIRD AVE
SIXTH AVE
FIFTH AVE
OLD RUFFORD RD
Edwinstowe
HIGH ST
BOY LA
WOODHEAD CL
FRIEND LA
MILL LA
Rainworth Water
HENTON RD
CARVER CL
BEARDSLEY RD
ABBEY RD
STATION LA
RUFFORD RD
GAITSKELL CRES
B6030
A614(T)
4
69
3
68
2
67
1
66
62
63
64

75
91

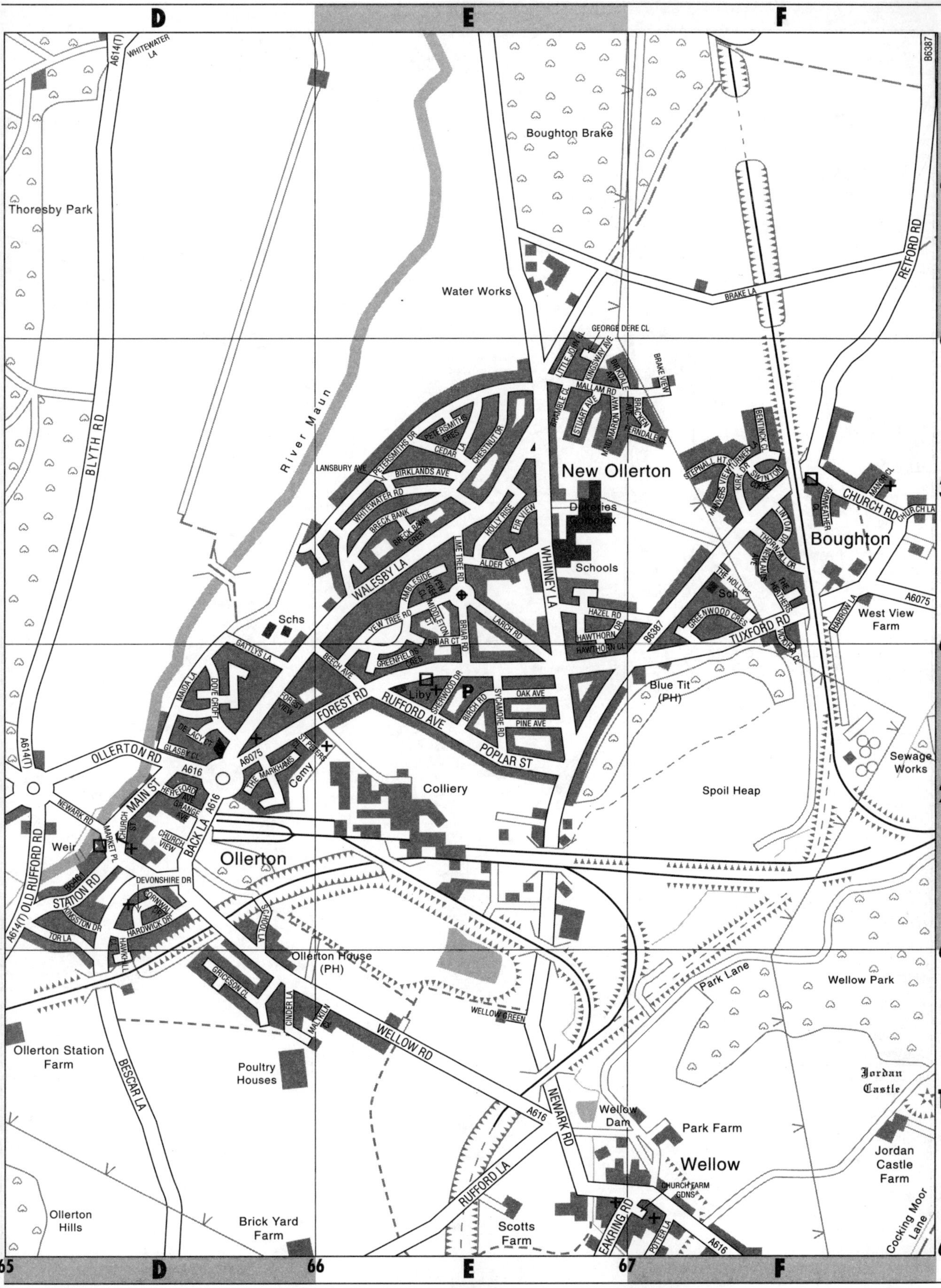
Boughton Brake
Thoresby Park
Water Works
River Maun
New Ollerton
Boughton
Schools
Schs
Sch
West View Farm
Blue Tit (PH)
Sewage Works
Spoil Heap
Colliery
Ollerton
Weir
Ollerton House (PH)
Park Lane
Wellow Park
Jordan Castle
Ollerton Station Farm
Poultry Houses
Wellow Dam
Park Farm
Wellow
Jordan Castle Farm
Ollerton Hills
Brick Yard Farm
Scotts Farm
Cocking Moor Lane
BLYTH RD
OLLERTON RD
WALESBY LA
FOREST RD
RUFFORD AVE
POPLAR ST
WHINNEY LA
TUXFORD RD
CHURCH RD
RETFORD RD
BRAKE LA
WELLOW RD
NEWARK RD
RUFFORD LA
BESCAR LA
OLD RUFFORD RD
EAKRING RD
BACK LA
MAIN ST
STATION RD
Liby
Cemy

77
64

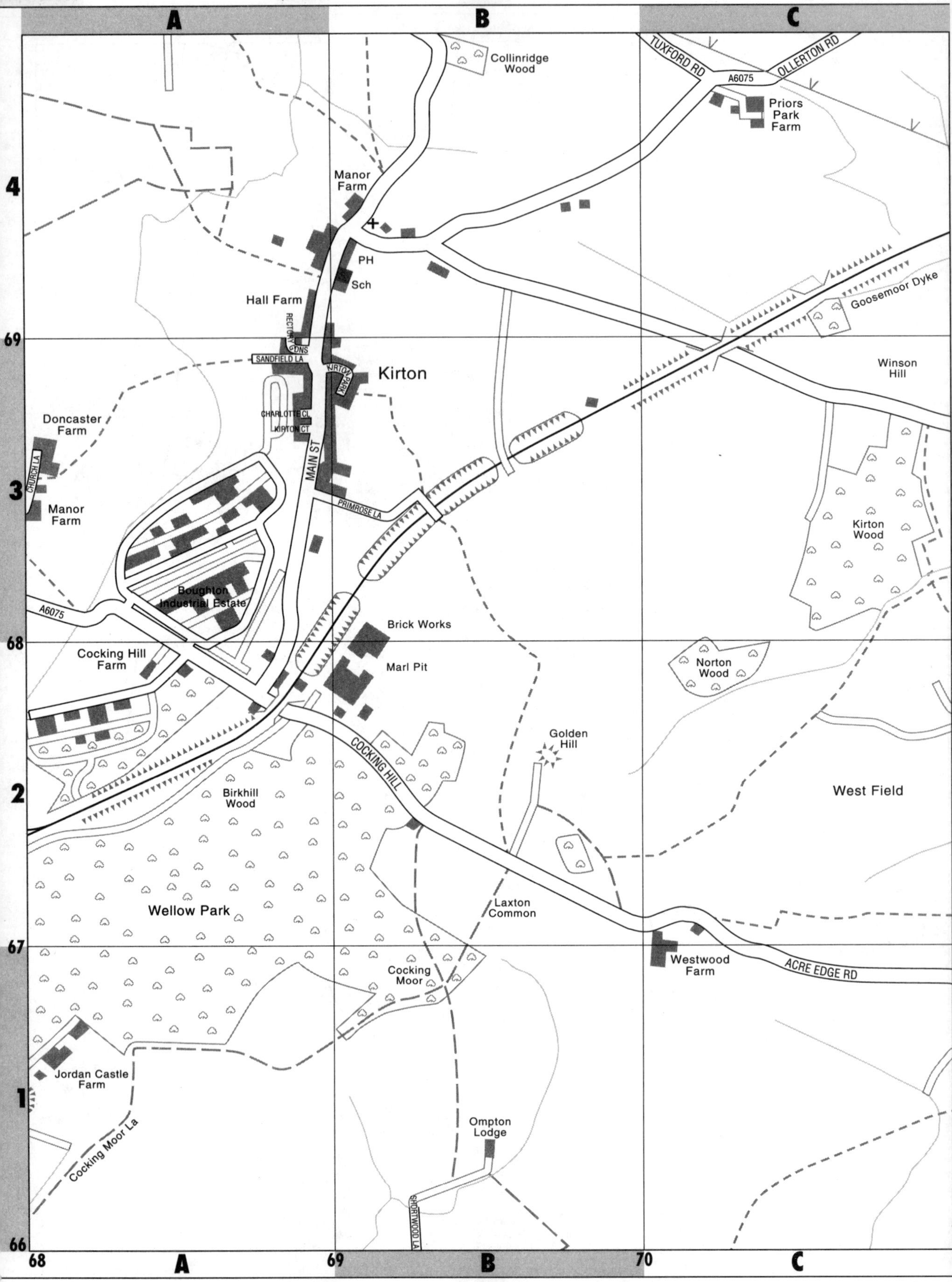
A
B
C
4
3
2
1
69
68
67
66
70
TUXFORD RD
OLLERTON RD
A6075
Collinridge Wood
Priors Park Farm
Manor Farm
PH
Sch
Hall Farm
RECTORY GDNS
SANDFIELD LA
KIRTON PARK
Kirton
CHARLOTTE CL
KIRTON CT
MAIN ST
PRIMROSE LA
Goosemoor Dyke
Winson Hill
Doncaster Farm
CHURCH LA
Manor Farm
Kirton Wood
A6075
Boughton Industrial Estate
Brick Works
Marl Pit
Cocking Hill Farm
Norton Wood
Golden Hill
COCKING HILL
Birkhill Wood
West Field
Wellow Park
Laxton Common
Cocking Moor
Westwood Farm
ACRE EDGE RD
Jordan Castle Farm
Cocking Moor La
Ompton Lodge
SPORTWOOD LA

77
93

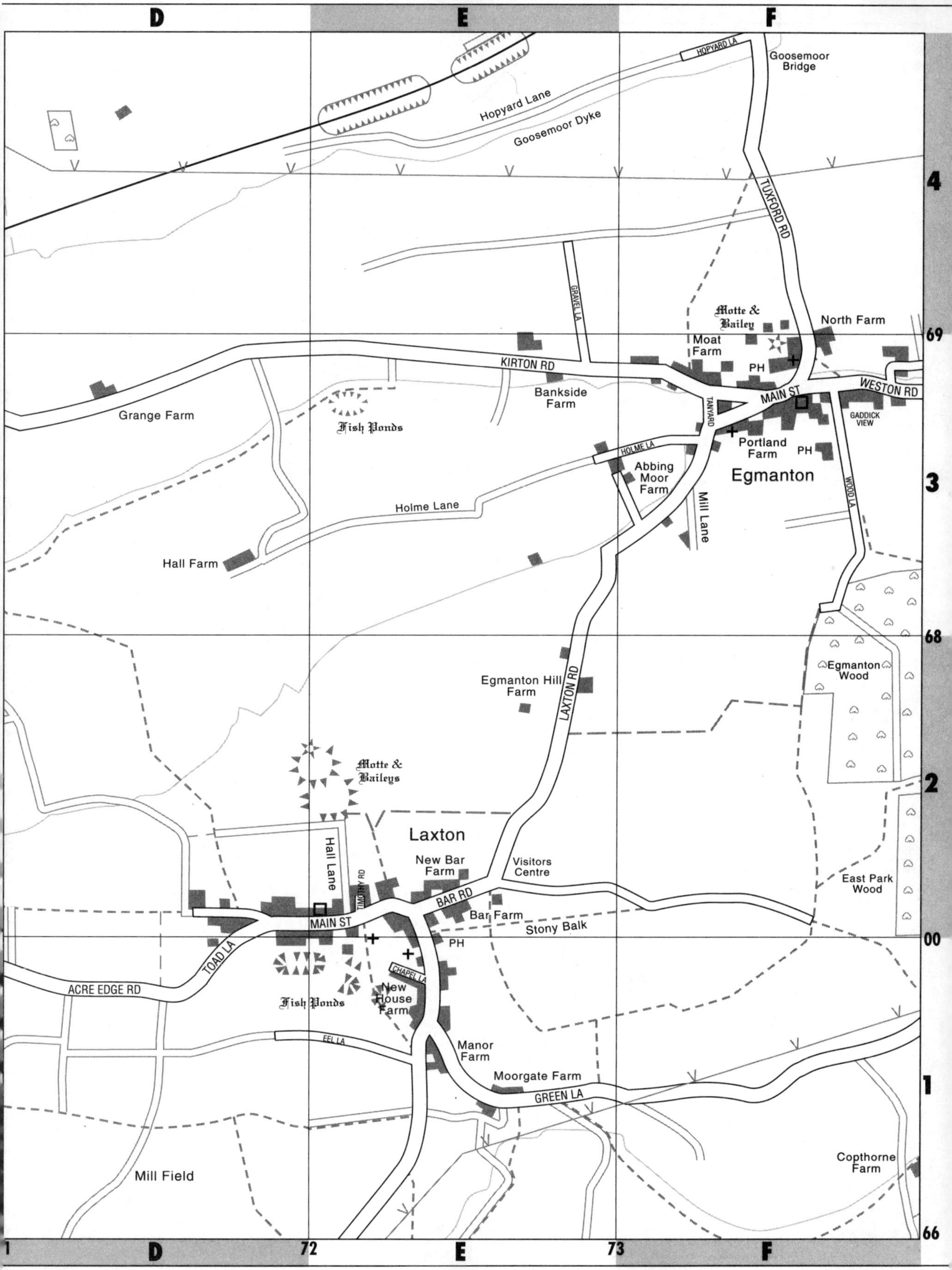
D
E
F
HOPYARD LA
Goosemoor Bridge
Hopyard Lane
Goosemoor Dyke
TUXFORD RD
GRAVEL LA
Motte & Bailey
North Farm
Moat Farm
PH
KIRTON RD
Bankside Farm
WESTON RD
MAIN ST
TANYARD
GADDICK VIEW
Grange Farm
Fish Ponds
Portland Farm
PH
HOLME LA
Abbing Moor Farm
Egmanton
Mill Lane
WOOD LA
Holme Lane
Hall Farm
Egmanton Hill Farm
LAXTON RD
Egmanton Wood
Motte & Baileys
Laxton
Hall Lane
TIMOTHY RD
New Bar Farm
Visitors Centre
East Park Wood
BAR RD
Bar Farm
MAIN ST
Stony Balk
PH
TOAD LA
CHAPEL LA
ACRE EDGE RD
New House Farm
Fish Ponds
EEL LA
Manor Farm
Moorgate Farm
GREEN LA
Copthorne Farm
Mill Field
4
69
3
68
2
00
1
66
1
72
73

79
66

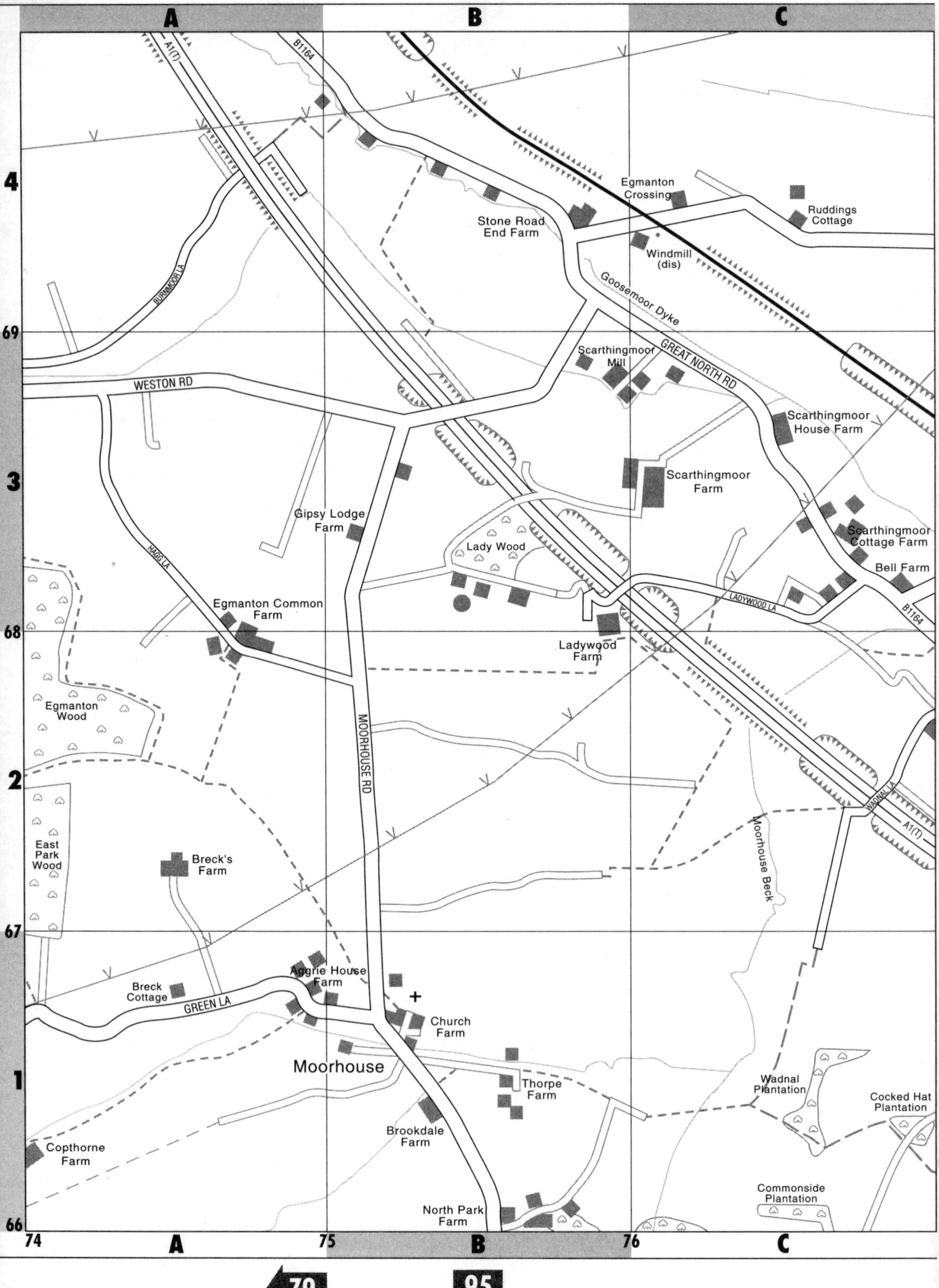
A
B
C
4
3
2
1
69
68
67
66
74
75
76
A1(T)
B1164
BURNMOOR LA
WESTON RD
Stone Road
End Farm
Egmanton
Crossing
Ruddings
Cottage
Windmill
(dis)
Goosemoor Dyke
GREAT NORTH RD
Scarthingmoor
Mill
Scarthingmoor
House Farm
Scarthingmoor
Farm
Gipsy Lodge
Farm
Lady Wood
Scarthingmoor
Cottage Farm
Bell Farm
LADYWOOD LA
HAGG LA
Egmanton Common
Farm
Ladywood
Farm
Egmanton
Wood
MOORHOUSE RD
East
Park
Wood
Breck's
Farm
WADNAL LA
Moorhouse Beck
Breck
Cottage
GREEN LA
Aggrie House
Farm
Church
Farm
Moorhouse
Thorpe
Farm
Wadnal
Plantation
Cocked Hat
Plantation
Brookdale
Farm
Copthorne
Farm
Commonside
Plantation
North Park
Farm

79
95

67
82

D
E
F
Skegby Manor
Waterloo Farm
Hanginghill La
SKEGBY RD
Thurber
The Ruddings Farm
Stonehill House
Sch
MILL LA
Square and Compass (Inn)
CAD LA
GRACEFIELD LA
Mount Pleasant
EASTGATE
Vic
TUXFORD RD
Church Farm
BROTTS LA
Trentman Lodge
Normanton on Trent
The Crown (PH)
Vines House Farm
HAWBUSH RD
Mount Pleasant Farm
SOUTH ST
BROTTS RD
Archway Farm
WESTON LA
Manor Farm
SOUTH LA
Border Farm
Moor Farm
BELL LA
Grassthorpe Beck
Moat
CHURCH WK
MAIN ST
MEADOW LA
Stud Farm
PH
COLLEY LA
Weston
WADNAL LA
Grassthorpe
INGRAM LA
COPPER HILL
TOWN ST
SILVER ST
TOWN LA
INFIELD LA
Grassthorpe Lane Crossing
GREAT NORTH RD
A1(T)
Mill Farm
Grange Farm
Lodge Plantation
Dunstall Lodge
Crow Park Farm
The Crest
GRASSTHORPE RD
Works
Cemy
BULHAM LA
CROW PARK AVE
SNELL CL
THE MEERINGS
STERNTHORPE CL
STATION RD
Rod Holt
Poplar Farm
B1164
4
69
3
68
2
67
1
66
77
78
79

96
82

81
68

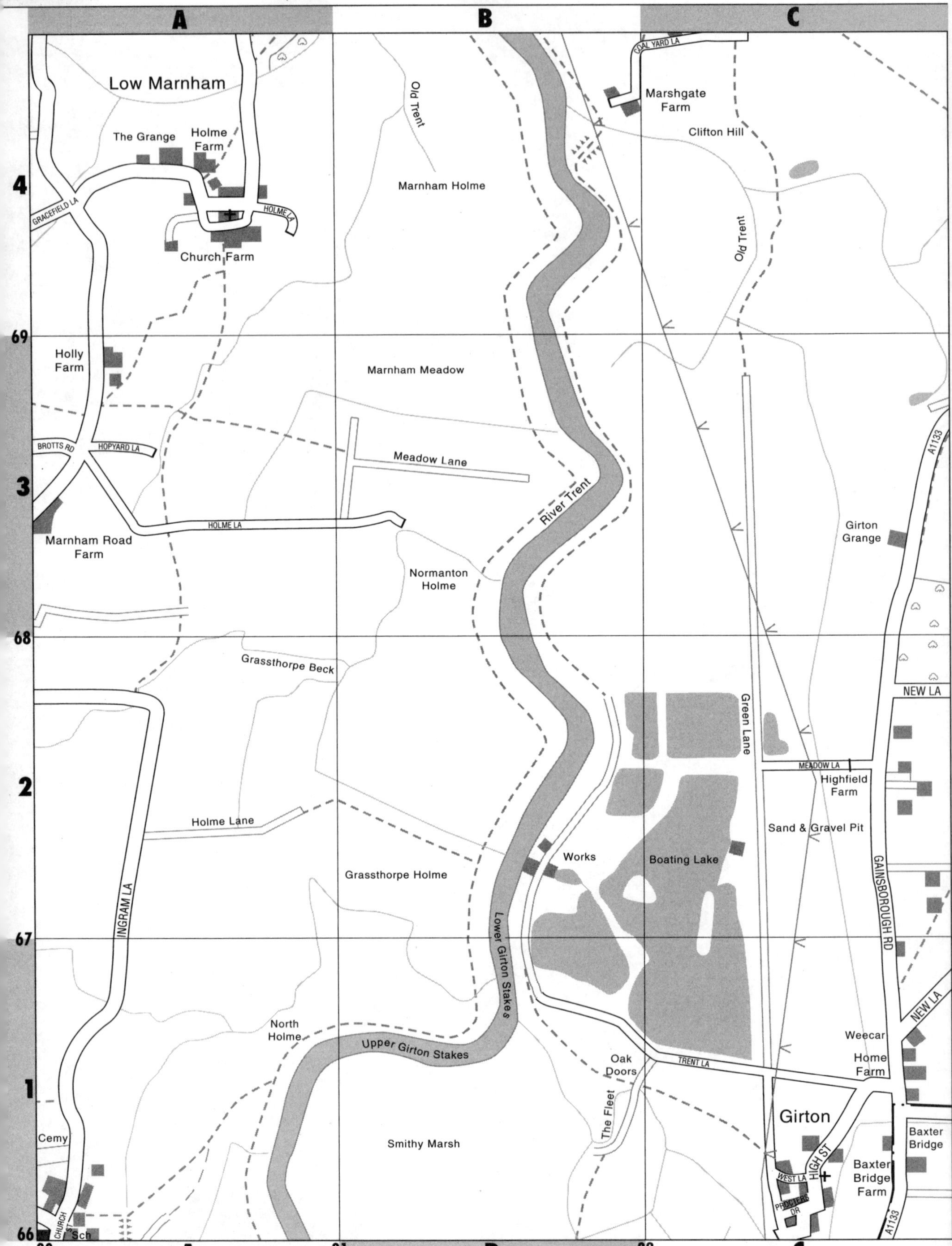
A
B
C
Low Marnham
The Grange
Holme Farm
Church Farm
GRACEFIELD LA
HOLME LA
Old Trent
Marnham Holme
COAL YARD LA
Marshgate Farm
Clifton Hill
4
69
Holly Farm
Marnham Meadow
BROTTS RD
HOPYARD LA
Meadow Lane
3
HOLME LA
Marnham Road Farm
River Trent
Girton Grange
A1133
Normanton Holme
68
Grassthorpe Beck
NEW LA
Green Lane
MEADOW LA
Highfield Farm
2
Holme Lane
Sand & Gravel Pit
Works
Boating Lake
Grassthorpe Holme
GAINSBOROUGH RD
INGRAM LA
67
Lower Girton Stakes
NEW LA
North Holme
Upper Girton Stakes
Weecar
Home Farm
Oak Doors
TRENT LA
1
Girton
The Fleet
Cemy
Smithy Marsh
Baxter Bridge
HIGH ST
WEST LA
Baxter Bridge Farm
PROCTERS DR
CHURCH ST
Sch
66
80
A
81
B
82
C

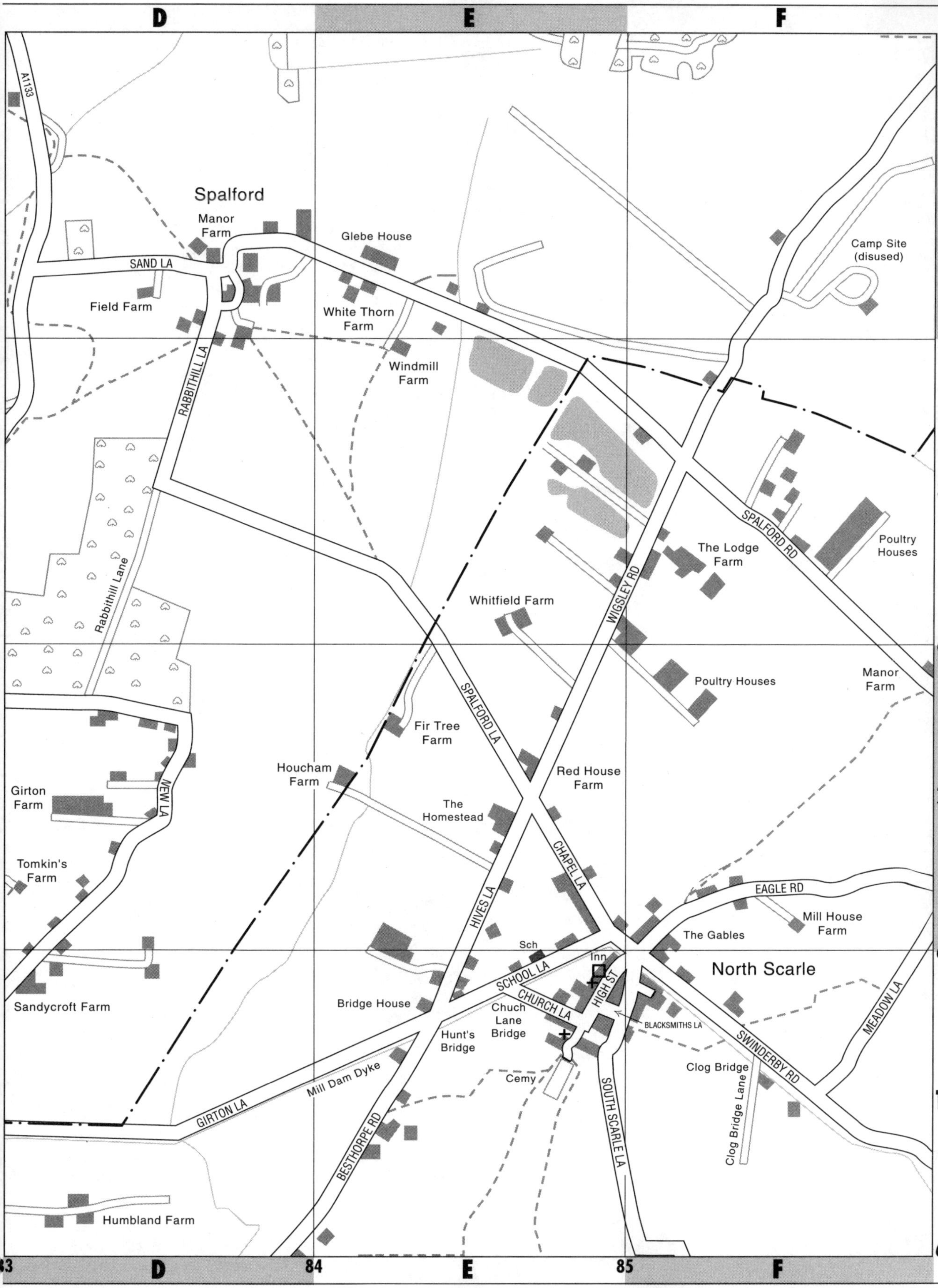
D
E
F
A1133
Spalford
Manor Farm
SAND LA
Field Farm
Glebe House
White Thorn Farm
Windmill Farm
Camp Site (disused)
RABBITHILL LA
Rabbithill Lane
SPALFORD RD
The Lodge Farm
Poultry Houses
Whitfield Farm
WIGSLEY RD
Poultry Houses
Manor Farm
SPALFORD LA
Fir Tree Farm
Houcham Farm
Red House Farm
NEW LA
Girton Farm
The Homestead
Tomkin's Farm
CHAPEL LA
HIVES LA
EAGLE RD
Mill House Farm
The Gables
Sch
Inn
North Scarle
SCHOOL LA
CHURCH LA
HIGH ST
BLACKSMITHS LA
Sandycroft Farm
Bridge House
Chuch Lane Bridge
Hunt's Bridge
MEADOW LA
SWINDERBY RD
Clog Bridge
Cemy
Mill Dam Dyke
GIRTON LA
BESTHORPE RD
SOUTH SCARLE LA
Clog Bridge Lane
Humbland Farm
4
69
3
68
2
67
1
66
83
84
85

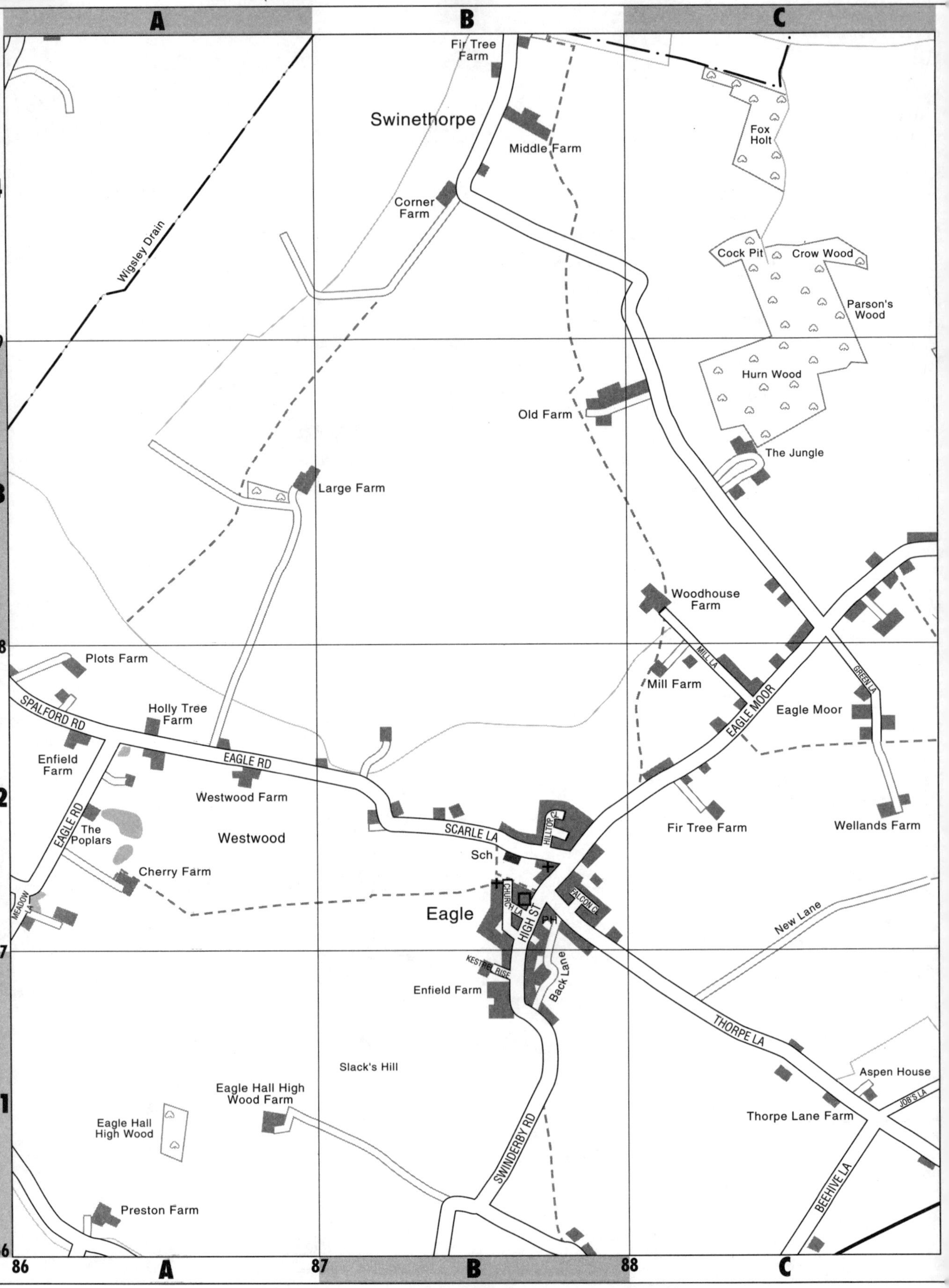
A
B
C
4
3
2
1
69
68
67
66
86
87
88
Fir Tree Farm
Swinethorpe
Middle Farm
Fox Holt
Corner Farm
Wigsley Drain
Cock Pit
Crow Wood
Parson's Wood
Hurn Wood
Old Farm
The Jungle
Large Farm
Woodhouse Farm
MILL LA
Mill Farm
GREEN LA
Plots Farm
Holly Tree Farm
SPALFORD RD
EAGLE RD
EAGLE MOOR
Eagle Moor
Enfield Farm
Westwood Farm
Fir Tree Farm
Wellands Farm
EAGLE RD
The Poplars
Westwood
SCARLE LA
HILLTOP CL
Sch
Cherry Farm
CHURCH LA
HIGH ST
FALCON CL
PH
MEADOW LA
Eagle
New Lane
KESTREL RISE
Back Lane
Enfield Farm
THORPE LA
Slack's Hill
Aspen House
Eagle Hall High Wood Farm
JOB'S LA
Eagle Hall High Wood
Thorpe Lane Farm
SWINDERBY RD
BEEHIVE LA
Preston Farm

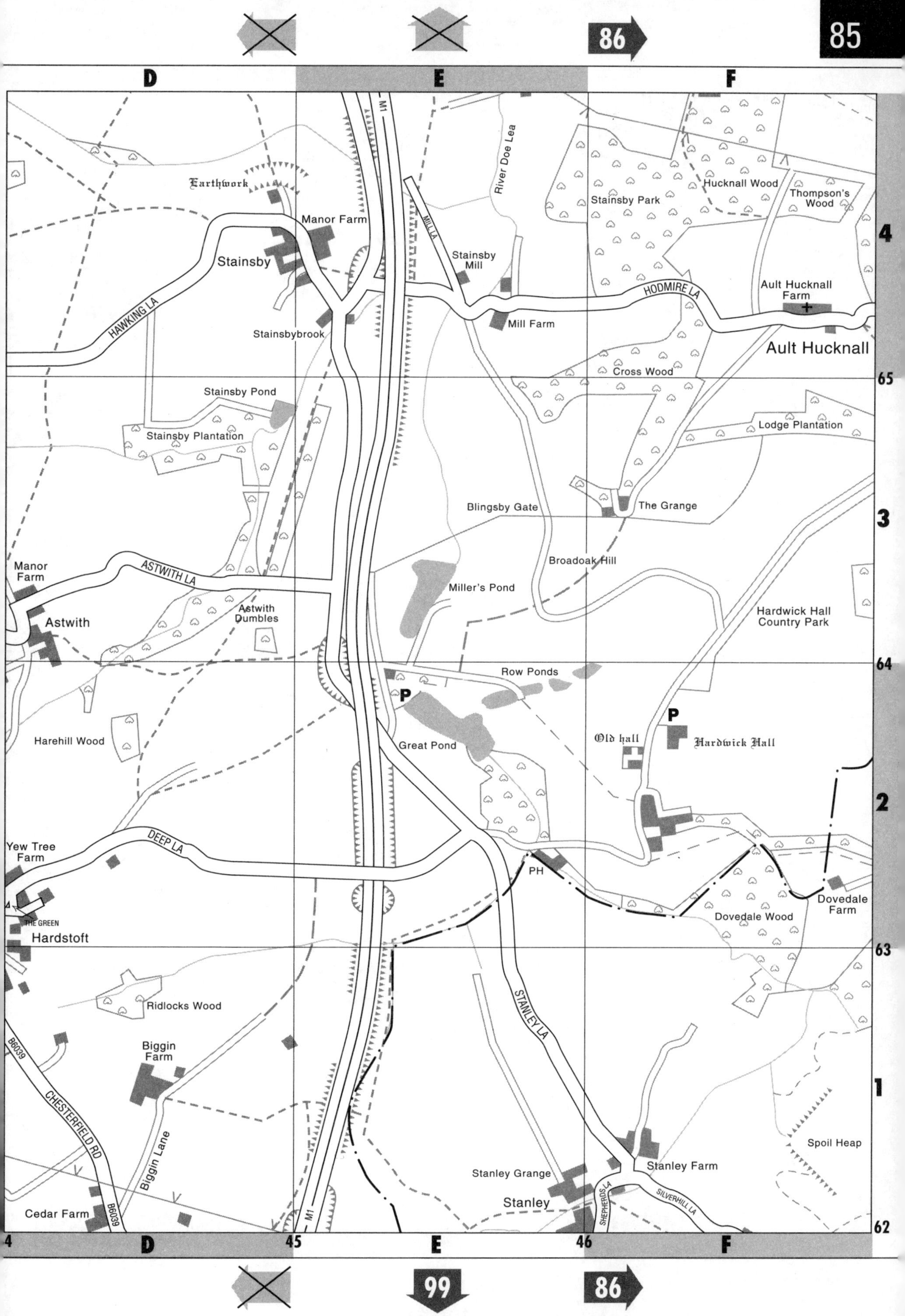
86
D
E
F
M1
River Doe Lea
Earthwork
Manor Farm
Stainsby
Mill La
Stainsby Mill
Stainsby Park
Hucknall Wood
Thompson's Wood
4
Hawking La
Stainsbybrook
Mill Farm
Hodmire La
Ault Hucknall Farm
Ault Hucknall
Cross Wood
65
Stainsby Pond
Stainsby Plantation
Lodge Plantation
Blingsby Gate
The Grange
3
Manor Farm
Astwith La
Broadoak Hill
Miller's Pond
Astwith
Astwith Dumbles
Hardwick Hall Country Park
64
Row Ponds
P
Harehill Wood
Great Pond
Old hall
Hardwick Hall
2
Yew Tree Farm
Deep La
PH
Dovedale Farm
The Green
Hardstoft
Dovedale Wood
63
Ridlocks Wood
Stanley La
B6039
Biggin Farm
1
Chesterfield Rd
Spoil Heap
Biggin Lane
Stanley Farm
Stanley Grange
Shepherds La
Silverhill La
Stanley
Cedar Farm
B6039
M1
62
4
D
45
E
46
F
99
86

85

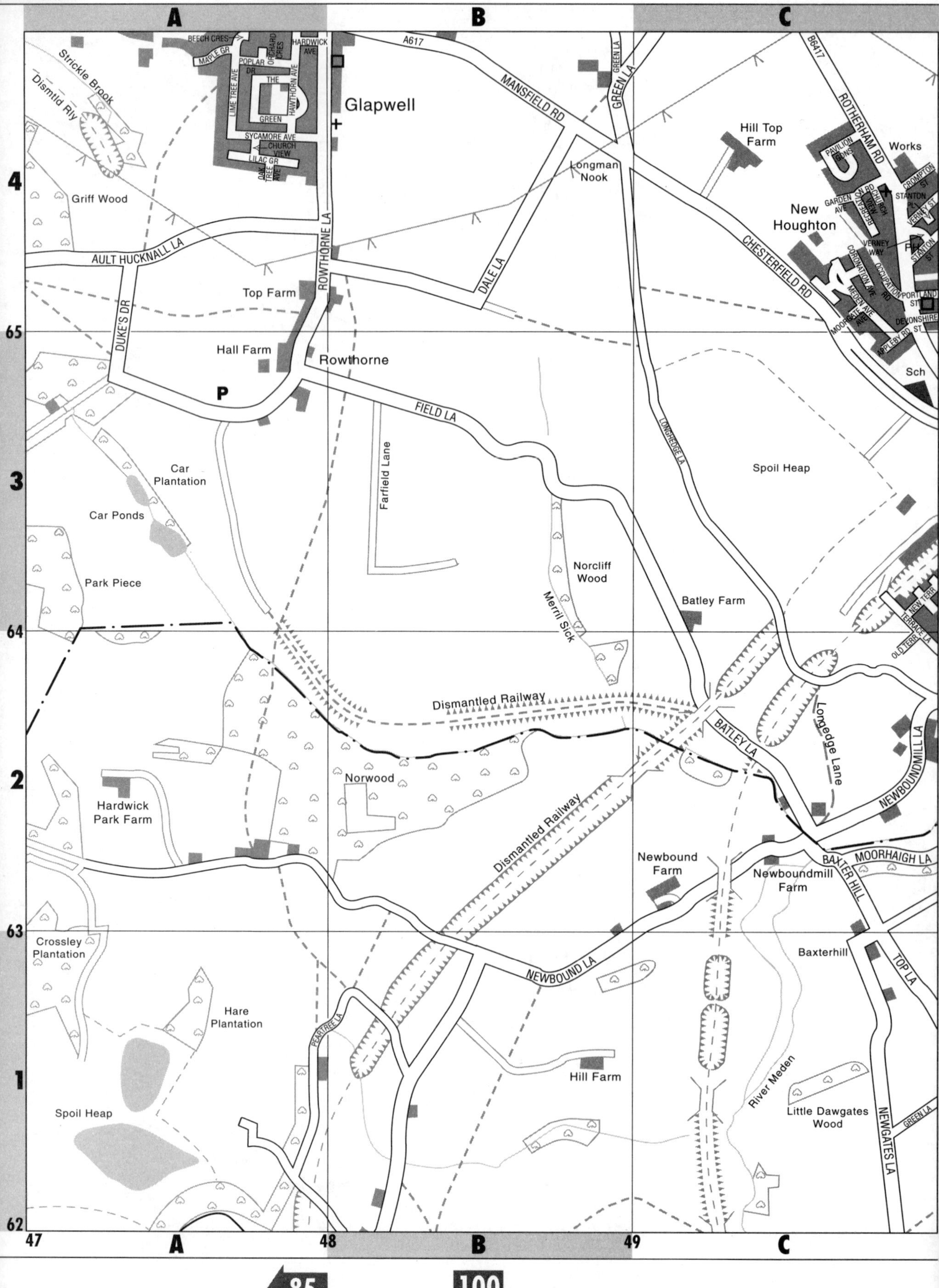
A
B
C
4
3
2
1
65
64
63
62
47
48
49
Glapwell
BEECH CRES
MAPLE GR
POPLAR DR
ORCHARD CRES
HARDWICK AVE
LIME TREE AVE
THE GREEN
HAWTHORN AVE
SYCAMORE AVE
CHURCH VIEW
LILAC GR
OAK TREE AVE
A617
MANSFIELD RD
GREEN LA
B6417
ROTHERHAM RD
Strickle Brook
Dismtld Rly
Griff Wood
AULT HUCKNALL LA
ROWTHORNE LA
DALE LA
Longman Nook
Hill Top Farm
Works
PAVILION GDNS
New Houghton
GARDEN AVE
CHURCH VIEW
STANTON PL
VERNEY ST
VERNEY WAY
PH
STANTON ST
CHESTERFIELD RD
CORONATION AVE
OCCUPATION RD
PORTLAND ST
MEDEN AVE
MOORGATE AVE
DEVONSHIRE ST
APPLEBY RD
CROMPTON ST
Sch
Top Farm
DUKE'S DR
Hall Farm
Rowthorne
P
FIELD LA
Farfield Lane
LONGHEDGE LA
Spoil Heap
Car Plantation
Car Ponds
Park Piece
Norcliff Wood
Merril Sick
Batley Farm
NEW TERR
TERRACE LA
OLD TERR
Dismantled Railway
BATLEY LA
Longedge Lane
NEWBOUNDMILL LA
Norwood
Hardwick Park Farm
Dismantled Railway
Newbound Farm
Newboundmill Farm
BAXTER HILL
MOORHAIGH LA
Crossley Plantation
NEWBOUND LA
Baxterhill
TOP LA
Hare Plantation
PEARTREE LA
Hill Farm
River Meden
Little Dawgates Wood
Spoil Heap
NEWGATES LA
GREEN LA

85

100

72
88

D E F

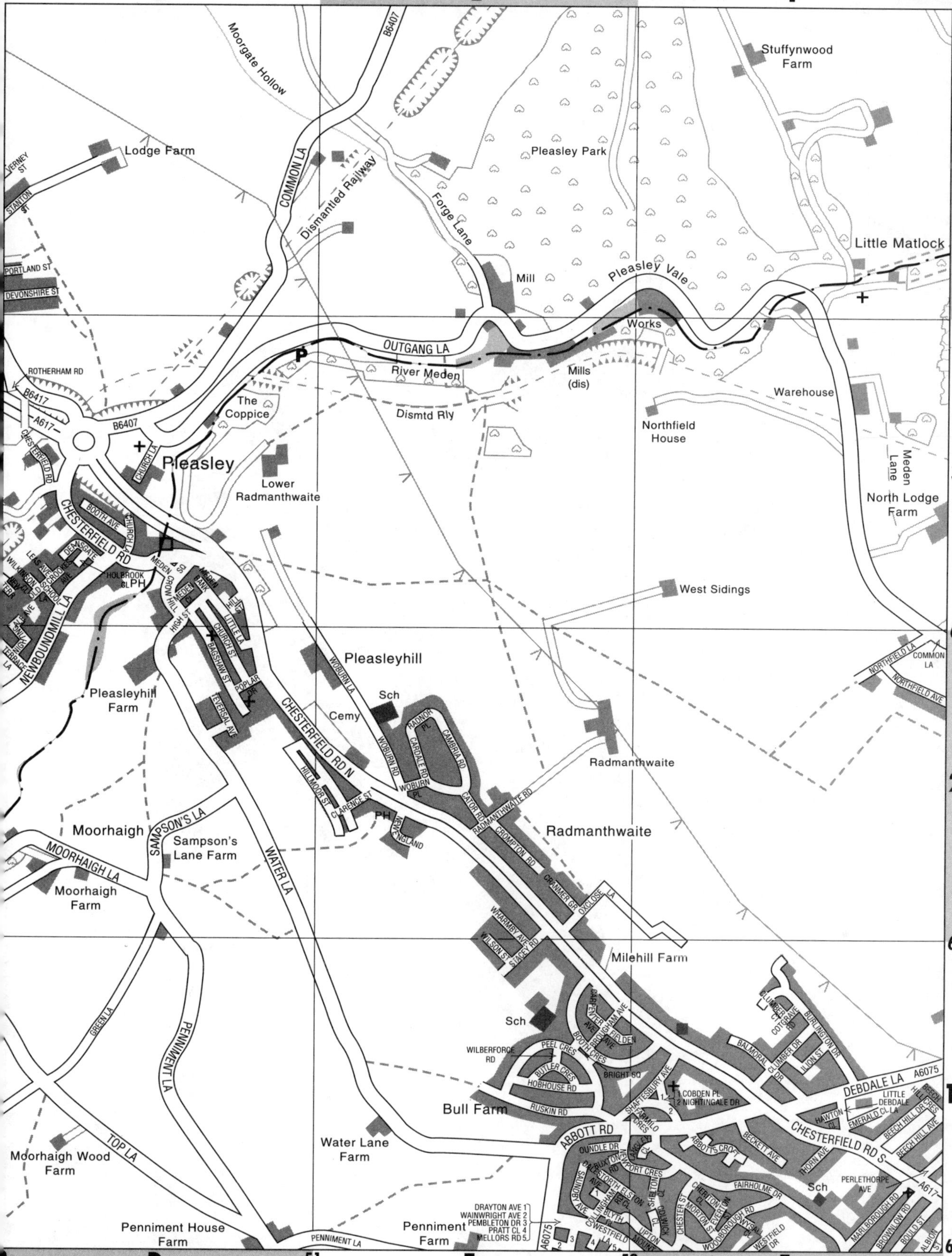


D E F

101
88

87
73

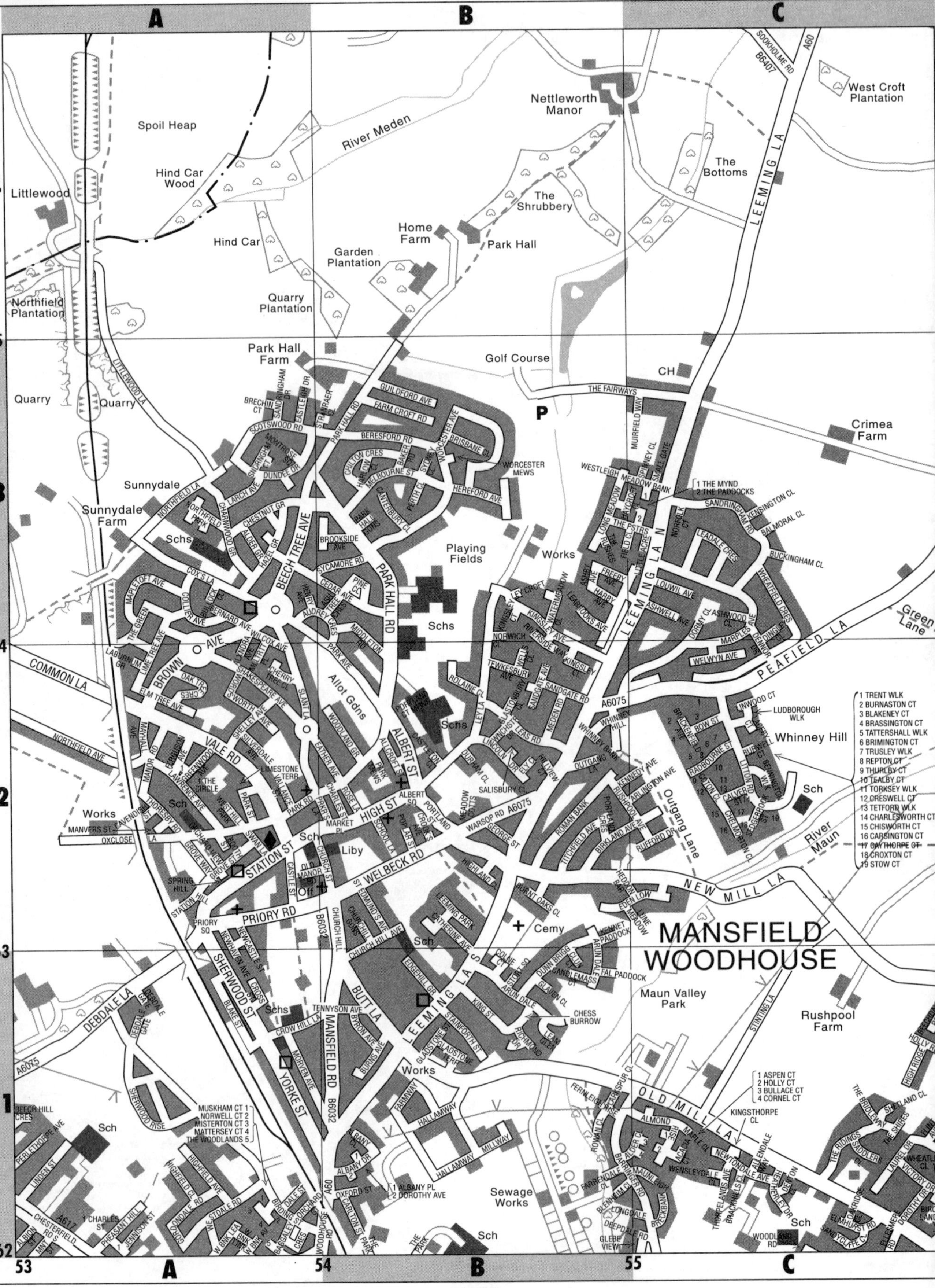
A
B
C
Spoil Heap
River Meden
Nettleworth Manor
West Croft Plantation
Littlewood
Hind Car Wood
Hind Car
The Shrubbery
The Bottoms
Home Farm
Park Hall
Garden Plantation
Quarry Plantation
Northfield Plantation
LEEMING LA
Park Hall Farm
Golf Course
CH
Quarry
THE FAIRWAYS
Crimea Farm
Sunnydale
Sunnydale Farm
Schs
Playing Fields
Works
BEECH TREE AVE
PARK HALL RD
Green Lane
PEAFIELD LA
COMMON LA
BROWN AVE
NORTHFIELD AVE
Allot Gdns
Whinney Hill
VALE RD
HIGH ST
WELBECK RD
WARSOP RD A6075
Outgang Lane
River Maun
Liby
Cemy
NEW MILL LA
PRIORY RD
MANSFIELD WOODHOUSE
Maun Valley Park
Rushpool Farm
DEBDALE LA
SHERWOOD ST
MANSFIELD RD
LEEMING LA
YORKE ST
OLD MILL LA
Sewage Works
A6075
A60
B6032
Sch
1 TRENT WLK
2 BURNASTON CT
3 BLAKENEY CT
4 BRASSINGTON CT
5 TATTERSHALL WLK
6 BRIMINGTON CT
7 TRUSLEY WLK
8 REPTON CT
9 THURLBY CT
10 TEALBY CT
11 TORKSEY WLK
12 CRESWELL CT
13 TETFORD WLK
14 CHARLESWORTH CT
15 CHISWORTH CT
16 CARSINGTON CT
17 CAYTHORPE CT
18 CROXTON CT
19 STOW CT
1 ASPEN CT
2 HOLLY CT
3 BULLACE CT
4 CORNEL CT
MUSKHAM CT 1
NORWELL CT 2
MISTERTON CT 3
MATTERSEY CT 4
THE WOODLANDS 5
1 ALBANY PL
2 DOROTHY AVE
1 THE MYND
2 THE PADDOCKS
65
64
63
62
4
3
2
1
53
54
55

87
102

74 90

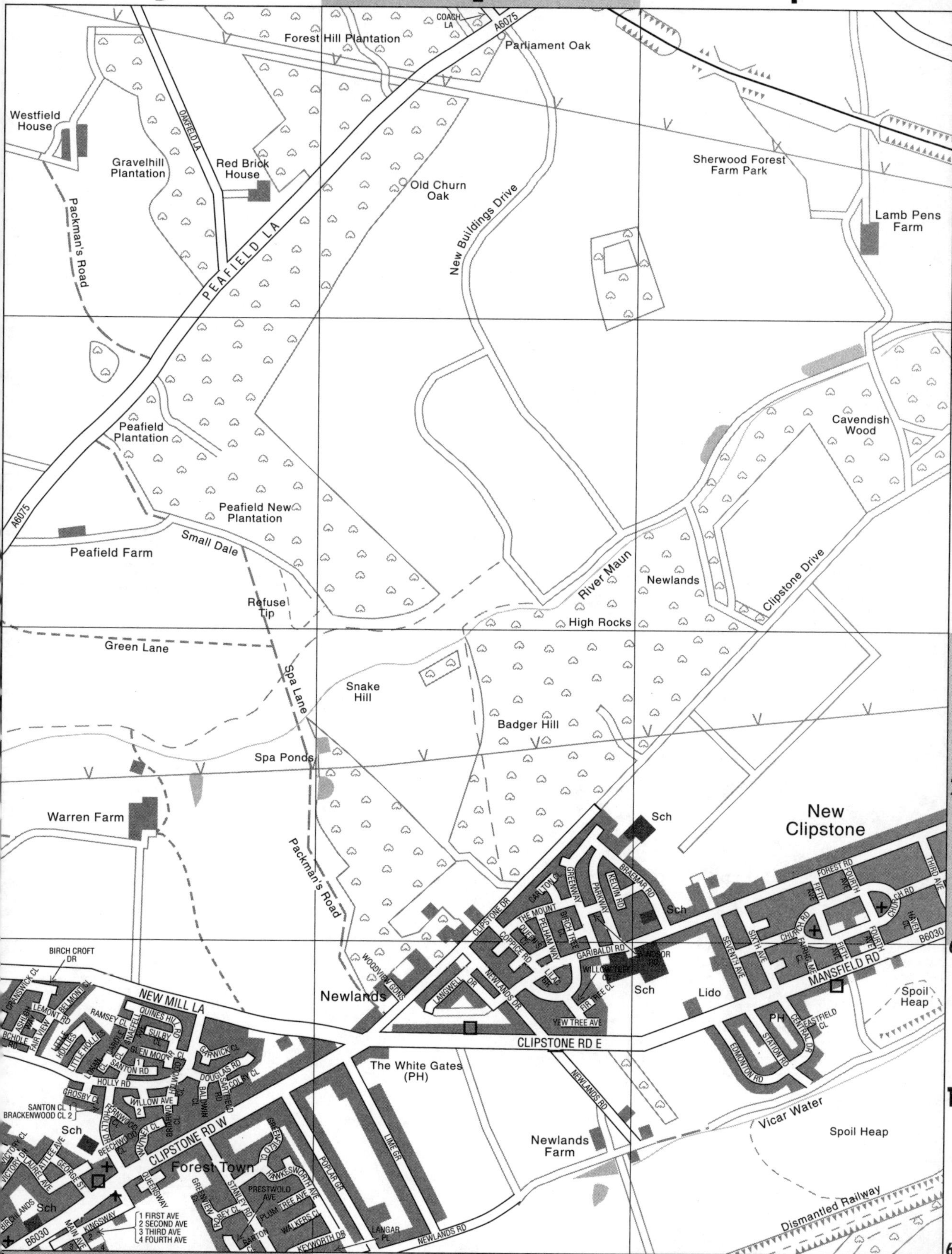
D
E
F
Forest Hill Plantation
COACH LA
A6075
Parliament Oak
Westfield House
Gravelhill Plantation
OAKFIELD LA
Red Brick House
Old Churn Oak
New Buildings Drive
Sherwood Forest Farm Park
Lamb Pens Farm
Packman's Road
PEAFIELD LA
4
65
Peafield Plantation
Cavendish Wood
3
A6075
Peafield New Plantation
Peafield Farm
Small Dale
River Maun
Newlands
Clipstone Drive
Refuse Tip
High Rocks
64
Green Lane
Spa Lane
Snake Hill
Badger Hill
Spa Ponds
2
Warren Farm
Sch
New Clipstone
Packman's Road
CLIPSTONE DR
Sch
MANSFIELD RD
B6030
63
BIRCH CROFT DR
Newlands
Sch
Lido
Spoil Heap
NEW MILL LA
PH
CLIPSTONE RD E
The White Gates (PH)
NEWLANDS RD
1
SANTON CL 1
BRACKENWOOD CL 2
Sch
Vicar Water
Spoil Heap
CLIPSTONE RD W
Newlands Farm
Forest Town
Sch
Dismantled Railway
1 FIRST AVE
2 SECOND AVE
3 THIRD AVE
4 FOURTH AVE
B6030
KEYWORTH DR
LANGAR PL
NEWLANDS RD
62
57
58
D
E
F

103 90

89 75

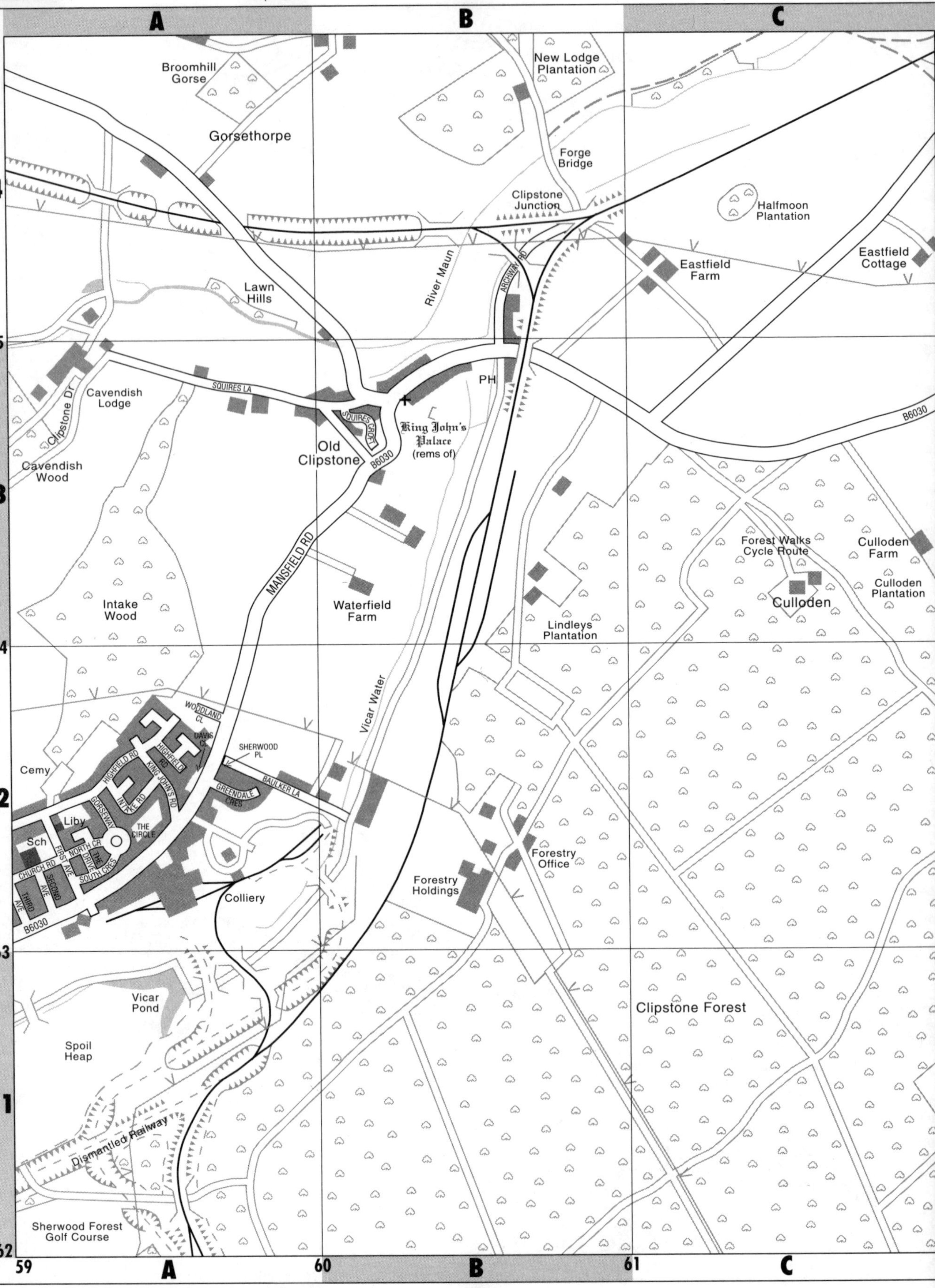
A
B
C
4
3
2
1
65
64
63
62
59
60
61
Broomhill Gorse
New Lodge Plantation
Gorsethorpe
Forge Bridge
Clipstone Junction
Halfmoon Plantation
River Maun
ARCHWAY RD
Eastfield Farm
Eastfield Cottage
Lawn Hills
SQUIRES LA
PH
Cavendish Lodge
Clipstone Dr
SQUIRES CROFT
King John's Palace (rems of)
Old Clipstone
B6030
Cavendish Wood
MANSFIELD RD
Forest Walks Cycle Route
Culloden Farm
Culloden Plantation
Culloden
Waterfield Farm
Intake Wood
Lindleys Plantation
Vicar Water
WOODLAND CL
DAVIS CL
SHERWOOD PL
HIGHFIELD RD
KING JOHN'S RD
BAULKER LA
GREENDALE CRES
Cemy
GORSEWAY
INTAKE RD
Liby
Sch
THE CIRCLE
NORTH CR
THE DRIVE
FIRST AVE
CHURCH RD
SOUTH CRES
SECOND AVE
THIRD AVE
Forestry Office
Forestry Holdings
Colliery
Vicar Pond
Clipstone Forest
Spoil Heap
Dismantled Railway
Sherwood Forest Golf Course

89 104

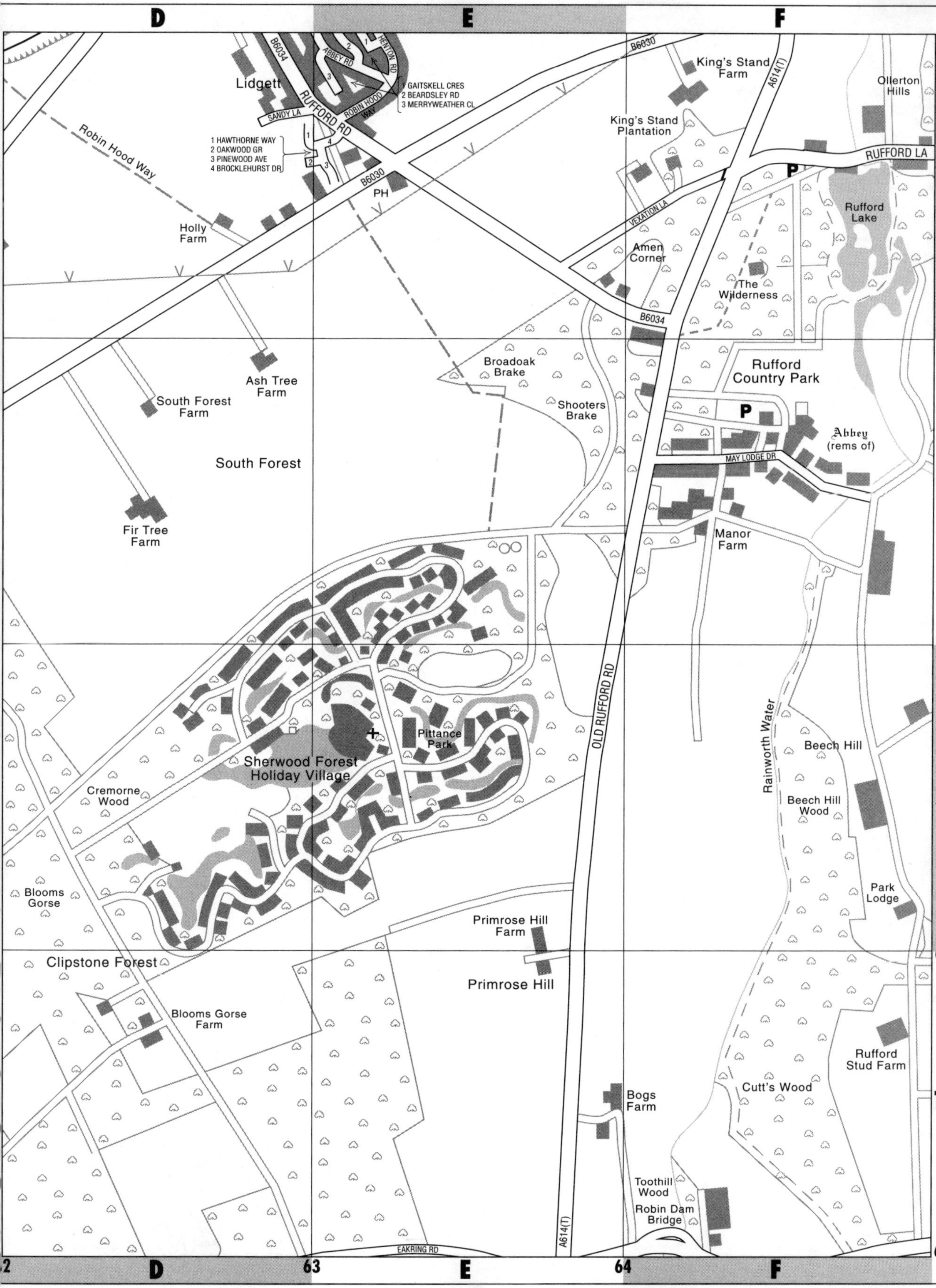
Lidgett
GAITSKELL CRES
BEARDSLEY RD
MERRYWEATHER CL
HAWTHORNE WAY
OAKWOOD GR
PINEWOOD AVE
BROCKLEHURST DR
SANDY LA
RUFFORD RD
ABBEY RD
HENTON RD
ROBIN HOOD WAY
B6034
B6030
Robin Hood Way
PH
Holly Farm
King's Stand Farm
King's Stand Plantation
Ollerton Hills
RUFFORD LA
Rufford Lake
VEXATION LA
Amen Corner
The Wilderness
A614(T)
Broadoak Brake
Ash Tree Farm
South Forest Farm
Rufford Country Park
Shooters Brake
Abbey (rems of)
MAY LODGE DR
South Forest
Fir Tree Farm
Manor Farm
OLD RUFFORD RD
Pittance Park
Sherwood Forest Holiday Village
Cremorne Wood
Rainworth Water
Beech Hill
Beech Hill Wood
Blooms Gorse
Park Lodge
Primrose Hill Farm
Primrose Hill
Clipstone Forest
Blooms Gorse Farm
Rufford Stud Farm
Cutt's Wood
Bogs Farm
Toothill Wood
Robin Dam Bridge
EAKRING RD

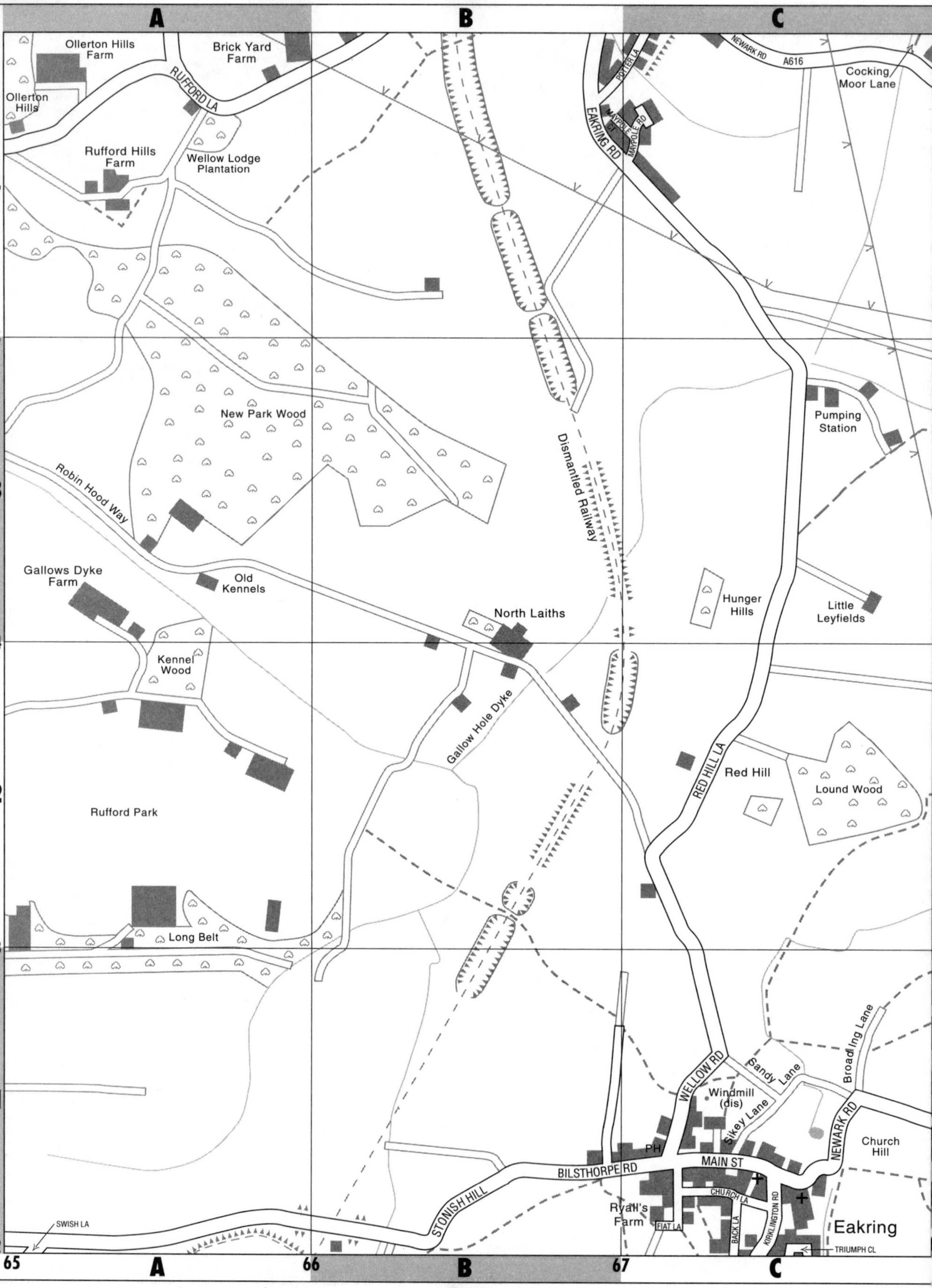
A
B
C
Ollerton Hills Farm
Brick Yard Farm
Ollerton Hills
RUFFORD LA
NEWARK RD
A616
Cocking Moor Lane
POTTER LA
MAYPOLE RD
EAKRING RD
Rufford Hills Farm
Wellow Lodge Plantation
4
65
New Park Wood
Pumping Station
Dismantled Railway
3
Robin Hood Way
Gallows Dyke Farm
Old Kennels
North Laiths
Hunger Hills
Little Leyfields
64
Kennel Wood
Gallow Hole Dyke
RED HILL LA
Red Hill
Lound Wood
2
Rufford Park
Long Belt
63
Broad Ing Lane
1
WELLOW RD
Sandy Lane
Windmill (dis)
Sikey Lane
NEWARK RD
Church Hill
PH
MAIN ST
BILSTHORPE RD
STONISH HILL
CHURCH LA
Ryall's Farm
FIAT LA
BACK LA
KIRKLINGTON RD
Eakring
TRIUMPH CL
SWISH LA
62
65
66
67

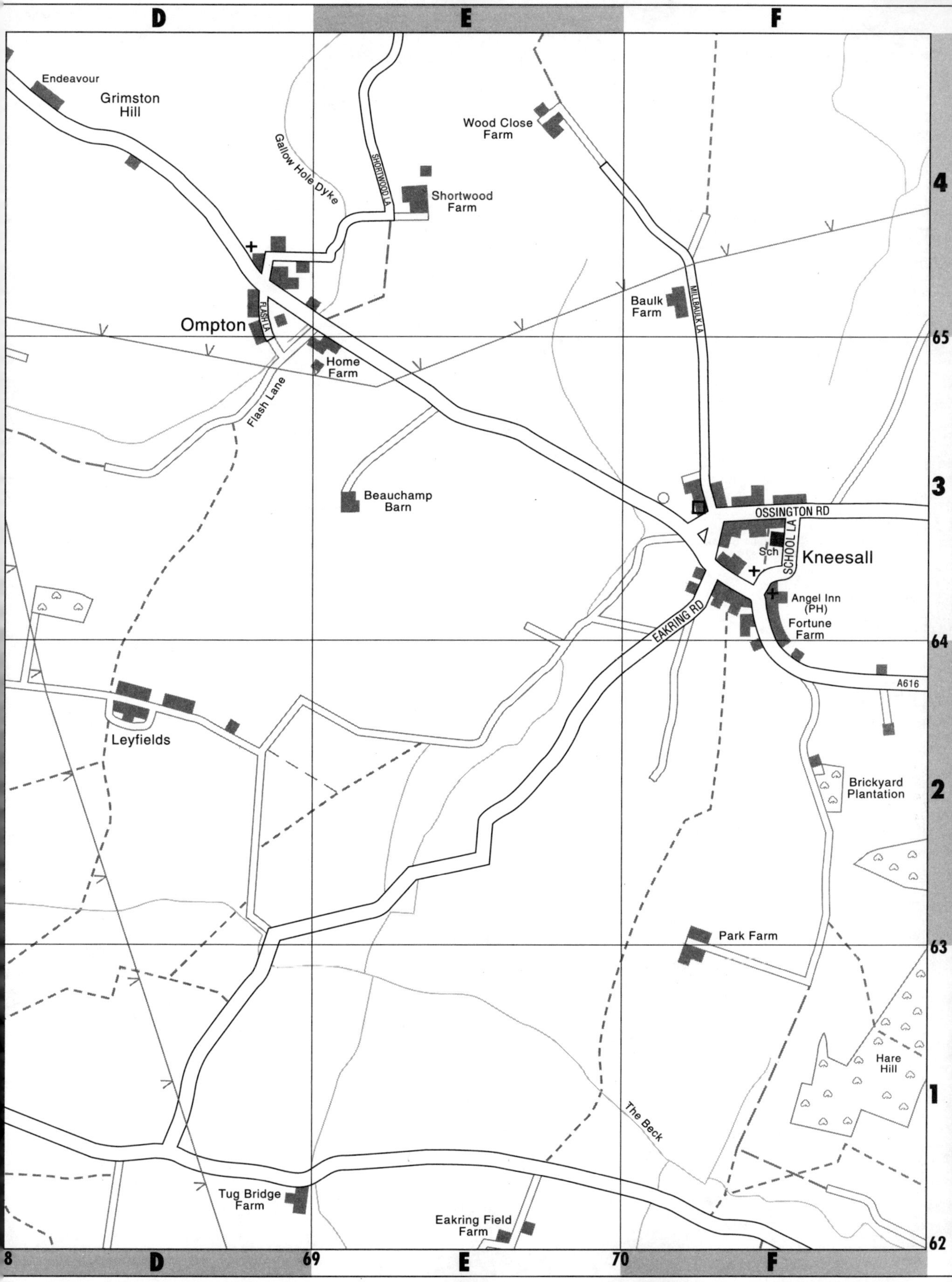
D
E
F
Endeavour
Grimston Hill
Gallow Hole Dyke
SHORTWOOD LA
Wood Close Farm
Shortwood Farm
4
Ompton
FLASH LA
Baulk Farm
MILLBAULK LA
Home Farm
65
Flash Lane
Beauchamp Barn
3
OSSINGTON RD
Sch
SCHOOL LA
Kneesall
Angel Inn (PH)
Fortune Farm
EAKRING RD
64
A616
Leyfields
Brickyard Plantation
2
Park Farm
63
Hare Hill
1
The Beck
Tug Bridge Farm
Eakring Field Farm
62
8
D
69
E
70
F

93
79

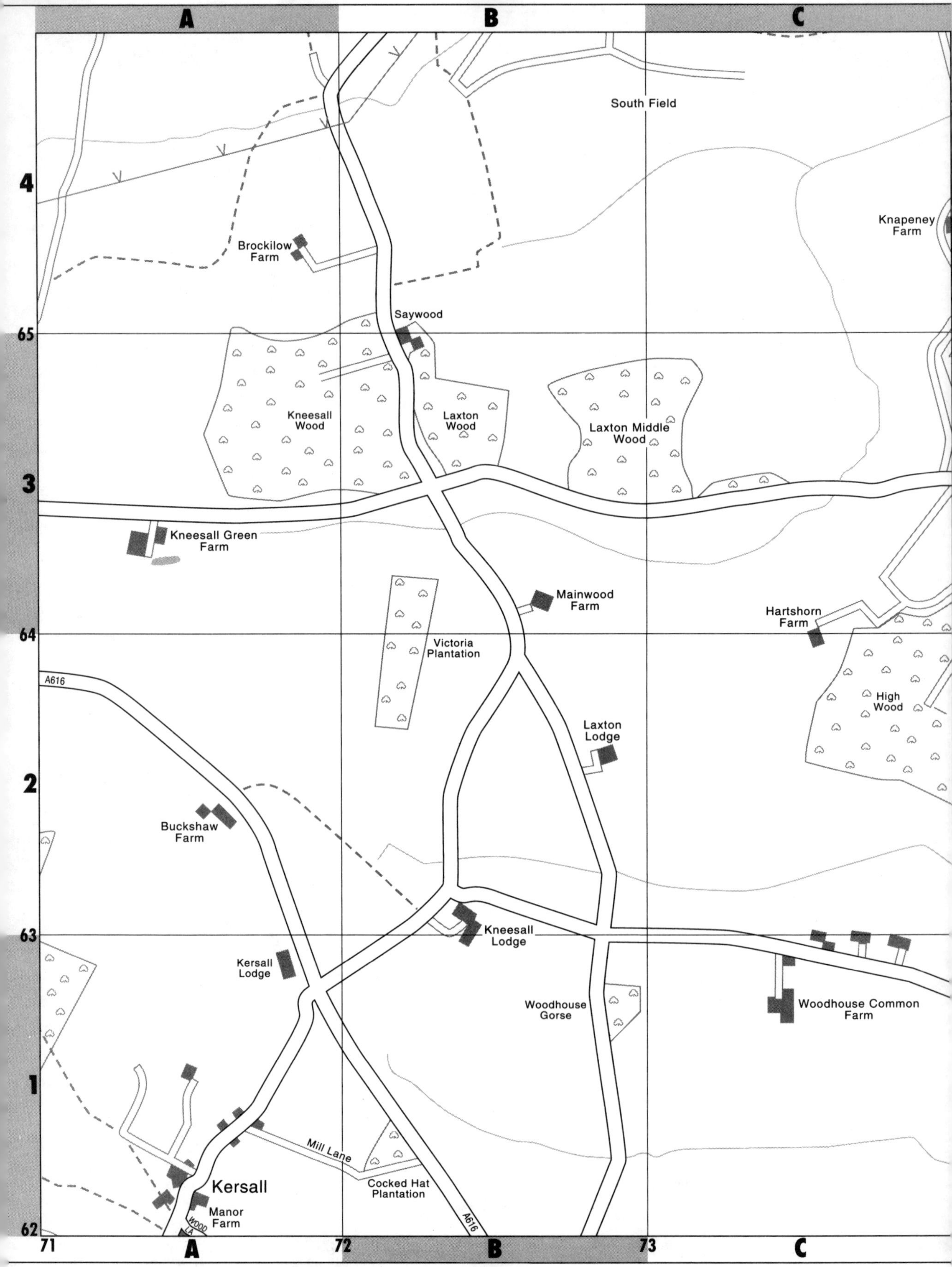
A
B
C
South Field
4
Knapeney Farm
Brockilow Farm
Saywood
65
Kneesall Wood
Laxton Wood
Laxton Middle Wood
3
Kneesall Green Farm
Mainwood Farm
Hartshorn Farm
64
Victoria Plantation
A616
High Wood
Laxton Lodge
2
Buckshaw Farm
63
Kneesall Lodge
Kersall Lodge
Woodhouse Gorse
Woodhouse Common Farm
1
Mill Lane
Kersall
Cocked Hat Plantation
Manor Farm
WOOD LA
A616
62
71
A
72
B
73
C

93
108

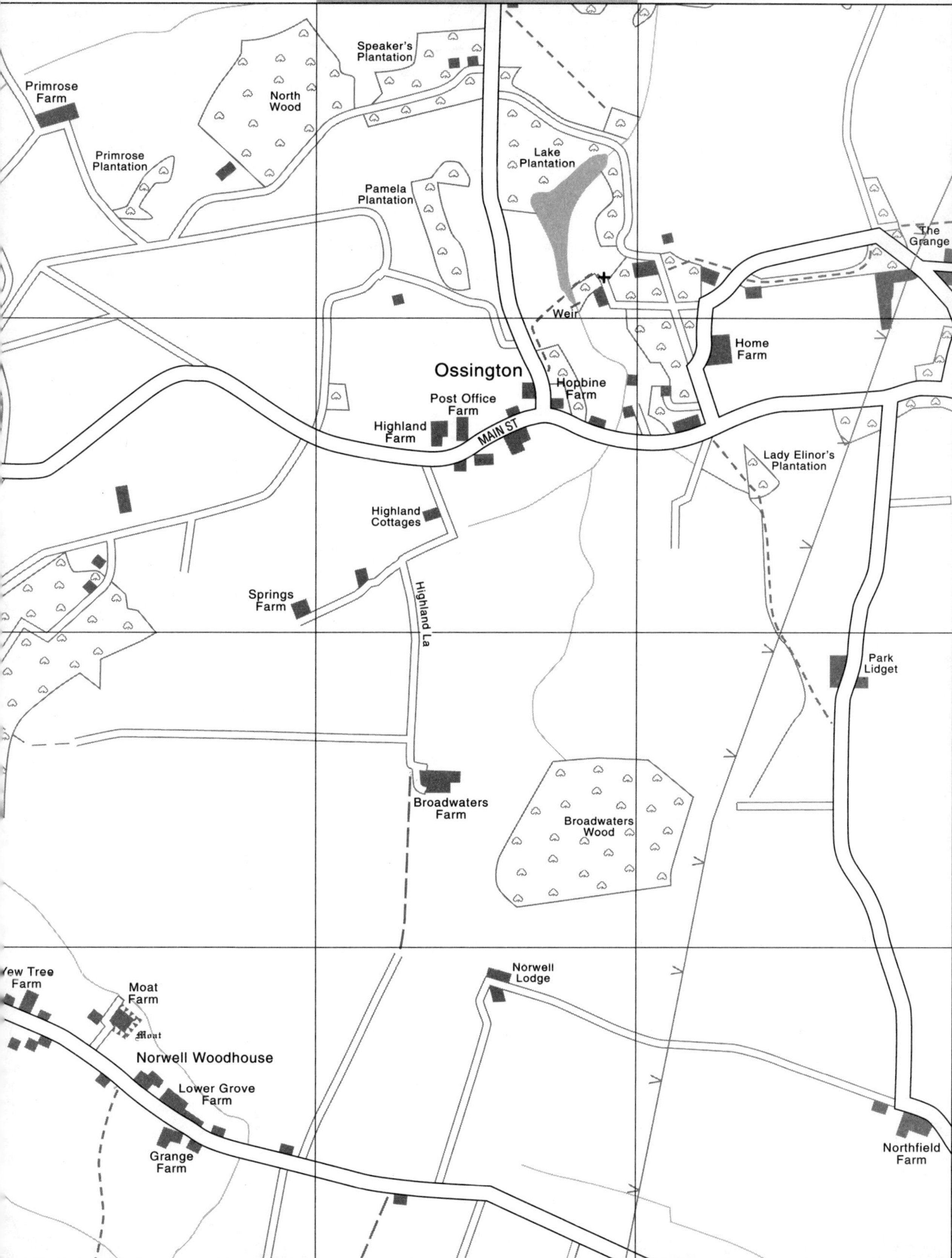
D
E
F
Primrose Farm
Primrose Plantation
North Wood
Speaker's Plantation
Lake Plantation
Pamela Plantation
The Grange
Weir
Home Farm
Ossington
Post Office Farm
Hopbine Farm
Highland Farm
MAIN ST
Lady Elinor's Plantation
Highland Cottages
Springs Farm
Highland La
Park Lidget
Broadwaters Farm
Broadwaters Wood
Yew Tree Farm
Moat Farm
Moat
Norwell Lodge
Norwell Woodhouse
Lower Grove Farm
Grange Farm
Northfield Farm
4
65
3
64
2
63
1
62
75
76

95
81

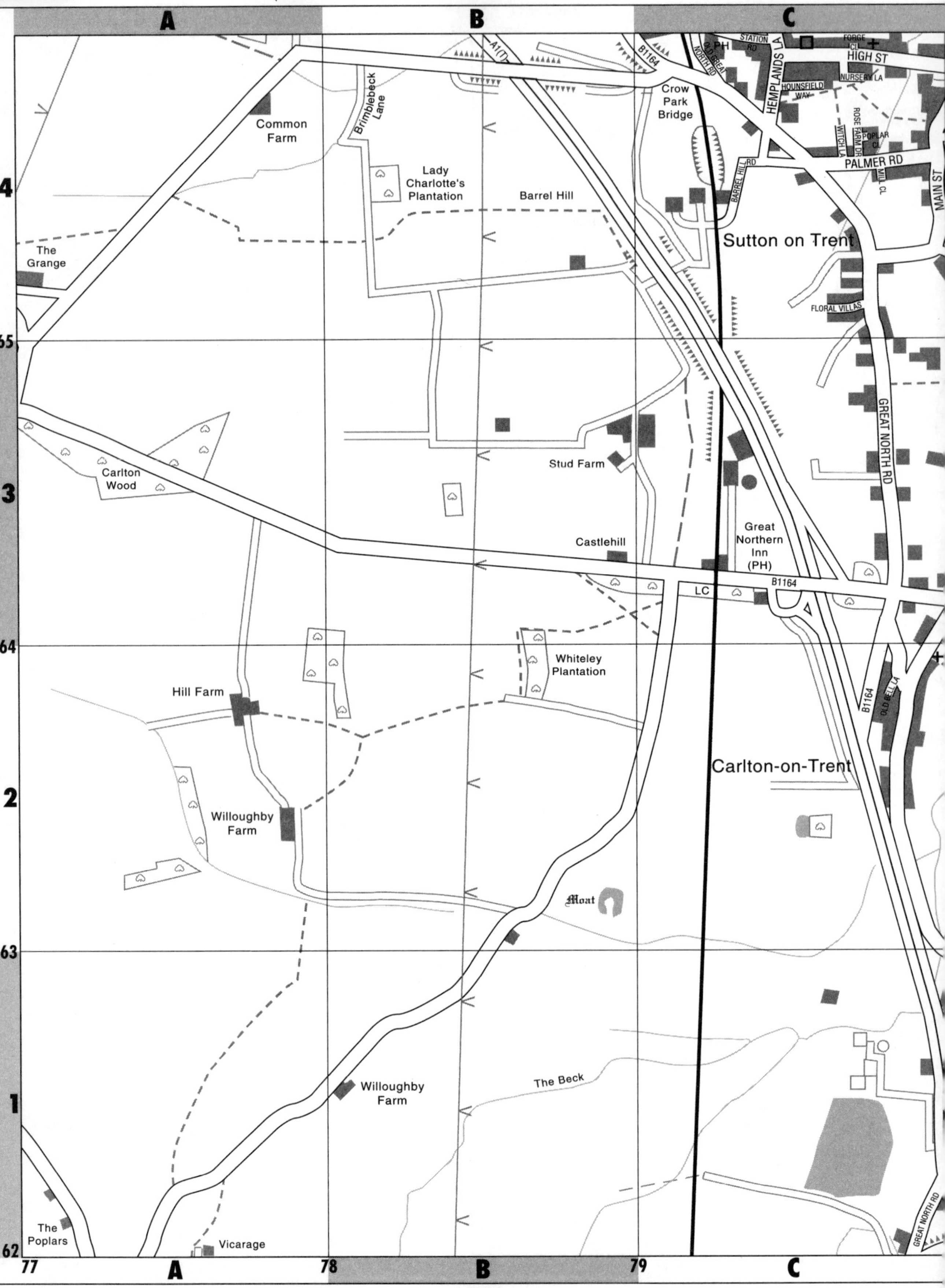
A
B
C
4
65
3
64
2
63
1
62
77
78
79
Common Farm
Brimblebeck Lane
Lady Charlotte's Plantation
Barrel Hill
Crow Park Bridge
A1(T)
B1164
HIGH ST
HEMPLANDS LA
STATION RD
FORGE CL
NURSERY LA
HOUNSFIELD WAY
ROSE FARM DR
POPLAR CL
WITCH LA
PALMER RD
MILL CL
MAIN ST
BARREL HILL RD
Sutton on Trent
The Grange
FLORAL VILLAS
GREAT NORTH RD
Carlton Wood
Stud Farm
Castlehill
Great Northern Inn (PH)
LC
Whiteley Plantation
Hill Farm
OLD BELL LA
Carlton-on-Trent
Willoughby Farm
Moat
The Beck
Willoughby Farm
The Poplars
Vicarage
GREAT NORTH RD

95
110

82
98

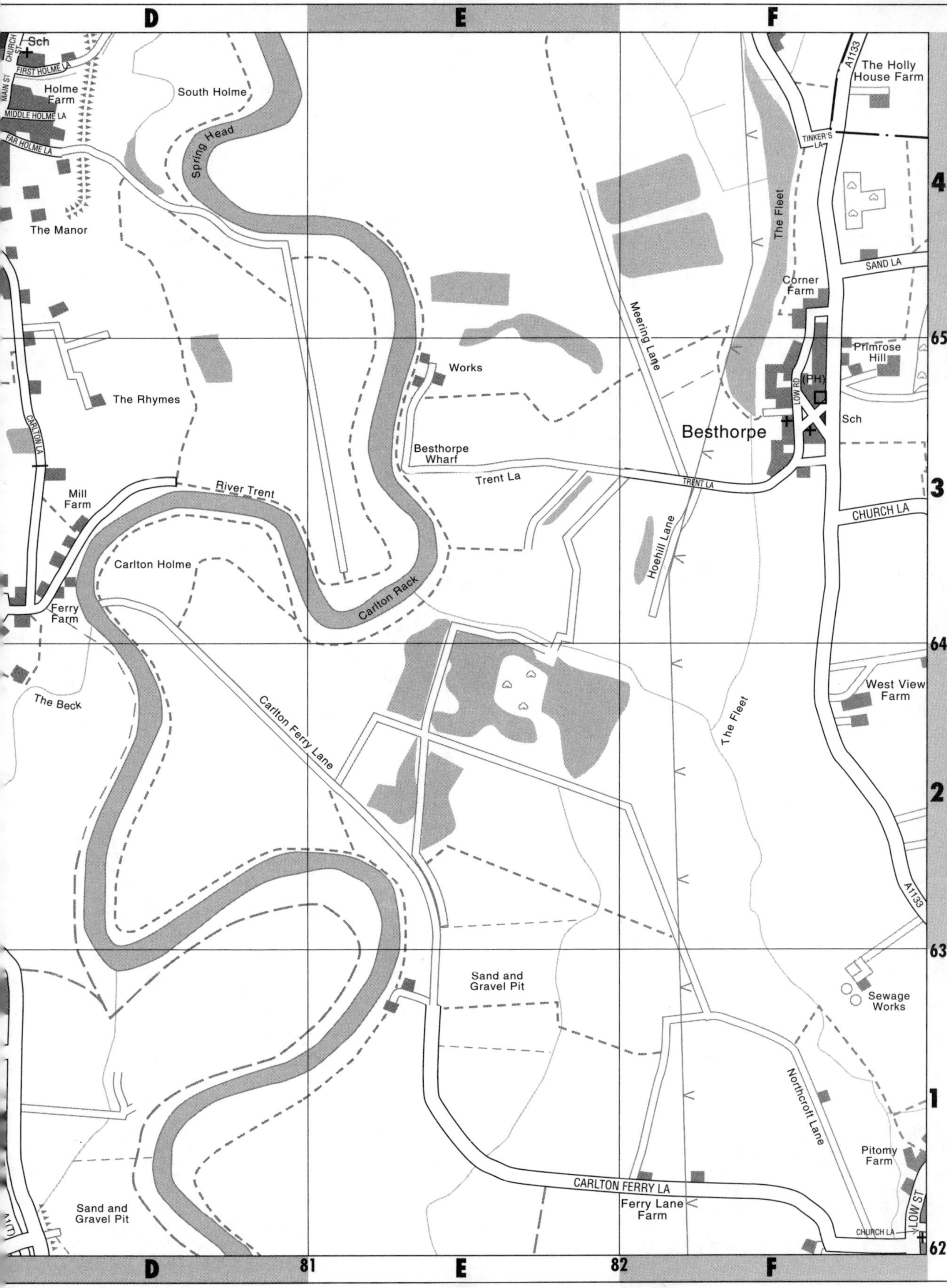
D
E
F
Sch
CHURCH ST
FIRST HOLME LA
MAIN ST
Holme Farm
MIDDLE HOLME LA
FAR HOLME LA
The Manor
South Holme
Spring Head
The Holly House Farm
A1133
TINKER'S LA
The Fleet
SAND LA
Corner Farm
Primrose Hill
Meering Lane
Works
The Rhymes
CARLTON LA
LOW RD
(PH)
Sch
Besthorpe
Besthorpe Wharf
Trent La
TRENT LA
Mill Farm
River Trent
CHURCH LA
Hoehill Lane
Carlton Holme
Carlton Rack
Ferry Farm
The Beck
Carlton Ferry Lane
West View Farm
The Fleet
Sand and Gravel Pit
Sewage Works
Northcroft Lane
Pitomy Farm
CARLTON FERRY LA
Ferry Lane Farm
Sand and Gravel Pit
CHURCH LA
LOW ST
A1(T)
4
65
3
64
2
63
1
62
81
82

111
98

97 83

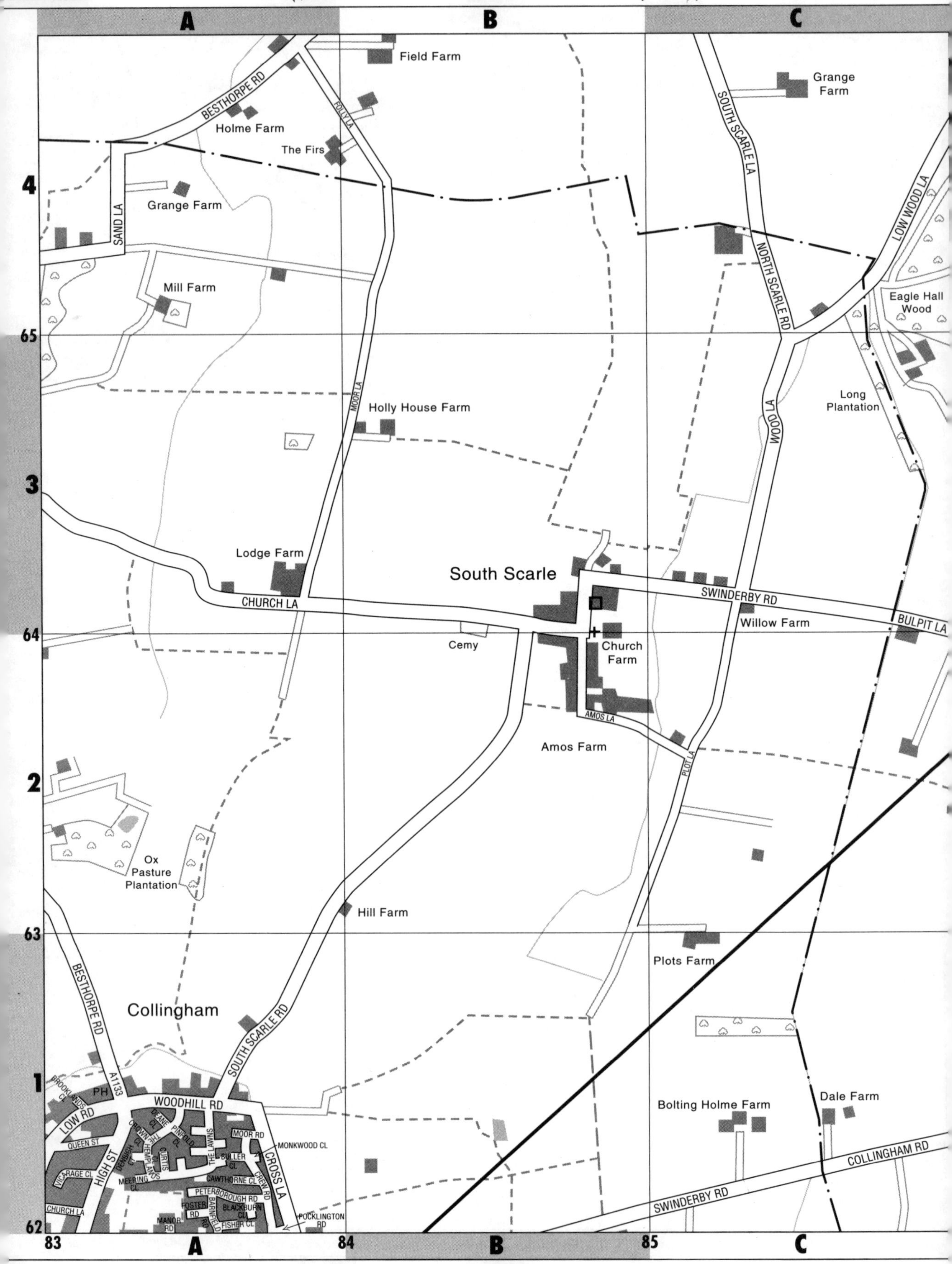
A
B
C
4
65
3
64
2
63
1
62
83
84
85
Field Farm
Grange Farm
BESTHORPE RD
FOLLY LA
Holme Farm
The Firs
SOUTH SCARLE LA
Grange Farm
SAND LA
LOW WOOD LA
NORTH SCARLE RD
Mill Farm
Eagle Hall Wood
MOOR LA
Holly House Farm
WOOD LA
Long Plantation
Lodge Farm
South Scarle
CHURCH LA
SWINDERBY RD
Willow Farm
BULPIT LA
Cemy
Church Farm
AMOS LA
Amos Farm
PLOT LA
Ox Pasture Plantation
Hill Farm
Plots Farm
Collingham
BESTHORPE RD
SOUTH SCARLE RD
A1133
BROOKLANDS CL
PH
WOODHILL RD
LOW RD
QUEEN ST
HIGH ST
VICARAGE CL
CHURCH LA
DEANE CL
PINFOLD CL
THE LAWNS
MOOR RD
MONKWOOD CL
BULLER CL
CROSS LA
CAWTHORNE CL
CREW RD
CURTIS CL
HEMPLANDS
MEERING CL
PETERBOROUGH RD
FOSTER RD
BARNFIELD RD
BLACKBURN CL
FISHER CL
MANOR RD
POCKLINGTON RD
Bolting Holme Farm
Dale Farm
SWINDERBY RD
COLLINGHAM RD

97 112

85
100

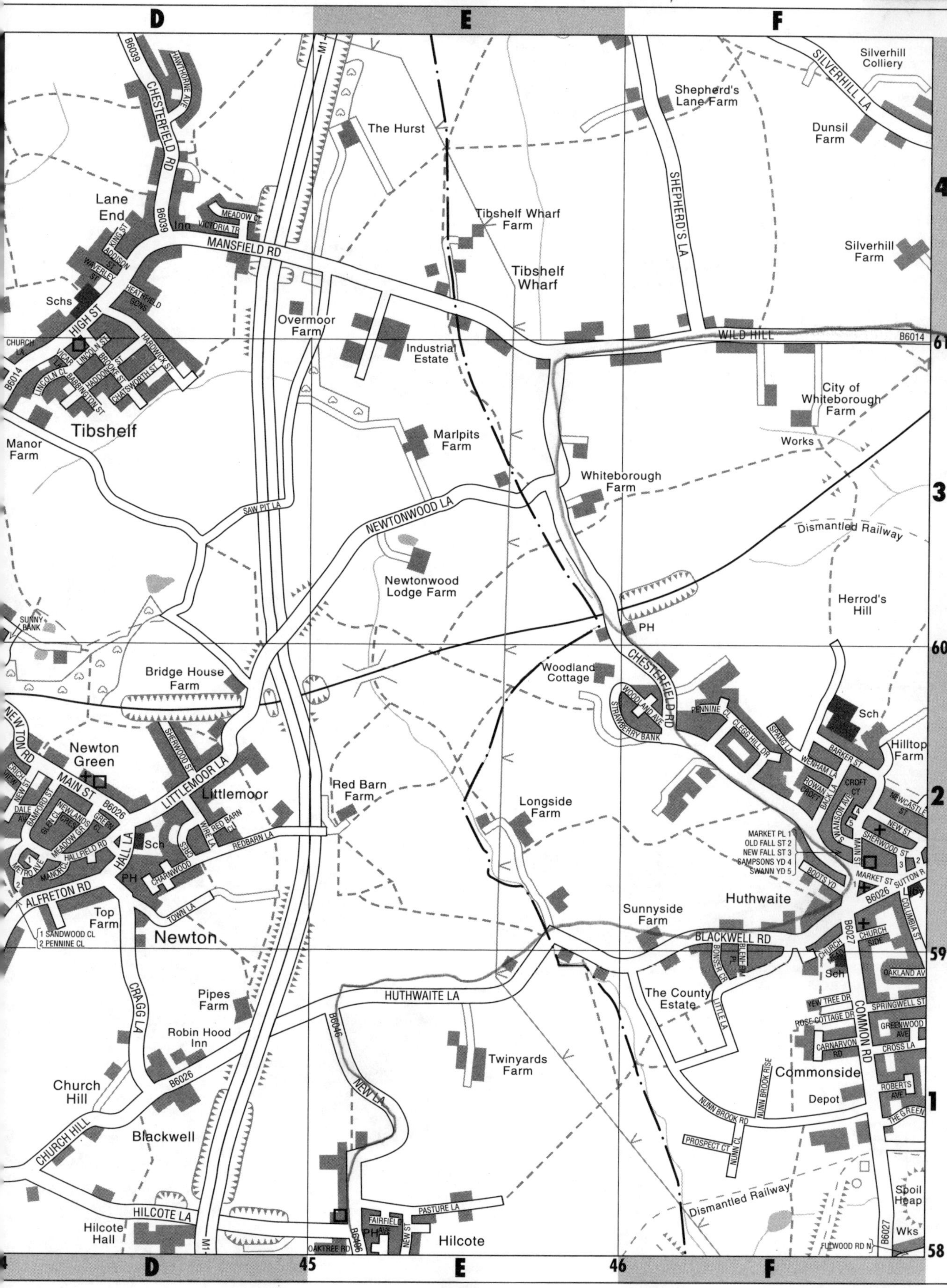


113
100

99
86

A
B
C
4
3
2
1
61
60
59
58
47
48
49
Spoil Heap
Silverhill Colliery
Fackley
Silverhill Cottages
Silverhill La
Fackley Farm
PH
Tibshelf Rd
B6014
Fackley Farm
Orchard Farm
LC
Teversal
Manor Farm
Coppy Wood
Dismantled Railway
Buttery La
Dawgates Wood
Dawgates Farm
Sewage Works
Dawgates La
River Meden
Fackley Rd
Carnarvon St
Crompton St
School
Liby
Mansfield Rd
Skegby
Sch
Woodside
Manor Rd
Buttery La
High Tor
Overdale Ave
Vicarage Cl
Greenland Rd
Wheatfield Way
Birchwood Dr
Birchwood Cl
The Crescent
Beech St
The Beeches
Oak St
Cedar Cl
Ash Gr
Hazel St
Elder St
Barker Ave
Headswood St
Leigh Dr
Station Yd
Old Rd
Low Rd
Back La
B6014
Forest Rd
Thoresby Cres
Welbeck Sq
Church View
Clumber Cres
Bridle Cl
Bluebell Cl
Briar Cl
Meden Bank
Hawthorne Cl
Wharf Rd
Fackley Rd
Victoria St
Albert St
New La
High St
Alexandra Terr
Morley St
Co-operative St
Institute St
Fackley Way
Greenacre
The Croft
Pasture Cl
The Copse
The Paddock
Brand La
Lime Tree Ave
West Hill
Gilcroft St
St Andrews St
Hall St
1 Longden Terr
2 Bainbridge Terr
3 Marshall Terr
4 Gardiner Terr
5 Cochrane Terr
Spring Wood Farm
Spring Wood
Stanton Hill
Miners Arms (PH)
Rose and Crown (PH)
Stubbinghill Farm
Dismantled Railway
Shepherds Oak
Rosemont Cl
Dismantled Railway
School
Stoneyford Rd
Vere Ave
Greenbank Dr
Quarrydale Ave
Quarrydale Dr
Beechdale Ave
Beechdale Cres
Deepdale Pk
Deepdale Gdns
Deepdale St
Queen St
Howard St
Alfred St
John St
Slater St
Holmecroft Ave
Lound House Cl
Lound House Rd
Chatsworth Cl
Anslow Ave
Lindholme Way
Roger Cl
Ashfield St
Leyton Ave
Farndale Cl
Sywell Cl
Farndale Rd
Buttermere
Saville Rd
Whitehead La
Stamper Cres
Rooley Lane
Spoil Heap
Cowpes Cl
Fern St
Glen St
Haddon St
Ashford Rise
Hathersage Way
Edale Ct
Milldale Wlk
Mount Pleasant
New Cross
Bath St
Edward Ave
Alexandra Ave
Lime Ave
Wolseley Ct
B6023
Morley St
New Cross St
Downing St
Brighton St
Offices
Russell St
North St
Stoney St
Outram St
Bowne St
Penn St
Scarcliffe St
Bentinck St
Bramley Ct
Welbeck St
Stanton Cres
Northwood Ave
Carsic Rd
The Oval
St Mary's Ct
Southwood Ave
Brandreth Ave
Brookfield Ave
Sowter Ave
Brierly Rd
Caunt's Cres
Carsfield Cl
Westbourne View
Percival Cl
Paling Cres
Davies Ave
Northfield Ave
Bishop St
Edwin St
Northern View
Priestsic Rd
Meden Cres
Highfield Rd
Far Croft
Rooley Dr
Rooley Ave
Evans Ave
Ashland Rd (W)
Wordsworth Ave
Coulton's Ave
Ashgate
Alder Way
Willow Cres
St Mary's Rd
Schs
Westbourne Rd
Jubilee Rd
Ridge Cl
Ashley Rd
Briefly Cotts
Haven Cl
Carsic La
Percival Cres
Cavendish St
York St
Langford St
Caton Cl
Starr Ave
Newcastle St
Parkside
Skegby Rd
Unwin St
North St
High St
Duke St
King St
Ashfield St
George St
Carnarvon Gr
Norwood Cl
B6026
Sutton Rd
Mill Cl
Beech Ave
Lime Ave
Crossley Ave
Cemy
Keats Ave
Windsor Ave
Foxhill Ave
Parkway
Crampton Ct
Siddalls Dr
Springwood View Cl
Riley Cl
Meadow Dr
Riley Ave
Burton Rd
Dunelm
Sch
Westbourne Cl
Huthwaite Rd
Columbia Ave
Ashmore Ave
Peveril Dr
Regent St
Oxford St
Pelham St
Douglas Rd
B6026
Cemy
Church Ave
Sch
Lammas Rd
Hack La
Church St
Church La
Church Hill
Liby
Idlewells Shopping Centre
Portland Sq
Portland St
Forest St
Station Rd
Albion Rd
Sch
Market St
Low St
Parliament St
1 Market Pl
2 Albert Sq
3 Victoria St
Station St
Hardwick St
Reform St
Union St
The Homelands
Hardwick La
Coburn St
Martyn Ave
Thornton St
Henry St
Nesbitt St
Taylor Cres
Willetts Ct
Limb Cres
Leamington Dr
Thompson Cres
Lansbury Rd
Kings Mill Rd E
Columbia St
Cross La
Mill La
The Green
Devonshire Cl
Warren Cl
Mosborough Rd
Refuse Tip
Greenwood Falls Farm
Works
Spoil Heap
Gill St
Twin Oaks Dr
Nursery Ave
Charnwood St
Frederick St
Alfreton Rd
Mapplewells Rd
Mapplewells Cres
Sch
Henning La
B6023
Dorgen Dr
Percy St
Clumber St
TA Centre
Willowbridge La
Grosvenor Ave
Bonser Gdns
Carsdale Ave
Dovedale Ave
Stevenson Cres
Beeley Ave
Luther Ave
High Pavement
Quarry Yard
Prospect Pl
Crasters Pl
Bank Ave
Cowpasture La
Coronation St
Mill Croft
Silk St
The Twitchell
SUTTON IN ASHFIELD
Kirkby Rd
Corene Ave
Leopold St
Tudor St
Playing Field
Stuart St
The Avenue
Leamington Hall
James William Turner Ave
Sherwood Rd
Barnes Cres
Collins Ave

99
114

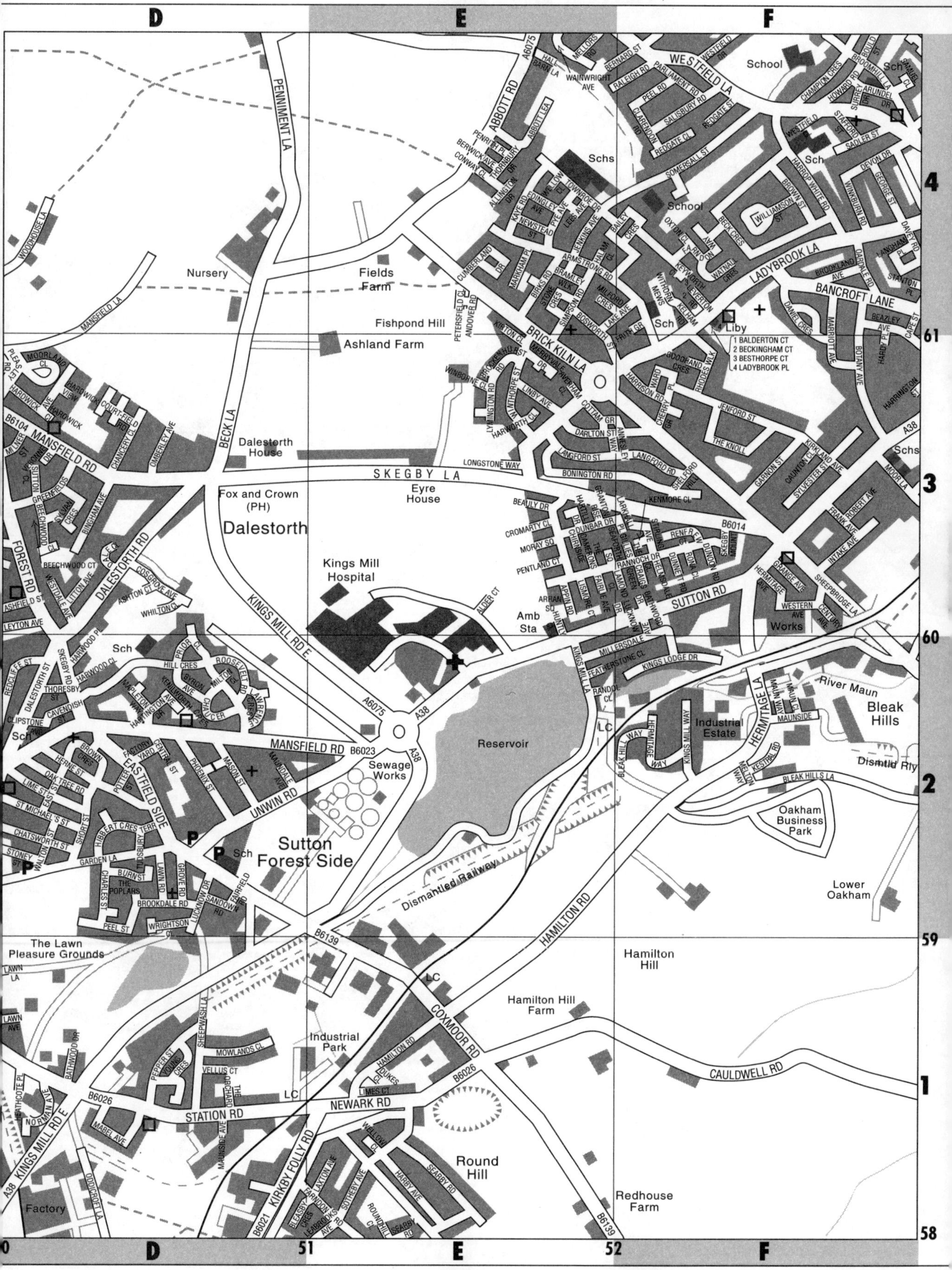
D
E
F
4
61
3
60
2
59
1
58
0
51
52
Nursery
Fields Farm
Fishpond Hill
Ashland Farm
Dalestorth House
Fox and Crown (PH)
Dalestorth
Eyre House
Kings Mill Hospital
Amb Sta
Reservoir
Sewage Works
Sutton Forest Side
Dismantled Railway
Industrial Estate
Bleak Hills
River Maun
Dismtld Rly
Oakham Business Park
Lower Oakham
Hamilton Hill
Hamilton Hill Farm
Industrial Park
Round Hill
Redhouse Farm
Factory
The Lawn Pleasure Grounds
Works
School
Schs
Sch
Liby
1 BALDERTON CT
2 BECKINGHAM CT
3 BESTHORPE CT
4 LADYBROOK PL
WESTFIELD LA
LADYBROOK LA
BANCROFT LANE
BRICK KILN LA
SKEGBY LA
PENNIMENT LA
BECK LA
MANSFIELD LA
MANSFIELD RD
B6104
KINGS MILL RD E
A6075
A38
B6023
B6014
SUTTON RD
UNWIN RD
EASTFIELD SIDE
FOREST RD
DALESTORTH RD
HAMILTON RD
COXMOOR RD
CAULDWELL RD
NEWARK RD
STATION RD
B6026
B6139
B6021
KIRKBY FOLLY RD
HERMITAGE LA
BLEAK HILLS LA
MAUNSIDE
LONGSTONE WAY
ABBOTT RD
WOODHOUSE LA
LC

101
88

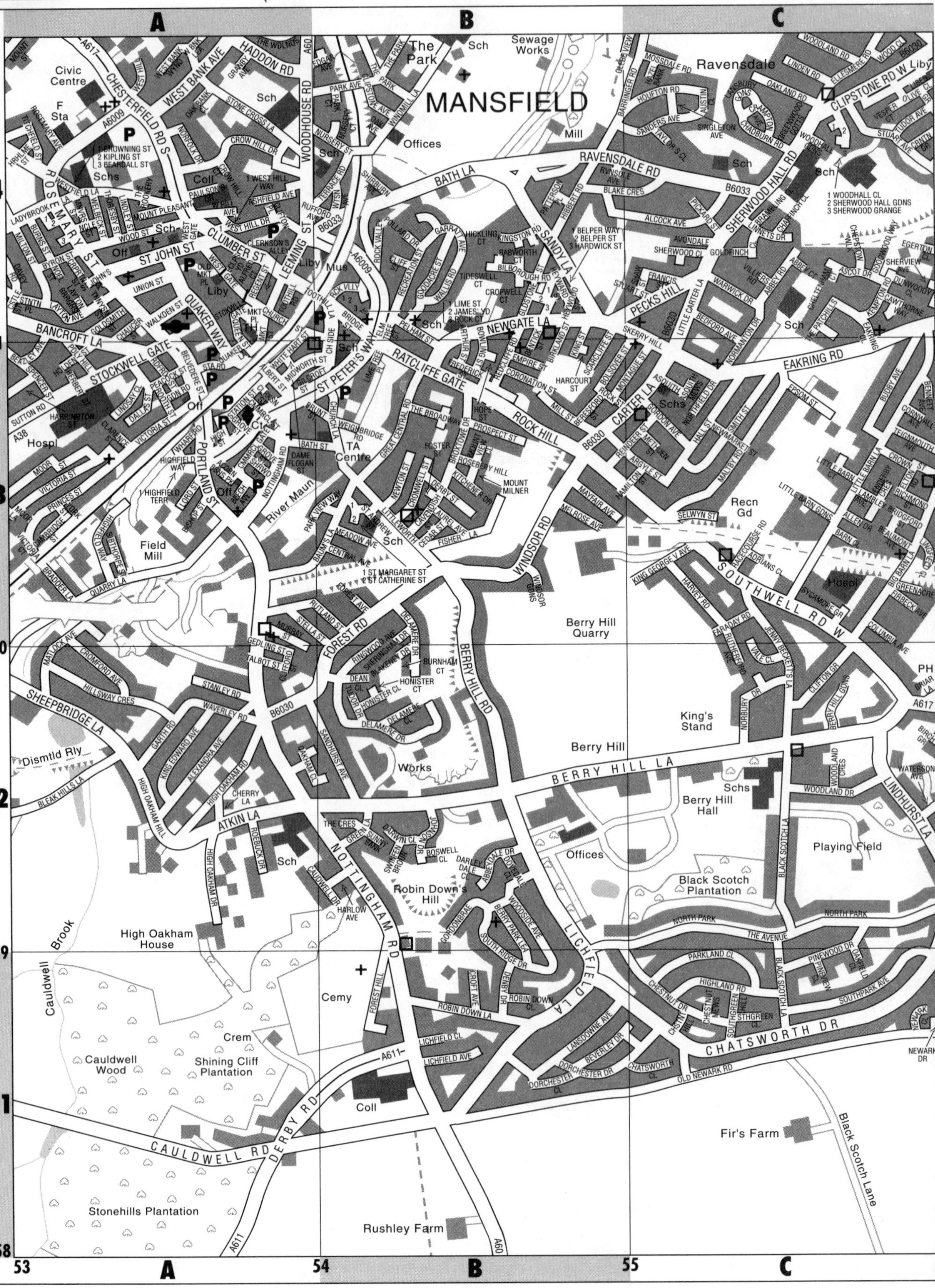


101
116

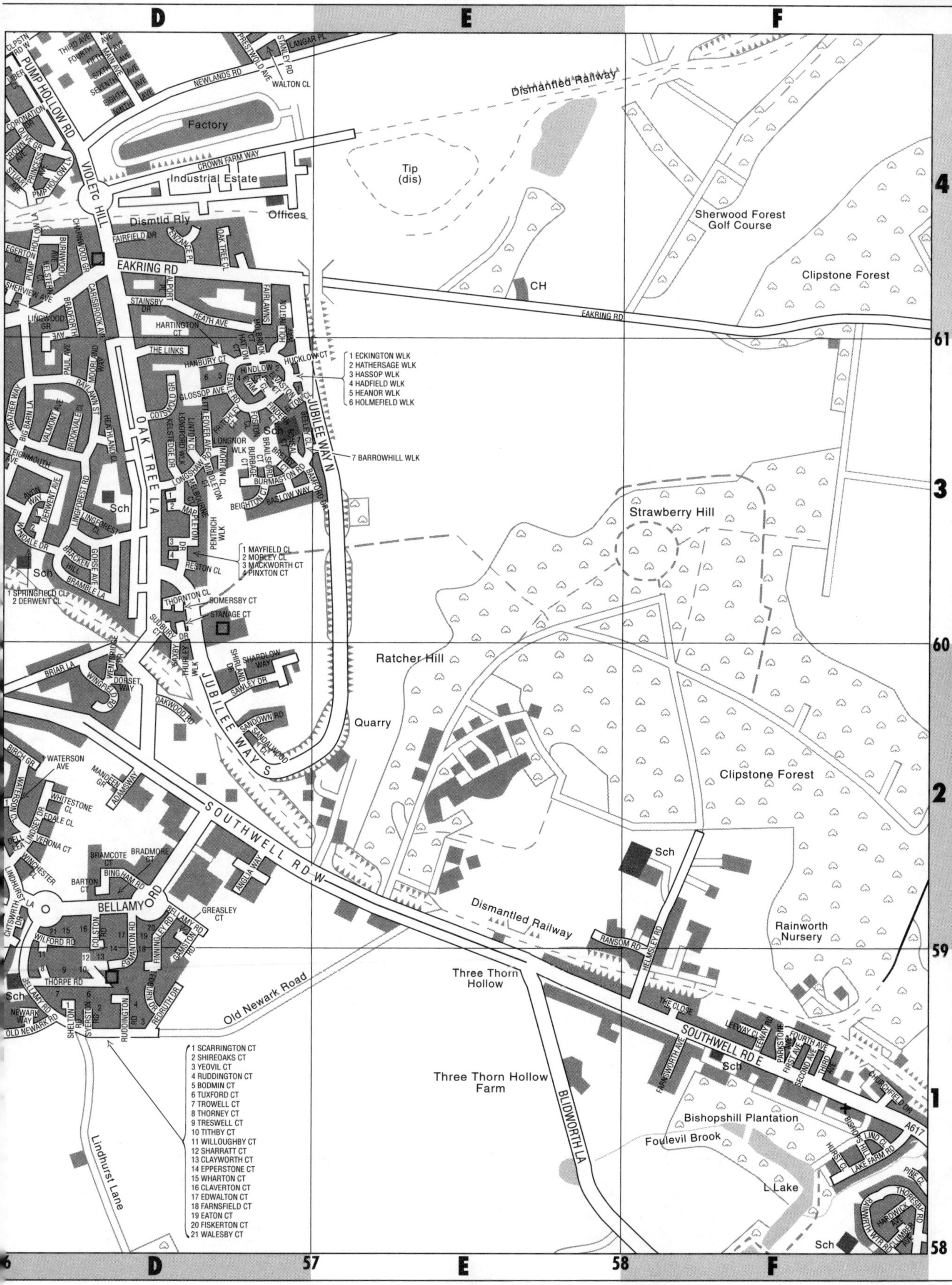
D
E
F
4
3
2
1
61
60
59
58
57
Factory
Industrial Estate
Offices
Dismtld Rly
Dismantled Railway
Tip (dis)
CH
EAKRING RD
Sherwood Forest Golf Course
Clipstone Forest
Strawberry Hill
Ratcher Hill
Quarry
Clipstone Forest
Sch
Rainworth Nursery
Three Thorn Hollow
Three Thorn Hollow Farm
Bishopshill Plantation
Foulevil Brook
Lake
Old Newark Road
Lindhurst Lane
SOUTHWELL RD W
SOUTHWELL RD E
BLIDWORTH LA
JUBILEE WAY N
JUBILEE WAY S
OAK TREE LA
VIOLET HILL
PUMP HOLLOW RD
NEWLANDS RD
CROWN FARM WAY
BELLAMY RD
A617
1 ECKINGTON WLK
2 HATHERSAGE WLK
3 HASSOP WLK
4 HADFIELD WLK
5 HEANOR WLK
6 HOLMEFIELD WLK
7 BARROWHILL WLK
1 MAYFIELD CL
2 MORLEY CL
3 MACKWORTH CT
4 PINXTON CT
1 SPRINGFIELD CL
2 DERWENT CL
1 SCARRINGTON CT
2 SHIREOAKS CT
3 YEOVIL CT
4 RUDDINGTON CT
5 BODMIN CT
6 TUXFORD CT
7 TROWELL CT
8 THORNEY CT
9 TRESWELL CT
10 TITHBY CT
11 WILLOUGHBY CT
12 SHARRATT CT
13 CLAYWORTH CT
14 EPPERSTONE CT
15 WHARTON CT
16 CLAVERTON CT
17 EDWALTON CT
18 FARNSFIELD CT
19 EATON CT
20 FISKERTON CT
21 WALESBY CT

103
90

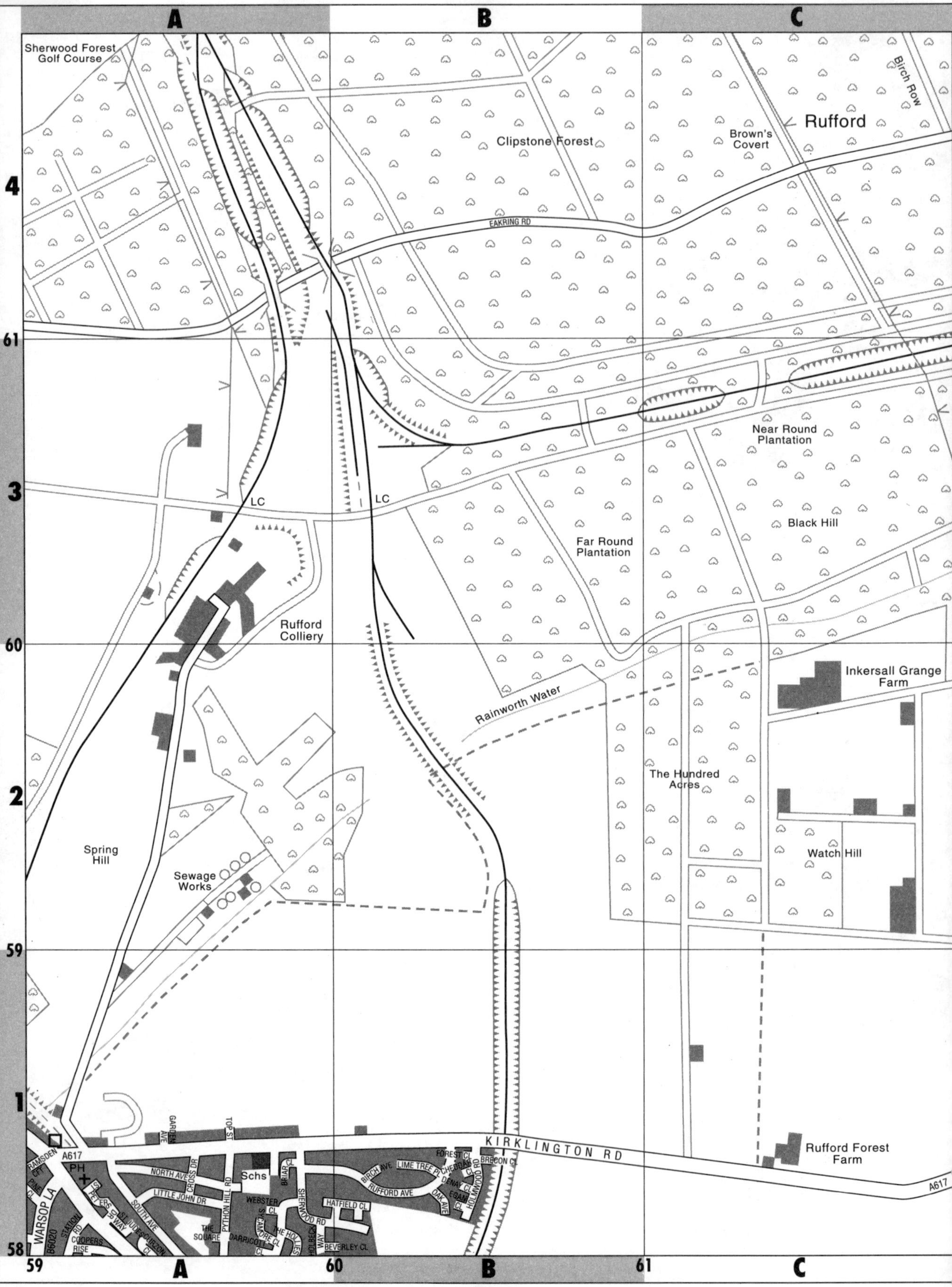


103
118

91
106

119
106

105
92

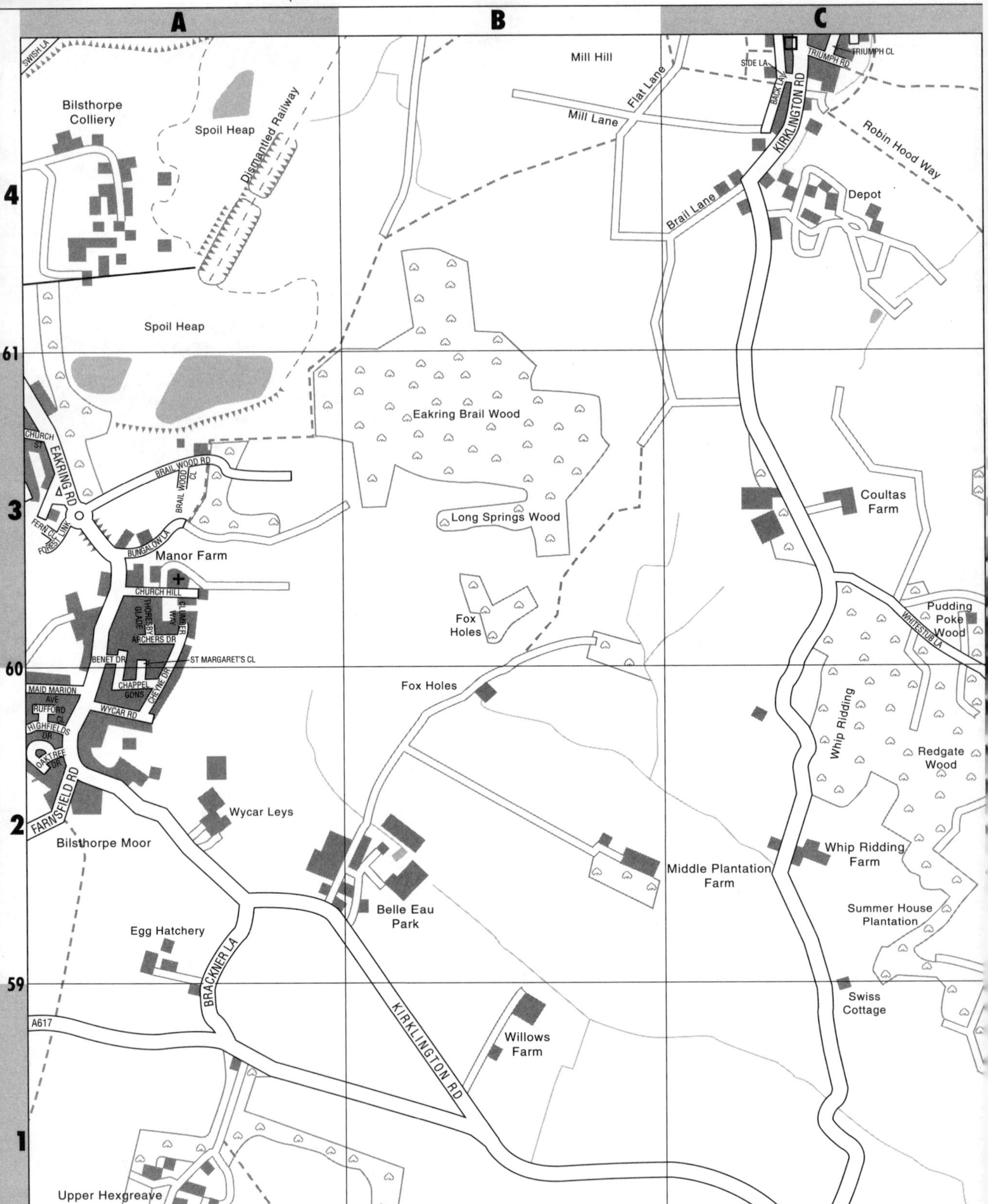


105
120

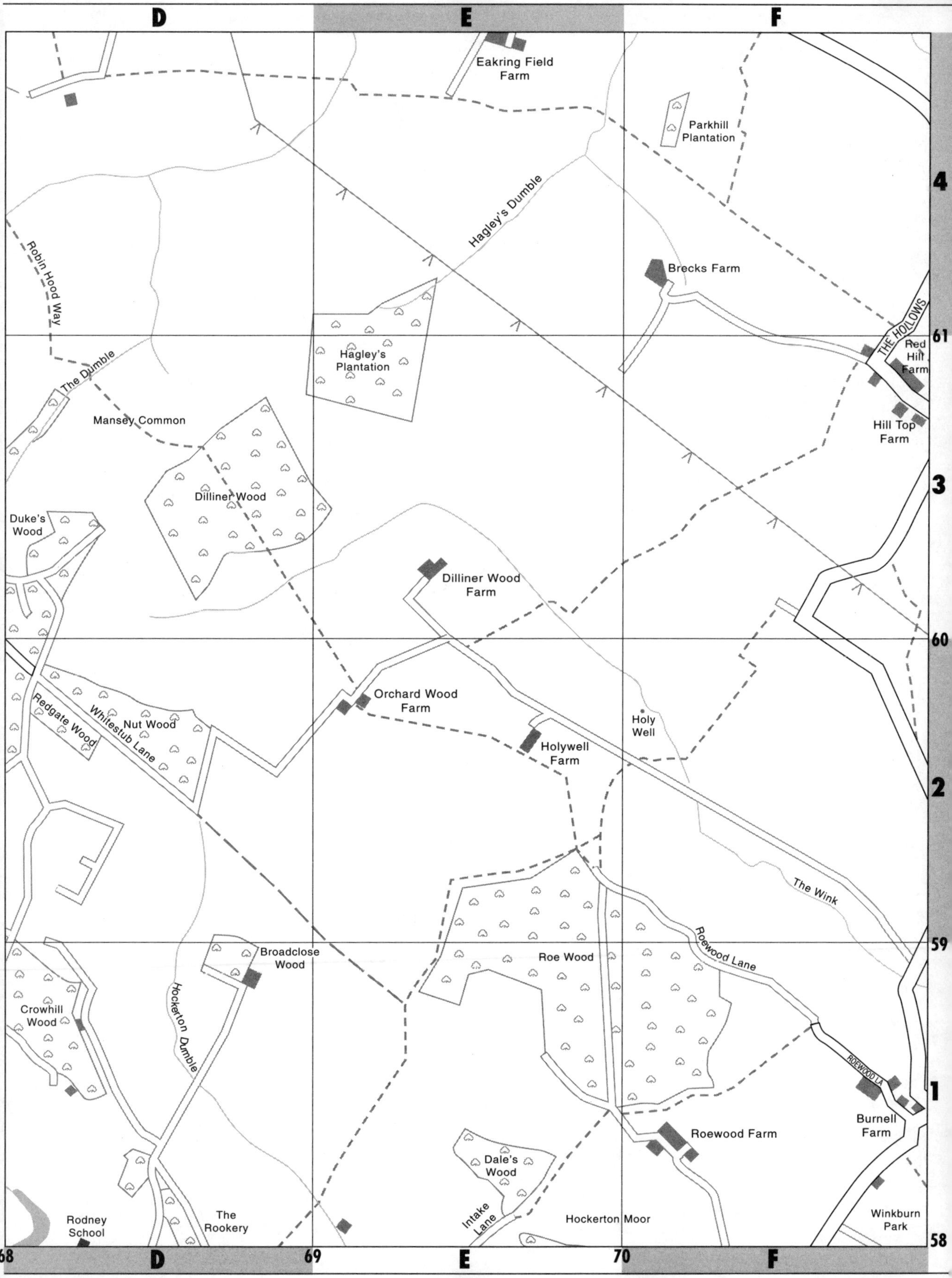
D
E
F
Eakring Field Farm
Parkhill Plantation
4
Robin Hood Way
Hagley's Dumble
Brecks Farm
THE HOLLOWS
61
Red Hill Farm
The Dumble
Hagley's Plantation
Mansey Common
Hill Top Farm
Dilliner Wood
3
Duke's Wood
Dilliner Wood Farm
60
Orchard Wood Farm
Redgate Wood
Whitestub Lane
Nut Wood
Holy Well
Holywell Farm
2
The Wink
Roe Wood
Roewood Lane
59
Broadclose Wood
Crowhill Wood
Hockerton Dumble
ROEWOOD LA
1
Burnell Farm
Roewood Farm
Dale's Wood
Intake Lane
Hockerton Moor
Winkburn Park
Rodney School
The Rookery
58
68
D
69
E
70
F

107
94

107
122

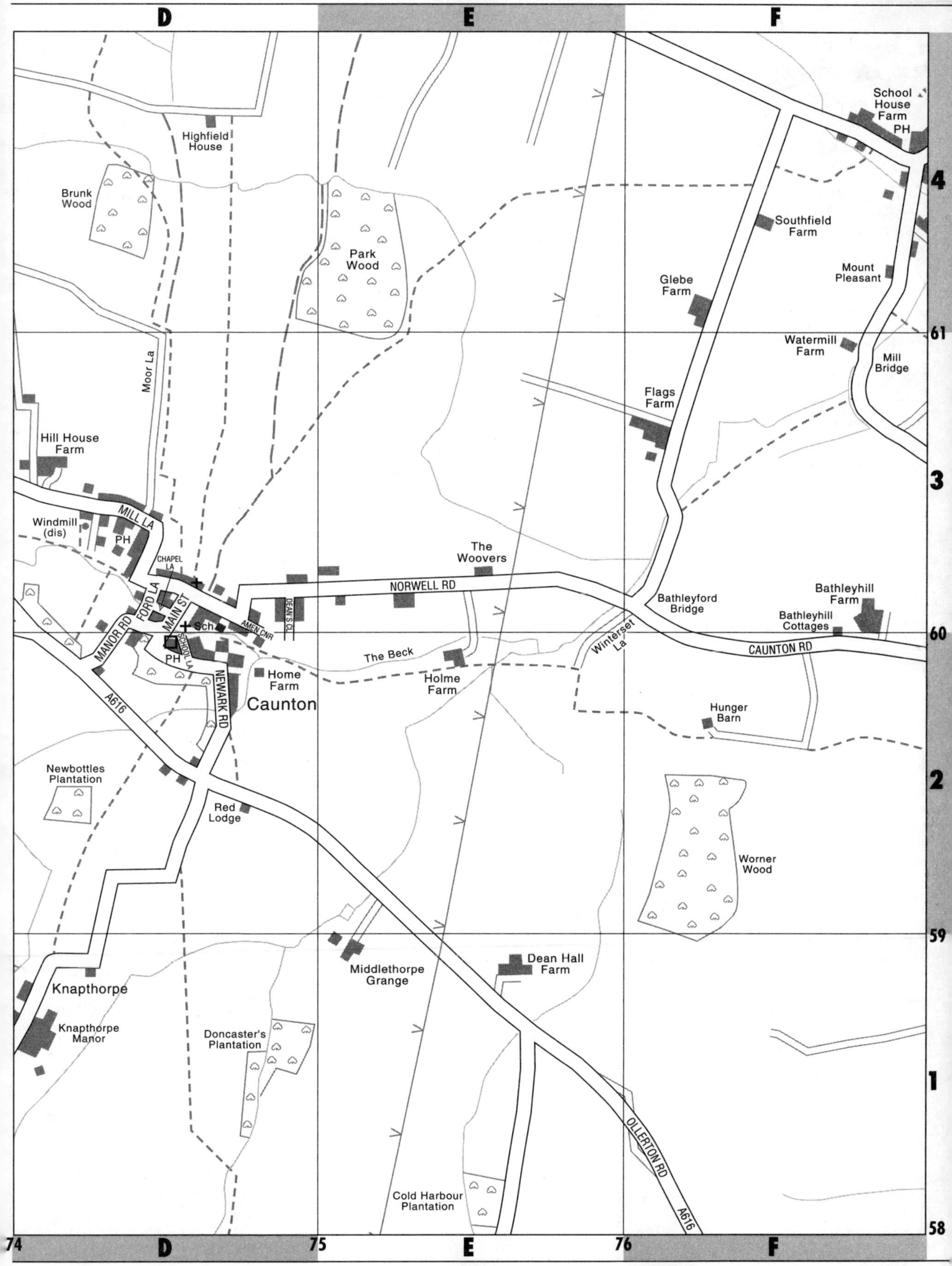
D
E
F
Highfield House
Brunk Wood
Park Wood
School House Farm
PH
Southfield Farm
Mount Pleasant
Glebe Farm
Watermill Farm
Mill Bridge
Flags Farm
Moor La
Hill House Farm
MILL LA
Windmill (dis)
PH
CHAPEL LA
FORD LA
MAIN ST
MANOR RD
Sch
PH
SCHOOL LA
AMEN CNR
DEAN'S CL
NEWARK RD
The Woovers
NORWELL RD
Bathleyford Bridge
Bathleyhill Farm
Bathleyhill Cottages
Winterset La
CAUNTON RD
The Beck
Home Farm
Holme Farm
Caunton
Hunger Barn
A616
Newbottles Plantation
Red Lodge
Worner Wood
Middlethorpe Grange
Dean Hall Farm
Knapthorpe
Knapthorpe Manor
Doncaster's Plantation
OLLERTON RD
A616
Cold Harbour Plantation
4
61
3
60
2
59
1
58
74
75
76

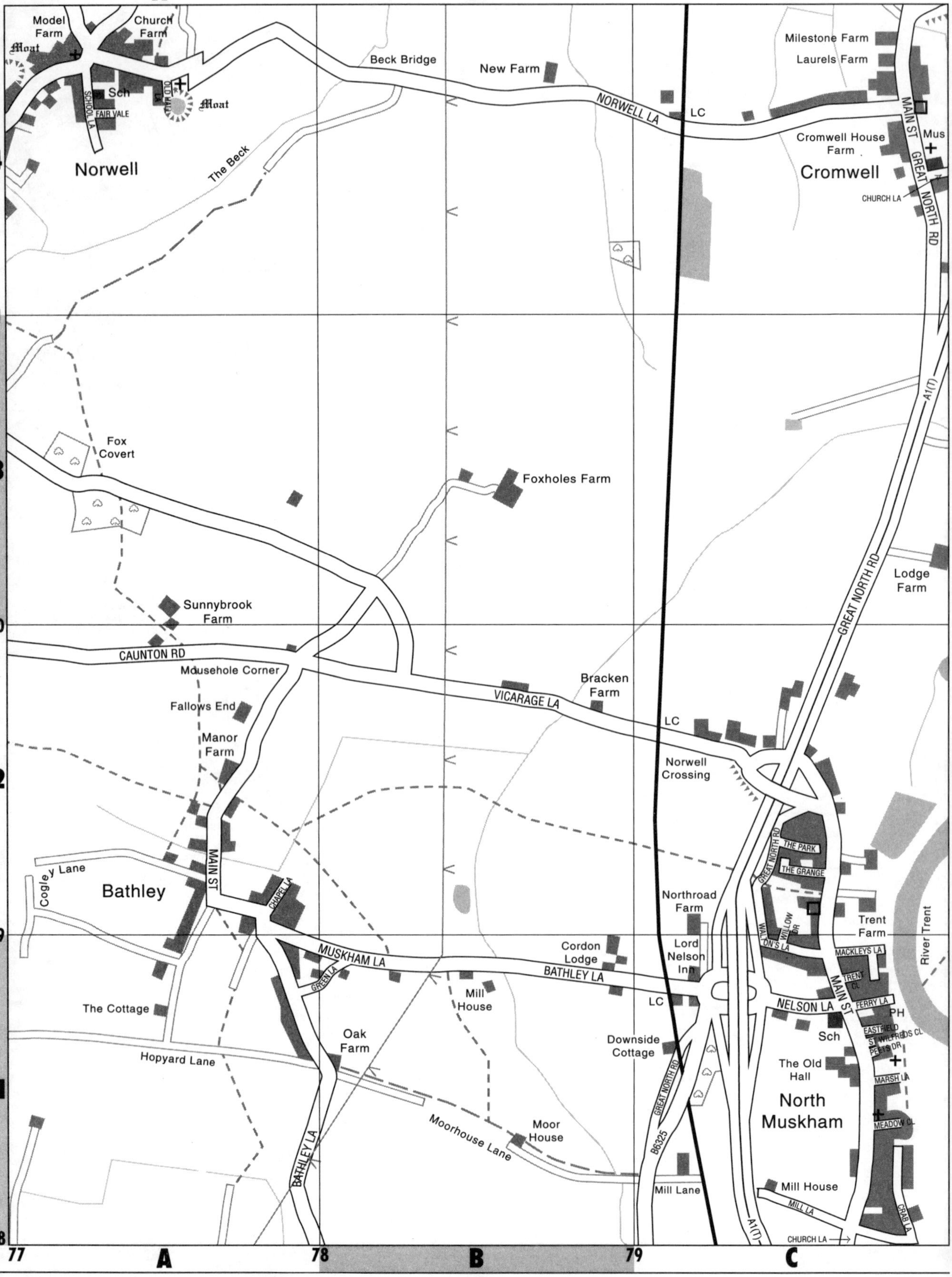
A
B
C
4
61
3
60
2
59
1
58
77
78
79
Model Farm
Church Farm
Moat
Sch
SCHOOL LA
FAIR VALE
OLD HALL
Norwell
The Beck
Beck Bridge
New Farm
NORWELL LA
LC
Milestone Farm
Laurels Farm
Cromwell House Farm
Mus
MAIN ST
GREAT NORTH RD
Cromwell
CHURCH LA
A1(T)
Fox Covert
Foxholes Farm
Lodge Farm
Sunnybrook Farm
CAUNTON RD
Mousehole Corner
Fallows End
Manor Farm
VICARAGE LA
Bracken Farm
Norwell Crossing
THE PARK
THE GRANGE
WILLOW DR
WALDON'S LA
Northroad Farm
Trent Farm
River Trent
Cogley Lane
Bathley
CHAPEL LA
Cordon Lodge
Lord Nelson Inn
MUSKHAM LA
GREEN LA
BATHLEY LA
Mill House
NELSON LA
MACKLEYS LA
TRENT CL
FERRY LA
PH
EASTFIELD
ST WILFREDS CL
PEETS DR
Sch
The Cottage
Oak Farm
Hopyard Lane
Downside Cottage
The Old Hall
MARSH LA
North Muskham
MEADOW CL
Moorhouse Lane
Moor House
B6325
Mill Lane
Mill House
MILL LA
CRAB LA
CHURCH LA

97
112

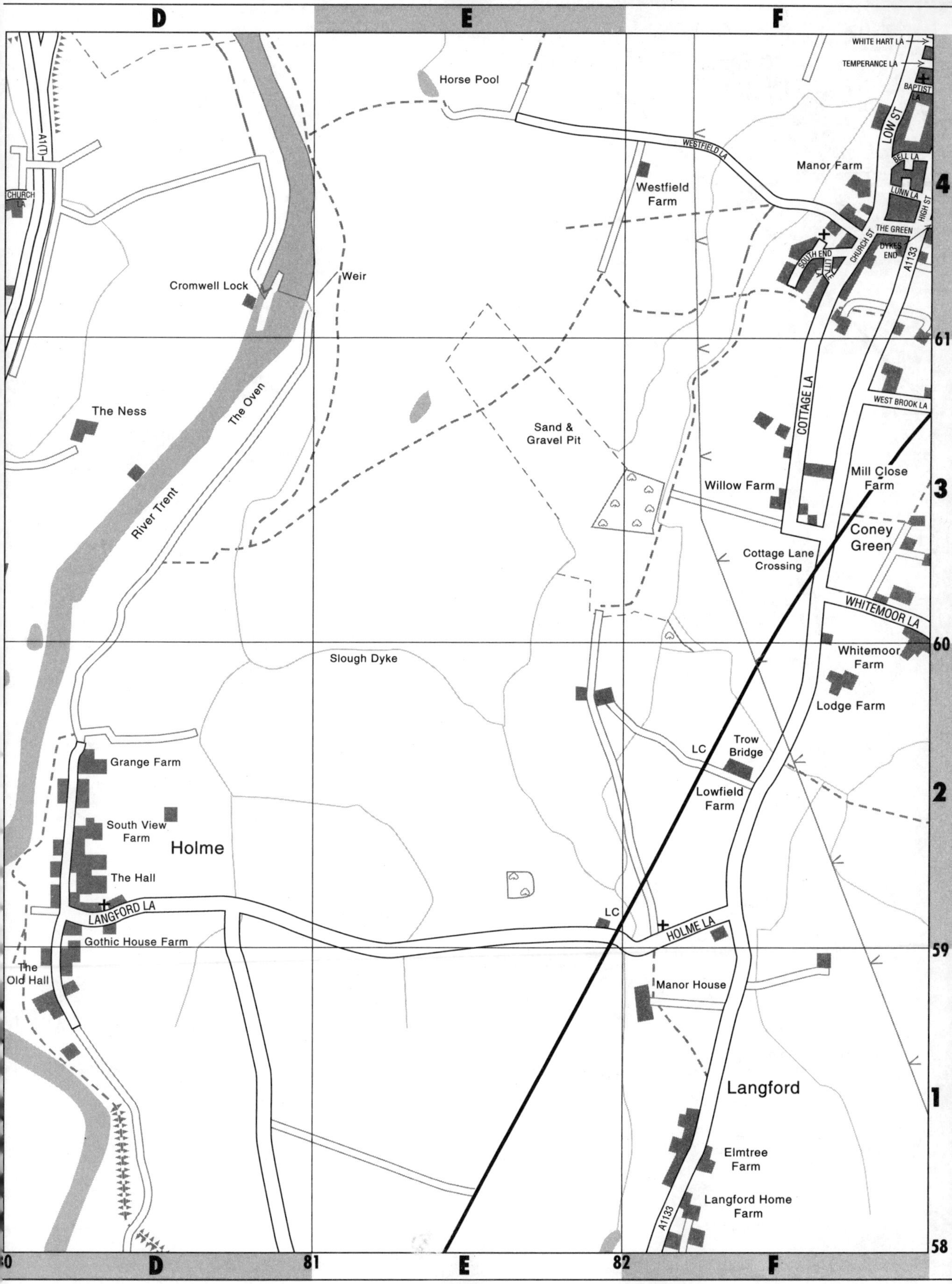


125
112

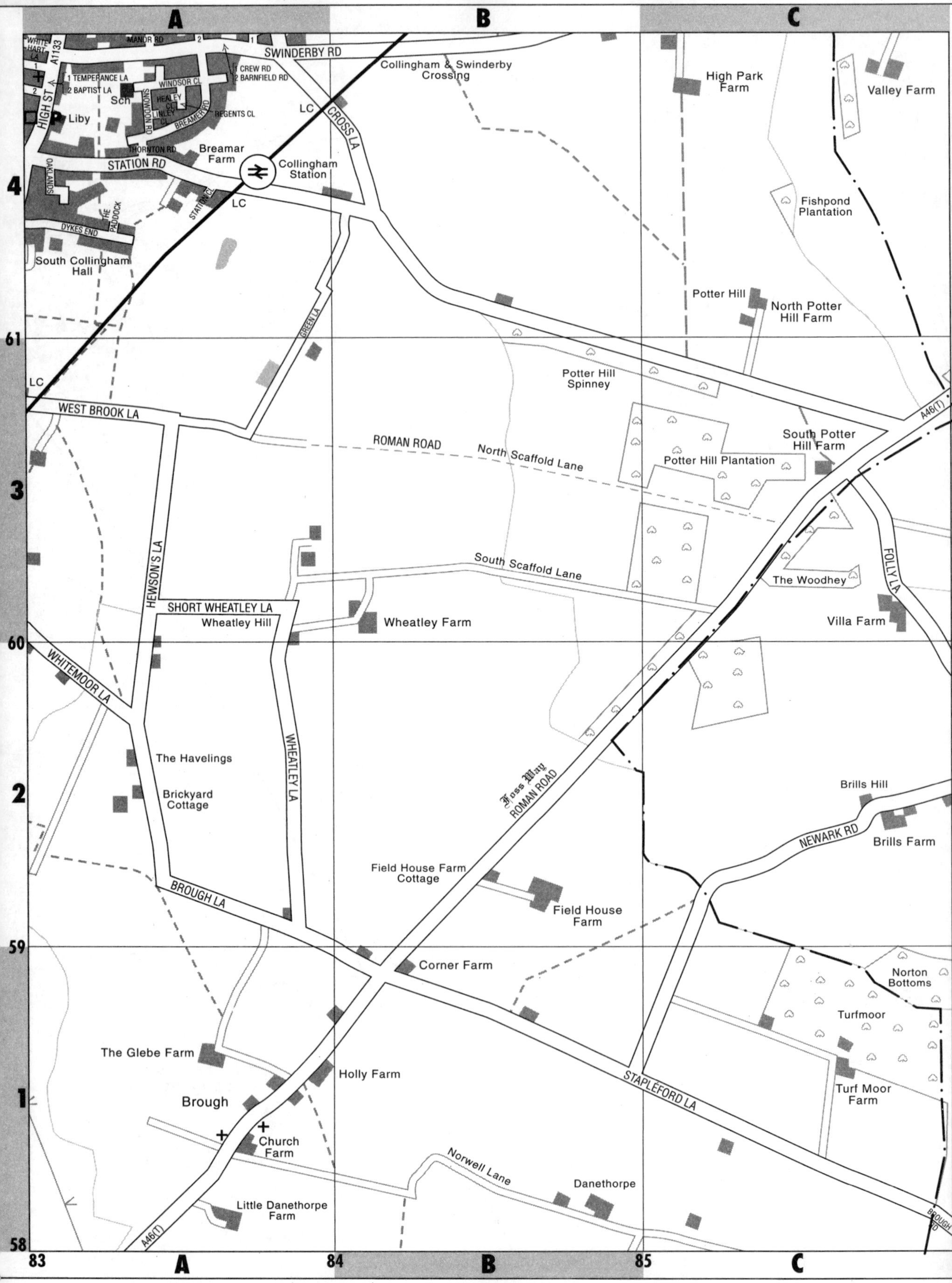
A
B
C
SWINDERBY RD
MANOR RD
WHITE HART LA
A1133
HIGH ST
1 TEMPERANCE LA
2 BAPTIST LA
1 CREW RD
2 BARNFIELD RD
WINDSOR CL
HEALEY CL
LINLEY CL
SNOWDON RD
BREAMER RD
REGENTS CL
Sch
Liby
THORNTON RD
STATION RD
OAKLANDS
THE PADDOCK
DYKES END
STATION CL
Collingham & Swinderby Crossing
LC
CROSS LA
Breamar Farm
Collingham Station
South Collingham Hall
High Park Farm
Valley Farm
Fishpond Plantation
Potter Hill
North Potter Hill Farm
GREEN LA
Potter Hill Spinney
WEST BROOK LA
ROMAN ROAD
North Scaffold Lane
South Potter Hill Farm
Potter Hill Plantation
A46(T)
South Scaffold Lane
The Woodhey
FOLLY LA
Villa Farm
HEWSON'S LA
SHORT WHEATLEY LA
Wheatley Hill
Wheatley Farm
WHITEMOOR LA
WHEATLEY LA
The Havelings
Brickyard Cottage
Foss Way
ROMAN ROAD
Brills Hill
NEWARK RD
Brills Farm
Field House Farm Cottage
Field House Farm
BROUGH LA
Corner Farm
Norton Bottoms
Turfmoor
The Glebe Farm
Holly Farm
STAPLEFORD LA
Turf Moor Farm
Brough
Church Farm
Norwell Lane
Danethorpe
Little Danethorpe Farm
BROUGH RD
4
61
3
60
2
59
1
58
83
84
85

99
114

128
114

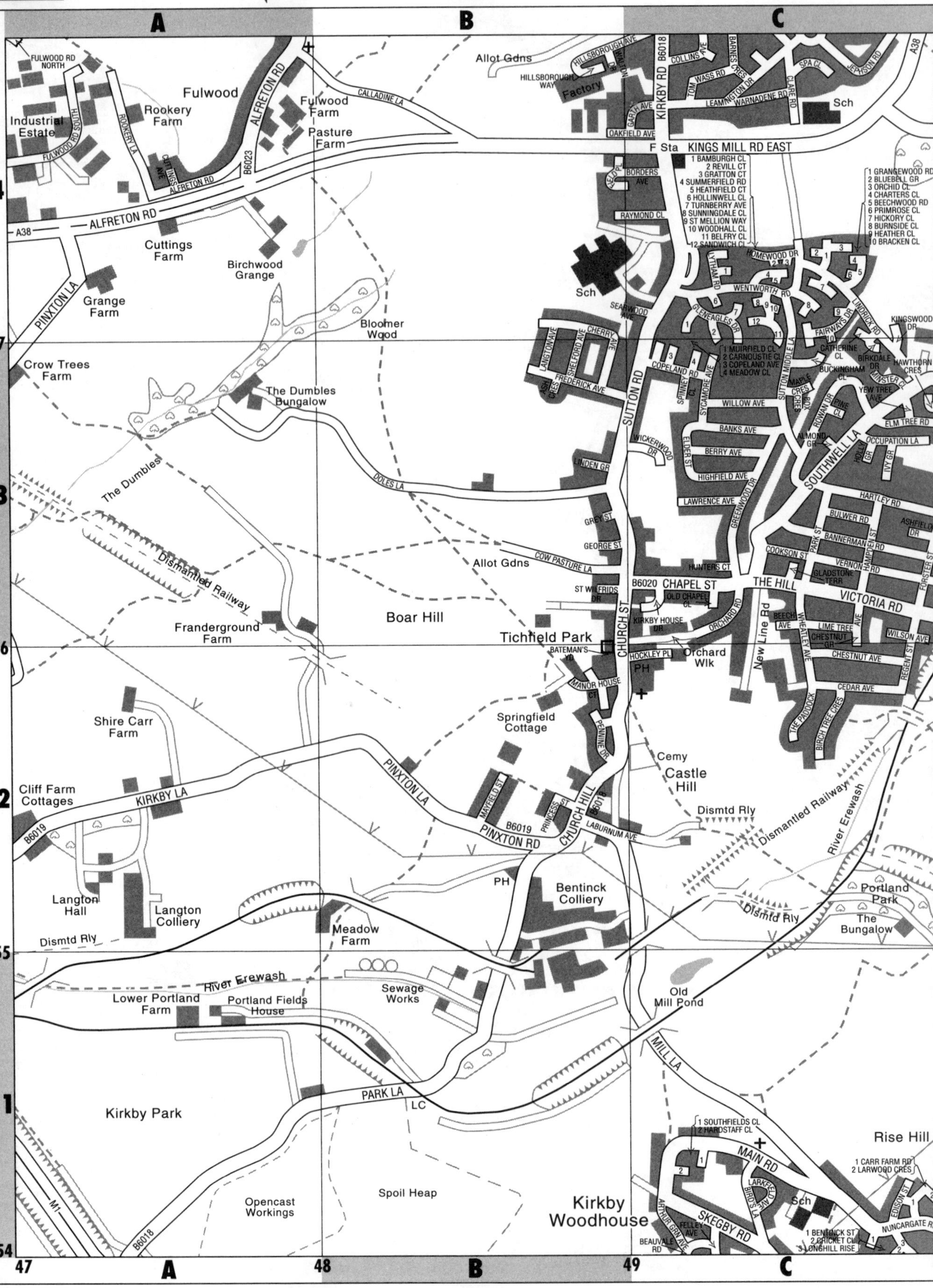
A
B
C
Fulwood
Industrial Estate
Rookery Farm
Fulwood Farm
Pasture Farm
ALFRETON RD
CALLADINE LA
Allot Gdns
Factory
KIRKBY RD B6018
KINGS MILL RD EAST
F Sta
Sch
Cuttings Farm
Birchwood Grange
Grange Farm
PINXTON LA
Bloomer Wood
Crow Trees Farm
The Dumbles Bungalow
The Dumbles
Dismantled Railway
DOLES LA
SUTTON RD
Allot Gdns
Boar Hill
Franderground Farm
CHAPEL ST
THE HILL
VICTORIA RD
Tichfield Park
CHURCH ST
Orchard Wlk
New Line Rd
PH
Springfield Cottage
Shire Carr Farm
Cemy
Castle Hill
Cliff Farm Cottages
KIRKBY LA
PINXTON RD
CHURCH HILL
Dismtd Rly
Dismantled Railway
River Erewash
Langton Hall
Langton Colliery
Meadow Farm
Bentinck Colliery
Portland Park
The Bungalow
Dismtd Rly
River Erewash
Lower Portland Farm
Portland Fields House
Sewage Works
Old Mill Pond
MILL LA
PARK LA
LC
Kirkby Park
Rise Hill
Opencast Workings
Spoil Heap
Kirkby Woodhouse
MAIN RD
SKEGBY RD
M1
B6018
47
48
49
A
B
C
54
1
55
2
56
3
57
4

101
116

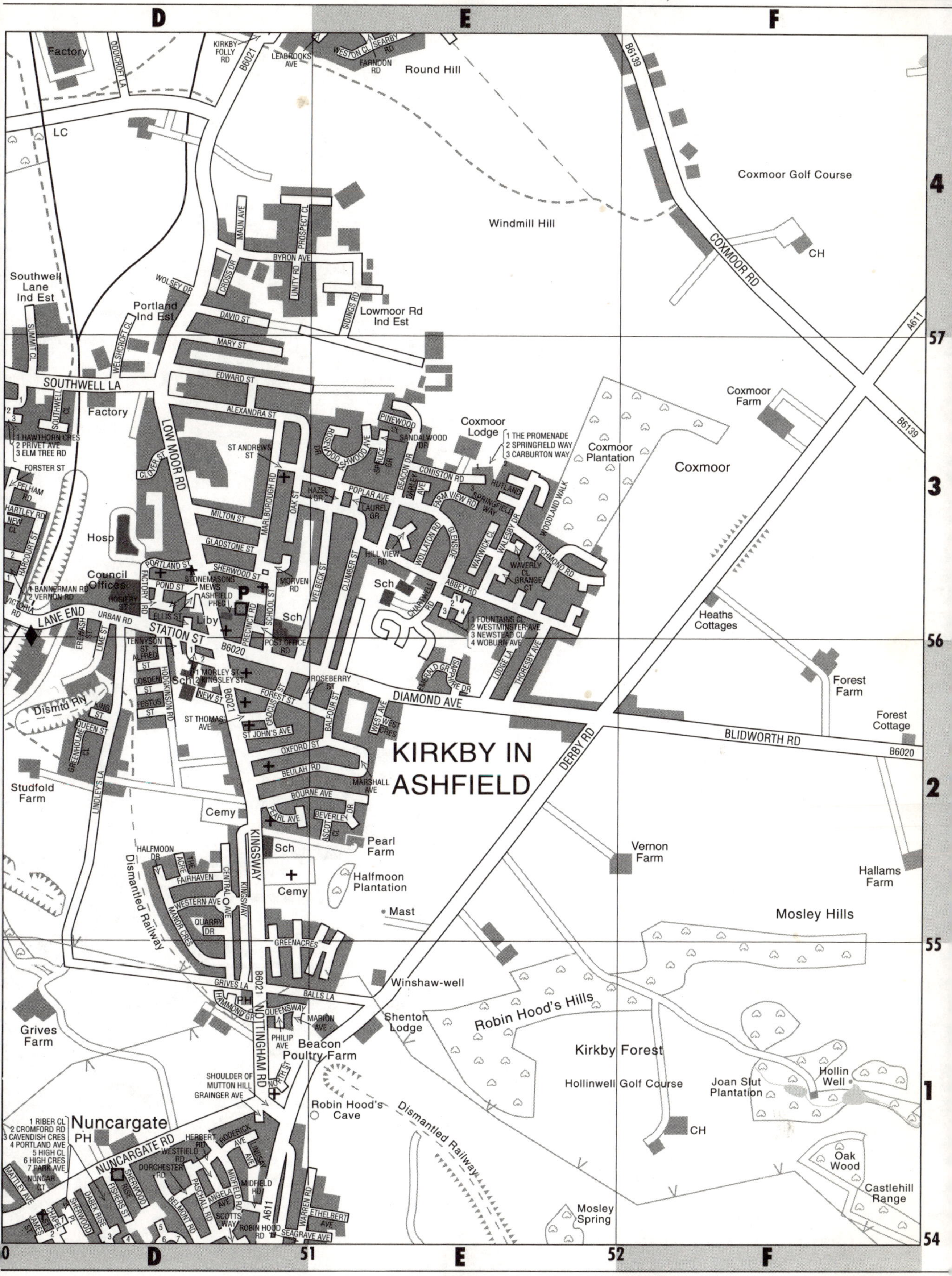


130
116

115
102

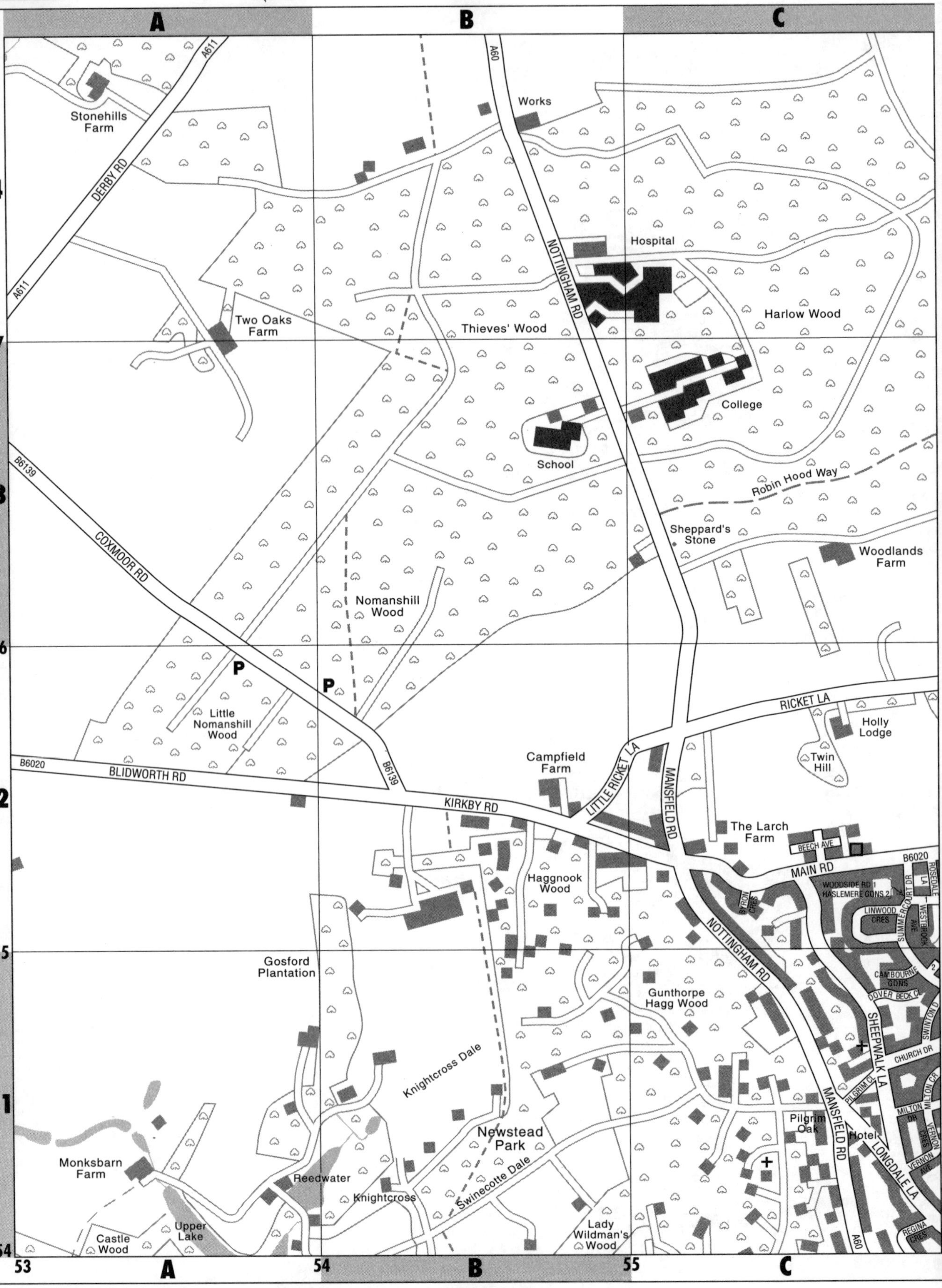


115
131

D
E
F
Lindhurst La
Lindhurst Farm
Rainworth
Sch
THORESBY RD
Rainworth Lodge
BLIDWORTH LA
The Archer (PH)
B6020
WARSOP LA
4
New Farm
Cottage Farm
57
Providence Farm
Moat
High Park
CROSS LA
Fountain Dale
Greenfields
Copt Hill Farm
Norwood Hill Close
MANSFIELD RD
B6020
Brick Kiln Hill
3
Robin Hood Way
NEW LA
Ling Farm
RICKET LA
Norwood Hill Farm
Redgate Farm
56
MARRIOTS LA
GROVE PARK
BUTLER DR
B6020
PH
Rock Farm
MAIN ST
PH
Silverland Farm
ROBIN HOOD TERR
SANDY LA
PH
Fishpool Farm
FISHPOOL RD
Tel Ex
2
MAIN RD
FIELD LA
Cottage Farm
THE BIRCHES
BRETTON RD
CROMFORD CL
CAROLINE CL
WOODSIDE RD
DOVERIDGE CT
ASHOVER CL
HADDON RD
LITTON CL
BRACKENFIELD RISE
HEREFORD RD
ASHFORD DR
WINSTER AVE
1 CHERNSIDE
2 STANLEY CL
3 CASTLETON
Schs
TIDESWELL CL
55
SWINTON RISE
WALTHAM RD
SOUTHVIEW GDNS
DENBURY RD
BOURNE DR
CHERITON DR
DOWNHAM GDNS
Bottom Farm
PH
CHURCH DR
WOODLAND RISE 1
RIDGEWOOD GR 2
HIGHFIELD CL
PH
Jackson's Hill
MILTON CRES
WOOD END DR
MAVIS AVE
LEA CL
LEA RD
CHAPEL LA
MILTON DR
BIRCH CL
1
Sch
BIRCHWOOD DR
CHEMSIDE CL
Ravenshead
Robin Hood Way
ROBIN GR
HEAVYTREES AVE
VERNON CRES
RIGG LA
DUNCAN AVE
SILVERWOOD AV
GORSE HILL
LONGDALE AVE
OAKWOOD DR
PRIORY AVE
BIRCHWOOD CL
BARBERS WOOD CL
ROWAN AVE
Blidworth Dale
CHESTNUT AVE
LONGDALE LA
REGINA CRES
QUARRY RD
FERN
54
6
D
57
E
58
F

117
104

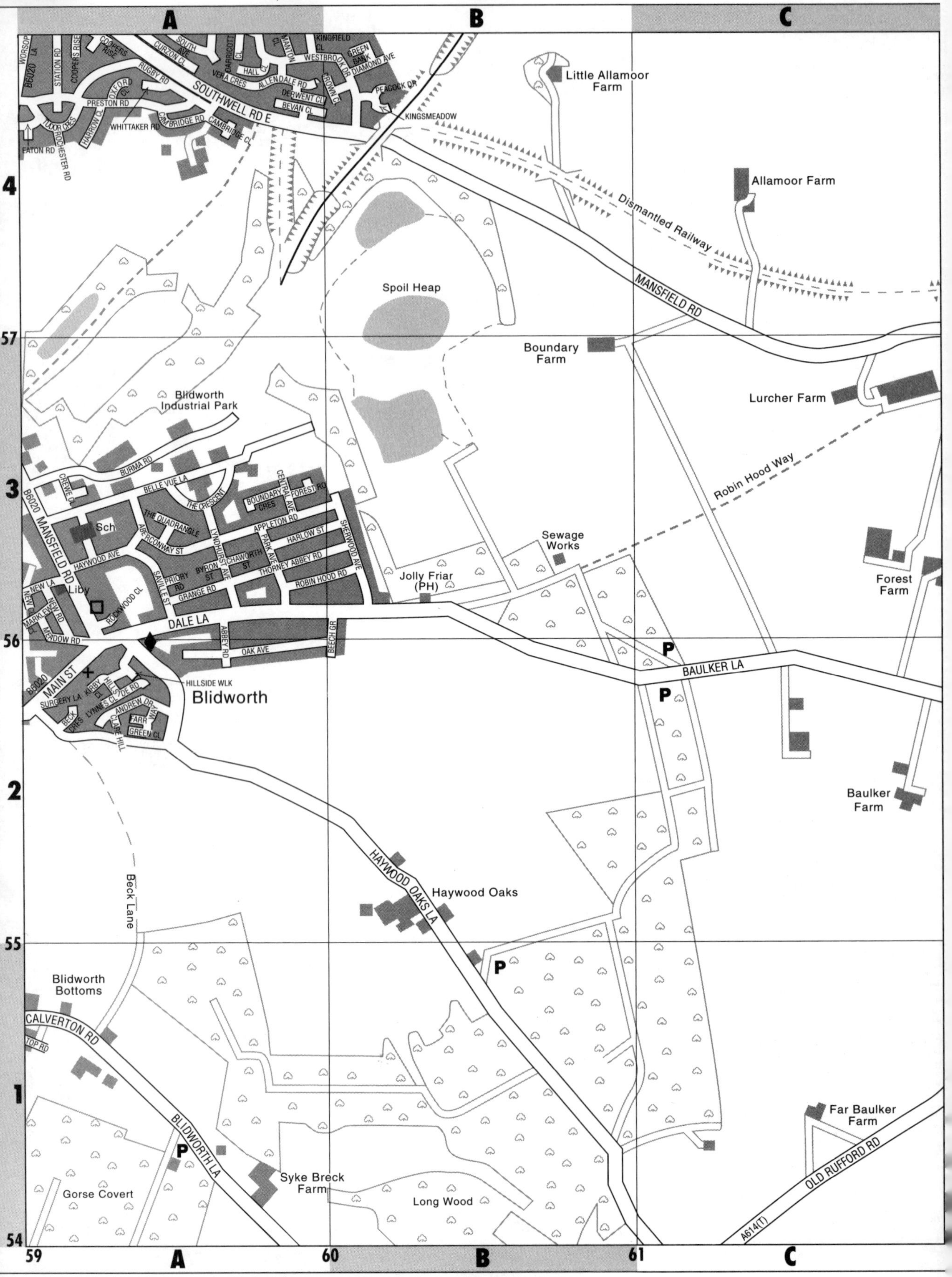


117
133

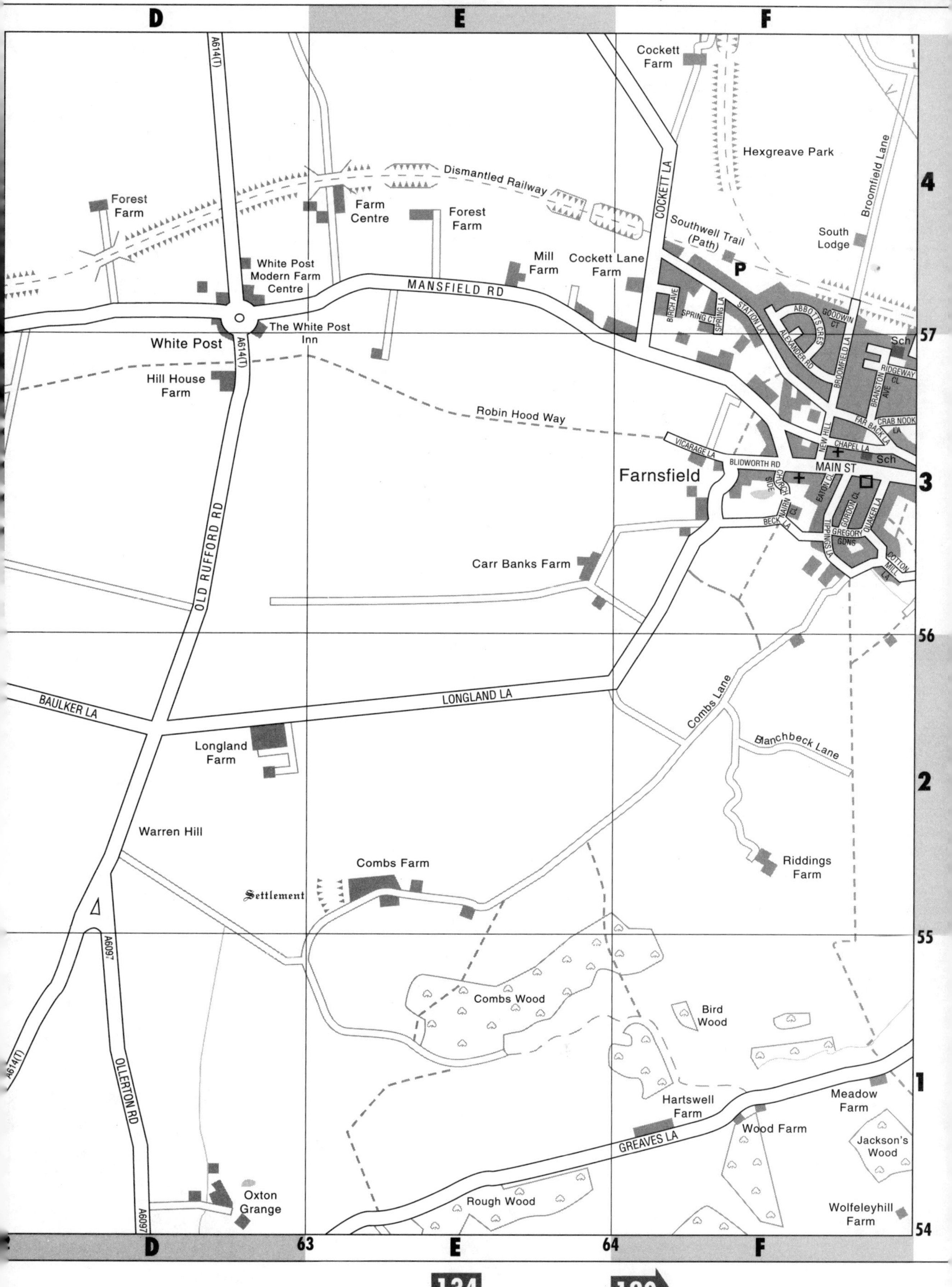
D
E
F
Cockett Farm
Hexgreave Park
Broomfield Lane
Dismantled Railway
Forest Farm
Farm Centre
Forest Farm
COCKETT LA
Southwell Trail (Path)
South Lodge
White Post Modern Farm Centre
Mill Farm
Cockett Lane Farm
MANSFIELD RD
A614(T)
The White Post Inn
White Post
Hill House Farm
Robin Hood Way
Sch
Farnsfield
MAIN ST
BLIDWORTH RD
VICARAGE LA
Carr Banks Farm
OLD RUFFORD RD
BAULKER LA
LONGLAND LA
Combs Lane
Blanchbeck Lane
Longland Farm
Warren Hill
Riddings Farm
Combs Farm
Settlement
Combs Wood
Bird Wood
OLLERTON RD
A6097
Hartswell Farm
Meadow Farm
Wood Farm
GREAVES LA
Jackson's Wood
Oxton Grange
Rough Wood
Wolfeleyhill Farm
4
57
3
56
2
55
1
54
63
64

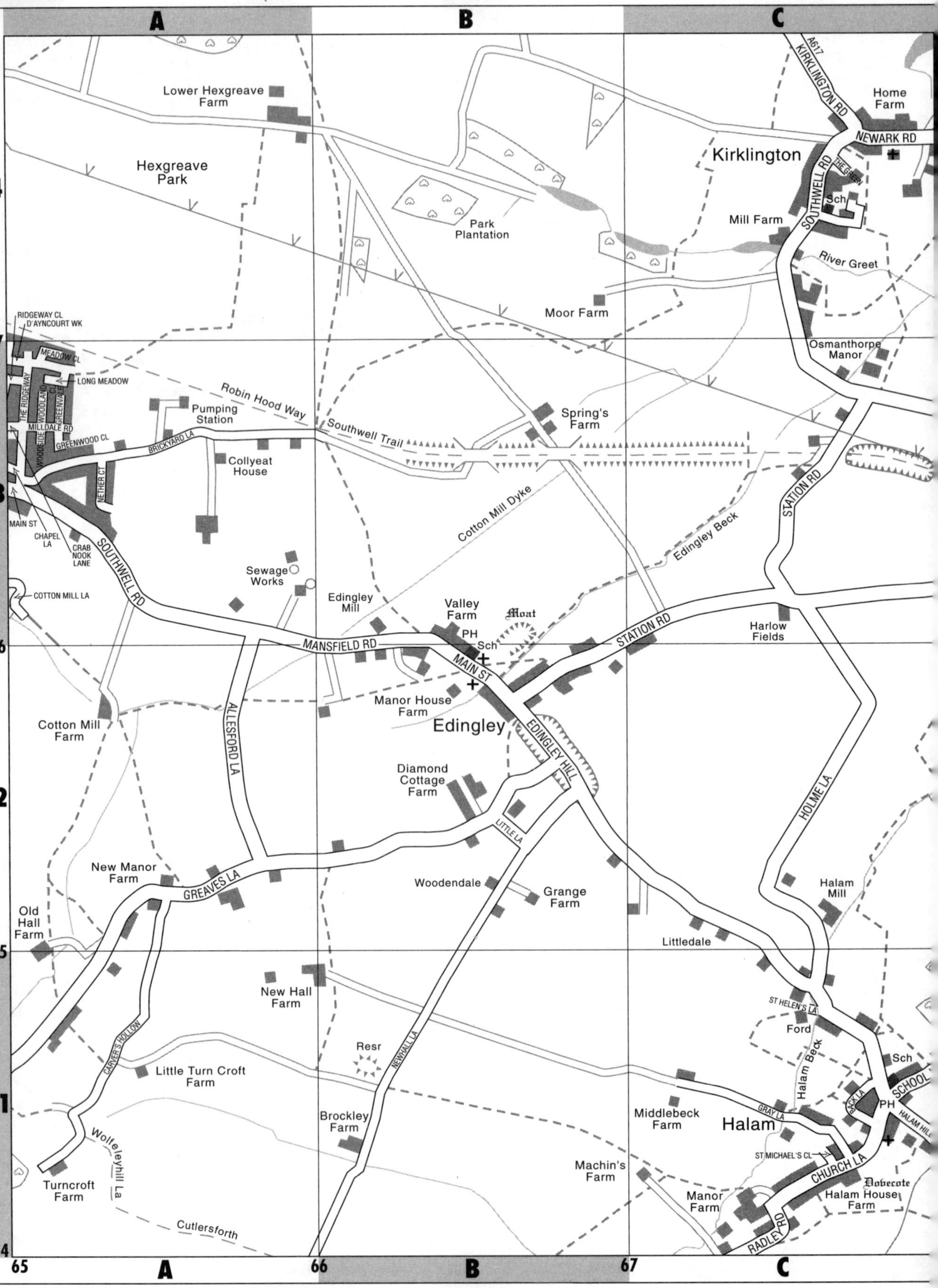
A
B
C
Lower Hexgreave Farm
Hexgreave Park
Park Plantation
Kirklington
Home Farm
NEWARK RD
KIRKLINGTON RD
A617
SOUTHWELL RD
THE GREEN
Sch
Mill Farm
River Greet
Moor Farm
Osmanthorpe Manor
RIDGEWAY CL
D'AYNCOURT WK
MEADOW CL
LONG MEADOW
THE RIDGEWAY
WOODLAND
GREENVALE
MILLDALE RD
WOODSIDE
GREENWOOD CL
Robin Hood Way
Pumping Station
Southwell Trail
Spring's Farm
BRICKYARD LA
Collyeat House
NETHER CT
MAIN ST
CHAPEL LA
CRAB NOOK LANE
SOUTHWELL RD
Cotton Mill Dyke
Edingley Beck
STATION RD
Sewage Works
COTTON MILL LA
Edingley Mill
Valley Farm
Moat
PH
Sch
MANSFIELD RD
MAIN ST
STATION RD
Harlow Fields
Manor House Farm
Edingley
Cotton Mill Farm
ALLESFORD LA
EDINGLEY HILL
Diamond Cottage Farm
HOLME LA
LITTLE LA
New Manor Farm
GREAVES LA
Woodendale
Grange Farm
Halam Mill
Old Hall Farm
Littledale
New Hall Farm
ST HELEN'S LA
Ford
Resr
NEWHALL LA
CARVER'S HOLLOW
Little Turn Croft Farm
Halam Beck
Sch
SCHOOL
BACK LA
PH
HALAM HILL
Middlebeck Farm
GRAY LA
Halam
Brockley Farm
Wolfeleyhill La
ST MICHAEL'S CL
Machin's Farm
CHURCH LA
Dovecote
Halam House Farm
Turncroft Farm
Manor Farm
RADLEY RD
Cutlersforth
4
57
3
56
2
55
1
54
65
66
67

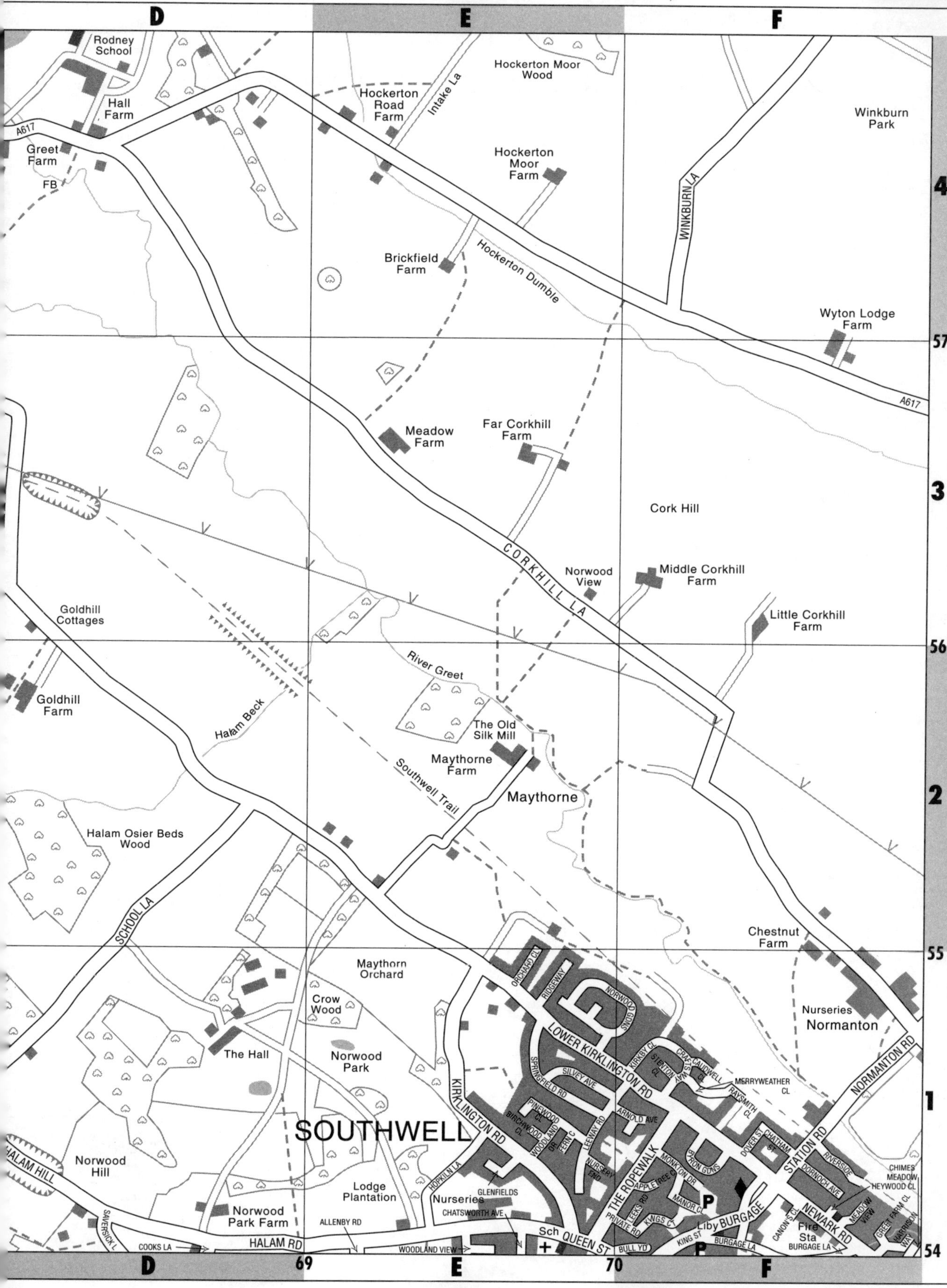
D
E
F
Rodney School
Hall Farm
A617
Greet Farm
FB
Hockerton Road Farm
Intake La
Hockerton Moor Wood
Hockerton Moor Farm
Winkburn Park
WINKBURN LA
4
Brickfield Farm
Hockerton Dumble
Wyton Lodge Farm
57
A617
Meadow Farm
Far Corkhill Farm
3
Cork Hill
CORKHILL LA
Norwood View
Middle Corkhill Farm
Goldhill Cottages
Little Corkhill Farm
56
River Greet
Goldhill Farm
Halam Beck
The Old Silk Mill
Maythorne Farm
Southwell Trail
Maythorne
2
Halam Osier Beds Wood
SCHOOL LA
Chestnut Farm
55
Maythorn Orchard
Crow Wood
ORCHARD CL
RIDGEWAY
NORWOOD GDNS
Nurseries
Normanton
NORMANTON RD
LOWER KIRKLINGTON RD
The Hall
Norwood Park
SPRINGFIELD RD
SILVEY AVE
KIRKBY CL
CAUDWELL CL
MERRYWEATHER CL
RAYSMITH CL
1
KIRKLINGTON RD
PINEWOOD CL
BIRCHWOOD CL
WOODLAND DR
FERN C
LEEWAY RD
ARNOLD AVE
SOUTHWELL
THE ROPEWALK
MONKTON DR
BYRON GDNS
DOVER ST
CHATHAM ST
STATION RD
RIVERSIDE
DORNOCH AVE
CHIMES MEADOW
HEYWOOD CL
HALAM HILL
Norwood Hill
Lodge Plantation
HOPKILN LA
Nurseries
GLENFIELDS
NURSERY END
APPLETREE CL
MANOR C
P
CHATSWORTH AVE
LEEKS RD
KINGS CT
PRIVATE RD
Liby
BURGAGE
CANON'S CL
NEWARK RD
MEADOW VIEW
GREET FARM CL
HARRISON WAY
Norwood Park Farm
SAVERSICK L
ALLENBY RD
Sch
Fire Sta
COOKS LA
HALAM RD
WOODLAND VIEW
QUEEN ST
BULL YD
KING ST
BURGAGE LA
54
69
70

121
108

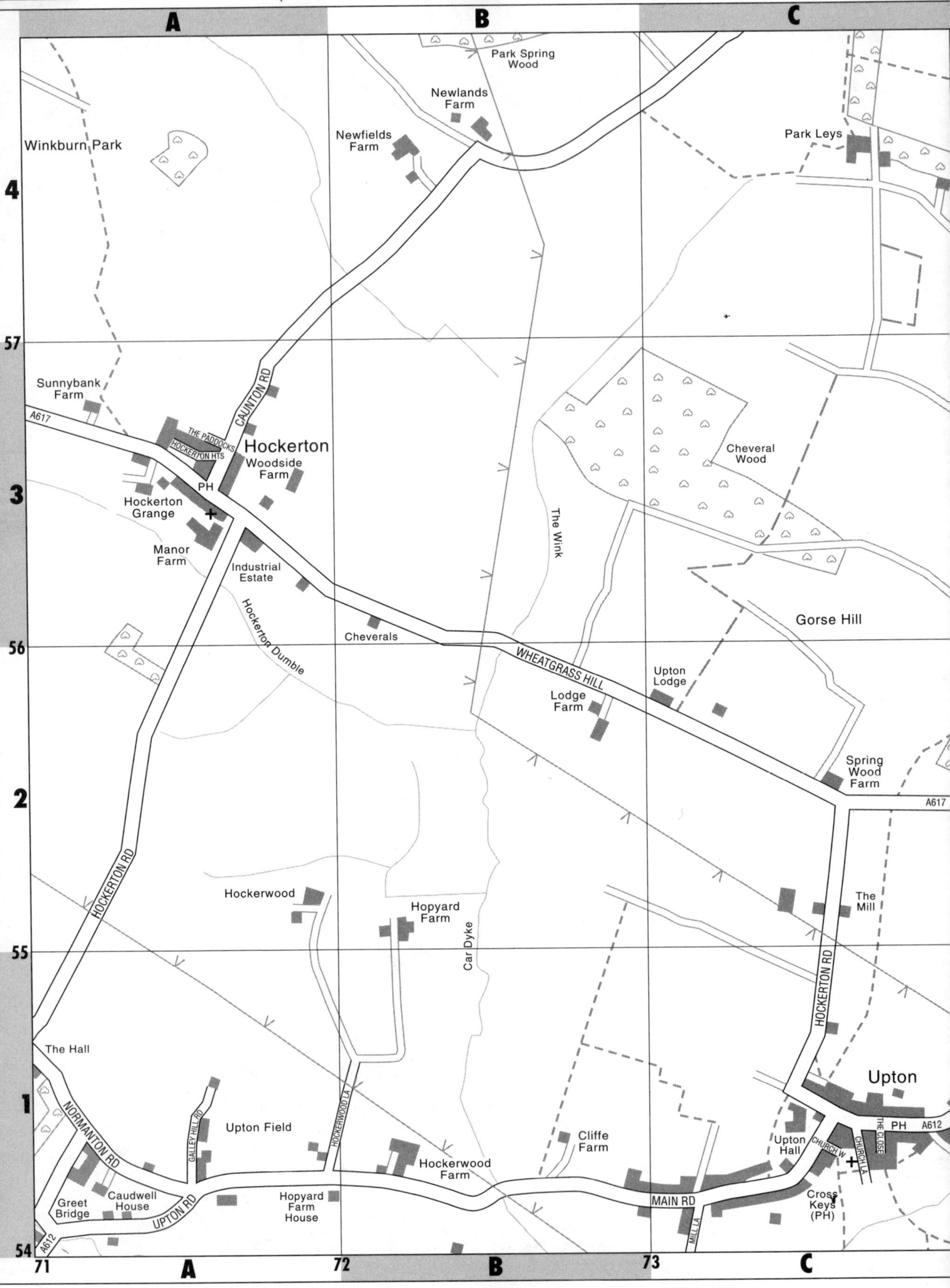


121
137

109
124

138
124

123
110

123
139

D
E
F
Winthorpe Lake
The Fleet
Winthorpe Crossing
Holme La
High Leys
Woodlands
Thoroughfare La
Sch
Hall Farm
Langford Hall
Lodge
A1133
A46(T)
A1(T)
Pocklington Cres
Branston Cl
Chapel La
Gainsborough Rd
The Drive
The Hall
PH
Hargon La
Drove La
Winthorpe
Spright Cl
The Spinney
Winthorpe Bridge
River Trent
Winthorpe Rack
Crankley Point
Bridge House
Fosse Way
Roman Road
Newark and Nottingham Agricultural Society's Showground
Airfield (disused)
Whinthorpe Rd
Sewage Works
LC
A17(T)
Stephen Rd
Alexander Ave
Pine Cl
Norman Ave
Primrose Ave
Hollies Ave
South Airfield Farm
Depot
North Airfield Farm
The Bungalow
Newark Crossing
Fleming Dr
Wolsey Rd
Meering Ave
Winthorpe Rd
Park Cres
Chestnut Ave
Cedar Ave
B6166
Lincoln Rd
Stanhope Ave
Gainsborough Dr
Clifton Cres
Middleton Rd
Pembroke Cres
Terry Ave
Telford Dr
Quibell's La
Seven Hills
Markham Ave
Hatchet's La
Newark Branch
Works
Yorke Dr
Fenton Cl
Rosewood Cl
Beaumont Wlk
Brunel Dr
Beaconfield Farm
The Nook
Malt Kiln
Trent La
Strawberry Hall La
Whittle Cl
Lincoln Road Bridge
Lincoln St
Farrar Cl
Trenchard Ave
Valiant Rd
Canberra Rd
Mitchell Ave
Hall Gdns
Parklands Cl
Pennswick Gr
Newark Rd
Harvey Ave
Sycamore Dr
Trent Way
Maun Gn
Derwent Way
Welland Cl
Witham
1 Alliance St
2 Summer's Rd
3 Newnham Rd
4 Meyrick Rd
North Gate
Currie
The Trust
Nursery Ct
Warburton Ct
George St
Depot
Newark Northgate Station
Northern Rd
Abbott's Way
Jessop Cl
Jessop Way
Stanley St
Cotswold
1 The Mount
2 Mount La
Lover's La
The Barn Ct
Mumby Cl
Queen's Ct
Queen's Rd
Appleton Gate
Cliff Nook La
Lawrence Pl
Amb Sta
Schs
Sleaford Rd
Lawrence St
Welbeck Ave
Newstead
Friary Rd
Magnus St
Wellington Rd
Works
Beacon Hill Rd
Greenways
4
57
3
56
2
55
1
54
81
82

125
112

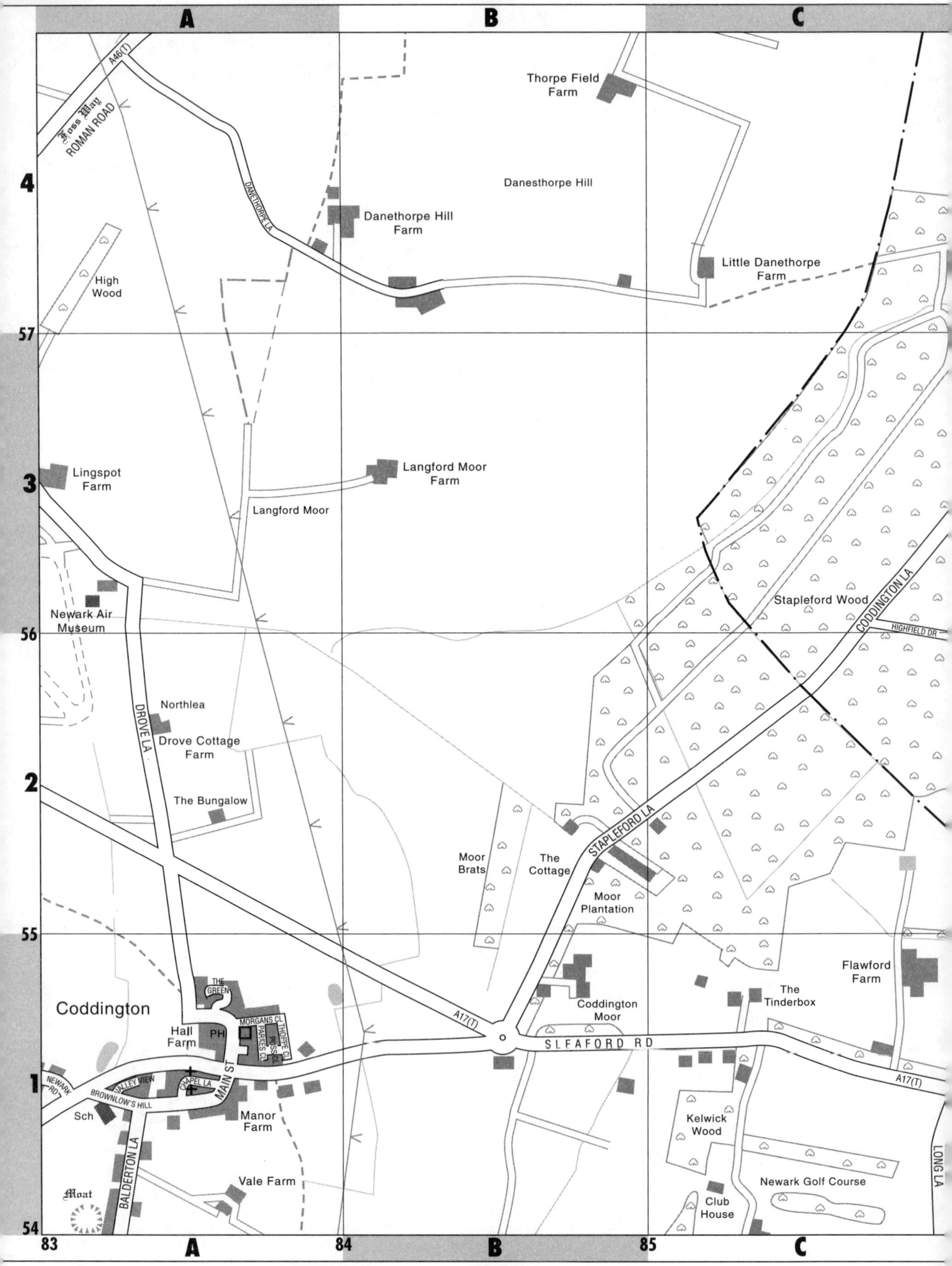


125
141

D
E
F
Stapleford Moor
BROUGH RD
Moor Farm
NEWARK RD
BRECKS LA
THE PADDOCKS
NORTON RD
The Hall
Church Lane
Sch
Poplar Tree Farm
Woodland View
Stapleford
The Laurels
Pailing's Ride
BROUGHTON RD
Moor Lane
Lodge Drive
CODDINGTON LA
Broughton Clays
57
Stapleford House
The Elms
Stapleford Wood
Clay Lane
3
Grange Drive
DANGER AREA
Stapleford Grange
River Witham
Top Covert Farm
56
HIGHFIELD DR
Highfield House
DANGER AREA
Top Covert
2
Stapleford Moor
DANGER AREA
Four Acres
55
Youle Dike
Hanley Farm
Whitegate House
1
SLEAFORD RD
Rifle Range
WOODGATE LA
Beckingham Training Camp
Sewage Works
Barnby Manor
A17(T)
College Plantation
SLEAFORD RD
54
D
87
E
88
F

A
B
C
Sewage Works
Hobsic Farm
HOBSIC LA
PH
Hall Green
Hillbank Farm
Commonside
COMMON SIDE
Hall Green Farm
River Erewash
Dismantled Railway
Crimea Farm
Pye Bridge Junction
CHURCH LA
HOMECROFT DR
STONEY LA
Rosemaryhill
Selston Green
Selston
Liby
FB
Sch
Pinfold Farm
MANSFIELD RD
B6018
Pye Bridge
B600
MAIN RD
ALFRETON RD
GREEN FARM RD
CRESCENT RD
Sleepy Hole
NOTTINGHAM RD
Dove Green
Golf Course
B6016
Ashes Farm
Allen's Green
Toadhole
LANGTON HOLLOW
Handstubbing
Barrows Green
SELSTON RD
Barrows Hill
Home Farm
Lea Farm
BARROWS HILL LA
Pye Hill
New Westwood
WAGSTAFF LA
PALMERSTON ST
Bagthorpe Brook
Bagthorpe
Manor Farm
Shepherds Rest (PH)
LOWER BAGTHORPE
Brookside Farm
Jacksdale
Gate Inn (PH)
Westwood
FLATTS LA
Wansley Hall
STATION LA
Westwood Farm
Yewtree Farm
Cromford Canal (disused)
MAIN RD
WILHALLOW LA
Underwood Green
Underwood Hill
Hole in the Wall (PH)
PLAINSPOT RD
Plain Spot
Plain Spot Farm
BRINSLEY HILL
HIGH ST
MAIN ST
Pollington House
New Brinsley
Oaktree Farm
EROAD LA
RED LA
WINTER CLOSES
WINDSMOOR RD
4
53
3
52
2
51
1
50
44
45
46

D
E
F
Kirkby Park
Spoil Heap
Kirkby Lane Farm
Kirkby Park's Farm
Bleak Hall Farm
Cemetery
Nuncargate
Annesley Woodhouse
Salmon Farm
FOREST RD
Boggs Farm
SALMON LA
Cuttail Brook
Two Dale Farm
PARK LA
B6018
M1
BRIDGE END AVE
MANSFIELD RD
WINDSOR RD
BOURNE AVE
MANITOBA WAY
SCHOOL RD
PORTLAND RD
CHAPEL ST
UNION ST
VICTORIA ST
NEWSTEAD CL
HARDWICK DR
ROYAL OAK DR
Sch
VICTORIA RD
UPPER MEXBOROUGH RD
HOLLAND CRES
CHATSWORTH AVE
DEETLETON CL
SHERWOOD WAY
FOREST CL
ANNESLEY LA
Selston Common
Annesley Lane End
Skegness
MELBOURNE ST
RECREATION ST
RAWSON ST
GILL ST
WILDE CRES
HOLLY HILL RD
PH
Woodnook
NOTTINGHAM RD
Davis's Bottom
Works
Alma
ALMA RD
Middlebrook Farm
Millington Springs
Junction 27
MANSFIELD RD
A608
Home Farm
Middlebrook Bridge
Middle Brook
MIDDLEBROOK RD
New Bagthorpe
SCHOOL RD
Sch
Shipton Hill Farm
Felley Priory Farm
Felley Priory
KENNEL LA
Audrey Wood
William Wood
Bagthorpe Plantation
ALFRETON RD
CHURCH LA
BEECH RD
SANDHILL RD
PH
MANSFIELD RD
WEAVER'S LA
OLD CHAPEL LA
DE MORGAN CL
WESTBOURNE RD
Friezeland
B600
America Farm
FELLEY MILL LA N
The Dumbles
Pamela's Larches
Underwood
FELLY MILL LA S
MAIN RD
CORDY LA
B600
Willeylane End
Willey Spring
Greasley Haggs
Felley Farm
Felley Mill
Haggs Farm
Park Springs
M1
4
53
3
52
2
51
1
50
48
49
D
E
F

129
115

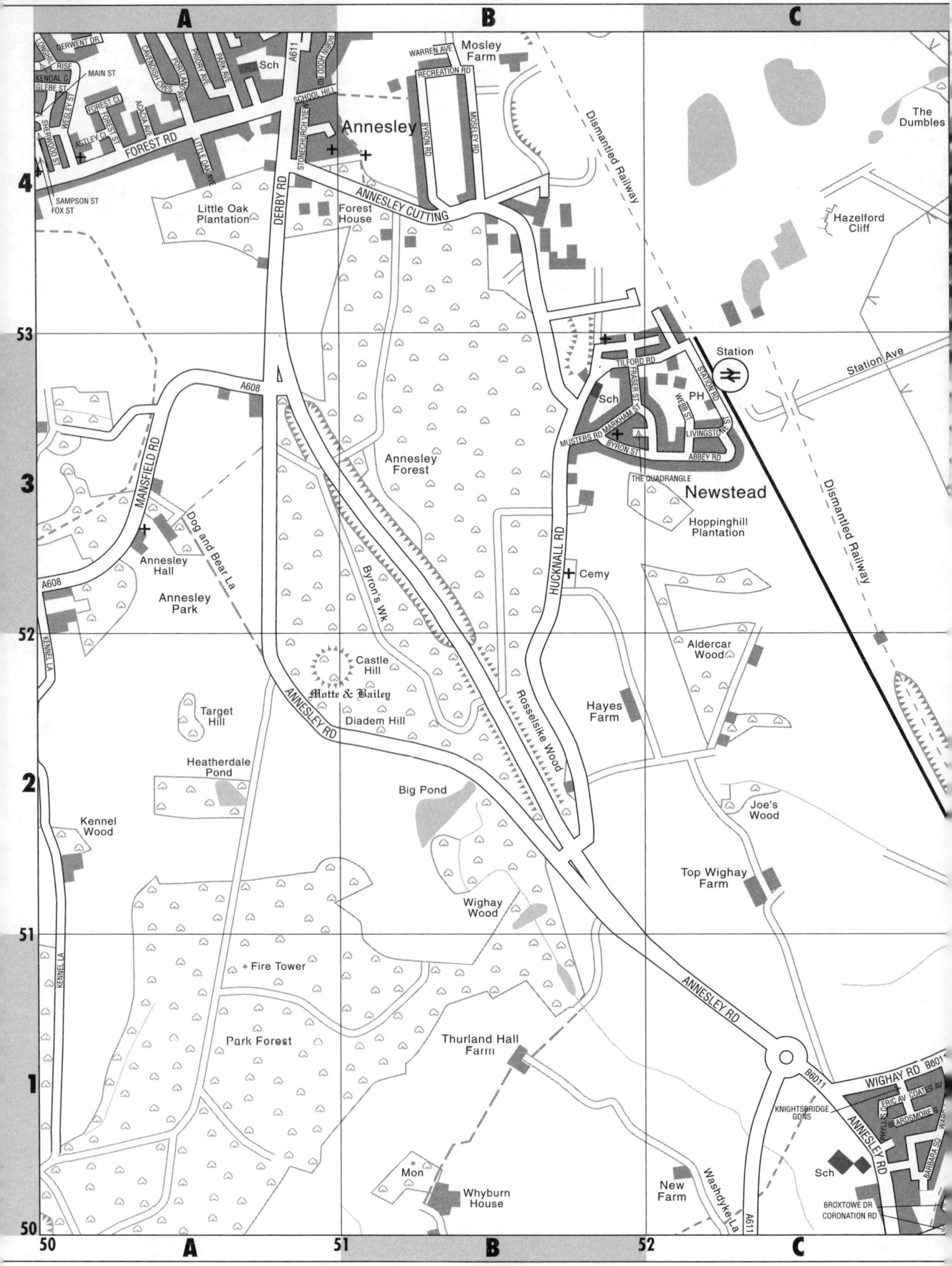


129
145

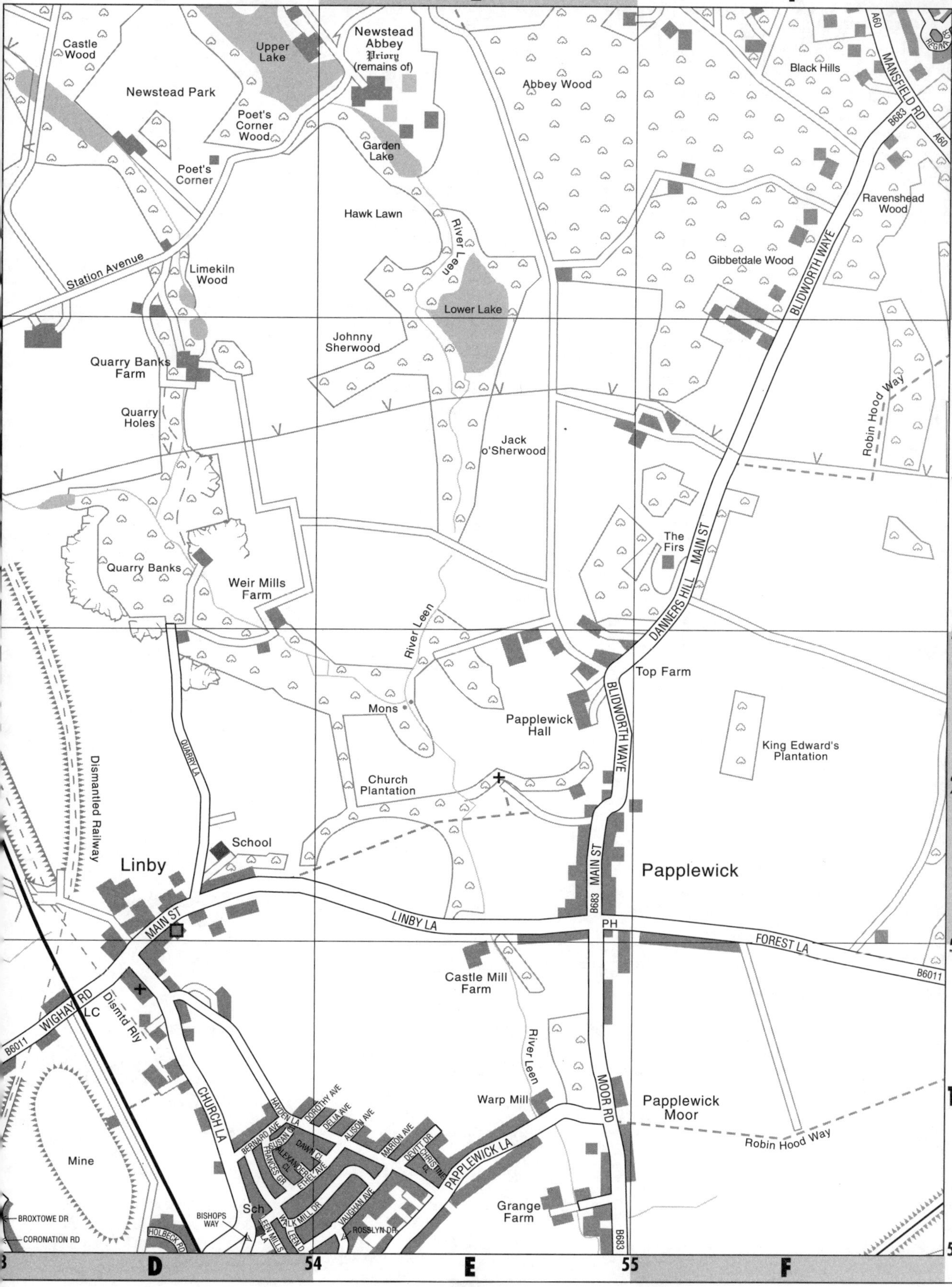
D
E
F
Castle Wood
Newstead Park
Upper Lake
Newstead Abbey Priory (remains of)
Abbey Wood
Black Hills
Poet's Corner Wood
Poet's Corner
Garden Lake
Hawk Lawn
River Leen
Ravenshead Wood
Gibbetdale Wood
Station Avenue
Limekiln Wood
Lower Lake
BLIDWORTH WAYE
MANSFIELD RD
A60
B683
Johnny Sherwood
Quarry Banks Farm
Quarry Holes
Jack o'Sherwood
Robin Hood Way
Quarry Banks
Weir Mills Farm
The Firs
DANNERS HILL
MAIN ST
Top Farm
Mons
Papplewick Hall
King Edward's Plantation
Church Plantation
QUARRY LA
Dismantled Railway
School
Linby
Papplewick
LINBY LA
PH
FOREST LA
B6011
Castle Mill Farm
WIGHAY RD
LC
Dismtd Rly
CHURCH LA
Warp Mill
MOOR RD
Papplewick Moor
PAPPLEWICK LA
Mine
Grange Farm
Sch
BISHOPS WAY
BROXTOWE DR
CORONATION RD
HOLBECK RD
ROSSLYN DR
VAUGHAN AVE
WALK MILL DR
LEEN MILLS LA
DOROTHY AVE
DELIA AVE
ALISON AVE
MARION AVE
DEVITT DR
CHRISTINE CL
BERNARD AVE
FRANCES GR
DAWN CL
ETHEL AVE
4
53
3
52
2
51
1
50
54
55

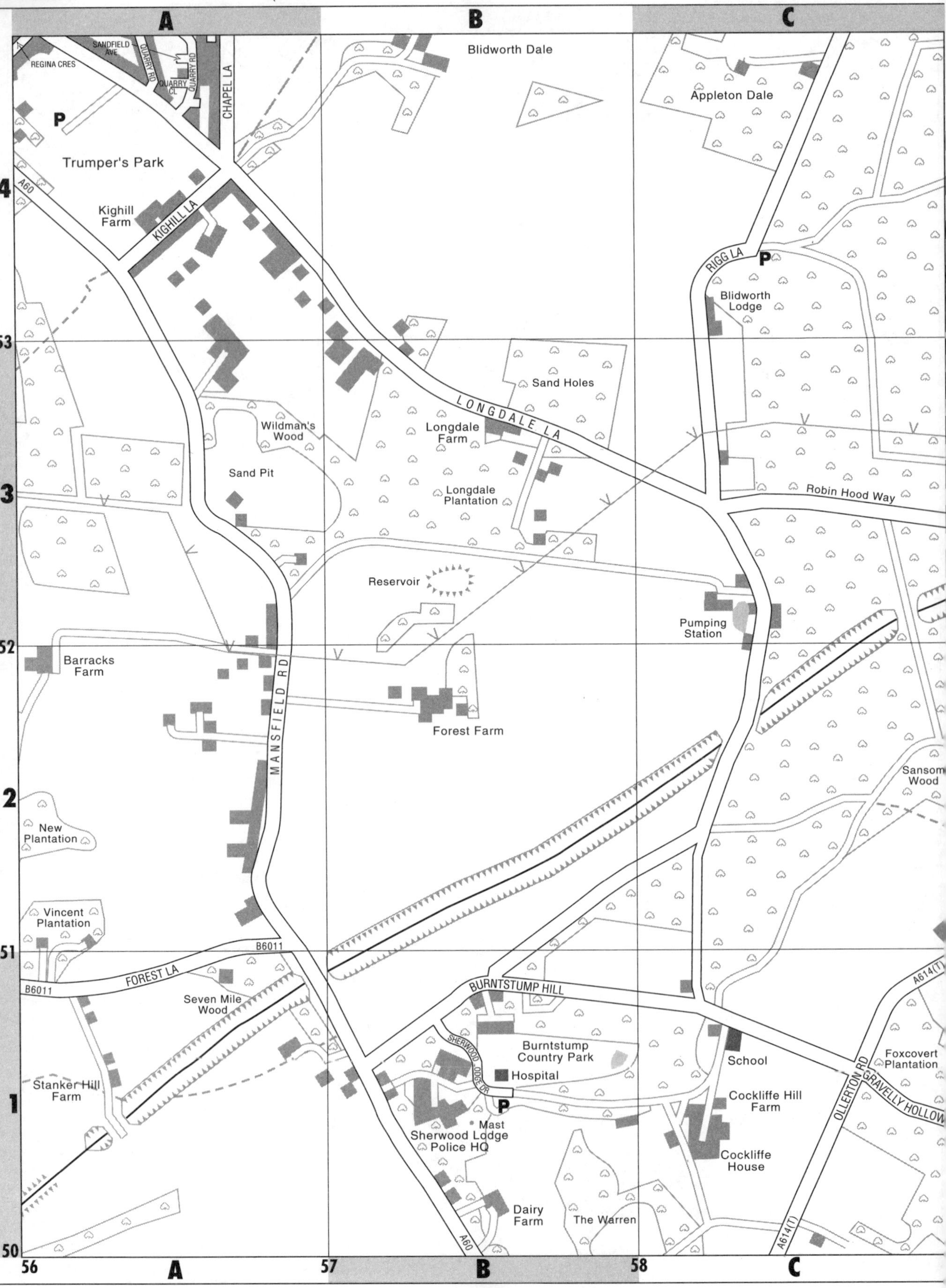
A
B
C
Blidworth Dale
Appleton Dale
SANDFIELD AVE
REGINA CRES
QUARRY RD
QUARRY CL
CHAPEL LA
Trumper's Park
A60
Kighill Farm
KIGHILL LA
RIGG LA
Blidworth Lodge
Sand Holes
LONGDALE LA
Wildman's Wood
Longdale Farm
Sand Pit
Longdale Plantation
Robin Hood Way
Reservoir
Pumping Station
Barracks Farm
MANSFIELD RD
Forest Farm
Sansom Wood
New Plantation
Vincent Plantation
B6011
FOREST LA
Seven Mile Wood
BURNTSTUMP HILL
A614(T)
Burntstump Country Park
Hospital
SHERWOOD LODGE DR
School
Foxcovert Plantation
OLLERTON RD
GRAVELLY HOLLOW
Stanker Hill Farm
Mast
Sherwood Lodge Police HQ
Cockliffe Hill Farm
Cockliffe House
Dairy Farm
The Warren
4
53
3
52
2
51
1
50
56
57
58

118
134

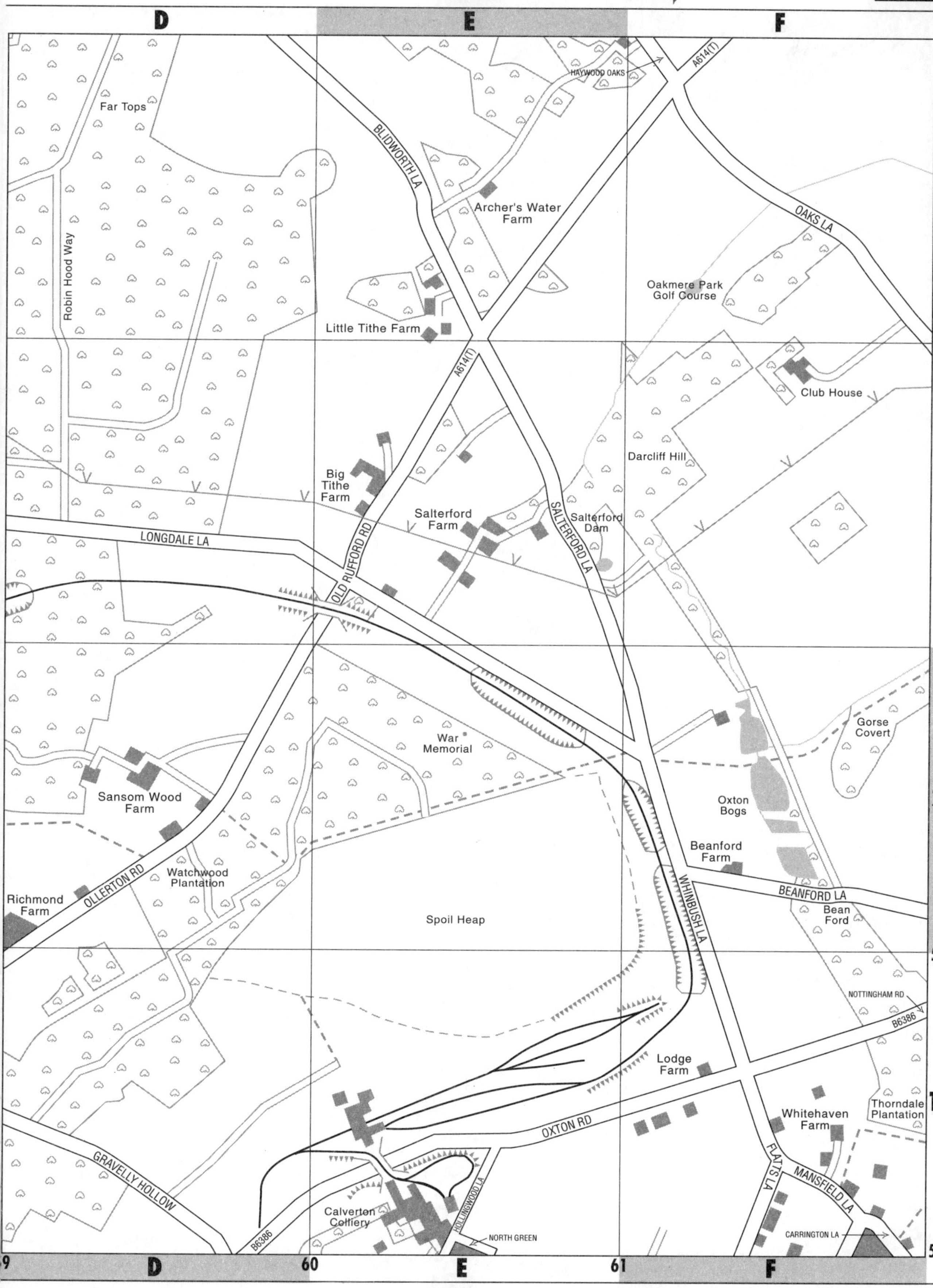


148
134

133
119

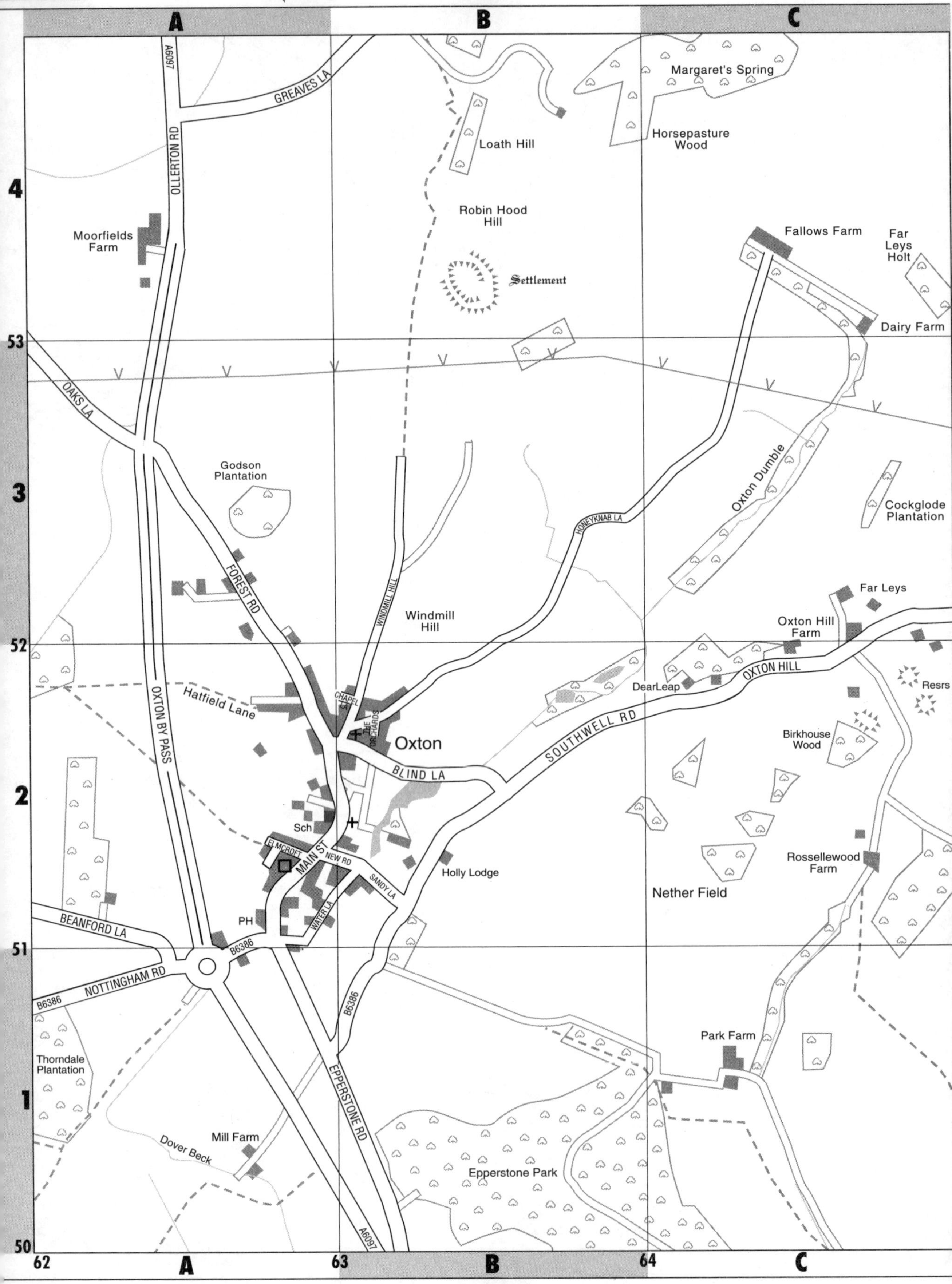


133
149

120
136

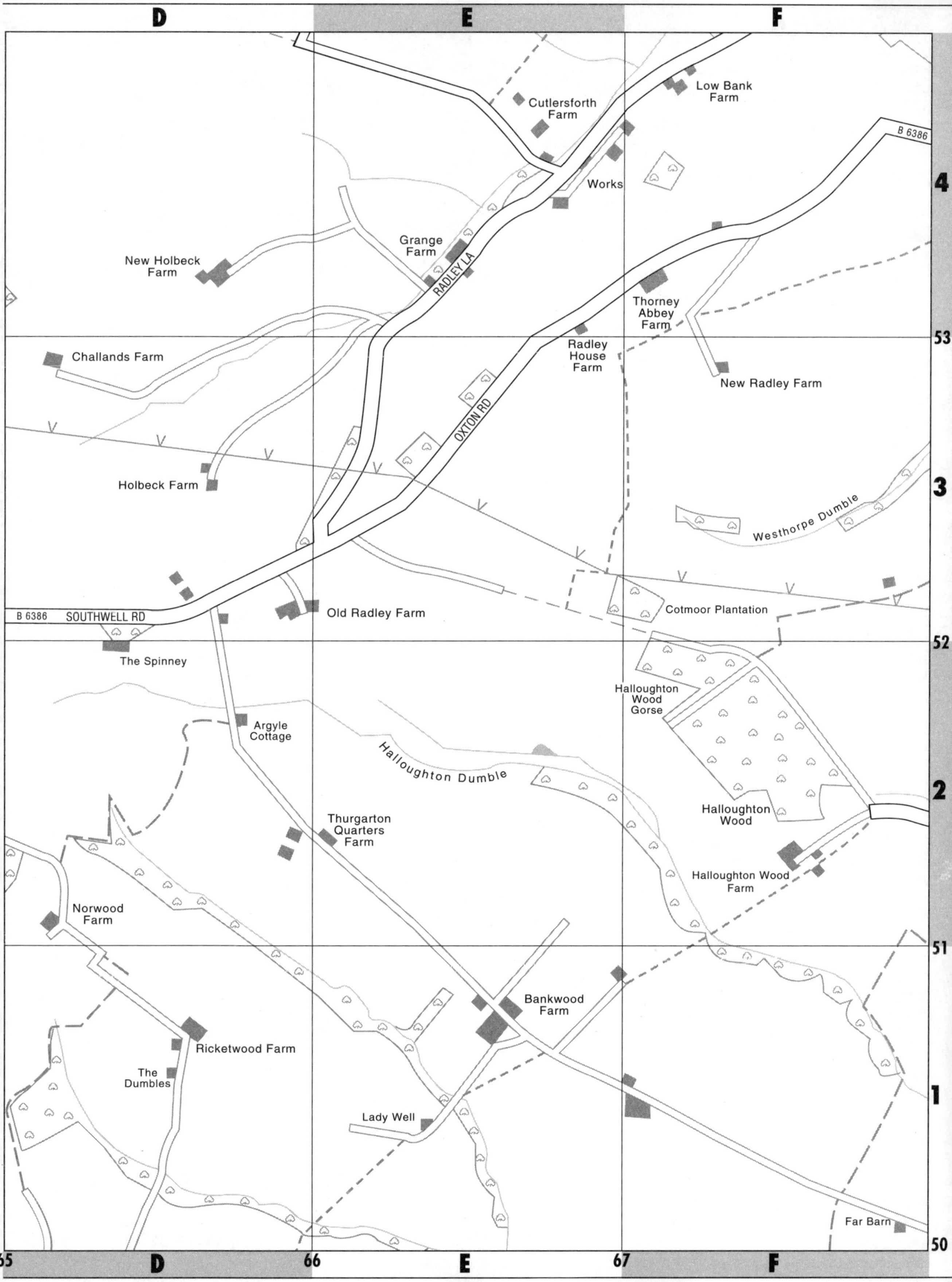


150
136

135 121

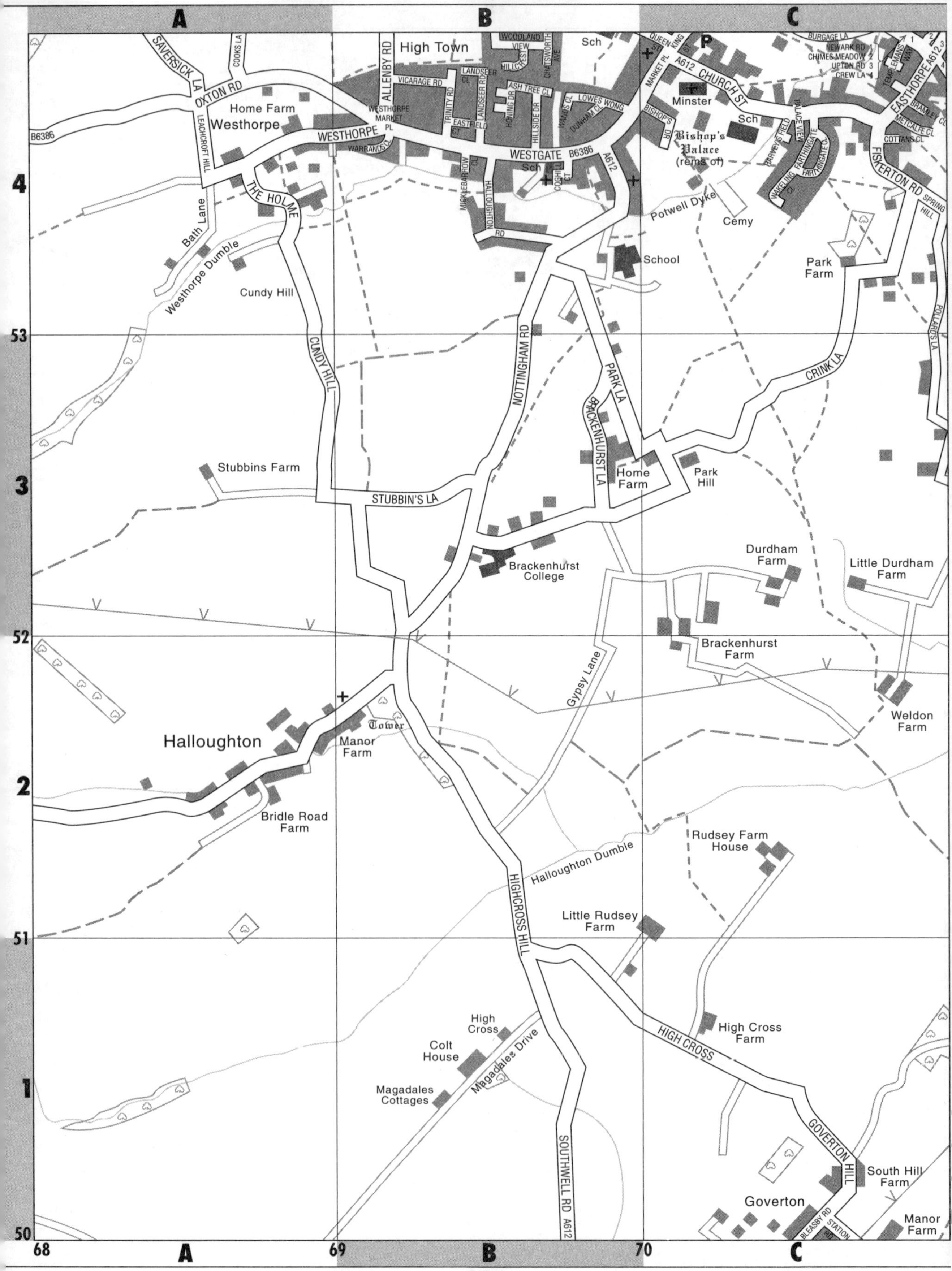


135 151

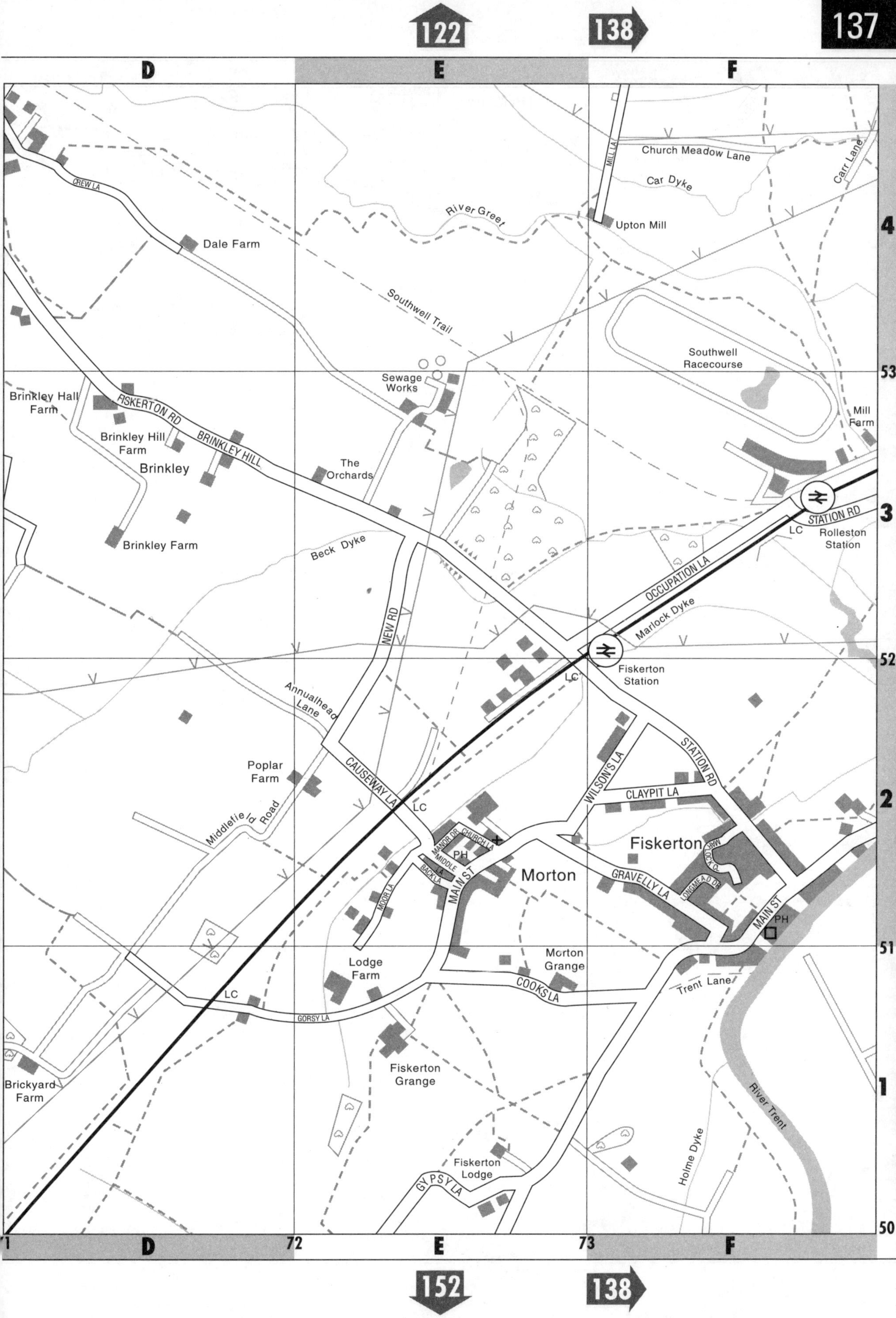
122
138
D
E
F
Church Meadow Lane
Car Dyke
Carr Lane
MILL LA
CREW LA
River Greet
Upton Mill
Dale Farm
Southwell Trail
Southwell Racecourse
Sewage Works
Brinkley Hall Farm
FISKERTON RD
BRINKLEY HILL
Brinkley Hill Farm
Brinkley
The Orchards
Mill Farm
STATION RD
LC
Rolleston Station
Brinkley Farm
Beck Dyke
OCCUPATION LA
Marlock Dyke
NEW RD
Fiskerton Station
Annualhead Lane
STATION RD
WILSON'S LA
CLAYPIT LA
Poplar Farm
CAUSEWAY LA
Middlefield Road
MANOR DR
CHURCH LA
PH
Fiskerton
Morton
MIDDLE LA
BACK LA
MAIN ST
MOOR LA
GRAVELLY LA
LONGMEAD DR
MAIN ST
Lodge Farm
Morton Grange
COOKS LA
Trent Lane
GORSY LA
Fiskerton Grange
Brickyard Farm
River Trent
Holme Dyke
Fiskerton Lodge
GYPSY LA
4
53
3
52
2
51
1
50
71
72
73
152
138

137
123

137
153

124
140

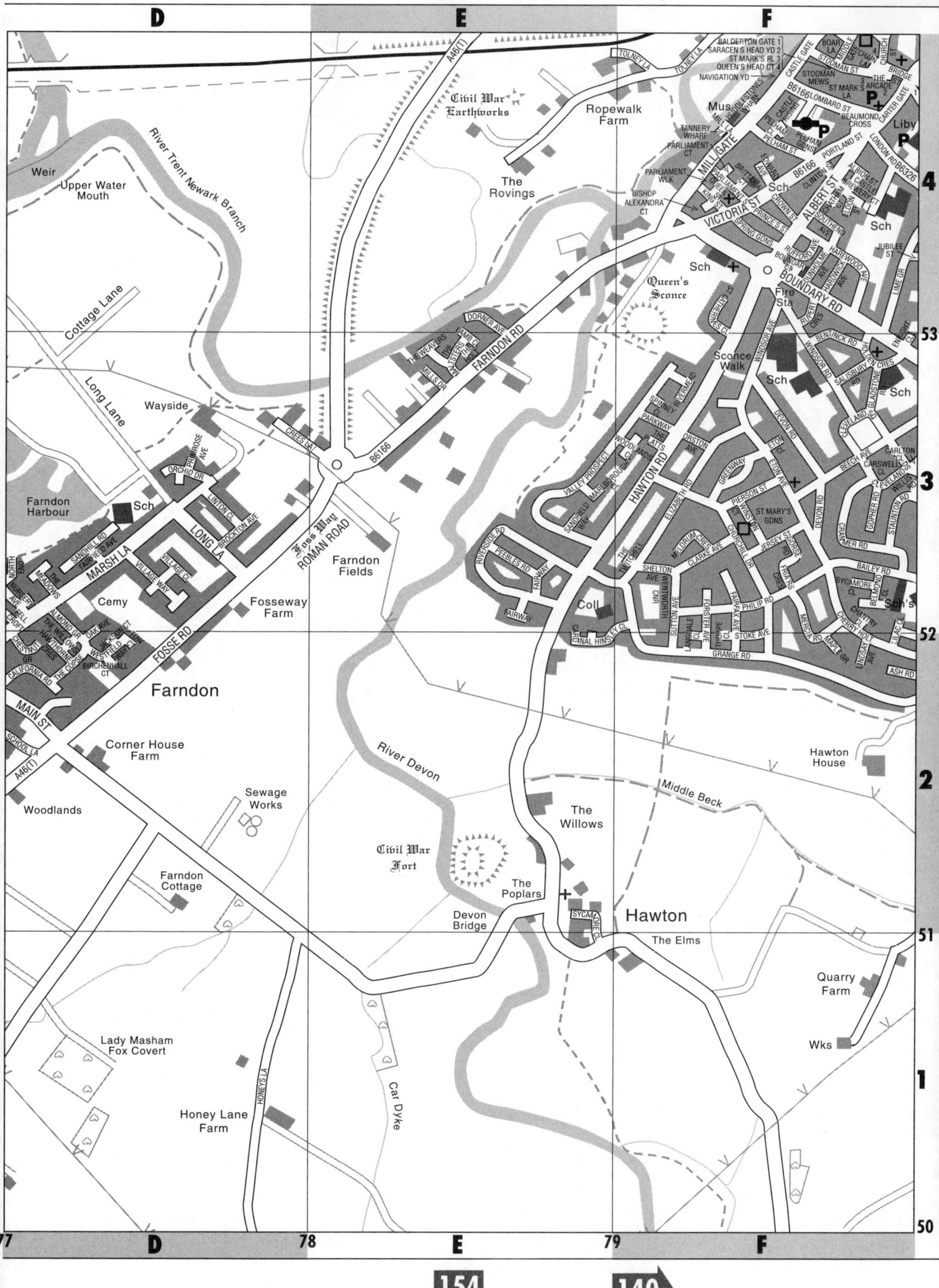


154
140

139
125

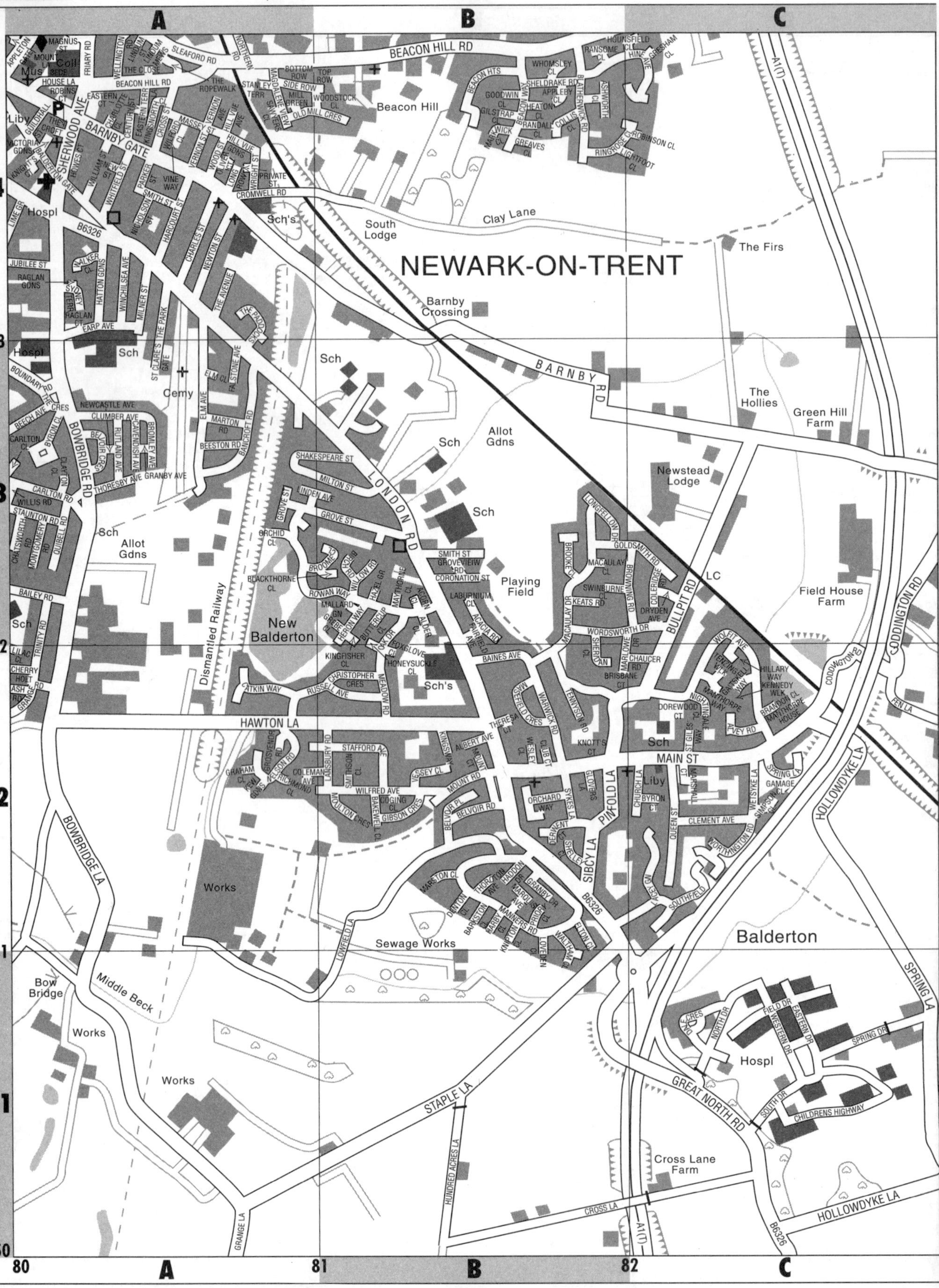


139
155

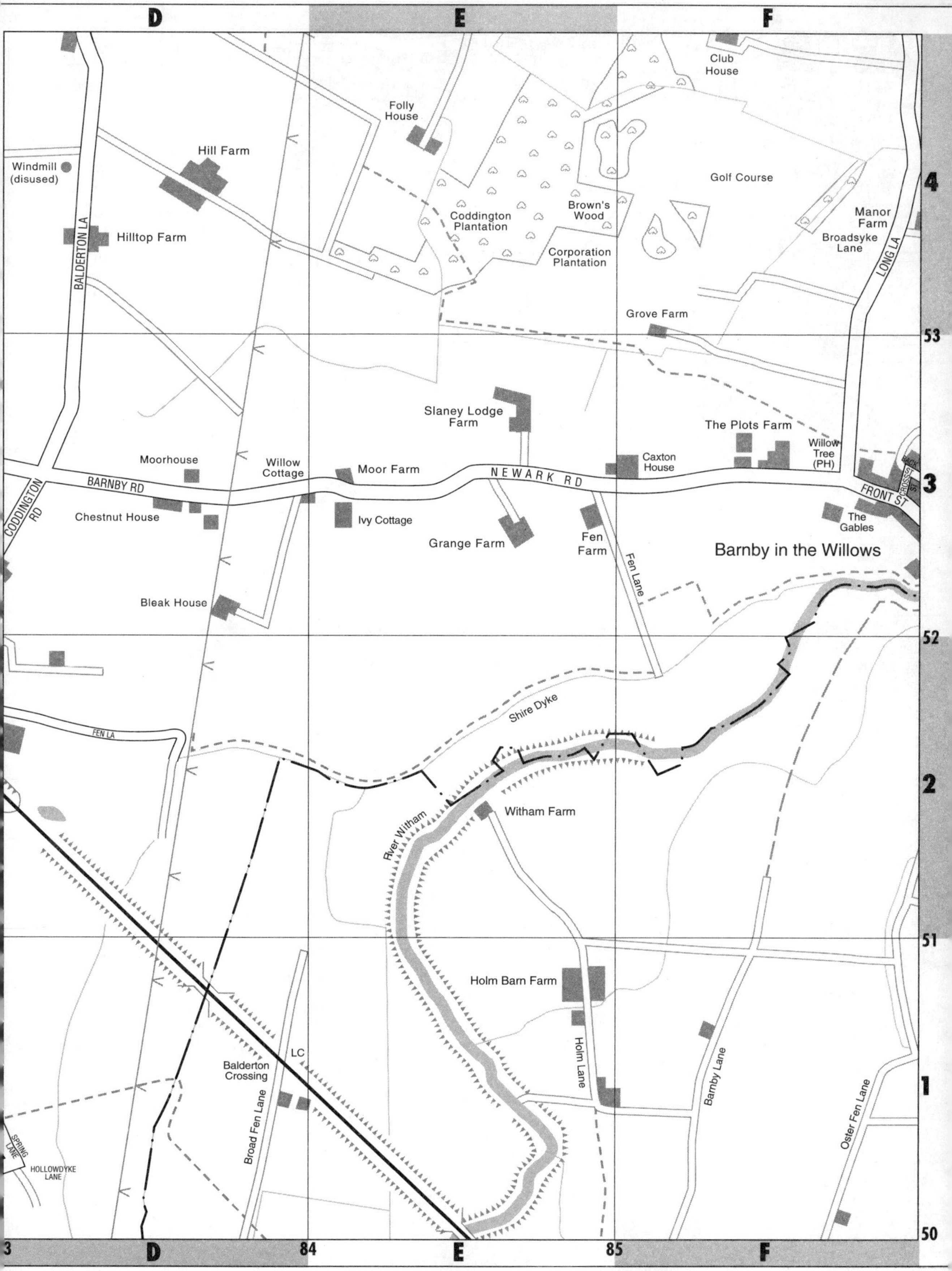

D
E
F
4
3
2
1
53
52
51
50
84
85
Club House
Folly House
Hill Farm
Windmill (disused)
Golf Course
Brown's Wood
Coddington Plantation
Corporation Plantation
Manor Farm
Broadsyke Lane
LONG LA
BALDERTON LA
Hilltop Farm
Grove Farm
Slaney Lodge Farm
The Plots Farm
Willow Tree (PH)
Moorhouse
Willow Cottage
Moor Farm
Caxton House
BARNBY RD
NEWARK RD
BACK ST
CROSS ST
FRONT ST
CODDINGTON RD
Chestnut House
Ivy Cottage
Grange Farm
Fen Farm
The Gables
Barnby in the Willows
Fen Lane
Bleak House
Shire Dyke
FEN LA
River Witham
Witham Farm
Holm Barn Farm
Holm Lane
Barnby Lane
Oster Fen Lane
LC
Balderton Crossing
Broad Fen Lane
SPRING LANE
HOLLOWDYKE LANE

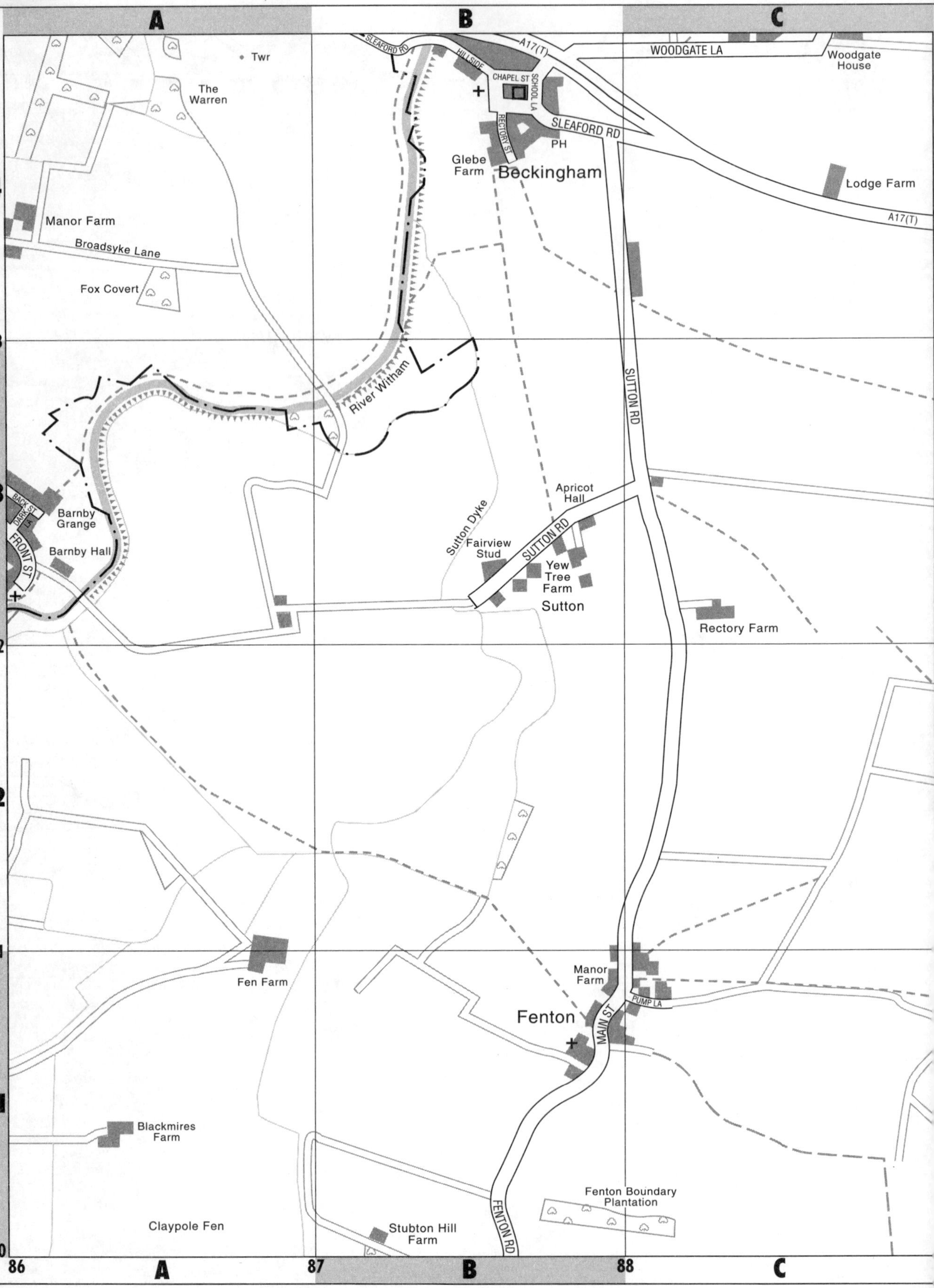
A
B
C
Twr
The Warren
SLEAFORD RD
HILLSIDE
A17(T)
WOODGATE LA
Woodgate House
CHAPEL ST
SCHOOL LA
RECTORY ST
SLEAFORD RD
PH
Glebe Farm
Beckingham
Lodge Farm
A17(T)
4
Manor Farm
Broadsyke Lane
Fox Covert
53
River Witham
SUTTON RD
3
BACK ST
DARK LA
FRONT ST
Barnby Grange
Barnby Hall
Apricot Hall
Sutton Dyke
Fairview Stud
SUTTON RD
Yew Tree Farm
Sutton
Rectory Farm
52
2
51
Fen Farm
Manor Farm
PUMP LA
Fenton
MAIN ST
1
Blackmires Farm
FENTON RD
Fenton Boundary Plantation
Claypole Fen
Stubton Hill Farm
50
86
87
88

D
E
F
4
49
3
48
2
47
1
46
45
Gin Farm
Dismtd Rly
Hobsic
Brinsley Gin
Lower Stoneyford Farm
BOAT LA
Inn
Stoneyford
The Moor
Hall Farm
Crowfields Farm
Brinsley
HALL LA
STONEY LA
CHURCH LA
BROAD LA
MOOR RD
CORDY LA
A608
Park Farm
New Farm
River Erewash
Coneygrey Plantation
Brinsley Brook
ALDERCAR LA
Crow Wood
A610
MANSFIELD RD
Hall Farm
Eastwood Hall
Aldercar
Sch
CROMFORD RD
UPPER DUNSTEAD RD
LOWER DUNSTEAD RD
Langley Mill
HALL RD
Nether Green Brook
EASTWOOD
GREENHILLS RD
DERBY RD
STATION RD
Langley Mill Station
MANSFIELD RD
Heanor
Bailey Grove
NOTTINGHAM RD
CHURCH ST
MILNHAY RD
Sewage Works
Erewash Canal
Works
Langley
HAND'S RD
LACEY FIELDS RD
BREACH RD
LEE LA
Lacey Fields Farm
TINSLEY RD
Cemy
CHEWTON ST

143
129

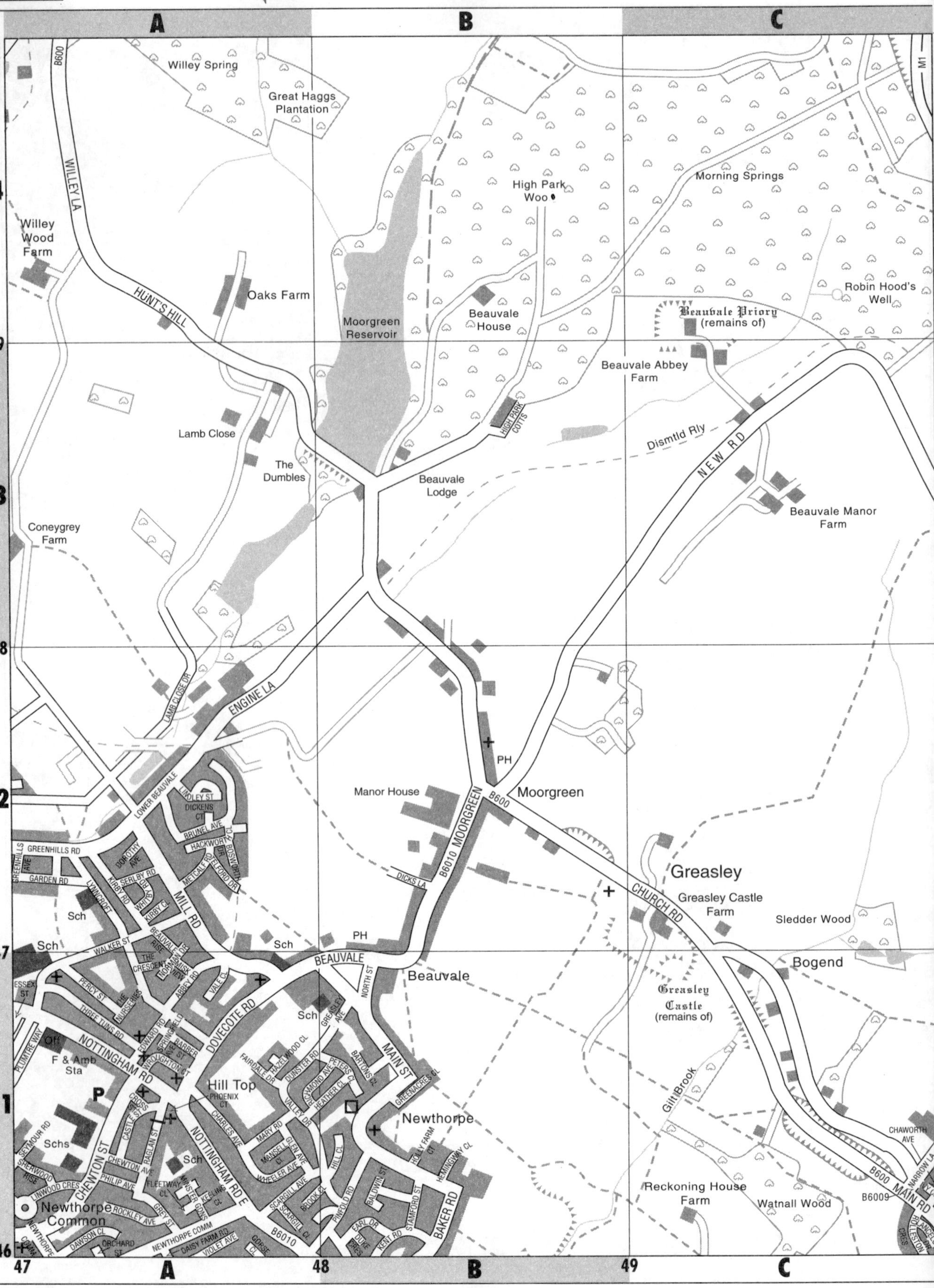


143
158

130
146

159
146

145
131

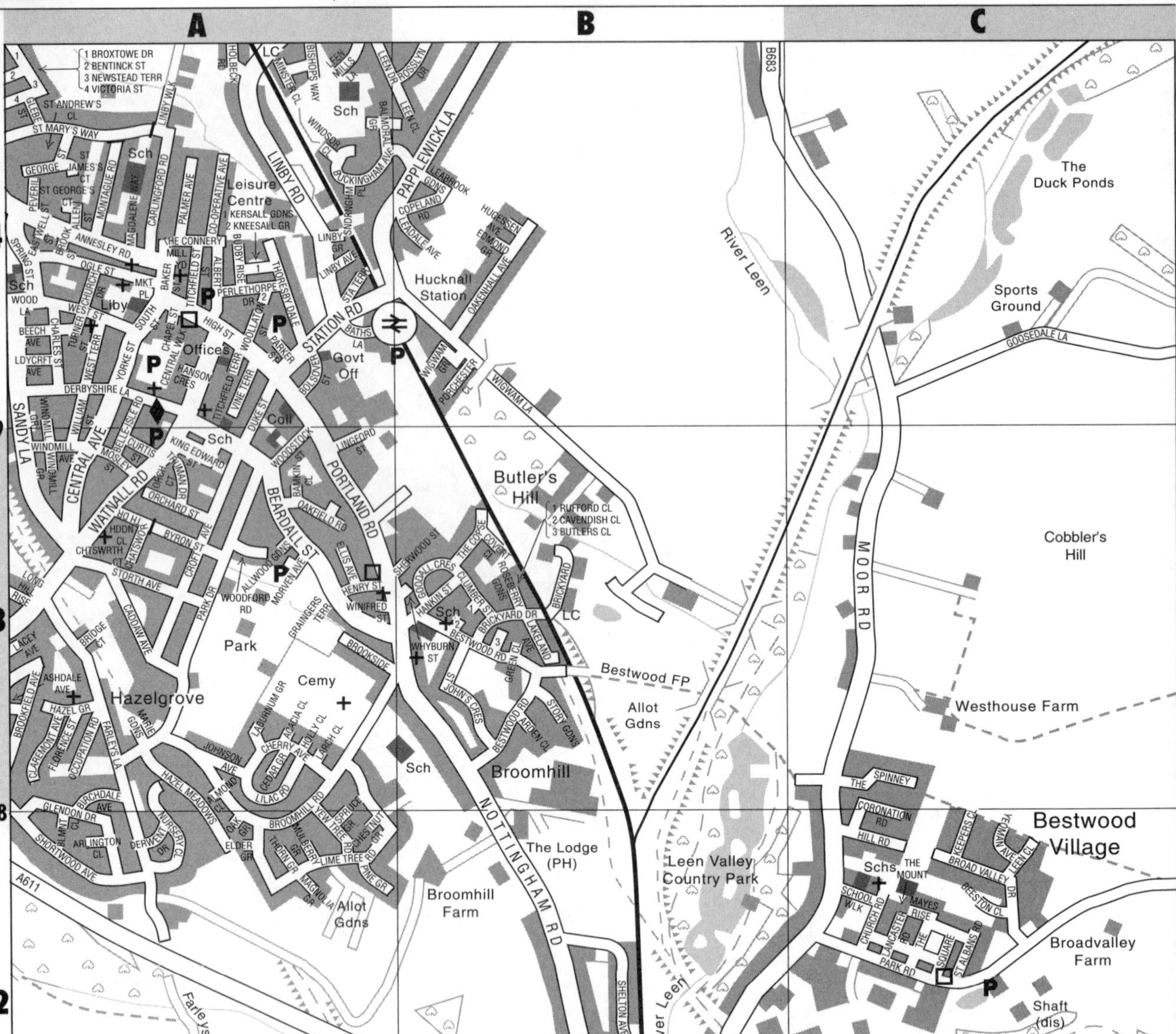


145
160

132
148

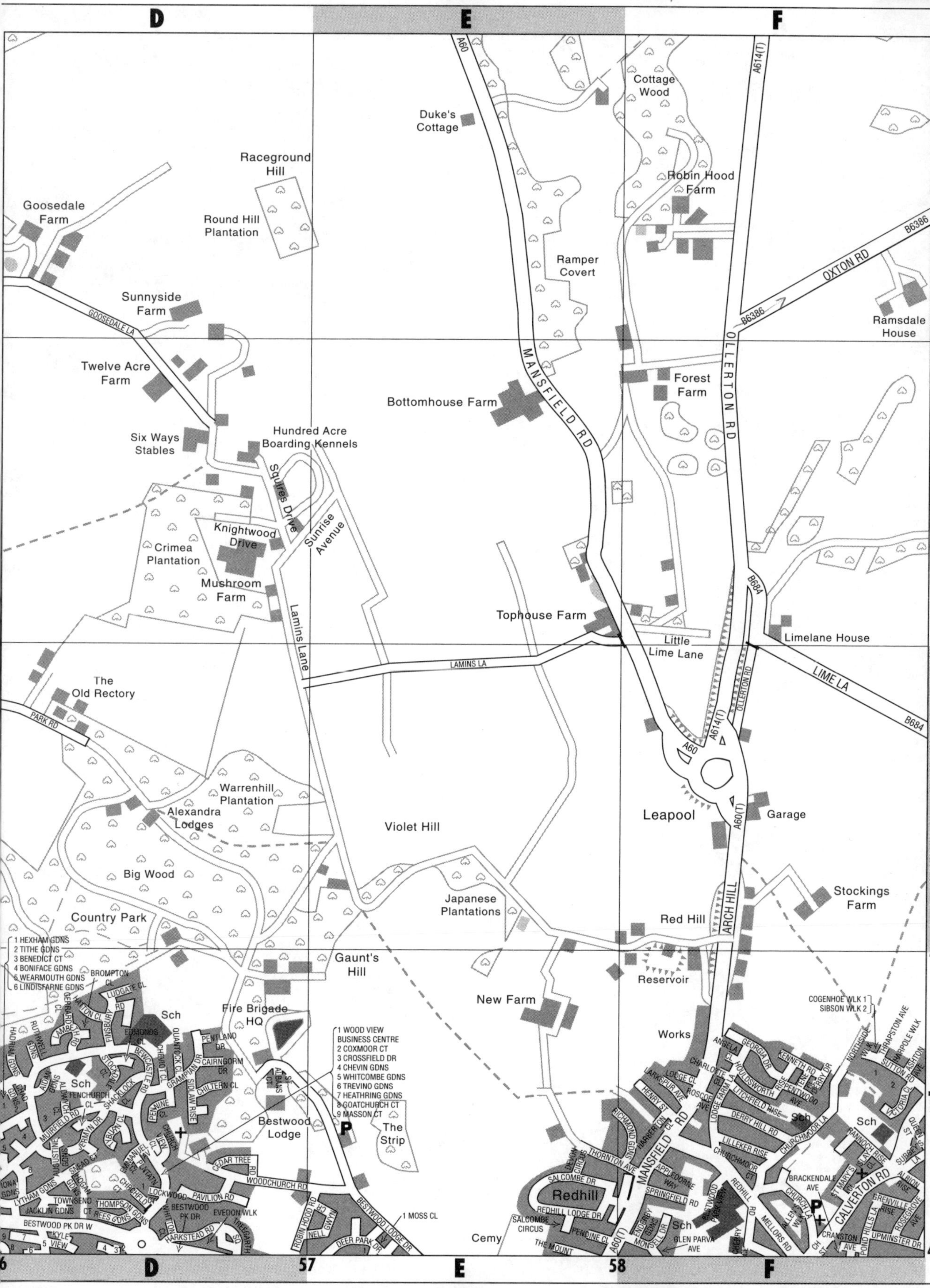


161
148

Sports Ground
Patching's Farm
OXTON RD
Golf Course
Club House
Hollingwood Lane
Hollinwood House
Waterworks Cottage
PARK RD
Schools
MAIN ST
COLLYER RD
MANSFIELD LA
Liby
School
Dark Lane
BONNER HILL
Bonner Hill
Leila's Plantation
Ramsdale Park
Abbey House
Ramsdale Hill
Spring Cottage
GEORGE'S LA
Lamp Wood
Spindle Lane
Fox Wood Settlement
Woodborough Park
Wood Farm
Dorket Head Farm
LIME LA
Dorket Head
Works
Clay Pit
Bank Farm
Arnold Lodge
WOODBOROUGH LA
BANK HILL
NOTTINGHAM RD
CALVERTON RD
Lambley House
Killisick Lane
Barn Farm
MAPPERLEY PLAINS
Travellers Rest (PH)
Fox Covert
Orchard Farm

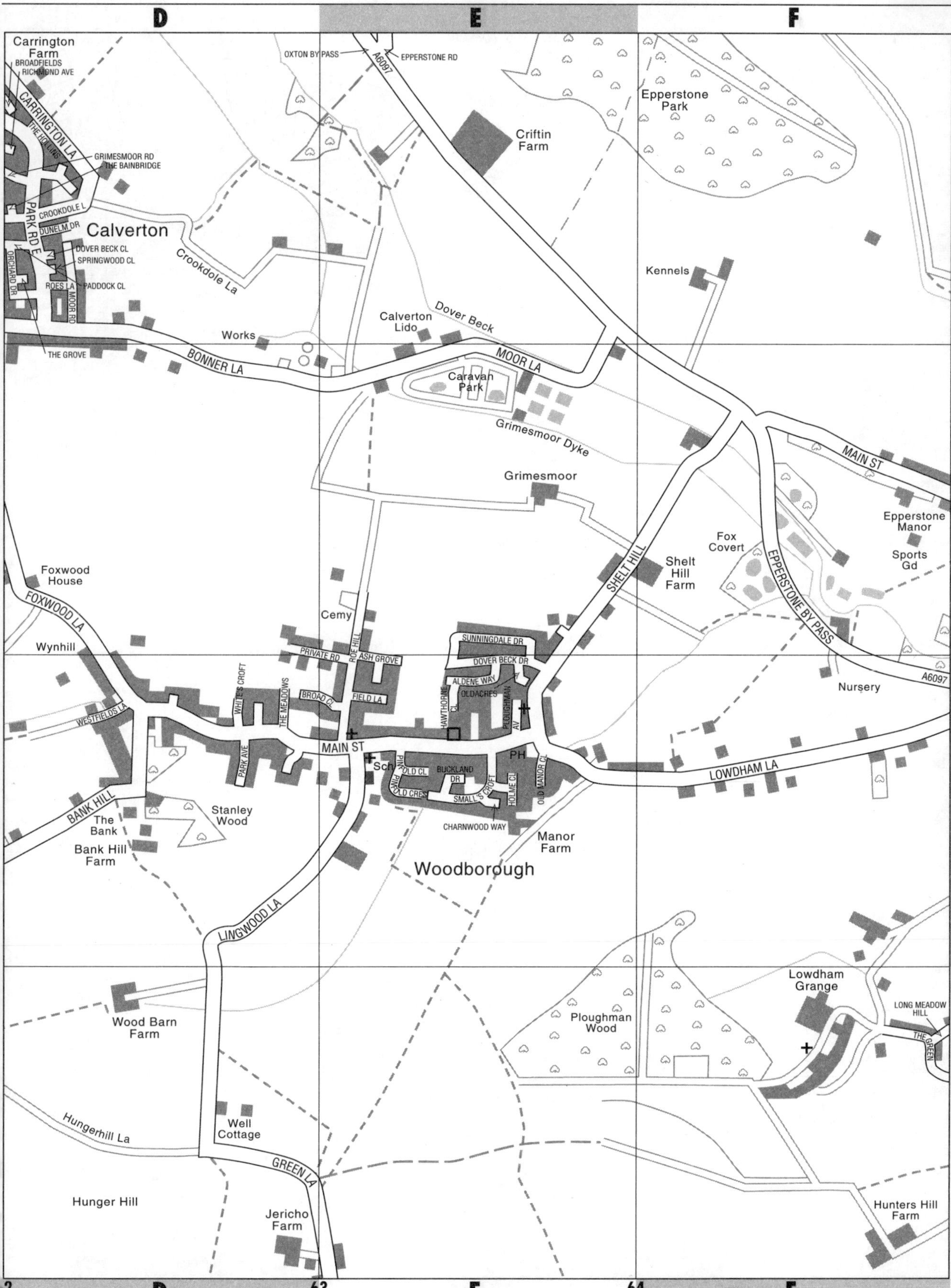
D
E
F
Carrington Farm
BROADFIELDS
RICHMOND AVE
CARRINGTON LA
THE HOLLINS
GRIMESMOOR RD
THE BAINBRIDGE
CROOKDOLE L
DUNELM DR
PARK RD E
Calverton
DOVER BECK CL
SPRINGWOOD CL
ORCHARD DR
ROES LA
PADDOCK CL
MOOR RD
THE GROVE
Crookdole La
Works
BONNER LA
OXTON BY PASS
EPPERSTONE RD
A6097
Criftin Farm
Epperstone Park
Kennels
Calverton Lido
Dover Beck
MOOR LA
Caravan Park
Grimesmoor Dyke
Grimesmoor
MAIN ST
Epperstone Manor
Sports Gd
Fox Covert
Shelt Hill Farm
SHELT HILL
EPPERSTONE BY PASS
Foxwood House
FOXWOOD LA
Cemy
Wynhill
PRIVATE RD
ROE HILL
ASH GROVE
SUNNINGDALE DR
DOVER BECK DR
ALDENE WAY
OLDACRES
HAWTHORNE CL
PLOUGHMAN AV
Nursery
WHITE'S CROFT
THE MEADOWS
BROAD CL
FIELD LA
WESTFIELDS LA
MAIN ST
Sch
PH
PARK AVE
PINFOLD CL
PINFOLD CRES
BUCKLAND DR
SMALL'S CROFT
HOLME CL
OLD MANOR CL
LOWDHAM LA
BANK HILL
The Bank
Stanley Wood
CHARNWOOD WAY
Manor Farm
Bank Hill Farm
Woodborough
LINGWOOD LA
Lowdham Grange
LONG MEADOW HILL
THE GREEN
Ploughman Wood
Wood Barn Farm
Well Cottage
Hungerhill La
GREEN LA
Hunger Hill
Jericho Farm
Hunters Hill Farm
4
49
3
48
2
47
1
46
62
63
64

149
135

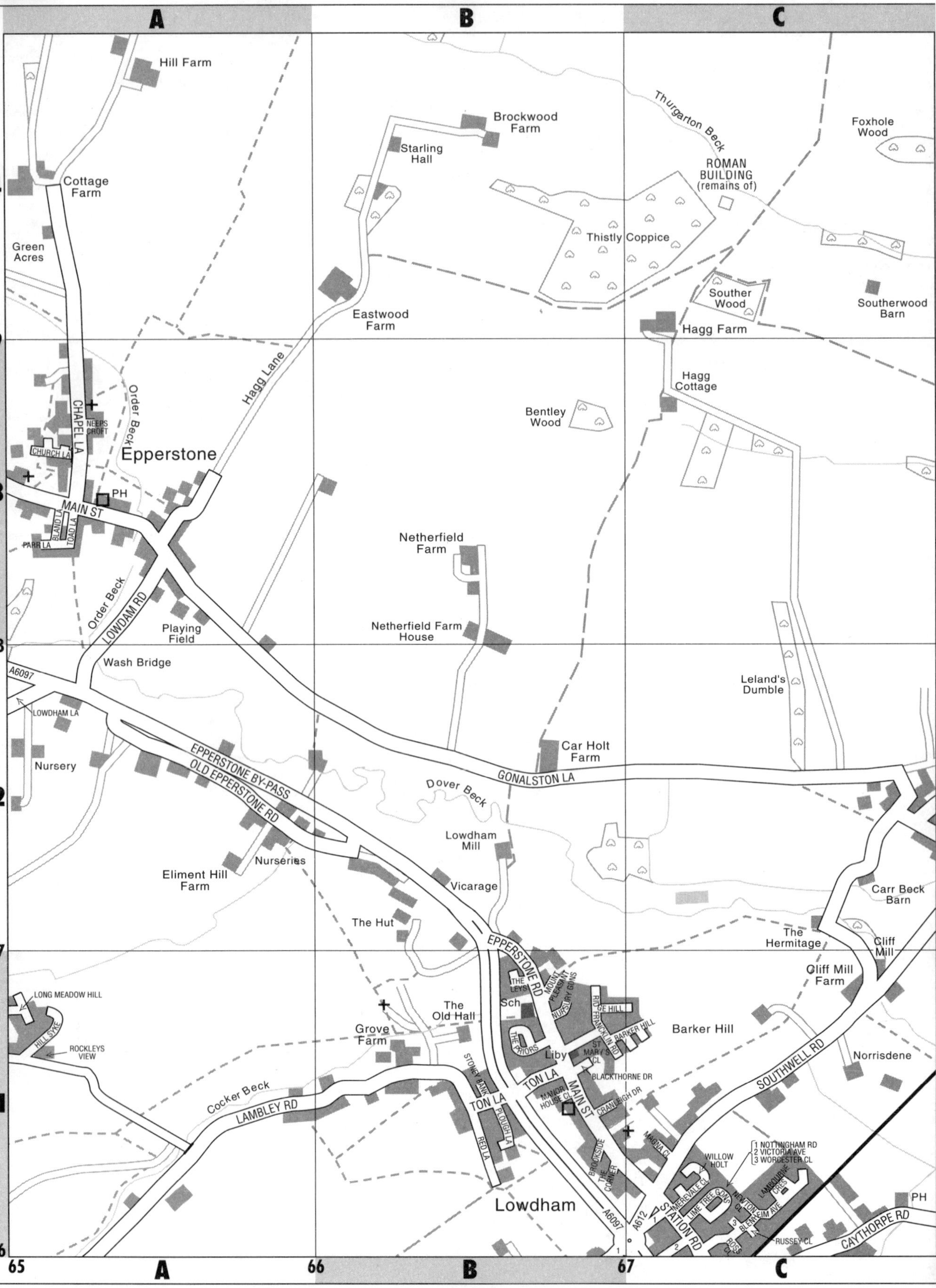


149
164

136 152

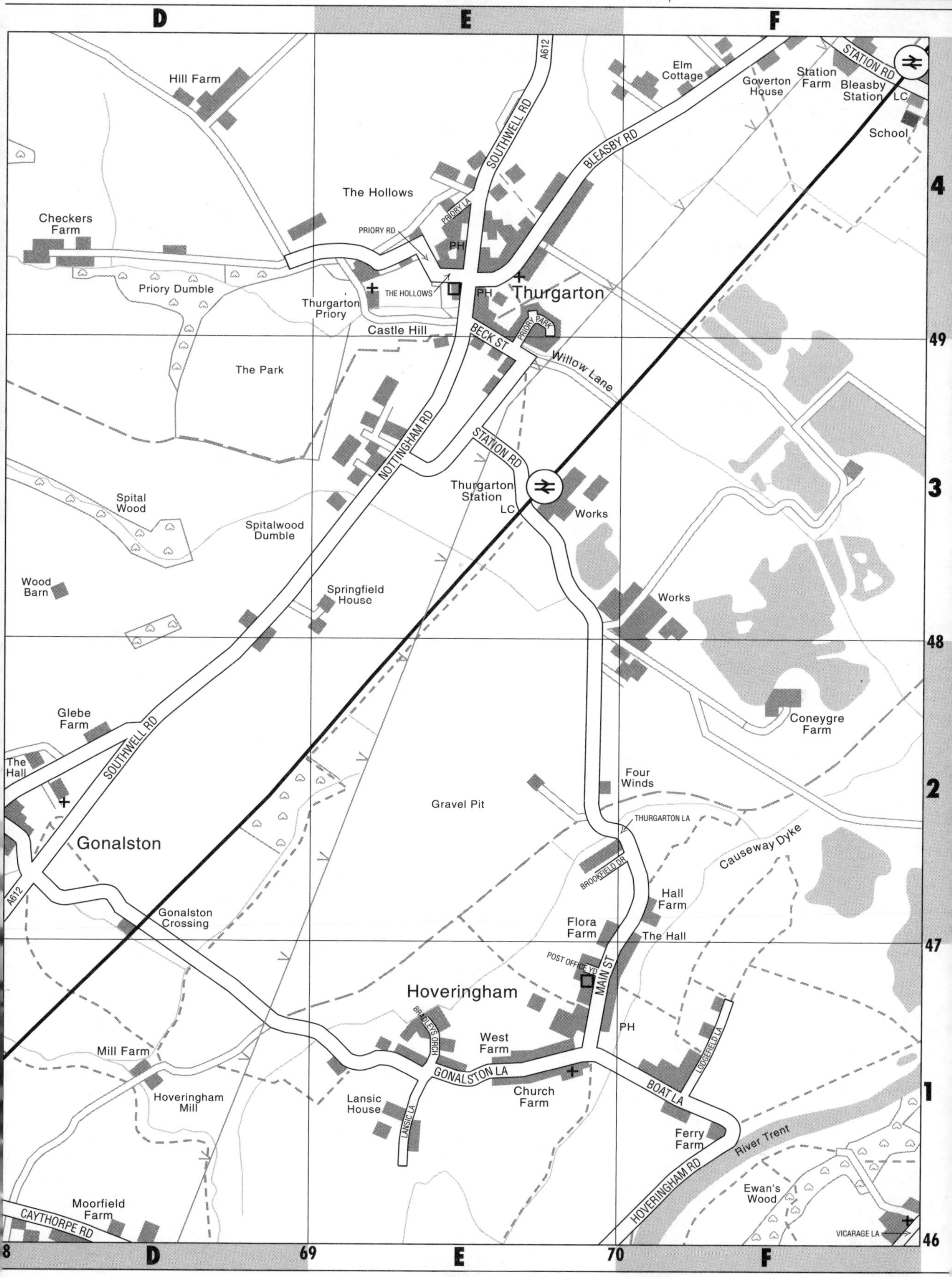


165 152

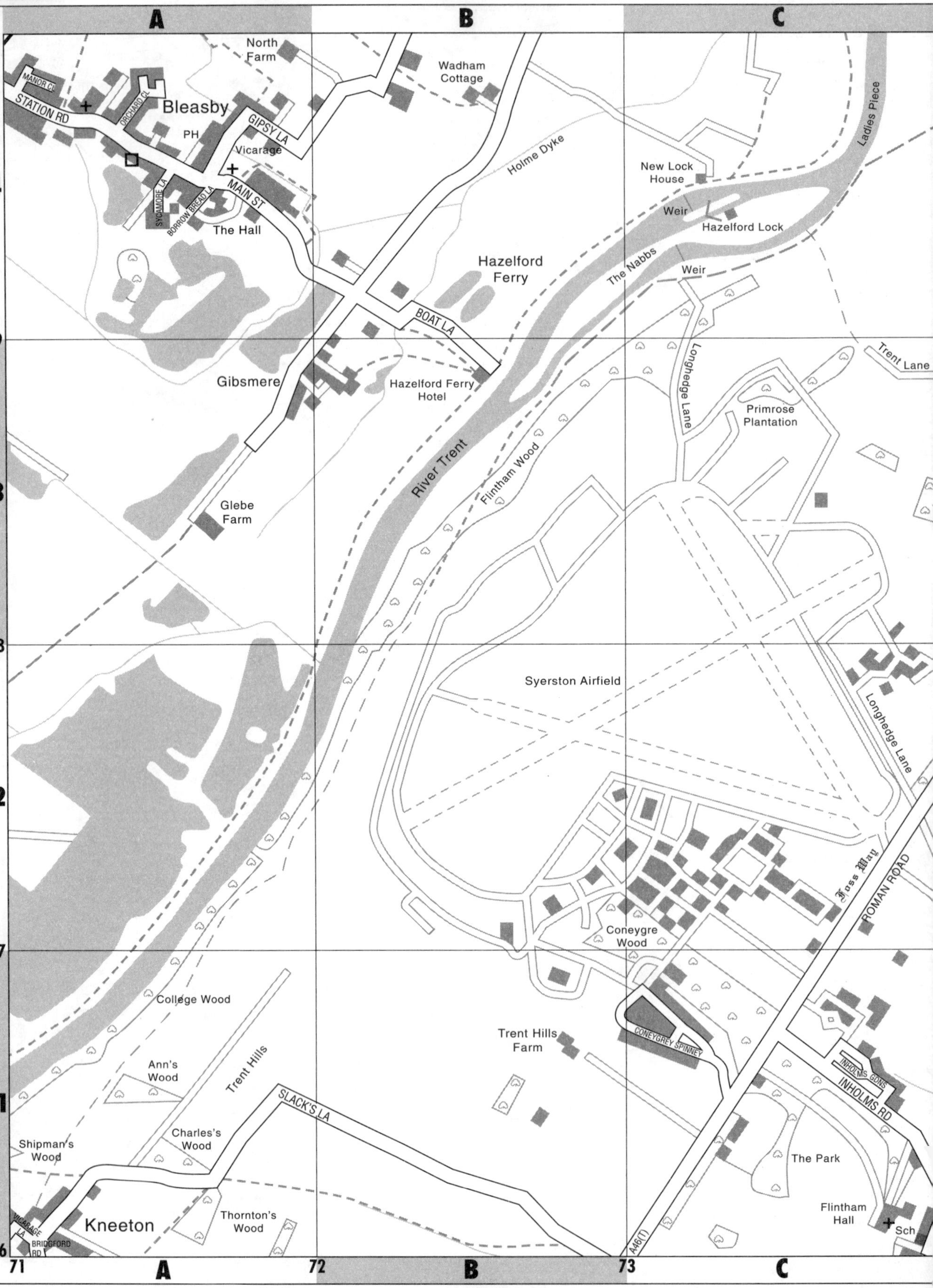
A
B
C
Bleasby
North Farm
Wadham Cottage
MANOR CL
STATION RD
ORCHARD CL
PH
GIPSY LA
Vicarage
SYCAMORE LA
BORROW BREAD LA
MAIN ST
The Hall
Holme Dyke
New Lock House
Weir
Hazelford Lock
Ladies Piece
Hazelford Ferry
The Nabbs
Weir
BOAT LA
Gibsmere
Hazelford Ferry Hotel
Longhedge Lane
Trent Lane
Primrose Plantation
River Trent
Flintham Wood
Glebe Farm
Syerston Airfield
Longhedge Lane
Foss Way
ROMAN ROAD
Coneygre Wood
College Wood
Trent Hills Farm
CONEYGREY SPINNEY
INHOLMS GDNS
INHOLMS RD
Ann's Wood
Trent Hills
SLACK'S LA
Charles's Wood
Shipman's Wood
The Park
Flintham Hall
Sch
Kneeton
Thornton's Wood
VICARAGE LA
BRIDGFORD RD
A46(T)
4
49
3
48
2
47
1
46
71
72
73

D
E
F
East Stoke
Hall Farm
PH
Sch
SCHOOL LA
A46(T)
HUMBER LA
BROWNLOW CL
Stoke Wood
Manor Farm
Grange Fram
The Old Vicarage
MOOR LA
Battle of Stoke Field 1487
ELSTON LA
Cedar Cottage
Mill Hill House
Fosse Way
ROMAN ROAD
Trent Lane
Elston Lodge Farm
Stoke Fields Farm
Elston Towers
LODGE LA
Lady Pit Farm
PINFOLD LA
LOW ST
THE SPINNEY
Elston Chapel
OLD CHAPEL LA
Codders Dyke
Elston
Sch
TOP ST
ELSTON HALL
THE GREEN
TOAD LA
CARRGATE LA
CENTRAL DR
WINSTON DR
DARWIN CL
PADDOCKS CL 1
THE PADDOCKS 2
MILL RD
PH
Sewage Works
The Windmill
Carrgate Lane
Syerston
GREENGATE
The Rookery
Low Farm
Croft House
HAWKSWORTH RD
Gundykes Plantation
BRECKS LA
MOOR LA
DOGHILL LA
Hawksworth Road
Lineham Plantation
LINEHAM LA
Ash Holt
Longhedge Lane
Sewage Works
Brecks Plantation
Hill Farm
Flintham
Sch
MAIN ST
WOOD'S LA
DEADWONG LA
4
49
3
48
2
47
1
46
75
76

153
139

153
168

140
156

169
156

155
141

A
B
C
4
3
2
1
49
48
47
46
83
84
85
Balderfields
Balderfield
Broad Fen Lane
Well Fen Lane
Barnby Lane
Cross Lane
Liberty Gates Crossing
Claypole
Brunts Farm
FB
Oster Fen Lane
LC
SHIRE LA
Piggery
Witham View
WELL FEN LA
CHAPEL LA
BARNBY LA
SCHOOL LA
RECTORY LA
Sch
TOWN ST
PH
BACK LA
COULBY CL
REDTHORN WAY
TINSLEY CL
STUBTON RD
Claypole Bridge
Hough Lane
Mill Road
DODDINGTON LA
Sandhills
Mill Farm
Weir
River Witham
Holmes Lane
The Willows
Doddington Bridge
Coach Road
Long Lane
CLAYPOLE LA
MANOR HOUSE LA
GREEN LA
Manor Farm
CLENSEY LA
Bridge Farm
MAIN ST
Red House Farm
HOUGHAM RD
GREAT NORTH RD
Syke Lane
The Wheatsheaf (PH)
Dry Doddington
Hill Farm
A1(T)

155

143
158

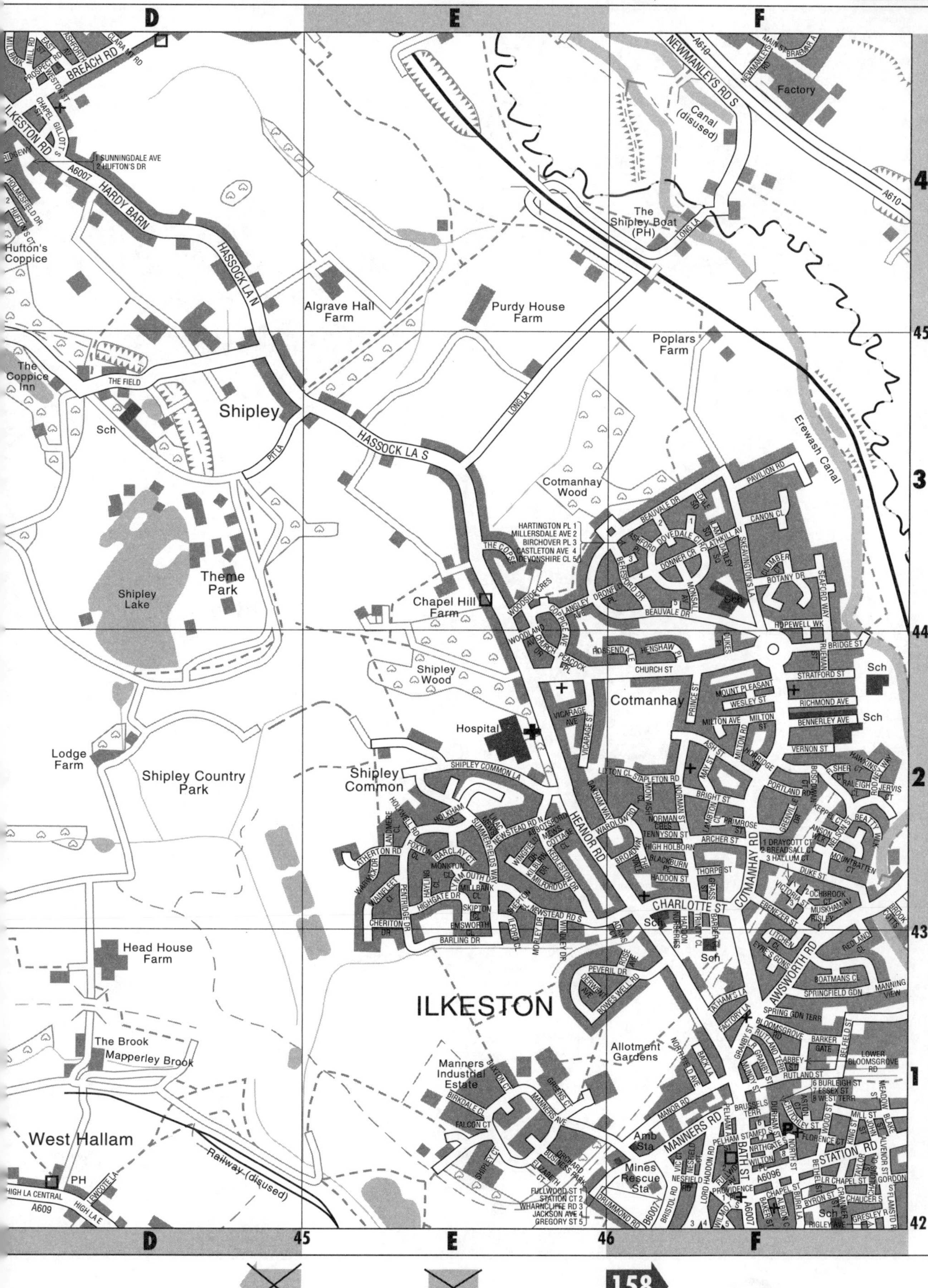
D
E
F
Factory
Canal (disused)
The Shipley Boat (PH)
Hufton's Coppice
Algrave Hall Farm
Purdy House Farm
Poplars Farm
The Coppice Inn
Shipley
Sch
Erewash Canal
Cotmanhay Wood
Theme Park
Shipley Lake
Chapel Hill Farm
Shipley Wood
Cotmanhay
Hospital
Lodge Farm
Shipley Country Park
Shipley Common
Head House Farm
ILKESTON
The Brook
Mapperley Brook
Manners Industrial Estate
Allotment Gardens
West Hallam
Railway (disused)
Amb Sta
Mines Rescue Sta
PH
HASSOCK LA N
HASSOCK LA S
HARDY BARN
HEANOR RD
CHARLOTTE ST
COTMANHAY RD
AWSWORTH RD
MANNERS RD
STATION RD
BATH ST
A6007
A6096
A610
A609
45
46
42
43
44
1
2
3
4

158

A
B
C
Newthorpe Common
Giltbrook
Reservoir
Rolleston Cres
NOTTINGHAM RD
BAKER RD
A610
Depot
Gilt Hill Farm
Sch
GILT HILL
B6010
MAWS LA
HARDY ST
EASTWOOD RD
Kimberley
Coll
MAIN ST
HIGH ST
Sewage Works
Hogs Head (PH)
GIN CLOSE WAY
A6096
AWSWORTH LA
Dismantled Railway
Grasscroft Farm
Swingate
MEADOW RD
STATION RD
Manor Farm
Sch
THE LANE
Awsworth
Babbington Hall
Babbington
BABBINGTON LA
Viaduct
Stenson's Lock
NEWTON'S LA
PH
WESTBY LA
Babbington House Farm
Swingate Farm
AWSWORTH RD
Cossall Common
Common Farm
Strelley Park Farm
Cossall Marsh
Spring Wood
River Erewash
Erewash Canal
CORONATION RD
Nottingham Canal (disused)
Turkey Fields Farm
Grange Farm
Almshouses
Cossall
Manor Farm
ROBINETTES LA
Oldmoor Farmhouse
CHURCH LA
Works
THE ROPEWORK SEEDBED CENTRE
MILL LA
DEAD LA
STATION RD
A6096
45
44
43
42
4
3
2
1
47
48
49

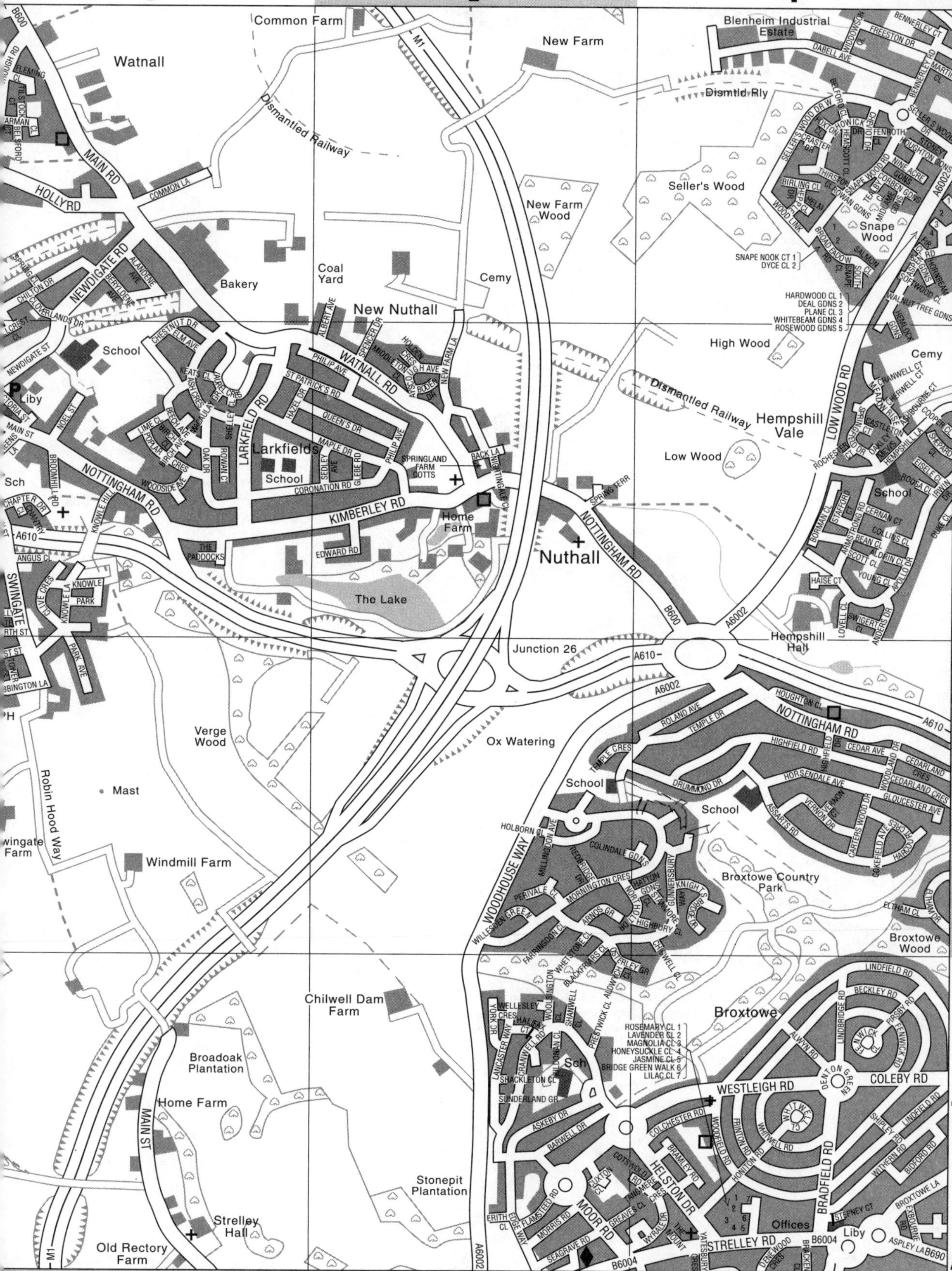
D
E
F
Watnall
Common Farm
New Farm
Blenheim Industrial Estate
Dismantled Railway
Dismtld Rly
Seller's Wood
New Farm Wood
Snape Wood
Bakery
Coal Yard
Cemy
New Nuthall
School
Liby
High Wood
Hempshill Vale
Low Wood
Larkfields
School
Springland Farm Cotts
Home Farm
Nuthall
The Lake
Junction 26
Hempshill Hall
Verge Wood
Ox Watering
Mast
Robin Hood Way
Windmill Farm
School
School
Broxtowe Country Park
Broxtowe Wood
Chilwell Dam Farm
Broxtowe
Broadoak Plantation
Home Farm
Sch
Stonepit Plantation
Strelley Hall
Old Rectory Farm
Offices
Liby
MAIN RD
HOLLY RD
NOTTINGHAM RD
KIMBERLEY RD
WATNALL RD
LARKFIELD RD
NEWDIGATE RD
LOW WOOD RD
WOODHOUSE WAY
WESTLEIGH RD
COLEBY RD
BRADFIELD RD
STRELLEY RD
MOOR RD
HELSTON DR
MAIN ST
M1
A610
A6002
B600
B6004
B690
4
45
3
44
2
43
1
42
51
52

159
146

159
172

D E F

Bestwood
Daybrook
Sherwood
Carrington
Woodthorpe
Mapperley
Mapperley Park
Sunrise Hill
Glade Hill
Hospitals
Playing Field
HM Prison
Council Offices
Dismantled Railway
Ambulance Sta
Leisure Centre
Cemy
RIDGEWAY
QUEENS BOWER RD
OXCLOSE LA
ARNOLD RD
VALLEY RD
EDWARDS LA
MANSFIELD RD
HUCKNALL RD
NOTTINGHAM RD
WOODTHORPE DR
MAPPERLEY RISE
WINCHESTER ST
WOODBOROUGH RD
PORCHESTER RD
THE WELLS ROAD
RANSOM RD
BRECK HILL RD
ARNO VALE RD
ARNOT HILL RD
HIGH ST
SANDFIELD RD
RAVENSWOOD RD
GELDING RD
COPPICE RD
HAYDN RD
A611
A60
A6514
B6004
B684
4
45
3
44
2
43
1
42
57
58

D E F

161
148

161
174

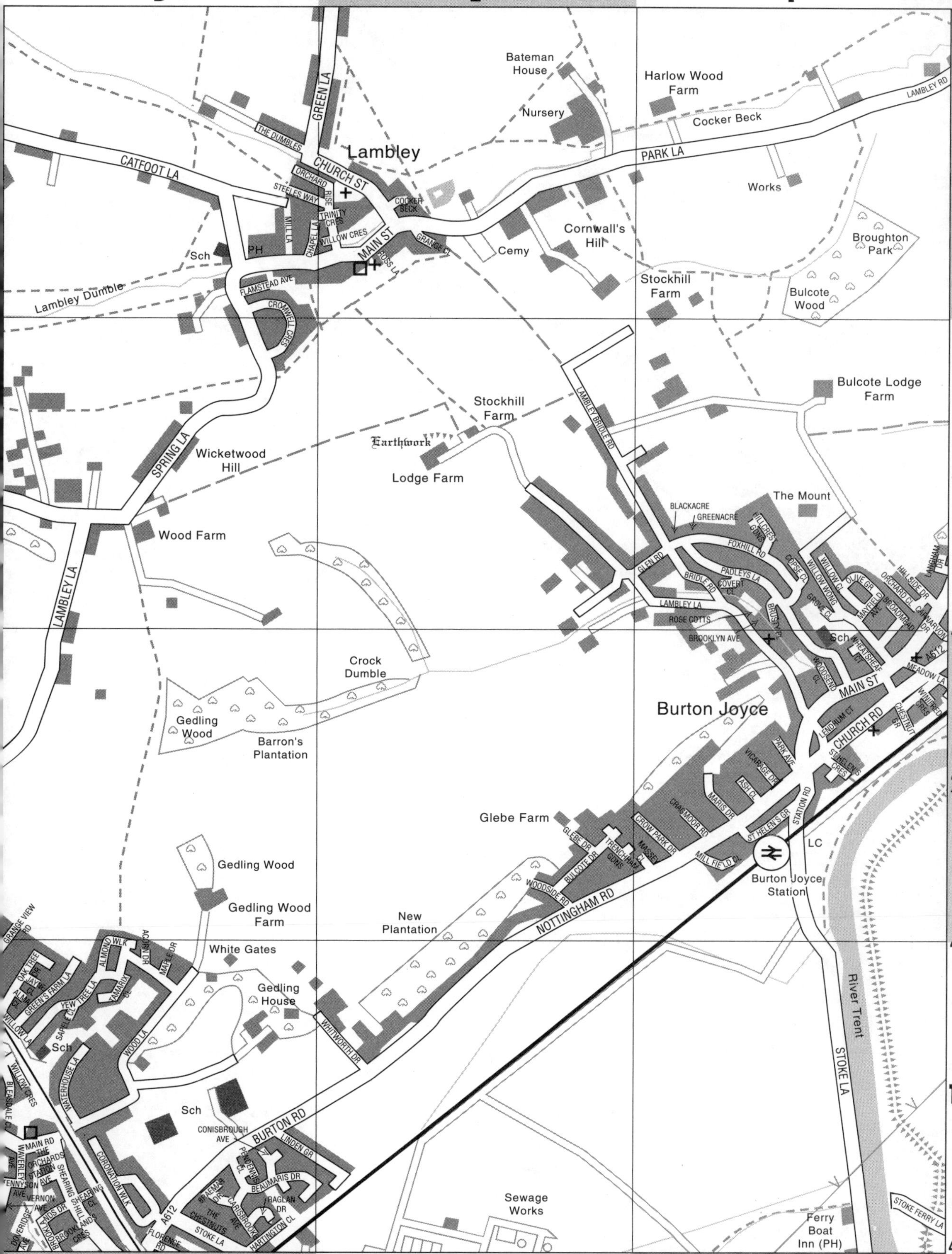
D
E
F
Bateman House
Harlow Wood Farm
Nursery
Cocker Beck
LAMBLEY RD
Lambley
GREEN LA
THE DUMBLES
CATFOOT LA
CHURCH ST
ORCHARD
STEELES WAY
RISE
TRINITY CRES
COCKER BECK
PARK LA
Works
MILL LA
CHAPEL LA
WILLOW CRES
MAIN ST
GRANGE CL
ROSS LA
Cemy
Cornwall's Hill
Broughton Park
Sch
PH
FLAMSTEAD AVE
CROMWELL CRES
Lambley Dumble
Stockhill Farm
Bulcote Wood
Bulcote Lodge Farm
Stockhill Farm
LAMBLEY BRIDLE RD
SPRING LA
Wicketwood Hill
Earthwork
Lodge Farm
The Mount
BLACKACRE
GREENACRE
HILLCREST GDNS
FOXHILL RD
GLEN RD
BRIDLE RD
PADLEYS LA
COVERT CL
COPSE CL
WILLOW CL
WILLOW WONG
OLIVE GR
ORCHARD CL
HILLSIDE DR
LAMBLEY LA
ROSE COTTS
BROOKLYN AVE
GROVE CL
MAYFIELD AVE
BROADMEAD
Wood Farm
LAMBLEY LA
Crock Dumble
Sch
WOODSEND CL
MAIN ST
MEADOW LA
A612
Burton Joyce
LENDRUM CT
CHURCH RD
CHESTNUT GR
ST HELEN'S CRES
Gedling Wood
Barron's Plantation
PARK AVE
VICARAGE DR
ASH CL
MARIS DR
STATION RD
Glebe Farm
GLEBE DR
TRENCHAM GDNS
CRAGMOOR RD
CROW PARK DR
MASSEY CL
ST HELEN'S GR
LC
MILL FIELD CL
Burton Joyce Station
Gedling Wood
BULCOTE DR
WOODSIDE RD
NOTTINGHAM RD
Gedling Wood Farm
New Plantation
GRANGE VIEW RD
ALMOND WLK
ACORN DR
MAPLE DR
White Gates
OAK TREE DR
TAMARIX CL
GREEN'S FARM LA
YEW TREE LA
SAPELE CL
Gedling House
River Trent
WOOD LA
Sch
WHITWORTH DR
WILLOW CRES
WATERHOUSE LA
STOKE LA
Sch
CONISBROUGH AVE
BURTON RD
LINDEN GR
MAIN RD
THE ORCHARDS
STATION AVE
WAVERLEY AVE
TENNYSON AVE
VERNON AVE
CORONATION WLK
BEAUMARIS DR
BRAEMAR DR
CARISBROOKE AVE
RAGLAN DR
THE CHESTNUTS
HARTINGTON CL
Sewage Works
STOKE FERRY LA
Ferry Boat Inn (PH)
A612
STOKE LA
FLORENCE RD
4
45
3
44
2
43
1
42
63
64

163
150

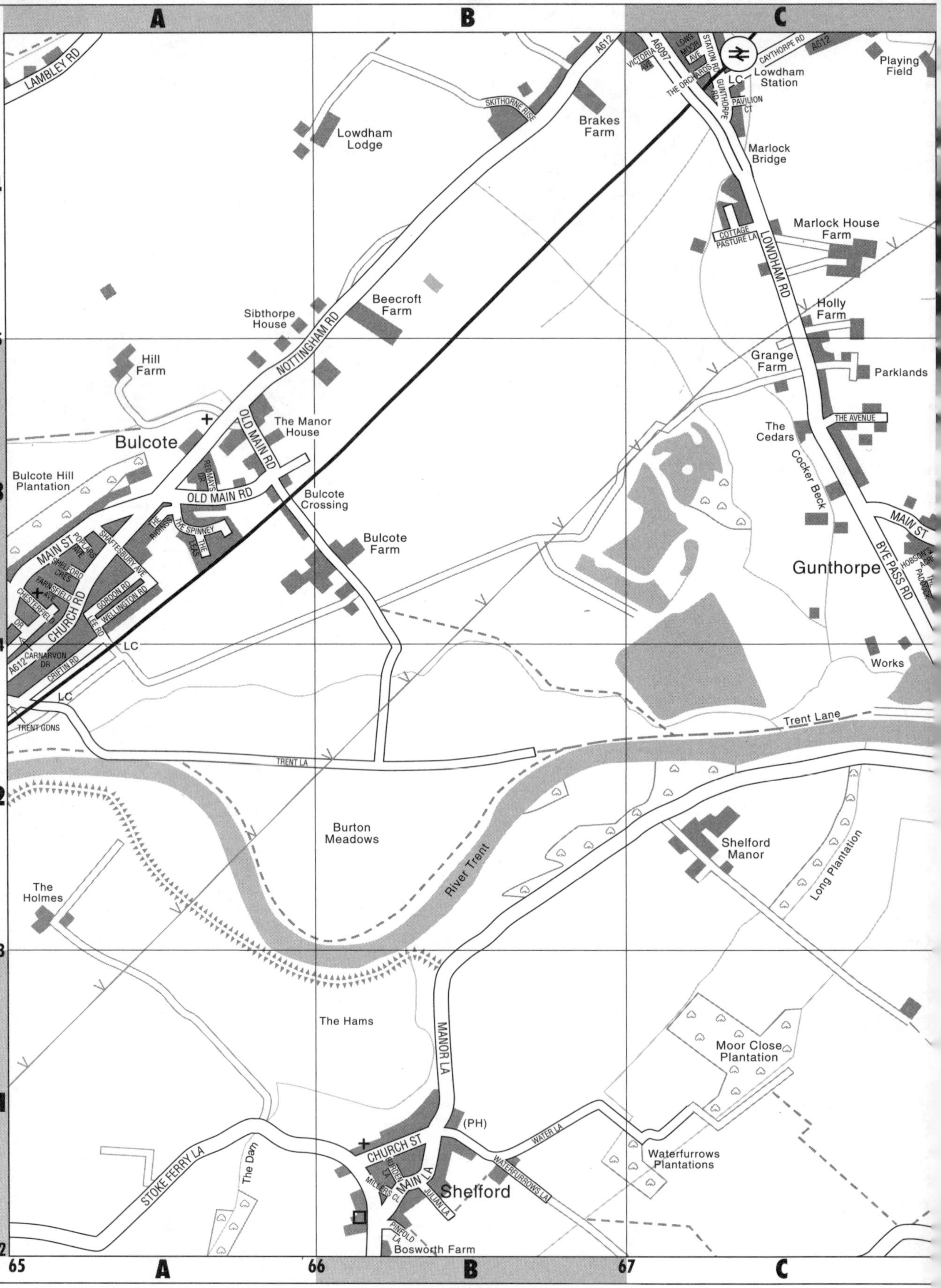


163
176

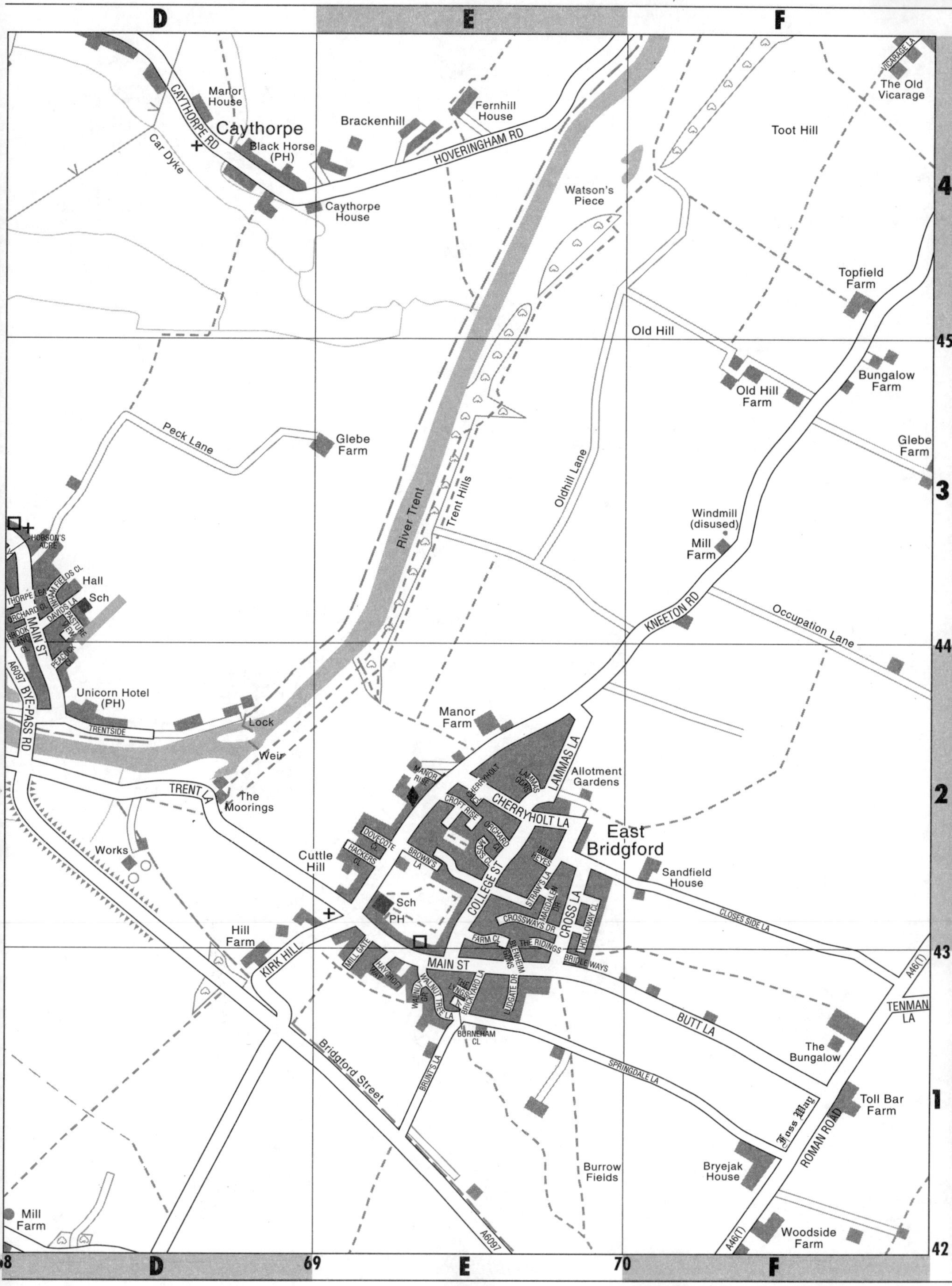

D
E
F
Caythorpe
Manor House
CAYTHORPE RD
Car Dyke
Black Horse (PH)
Brackenhill
Fernhill House
HOVERINGHAM RD
Caythorpe House
The Old Vicarage
VICARAGE LA
Toot Hill
Watson's Piece
Topfield Farm
Old Hill
Old Hill Farm
Bungalow Farm
Glebe Farm
Peck Lane
Glebe Farm
River Trent
Trent Hills
Oldhill Lane
Windmill (disused)
Mill Farm
KNEETON RD
Occupation Lane
HOBSON'S ACRE
Hall
Sch
MAIN ST
A6097 BYE-PASS RD
Unicorn Hotel (PH)
TRENTSIDE
Lock
Weir
Manor Farm
LAMMAS LA
Allotment Gardens
CHERRY HOLT LA
East Bridgford
TRENT LA
The Moorings
Works
Cuttle Hill
COLLEGE ST
CROSS LA
Sandfield House
CLOSES SIDE LA
Sch
PH
Hill Farm
KIRK HILL
MAIN ST
BUTT LA
TENMAN LA
A46(T)
The Bungalow
Bridgford Street
BRUNT'S LA
SPRINGDALE LA
Foss Way
ROMAN ROAD
Toll Bar Farm
Burrow Fields
Bryejak House
Mill Farm
Woodside Farm
A6097
4
45
3
44
2
43
1
42
69
70

165
152

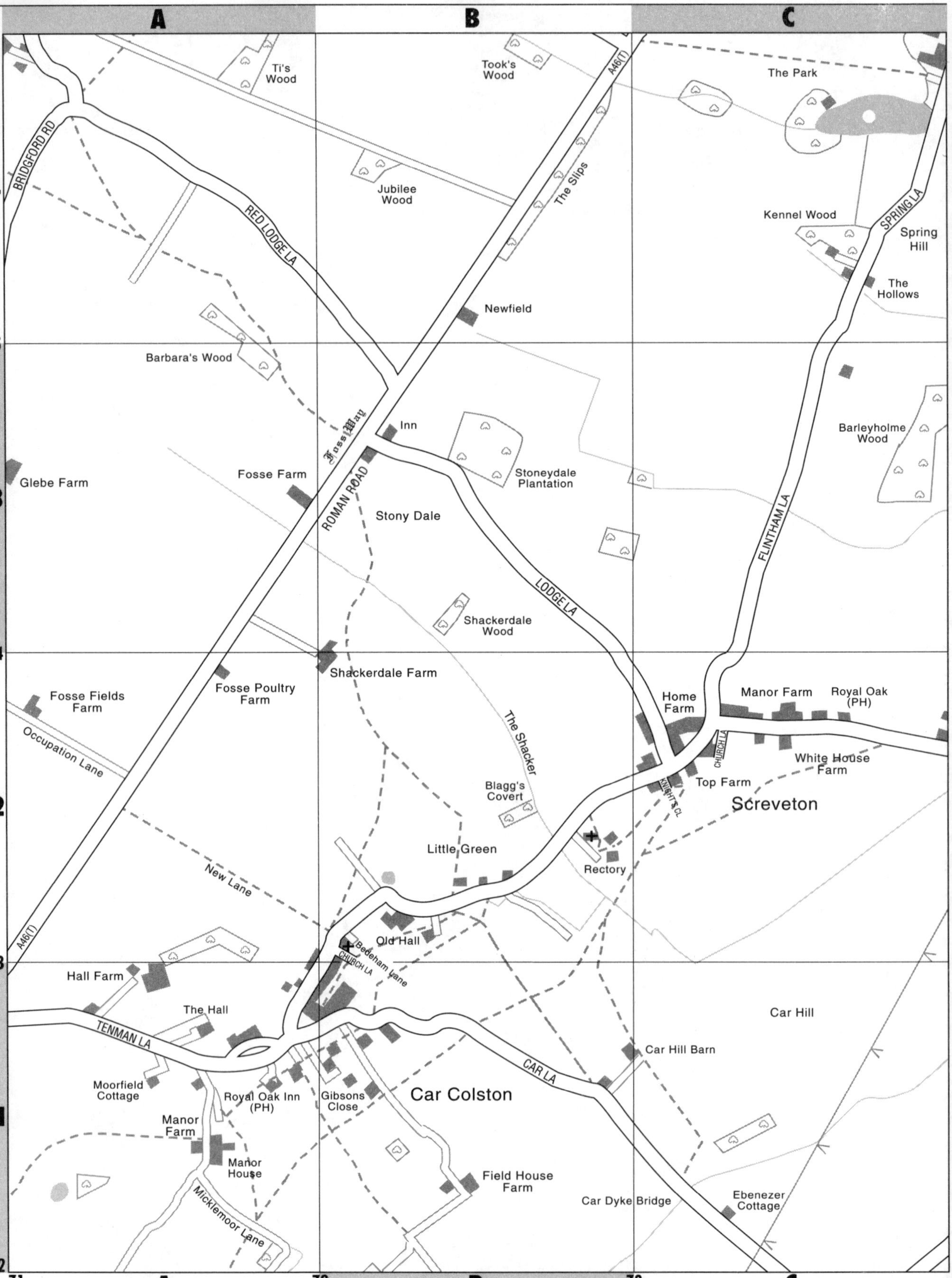


165
178

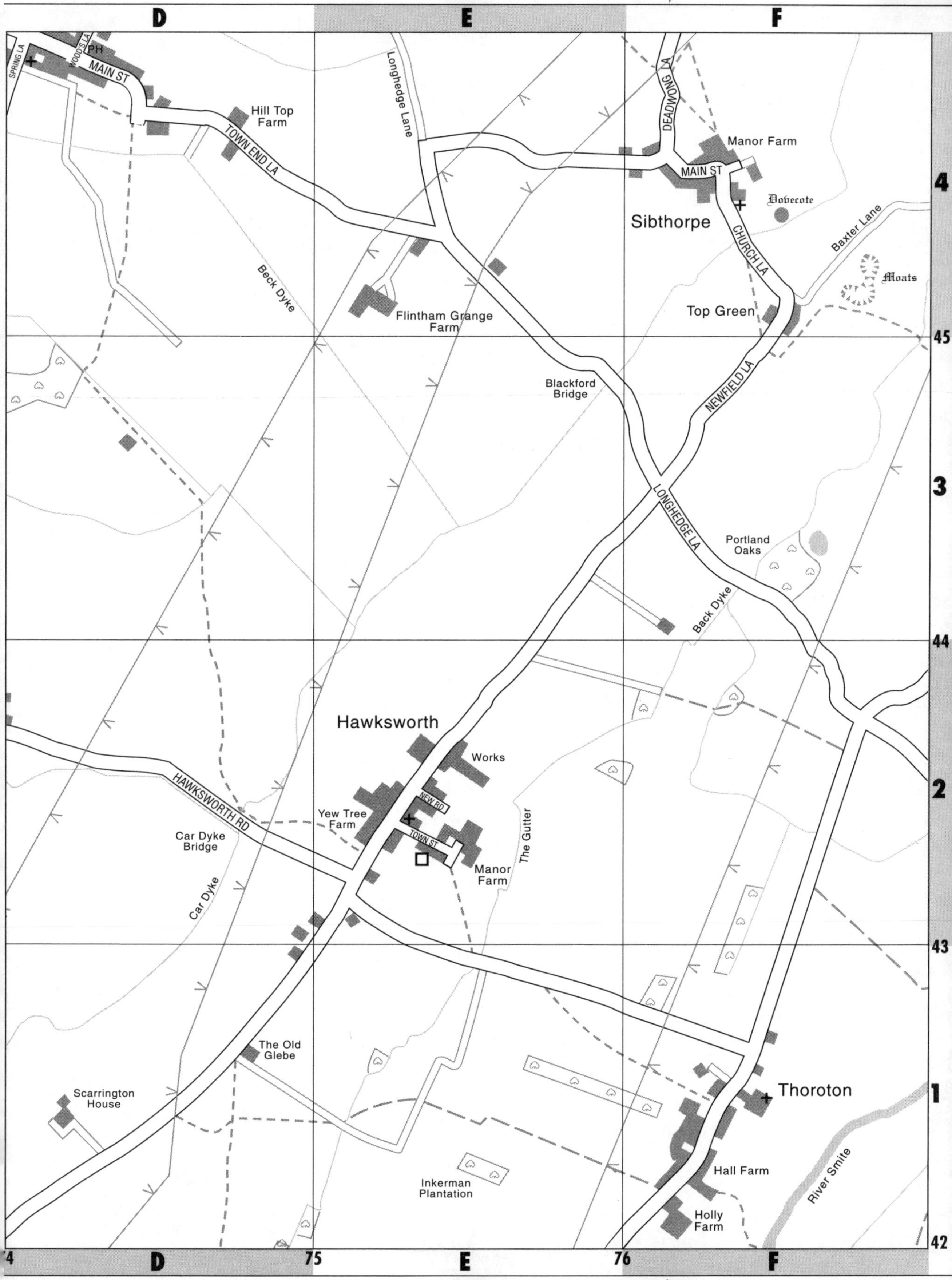
D
E
F
SPRING LA
WOOD'S LA
PH
MAIN ST
Hill Top Farm
TOWN END LA
Longhedge Lane
DEADWONG LA
Manor Farm
MAIN ST
Dovecote
Sibthorpe
CHURCH LA
Baxter Lane
Moats
Top Green
Beck Dyke
Flintham Grange Farm
Blackford Bridge
NEWFIELD LA
LONGHEDGE LA
Portland Oaks
Back Dyke
Hawksworth
Works
NEW RD
Yew Tree Farm
TOWN ST
Manor Farm
The Gutter
HAWKSWORTH RD
Car Dyke Bridge
Car Dyke
The Old Glebe
Scarrington House
Thoroton
Inkerman Plantation
Hall Farm
Holly Farm
River Smite
4
45
3
44
2
43
1
42
74
75
76

167
154

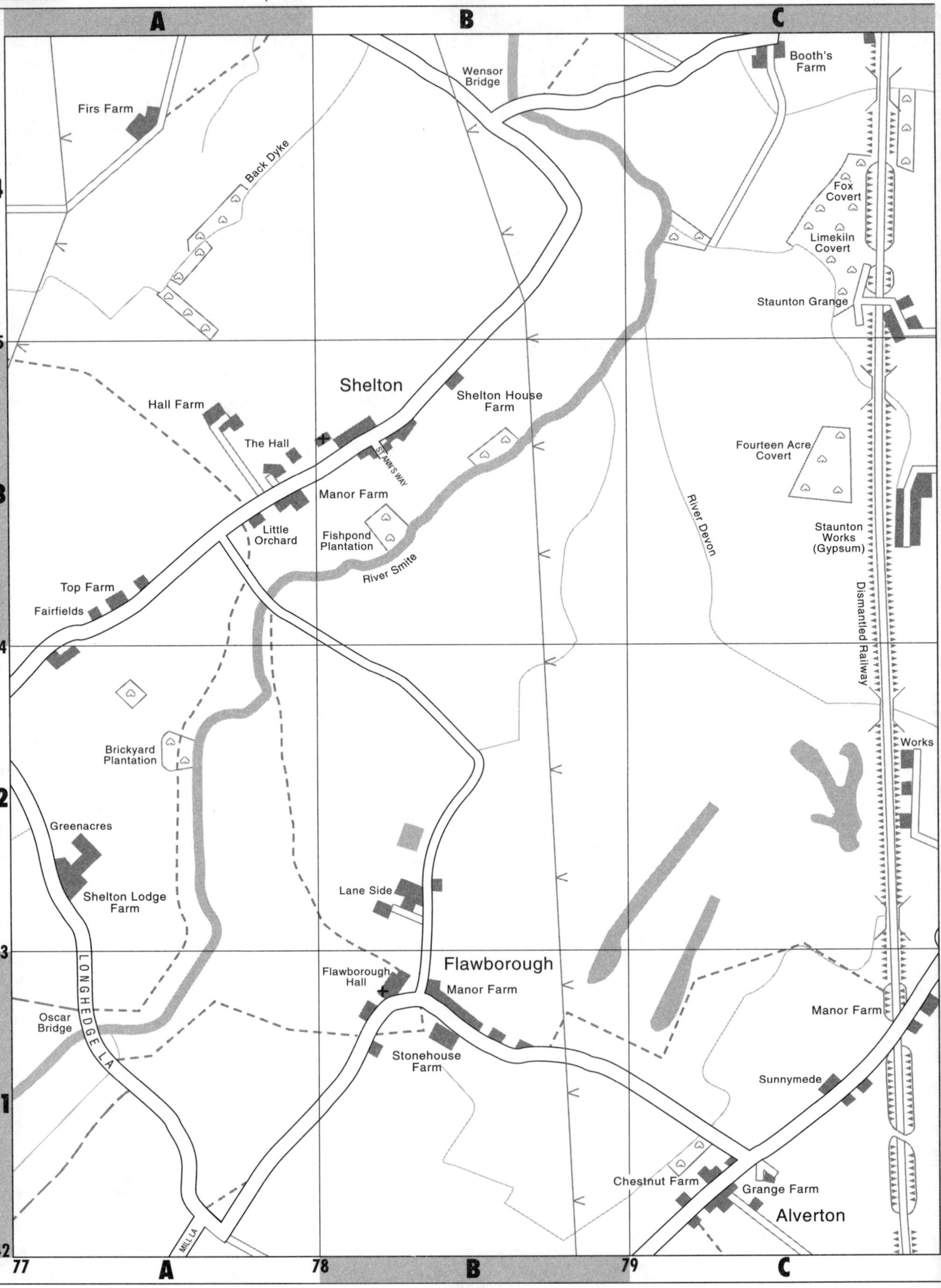


167
180

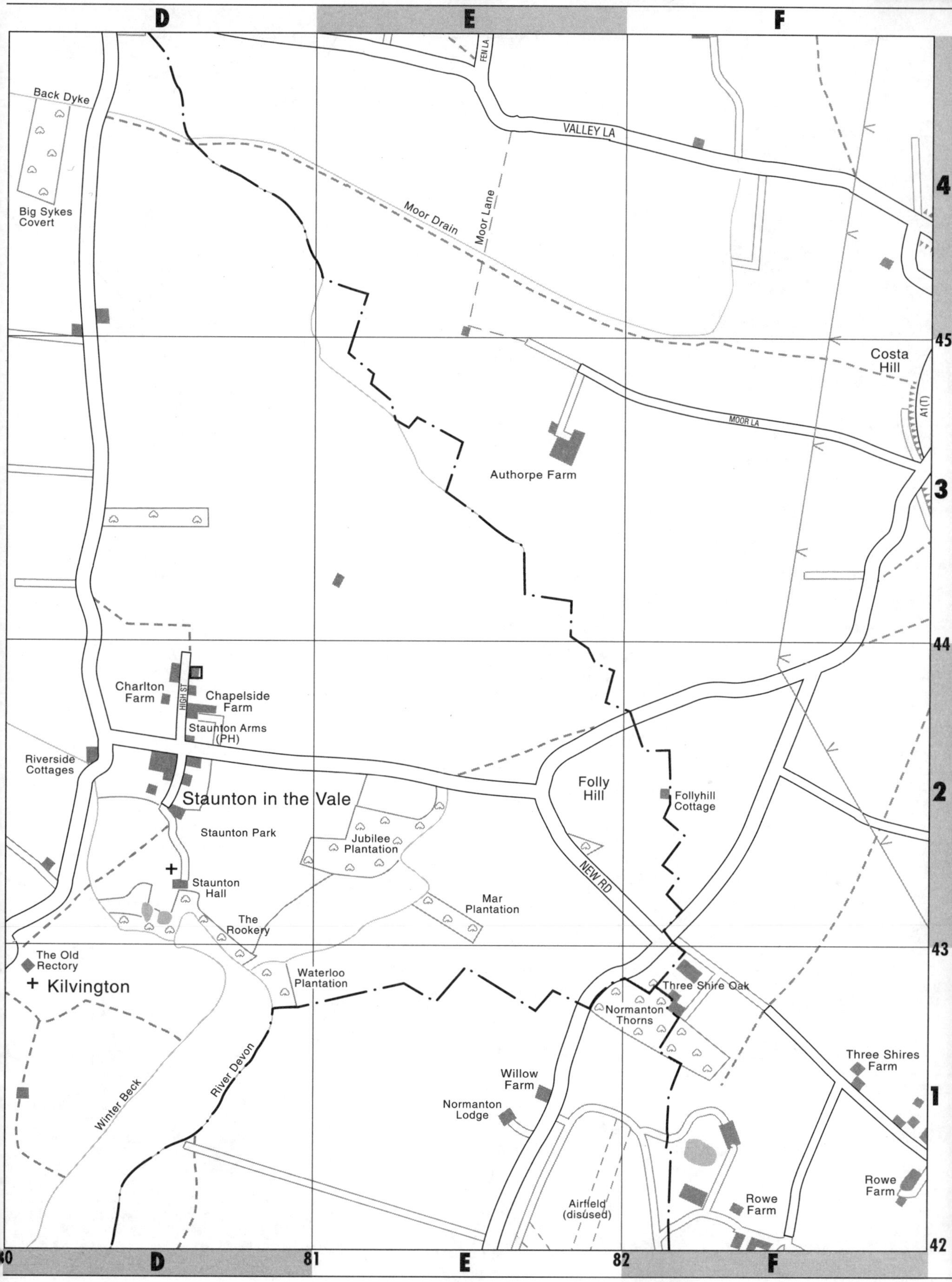
D
E
F
FEN LA
Back Dyke
VALLEY LA
Big Sykes Covert
Moor Drain
Moor Lane
4
45
Costa Hill
MOOR LA
A1(T)
Authorpe Farm
3
44
Charlton Farm
HIGH ST
Chapelside Farm
Staunton Arms (PH)
Riverside Cottages
Folly Hill
Follyhill Cottage
2
Staunton in the Vale
Staunton Park
Jubilee Plantation
Staunton Hall
NEW RD
Mar Plantation
The Rookery
43
The Old Rectory
Kilvington
Waterloo Plantation
Three Shire Oak
Normanton Thorns
Three Shires Farm
Willow Farm
Winter Beck
River Devon
Normanton Lodge
1
Rowe Farm
Airfield (disused)
Rowe Farm
42
81
82

158

A
B
C
4
41
3
40
2
39
1
38
47
48
49
Cemy
Larklands
Sch
Schs
Gallows Inn
Lock
River Erewash
Robbinetts Arm (dis)
Oldmoor Wood
Shortwood Farm
Field House
Meadow Farm
Robin Hood Way
Trowell Service Area
Trowell Moor
Moor Cottages
Shortwood House
Grange Wood
Uplands Farm
Trowell
Nottingham Canal (disused)
Trowell Junction
NOTTINGHAM RD
Trowell Hall
Potter's Plantation
Factories
Hallam Fields Lock
Hallam Fields
Sewage Works
Crompton Road Industrial Estate
Erewash Canal
Swancar Farm
Dismtd Rly
Works
Stanton Works
Field Farm
Stapleford Hill
Junction Lock
LC
Stanton- by- Dale
PH
Golf Course
CH
Stanton Gate
M1
A609
A6007
A6002
B6003
B6004
ILKESTON RD
STAPLEFORD RD
TROWELL RD
COSSALL RD
CORPORATION RD
HALLAM FIELDS RD
CROMPTON RD
LOW'S LA
SEVEN OAKS RD
GOLF CLUB RD
QUARRY HILL
MOORBRIDGE LA
PASTURE RD
HICKINGS LA
WATERLOO LA
DEAD LA
STONEY LA
FURNACE RD
KINGSWAY
LONGFIELD LA
KINGSTON AVE
HEXHAM AVE
1 NEWDIGATE ST
2 STANHOPE ST
3 LITTLE HALAM LA
1 SHERIDAN CT
2 ADELAIDE CL
3 CANBERRA CL
4 DRYDEN CT
P

182

159
172

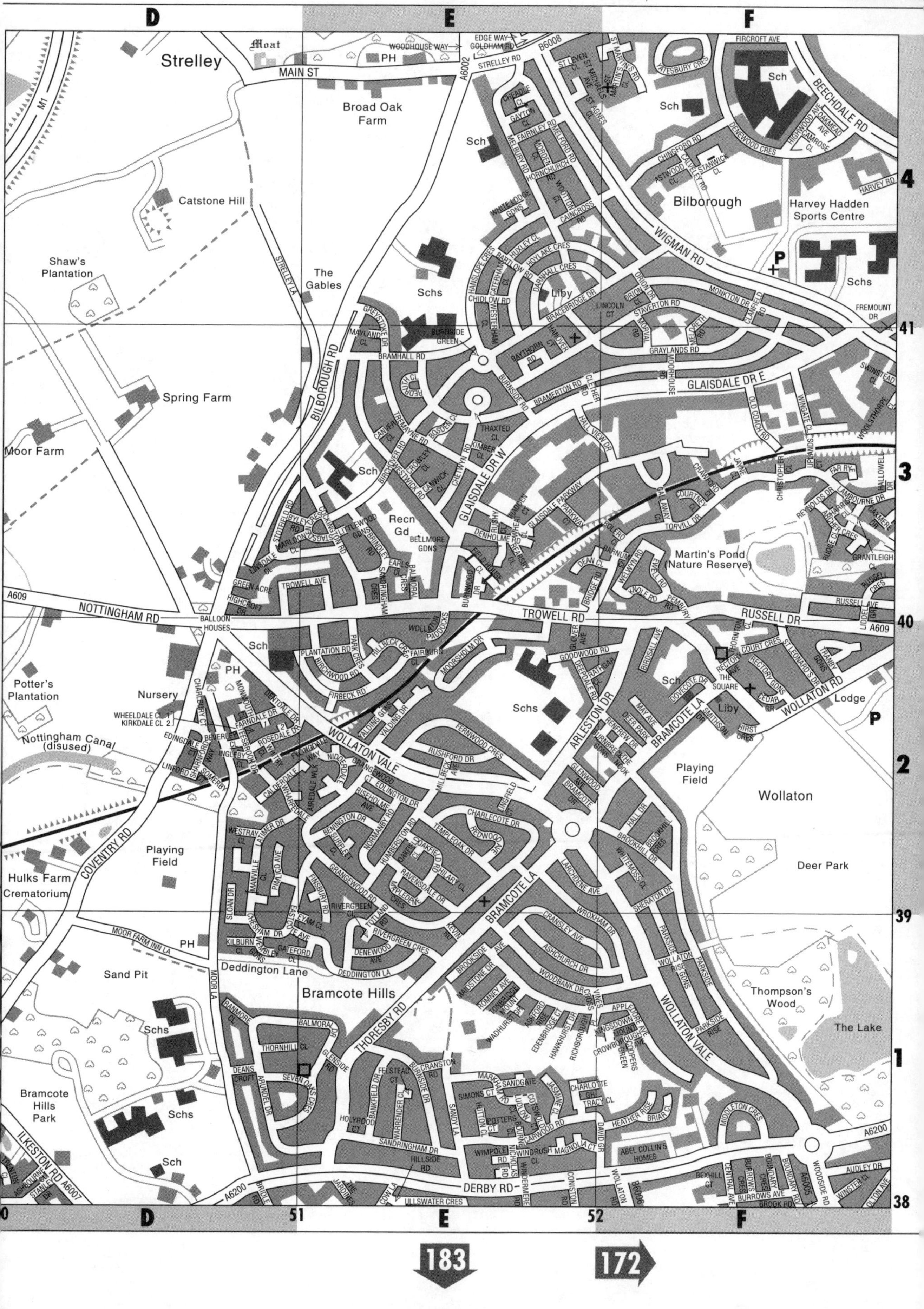


183
172

171
160

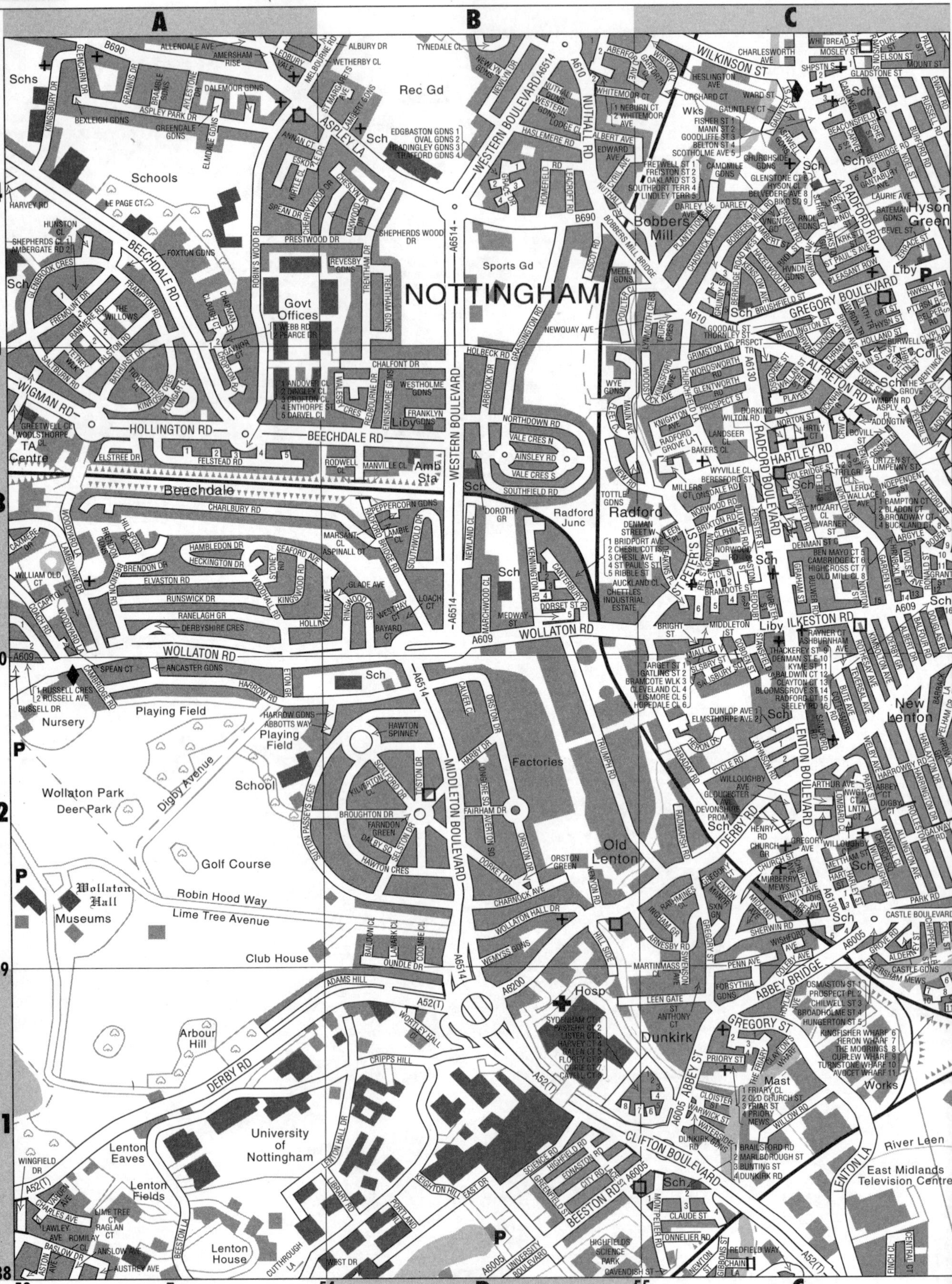


171
184

D
E
F
Alexandra Park
Hungerhill Gdns
St Ann's
Sneinton
Meadows
Nottingham Midland Station
Castle
Shire Hall
Sports Ground
Meadow Lane Lock
Trent Bridge
County Hall
Cricket Gd
Football Gd
Recn Gd
Cemy
GREGORY BVD
MANSFIELD RD
WOODBOROUGH RD
MAGDALA RD
WAVERLEY ST
MILTON ST
CANAL ST
STATION ST
QUEEN'S RD
LONDON RD
CARLTON RD
MANVERS ST
LADY BAY BRIDGE
RADCLIFFE RD
TRENT BVD
DALESIDE RD
CASTLE BVD
QUEENS DR
SHERWOOD RISE
FOREST RD E
DERBY RD
River Trent
Nottingham Canal
4
41
3
40
2
39
1
38
6
57
58

173
162

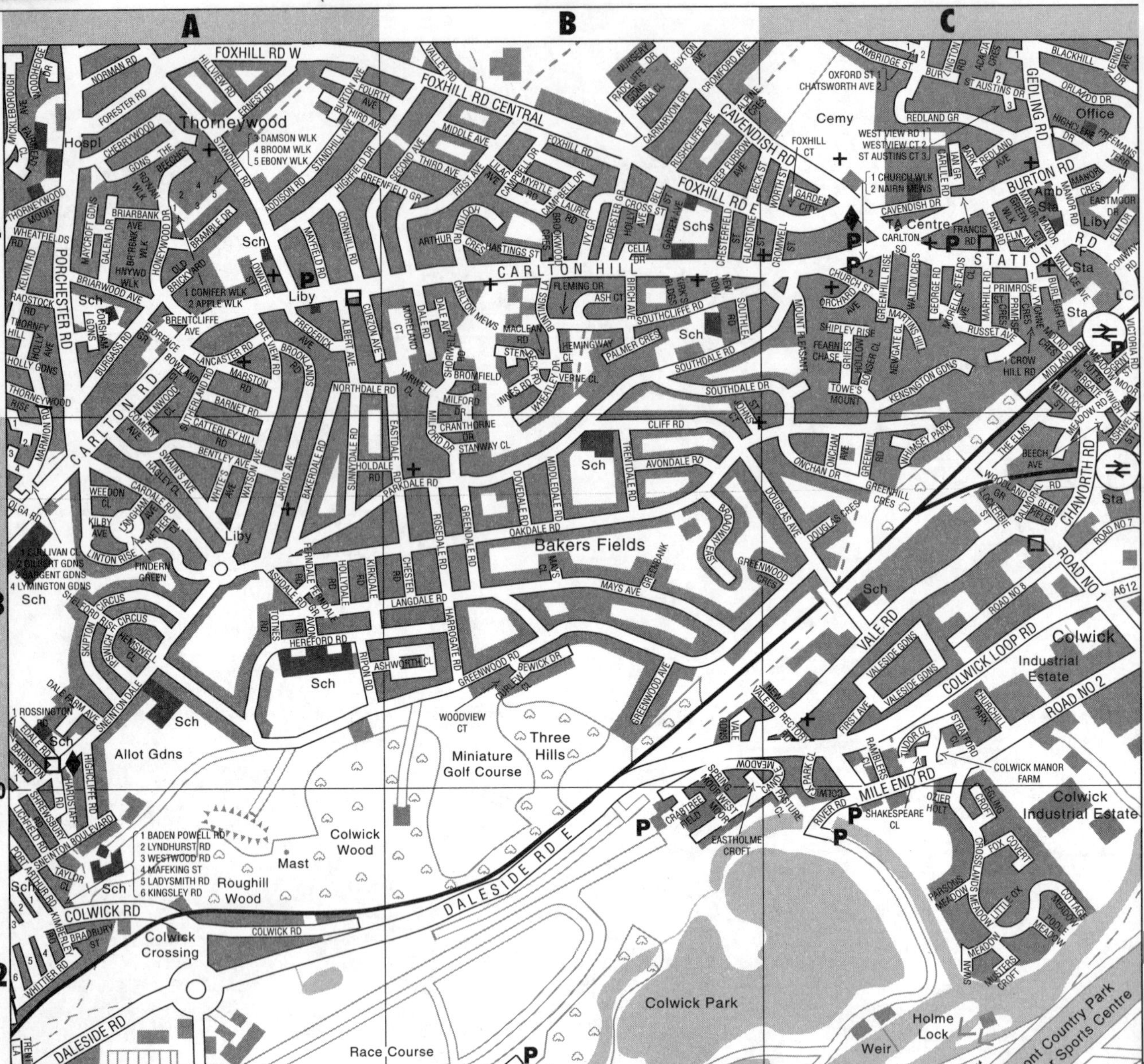


173
186

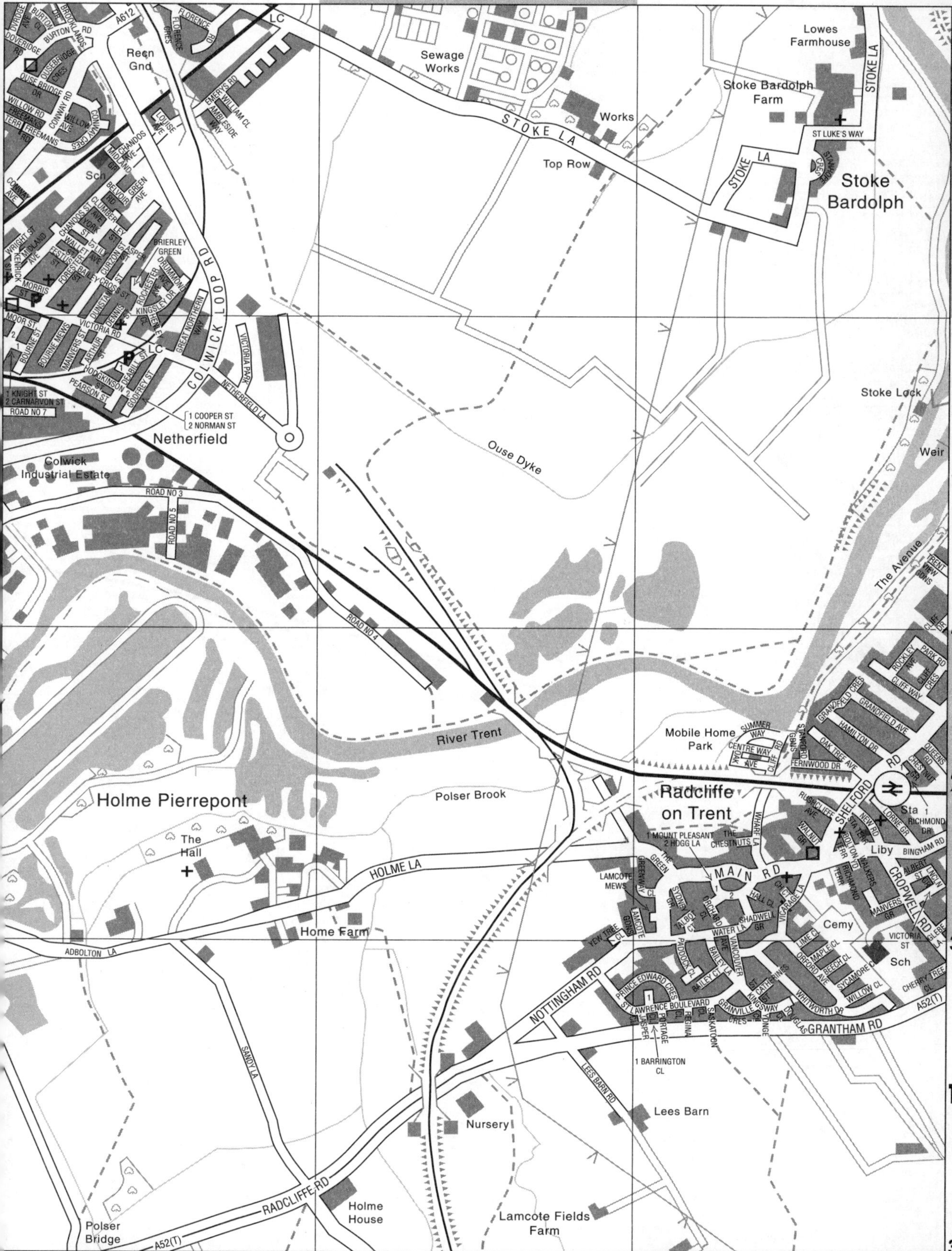
D
E
F
Sewage Works
Lowes Farmhouse
Stoke Bardolph Farm
Works
STOKE LA
Top Row
ST LUKE'S WAY
Stoke Bardolph
Recn Gnd
Sch
Netherfield
COLWICK LOOP RD
VICTORIA PARK
NETHERFIELD LA
Colwick Industrial Estate
ROAD NO 3
ROAD NO 5
ROAD NO 4
Ouse Dyke
Stoke Lock
Weir
The Avenue
River Trent
Mobile Home Park
Radcliffe on Trent
Polser Brook
Holme Pierrepont
The Hall
HOLME LA
Home Farm
ADBOLTON LA
MAIN RD
SHELFORD RD
CROPWELL RD
Liby
Sta
Cemy
Sch
NOTTINGHAM RD
GRANTHAM RD
A52(T)
SANDY LA
LEES BARN RD
Lees Barn
Nursery
RADCLIFFE RD
Holme House
Lamcote Fields Farm
Polser Bridge
1 COOPER ST
2 NORMAN ST
1 KNIGHT ST
2 CARNARVON ST
ROAD NO 7
1 MOUNT PLEASANT
2 HOGG LA
1 BARRINGTON CL
1 RICHMOND DR
4
41
3
40
2
39
1
38
63
64

175
164

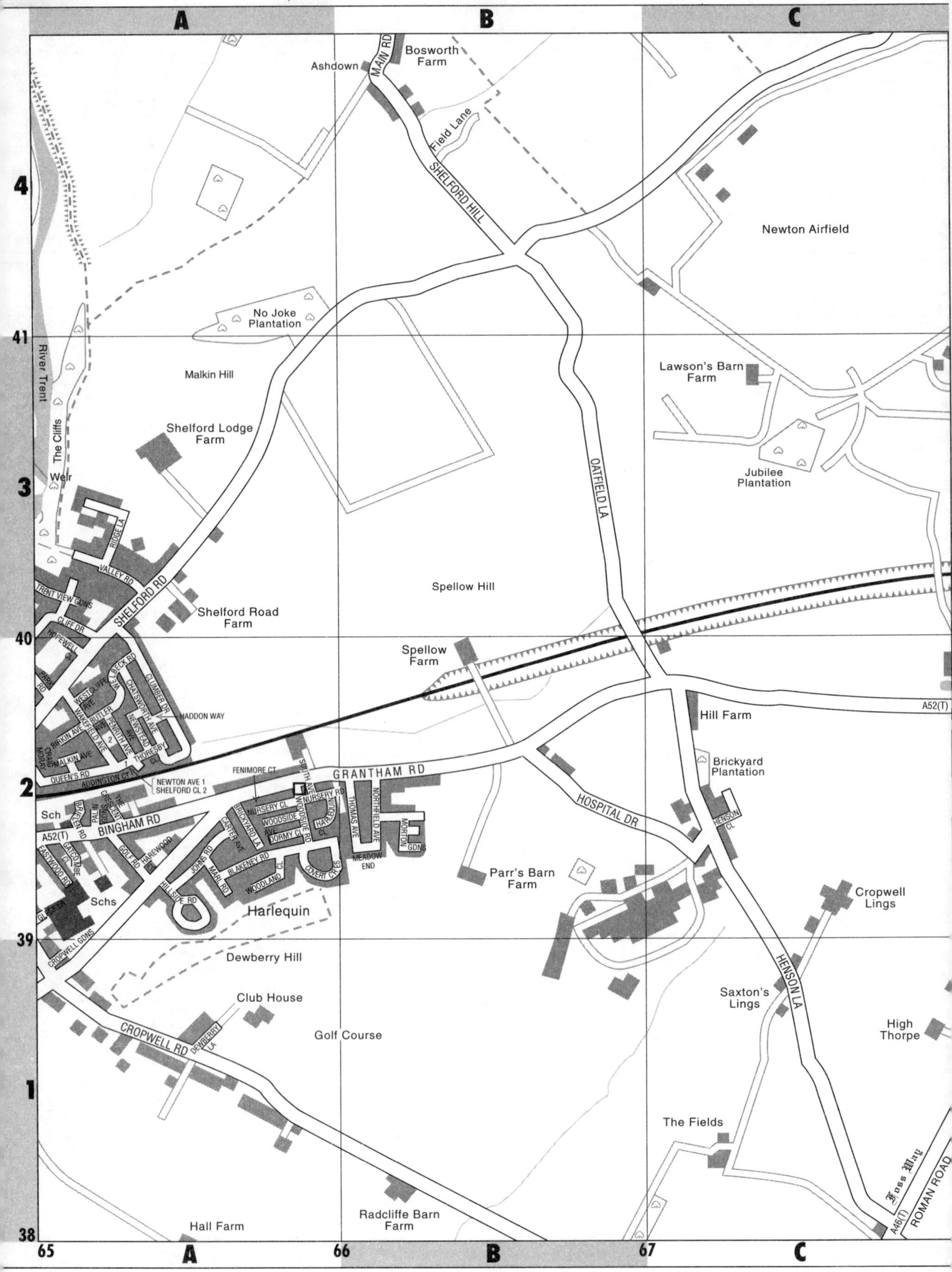


175
188

165
178

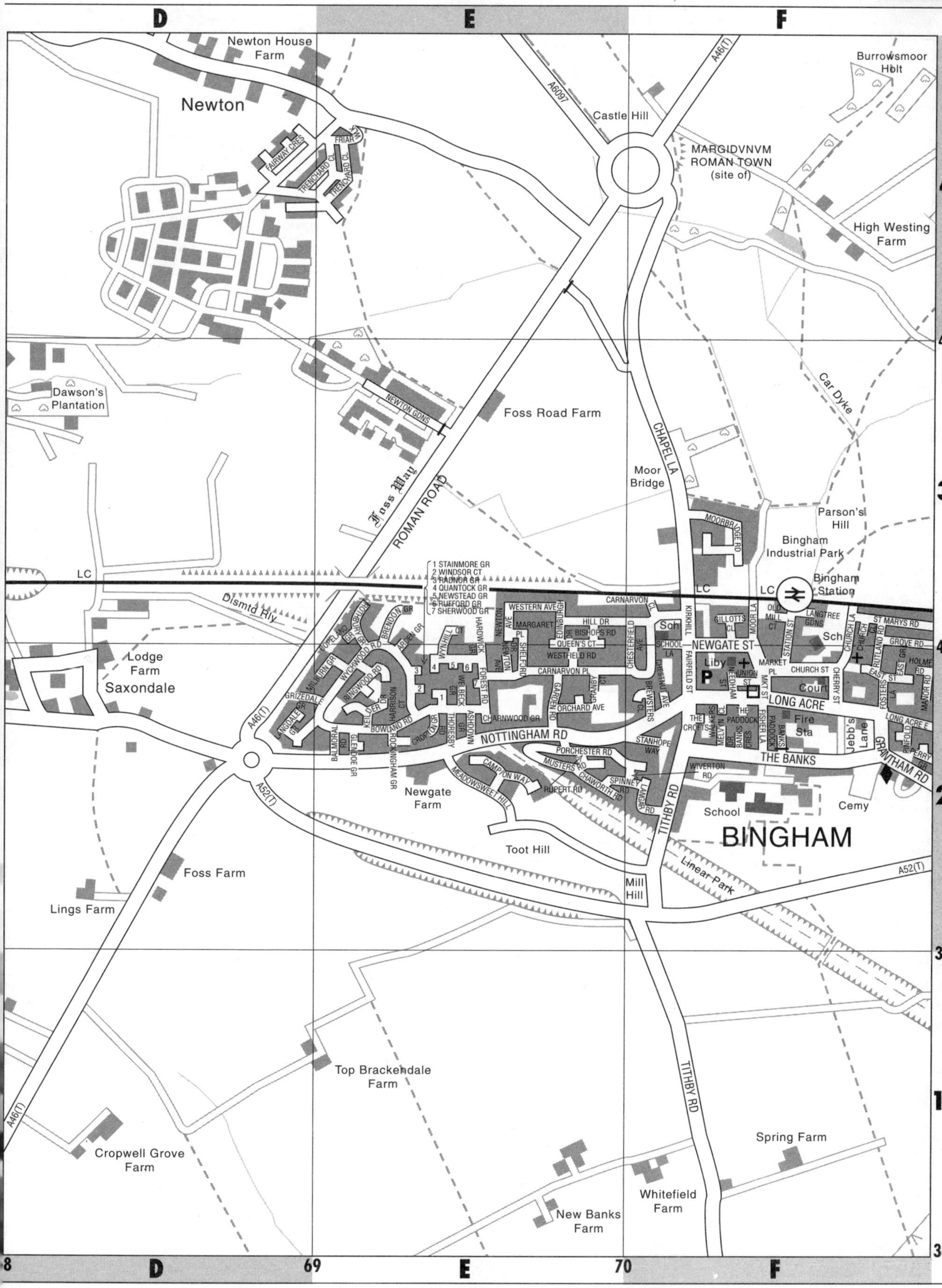


189
178

177
166

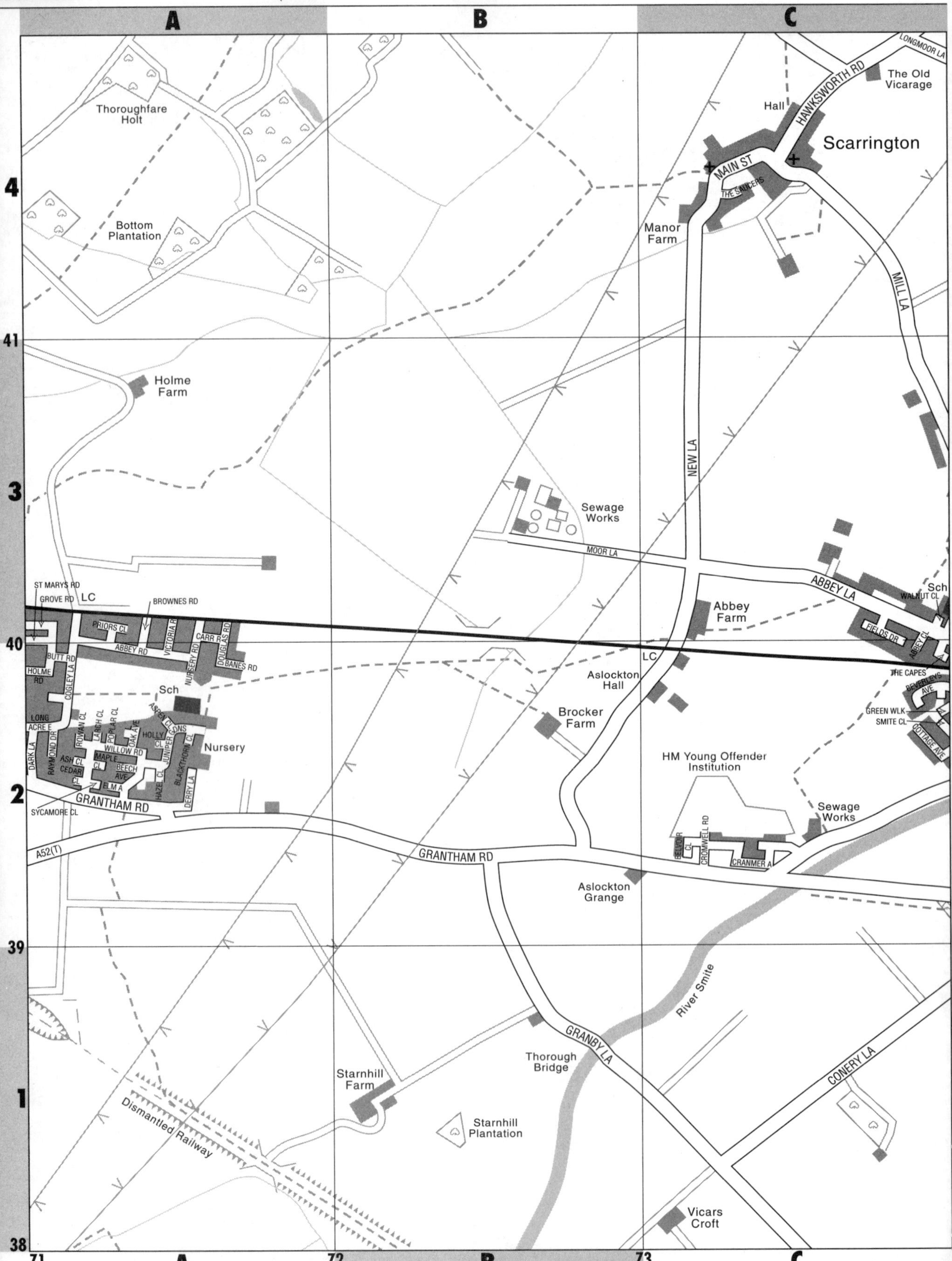


177
190

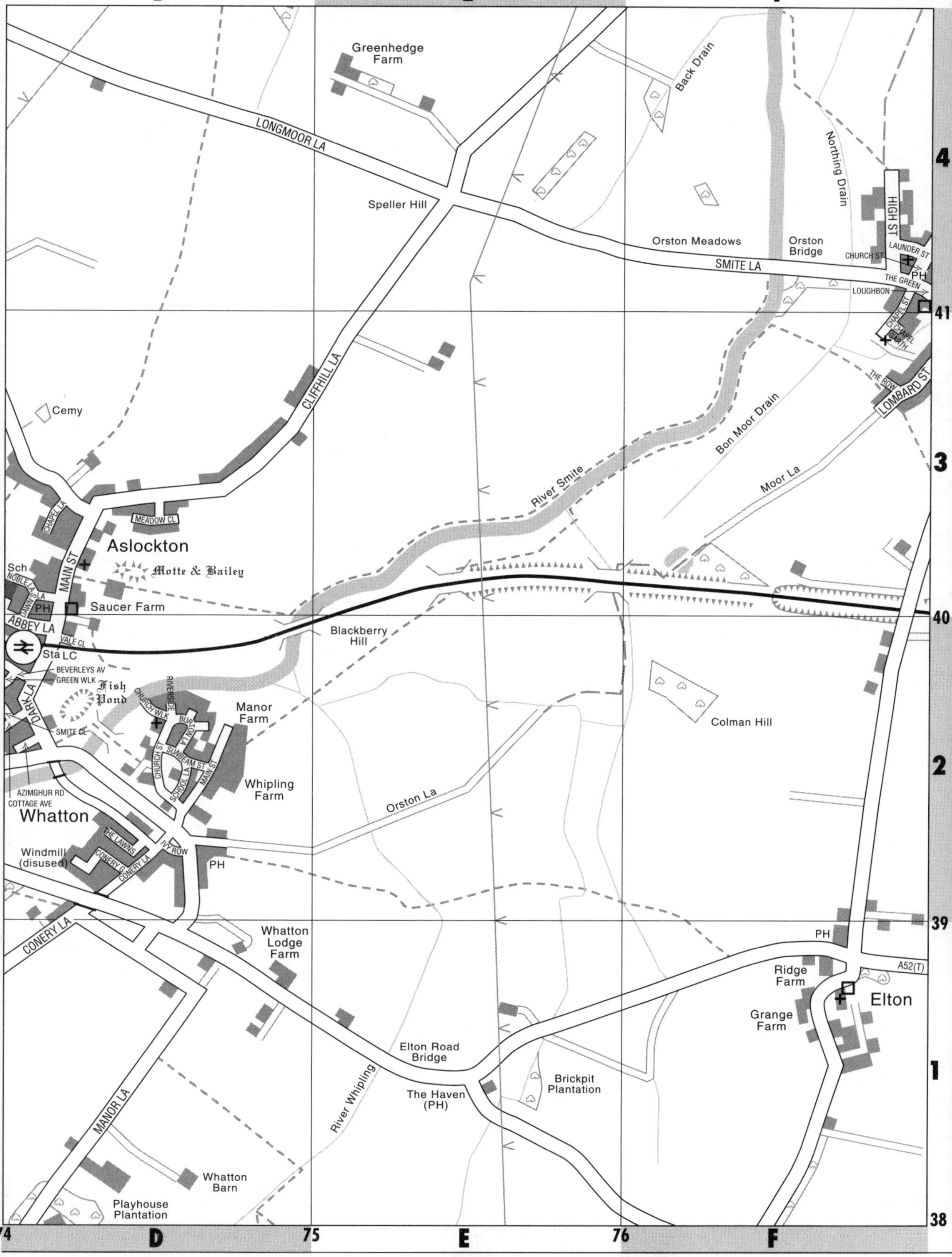
D
E
F
Greenhedge Farm
LONGMOOR LA
Back Drain
Speller Hill
Northing Drain
HIGH ST
Orston Meadows
Orston Bridge
SMITE LA
CHURCH ST
LAUNDER ST
PH
THE GREEN
LOUGHBON
CHAPEL ST
CHAPEL GARTH
THE ROW
LOMBARD ST
CLIFFHILL LA
Cemy
Bon Moor Drain
River Smite
Moor La
CHAPEL LA
MEADOW CL
Aslockton
Motte & Bailey
Sch
NOBLE LA
DAWN'S LA
MAIN ST
PH
Saucer Farm
ABBEY LA
VALE CL
Sta LC
Blackberry Hill
BEVERLEYS AV
GREEN WLK
Fish Pond
RIVERSIDE
CHURCH WLK
BURTON LA
Manor Farm
Colman Hill
DARK LA
SMITE CL
CHURCH ST
SUNBEAM ST
SCHOOL LA
MAIN ST
Whipling Farm
AZIMGHUR RD
COTTAGE AVE
Whatton
Orston La
THE LAWNS
IVY ROW
Windmill (disused)
CONERY G
CONERY LA
PH
CONERY LA
Whatton Lodge Farm
PH
A52(T)
Ridge Farm
Elton
Grange Farm
Elton Road Bridge
River Whipling
The Haven (PH)
Brickpit Plantation
MANOR LA
Whatton Barn
Playhouse Plantation
4
3
2
1
41
40
39
38
74
75
76

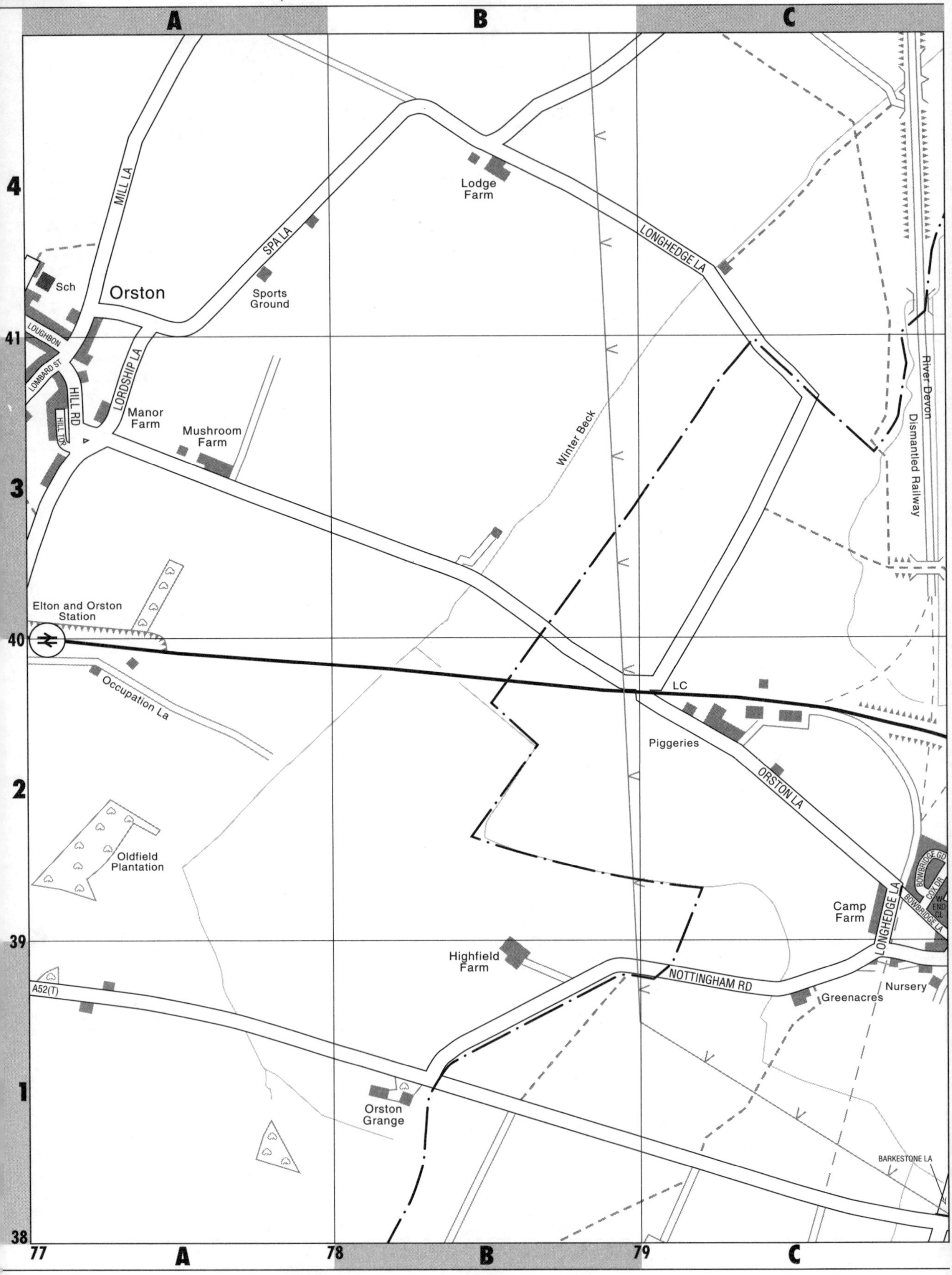
A
B
C
4
3
2
1
41
40
39
38
77
78
79
Orston
Sch
MILL LA
SPA LA
Sports Ground
Lodge Farm
LONGHEDGE LA
LOUGHBON
LOMBARD ST
HILL RD
HILL TOR
LORDSHIP LA
Manor Farm
Mushroom Farm
Winter Beck
River Devon
Dismantled Railway
Elton and Orston Station
Occupation La
LC
Piggeries
ORSTON LA
Oldfield Plantation
BOWBRIDGE GD
COX DR
BOWBRIDGE LA
Camp Farm
LONGHEDGE LA
Highfield Farm
NOTTINGHAM RD
Nursery
Greenacres
A52(T)
Orston Grange
BARKESTONE LA

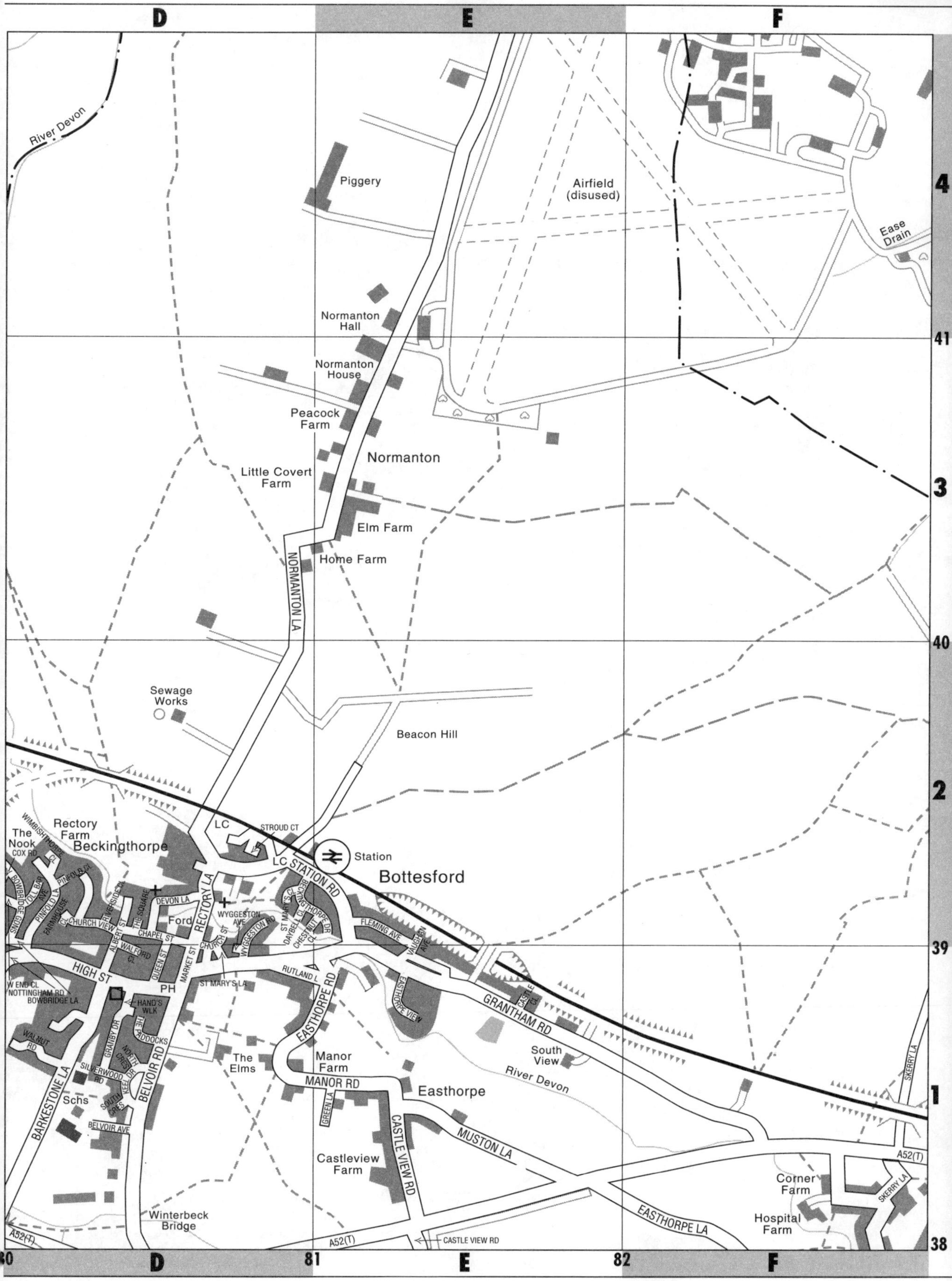
D
E
F
4
41
3
40
2
39
1
38
80
81
82
River Devon
Piggery
Airfield
(disused)
Ease
Drain
Normanton
Hall
Normanton
House
Peacock
Farm
Normanton
Little Covert
Farm
Elm Farm
Home Farm
NORMANTON LA
Sewage
Works
Beacon Hill
LC
STROUD CT
Station
Bottesford
Rectory
Farm
The
Nook
Beckingthorpe
COX RD
WIMBISH
TOLL BAR
AVE
PINFOLD CL
PINFOLD LA
BOWBRIDGE GDNS
FARMHOUSE
CHURCH VIEW
RIVERSIDE CL
THE SQUARE
DEVON LA
Ford
RECTORY LA
WYGGESTON
AVE
WYGGESTON RD
CHAPEL ST
ALBERT ST
WALFORD
CL
QUEEN ST
MARKET ST
CHURCH ST
ST MARY'S CL
DAYBELL CL
CHESTNUT CL
BECKINGTHORPE DR
STATION RD
FLEMING AVE
VAUGHAN AVE
HIGH ST
W END CL
NOTTINGHAM RD
BOWBRIDGE LA
PH
ST MARY'S LA
RUTLAND L
EASTHORPE RD
EASTHORPE VIEW
GRANTHAM RD
CASTLE CL
HAND'S
WLK
THE PADDOCKS
GRANBY DR
NORTH
CRES
WALNUT
RD
SILVERWOOD
RD
BELVOIR RD
The
Elms
Manor
Farm
MANOR RD
South
View
River Devon
Easthorpe
BARKESTONE LA
Schs
SOUTH
CRES
BELVOIR AVE
GREEN LA
CASTLE VIEW RD
MUSTON LA
SKERRY LA
A52(T)
Castleview
Farm
Corner
Farm
Hospital
Farm
EASTHORPE LA
Winterbeck
Bridge
CASTLE VIEW RD

170

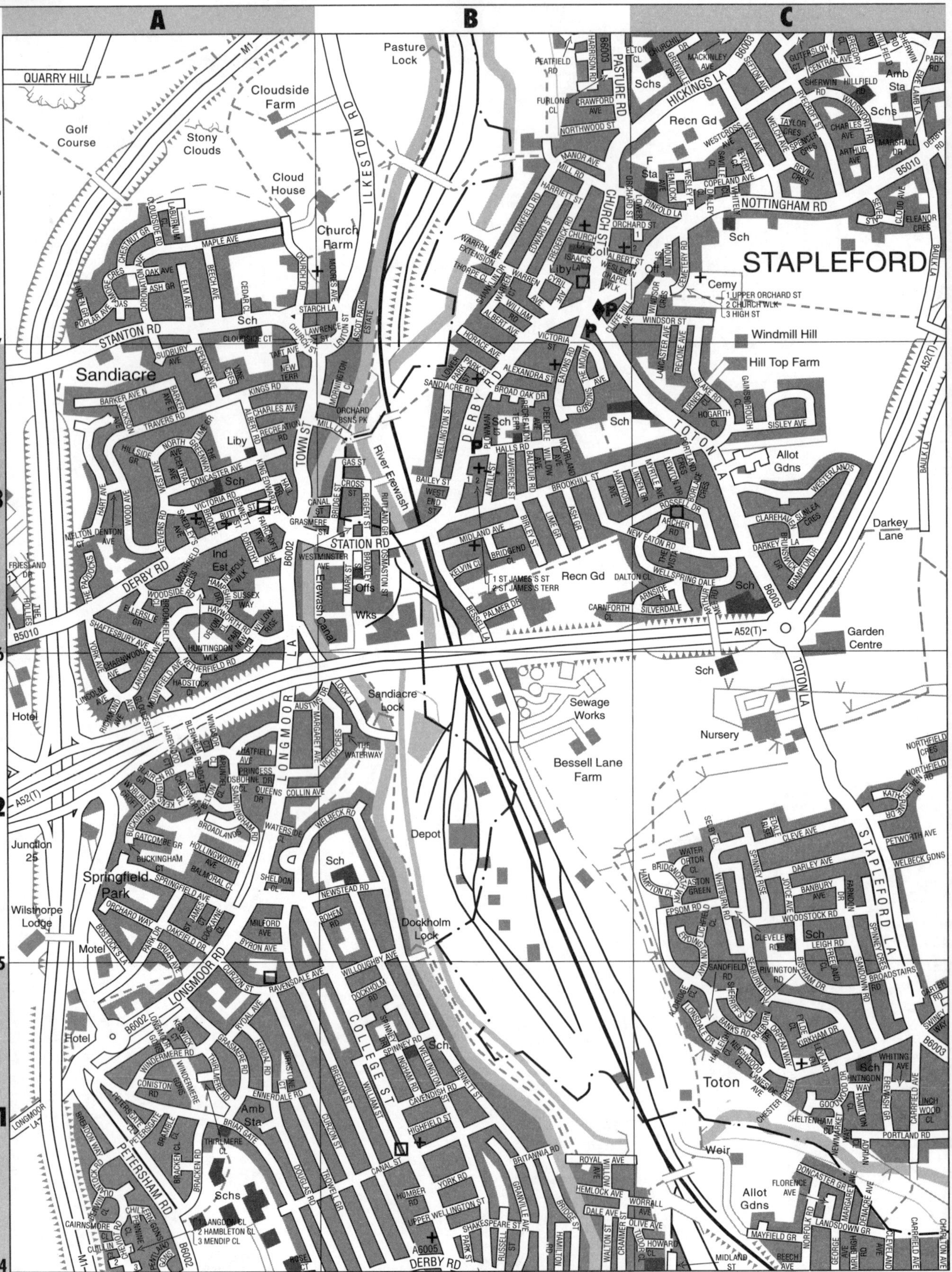
A
B
C
STAPLEFORD
Sandiacre
Toton
Springfield Park
Quarry Hill
Golf Course
Stony Clouds
Cloudside Farm
Cloud House
Church Farm
Pasture Lock
Sandiacre Lock
Dockholm Lock
Erewash Canal
River Erewash
Sewage Works
Bessell Lane Farm
Depot
Windmill Hill
Hill Top Farm
Allot Gdns
Darkey Lane
Garden Centre
Nursery
Recn Gd
Junction 25
Wilsthorpe Lodge
Motel
Hotel
Weir
Cemy
Ind Est
ILKESTON RD
STANTON RD
DERBY RD
STATION RD
TOWN ST
LONGMOOR LA
LONGMOOR RD
COLLEGE ST
PETERSHAM RD
NOTTINGHAM RD
HICKINGS LA
PASTURE RD
CHURCH ST
TOTON LA
STAPLEFORD LA
A52(T)
B5010
B6002
B6003
A6005
M1
4
37
3
36
2
35
1
34
47
48
49
1 UPPER ORCHARD ST
2 CHURCH WLK
3 HIGH ST
1 ST JAMES'S ST
2 ST JAMES'S TERR
1 LANGDON CL
2 HAMBLETON CL
3 MENDIP CL

193

171
184

194
184

183
172

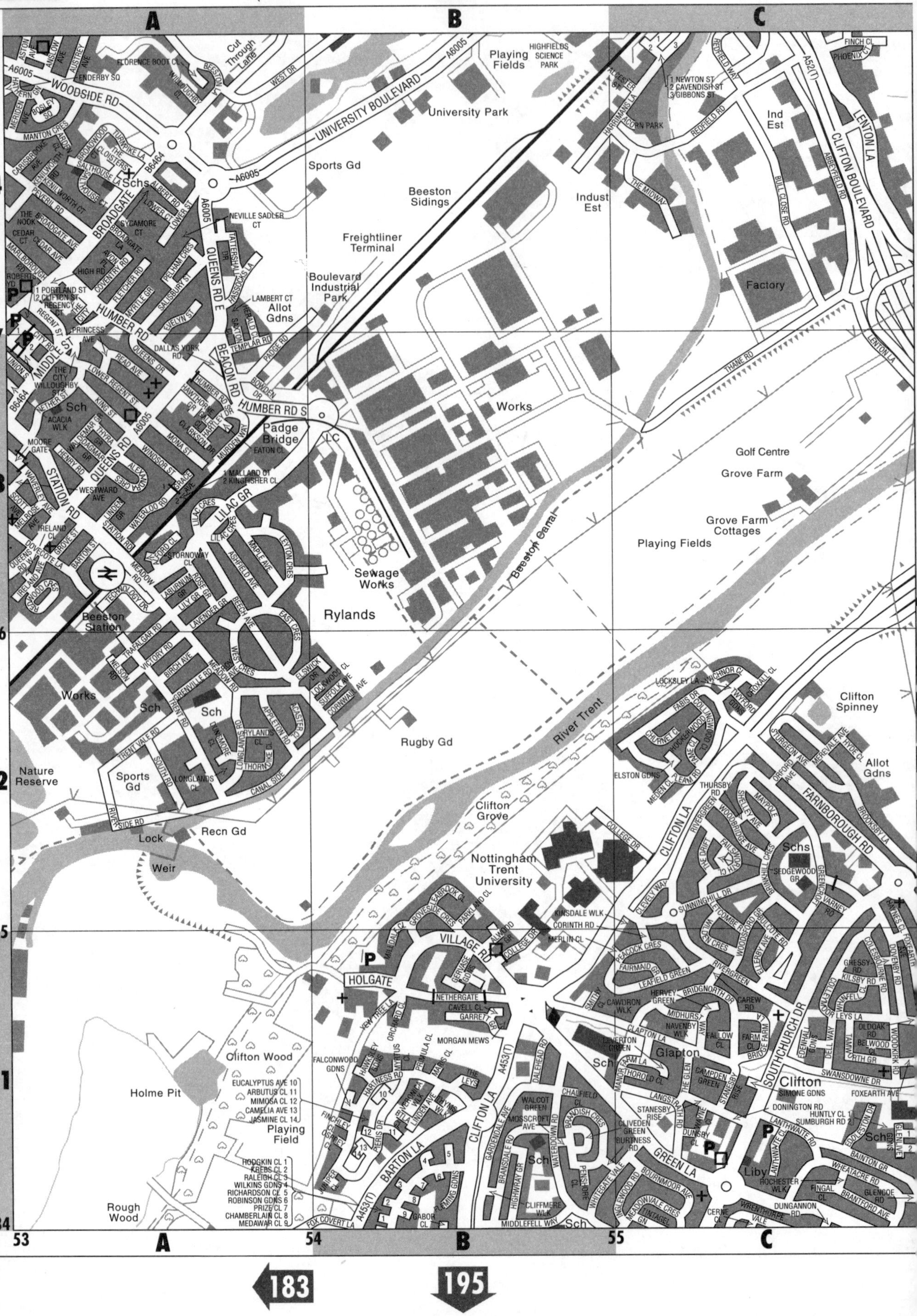


183
195

D E F

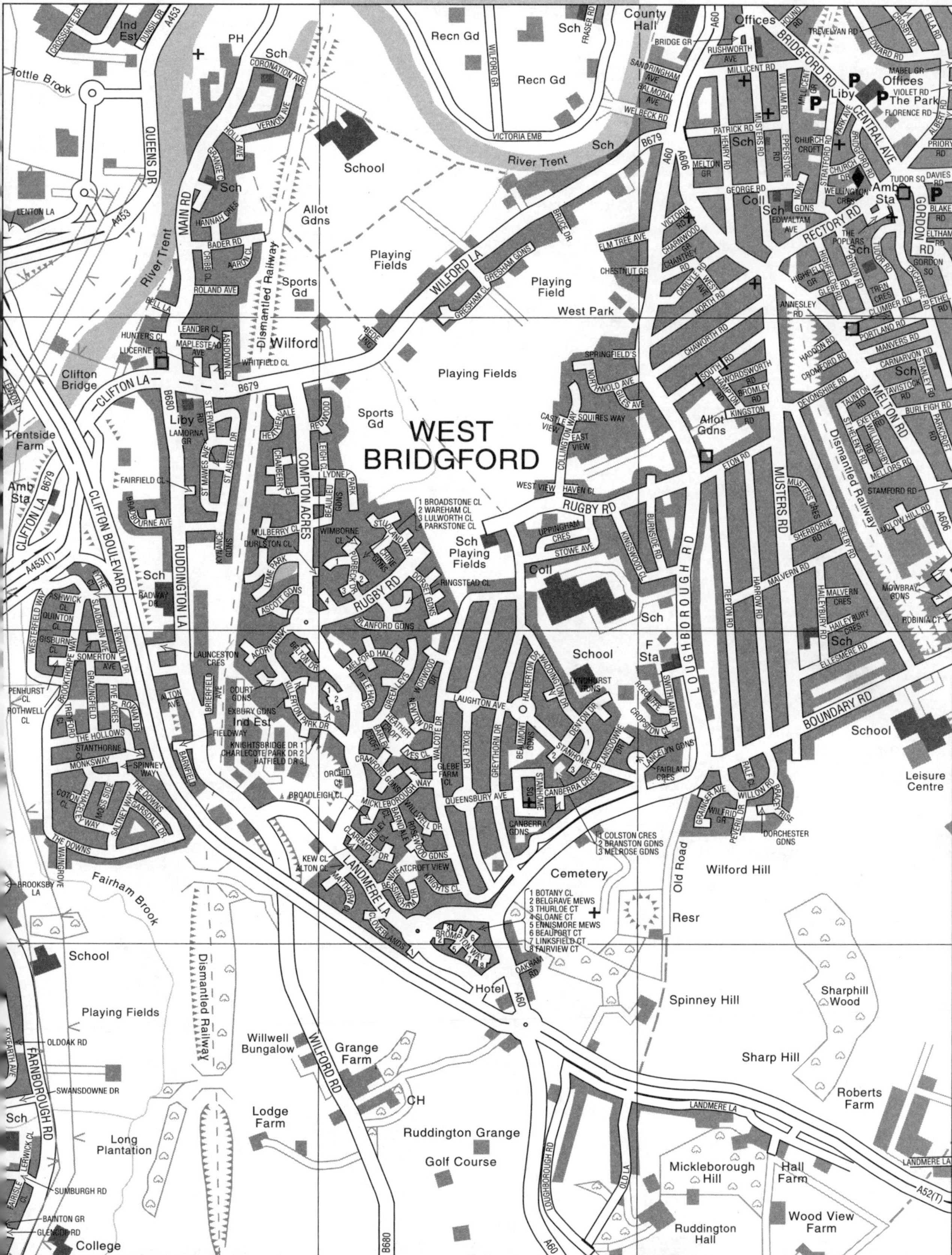


4
37
3
36
2
35
1
34

D 57 E 58 F

185
174

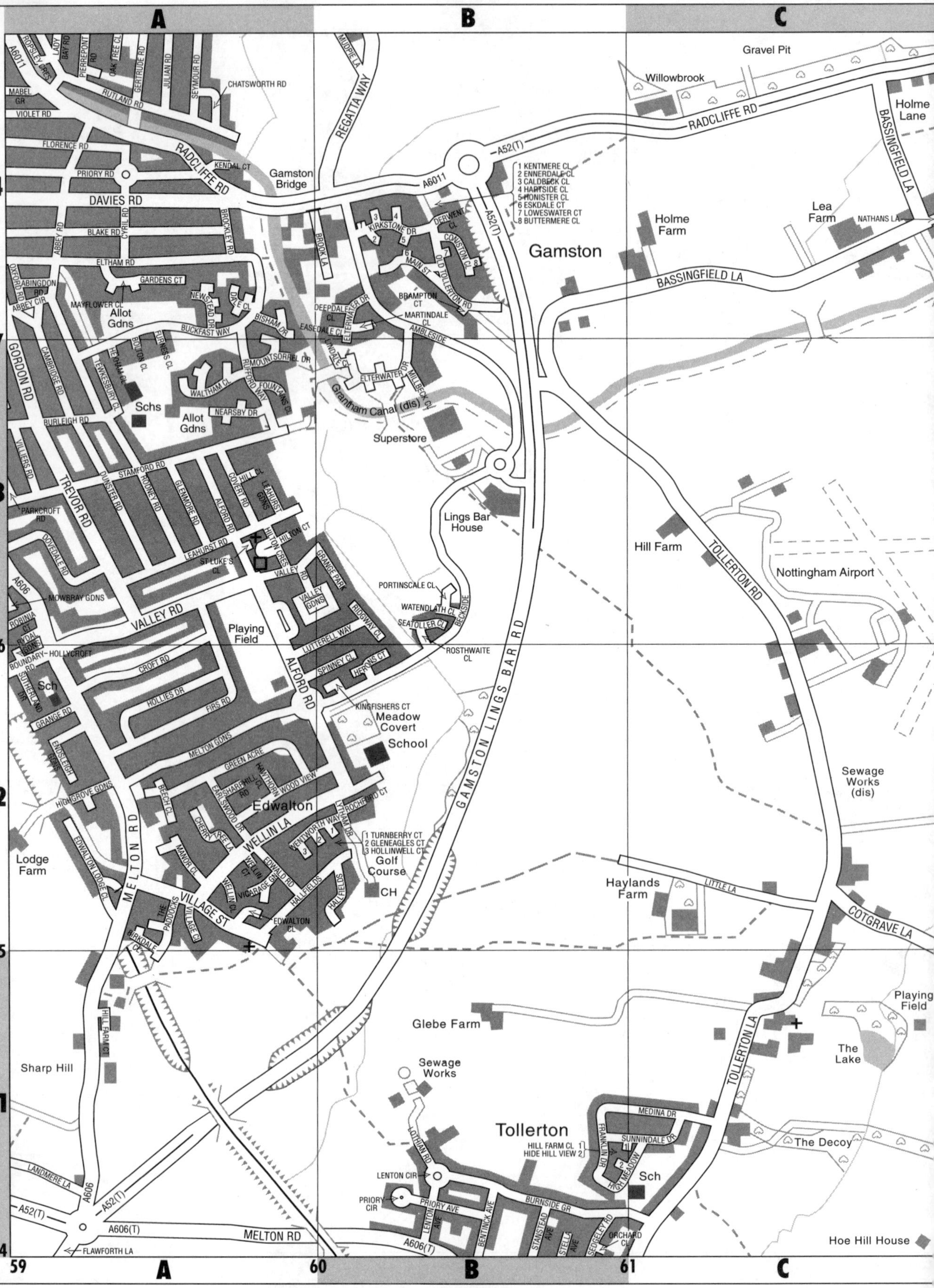


185
197

D
E
F
Sch
RADCLIFFE RD
A52(T)
Caravan Site
Sewage Works
Thornton's Holt Farm
Shepherd's (PH)
North Farm
Polser Brook
Bassingfield
Nursery
Cotgrave Place
Slag Heap
Cotgrave Bridge
Grantham Canal (dis)
Cotgrave Colliery
Slag Heap
Thurlbeck Dyke
Peashill Farm
Windmill Hill
MAIN RD
MILL LA
CHICHESTER DR
MORKINSHIRE CRES
MORKINSHIRE LA
BINGHAM RD
THE PARK
PINFOLD CL
HOLLYGATE LA
EAST ACRES
THURMAN DR
Sewage Works
CHURCH LA
THE CROSS
Sch
BINGHAM RD
LAWRENCE CL
COLSTON GATE
MILLER HIVES CL
CANDLEBY CT
CHAPEL LA
SCOTLAND BANK
RIVERMEAD
HALLS CL
PLUMTREE RD
SCRIMSHIRE LA
CHERRY ORCH
RISEGATE
RISEGATE GDNS
THE PRECINCT
RECTORY LA
WOODGATE LA
WOODGATE CL
BAKER'S HOLLOW
CANDLEBY LA
AVONDALE
CANDLEBY CL
1 LANGLANDS
MENSING AVE
GREEN PLATT
BROAD MEER
FOREST CL
Schs
GREENFIELDS DR
PLUMTREE RD
WHITE FURROWS
DAISY CL
FERN LEA AVE
HAWTHORN AVE
WOODLAND CL
ASH LEA CL
CARTBRIDGE
COTGRAVE LA
BARN CL
MANNS LEYS
CORN CL
SPINNEY CL
OWTHORPE RD
RING LEAS
MANORWOOD RD
TOFT CL
MILLERS BRIDGE 1
INGLEBY CL 2
BONNY MEAD
THE DIAL
DALESIDE
FOX HILL
WESTWAY
THE WARREN
RUNCIE CL
GRIPPS COMM
WOULDS FIELD
KINGSTON DR
SAXON WAY
WARWICK GDNS
COTGRAVE RD
Brickyard Plantation
Tollerton Wood
Mill Lane
Scotton's Hill
Manor Farm
GILLIVER LA
Clipston
Blackberry Farm
Wolds Lane
CHURCH GATE
Hoehill Farm
4
37
3
36
2
35
1
34
63
64
D
E
F

187
176

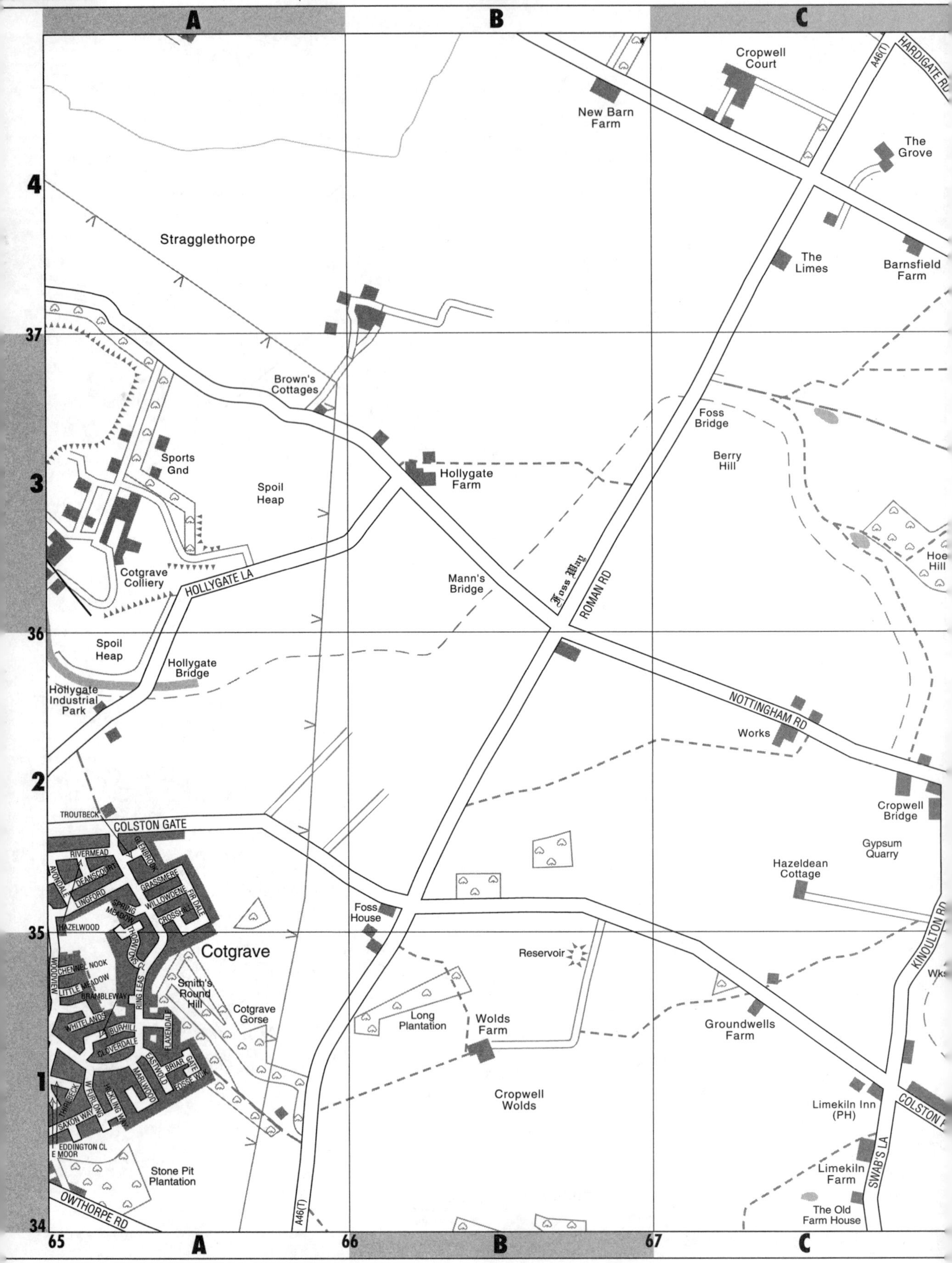


187
199

177 190

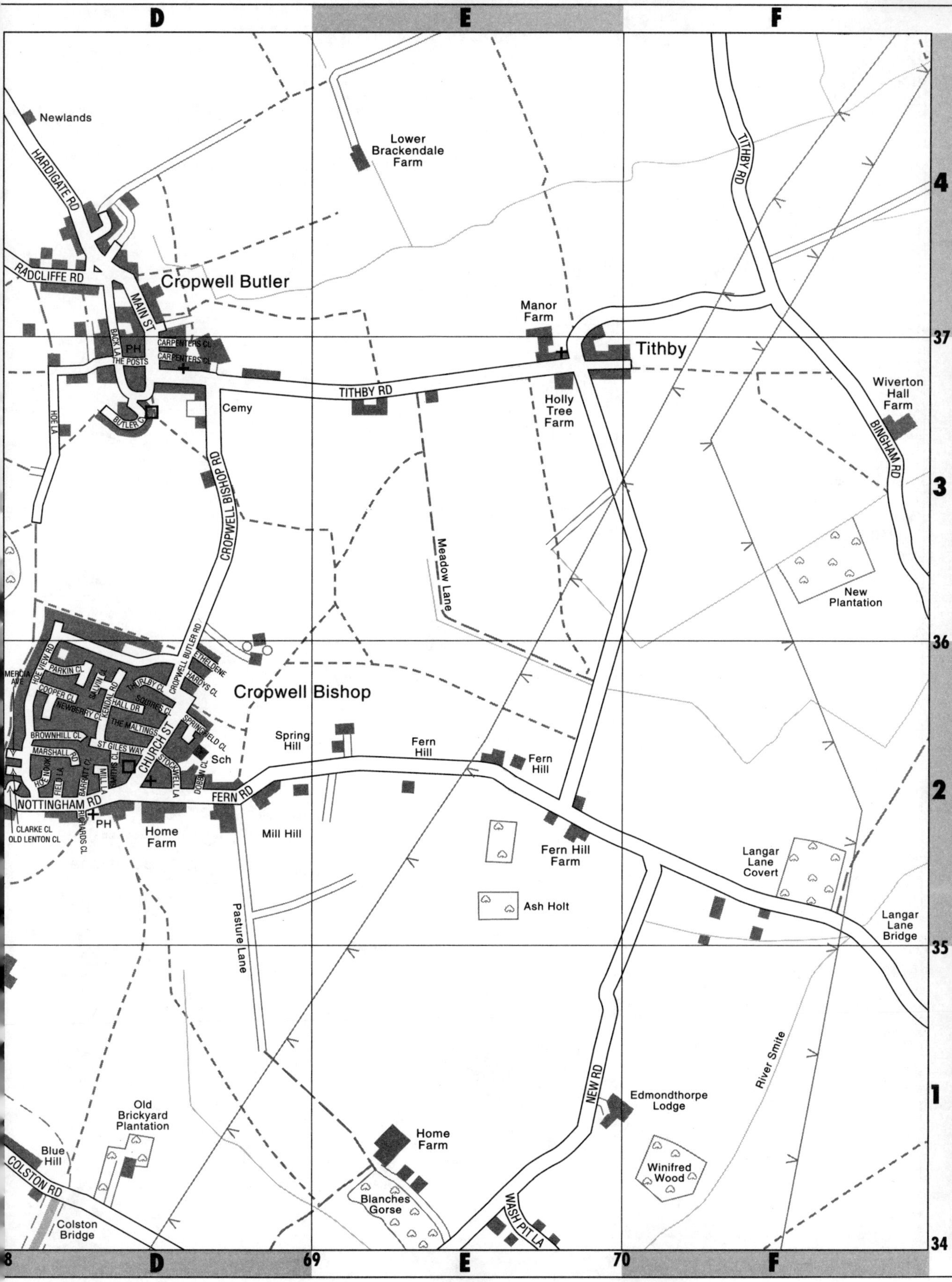


200 190

189
178

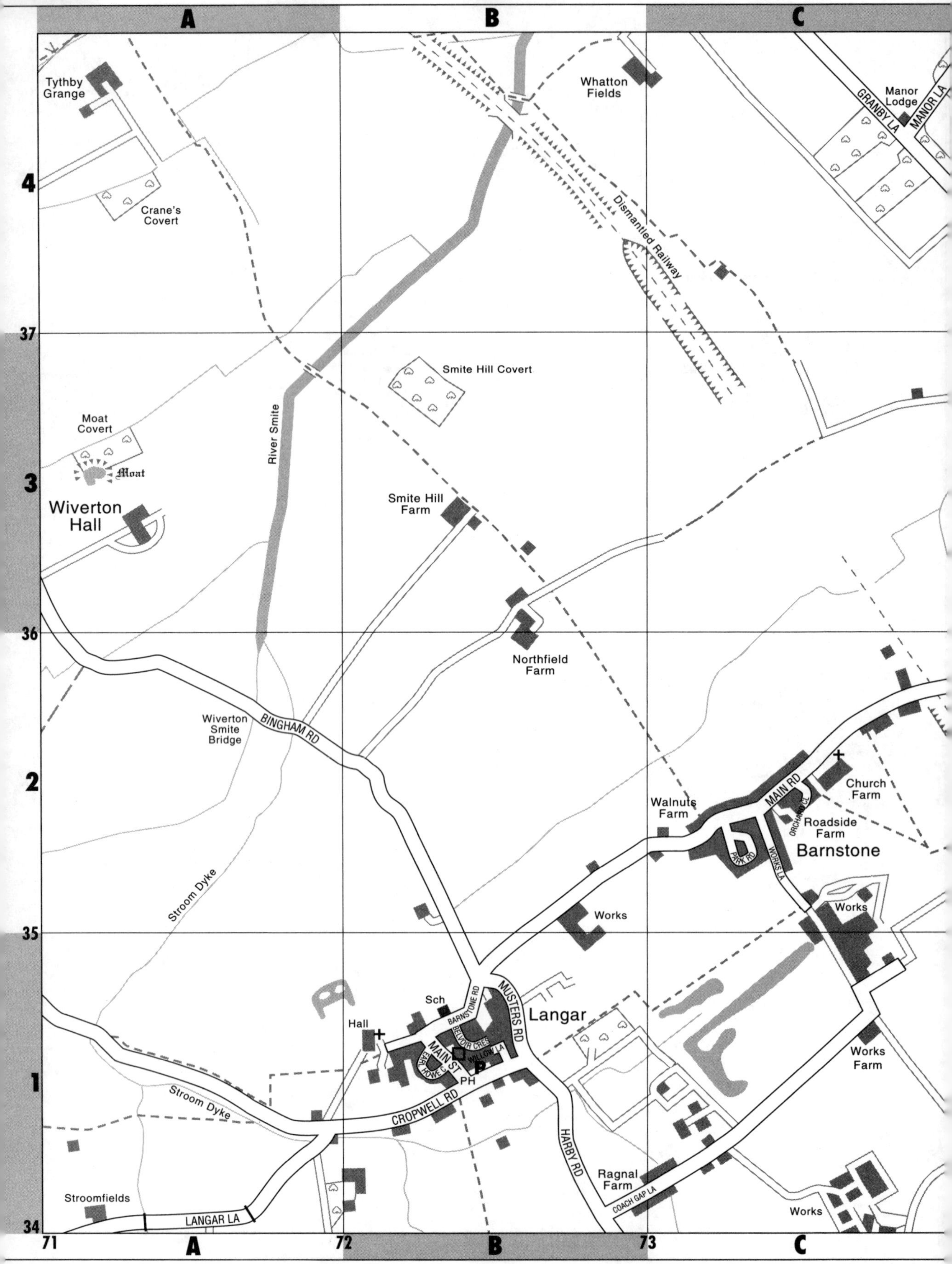


189
201

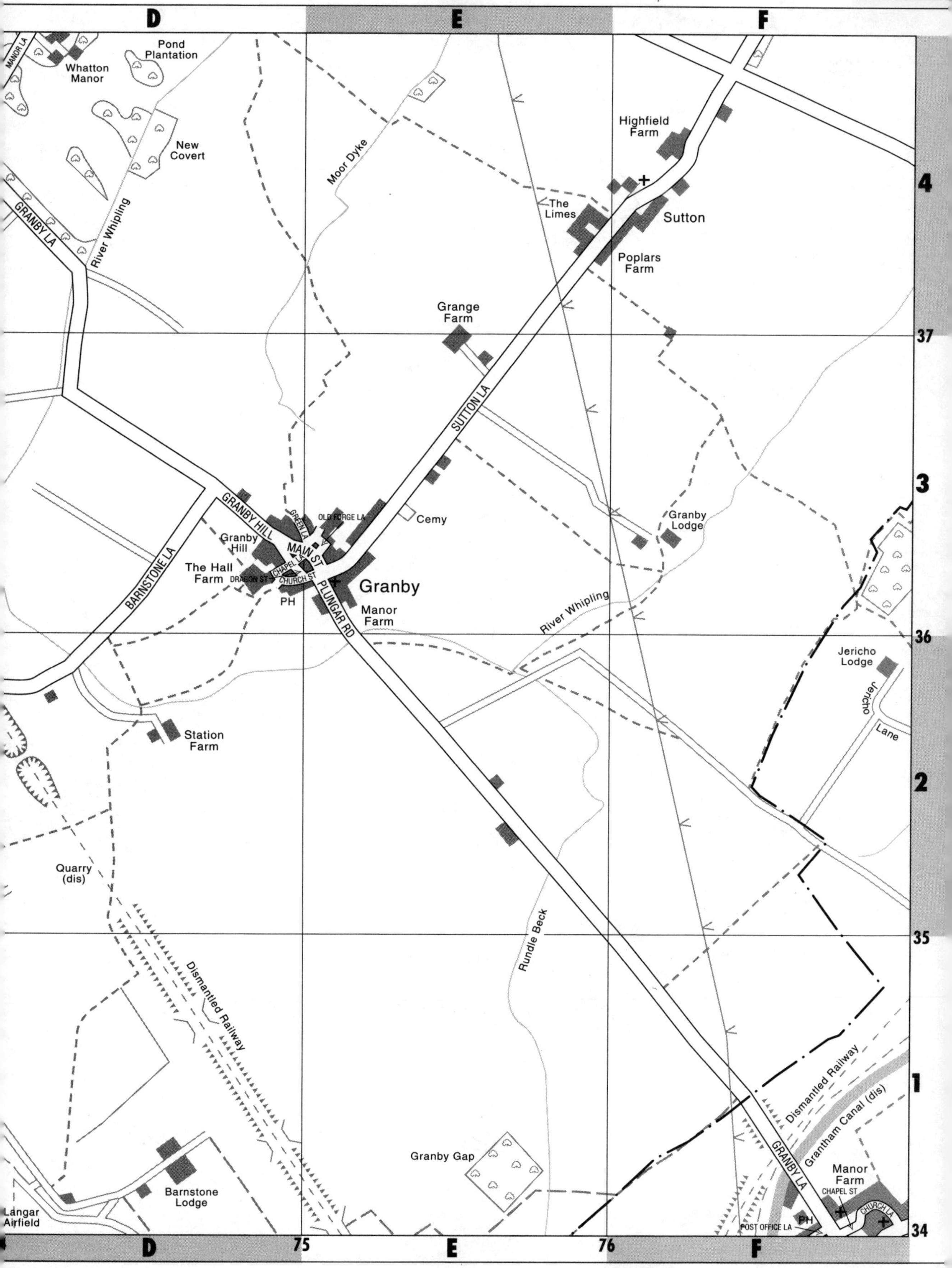
D
E
F
Pond Plantation
Whatton Manor
MANOR LA
New Covert
GRANBY LA
River Whipling
Moor Dyke
Highfield Farm
The Limes
Sutton
Poplars Farm
Grange Farm
SUTTON LA
GRANBY HILL
GREEN LA
OLD FORGE LA
MAIN ST
Cemy
Granby Lodge
Granby Hill
The Hall Farm
DRAGON ST
CHAPEL LA
CHURCH ST
PH
Granby
PLUNGAR RD
Manor Farm
BARNSTONE LA
River Whipling
Jericho Lodge
Jericho Lane
Station Farm
Quarry (dis)
Rundle Beck
Dismantled Railway
Granby Gap
Barnstone Lodge
Langar Airfield
Dismantled Railway
Grantham Canal (dis)
GRANBY LA
Manor Farm
CHAPEL ST
CHURCH LA
PH
POST OFFICE LA
4
37
3
36
2
35
1
34
75
76

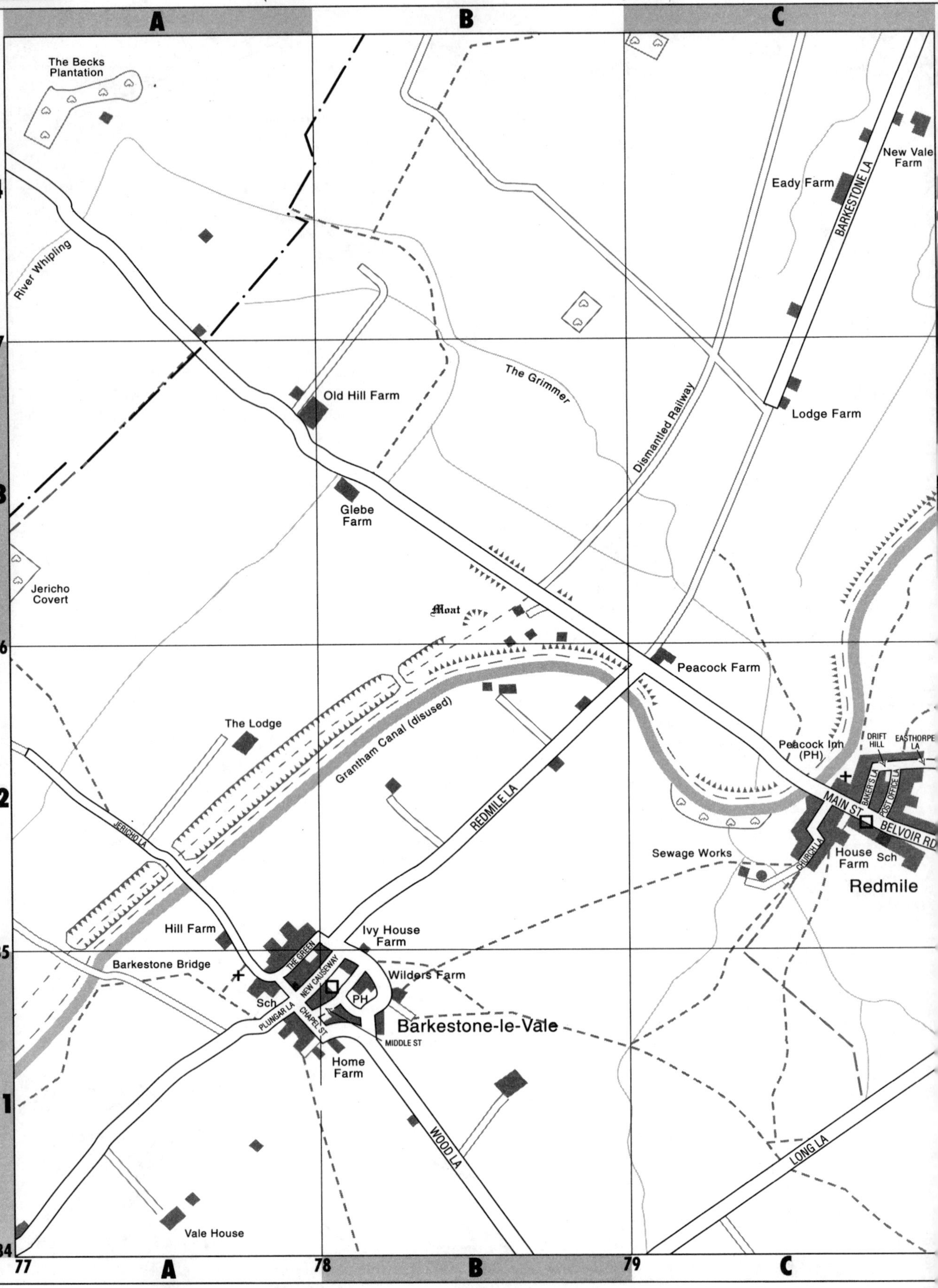
A
B
C
4
37
3
36
2
35
1
34
77
78
79
The Becks Plantation
River Whipling
Jericho Covert
Old Hill Farm
Glebe Farm
The Grimmer
Dismantled Railway
Eady Farm
New Vale Farm
BARKESTONE LA
Lodge Farm
Moat
Peacock Farm
The Lodge
Grantham Canal (disused)
REDMILE LA
Peacock Inn (PH)
DRIFT HILL
EASTHORPE LA
BAKER'S LA
POST OFFICE LA
MAIN ST
BELVOIR RD
CHURCH LA
House Farm
Sch
Sewage Works
Redmile
JERICHO LA
Hill Farm
Ivy House Farm
Barkestone Bridge
THE GREEN
NEW CAUSEWAY
Wilders Farm
Sch
PH
PLUNGAR LA
CHAPEL ST
Barkestone-le-Vale
MIDDLE ST
Home Farm
WOOD LA
LONG LA
Vale House

182
194

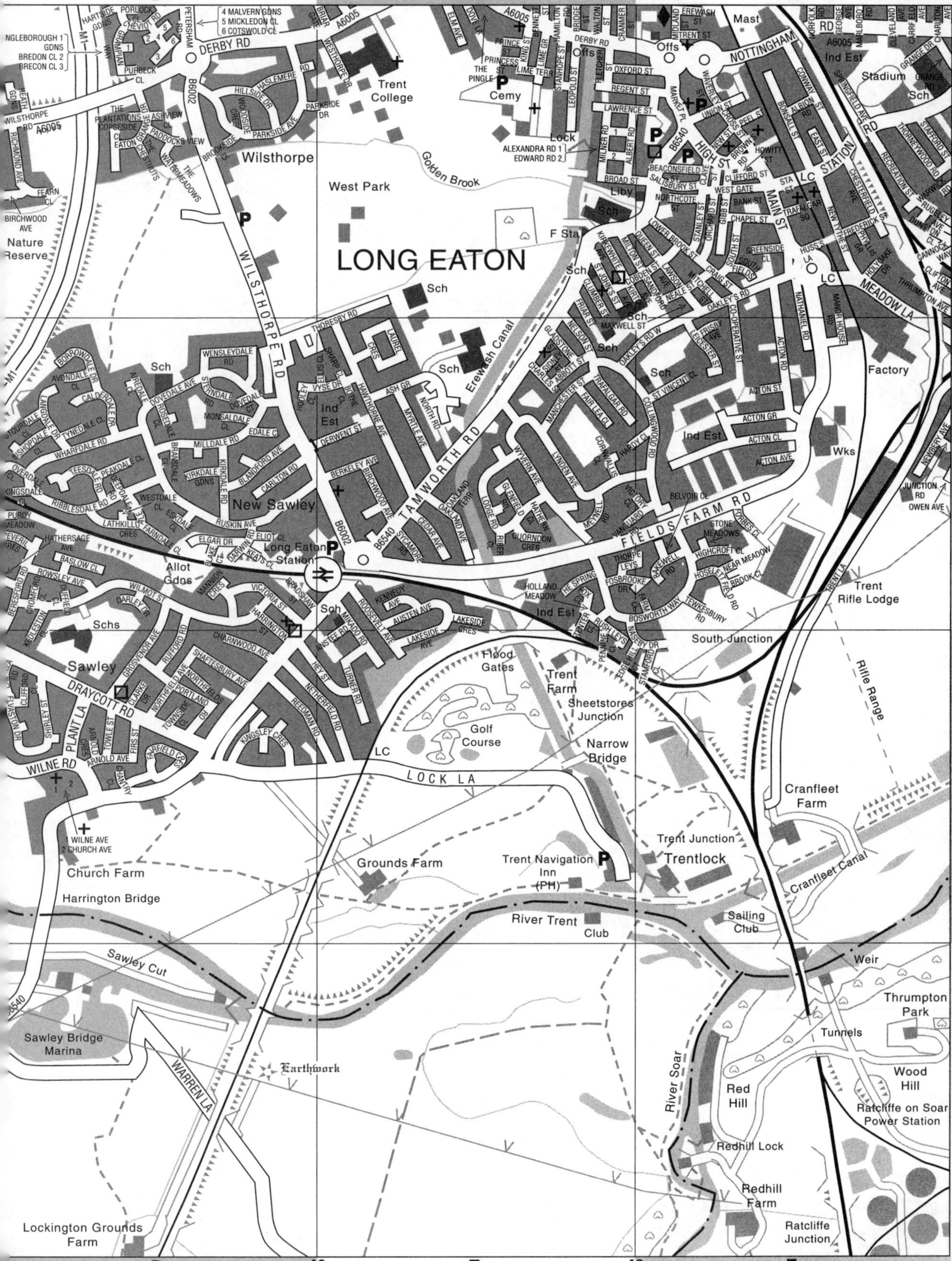


203
194

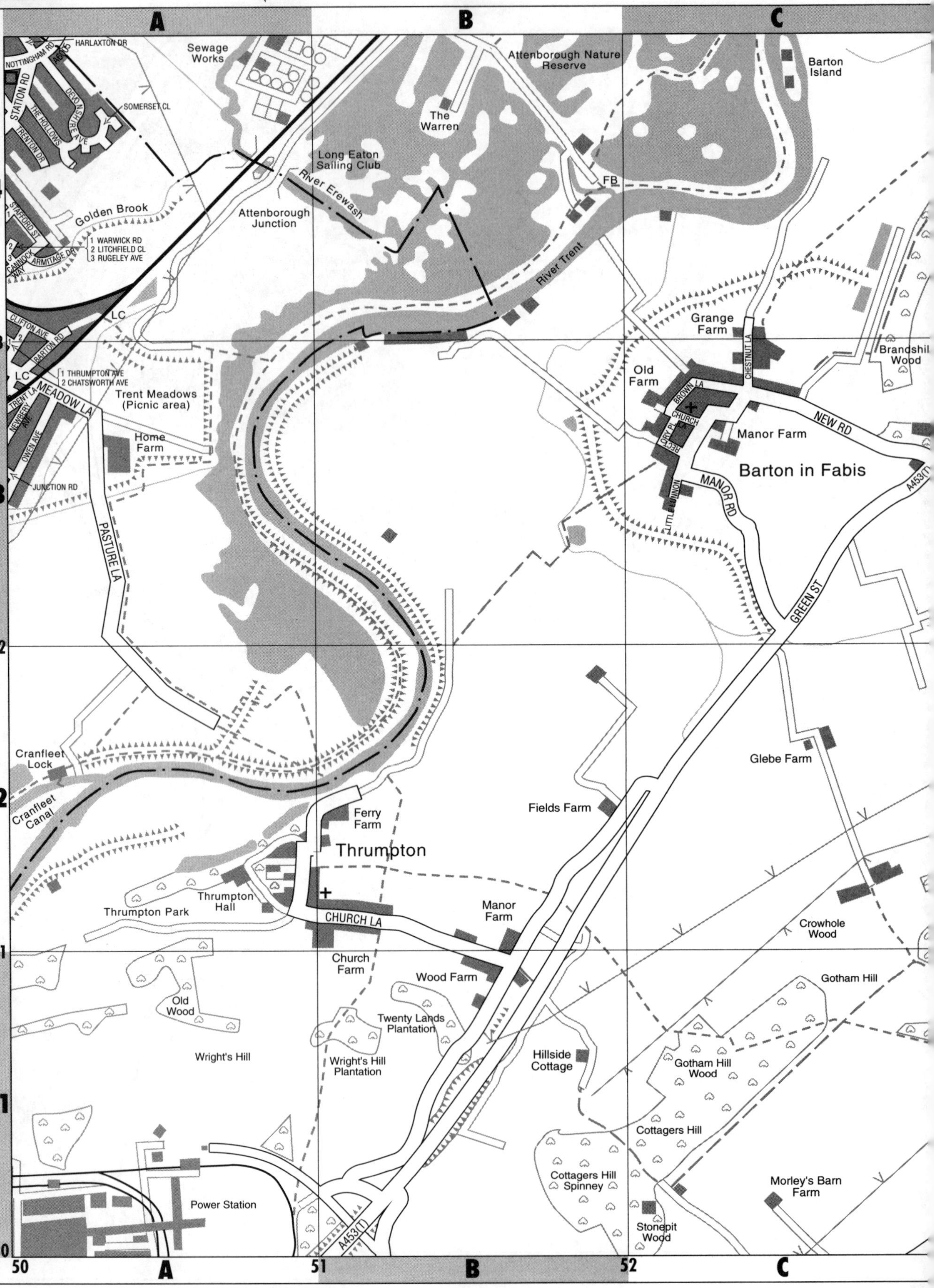
A
B
C
Sewage Works
Attenborough Nature Reserve
Barton Island
HARLAXTON DR
NOTTINGHAM RD
STATION RD
THE HOLLOWS
DEVONSHIRE AVE
SOMERSET CL
TRENTON DR
The Warren
Long Eaton Sailing Club
River Erewash
FB
Attenborough Junction
Golden Brook
STAFFORD ST
1 WARWICK RD
2 LITCHFIELD CL
3 RUGELEY AVE
CANNOCK WAY
ARMITAGE DR
River Trent
LC
CLIFTON AVE
BARTON RD
Grange Farm
CHESTNUT LA
Brandshill Wood
1 THRUMPTON AVE
2 CHATSWORTH AVE
MEADOW LA
TRENT LA
Trent Meadows
(Picnic area)
Old Farm
BROWN LA
CHURCH LA
NEW RD
Manor Farm
NEWBERY AVE
OWEN AVE
Home Farm
Barton in Fabis
JUNCTION RD
MANOR RD
LITTLE LUNNON
A453(T)
PASTURE LA
GREEN ST
Cranfleet Lock
Glebe Farm
Cranfleet Canal
Ferry Farm
Fields Farm
Thrumpton
Thrumpton Hall
Thrumpton Park
CHURCH LA
Manor Farm
Crowhole Wood
Church Farm
Wood Farm
Gotham Hill
Old Wood
Twenty Lands Plantation
Wright's Hill
Wright's Hill Plantation
Hillside Cottage
Gotham Hill Wood
Cottagers Hill
Cottagers Hill Spinney
Morley's Barn Farm
Power Station
Stonepit Wood
A453(T)
4
33
3
32
2
31
1
30
50
51
52

184
196

D E F

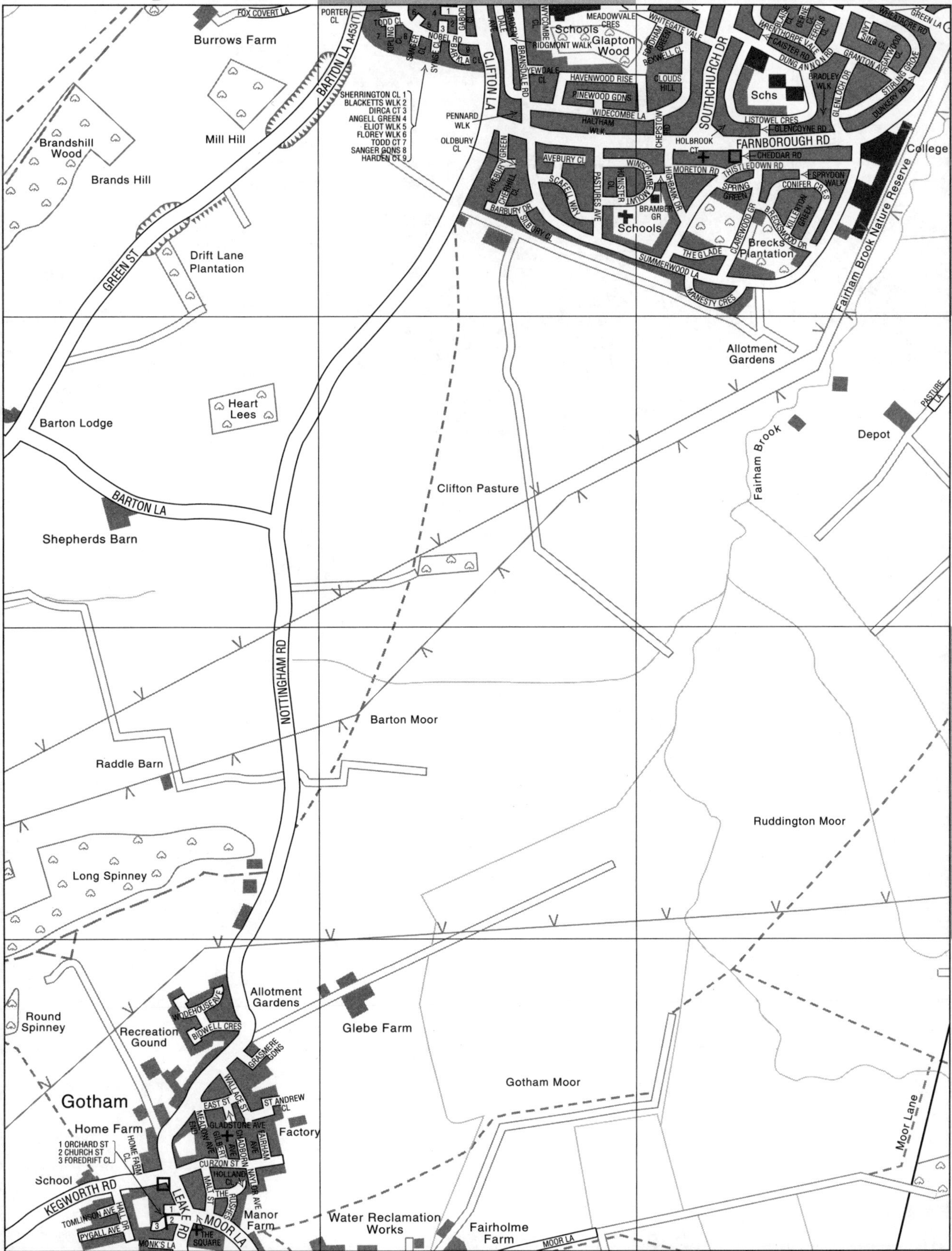


D E F

205
196

195
185

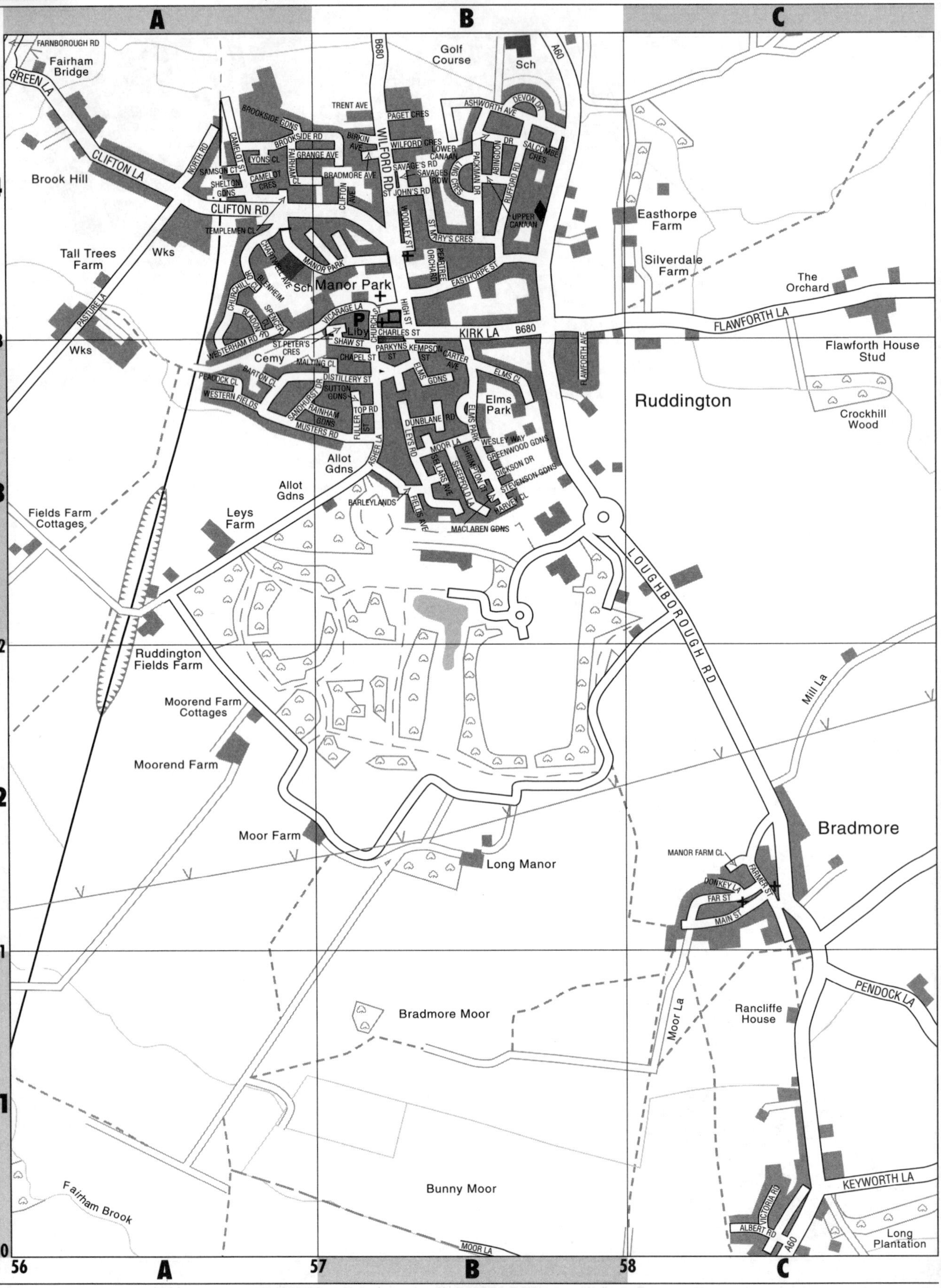


195
206

D
E
F
FLAWFORTH LA
Shire Farm
Barn Farm
Flawford House
Blackcliffe Hill
BRADMORE LA
BENTINCK AVE
A606(T)
STANSTEAD AV
STELLA GR
STELLA AVE
SEDGELEY R
MUIR AVE
TOLLERTON LA
MELTON RD
MAIN RD
COTGRAVE RD
CLIPSTON LA
THE LEYS
Hall Farm
CHURCH LA
OLD MELTON RD
FELLOWS YD
BRADLEYS YD
PH
Plumtree
The Poplars
Chestnut Farm
STATION RD
Plumtree Park
PARK RD
PARK AVE
GREEN CL
POPLARS CL
PARKSIDE
PLATT LA
NICKER HILL
Sch
HILLCREST RD
BEAUMONT CL
BELVEDERE CL
BROCKDALE GDNS
BRIAR CL
ROSE GR
VILLA RD
NORMANTON LA
LOWLANDS DR
COVERT CL
RANCLIFFE AVE
DELVILLE AVE
HIGHBURY RD
HIGHFIELD RD
ABBOT CL
CROSSDALE DR
FRANKLYN GDNS
CLIFFORD CL
ADAMS HILL
BISHOPS CL
SIDMOUTH CL
DEBDALE LA
WYNBRECK DR
LYNCOMBE GDNS
WOLDS RISE
SPINNEY RD
GORSE RD
HAYES RD
PLANTATION RD
THELDA AVE
DALE RD
NOTTINGHAM RD
ASHLEY CRES
ASHLEY RD
WALTON DR
CRANTOCK GDNS
RANNOCK GDNS
CHERRY HILL
MOUNT PLEASANT
HIGH VIEW AVE
WOLDS DR
Cotton's Plantation
INTAKE RD
FAIRHAM RD
CROFT RD
MANOR RD
ROSE HILL
CHURCH DR
Sch
Liby
FAIRWAY
PARK AVE W
PARK AVE E
PARK AVE
CHARNWOOD AVE
WEST CL
EAST CL
ELM AVE
ELM CL
WINDMILL CT
BEECH AVE
LAUREL AVE
LIMETREE AVE
ASH GR
Greenhays Farm
Woodfields
Rancliffe Wood
BUNNY LA
ROSELAND CL
HAWTHORN CL
COMMERCIAL RD
THE SQUARE
PH
SELBY LA
Keyworth
Hillside Farm
WRIGHTS ORCHARD
HOLMSFIELD
FAR PASTURE CL
BROOK VIEW DR
BROOK VIEW CT
MAIN ST
CEDAR DR
BARROW SLADE
PH
Holly Farm
PENDOCK LA
KEYWORTH LA
Wheatcroft Farm
Sewage Works
WYSALL RD
Long Plantation
Bunny Park
LINGS LA
New Holme Farm
Lings Lane Farm
4
33
3
32
2
31
1
30
59
60
61

197
187

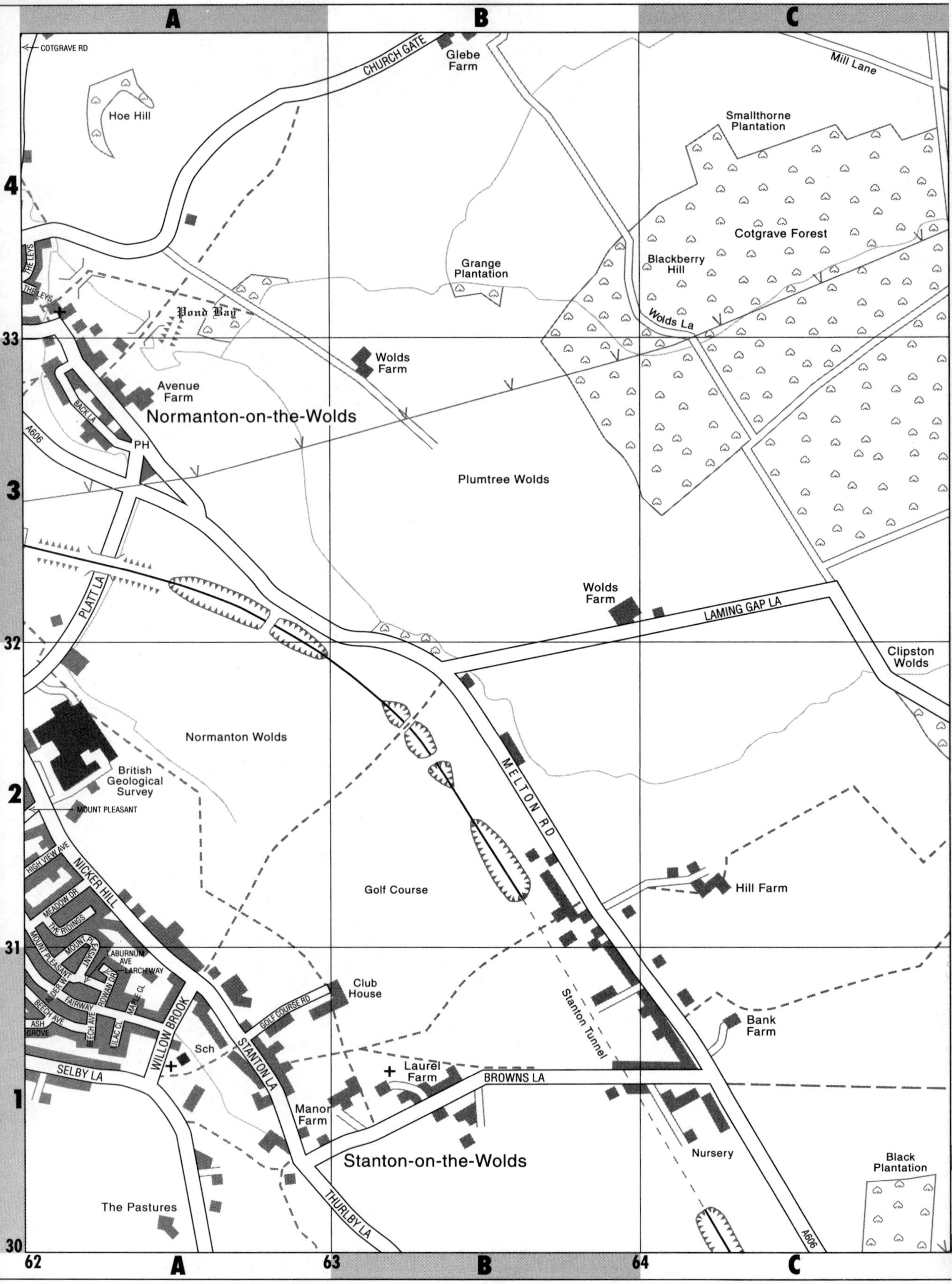


197
208

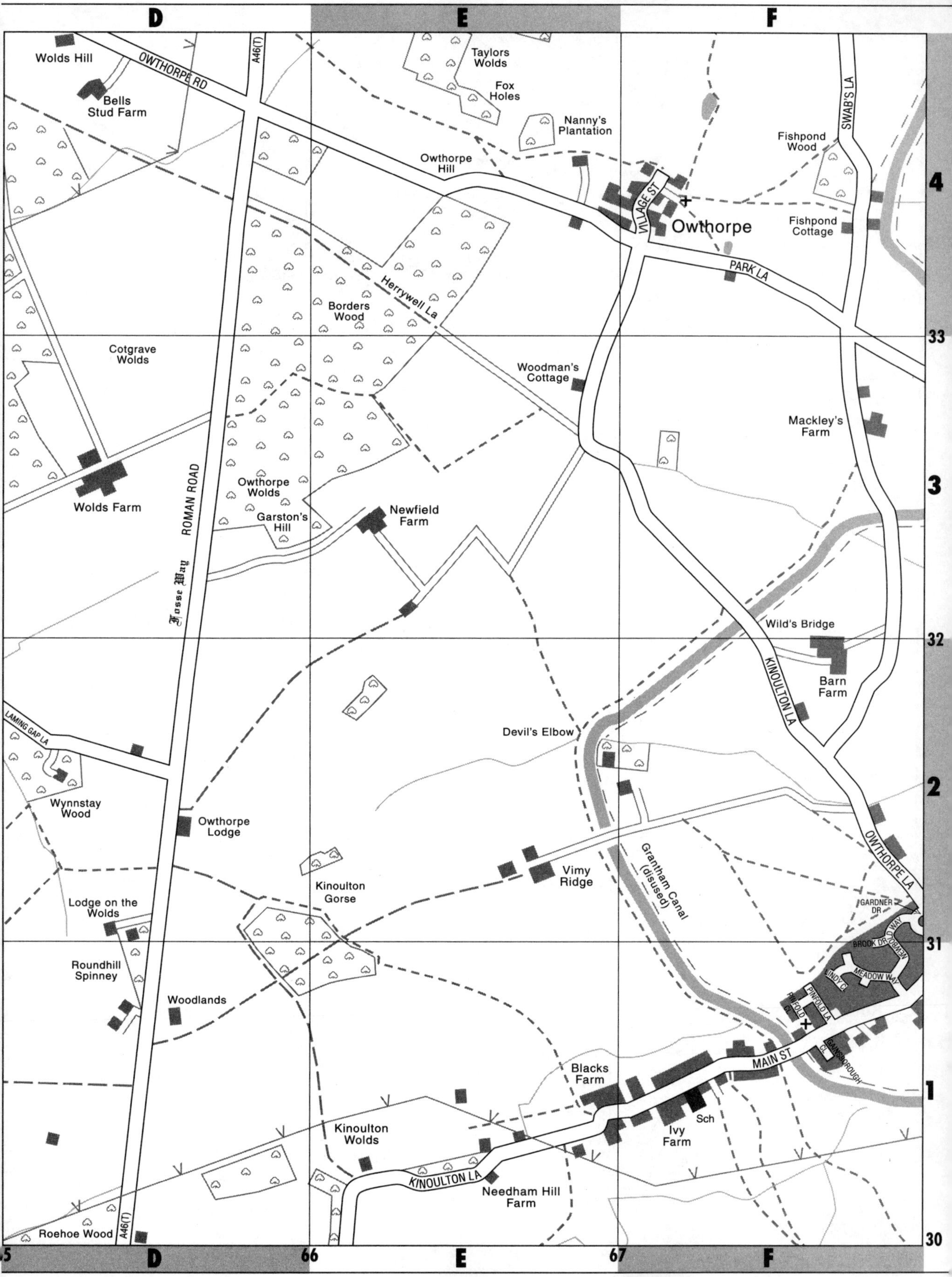
D
E
F
Wolds Hill
OWTHORPE RD
A46(T)
Bells
Stud Farm
Taylors
Wolds
Fox
Holes
Nanny's
Plantation
SWAB'S LA
Fishpond
Wood
Owthorpe
Hill
VILLAGE ST
Owthorpe
Fishpond
Cottage
PARK LA
Herrywell La
Borders
Wood
Cotgrave
Wolds
Woodman's
Cottage
Mackley's
Farm
Wolds Farm
ROMAN ROAD
Owthorpe
Wolds
Garston's
Hill
Newfield
Farm
Fosse Way
Wild's Bridge
KINOULTON LA
Barn
Farm
LAMING GAP LA
Devil's Elbow
Wynnstay
Wood
Owthorpe
Lodge
Grantham Canal
(disused)
OWTHORPE LA
Vimy
Ridge
Kinoulton
Gorse
Lodge on the
Wolds
GARDNER
DR
BROOK DR
MEADOW WAY
PINFOLD LA
PINFOLD CL
Roundhill
Spinney
Woodlands
MAIN ST
GAINSBOROUGH CL
Blacks
Farm
Sch
Ivy
Farm
Kinoulton
Wolds
KINOULTON LA
Needham Hill
Farm
Roehoe Wood
A46(T)
4
33
3
32
2
31
1
30
65
66
67

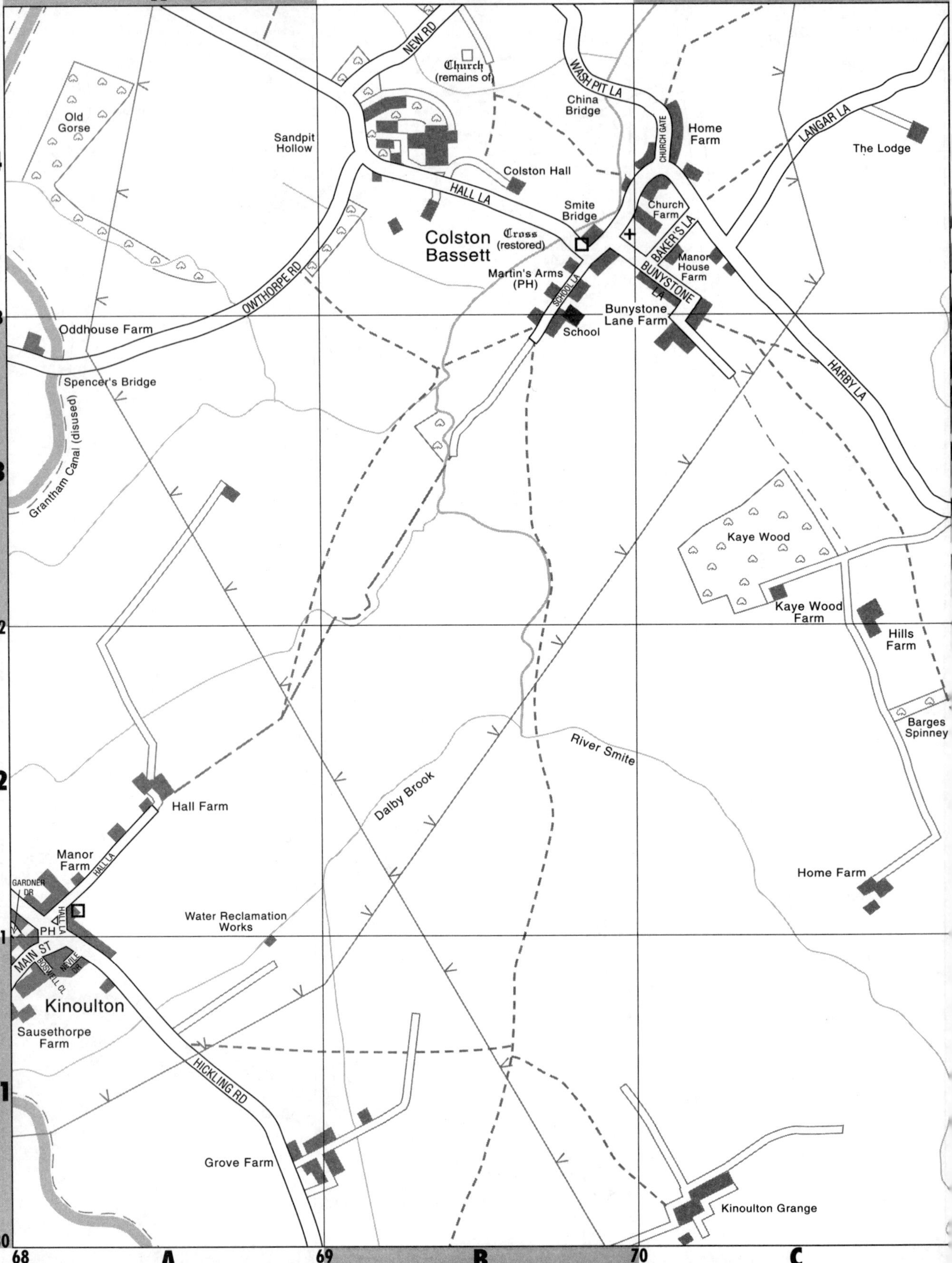
A
B
C
Old Gorse
Sandpit Hollow
NEW RD
Church (remains of)
WASH PIT LA
China Bridge
CHURCH GATE
Home Farm
LANGAR LA
The Lodge
4
Colston Hall
HALL LA
Smite Bridge
Church Farm
Colston Bassett
Cross (restored)
BAKER'S LA
Manor House Farm
Martin's Arms (PH)
SCHOOL LA
BUNYSTONE LA
OWTHORPE RD
33
Oddhouse Farm
Bunystone Lane Farm
School
Spencer's Bridge
HARBY LA
Grantham Canal (disused)
3
Kaye Wood
Kaye Wood Farm
Hills Farm
32
Barges Spinney
River Smite
2
Hall Farm
Dalby Brook
Manor Farm
HALL LA
GARDNER DR
Home Farm
Water Reclamation Works
PH
31
MAIN ST
BOSWELL CL
NEVILE DR
Kinoulton
Sausethorpe Farm
HICKLING RD
1
Grove Farm
Kinoulton Grange
30
68
69
70

190
202

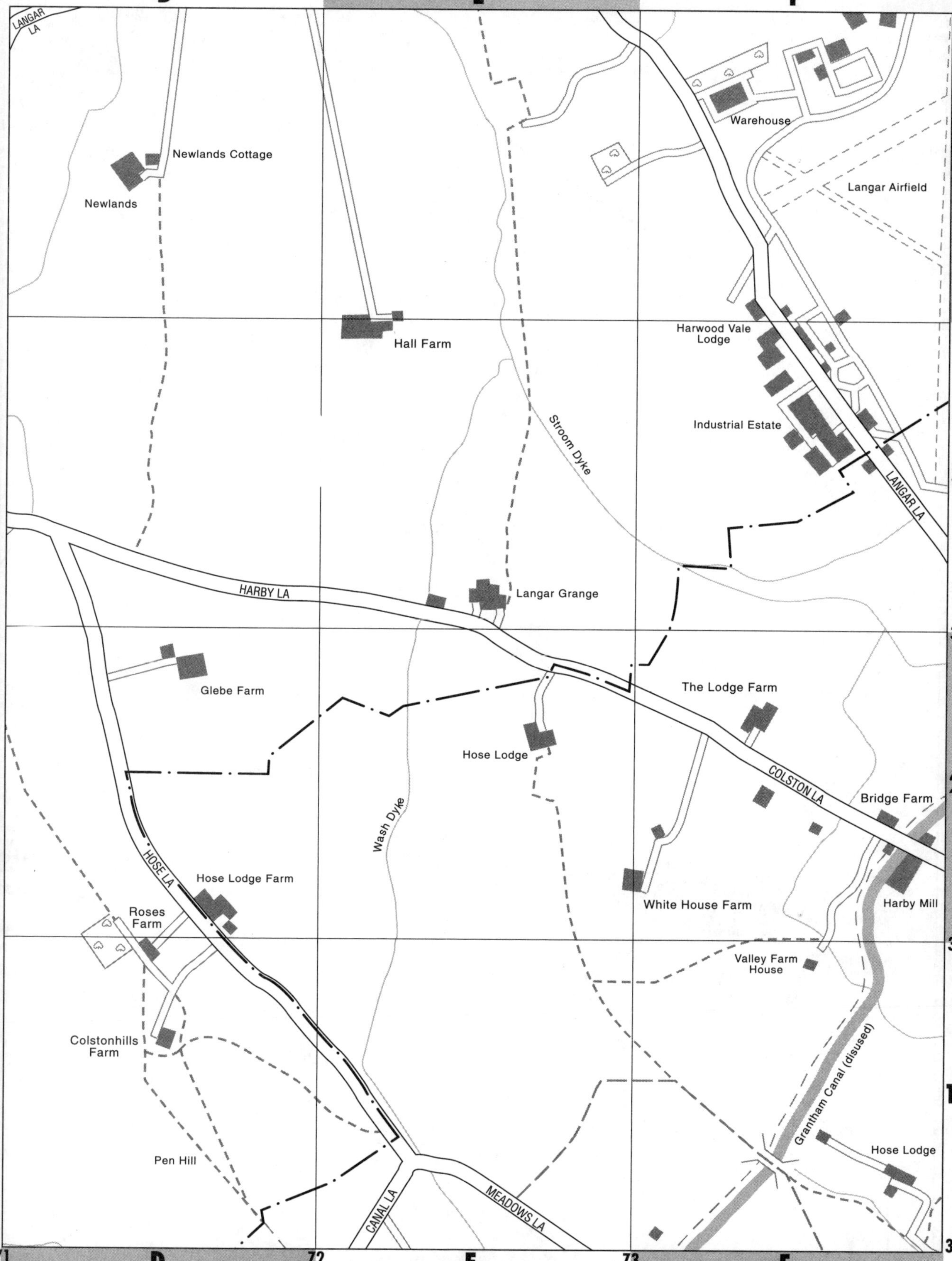


211
202

201
191

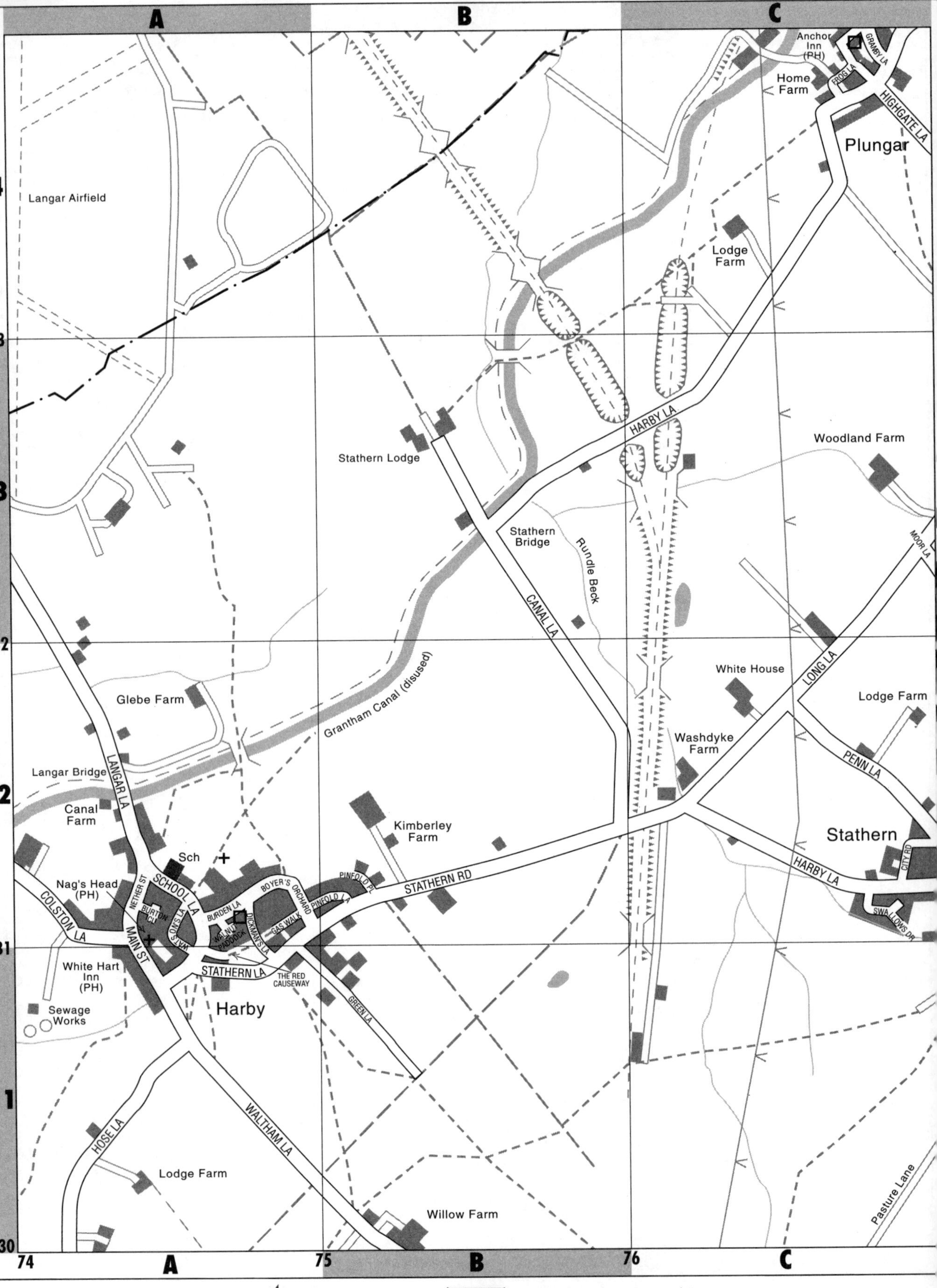
A
B
C
4
33
3
32
2
31
1
30
74
75
76
Langar Airfield
Anchor Inn (PH)
GRANBY LA
FROG LA
HIGHGATE LA
Home Farm
Plungar
Lodge Farm
HARBY LA
Woodland Farm
Stathern Lodge
Stathern Bridge
Rundle Beck
CANAL LA
MOOR LA
White House
LONG LA
Lodge Farm
Glebe Farm
Grantham Canal (disused)
Washdyke Farm
PENN LA
Langar Bridge
LANGAR LA
Canal Farm
Kimberley Farm
Stathern
Sch
Nag's Head (PH)
NETHER ST
SCHOOL LA
BOYER'S ORCHARD
PINFOLD PL
STATHERN RD
HARBY LA
CITY RD
COLSTON LA
BURTON CL
BURDEN LA
PINFOLD LA
SWALLOWS DR
MAIN ST
WALNUT PADDOCK
DICKMAN'S LA
GAS WALK
White Hart Inn (PH)
STATHERN LA
THE RED CAUSEWAY
GREEN LA
Sewage Works
Harby
HOSE LA
WALTHAM LA
Lodge Farm
Willow Farm
Pasture Lane

201

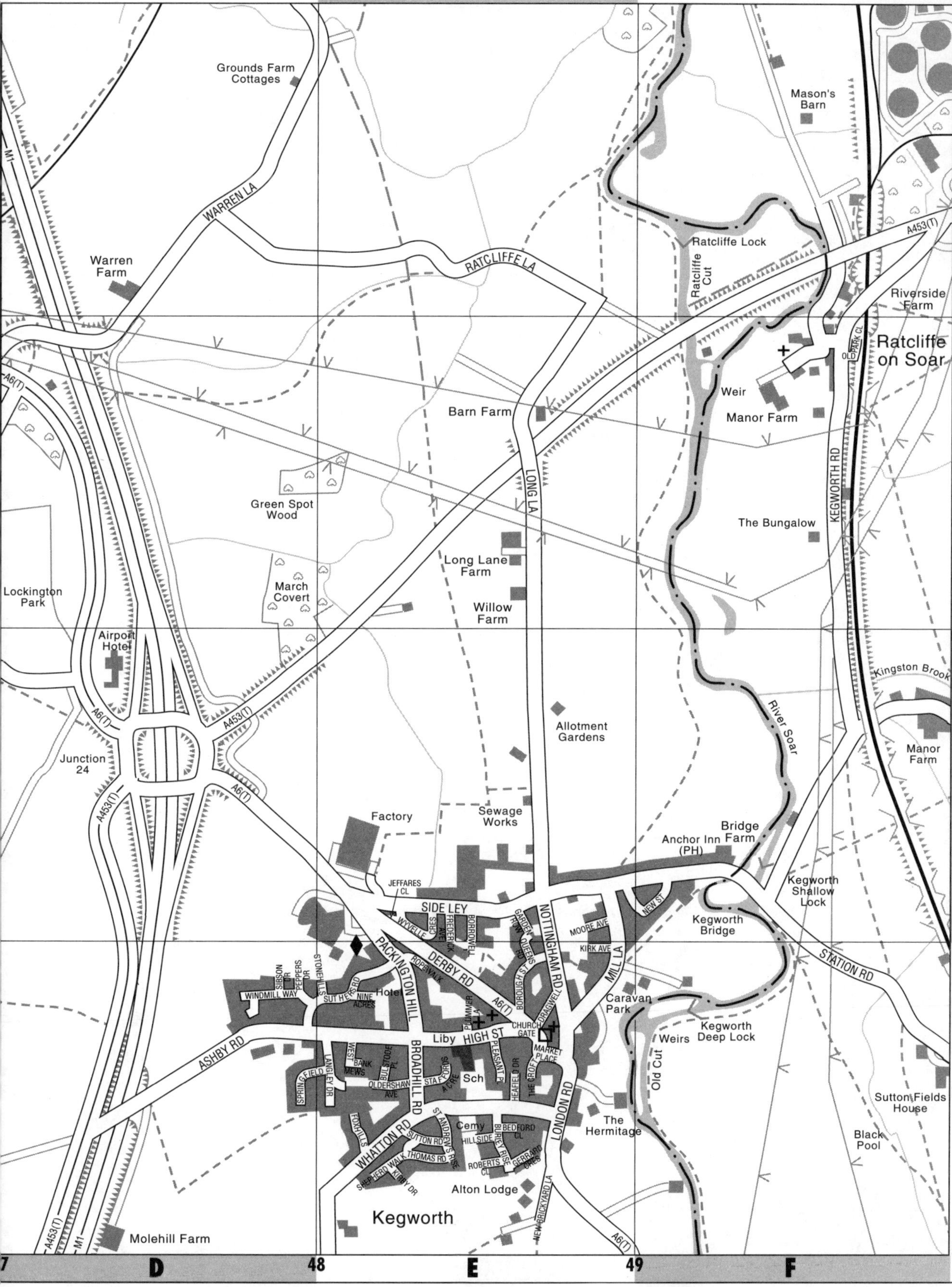
D
E
F
Grounds Farm Cottages
Mason's Barn
WARREN LA
Warren Farm
RATCLIFFE LA
Ratcliffe Lock
Ratcliffe Cut
Riverside Farm
Ratcliffe on Soar
Weir
Manor Farm
Barn Farm
LONG LA
KEGWORTH RD
Green Spot Wood
The Bungalow
Long Lane Farm
Lockington Park
March Covert
Willow Farm
Airport Hotel
Kingston Brook
River Soar
Allotment Gardens
Junction 24
Manor Farm
Factory
Sewage Works
Bridge Farm
Anchor Inn (PH)
Kegworth Shallow Lock
JEFFARES CL
SIDE LEY
NOTTINGHAM RD
Kegworth Bridge
PACKINGTON HILL
DERBY RD
MILL LA
STATION RD
WINDMILL WAY
Hotel
Caravan Park
HIGH ST
ASHBY RD
Liby
Weirs
Kegworth Deep Lock
Old Cut
BROADHILL RD
Sch
LONDON RD
Sutton Fields House
Cemy
The Hermitage
WHATTON RD
Black Pool
Alton Lodge
Kegworth
Molehill Farm
A453(T)
A6(T)
M1
4
3
2
1
29
28
27
26
48
49

203
194

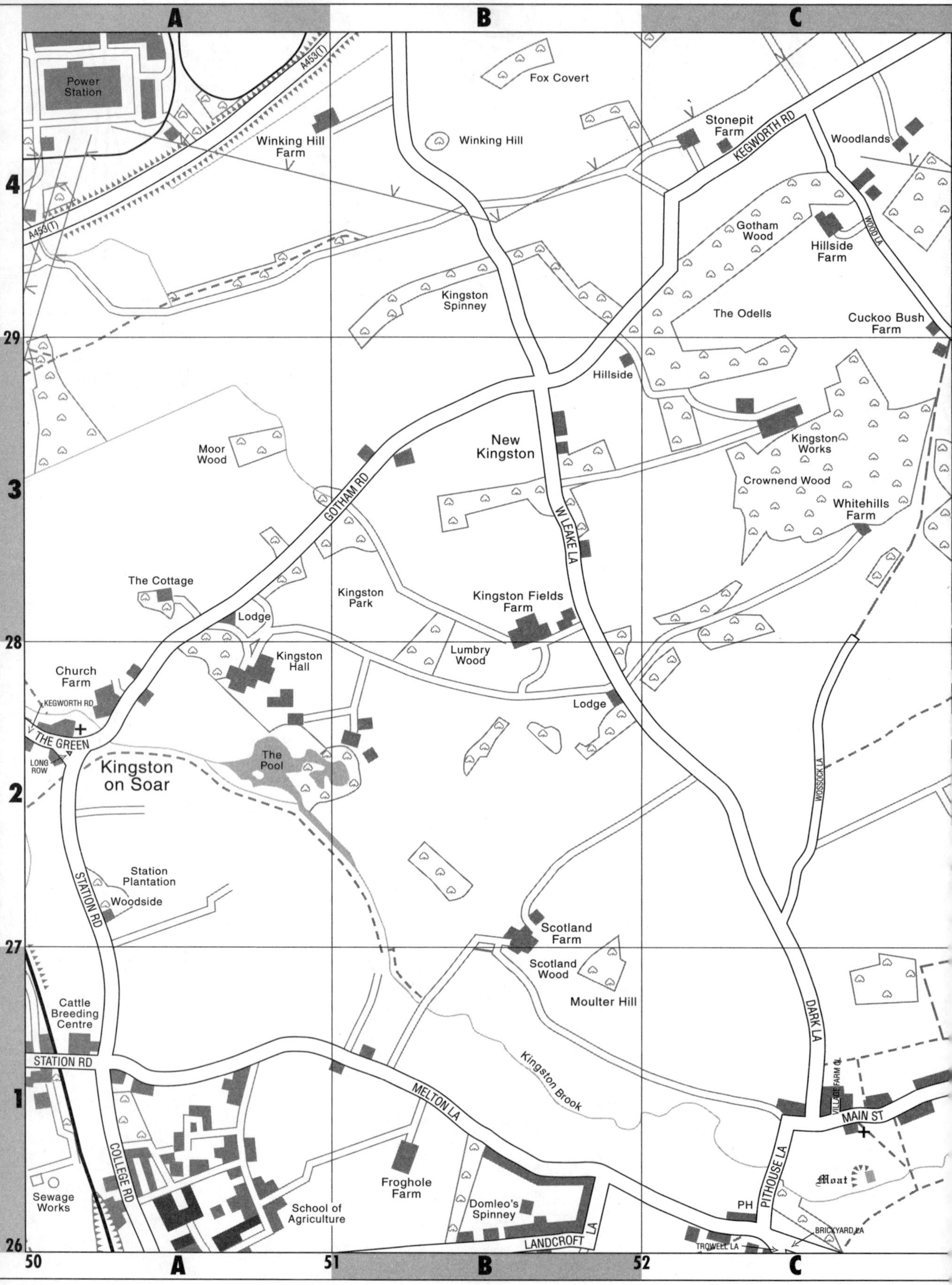


203
213

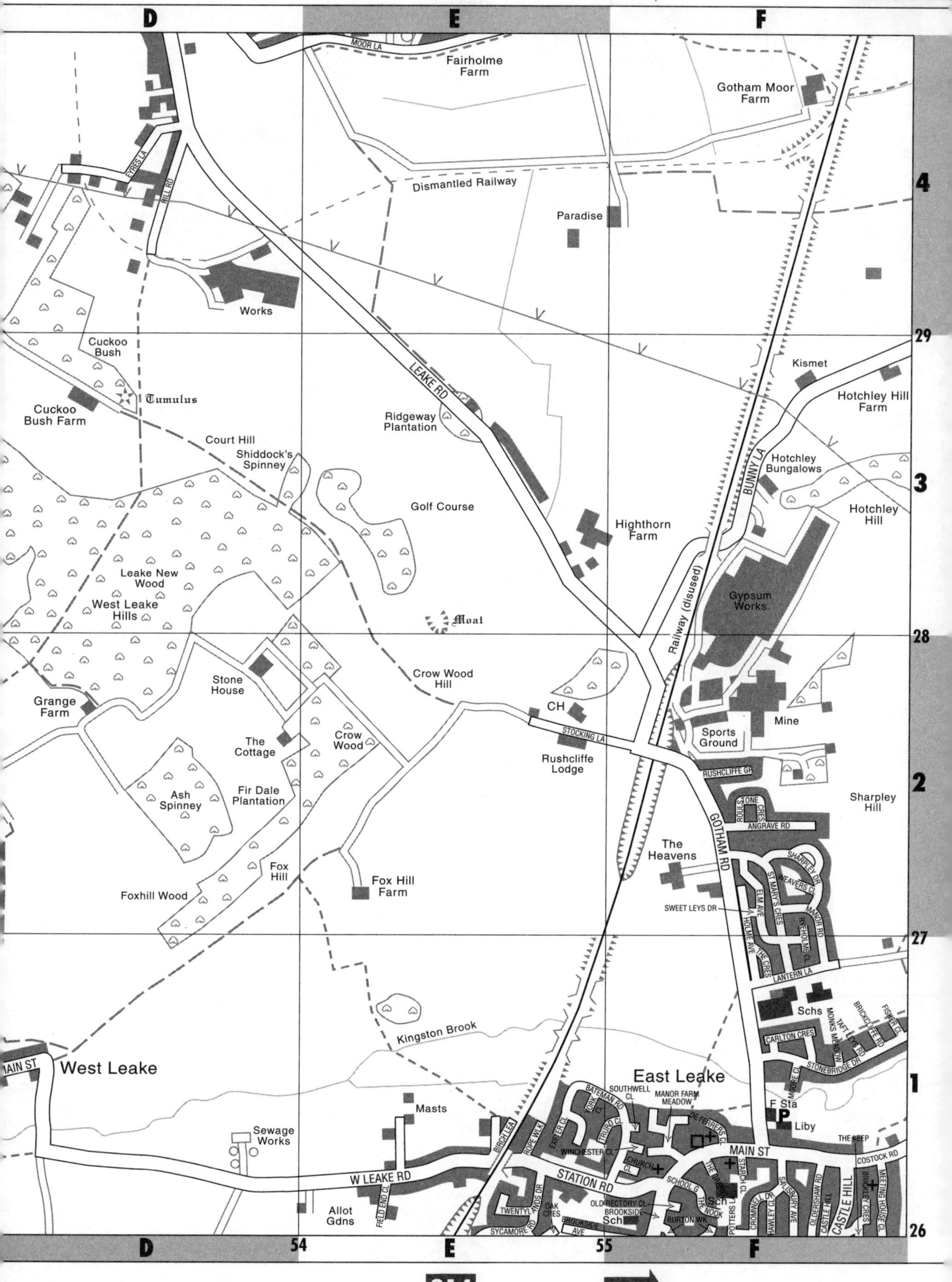
195
206
D
E
F
MOOR LA
Fairholme Farm
Gotham Moor Farm
EYRES LA
HILL RD
Dismantled Railway
Paradise
4
Works
Cuckoo Bush
29
Kismet
Hotchley Hill Farm
Cuckoo Bush Farm
Tumulus
LEAKE RD
Ridgeway Plantation
Court Hill
Shiddock's Spinney
BUNNY LA
Hotchley Bungalows
3
Hotchley Hill
Golf Course
Highthorn Farm
Leake New Wood
West Leake Hills
Railway (disused)
Gypsum Works
Moat
28
Crow Wood Hill
Stone House
Grange Farm
CH
Mine
The Cottage
Crow Wood
STOCKING LA
Sports Ground
Rushcliffe Lodge
RUSHCLIFFE GR
2
Ash Spinney
Fir Dale Plantation
ROULSTONE CRES
ANGRAVE RD
Sharpley Hill
GOTHAM RD
The Heavens
SHARPLEY DR
Fox Hill
Fox Hill Farm
WEAVERS CL
ST MARY'S CRES
ELM AVE
Foxhill Wood
SWEET LEYS DR
RYEHOLME CL
MANOR RD
HOLME AVE
THE CRES
27
LANTERN LA
Schs
MONKS MEAD
TAFT LEYS RD
BRICKCLIFFE RD
FISHER CL
Kingston Brook
CARLTON CRES
STONEBRIDGE DR
MAIN ST
West Leake
East Leake
1
BATEMAN RD
SOUTHWELL CL
MANOR FARM MEADOW
MOORE CL
F Sta
P
Liby
Masts
DE FERRERS CL
YORK CL
EXETER CL
TRURO CL
ROPE WLK
BIRCH LEA
Sewage Works
WINCHESTER CL
MAIN ST
THE KEEP
CHURCH CL
COSTOCK RD
W LEAKE RD
STATION RD
SCHOOL G
THE BRICKS
STARCH CL
SALISBURY AVE
OLDERSHAW RD
CASTLE HILL
BRICKLEY CRES
MEETING HOUSE CL
FIELD END CL
Allot Gdns
TWENTYLANDS DR
OAK CRES
OLD RECTORY CL
BROOKSIDE
Sch
THE NOOK
Sch
BURTON WK
POTTERS LA
CROMWELL DR
HAWLEY CL
SYCAMORE RD
BROOKSIDE AVE
26
D
54
E
55
F

214
206

205
196

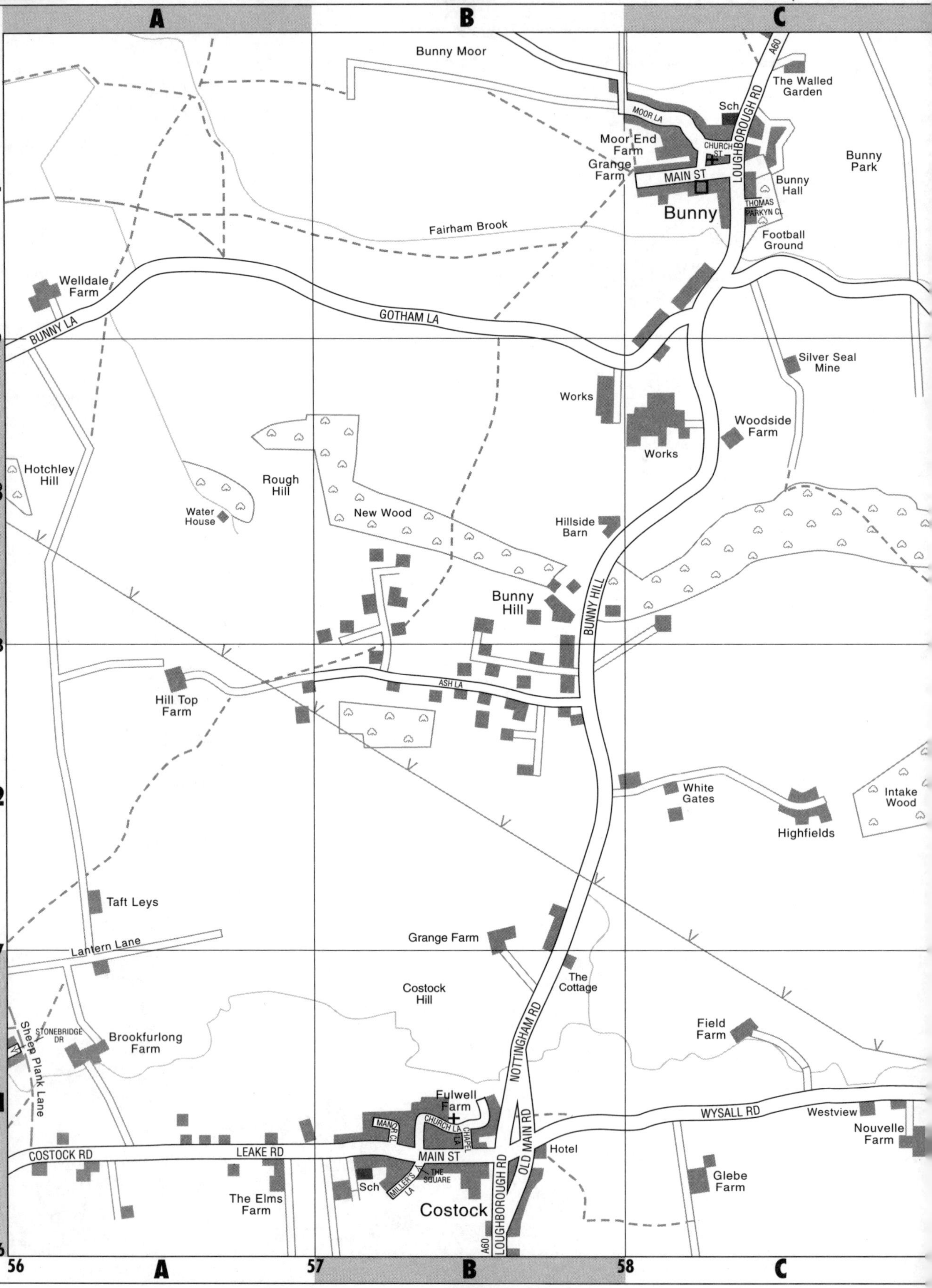


205
215

197
208

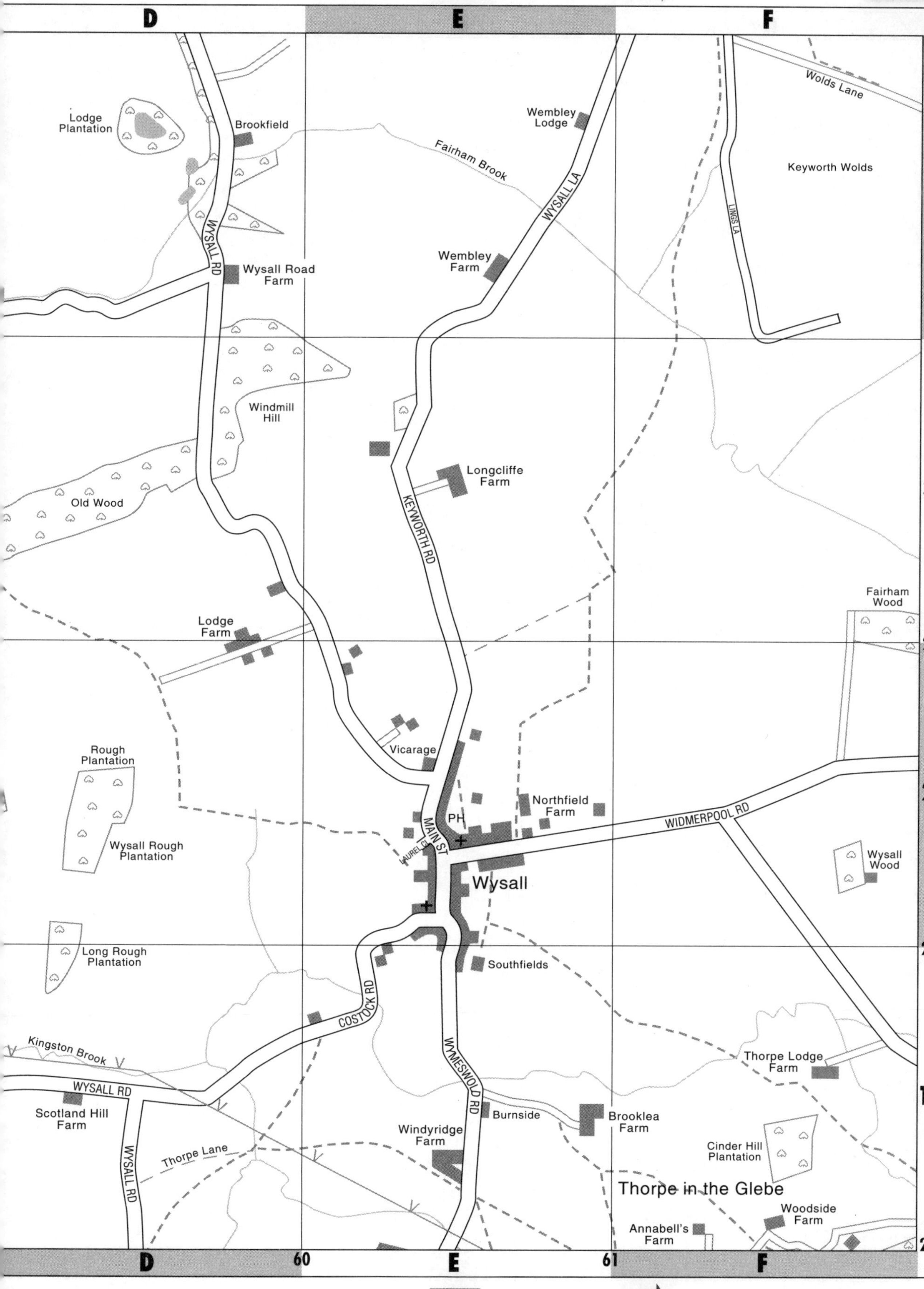


216
208

207
198

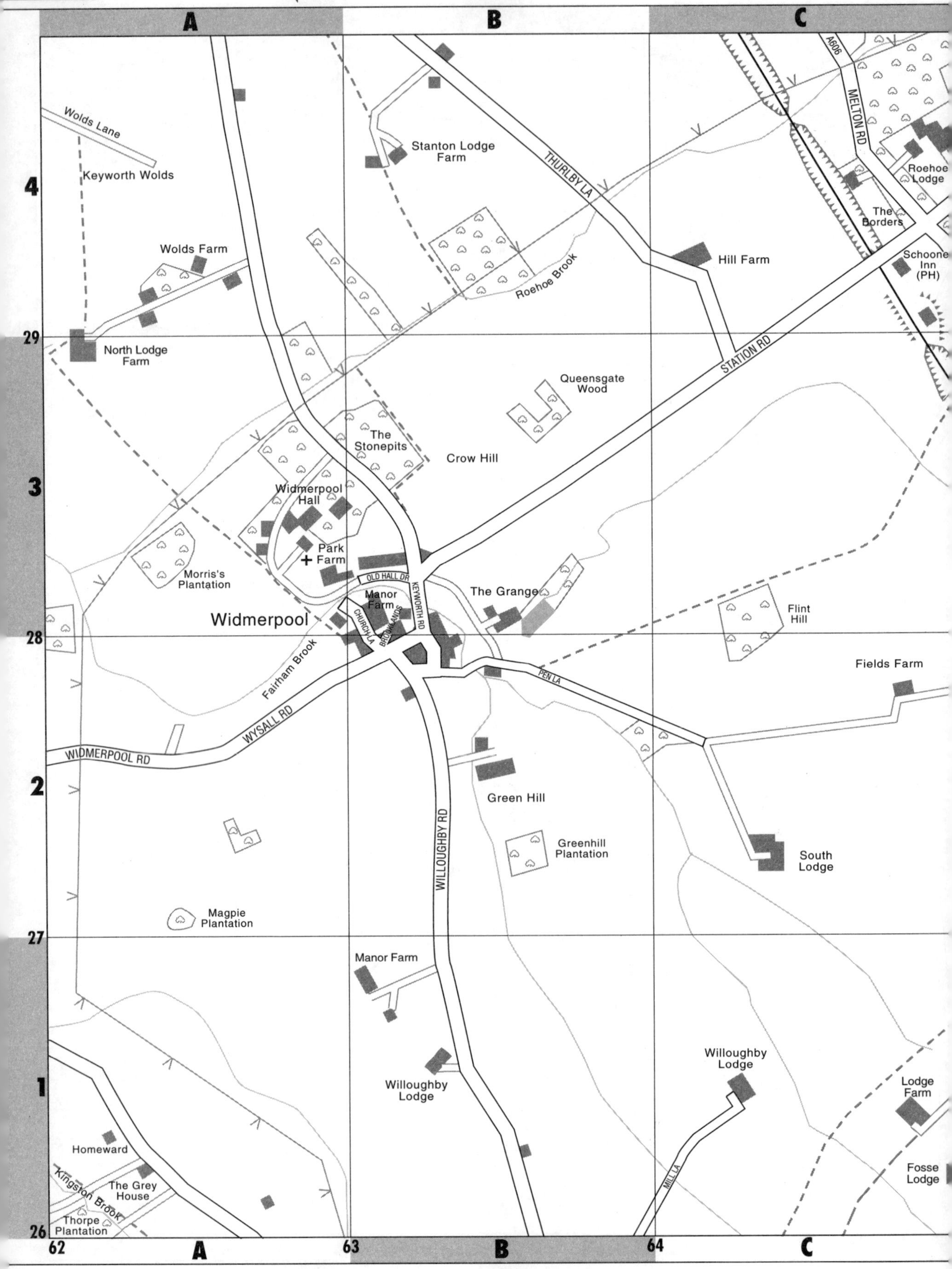


207
217

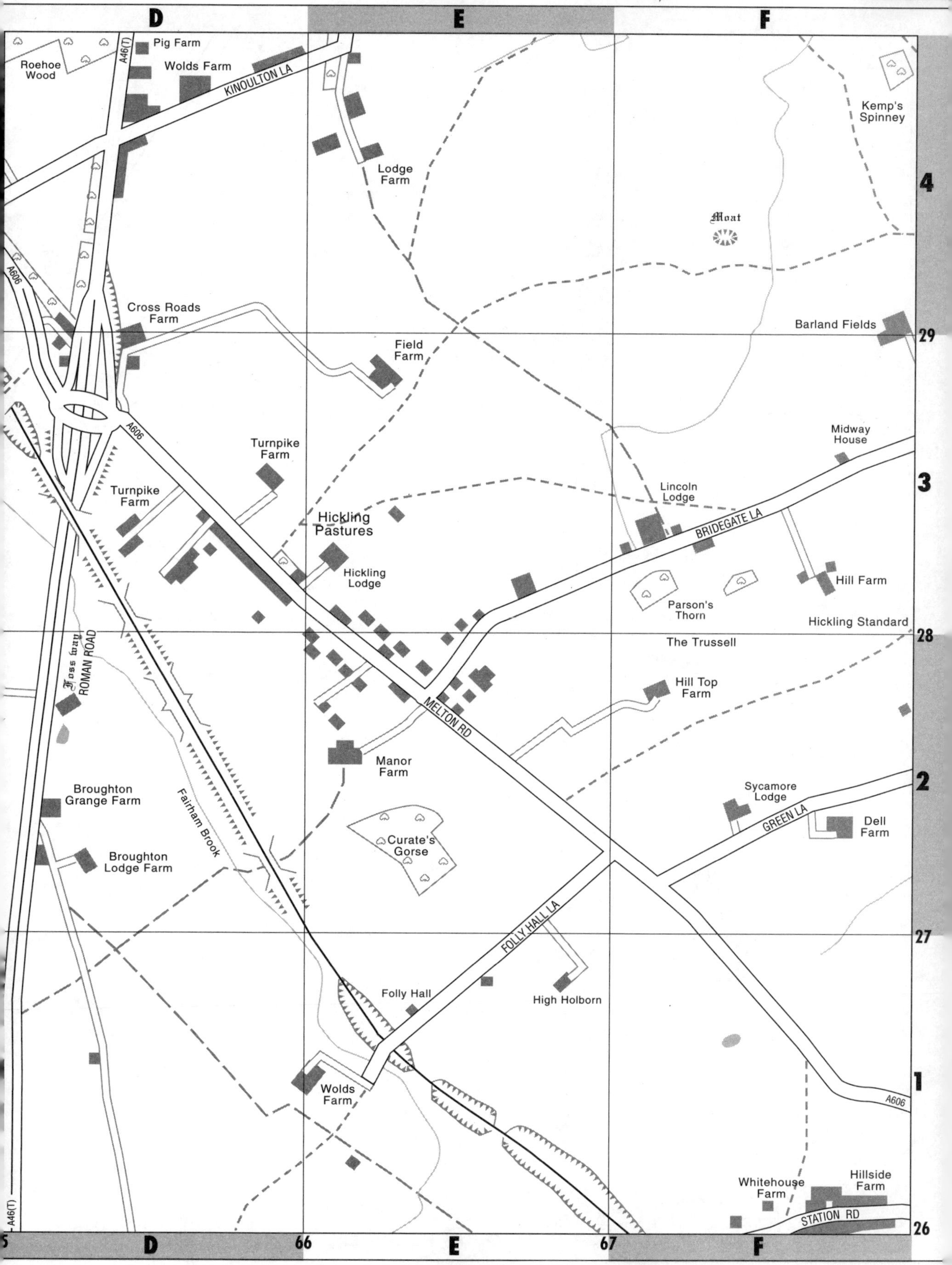
D
E
F
Roehoe Wood
Pig Farm
Wolds Farm
KINOULTON LA
A46(T)
Lodge Farm
Kemp's Spinney
4
Moat
A606
Cross Roads Farm
Field Farm
Barland Fields
29
A606
Midway House
Turnpike Farm
Turnpike Farm
3
Lincoln Lodge
Hickling Pastures
BRIDEGATE LA
Hickling Lodge
Hill Farm
Parson's Thorn
Hickling Standard
28
The Trussell
Foss Way
ROMAN ROAD
Hill Top Farm
MELTON RD
Manor Farm
2
Broughton Grange Farm
Sycamore Lodge
Fairham Brook
GREEN LA
Dell Farm
Curate's Gorse
Broughton Lodge Farm
FOLLY HALL LA
27
Folly Hall
High Holborn
1
Wolds Farm
A606
Whitehouse Farm
Hillside Farm
A46(T)
STATION RD
26
5
66
67

209
200

209
219

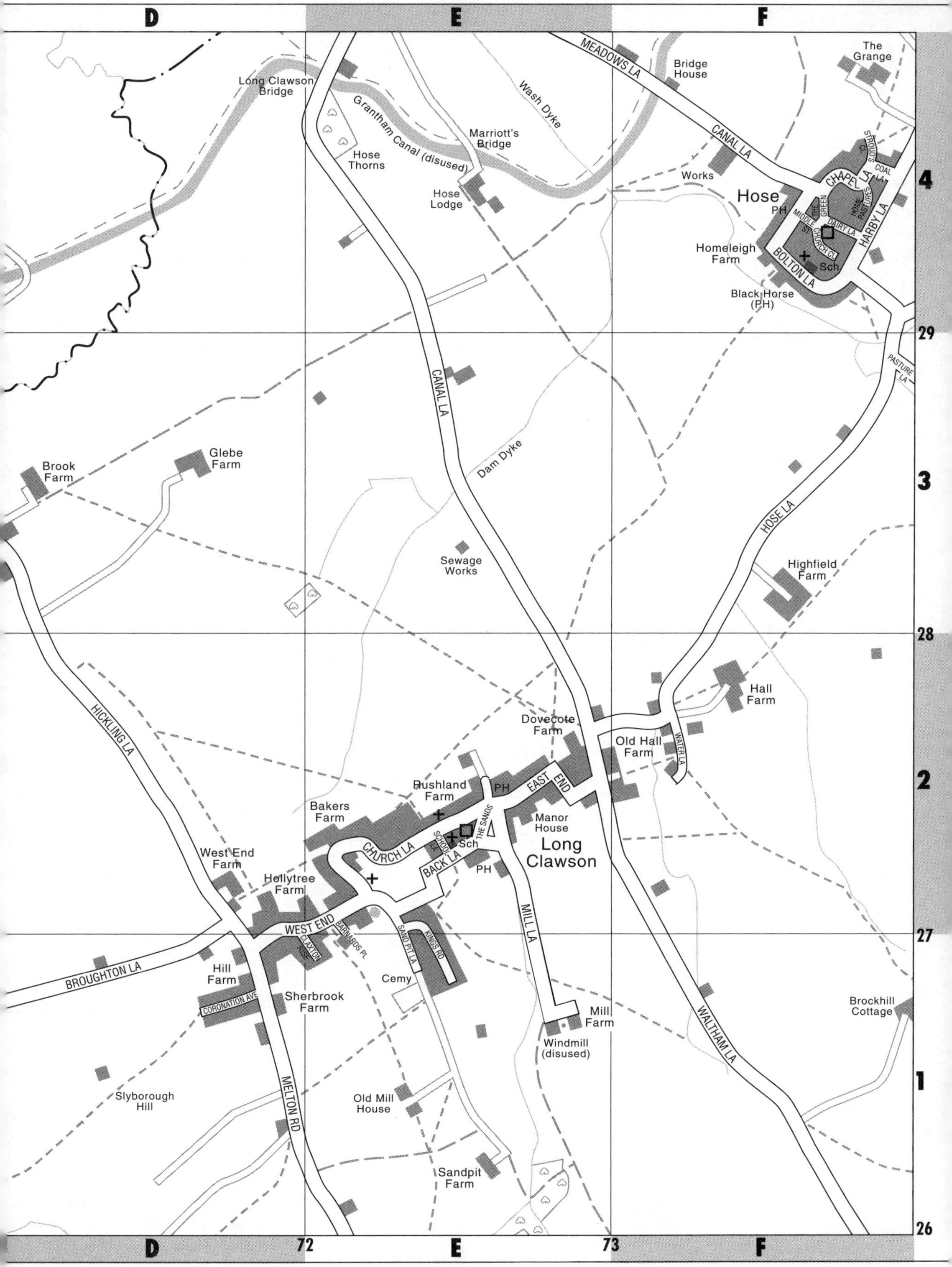
Long Clawson Bridge
Grantham Canal (disused)
Hose Thorns
Marriott's Bridge
Wash Dyke
MEADOWS LA
Bridge House
The Grange
CANAL LA
Works
Hose Lodge
Hose
PH
CHAPEL LA
STROUDS CL
COAL LA
HOME PASTURES
HARBY LA
THE GREEN
MIDDLE ST
DAIRY LA
CHURCH CL
Homeleigh Farm
BOLTON LA
Sch
Black Horse (PH)
PASTURE LA
CANAL LA
Brook Farm
Glebe Farm
Dam Dyke
HOSE LA
Sewage Works
Highfield Farm
HICKLING LA
Hall Farm
Dovecote Farm
Old Hall Farm
WATER LA
Rushland Farm
PH
EAST END
Bakers Farm
SCHOOL LA
THE SANDS
Sch
Manor House
Long Clawson
West End Farm
CHURCH LA
BACK LA
PH
Hollytree Farm
MILL LA
WEST END
CLAXTON RISE
BARNARDS PL
SAND PIT LA
KINGS RD
BROUGHTON LA
Hill Farm
Cemy
CORONATION AVE
Sherbrook Farm
Mill Farm
Brockhill Cottage
WALTHAM LA
Windmill (disused)
Slyborough Hill
MELTON RD
Old Mill House
Sandpit Farm
D
E
F
4
29
3
28
2
27
1
26
72
73

203

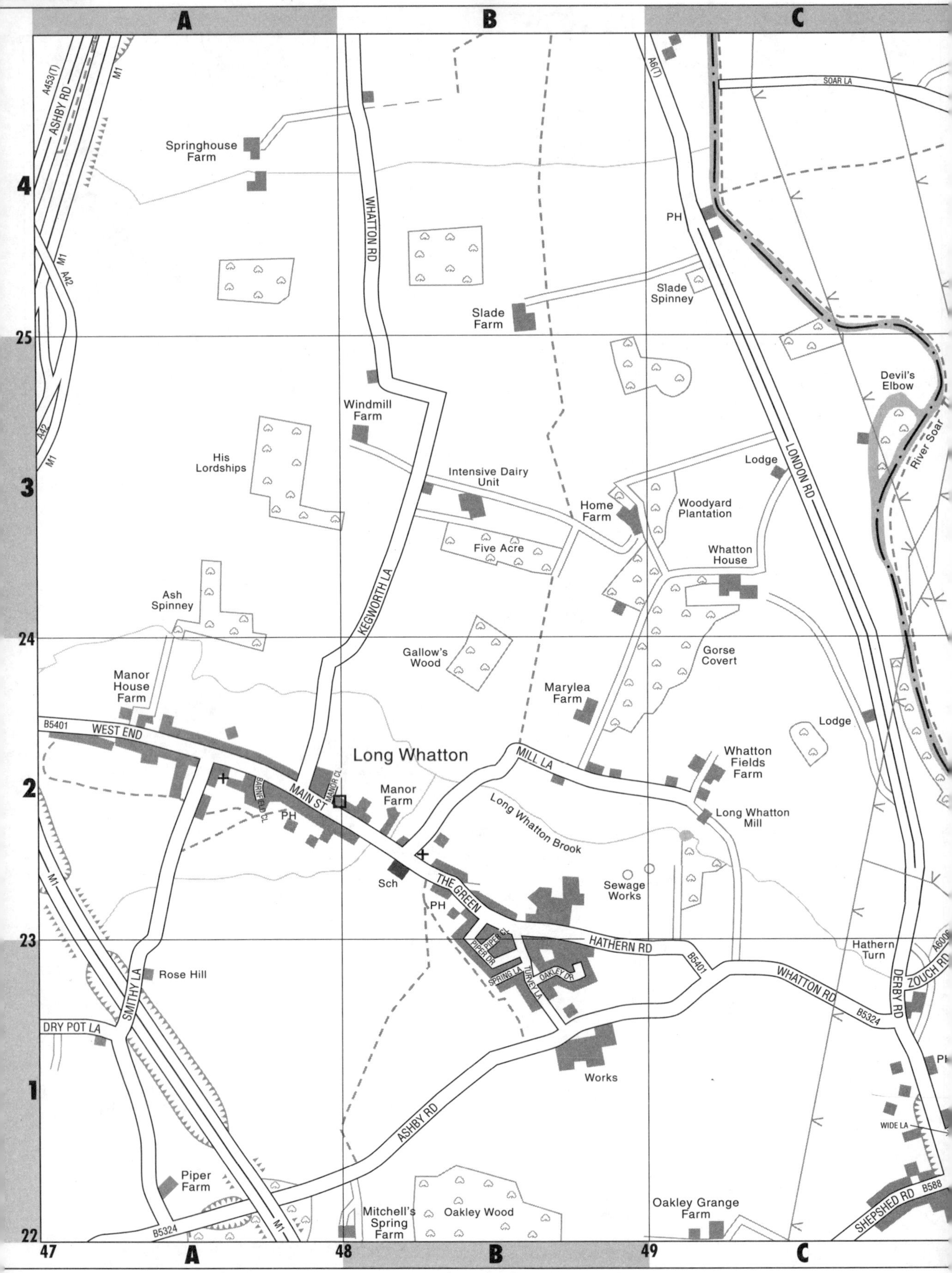

A
B
C
Springhouse Farm
Slade Farm
Slade Spinney
PH
Windmill Farm
His Lordships
Intensive Dairy Unit
Five Acre
Home Farm
Woodyard Plantation
Whatton House
Lodge
Devil's Elbow
River Soar
Ash Spinney
Gallow's Wood
Gorse Covert
Manor House Farm
Marylea Farm
Lodge
Long Whatton
Manor Farm
Whatton Fields Farm
Long Whatton Mill
Long Whatton Brook
Sch
PH
Sewage Works
Hathern Turn
Rose Hill
Works
Piper Farm
Mitchell's Spring Farm
Oakley Wood
Oakley Grange Farm
ASHBY RD
A453(T)
M1
A42
WHATTON RD
KEGWORTH LA
A6(T)
SOAR LA
LONDON RD
B5401
WEST END
MAIN ST
MANOR CL
BARNFIELD CL
MILL LA
THE GREEN
PIPER CL
PIPER DR
SPRING LA
TURVEY LA
OAKLEY DR
HATHERN RD
WHATTON RD
B5324
DERBY RD
ZOUCH RD
A6006
SMITHY LA
DRY POT LA
WIDE LA
SHEPSHED RD
B588
4
25
3
24
2
23
1
22
47
48
49

204
214

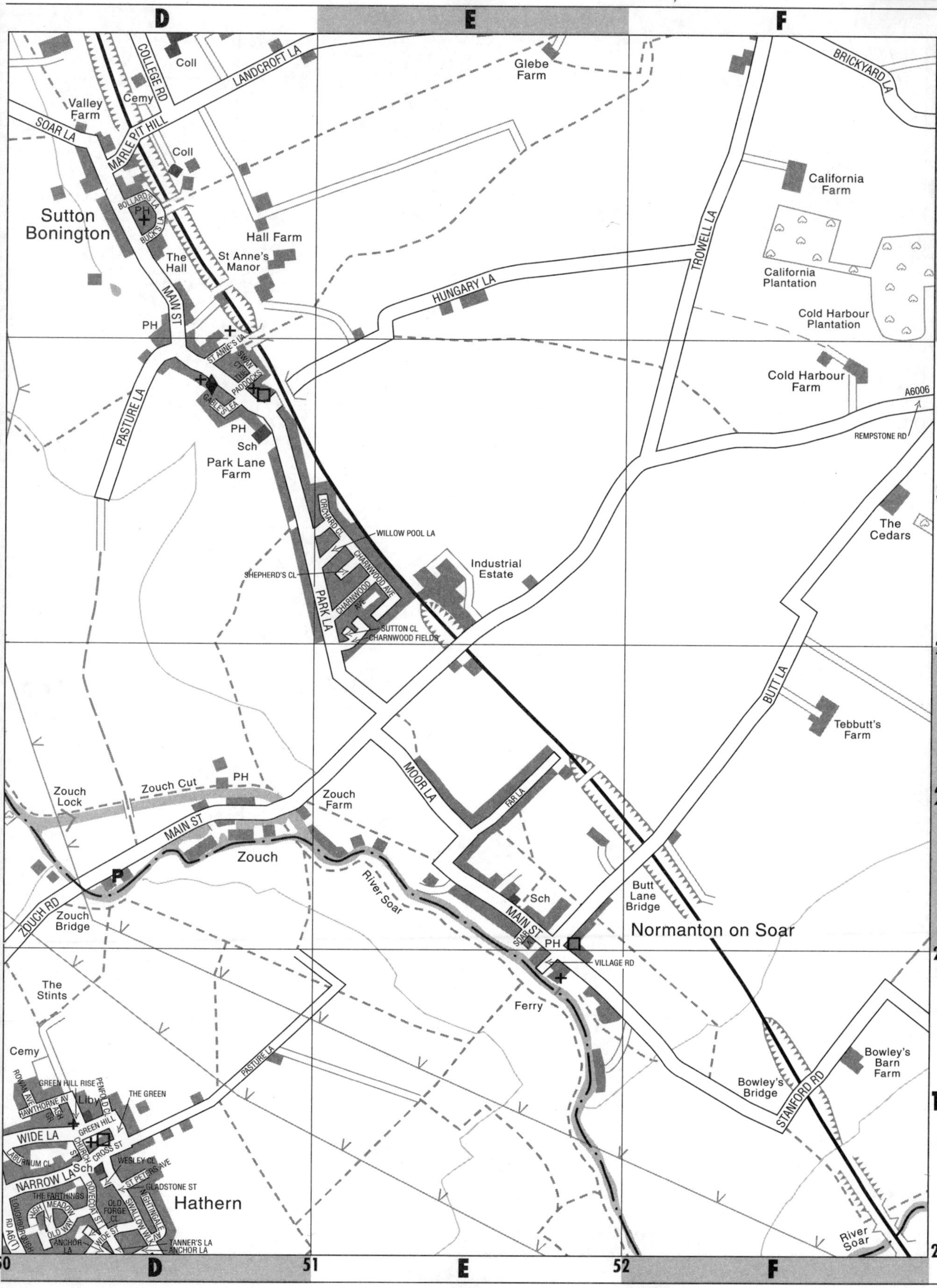
D
E
F
Coll
COLLEGE RD
LANDCROFT LA
Glebe Farm
BRICKYARD LA
Valley Farm
Cemy
SOAR LA
MARLE PIT HILL
Coll
California Farm
4
BOLLARDS LA
PH
BUCK'S LA
Sutton Bonington
Hall Farm
TROWELL LA
The Hall
St Anne's Manor
California Plantation
MAIN ST
HUNGARY LA
Cold Harbour Plantation
PH
ST ANNE'S LA
SWAN CT
THE PADDOCKS
GABLES LEA
25
Cold Harbour Farm
A6006
PASTURE LA
PH
Sch
REMPSTONE RD
Park Lane Farm
3
The Cedars
ORCHARD CL
WILLOW POOL LA
CHARNWOOD AVE
SHEPHERD'S CL
Industrial Estate
CHARNWOOD AVE
PARK LA
SUTTON CL
CHARNWOOD FIELDS
24
BUTT LA
Tebbutt's Farm
MOOR LA
PH
Zouch Lock
Zouch Cut
Zouch Farm
FAR LA
2
MAIN ST
Zouch
River Soar
P
Sch
Butt Lane Bridge
ZOUCH RD
Zouch Bridge
MAIN ST
SOAR LA
PH
Normanton on Soar
VILLAGE RD
23
The Stints
Ferry
Cemy
PASTURE LA
Bowley's Barn Farm
Bowley's Bridge
STANFORD RD
ROWAN AVE
GREEN HILL RISE
PENFOLD CL
HAWTHORNE AV
ASH GR
Liby
THE GREEN
1
WIDE LA
GREEN HILL
CHURCH ST
CROSS ST
LABURNUM CL
WESLEY CL
NARROW LA
Sch
ST PETERS AVE
GLADSTONE ST
THE FARTHINGS
HIGH MEADOW
OLD FORGE CL
NIGHTINGALE
Hathern
DOVECOTE ST
SWALLOW WALK
LOUGHBOROUGH RD A6(T)
OLD WAY
ANCHOR LA
WIDE ST
TANNER'S LA
ANCHOR LA
River Soar
22
50
51
52

214

213
205

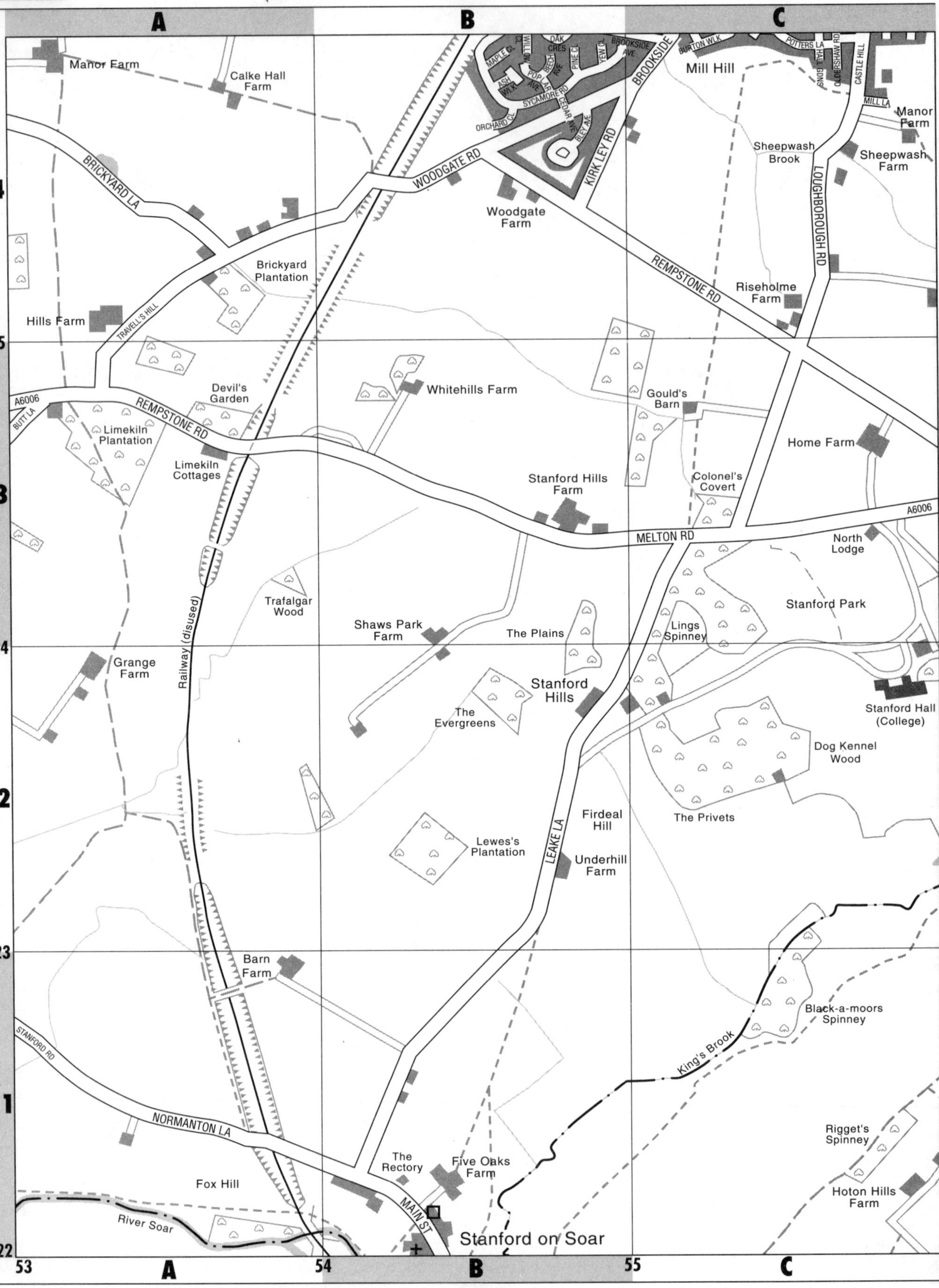


213
220

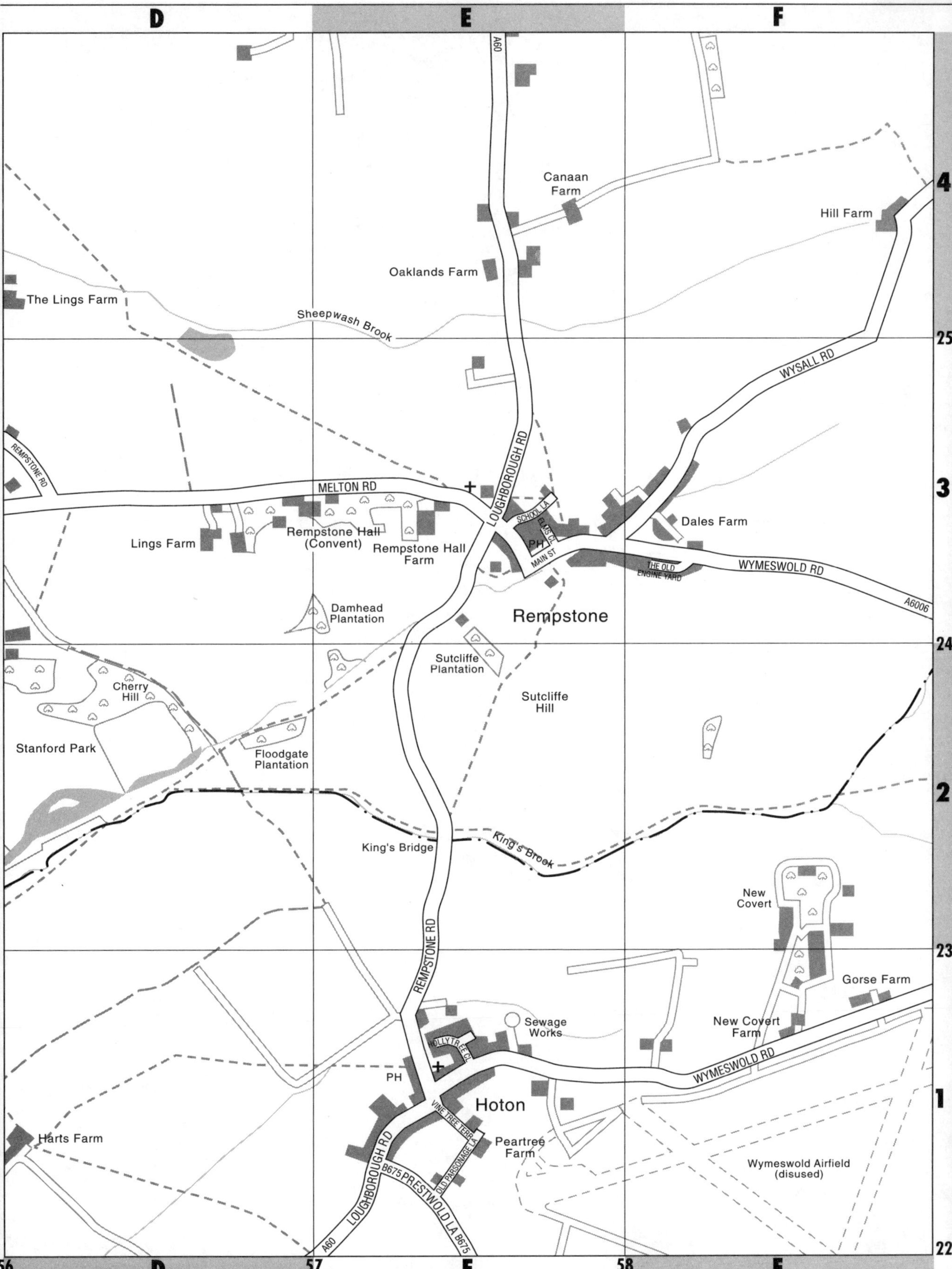
D
E
F
A60
Canaan Farm
Hill Farm
Oaklands Farm
The Lings Farm
Sheepwash Brook
WYSALL RD
REMPSTONE RD
MELTON RD
LOUGHBOROUGH RD
SCHOOL LA
ELMS CL
PH
MAIN ST
Dales Farm
Lings Farm
Rempstone Hall (Convent)
Rempstone Hall Farm
THE OLD ENGINE YARD
WYMESWOLD RD
A6006
Damhead Plantation
Rempstone
Sutcliffe Plantation
Sutcliffe Hill
Cherry Hill
Stanford Park
Floodgate Plantation
King's Bridge
King's Brook
New Covert
REMPSTONE RD
Gorse Farm
Sewage Works
New Covert Farm
HOLLYTREE CL
WYMESWOLD RD
PH
Hoton
VINE TREE TERR
Harts Farm
Peartree Farm
OLD PARSONAGE LA
Wymeswold Airfield (disused)
B675 PRESTWOLD LA B675
LOUGHBOROUGH RD
A60
4
25
3
24
2
23
1
22
56
57
58

215
207

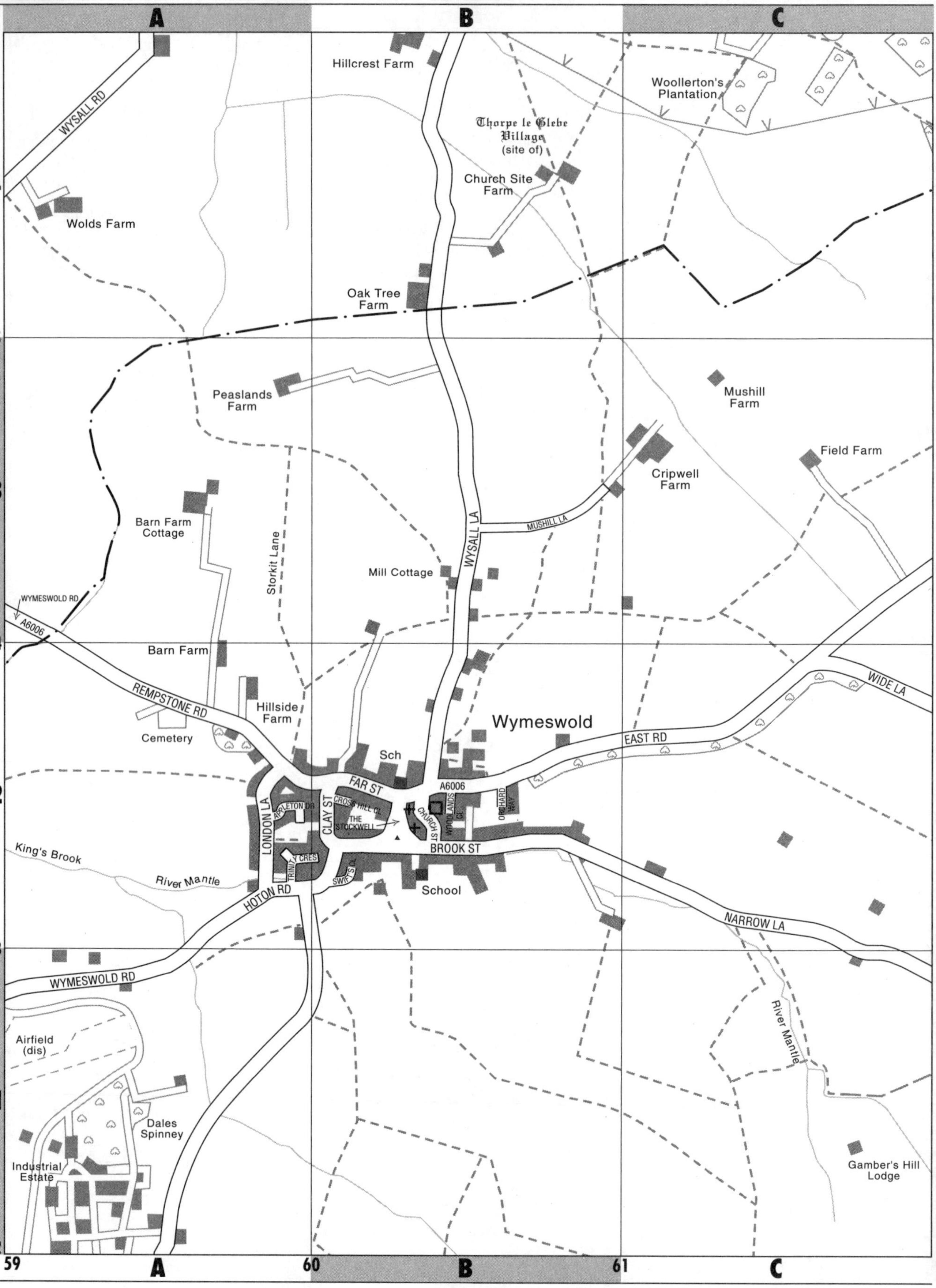
A
B
C
4
25
3
24
2
23
1
22
59
60
61
WYSALL RD
Hillcrest Farm
Woollerton's Plantation
Thorpe le Glebe Village (site of)
Church Site Farm
Wolds Farm
Oak Tree Farm
Peaslands Farm
Mushill Farm
Field Farm
Cripwell Farm
Barn Farm Cottage
Storkit Lane
MUSHILL LA
WYSALL LA
Mill Cottage
WYMESWOLD RD
A6006
Barn Farm
REMPSTONE RD
Hillside Farm
Cemetery
Wymeswold
WIDE LA
EAST RD
Sch
FAR ST
A6006
ORCHARD WAY
WOODLANDS CL
CHURCH ST
CROSS HILL CL
THE STOCKWELL
APPLETON DR
CLAY ST
LONDON LA
TRINITY CRES
SWIFTS CL
BROOK ST
King's Brook
River Mantle
HOTON RD
School
NARROW LA
WYMESWOLD RD
River Mantle
Airfield (dis)
Dales Spinney
Industrial Estate
Gamber's Hill Lodge

215

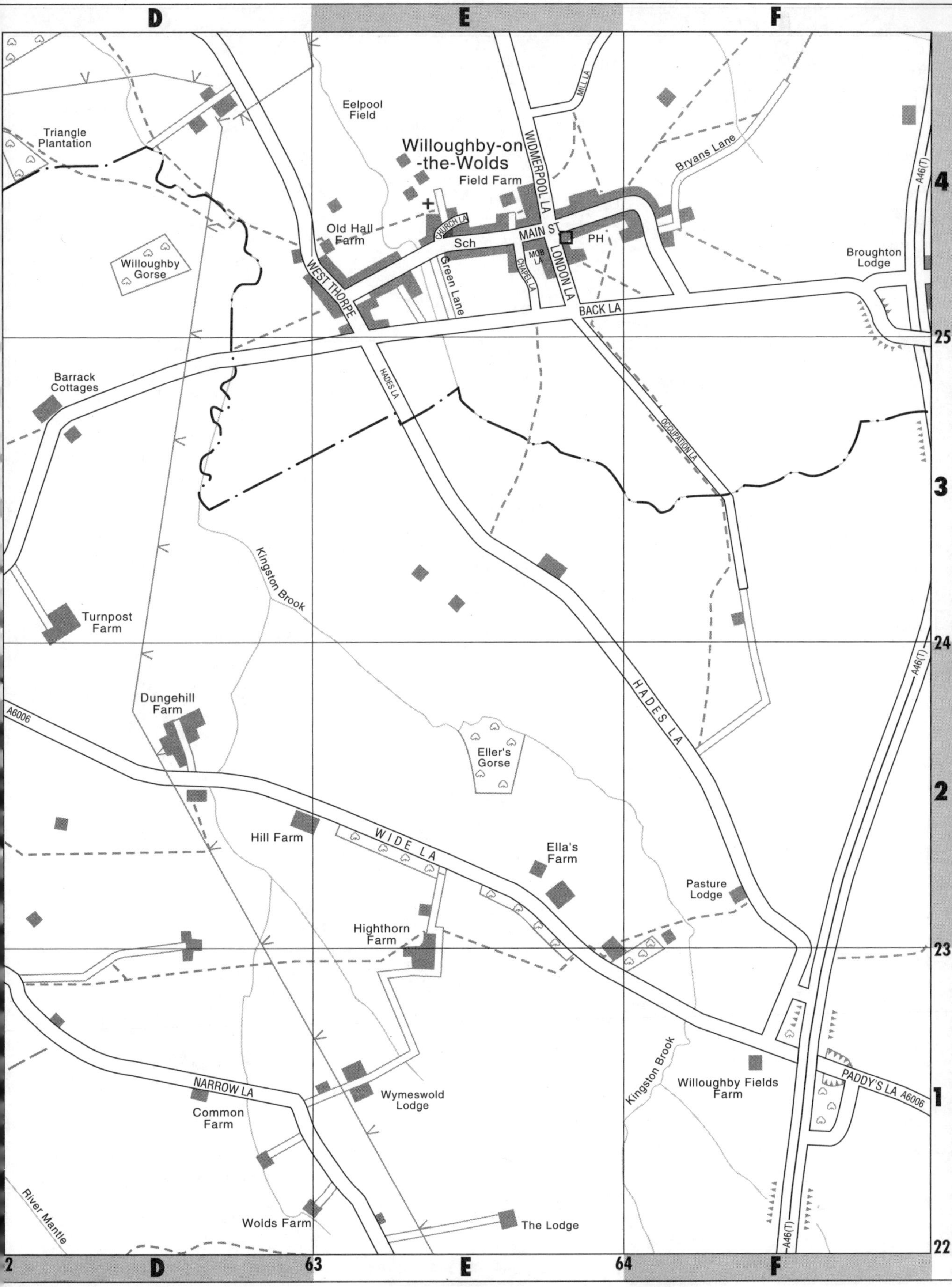
D
E
F
Triangle Plantation
Eelpool Field
Willoughby-on-the-Wolds
Field Farm
WIDMERPOOL LA
MILL LA
Bryans Lane
A46(T)
Old Hall Farm
CHURCH LA
Sch
MAIN ST
PH
Willoughby Gorse
WEST THORPE
Green Lane
MOB LA
CHAPEL LA
LONDON LA
BACK LA
Broughton Lodge
Barrack Cottages
HADES LA
OCCUPATION LA
Kingston Brook
Turnpost Farm
Dungehill Farm
A6006
HADES LA
Eller's Gorse
Hill Farm
WIDE LA
Ella's Farm
Pasture Lodge
Highthorn Farm
NARROW LA
Common Farm
Wymeswold Lodge
Kingston Brook
Willoughby Fields Farm
PADDY'S LA A6006
River Mantle
Wolds Farm
The Lodge
A46(T)
25
24
23
22
4
3
2
1
62
63
64

A
B
C
Manor Barn Farm
A46(T)
STATION RD
Brookside Cottage
Manor Farm
4
The Willoughby Hotel
Top Cottage
Fairham Brook
Longcliff Hill
25
Dalby Brook
3
Wad House
Spruce Haven
NOTTINGHAM LA
Dalby Lodges
Beazley's Farm
North Lodge
North Lodge Farm
24
Sch
STATION LA
LONGCLIFF HILL
HAWTHORN CL
DEBDALE HILL
CROFT
Old Dalby
PH
GDNS
CHAPEL LA
MAIN RD
PARADISE LA
Wood's Hill
Vale View Farm
CHURCH LA
2
WOOD HILL
Woodhill Farm
Hall Plantation
Fishpond Plantation
Hill Top Farm
Thorney Hollow
23
Yard Farm
Old Dalby Wood
Upper Grange Farm
LAWN LA
Grange Cottages
Wavendon Grange
GIBSON'S LA
Home Lodge Farm
Dalby Wolds
Old Dalby Grange
Old Dalby Wood House
1
A6006
Lower Grange Farm
Bridgets Covert
SIX HILLS LA
PADDY'S LA
Lodge Farm
22
65
66
67

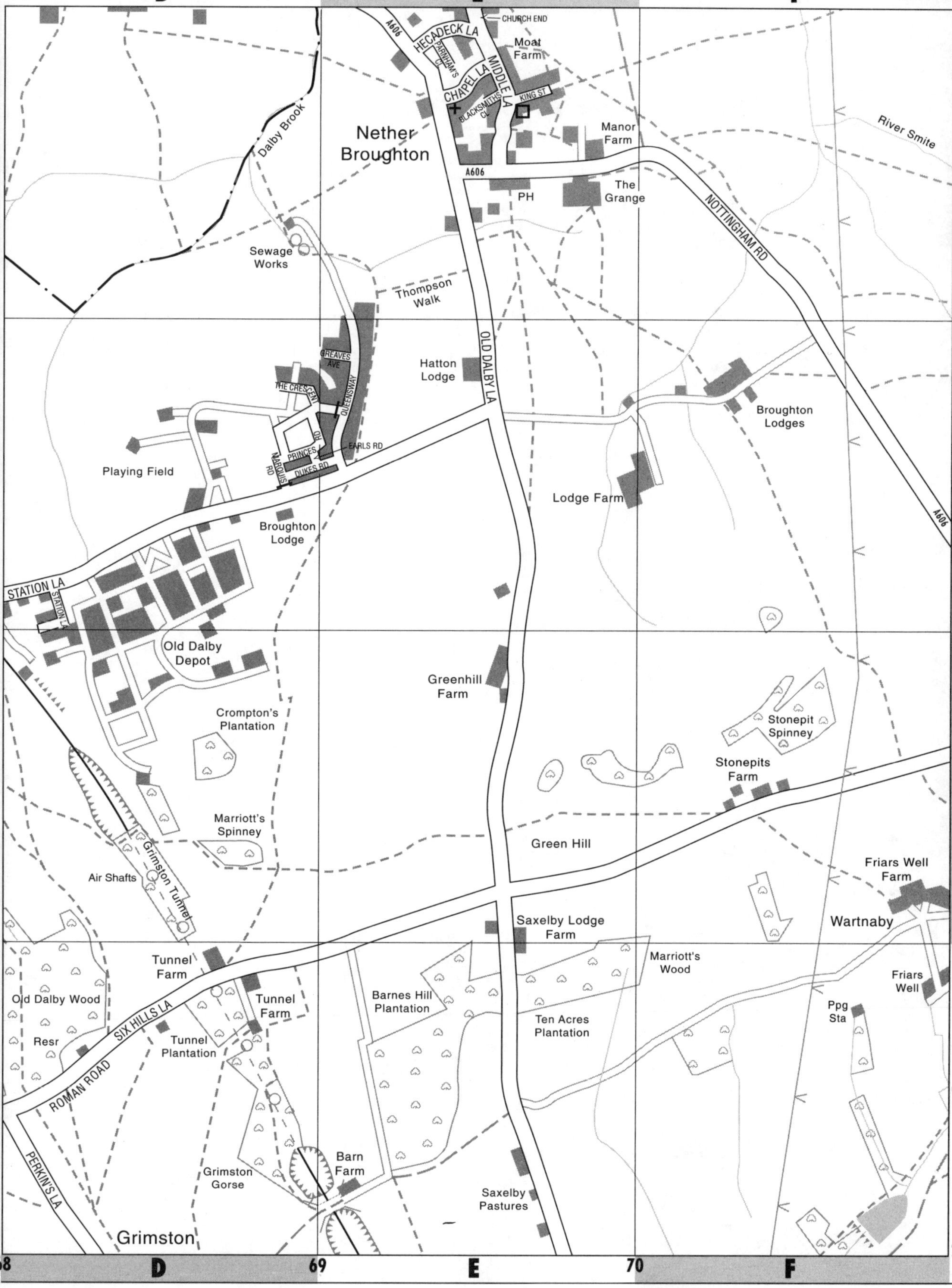
D
E
F
CHURCH END
A606
HECADECK LA
PARNHAM'S CL
Moat Farm
CHAPEL LA
MIDDLE LA
KING ST
BLACKSMITHS CL
Nether Broughton
Dalby Brook
Manor Farm
River Smite
A606
The Grange
PH
NOTTINGHAM RD
Sewage Works
Thompson Walk
OLD DALBY LA
Hatton Lodge
GREAVES AVE
QUEENSWAY
THE CRESCENT
Broughton Lodges
EARLS RD
PRINCES
DUKES RD
MARQUIS RD
Playing Field
Lodge Farm
Broughton Lodge
STATION LA
Old Dalby Depot
Greenhill Farm
Crompton's Plantation
Stonepit Spinney
Stonepits Farm
Marriott's Spinney
Green Hill
Grimston Tunnel
Air Shafts
Friars Well Farm
Saxelby Lodge Farm
Wartnaby
Tunnel Farm
Marriott's Wood
Old Dalby Wood
Tunnel Farm
Barnes Hill Plantation
Friars Well
SIX HILLS LA
Ppg Sta
Ten Acres Plantation
Resr
Tunnel Plantation
ROMAN ROAD
PERKIN'S LA
Barn Farm
Grimston Gorse
Saxelby Pastures
Grimston
4
25
3
24
2
23
1
22
68
69
70

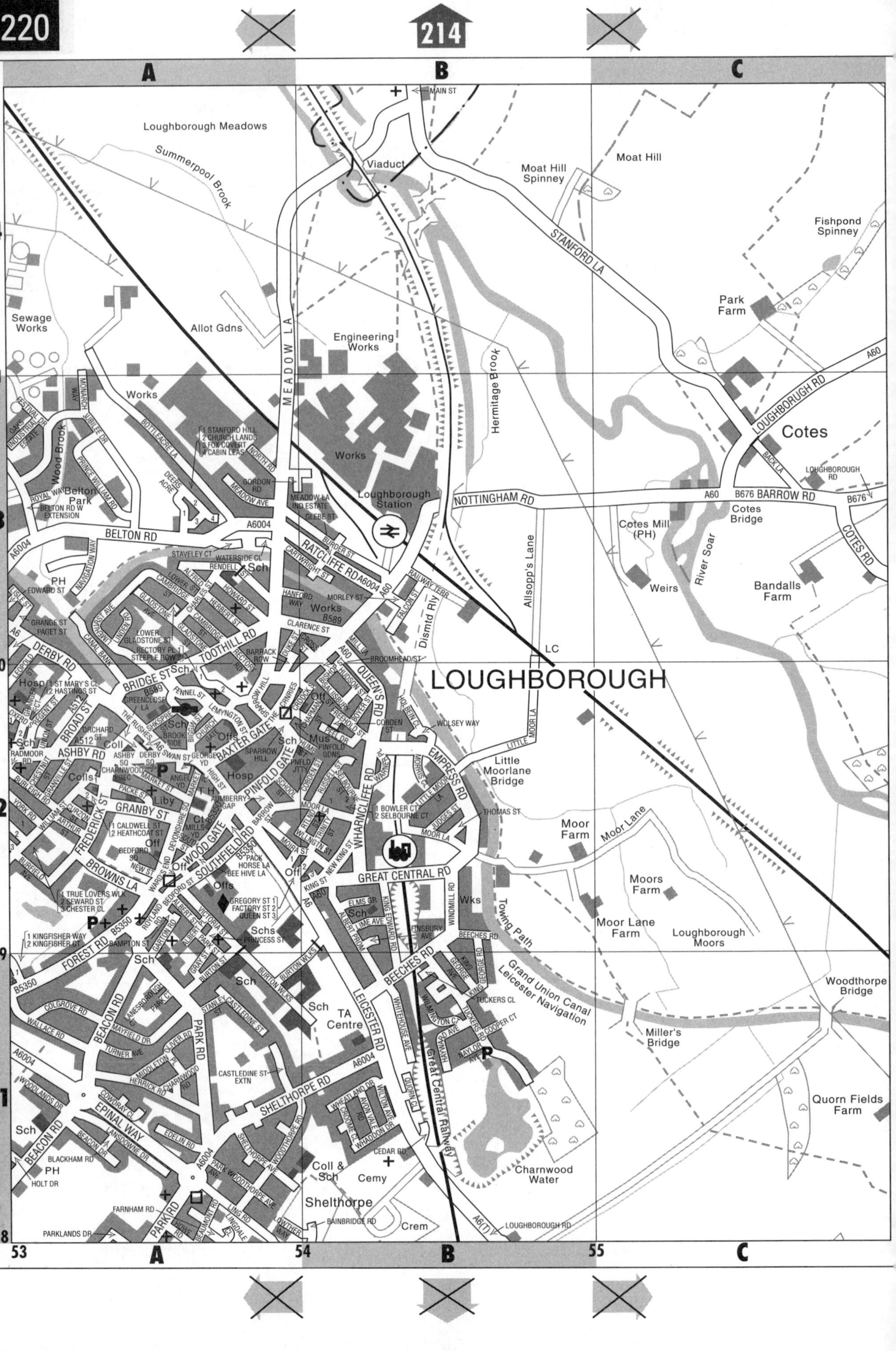
214
A
B
C
4
3
2
1
21
20
19
18
53
54
55
Loughborough Meadows
Summerpool Brook
Viaduct
Moat Hill
Moat Hill Spinney
Fishpond Spinney
STANFORD LA
Sewage Works
Allot Gdns
Engineering Works
Park Farm
Works
MEADOW LA
Hermitage Brook
LOUGHBOROUGH RD
Cotes
A60
Loughborough Station
NOTTINGHAM RD
B676 BARROW RD
Cotes Bridge
Cotes Mill (PH)
COTES RD
BELTON RD
Belton Park
Wood Brook
A6004
RATCLIFFE RD
River Soar
Weirs
Bandalls Farm
Allsopp's Lane
Dismtd Rly
LC
LOUGHBOROUGH
TOOTHILL RD
DERBY RD
BRIDGE ST
QUEEN'S RD
Little Moorlane Bridge
EMPRESS RD
ASHBY RD
BAXTER GATE
PINFOLD GATE
WHARNCLIFFE RD
Moor Farm
Moor Lane
GRANBY ST
WOOD GATE
SOUTHFIELD RD
GREAT CENTRAL RD
Moors Farm
Moor Lane Farm
Loughborough Moors
Towing Path
FOREST RD
BEECHES RD
Grand Union Canal Leicester Navigation
Woodthorpe Bridge
Miller's Bridge
TA Centre
LEICESTER RD
PARK RD
BEACON RD
Great Central Railway
SHELTHORPE RD
EPINAL WAY
Charnwood Water
Quorn Fields Farm
Cemy
Coll & Sch
Shelthorpe
Crem
LOUGHBOROUGH RD

USER'S NOTES

# EXPLANATION OF THE STREET INDEX REFERENCE SYSTEM

Street names are listed alphabetically and show the locality, the page number and a reference to the square in which the name falls on the map page.

| | |
|---|---|
| Example: | Southlands Dr. Mort.......................................................15 D2 |
| Southlands Dr | This is the full street name, which may have been abbreviated on the map. |
| Mort | This is the abbreviation for the town, village or locality in which the street falls. |
| 15 | This is the page number of the map on which the street name appears. |
| D2 | The letter and figure indicate the square on the map in which the centre of the street falls. The square can be found at the junction of the vertical column carrying the appropriate letter and the horizontal row carrying the appropriate figure. |

## ABBREVIATIONS USED IN THE INDEX

Road Names

Approach....................................App
Avenue........................................Ave
Boulevard....................................Bvd
Broadway....................................Bwy
By-Pass....................................By-Ps
Causeway.................................Cswy
Common..................................Comm
Corner..........................................Cnr
Cottages....................................Cotts
Court.............................................Ct
Crescent....................................Cres
Drive.............................................Dri
Drove............................................Dro
East.................................................E
Gardens.....................................Gdns
Grove.............................................Gr
Heights.........................................Hts
Lane..............................................La
North...............................................N
Orchard......................................Orch
Parade..........................................Par
Passage.......................................Pas
Place...............................................Pl
Pleasant.....................................Plea
Precinct......................................Prec
Promenade................................Prom
Road..............................................Rd
South...............................................S
Square...........................................Sq
Street,Saint....................................St
Terrace........................................Terr
Walk.............................................Wlk
West...............................................W
Yard...............................................Yd

## Key to abbreviations of Town, Village and Rural locality names used in the index of street names.

| Locality | Abbreviation | Page | Grid |
|---|---|---|---|
| Aldercar | Ald | 143 | D2 |
| Allt Hucknall | Al Hu | 85 | F4 |
| Alverton | Alv | 168 | C1 |
| Annesley Woodhouse | Ann Wo | 129 | F4 |
| Arnold | Arn | 162 | A4 |
| Askham | Askh | 51 | F1 |
| Aslockton | Aslo | 179 | D3 |
| Austerfield | Aust | 3 | E1 |
| Averham | Aver | 123 | F1 |
| Awsworth | Awsw | 158 | B2 |
| Babworth | Babw | 39 | D1 |
| Balderton | Bald | 140 | C2 |
| Barkestone-le-Vale | B-le-V | 192 | B1 |
| Barnby in the Willows | B in W | 141 | F3 |
| Barnby Moor | Ba Mo | 28 | B3 |
| Barnstone | Barns | 190 | C2 |
| Barton in Fabis | B in F | 194 | C3 |
| Bathley | Bath | 110 | A2 |
| Bawtry | Baw | 10 | A4 |
| Beckingham | Beck | 14 | A1 |
| Beckingham | Beckin | 142 | B4 |
| Beeston | Bees | 183 | E4 |
| Besthorpe | Best | 97 | F3 |
| Bestwood Village | Bes Vil | 146 | C2 |
| Bevercotes | Bev | 64 | B3 |
| Bilsthorpe | Bils | 105 | F3 |
| Bingham | Bing | 177 | F2 |
| Bircotes | Bir | 9 | E2 |
| Blaxton | Blax | 1 | A1 |
| Bleasby | Bleas | 152 | A4 |
| Blidworth | Blid | 118 | A2 |
| Blyth | Blyth | 18 | A2 |
| Blyton | Blyt | 15 | F4 |
| Bole | Bole | 23 | F1 |
| Bothamsall | Both | 63 | F4 |
| Bottesford | Bott | 181 | E2 |
| Boughton | Boug | 77 | F3 |
| Bradmore | Brad | 196 | C2 |
| Brampton | Bram | 44 | B2 |
| Brinsley | Brin | 143 | F3 |
| Broadholme | Broad | 57 | D1 |
| Broxholme | Brox | 57 | F3 |
| Budby | Budby | 61 | F1 |
| Bulcote | Bulc | 164 | A3 |
| Bunny | Bunny | 206 | C4 |
| Burton Joyce | Bu Jo | 163 | F2 |
| Calverton | Calv | 149 | D4 |
| Car Colston | Car Co | 166 | B1 |
| Carlton | Carl | 162 | B1 |
| Carlton in Lindrick | C in L | 25 | F3 |
| Carlton on Trent | C on T | 96 | C2 |
| Caunton | Caun | 109 | D2 |
| Caythorpe | Cayt | 165 | D4 |
| Clarborough | Clar | 30 | C2 |
| Claypole | Clayp | 156 | B4 |
| Clayworth | Clay | 21 | E3 |
| Clipston | Clip | 187 | E1 |
| Coddington | Codd | 126 | A1 |
| Collingham | Coll | 98 | A1 |
| Colston Bassett | Co Ba | 200 | B4 |
| Cossall | Coss | 158 | B1 |
| Costock | Cost | 206 | B1 |
| Cotes | Cotes | 220 | C3 |
| Cotgrave | Cotg | 188 | A1 |
| Cotham | Coth | 154 | C2 |
| Cottam | Cott | 43 | E3 |
| Cromwell | Crom | 110 | C4 |
| Cropwell Bishop | Cr Bi | 189 | D2 |
| Cropwell Butler | Cr Bu | 189 | D4 |
| Cuckney | Cuck | 60 | A2 |
| Darlton | Darl | 67 | D4 |
| Dry Doddington | Dry Do | 156 | C1 |
| Dunham on Trent | D on T | 54 | B1 |
| Eagle | Eagle | 84 | B2 |
| Eakring | Eakr | 92 | C1 |
| East Bridgeford | E Brid | 165 | F2 |
| East Drayton | E Dray | 53 | D2 |
| East Leake | E Lea | 205 | F1 |
| East Markham | E Mark | 65 | F3 |
| East Stockwith | E Stock | 7 | F1 |
| East Stoke | E Sto | 153 | E4 |
| Eastwood | East | 143 | F2 |
| Eaton | Eaton | 40 | A1 |
| Edingley | Edin | 120 | B2 |
| Edwinstowe | Edwin | 76 | A1 |
| Egmanton | Egma | 79 | F3 |
| Elkersley | Elk | 50 | A2 |
| Elmton | Elmt | 58 | A4 |
| Elston | Elst | 153 | F3 |
| Elton | Elton | 179 | F1 |
| Epperstone | Epp | 150 | A3 |
| Everton | Ever | 11 | D2 |
| Farndon | Farn | 139 | D2 |
| Farnsfield | Farns | 119 | F3 |
| Fenton | Fent | 55 | E3 |
| Fenton | Fenton | 141 | B1 |
| Finningley | Finn | 1 | A2 |
| Firbeck | Fir | 16 | A3 |
| Fiskerton | Fisk | 137 | F2 |
| Flawborough | Flaw | 168 | B1 |
| Fledborough | Fled | 68 | B3 |
| Flintham | Flint | 153 | D1 |
| Gainsborough | Gain | 24 | C3 |
| Gamston | Gam | 186 | B4 |
| Gamston | Gams | 51 | D3 |
| Girton | Girt | 82 | C1 |
| Glapwell | Glap | 86 | B4 |
| Gonalston | Gona | 151 | D2 |
| Gotham | Goth | 195 | D1 |
| Granby | Gran | 191 | E3 |
| Grassthorpe | Grass | 81 | F2 |
| Greasley | Greas | 144 | C2 |
| Grimston | Grim | 219 | D1 |
| Gringley on the Hill | G on H | 12 | B1 |
| Grove | Grove | 40 | C2 |
| Gunthorpe | Gunt | 164 | C3 |
| Halam | Halam | 120 | C1 |
| Halloughton | Hall | 136 | A2 |
| Harby | Harb | 202 | A1 |
| Harby | Harby | 70 | C1 |
| Hardwick | Hardw | 56 | A3 |
| Harworth | Har | 8 | C3 |
| Hathern | Hath | 213 | D1 |
| Haughton | Haug | 63 | F3 |
| Hawksworth | Hawk | 167 | E2 |
| Hawton | Hawt | 139 | F2 |
| Haxey | Haxey | 6 | B4 |
| Hayton | Hayt | 30 | B3 |
| Headon | Head | 52 | A4 |
| Heanor | Hean | 143 | D1 |
| Hickling | Hick | 210 | A4 |
| High Marnham | H Marn | 68 | A1 |
| Hockerton | Hock | 122 | A3 |
| Hodsock | Hod | 26 | C4 |
| Holbeck | Holb | 59 | E4 |
| Holme | Holme | 111 | D2 |
| Holme Pierrepont | Ho Pi | 175 | D2 |
| Hose | Hose | 211 | F4 |
| Hoton | Hoton | 215 | E1 |
| Hoveringham | Hover | 151 | E1 |
| Hucknall | Huck | 145 | F3 |
| Ilkeston | Ilk | 157 | E1 |
| Kegworth | Kegw | 203 | E1 |
| Kelham | Kelh | 124 | A2 |
| Kersall | Kers | 94 | A1 |
| Kettlethorpe | Kettl | 55 | E2 |
| Keyworth | Keyw | 197 | F1 |
| Kilvington | Kilv | 169 | D1 |
| Kimberley | Kim | 158 | C3 |
| Kingston on Soar | K on S | 204 | A2 |
| Kinoulton | Kinou | 200 | A1 |
| Kirkby-in-Ashfield | K-in-A | 115 | E2 |
| Kirklington | Kirk | 120 | C4 |
| Kirton | Kirt | 78 | B3 |
| Kneesall | Knee | 93 | F3 |
| Kneeton | Kneet | 152 | A1 |
| Lambley | Lamb | 163 | E4 |
| Laneham | Lane | 54 | B3 |
| Langar | Lang | 190 | B1 |
| Langford | Langf | 111 | F1 |
| Langley Mill | La Mi | 143 | D2 |
| Langold | Lan | 16 | C2 |
| Laxton | Lax | 79 | E2 |
| Lea | Lea | 24 | C1 |
| Letwell | Let | 16 | A2 |
| Linby | Linby | 131 | D2 |
| Long Clawson | Lo Cl | 211 | E2 |
| Long Eaton | Lo Ea | 193 | E4 |
| Long Whatton | Lo Wh | 212 | B2 |
| Loughborough | Lough | 220 | B2 |
| Lound | Lound | 29 | E4 |
| Low Marnham | L Marn | 82 | A4 |
| Lowdham | Lowd | 150 | B1 |
| Maltby | Malt | 16 | A4 |
| Mansfield | Mans | 102 | B4 |
| Maplebeck | Mapl | 108 | A3 |
| Market Warsop | Mar War | 74 | B2 |
| Marton | Mart | 44 | A4 |
| Mattersey | Matt | 20 | B4 |
| Misson | Miss | 4 | A1 |
| Misterton | Mist | 6 | C1 |
| Morton | Mort | 15 | D2 |
| Morton | Morton | 137 | E2 |
| Nether Broughton | Ne Br | 219 | E4 |
| Nether Langwith | Ne La | 59 | D1 |
| New Clipstone | N Clip | 89 | F4 |
| Newark-on-Trent | N-on-T | 140 | B4 |
| Newstead | News | 130 | C3 |
| Newton | New | 177 | D4 |
| Newton | Newt | 99 | D2 |
| Newton on Trent | Ne on T | 55 | D1 |
| Normanton on Soar | N on S | 213 | F2 |
| Normanton on Trent | Nor on T | 81 | E3 |
| Normanton-on-the-Wolds | N-on-W | 198 | A3 |
| North Clifton | N Clift | 68 | C3 |
| North Leverton with Habblesthorpe | N Le Ha | 42 | B4 |
| North Muskham | N Musk | 110 | C1 |
| North Scarle | N Sca | 83 | F1 |
| North Wheatley | N Whea | 31 | E4 |
| Norton | Nort | 60 | B3 |
| Norwell | Norw | 110 | A4 |
| Nottingham | Nott | 172 | C4 |
| Nuthall | Nuth | 159 | E3 |
| Old Dalby | Ol Da | 218 | C2 |
| Oldcotes | Old | 17 | D3 |
| Ollerton | Oll | 77 | D2 |
| Ompton | Omp | 93 | D4 |
| Orston | Orst | 180 | A4 |
| Ossington | Oss | 95 | E3 |
| Owthorpe | Owth | 199 | F4 |
| Oxton | Oxt | 134 | B2 |
| Papplewick | Papp | 131 | F2 |
| Perlethorpe | Perl | 62 | C2 |
| Pinxton | Pinx | 113 | E1 |
| Pleasley | Plea | 87 | D3 |
| Plumtree | Plum | 197 | F3 |
| Plungar | Plun | 202 | C4 |
| Radcliffe on Trent | R on T | 175 | F2 |
| Ragnall | Ragn | 68 | A4 |
| Rainworth | Rain | 117 | F4 |
| Rampton | Ramp | 42 | C1 |
| Ranskill | Ran | 19 | D2 |
| Ratcliffe on Sour | R on S | 203 | F3 |
| Ravenshead | Raven | 117 | D1 |
| Redmile | Redm | 192 | C2 |
| Rempstone | Remp | 215 | E3 |
| Retford | Ret | 39 | F4 |
| Rhodesia | Rhod | 35 | D3 |
| Rolleston | Roll | 138 | A3 |
| Ruddington | Rudd | 196 | C3 |
| Rufford | Ruff | 104 | C4 |
| Sandiacre | Sand | 182 | A3 |
| Saundby | Saun | 23 | E3 |
| Saxilby | Sax | 56 | C2 |
| Scaftworth | Scaf | 10 | B2 |
| Scarcliffe | Scarc | 72 | A3 |
| Scarrington | Scarr | 178 | C4 |
| Screveton | Screv | 166 | C2 |
| Scrooby | Scro | 9 | F1 |
| Selston | Sels | 128 | C4 |
| Shelford | Shel | 164 | B1 |
| Shelton | Shelt | 168 | B3 |
| Shipley | Ship | 157 | D3 |
| Shirebrook | Shireb | 72 | B2 |
| Shireoaks | Shire | 34 | C3 |
| Sibthorpe | Sibt | 167 | F4 |
| Skellingthorpe | Skel | 71 | F2 |
| South Clifton | S Clift | 68 | C1 |
| South Leverton | S Lev | 42 | B3 |
| South Muskham | S Musk | 124 | B4 |
| South Normanton | S Norm | 113 | D4 |
| South Scarle | S Sca | 98 | B3 |
| South Wheatley | S Whea | 31 | F4 |
| Southwell | South | 121 | E1 |
| Spalford | Spal | 83 | D4 |
| Stanford on Soar | S on S | 214 | B1 |
| Stanton-by-Dale | S-by-D | 170 | A1 |
| Stanton-on-the-Wolds | S-on-W | 198 | B1 |
| Stapleford | Stap | 182 | C4 |
| Stapleford | Staple | 127 | E4 |
| Stathern | Stat | 202 | C2 |
| Staunton in the Vale | S in V | 169 | D2 |
| Staythorpe | Stay | 138 | B4 |
| Stoke Bardolph | St Ba | 175 | F4 |
| Strelley | Stre | 171 | D4 |
| Sturton Le Steeple | S Le S | 32 | B3 |
| Styrrup | Styr | 8 | B1 |
| Sutton Bonington | Su Bo | 213 | D4 |
| Sutton in Ashfield | S in A | 100 | B1 |
| Sutton on Trent | S on T | 96 | C4 |
| Sutton-cum-Lound | Sutt | 28 | C3 |
| Swinethorpe | Swine | 84 | B4 |
| Syerston | Syer | 153 | E2 |
| Thonock | Thon | 15 | F2 |
| Thorney | Thor | 69 | F4 |
| Thoroton | Thoro | 167 | F1 |
| Thorpe | Thorpe | 138 | C1 |
| Thorpe in the Glebe | T in G | 207 | F1 |
| Thorpe Salvin | Th Sa | 34 | A3 |
| Thrumpton | Thrum | 194 | B2 |
| Thurgarton | Thur | 151 | E4 |
| Tibshelf | Tibs | 99 | D3 |
| Tickhill | Tick | 8 | A4 |
| Tithby | Tith | 189 | F3 |
| Tollerton | Toll | 186 | B1 |
| Torksey | Tork | 44 | A1 |
| Torworth | Torw | 19 | D1 |
| Treswell | Tres | 42 | B2 |
| Trowell | Trow | 170 | B3 |
| Tuxford | Tux | 66 | A1 |
| Upper Broughton | Up Br | 210 | A1 |
| Upton | Upt | 52 | A3 |
| Upton | Upton | 122 | C1 |
| Walesby | Wale | 64 | A1 |
| Walkeringham | Walker | 13 | F3 |
| Walkerith | Walk | 14 | B3 |
| Wallingwells | Wall | 25 | E3 |
| Wellow | Wellow | 92 | C4 |
| West Bridgford | W Brid | 185 | E3 |
| West Burton | W Burt | 32 | B4 |
| West Drayton | W Dray | 51 | D1 |
| West Hallam | We Ha | 157 | D1 |
| West Leake | W Lea | 205 | D1 |
| West Markham | W Mark | 65 | D3 |
| West Stockwith | W Sto | 7 | E1 |
| Weston | West | 81 | D2 |
| Whatton | What | 179 | D2 |
| Whitwell | Whit | 45 | D3 |
| Widmerpool | Widm | 208 | A3 |
| Wigsley | Wig | 70 | A1 |
| Willoughby-on-the-Wold | W-on-W | 217 | E4 |
| Winkburn | Wink | 108 | A1 |
| Winthorpe | Wint | 125 | E3 |
| Wiseton | Wise | 21 | D4 |
| Wiverton Hall | Wi Ha | 190 | A3 |
| Woodbeck | Wood | 53 | D4 |
| Woodborough | Woodb | 149 | E2 |
| Woodsetts | Woods | 25 | D1 |
| Worksop | Work | 36 | A2 |
| Wroot | Wroot | 2 | A4 |
| Wymeswold | Wyme | 216 | B2 |
| Wysall | Wys | 207 | E2 |

1st Ave. Nott 173 D4
2nd Ave. Nott 173 D4
3rd Ave. Nott 173 D4
4th Ave. Nott 173 D4

A'court St. Nott 172 C3
Aaron Cl. Nott 185 D4
Abba Cl. Kim 158 C4
Abbey Bridge. Nott 172 C1
Abbey Cir. W Brid 186 A4
Abbey Cl. Aslo 178 C3
Abbey Cl. Huck 145 F4
Abbey Ct. Bees 183 F4
Abbey Ct. Mans 102 C4
Abbey Ct. Nott 172 C2
Abbey Dr. Bees 183 F4
Abbey Gr. Nott 173 F4
Abbey La. Aslo 178 C3
Abbey Rd. Bees 183 F4
Abbey Rd. Bing 178 A2
Abbey Rd. Blid 118 A3
Abbey Rd. East 144 A1
Abbey Rd. Edwin 91 E4
Abbey Rd. K-in-A 115 E3
Abbey Rd. Mans 102 C4
Abbey Rd. Matt 20 B4
Abbey Rd. News 130 C3
Abbey Rd. W Brid 186 A4
Abbey St. Ilk 157 F1
Abbey St. Nott 172 C1
Abbey St. Work 35 F1
Abbeydale Dr. Mans 102 B2
Abbeyfield Rd. Nott 184 C4
Abbot Cl. Keyw 197 F2
Abbot St. Awsw 158 B2
Abbots Cl. Arn 161 E3
Abbots Dr. Huck 145 F3
Abbots Rd. Huck 145 F3
Abbots Wlk. Huck 145 F3
Abbotsbury Cl. Nott 146 C1
Abbotsford Dr. Nott 173 E3
Abbotsford Mews. Ilk 157 E2
Abbott Lea. Mans 101 E4
Abbott Rd. Mans 101 E4
Abbott St. Lo Ea 193 E3
Abbott's Way. N-on-T 125 D1
Abbotts Cres. Farns 119 F4
Abbotts Croft. Mans 87 F1
Abbotts Way. Nott 172 B2
Abel Collin's Homes. Bees 171 F1
Abercarn Cl. Nott 160 A4
Aberconway St. Blid 118 A3
Aberdeen St. Nott 173 F3
Aberford Ave. Nott 172 B4
Abingdon Dr. Rudd 196 B4
Abingdon Gdns. Arn 162 A3
Abingdon Gdns. Bees 183 E2
Abingdon Rd. W Brid 186 A4
Abingdon Sq. Nott 160 A1
Abington Ave. S in A 100 C3
Acacia Ave. Ann Wo 130 A4
Acacia Ave. Gain 15 E1
Acacia Cl. Huck 146 A3
Acacia Cres. Carl 162 C1
Acacia Ct. Mans 88 C1
Acacia Rd. Bald 140 B3
Acacia Wlk. Bees 183 F3
Academy Cl. Nott 160 C2
Acaster Cl. Bees 184 A2
Acer Cl. Pinx 113 E2
Ackford Dr. Work 35 E2
Acland St. Gain 15 E1
Acle Gdns. Nott 146 A1
Acle Gdns. Nott 160 A4
Acorn Ave. Greas 158 B4
Acorn Bank. W Brid 185 D2
Acorn Bsns Park. Mans 102 A3
Acorn Cl. Bald 140 B3
Acorn Dr. Carl 163 D1
Acorn Park. Nott 184 C4
Acorn Ridge. Shireb 72 B3
Acre Edge Rd. Lax 78 C1
Acre The. K-in-A 115 D2
Acreage La. Shireb 72 C1
Acton Ave. Lo Ea 193 F3
Acton Ave. Nott 160 B2
Acton Cl. Lo Ea 193 F3
Acton Gr. Lo Ea 193 F3
Acton Rd. Arn 161 F4
Acton Rd. Lo Ea 193 F3
Acton St. Lo Ea 193 F3
Adam St. Ilk 170 A3
Adams Ct. Ilk 157 F2
Adams Hill. Keyw 197 F2
Adams Hill. Nott 172 B1
Adams Way. Mart 44 B4
Adamsway. Mans 103 D2
Adbolton Ave. Carl 162 C1
Adbolton Gr. W Brid 174 A1
Adbolton La. Ho Pi 174 C1
Adderley Cl. Nott 161 D3
Addington Ct. R on T 176 A2
Addington Rd. Nott 172 C3
Addison Dr. Huck 145 F4
Addison Rd. Carl 174 A4
Addison St. Nott 173 D3
Addison St. Tibs 99 D4
Addison Villas. East 143 F1
Adel Dr. Carl 162 C1
Adelaide Cl. Gain 24 C3
Adelaide Cl. Staple 170 C1
Adelaide Gr. Nott 160 C4
Adenburgh Dr. Bees 183 E1
Adrian Cl. Bees 182 C1
Adrians Cl. Mans 102 C3
Aegir Cl. Gain 24 C3
Aeneas Ct. Nott 173 D4
Agnes Villas. Nott 161 F1
Aidan Gdns. Bes Vil 147 D1
Ainsdale Cres. Nott 160 A2
Ainsdale Green. Ret 39 E2
Ainsley Rd. Nott 172 B3
Ainsworth Dr. Nott 173 D1
Aintree Cl. Kim 158 C4
Airedale Ave. Tick 8 A4
Airedale Cl. Lo Ea 193 D3
Airedale Ct. Bees 183 D2
Airedale Wlk. Nott 171 E2
Airedale. Work 36 A4
Aisby Wlk. Gain 24 C4
Aitchison Ave. Huck 145 F4
Alandale Ave. Shireb 72 C3
Alandale. Bils 105 F3
Alandene Rd. Kim 159 D4
Albany Cl. Arn 161 F4
Albany Cl. Huck 145 E3
Albany Cl. Mans 88 B1
Albany Ct. Staple 170 C1
Albany Dr. Mans 88 B1
Albany Pl. Mans 88 B1
Albany Rd. Nott 173 D4
Albany Sq. Nott 173 D2
Albany St. Gain 15 E1
Albany St. Ilk 170 A3
Albemarle Rd. Arn 161 E2
Albert Ave. Bald 140 B2
Albert Ave. Carl 174 A4
Albert Ave. Nott 172 B4
Albert Ave. Nuth 159 E3
Albert Ave. Sels 128 A2
Albert Ave. Staple 182 B4
Albert Ball Cl. Nott 160 C4
Albert Dr. Nott 172 C3
Albert Pl. Lough 220 A2
Albert Prom. Lough 220 B2
Albert Rd. Bees 184 A4
Albert Rd. Bunn 196 C1
Albert Rd. Hello 173 A2
Albert Rd. Lo Ea 193 E4
Albert Rd. Nott 172 C2
Albert Rd. Ret 39 F3
Albert Rd. Sand 182 A3
Albert Rd. W Brid 185 F4
Albert Sq. S in A 100 C1
Albert St. Bott 181 D2
Albert St. Carl 162 C1
Albert St. East 143 F2
Albert St. Huck 146 A4
Albert St. Lough 220 A2
Albert St. Mans 88 B2
Albert St. Mans 102 A3
Albert St. Mar War 74 A3
Albert St. N-on-T 139 F4
Albert St. Nott 173 E2
Albert St. R on T 175 F2
Albert St. S in A 100 B3
Albert St. S Norm 113 D3
Albert St. Staple 182 B4
Albert St. Work 35 F2
Alberta Ave. Sels 129 D4
Alberta Terr. Nott 173 D4
Albine Rd. Shireb 72 C3
Albion Centre The. Ilk 157 F1
Albion Cl. Work 35 F2
Albion Rd. Lo Ea 193 F4
Albion Rd. S in A 100 C1
Albion Rise. Nott 147 F1
Albion St. Bees 183 F4
Albion St. Mans 87 F1
Albion St. N-on-T 139 F4
Albion St. Nott 173 E2
Albion Terr. Mist 7 D1
Albury Dr. Nott 160 A1
Alcester St. Nott 184 C4
Alcock Ave. Mans 102 C4
Aldene Ct. Bees 183 E3
Aldene Way. Woodb 149 E2
Alder Cl. Bald 140 B3
Alder Cl. Mans 88 C1
Alder Cl. Shireb 72 B3
Alder Cl. Work 35 F1
Alder Ct. Mans 101 E3
Alder Gdns. Nott 160 A4
Alder Gr. Mans 88 A3
Alder Gr. Oll 77 E3
Alder Way. Keyw 198 A1
Alder Way. S in A 100 B2
Alder Way. Shireb 72 B2
Aldercar La. Ald 143 D3
Aldermens Cl. Nott 173 E1
Alderney St. Nott 172 C2
Alderson Cl. Tick 8 A4
Alderson Dr. Tick 8 A4
Alderson Rd. Work 35 F1
Alderton Rd. Nott 161 E3
Aldgate Cl. Nott 160 A4
Aldred St E. Work 36 A1
Aldred St W. Work 36 A1
Aldred St. Work 36 A1
Aldred's La. Hean 143 D1
Aldridge Cl. Bees 182 C1
Aldrin Cl. Nott 159 F3
Aldworth Cl. Nott 161 E3
Aldwych Cl. Bes Vil 147 D1
Aldwych Cl. Nott 159 E1
Alec Rose Gr. Gain 24 C4
Alexander Ave. N-on-T 125 D2
Alexander Ave. Sels 128 B4
Alexander Cl. Huck 131 D1
Alexander Rd. Farns 119 F3
Alexander St. East 143 F1
Alexander Terr. Pinx 113 E1
Alexandra Ave. Mans 88 A3
Alexandra Ave. Mans 102 A2
Alexandra Ave. S in A 100 C2
Alexandra Cres. Bees 184 A3
Alexandra Rd. Har 9 D2
Alexandra Rd. Lo Ea 193 E4
Alexandra St. K-in-A 115 D3
Alexandra St. Mar War 74 A3
Alexandra St. Nott 173 D4
Alexandra St. Staple 182 B3
Alexandra Terr. S in A 100 B3
Alford Cl. Bees 184 A3
Alford Rd. W Brid 186 A3
Alfred Ave. Carl 162 A1
Alfred Cl. Nott 173 E3
Alfred Ct. Mans 102 A4
Alfred St Central. Nott 173 E3
Alfred St N. Nott 173 E3
Alfred St S. Nott 173 F3
Alfred St. Gain 15 E1
Alfred St. K-in-A 115 D2
Alfred St. Lough 220 A3
Alfred St. Pinx 113 E2
Alfred St. S in A 100 C2
Alfreton Rd. Newt 99 D2
Alfreton Rd. Nott 172 C3
Alfreton Rd. Pinx 113 E2
Alfreton Rd. S in A 100 B1
Alfreton Rd. S Norm 113 D3
Alfreton Rd. Sels 128 B4
Alfreton Rd. Sels 129 D2
Alison Ave. Huck 131 E1
Alison Wlk. Nott 173 E3
All Hallow Cl. Ret 39 F2
All Hallows Dr. Carl 162 C1
All Hallows St. Ret 39 F2
All Saints' St. Nott 173 D3
All Saints' Terr. Nott 173 D3
Allcroft St. Mans 88 B2
Allen Dr. Mans 102 C3
Allen St. Huck 146 A4
Allen St. Work 35 F1
Allen's Green Ave. Sels 128 C3
Allen's Wlk. Nott 147 F1
Allenby Rd. South 136 B4
Allendale Ave. Bees 183 E1
Allendale Ave. Nott 160 A1
Allendale Rd. Rain 118 A4
Allendale Way. Mans 88 C1
Allesford La. Edin 120 A2
Alliance St. N-on-T 125 D1
Allington Ave. Nott 172 C2
Allington Dr. Mans 101 E4
Allison Ave. Ret 40 A2
Allison Gdns. Bees 183 E2
Allsopp Dr. Work 35 F3
Allwood Gdns. Huck 146 A3
Alma Cl. Carl 163 D1
Alma Cl. Nott 173 E3
Alma Hill. Kim 158 C4
Alma Rd. Nott 173 F3
Alma Rd. Ret 40 A4
Alma Rd. Sels 128 C3
Alma Rd. Sels 129 D3
Alma St. Nott 173 D4
Almond Ave. Shireb 72 C3
Almond Cl. Huck 146 A3
Almond Cl. Kim 158 C4
Almond Cl. Sax 57 D2
Almond Gr. Farn 139 D3
Almond Gr. K-in-A 114 C3
Almond Gr. Work 35 F1
Almond Rise. Mans 88 C1
Almond Wlk. Carl 163 D2
Alnwick Cl. Nott 160 B3
Alpha Terr. Nott 173 D3
Alpine Cres. Carl 174 B4
Alpine St. Nott 160 C1
Alport Pl. Mans 103 D4
Althea Ct. Nott 161 D1
Althorpe St. Nott 173 D3
Alton Ave. Nott 185 D2
Alton Cl. W Brid 185 E2
Alum Ct. Nott 160 C4
Alvenor St. Ilk 157 F1
Alverstone Rd. Nott 161 E1
Alvey Rd. Bald 140 C2
Alwood Gr. Nott 184 B1
Alwyn Rd. Nott 159 F1
Amanda Ave. C in L 25 F3
Amanda Rd. Har 8 C2
Amber Dr. Hean 143 D1
Amber Hill. Nott 161 D4
Ambergate Rd. Nott 172 A4
Amberley St. Nott 173 D2
Ambleside Dr. East 143 E2
Ambleside Grange. Work 35 F4
Ambleside Rd. Nott 160 A1
Ambleside Way. Carl 175 D4
Ambleside. Gam 186 B4
Ambleside. Oll 77 E3
Amcott Ave. Mist 14 A4
Amcott Way. Ret 39 F4
Amen Cnr. Caun 109 D3
Amersham Rise. Nott 160 A1
Amesbury Circ. Nott 160 A2
Amos La. S Sca 98 B2
Ampthill Rise. Nott 161 D2
Anastasia Cl. Gain 15 E2
Ancaster Gdns. Nott 172 A2
Anchor La. Hath 213 D1
Anchor Rd. East 143 E1
Anders Dr. Nott 159 F3
Anderson Cres. Bees 183 F4
Anderson Ct. Nott 161 D4
Andover Cl. Nott 172 A3
Andover Rd. Mans 101 E4
Andover Rd. Nott 160 C3
Andrew Ave. Carl 162 A1
Andrew Ave. Ilk 170 A4
Andrew Dr. Blid 118 A2
Andrews Dr. La Mi 143 D2
Anfield Cl. Bees 183 D1
Anford Cl. Nott 160 A3
Angel Alley. Nott 173 E2
Angel Row. Nott 173 E2
Angel Yd. Lough 220 A2
Angela Ave. Ann Wo 115 D1
Angela Cl. Nott 147 F1
Angell Green. Nott 195 E4
Anglia Way. Mans 103 D2
Angrave Cl. Nott 173 F4
Angus Cl. Arn 148 A1
Angus Cl. Kim 159 D3
Anmer Cl. Nott 173 D1
Annan Ct. Nott 172 A4
Anne's Cl. Carl 162 A1
Annesley Cutting. Ann Wo 130 B4
Annesley Gr. Nott 173 E3
Annesley La. Sels 129 D3
Annesley Rd. Ann Wo 130 A2
Annesley Rd. Huck 130 C1
Annesley Rd. Huck 145 F4
Annesley Rd. Linby 130 C1
Annesley Rd. W Brid 185 F4
Annesley Way. Mans 101 E3
Anslow Ave. Nott 184 A4
Anslow Ave. S in A 100 C3
Anson Wlk. Ilk 157 F2
Anstee Rd. Lo Ea 193 E3
Anstey Rise. Nott 173 F3
Anston Ave. Work 35 F3
Antill St. Staple 182 B3
Apley Cl. Gain 24 C4
Apollo Dr. Nott 159 F3
Appin Rd. Mans 101 E3
Apple Tree La. Carl 162 C1
Apple Wlk. Carl 174 A4
Appleby Cl. N-on-T 140 B4
Appleby Rd. Plea 86 C3
Appledore Ave. Bees 171 F1
Appledore Ave. Nott 171 F1
Appledorne Way. Nott 147 F1
Appleton Dr. Wyme 216 B3
Appleton Gate. N-on-T 125 D1
Appleton Rd. Bees 184 A2
Appleton Rd. Blid 118 A3
Appleton St. Mar War 74 A2
Appletree Cl. South 121 F1
Applewood Gr. Nott 161 E2
Arboretum St. Nott 173 D3
Arbrook Dr. Nott 172 B3
Arbutus Cl. Nott 184 B1
Arcade The. N-on-T 139 F4
Arcadia Ave. Shireb 72 C3
Arch Hill. Bes Vil 147 F2
Archdale Rd. Nott 161 E3
Archer Cres. Nott 171 F3
Archer Rd. Staple 182 C3
Archer St. Ilk 157 F2
Archers Dr. Bils 106 A3
Archway Rd. N Clip 90 B4
Arden Cl. Huck 146 B3
Arden Cl. Nott 184 A4
Arden Gr. Bing 177 E3
Ardleigh Cl. Nott 146 B1
Ardsley Cl. Hean 143 D1
Argosy Cl. Baw 9 F4
Argyle Cl. Mar War 73 F2
Argyle St. La Mi 143 E2
Argyle St. Mans 102 B3
Argyle St. Nott 172 C3
Ariel Cl. Nott 160 C3
Arkers Cl. Nott 160 B2
Arklow Cl. Nott 160 A1
Arkwright St N. Nott 173 E1
Arkwright St S. Nott 173 E1
Arkwright St. Gain 15 E1
Arkwright Wlk. Nott 173 E1
Arleston Dr. Nott 171 E2
Arlington Ave. Mans 88 C2
Arlington Cl. Huck 146 A2
Arlington Dr. Nott 161 E1
Arlington Way. Ret 39 F4
Armadale Cl. Arn 162 B4
Armfield Rd. Arn 162 B3
Armitage Dr. Lo Ea 194 A4
Armstrong Rd. Mans 101 E4
Armstrong Rd. Mans 101 F4
Armstrong Rd. Nott 159 F3
Armstrong Rd. Ret 39 F4
Arndale Rd. Nott 161 E3
Arne Ct. Nott 173 E1
Arnesby Rd. Nott 172 C2
Arno Ave. Nott 173 D4
Arno Vale Gdns. Arn 161 F3
Arno Vale Rd. Arn 161 F3
Arnold Ave. Lo Ea 193 D2
Arnold Ave. Ret 40 A2
Arnold Ave. South 121 F1
Arnold Cres. Lo Ea 193 D2
Arnold La. Carl 162 B2
Arnold Rd. Nott 161 D3
Arnos Gr. Nuth 159 E2
Arnot Hill Rd. Arn 161 F3
Arnside Cl. Nott 161 D3
Arnside Rd. Nott 161 D3
Arnside. Staple 182 C3
Arran Cl. Staple 170 C1
Arran Sq. Mans 101 E3
Arthur Ave. Nott 172 C2
Arthur Ave. Staple 182 C4
Arthur Cres. Carl 174 B4
Arthur Green Ave. Ann Wo 114 C1
Arthur Mee Rd. Staple 182 C3
Arthur Rd. Gain 15 F1
Arthur Short Cl. Whit 45 D3
Arthur St. Carl 175 D3
Arthur St. Mans 102 B3
Arthur St. Nott 173 D3
Arthur St. Pinx 113 E2
Artic Way. Kim 158 B4
Arum Croft. Ret 39 E2
Arun Dale. Mans 88 B1
Arundel Cl. Gain 15 F1
Arundel Cl. Sand 182 A2
Arundel Dr. Bees 171 D1
Arundel Dr. C in L 25 F3
Arundel Dr. Mans 101 F4
Arundel Dr. Ran 19 D3
Arundel St. Nott 173 D3
Arundel Way. Ret 39 E4
Arundel Wlk. Har 9 D3
Ascot Ave. Kim 158 C4
Ascot Cl. K-in-A 115 E2
Ascot Dr. Arn 161 E4
Ascot Dr. Huck 145 E3
Ascot Dr. Mans 102 C4
Ascot Park Est. Sand 182 B4
Ascot Rd. Nott 172 B4
Ascott Gdns. W Brid 185 D3
Ash Cl. Bing 178 A2
Ash Cl. Bu Jo 163 F2
Ash Cl. Huck 145 E3
Ash Cl. Pinx 113 E1
Ash Cl. Work 35 F1
Ash Cres. K-in-A 114 B3
Ash Cres. Kim 159 D3
Ash Ct. Carl 174 B4
Ash Gr. Brin 143 E4
Ash Gr. Gain 15 E1
Ash Gr. Hath 213 D1
Ash Gr. Keyw 198 A1
Ash Gr. Lo Ea 193 E3
Ash Gr. S in A 100 B4
Ash Gr. Sand 182 A4
Ash Gr. Sels 128 C4
Ash Gr. Shireb 72 C3
Ash Gr. Staple 182 B3
Ash Grove. Woodb 149 E3
Ash La. Cost 206 B2
Ash Lea Cl. Cotg 187 F1
Ash Mount Rd. La Mi 143 D2
Ash Rd. N-on-T 139 F2
Ash St. Ilk 157 F2
Ash Tree Ave. Baw 9 F4
Ash Tree Cl. South 136 B4
Ash Tree Cres. Mans 88 B3
Ash Tree Sq. Bees 183 D4
Ash Vale Rd. Wale 64 A1
Ash Villas. Nott 161 D1
Ash Wlk. E Lea 214 B4
Ashbourne Cl. Bees 171 D1
Ashbourne Ct. Nott 159 F3
Ashbourne Rd. Sels 129 D1
Ashbourne St. Nott 173 D3
Ashbourne St. Scarc 72 C2
Ashburnham Ave. Nott 172 C2
Ashburnham Ave. Nott 172 C2
Ashby Ave. Mans 88 B3
Ashby Rd. Kegw 203 D1
Ashby Rd. Kegw 212 A4
Ashby Rd. Lo Wh 212 B1
Ashby Rd. Lough 220 A2
Ashby Sq. Lough 220 A2
Ashchurch Dr. Nott 171 E1
Ashcroft Rd. Gain 24 B3
Ashcroft. Ret 39 E2

Ashdale Ave. Huck ........ 146 A3
Ashdale Rd. Arn ........ 162 A4
Ashdale Rd. Ilk ........ 170 A3
Ashdale Rd. Nott ........ 174 A3
Ashdown Cl. Nott ........ 185 D3
Ashdown Gr. Bing ........ 177 E2
Ashdown Way. Mist ........ 6 C1
Ashe Cl. Arn ........ 162 A4
Asher La. Rudd ........ 196 B3
Ashfield Ave. Bees ........ 184 A3
Ashfield Ave. Mans ........ 102 A4
Ashfield Dr. K-in-A ........ 114 C3
Ashfield Prec. K-in-A ........ 115 D3
Ashfield Rd. Nott ........ 173 F2
Ashfield Rd. S in A ........ 100 A2
Ashfield St. S in A ........ 101 D3
Ashford Dr. Raven ........ 117 D2
Ashford Pl. Ilk ........ 157 F3
Ashford Rise. Nott ........ 171 E1
Ashford Rise. S in A ........ 100 B2
Ashforth Ave. Hean ........ 143 D1
Ashforth St. Nott ........ 173 E3
Ashgate. S in A ........ 100 B2
Ashington Dr. Arn ........ 148 A1
Ashland Rd (W). S in A ........ 100 A2
Ashland Rd. S in A ........ 100 B2
Ashlands Cl. S in A ........ 100 A2
Ashlea. Mist ........ 6 C1
Ashleigh Way. Mans ........ 89 D1
Ashley Cl. Bees ........ 183 E3
Ashley Cres. Keyw ........ 197 F2
Ashley Ct. Work ........ 35 F3
Ashley Gr. Huck ........ 145 F4
Ashley La. Tres ........ 41 F1
Ashley La. Wood ........ 41 F1
Ashley Rd. Keyw ........ 197 F2
Ashley Rd. Work ........ 35 F3
Ashley St. Nott ........ 173 F3
Ashley Terr. Work ........ 35 F2
Ashling St. Nott ........ 173 E1
Ashmore Ave. S in A ........ 100 B1
Ashover Cl. Nott ........ 173 F4
Ashover Cl. Raven ........ 117 D2
Ashton Ave. Nott ........ 147 F1
Ashton Ct. S in A ........ 101 D3
Ashvale Rd. Tux ........ 66 A1
Ashview Cl. Lo Ea ........ 193 D4
Ashville Cl. Nott ........ 173 D1
Ashwater Dr. Carl ........ 162 B3
Ashwell Ave. Mans ........ 88 C3
Ashwell Gdns. Nott ........ 172 C4
Ashwell St. Carl ........ 174 C3
Ashwick Cl. Nott ........ 185 D3
Ashwood Ave. K-in-A ........ 115 E3
Ashwood Cl. Mans ........ 88 C3
Ashworth Ave. Rudd ........ 196 B4
Ashworth Cl. N-on-T ........ 140 B4
Ashworth Cl. Nott ........ 174 B3
Ashworth Cres. Carl ........ 162 A1
Ashworth Cres. N Le Ha ........ 32 B1
Askeby Dr. Nott ........ 159 E1
Askew La. Mar War ........ 74 A2
Askham La. Upt ........ 52 A3
Askham Rd. Ashkh ........ 51 F1
Askham Rd. E Mark ........ 51 F1
Aslockton Dr. Nott ........ 160 B1
Aspen Cl. Bing ........ 178 A2
Aspen Cl. Kettl ........ 55 D2
Aspen Cl. Tux ........ 66 A1
Aspen Cl. Wale ........ 64 A1
Aspen Ct. Mans ........ 88 C1
Aspen Ct. Tux ........ 66 A1
Aspen Rd. Nott ........ 159 F4
Asper St. Carl ........ 175 D4
Aspinall Ct. Nott ........ 172 B3
Aspley La. Nott ........ 172 B4
Aspley Park Dr. Nott ........ 172 A4
Aspley Pl. Nott ........ 172 C3
Aspley Rd. S in A ........ 100 B2
Asquith Mews. Mans ........ 102 C3
Asquith St. Gain ........ 15 D1
Asquith St. Mans ........ 102 C3
Assarts Rd. Nuth ........ 159 F2
Astcote Cl. Hean ........ 143 D1
Aster Rd. Nott ........ 173 F4
Astle Ct. Arn ........ 162 B3
Astley Cl. Ann Wo ........ 130 A4
Astley Dr. Nott ........ 161 F1
Aston Ave. Nott ........ 172 A1
Aston Ct. Ilk ........ 157 F1
Aston Dr. Nott ........ 146 B1
Aston Green. Bees ........ 182 C2
Astral Gr. Huck ........ 145 E2
Astrid Gdns. Nott ........ 160 C3
Astwith La. Al Hu ........ 85 D3
Astwood Cl. Nott ........ 171 F4
Athelstan Rd. Work ........ 35 F1
Atherfield Gdns. East ........ 143 F2
Atherton Rd. Ilk ........ 157 E2
Atherton Rd. Ship ........ 157 E2
Atherton Rise. Nott ........ 160 A2
Athorpe Gr. Nott ........ 160 C2
Atkin La. Mans ........ 102 A2
Attenborough La. Bees ........ 183 E1
Attenborough La. Bees ........ 183 E2
Attercliffe Terr. Nott ........ 173 E1
Attewell Rd. Awsw ........ 158 A3
Attlee Ave. Mans ........ 89 D1
Aubrey Rd. Nott ........ 161 D1
Auckland Cl. Nott ........ 172 C3
Auckland Rd. Huck ........ 145 E3
Auckland Rd. Ret ........ 39 E4
Audley Dr. Nott ........ 171 F1
Audon Ave. Bees ........ 183 F3
Audrey Cres. Mans ........ 88 B3
Augustine Gdns. Bes Vil ........ 147 D1
Ault Hucknall La. Al Hu ........ 86 A4
Aumberry Gap. Lough ........ 220 A2
Aurillac Way. Ret ........ 29 E1
Austen Ave. Lo Ea ........ 193 E3
Austen Ave. Nott ........ 173 D4
Austin Cl. Mans ........ 102 C4
Austin St. Nott ........ 160 B4
Austin St. Shireb ........ 73 D2
Austins Dr. Sand ........ 182 A2
Austrey Ave. Nott ........ 184 A4
Avalon Cl. Nott ........ 160 C3
Ave A. Nott ........ 173 E2
Ave B. Nott ........ 173 E2
Ave C. Nott ........ 173 E2
Ave D. Nott ........ 173 E2
Ave E. Nott ........ 173 F3
Avebury Cl. Nott ........ 195 E4
Avenue Cl. Nott ........ 160 C4
Avenue Rd. Ret ........ 39 F3
Avenue The. Calv ........ 148 C4
Avenue The. Gain ........ 15 F1
Avenue The. Gunt ........ 164 C3
Avenue The. Mans ........ 102 C2
Avenue The. N-on-T ........ 140 A4
Avenue The. S in A ........ 100 C1
Averham Cl. Mans ........ 101 E3
Averton Sq. Nott ........ 172 B2
Aviemore Cl. Arn ........ 162 A4
Avocet Wharf. Nott ........ 172 C1
Avon Ave. Huck ........ 145 F2
Avon Cl. Ann Wo ........ 129 F4
Avon Gdns. W Brid ........ 185 F4
Avon Pl. Bees ........ 184 A4
Avon Rd. Carl ........ 162 C1
Avon Rd. Nott ........ 174 A3
Avon Rise. Ret ........ 40 A4
Avon Vale Rd. Lough ........ 220 B1
Avon Way. Mans ........ 103 D3
Avon Way. Work ........ 35 F4
Avonbridge Cl. Arn ........ 148 B1
Avondale Cl. Lo Ea ........ 193 D3
Avondale Rd. Carl ........ 174 B3
Avondale. Cotg ........ 188 A2
Avondale. Mans ........ 102 C4
Avonlea Cl. Ilk ........ 170 A3
Awsworth La. Awsw ........ 158 B2
Awsworth La. Awsw ........ 158 B3
Awsworth La. Kim ........ 158 B3
Awsworth Rd. Ilk ........ 157 F1
Axford Cl. Carl ........ 162 C1
Aylesham Ave. Arn ........ 161 F3
Aylestone Dr. Nott ........ 172 A4
Ayr St. Nott ........ 173 D3
Ayscough Ave. Nuth ........ 159 E3
Ayton Cl. Nott ........ 173 D1
Azalea Ct. Greas ........ 158 B4
Azimghur Rd. What ........ 179 D2

Babbacombe Way. Huck ........ 145 E3
Babbington Cres. Carl ........ 162 C1
Babbington La. Kim ........ 158 C2
Babbington St. Tibs ........ 99 D3
Babington Ct. Bees ........ 183 E3
Babworth Cres. Ret ........ 39 E3
Babworth Ct. Mans ........ 102 B4
Babworth Rd. Babw ........ 39 E3
Babworth Rd. Ret ........ 39 E3
Back La. Clayp ........ 156 B3
Back La. Cotes ........ 220 C3
Back La. Cr Bu ........ 189 D3
Back La. E Mark ........ 66 A4
Back La. Eakr ........ 106 C4
Back La. Halam ........ 120 C1
Back La. Ilk ........ 157 F1
Back La. Lo Cl ........ 211 E2
Back La. Miss ........ 4 A1
Back La. Morton ........ 137 E2
Back La. N-on-W ........ 198 A3
Back La. Nuth ........ 159 E3
Back La. Oll ........ 77 D2
Back La. Ran ........ 19 D2
Back La. S in A ........ 99 F2
Back La. S in A ........ 100 C3
Back La. Th Sa ........ 34 A3
Back La. W-on-W ........ 217 E3
Back St. B in W ........ 142 A3
Back St. E Stock ........ 7 F1
Back St. S Clift ........ 68 C1
Back Terr. Ret ........ 39 F4
Bacon Cl. Greas ........ 158 A4
Bacon St. Gain ........ 24 B3
Bacton Ave. Nott ........ 160 A4
Bacton Gdns. Nott ........ 160 A4
Baden Powell Rd. Nott ........ 174 A2
Bader Rise. Matt ........ 20 A4
Bader. Nott ........ 185 D4
Badger Cl. Huck ........ 145 E3
Baggaley Cres. Mans ........ 88 A1
Bagnall Ave. Arn ........ 161 E4
Bagnall Rd. Nott ........ 160 B2
Bagshaw St. Mans ........ 87 D2
Baildon Cl. Nott ........ 172 B2
Bailey Brook Cres. La Mi ........ 143 D2
Bailey Brook Ind Est. Hean ........ 143 D1
Bailey Cl. Arn ........ 161 E4
Bailey Cres. Mans ........ 101 F4
Bailey Ct. R on T ........ 175 F1
Bailey Grove Rd. East ........ 143 E1
Bailey La. R on T ........ 175 F1
Bailey Rd. N-on-T ........ 139 F3
Bailey St. Carl ........ 175 D4
Bailey St. Nott ........ 160 C1
Bailey St. Staple ........ 182 B3
Bainbridge Rd. Lough ........ 220 B1
Bainbridge Rd. Mar War ........ 74 A2
Bainbridge Terr. S in A ........ 100 B3
Bainbridge The. Calv ........ 149 D4
Baines Ave. Bald ........ 140 B2
Baines Rd. Gain ........ 24 C4
Bainton Gr. Nott ........ 184 C1
Baker Ave. Arn ........ 148 A1
Baker La. Cuck ........ 60 A1
Baker Rd. Greas ........ 144 B1
Baker Rd. Mans ........ 88 B3
Baker St. Huck ........ 146 A4
Baker St. Ilk ........ 157 F1
Baker St. Nott ........ 173 D4
Baker's Hollow. Cotg ........ 187 F2
Baker's La. Co Ba ........ 200 C4
Baker's La. Redm ........ 192 C2
Bakerdale Rd. Nott ........ 174 A3
Bakers Cl. Nott ........ 172 C3
Bakewell Ave. Carl ........ 162 C1
Bakewell Cl. Bald ........ 140 B2
Bakewell Dr. Nott ........ 160 C4
Bakewell Rd. Lo Ea ........ 193 F3
Bala Dr. Nott ........ 161 D4
Balderton Ct. Mans ........ 101 F4
Balderton Gate. N-on-T ........ 140 A4
Balderton La. Codd ........ 141 D4
Baldwin Cl. Mans ........ 89 D1
Baldwin Ct. Nott ........ 172 C3
Baldwin St. Greas ........ 144 B1
Baldwin St. Nott ........ 173 D3
Balfour Rd. Nott ........ 172 C3
Balfour Rd. Staple ........ 182 B3
Balfour St. Gain ........ 15 E1
Balfour St. K-in-A ........ 115 E2
Balfron Gdns. Nott ........ 173 D1
Ball Hill. S Norm ........ 113 E3
Ball St. Nott ........ 173 F4
Ballantrae Cl. Arn ........ 162 A4
Ballerat Cres. Nott ........ 160 C4
Balloon Houses. Nott ........ 171 D2
Balls La. K-in-A ........ 115 E1
Balmoral Ave. W Brid ........ 185 F4
Balmoral Cl. C in L ........ 25 F3
Balmoral Cl. Mans ........ 88 C3
Balmoral Cl. Sand ........ 182 A2
Balmoral Cres. Nott ........ 171 E3
Balmoral Ct. Har ........ 9 D3
Balmoral Ct. Har ........ 9 D3
Balmoral Dr. Bees ........ 171 E1
Balmoral Dr. Mans ........ 87 F1
Balmoral Gr. Huck ........ 146 A4
Balmoral Rd. Bing ........ 177 E2
Balmoral Rd. Carl ........ 174 C3
Balmoral Rd. Nott ........ 173 D3
Bamburgh Cl. K-in-A ........ 114 C4
Bamford Dr. Mans ........ 103 D3
Bamford St. Newt ........ 99 D2
Bamkin Cl. Huck ........ 146 A3
Bampton Ct. Nott ........ 172 C3
Bampton St. Lough ........ 220 A2
Banbury Ave. Bees ........ 182 C2
Bancroft La. Mans ........ 101 F4
Bancroft Rd. N-on-T ........ 140 A3
Bancroft St. Nott ........ 160 B4
Banes Rd. Bing ........ 178 A2
Bangor Wlk. Nott ........ 173 E4
Bank Ave. S in A ........ 100 C1
Bank End Rd. Fin ........ 1 B2
Bank End Rd. Mis ........ 1 B2
Bank Hill. Lamb ........ 149 D2
Bank Hill. Woodb ........ 149 D2
Bank Pl. Nott ........ 173 E2
Bank Side. Ret ........ 39 F2
Bank St. La Mi ........ 143 E2
Bank St. Lo Ea ........ 193 F4
Bankfield Dr. Bees ........ 171 E1
Banks Ave. K-in-A ........ 114 C3
Banks Cl. Arn ........ 162 A3
Banks Cres. Bing ........ 177 F2
Banks Paddock. Bing ........ 177 F2
Banks Rd. Bees ........ 182 C1
Banks The. Bing ........ 177 F2
Bankwood Cl. Nott ........ 160 A1
Bannerman Rd. K-in-A ........ 114 C3
Bannerman Rd. Nott ........ 160 B3
Baptist La. Coll ........ 111 F4
Bar Gate. N-on-T ........ 124 C1
Bar La. Nott ........ 160 B1
Bar Lane Ind Park. Nott ........ 160 B1
Bar Rd N. Beck ........ 23 E4
Bar Rd S. Beck ........ 23 E4
Bar Rd. Beck ........ 23 E4
Bar Rd. Lax ........ 79 E2
Barbara Sq. Huck ........ 130 C1
Barber Cl. Ilk ........ 157 F2
Barber St. East ........ 144 A1
Barbers Wood Cl. Raven ........ 117 D1
Barbury Dr. Nott ........ 195 E4
Barclay Ct. Ship ........ 157 E2
Barden Rd. Arn ........ 162 A2
Bardfield Gdns. Nott ........ 146 B1
Bardney Dr. Nott ........ 160 A4
Bardsey Gdns. Nott ........ 161 D4
Barent Cl. Nott ........ 160 C3
Barent Wlk. Nott ........ 160 C3
Barker Ave E. Sand ........ 182 A3
Barker Ave N. Sand ........ 182 A3
Barker Ave. S in A ........ 100 B4
Barker Ave. Sels ........ 128 A2
Barker Gate. Huck ........ 145 F4
Barker Gate. Ilk ........ 157 F1
Barker Gate. Nott ........ 173 E2
Barker Hades Rd. Let ........ 16 A2
Barker Hill. Lowd ........ 150 C1
Barker St. S in A ........ 99 F2
Barker's La. Bees ........ 183 F2
Barkestone La. Bott ........ 181 D1
Barkestone La. Bott ........ 192 C4
Barkla Cl. Nott ........ 195 E4
Barkston Cl. Bald ........ 140 B2
Barley Brook Dr. La Mi ........ 143 D2
Barley Brook Wlk. La Mi ........ 143 D2
Barley Cft. S Norm ........ 113 D2
Barley Croft. W Brid ........ 185 E2
Barley Dale Dr. Staple ........ 170 B1
Barleylands. Rudd ........ 196 B3
Barling Dr. Ship ........ 157 E1
Barlock Rd. Nott ........ 160 C2
Barlow Dr (N). Awsw ........ 158 A2
Barlow Dr (S). Awsw ........ 158 A2
Barn Cl. Cotg ........ 187 F1
Barn Cl. Mans ........ 102 C3
Barn Cl. Work ........ 36 A4
Barn Croft. Bees ........ 183 D3
Barnards Pl. Lo Cl ........ 211 E2
Barnby Gate. N-on-T ........ 140 A4
Barnby La. Clayp ........ 156 B4
Barnby Rd. Bald ........ 140 B3
Barnby Rd. N-on-T ........ 140 B3
Barnby Wlk. Nott ........ 161 D2
Barndale Cl. Nott ........ 185 E2
Barnes Cres. S in A ........ 114 C4
Barnes Ct. Ret ........ 29 E1
Barnes Rd. Nott ........ 160 C4
Barnet Rd. Nott ........ 174 A4
Barnfield Cl. Lo Wh ........ 212 A2
Barnfield Rd. Coll ........ 98 A1
Barnfield. Nott ........ 185 D2
Barnsley Terr. Nott ........ 173 E1
Barnston Rd. Nott ........ 174 A3
Barnstone La. Gran ........ 191 D3
Barnum Cl. Nott ........ 171 F3
Barons Cl. Carl ........ 162 C1
Barra Mews. Nott ........ 173 D1
Barrack La. Nott ........ 172 C2
Barrack Row. Lough ........ 220 A3
Barratt Cl. Bees ........ 183 E1
Barratt Cl. Cr Bi ........ 189 D2
Barratt Cres. Bees ........ 183 E1
Barratt La. Bees ........ 183 E1
Barrel Hill Rd. S on T ........ 96 C4
Barrhead Cl. Nott ........ 146 C1
Barringer Rd. Mans ........ 102 C4
Barrington Cl. R on T ........ 175 F1
Barrow Rd. Cotes ........ 220 C3
Barrow Slade. Keyw ........ 197 F1
Barrow St. Lough ........ 220 A2
Barrowhill Wlk. Mans ........ 103 D3
Barrows Hill La. Sels ........ 128 B3
Barry St. Nott ........ 160 A4
Barrydale Ave. Bees ........ 183 F3
Bartlow Rd. Nott ........ 171 E4
Bartlow Rd. Nott ........ 171 E4
Barton Cl. Mans ........ 89 D1
Barton Cl. Rudd ........ 196 A3
Barton La. B in F ........ 195 D3
Barton La. Bees ........ 183 E1
Barton La. Nott ........ 184 B1
Barton Rd. Lo Ea ........ 194 A3
Barton St. Bees ........ 184 A3
Bartons Cl. Greas ........ 144 B1
Barwell Dr. Nott ........ 159 E1
Basa Cres. Nott ........ 160 C4
Basford Rd. Nott ........ 160 B1
Baskin La. Bees ........ 183 E2
Baslow Ave. Carl ........ 162 C1
Baslow Cl. Lo Ea ........ 193 D3
Baslow Dr. Nott ........ 172 A1
Baslow Way. Mans ........ 103 D3
Bassett Cl. Kim ........ 158 C4
Bassett Rd. Kim ........ 158 C4
Bassett The. Shireb ........ 72 B3
Bassingfield La. Gam ........ 186 C4
Bassingfield La. Ho Pi ........ 186 C4
Baston St. Nott ........ 172 C3
Bateman Gdns. Nott ........ 172 C4
Bateman Rd. E Lea ........ 205 F1
Bateman's Yd. K-in-A ........ 114 B2
Bath La. Mans ........ 102 B4
Bath La. Mar War ........ 73 E1
Bath St. Ilk ........ 157 F1
Bath St. Mans ........ 102 A3
Bath St. Nott ........ 173 E3
Bath St. S in A ........ 100 C2
Bathley La. S Musk ........ 110 A1
Bathley La. S Musk ........ 124 A4
Bathley St. Nott ........ 173 E1
Baths La. Huck ........ 146 A4
Bathurst Dr. Nott ........ 172 A3
Bathurst Terr. Scarc ........ 58 C1
Bathwood Dr. Mans ........ 101 F3
Bathwood Dr. S in A ........ 101 D1
Batley La. Al Hu ........ 86 C2
Baulk La. Bees ........ 182 C3
Baulk La. Bees ........ 182 C4
Baulk La. Har ........ 8 C3
Baulk La. Torw ........ 19 D1
Baulk La. Work ........ 35 F3
Baulk The. Clar ........ 40 C4
Baulk The. Work ........ 35 F3
Baulker La. Blid ........ 118 C2
Baulker La. Farns ........ 119 D2
Baulker La. N Clip ........ 90 A2
Baum's La. Mans ........ 102 B3
Bawtry Cl. Har ........ 8 C2
Bawtry Rd. Aust ........ 10 B4
Bawtry Rd. Blyth ........ 18 A3
Bawtry Rd. Ever ........ 11 D2
Bawtry Rd. Har ........ 9 D3
Bawtry Rd. Miss ........ 4 A2
Bawtry Rd. Tick ........ 8 B4
Bawtry Wlk. Nott ........ 173 F3
Baxter Hill. Mans ........ 86 C2
Baxter St. Lough ........ 220 A2
Bayard Ct. Nott ........ 172 B3
Bayard St. Gain ........ 15 E1
Bayliss Rd. Carl ........ 162 B2
Bayswater Rd. Kim ........ 158 C4
Baythorn Rd. Nott ........ 171 E3
Beacon Dr. K-in-A ........ 115 E3
Beacon Dr. Lough ........ 220 A1
Beacon Hill Dr. Huck ........ 145 E3
Beacon Hill Rd. G on H ........ 13 D1
Beacon Hill Rd. N-on-T ........ 140 B4
Beacon Hill Rise. Nott ........ 173 F3
Beacon Hts. N-on-T ........ 140 B4
Beacon Rd. Bees ........ 184 A3
Beacon Rd. Lough ........ 220 A1
Beacon Way. N-on-T ........ 140 B4
Beaconsfield St. Lo Ea ........ 193 F4
Beaconsfield St. Nott ........ 172 C4
Bean Ave. Work ........ 36 A2
Bean Cl. Nott ........ 159 F3
Beanford La. Calv ........ 133 F2
Beanford La. Oxt ........ 134 A2
Beardall St. Huck ........ 146 A3
Beardall St. Mans ........ 102 A4
Beardsall's Row. Ret ........ 39 F4
Beardsley Gdns. Nott ........ 173 D1
Beardsley Rd. Edwin ........ 76 B1
Beardsmore Gr. Huck ........ 130 C1
Beast Market Hill. N-on-T ........ 124 C1
Beast Market Hill. Nott ........ 173 E2
Beatty Wlk. Ilk ........ 157 F2
Beauclerk Dr. Nott ........ 160 C4
Beaufit La. Pinx ........ 113 F1
Beaufort Ct. W Brid ........ 185 E2
Beaufort Dr. Bees ........ 183 E3
Beaufort St. Gain ........ 15 E2
Beaulieu Gdns. W Brid ........ 185 E3
Beauly Dr. Mans ........ 101 E3
Beaumaris Dr. Bees ........ 183 D2
Beaumaris Dr. Carl ........ 163 D1
Beaumond Cross. N-on-T ........ 139 F4
Beaumont Ave. Mans ........ 102 C3
Beaumont Cl. Keyw ........ 197 F2
Beaumont Cl. Staple ........ 170 C1
Beaumont Gdns. W Brid ........ 185 E2
Beaumont Rd. Lough ........ 220 A1
Beaumont Rise. Work ........ 35 E2
Beaumont St. Gain ........ 24 B4
Beaumont St. Nott ........ 173 F2
Beaumont Wlk. N-on-T ........ 125 D1
Beauvale Cres. Huck ........ 145 F3
Beauvale Dr. Ilk ........ 157 F3
Beauvale Rd. Ann Wo ........ 114 C1
Beauvale Rd. Huck ........ 145 F3
Beauvale Rd. Nott ........ 173 E1
Beauvale Rise. East ........ 144 A2
Beauvale. East ........ 144 B1
Beaver Pl. Work ........ 35 F2
Beazley Ave. Mans ........ 101 F4
Beck Ave. Calv ........ 148 C4
Beck Cres. Blid ........ 118 A2
Beck Cres. Mans ........ 101 F4
Beck La. Clay ........ 21 F2
Beck La. Farns ........ 119 F3
Beck La. Mans ........ 101 D3
Beck St. Carl ........ 174 C4
Beck St. Nott ........ 173 E3
Beck St. Thur ........ 151 E4
Beckenham Rd. Nott ........ 172 C3
Beckett Ave. C in L ........ 25 F4
Beckett Ave. Gain ........ 15 F1
Beckett Ave. Mans ........ 87 F1
Beckett Ct. Carl ........ 162 B2
Beckford Rd. Nott ........ 173 F2
Beckhampton Rd. Nott ........ 161 D4
Beckingham Ct. Mans ........ 101 F4
Beckingham Rd. Walker ........ 14 A2

Beckingthorpe Dr. Bott 181 D2
Beckland Hill. E Mark 65 F3
Beckley Rd. Nott 159 F1
Beckside. W Brid 186 B3
Bed Hill La. Ruff 92 C2
Bedale Ct. Bees 183 D2
Bedale Rd. Nott 161 E3
Bedale. Work 36 A4
Bede House La. N-on-T 140 A4
Bede Ling. W Brid 185 E3
Bedford Ave. Mans 102 C4
Bedford Cl. Kegw 203 E1
Bedford Ct. Baw 9 F4
Bedford Ct. Staple 170 C1
Bedford Gr. Nott 160 B3
Bedford Row. Nott 173 E3
Bedford Sq. Lough 220 A2
Bedford St. Lough 220 A2
Bedlington Gdns. Nott 161 F1
Bee Hive La. Lough 220 A2
Beech Ave. Arn 162 A2
Beech Ave. Bees 184 A3
Beech Ave. Bing 178 A2
Beech Ave. Carl 174 C3
Beech Ave. E Lea 214 B4
Beech Ave. Gain 15 F1
Beech Ave. Huck 146 A4
Beech Ave. K-in-A 114 C3
Beech Ave. Keyw 198 A1
Beech Ave. Kim 159 D3
Beech Ave. Lo Ea 182 C1
Beech Ave. Mans 102 A3
Beech Ave. Nott 173 D4
Beech Ave. Oll 77 E2
Beech Ave. Pinx 113 F2
Beech Ave. Raven 116 C2
Beech Ave. S in A 100 A2
Beech Ave. Sand 182 A4
Beech Ave. Tick 8 A4
Beech Ave. Work 35 F3
Beech Cl. G on H 12 C1
Beech Cl. Nott 160 B2
Beech Cl. R on T 175 F1
Beech Cl. W Brid 186 A2
Beech Cres. Glap 86 A4
Beech Ct. Arn 162 A2
Beech Ct. Sels 129 D2
Beech Gr. Blid 118 B3
Beech Gr. C in L 25 F4
Beech Gr. S Norm 113 D3
Beech Hill Ave. Mans 87 F1
Beech Hill Cres. Mans 87 F1
Beech Hill Dr. Mans 87 F1
Beech Rd. Har 9 D3
Beech Rd. Sels 129 D2
Beech St. S in A 100 B4
Beech Tree Ave. Mans 88 A3
Beech Wlk. Elk 50 A2
Beecham Ave. Nott 173 F3
Beechcroft. Work 36 A3
Beechdale Ave. S in A 100 C2
Beechdale Cres. S in A 100 C2
Beechdale Rd. Mans 89 D1
Beechdale Rd. Nott 172 A4
Beecher La. Beck 14 A1
Beeches Rd. Lough 220 B1
Beeches The. Carl 174 A4
Beeches The. S in A 100 B4
Beeches The. Tux 65 F1
Beechways. Ret 39 E2
Beechwood Cl. Mans 89 D1
Beechwood Cl. S in A 101 D3
Beechwood Cres. Babw 37 F3
Beechwood Ct. S in A 101 D3
Beechwood Dr. Babw 38 B3
Beechwood Rd. Arn 162 A4
Beechwood Rd. K-in-A 114 C4
Beehive La. Eagle 84 C1
Beehive St. Ret 39 F3
Beeley Ave. S in A 100 C1
Beeley Cl. Mans 103 D3
Beeston Cl. Bes Vil 146 C2
Beeston Ct. Nott 160 B3
Beeston Fields Dr. Bees 183 E4
Beeston La. Nott 184 A4
Beeston Rd. N-on-T 140 A3
Beeston Rd. Nott 172 B1
Behay Gdns. Stay 138 B4
Beighton Ct. Mans 103 D3
Beighton St. S in A 100 C2
Belconnen Rd. Nott 161 D3
Belfmoor Cl. Whit 45 D3
Belford Cl. Nott 159 F4
Belfry Cl. K-in-A 114 C4
Bell La. Coll 111 F4
Bell La. Nott 185 D4
Bell La. West 81 D3
Bell St. Carl 174 B4
Bellamy Rd. Mans 103 D1
Bellar Gate. Nott 173 E2
Belle Vue La. Blid 118 A3
Belle-isle Rd. Huck 146 A4
Belleville Dr. Nott 161 D4
Bellevue Ct. Nott 173 F3
Bellmore Gdns. Nott 171 E3
Bells La. Nott 160 A2
Bellsfield Cl. Whit 45 D3
Belmond Cl. N-on-T 139 F3
Belmont Ave. Nott 160 B4
Belmont Cl. Bees 183 D2
Belmont Cl. Huck 146 A2
Belmont Cl. Mans 89 D1
Belmont Rd. Ann Wo 115 D1
Belper Ave. Carl 162 B1
Belper Cres. Carl 162 B1
Belper Rd. Nott 172 C4
Belper St. Mans 102 B4
Belper Way. Mans 102 B4
Belsay Rd. Nott 161 D4
Belsford Ct. Greas 159 D4
Belt Rd The. Gain 15 F2
Belton Cl. Sand 182 A2
Belton Dr. W Brid 185 D2
Belton Rd W Ext. Lough 220 A3
Belton Rd. Lough 220 A3
Belton St. Nott 172 C4
Belvedere Ave. Nott 172 C4
Belvedere St. Mans 102 A3
Belvoir Ave. Bott 181 D1
Belvoir Cl. Aslo 178 C2
Belvoir Cl. Lo Ea 193 F3
Belvoir Cres. N-on-T 140 A3
Belvoir Hill. Nott 173 F2
Belvoir Pl. Bald 140 B2
Belvoir Rd. Bald 140 B2
Belvoir Rd. Bott 181 D1
Belvoir Rd. Carl 175 D4
Belvoir Rd. Redm 192 C2
Belvoir Rd. W Brid 174 A1
Belvoir St. Huck 145 F4
Belvoir St. Nott 161 F1
Belvoir Terr. Mort 15 D2
Belward St. Nott 173 E2
Belwood Cl. Nott 184 C1
Bembridge Ct. Bees 183 D4
Bembridge Dr. Nott 161 D3
Bembridge. Work 36 A3
Ben Mayo Ct. Nott 172 C3
Ben St. Nott 172 C3
Benedict Ct. Bes Vil 147 D1
Benet Dr. Bils 106 A3
Benington Dr. Nott 171 E2
Benner Ave. Ilk 170 A3
Bennerley Ave. Ilk 157 F2
Bennerley Ct. Nott 159 F4
Bennerley Rd. Nott 159 F4
Bennett Ave. Mans 102 C3
Bennett Rd. Carl 162 A2
Bennett St. Lo Ea 182 B1
Bennett St. Nott 161 F1
Bennett St. Sand 182 A3
Benneworth Cl. Huck 145 F3
Bennington Wlk. Mans 88 C2
Bentick St. Mans 102 B4
Bentinck Ave. Toll 186 B1
Bentinck Cl. Boug 77 F3
Bentinck Ct. Nott 173 F2
Bentinck Rd. Carl 162 B1
Bentinck Rd. N-on-T 139 F3
Bentinck St. Ann Wo 114 C1
Bentinck St. Ann Wo 129 F4
Bentinck St. Huck 145 F4
Bentinck St. S in A 100 C2
Bentinck Terr. Mar War 74 A2
Bentley Ave. Nott 174 A3
Bentwell Ave. Arn 162 A4
Beresford Dr. Ilk 157 F3
Beresford Rd. Lo Ea 193 D3
Beresford Rd. Mans 88 B3
Beresford St. Mans 102 B3
Beresford St. Nott 172 C3
Berkeley Ave. Lo Ea 193 E3
Berkeley Ave. Nott 173 E4
Bernard Ave. Huck 131 D1
Bernard Ave. Mans 88 A3
Bernard St. Mans 101 F4
Bernard St. Nott 161 D1
Bernisdale Cl. Nott 146 C1
Berridge Rd. Nott 172 C4
Berridge Rd. Nott 173 D4
Berridge Road West. Nott 172 C4
Berriedale Cl. Arn 162 B4
Berristow La. S Norm 113 E4
Berry Ave. K-in-A 114 C3
Berry Hill Gdns. Mans 102 C2
Berry Hill Gr. Carl 162 C1
Berry Hill La. Mans 102 B2
Berry Hill Rd. Mans 102 B2
Berry Park Lea. Mans 102 B2
Berwick Ave. Mans 101 E4
Berwick Cl. Nott 161 E3
Berwin Cl. Lo Ea 182 A1
Beryldene Ave. Kim 159 D4
Bescar La. Oll 77 D1
Bescoby St. Ret 39 F4
Besecar Ave. Carl 162 C1
Besecar Cl. Carl 162 C1
Bessell La. Bees 182 B3
Bessell La. Staple 182 B3
Bessingham Dr. W Brid 185 E2
Besthorpe Ct. Mans 101 F4
Besthorpe Rd. Coll 98 A1
Besthorpe Rd. N Sca 83 E1
Bestwick Ave. Hean 143 D1
Bestwood Ave. Arn 161 F4
Bestwood Cl. Arn 161 F4
Bestwood Lodge Dr. Bes Vil 161 E4
Bestwood Lodge Dr. Nott 161 E4
Bestwood Park Dr W. Nott 146 C1
Bestwood Park Dr. Nott 161 D4
Bestwood Park View. Nott 147 F1
Bestwood Rd. Huck 146 B3
Bestwood Rd. Nott 146 B1
Bestwood Rd. Pinx 113 F1
Bestwood Terr. Nott 160 B4
Bethel Gdns. Huck 145 E3
Bethel St. Ilk 157 F1
Bethel Terr. Shire 34 C3
Bethnal Wlk. Nott 160 A4
Betula Cl. Nott 184 B1
Beulah Rd. K-in-A 115 D2
Bevan Cl. Rain 118 A4
Bevel St. Nott 172 C4
Bevercotes Rd. Tux 65 E2
Beverley Cl. Nott 171 D2
Beverley Cl. Rain 104 B1
Beverley Dr. Codd 125 F1
Beverley Dr. K-in-A 115 E2
Beverley Dr. Kim 158 C4
Beverley Dr. Mans 102 B1
Beverley Gdns. Carl 162 C1
Beverley Rd. Har 9 D2
Beverley Sq. Nott 173 F3
Beverley Wlk. C in L 25 F4
Beverleys Ave. Aslo 178 C2
Bewcastle Rd. Bes Vil 147 D1
Bewcastle Rd. Nott 147 D1
Bewick Dr. Nott 174 B3
Bexhill Ct. Bees 171 F1
Bexwell Cl. Nott 195 F4
Biant Cl. Nott 160 A2
Bidford Rd. Nott 159 F1
Bidwell Cres. Goth 195 D1
Big Barn La. Mans 102 C3
Big La. Clar 30 B2
Biggin St. Lough 220 A2
Bigsby Rd. Ret 30 A1
Biko Sq. Nott 172 C4
Bilberry Wlk. Nott 173 F4
Bilbie Wlk. Nott 173 E3
Bilborough Rd. Nott 171 E3
Bilborough Rd. Stre 171 E3
Bilby Gdns. Nott 173 F3
Billesdon Dr. Nott 160 C2
Billingsley Ave. Pinx 113 E2
Bilsthorpe Rd. Eakr 92 B1
Bingham Ave. S in A 101 D3
Bingham Rd. Cotg 187 F2
Bingham Rd. Mans 103 D2
Bingham Rd. Nott 161 E1
Bingham Rd. R on T 176 A2
Bingham Rd. Wi Ha 189 F3
Birch Ave. Bees 184 A2
Birch Ave. Carl 174 B4
Birch Ave. Farns 119 F4
Birch Ave. Ilk 170 A4
Birch Ave. Kim 159 D3
Birch Ave. Rain 104 B1
Birch Cl. Kim 159 D3
Birch Cl. Ramp 42 C1
Birch Cl. Raven 117 D1
Birch Croft Dr. Mans 89 D1
Birch Ct. Tux 65 F1
Birch Gr. Gain 15 E1
Birch Gr. Mans 103 D2
Birch Gr. Shireb 72 B3
Birch Lea. Arn 161 E4
Birch Lea. E Lea 205 E1
Birch Pas. Nott 173 D3
Birch Rd. Bald 140 B3
Birch Rd. Oll 77 E2
Birch Rd. Whit 45 E3
Birch St. Mar War 73 F3
Birch Tree Cl. Mans 89 E2
Birch Tree Cres. K-in-A 114 C2
Birchdale Ave. Huck 146 A3
Birchen Holme. S Norm 113 D2
Birchenhall Ct. Farn 139 D2
Birches The. Raven 117 D2
Birchfield Rd. Arn 148 A1
Birchlands. Mans 88 C1
Birchover Pl. Ilk 157 F3
Birchover Rd. Nott 171 E3
Birchwood Ave. Lo Ea 193 D4
Birchwood Ave. Lo Ea 193 E3
Birchwood Cl. Raven 117 D1
Birchwood Cl. S in A 100 C3
Birchwood Cl. S Norm 113 D2
Birchwood Cl. South 121 E1
Birchwood Dr. Raven 117 D1
Birchwood Dr. S in A 100 B4
Birchwood Rd. Nott 171 E2
Bird's La. Ann Wo 114 C1
Birdcroft La. Walker 14 A3
Birding St. Mans 88 A1
Birdsall Ave. Nott 171 F2
Birkdale Ave. Boug 77 E3
Birkdale Cl. Ilk 157 E1
Birkdale Cl. W Brid 186 A2
Birkdale Dr. K-in-A 114 C3
Birkdale Gr. Ret 39 E2
Birkdale Way. Nott 160 C4
Birkdale. Work 36 A3
Birkin Ave. Bees 183 D1
Birkin Ave. Nott 172 C4
Birkin Ave. R on T 176 A2
Birkin Ave. Rudd 196 B4
Birkland Ave. Arn 162 A2
Birkland Ave. Mans 88 B2
Birkland Ave. Mar War 74 A2
Birkland Ave. Nott 173 E3
Birkland Dr. Edwin 76 A1
Birkland St. Mans 102 B4
Birklands Ave. Oll 77 E3
Birklands Ave. Work 36 B1
Birklands Cl. Mar War 74 A3
Birks Cl. Whit 45 E3
Birks Rd. Mans 101 E4
Birley St. Staple 182 B3
Birling Cl. Nott 159 F4
Birrel St. Gain 15 D1
Birrell Rd. Nott 173 D4
Bisham Dr. W Brid 186 A4
Bishop Alexandra Ct. N-on-T 139 F4
Bishop St. East 143 F1
Bishop St. Lough 220 B2
Bishop St. Mans 102 A3
Bishop St. S in A 100 C2
Bishop's Dr. South 136 C4
Bishop's Wlk. Mar War 74 A3
Bishopdale Cl. Lo Ea 193 D3
Bishopdale. Work 36 A4
Bishopfield La. Ran 19 D3
Bishops Cl. Keyw 197 F2
Bishops Hill. Mans 103 F1
Bishops Rd. Bing 177 E3
Bishops Way. Huck 146 A4
Bispham Dr. Bees 182 C1
Black La. Swine 71 F1
Black Scotch La. Mans 102 C2
Blackacre. Lamb 163 F3
Blackburn Cl. Coll 98 A1
Blackburn Pl. Ilk 157 F2
Blackcliff Field Cl. Whit 45 D3
Blacketts Wlk. Nott 195 E4
Blackfriars Cl. Nuth 159 E2
Blackham Rd. Lough 220 A1
Blackhill Dr. Carl 174 C4
Blackrod Cl. Bees 183 D1
Blacksmith La. Kelh 124 A2
Blacksmith La. Torw 19 D1
Blacksmiths Cl. Ne Br 219 E4
Blacksmiths La. N Sca 83 E1
Blackstone Wlk. Nott 173 E1
Blackstope La. Ret 40 A4
Blackthorn Cl. Bing 178 A2
Blackthorne Cl. Bald 140 A3
Blackthorne Dr. East 143 E1
Blackthorne Dr. Lowd 150 B1
Blackwell Rd. S in A 99 F2
Bladon Cl. Nott 161 F1
Bladon Ct. Nott 172 C3
Bladon Rd. Rudd 196 A4
Blair Ct. Nott 173 E1
Blair Gr. Sand 182 A2
Blaise Cl. Nott 195 F4
Blake Cl. Arn 162 A4
Blake Cres. Mans 102 C4
Blake Ct. Lo Ea 193 D3
Blake Rd. Staple 182 C3
Blake Rd. W Brid 186 A4
Blake St. Ilk 157 F1
Blake St. Mans 88 A1
Blakeney Ct. Mans 88 C2
Blakeney Dr. Mans 102 B2
Blakeney Rd. R on T 176 A2
Blakeney Wlk. Arn 161 F3
Bland La. Epp 150 A3
Blandford Ave. Lo Ea 193 D3
Blandford Gdns. W Brid 185 E3
Blandford Rd. Bees 183 E3
Blankney Cl. Sax 57 D2
Blankney St. Nott 160 C2
Blantyre Ave. Nott 146 C1
Blatherwick Rd. N-on-T 140 B4
Blatherwick's Yd. Arn 161 F4
Bleachers Yd. Nott 160 C1
Bleak Hill Way. Mans 101 F2
Bleak Hills La. Mans 101 F2
Bleasby Cres. S in A 101 D1
Bleasby Rd. Bleas 151 E4
Bleasby Rd. Thur 151 E4
Bleasby St. Nott 173 F2
Bleasdale Cl. Carl 163 D1
Blenheim Ave. Carl 162 B1
Blenheim Ave. Lowd 150 C1
Blenheim Cl. Mans 88 B1
Blenheim Cl. Rudd 196 A4
Blenheim Dr. Bees 183 E3
Blenheim Gdns. E Brid 165 E1
Blenheim La. Huck 145 F1
Blenheim La. Stre 145 F1
Blenheim Pl. S in A 99 F2
Blenhiem Ct. Sand 182 A2
Bley Ave. E Lea 214 B4
Blidworth La. Blid 133 E4
Blidworth La. Mans 103 E1
Blidworth La. Rain 117 F4
Blidworth La. Raven 103 E1
Blidworth Rd. Farns 119 F3
Blidworth Rd. K-in-A 115 F2
Blidworth Waye. Papp 131 E2
Blidworth Waye. Raven 131 F4
Blind La. Oxt 134 B2
Bloomgrove Rd. Ilk 157 F1
Bloomsgrove St. Nott 172 C3
Blue Bell Hill Rd. Nott 173 F3
Blue Bell Yd. Tux 65 F2
Bluebell Cl. Huck 145 E3
Bluebell Cl. S in A 100 A3
Bluebell Cl. Sels 128 C1
Bluebell Gr. K-in-A 114 C4
Bluecoat Cl. Nott 173 E3
Bluecoat St. Nott 173 E3
Blundell Cl. Nott 173 F4
Blyth Cl. Mans 87 E1
Blyth Gdns. Nott 161 F1
Blyth Gr. Work 36 A3
Blyth Rd. Babw 48 C2
Blyth Rd. Bir 8 C2
Blyth Rd. Elk 48 C2
Blyth Rd. Hod 27 F3
Blyth Rd. Old 16 C3
Blyth Rd. Oll 77 D3
Blyth Rd. Perl 63 D2
Blyth Rd. Ran 19 D2
Blyth Rd. Styr 8 C2
Blyth Rd. Styr 18 A4
Blyth Rd. Tick 8 C3
Blyth Rd. Work 36 A3
Blyth St. Nott 161 F1
Blyton Rd. Thon 15 E2
Blyton Wlk. Nott 161 D4
Boar La. N-on-T 139 F4
Boat La. Ald 143 D4
Boat La. E Sto 152 B4
Boat La. Hover 151 F1
Boatmans Cl. Ilk 157 F1
Bobbers Mill Bridge. Nott 172 B4
Bobbers Mill Rd. Nott 172 C4
Boden Dr. Nuth 159 E3
Boden St. Nott 172 C3
Bodmin Ave. Huck 145 E3
Bodmin Ct. Mans 103 D1
Bodmin Dr. Nott 160 B1
Bohem Rd. Lo Ea 182 B2
Bold Cl. Nott 160 A4
Bolero Cl. Nott 171 F3
Bolham La. Ret 29 F1
Bolingey Way. Huck 145 E3
Bollard's La. Su Bo 213 D4
Bolsover St. Huck 146 A4
Bolsover St. Mans 102 B3
Bolton Ave. Bees 183 E2
Bolton Cl. W Brid 186 A4
Bolton La. Hose 211 F4
Bolton Terr. R on T 175 F2
Bond St. Arn 161 F4
Bond St. Nott 173 F2
Bonemill La. Clar 30 B1
Bonemill La. Work 35 E3
Bonetti Cl. Arn 162 B3
Boniface Gdns. Bes Vil 147 D1
Bonington Dr. Arn 161 F4
Bonington Rd. Arn 162 A2
Bonington Rd. Mans 101 F3
Bonner Hill. Calv 148 C3
Bonner La. Calv 149 D3
Bonner's Rd. Awsw 158 B2
Bonnington Cl. Nott 160 A3
Bonnington Cres. Nott 161 E2
Bonny Mead. Cotg 187 F1
Bonsal Ct. Mans 103 D3
Bonsall St. Lo Ea 193 F4
Bonser Cl. Carl 174 C4
Bonser Cres. S in A 99 F1
Bonser Gdns. S in A 100 B1
Booth Ave. Plea 87 D3
Booth Cl. Nott 173 E3
Booth Cres. Mans 87 E1
Booth St. Mans 88 A2
Boots Yd. S in A 99 F2
Borders Ave. K-in-A 114 C4
Borlace Cres. Staple 182 C3
Borman Cl. Nott 159 F3
Borough St. Kegw 203 E1
Borrow Bread La. Bleas 152 A4
Borrowdale Dr. Lo Ea 193 D3
Borrowell. Kegw 203 E2
Boscowan Ct. Ilk 157 F2
Bosden Cl. Nott 171 E3
Bosley Sq. Nott 184 A4
Bostock's La. Sand 182 A2
Boston St. Nott 173 E3
Boswell Cl. Kinou 200 A1
Boswell Cl. Mans 102 B2
Bosworth Dr. Greas 144 A2
Bosworth St. Mans 101 E4
Bosworth Way. Lo Ea 193 F3
Bosworth Wlk. Nott 173 D1
Botany Ave. Mans 101 F3
Botany Ave. Nott 173 F4
Botany Cl. W Brid 185 E1
Botany Dr. Ilk 157 F3
Bothe Cl. Lo Ea 193 E3
Bottle La. Nott 173 E2
Bottleacre La. Lough 220 A3
Bottom Green. Up Br 210 A1
Bottom Row. N-on-T 140 A4
Boughton Cl. S in A 100 C3

Boughton Ind Est. Kirton ...... 78 A3
Boughton Rd. Rhod ............. 35 D3
Bould St. Mans ..................... 87 F1
Boundary Cl. Shireb ............ 72 C3
Boundary Cres. Bees ......... 171 F1
Boundary Cres. Blid ........... 118 A3
Boundary Ct. N-on-T .......... 139 F4
Boundary La. East ............ 143 E2
Boundary Rd. Bees ............ 183 F4
Boundary Rd. N-on-T ......... 139 F4
Boundary Rd. W Brid ......... 185 F2
Boundary Row. Work ........... 35 F1
Boundary Wlk. Scarc ........... 58 C1
Bourne Ave. K-in-A ........... 115 D2
Bourne Ave. Sels .............. 129 D4
Bourne Cl. Bees ................ 171 E1
Bourne Dr. Raven .............. 117 D1
Bourne Mews. Carl ............ 175 D3
Bourne St. Carl ................. 175 D3
Bournmoor Ave. Nott ......... 184 C1
Bovill St. Nott ..................... 172 C3
Bovington Ct. Ret ................ 29 F1
Bow St. Mans ....................... 88 C2
Bowbridge Gdns. Bott ........ 181 D2
Bowbridge La. Bald ............ 140 A2
Bowbridge La. Bott ............. 180 C2
Bowbridge Rd. N-on-T ....... 140 A3
Bowden Dr. Bees .............. 184 A3
Bowers Ave. Nott ............... 173 E4
Bowes Well Rd. Ilk ............ 157 F1
Bowland Cl. Nott ............... 174 A4
Bowland Rd. Bing .............. 177 E2
Bowler Ct. Lough .............. 220 B2
Bowling Green Rd. Gain ...... 15 D1
Bowling St. Mans ............... 102 B3
Bowlwell Ave. Nott ............. 160 C4
Bowne St. S in A ............... 100 C2
Bowness Ave. Nott ............ 160 B1
Box Cres. K-in-A ............... 114 C3
Boxley Dr. W Brid .............. 185 E2
Boy La. Edwin ..................... 76 A1
Boyce Gdns. Nott .............. 161 F1
Boycroft Ave. Nott ............. 173 F4
Boyd Cl. Arn ...................... 148 A1
Boyer St. Lough ................ 220 B2
Boyer's Orchard. Harb ........ 202 A2
Boynton Dr. Nott ................ 161 F1
Bracadale Rd. Nott ............ 146 C1
Bracebridge Ave. Work ........ 36 A2
Bracebridge Ct. Work .......... 36 A1
Bracebridge Dr. Nott .......... 171 E4
Bracebridge. Work .............. 36 A2
Bracey Rise. W Brid ........... 185 F2
Bracken Ave. Boug .............. 77 F3
Bracken Cl. Carl ................. 162 B1
Bracken Cl. Gain ................. 15 D2
Bracken Cl. K-in-A ............. 114 C4
Bracken Cl. Lo Ea .............. 182 A1
Bracken Cl. Mar War ........... 74 B2
Bracken Cl. Nott ................ 159 F1
Bracken Hill La. Miss ............ 4 A3
Bracken Hill. Mans ............. 103 D3
Bracken La. Ret .................. 40 A3
Bracken Rd. Lo Ea ............. 182 A1
Brackendale Ave. Arn ......... 161 F4
Brackendale Dr. Wale .......... 64 A1
Brackenfield Ave. Mans ....... 88 C2
Brackenfield Dr. Greas ...... 158 A4
Brackenfield Rise. Raven ... 117 D2
Brackenhurst La. South ..... 136 B3
Brackenwood Cl. Mans ........ 89 D1
Brackhills Cl. Mans ............. 88 C1
Bracknell Cres. Nott ........... 160 B1
Brackner La. Kirk ............... 106 A2
Bracton Dr. Nott ................ 173 F3
Bradbourne Ave. Nott ........ 185 D3
Bradbury St. Nott .............. 174 A2
Bradden Ave. Staple .......... 170 C1
Bradder La. Mans .............. 102 A3
Bradfield Rd. Nott .............. 159 F1
Bradforth Ave. Mans .......... 103 D4
Bradgate Cl. Sand ............. 182 A2
Bradgate Rd. Nott .............. 173 D4
Bradley St. Sand ............... 182 B3
Bradley Wlk. Nott ............... 195 F4
Bradley. Nott ...................... 195 F4
Bradleys Orch. Hover ......... 151 E1
Bradman Gdns. Arn ........... 162 A3
Bradmore Ave. Rudd .......... 196 B4
Bradmore Ct. Mans ............ 103 D2
Bradmore La. Plum ............ 197 E3
Bradmore Rise. Nott .......... 161 E2
Bradshaw St. Lo Ea ........... 193 D3
Bradwell Cl. Greas ............. 158 B4
Bradwell Dr. Nott ............... 161 D4
Braemar Ave. East ............ 143 F1
Braemar Dr. Carl ............... 163 D1
Braemar Rd. Mans ............... 89 F2
Braemar Rd. Nott ............... 160 B4
Brail Wood Cl. Bils ............. 106 A3
Brail Wood Rd. Bils ............ 106 A3
Brailsford Ct. Mans ............ 103 D3
Brailsford Rd. Nott ............. 172 C1
Brake La. Boug .................... 77 F4
Brake Rd. Wale .................... 63 F1
Brake View. Boug ................ 77 F3
Bramber Gr. Nott ............... 195 F4
Bramble Cl. Bees ............... 183 E1
Bramble Cl. Boug ................. 77 E3
Bramble Cl. Lo Ea .............. 182 A1
Bramble Cl. Nott ................ 160 B2
Bramble Cl. Shireb ............... 72 C3
Bramble Ct. Carl ................ 162 C1
Bramble Dr. Carl ................ 174 A4
Bramble Gdns. Nott ........... 172 A4
Bramble La. Mans .............. 103 D3
Bramble Rd. Ret .................. 40 A2
Bramble Way. Har .................. 8 C2
Brambles The. Wale ............ 64 A1
Brambleway. Cotg .............. 188 A1
Brambling Cl. Mans ............ 102 C4
Bramcote Ave. Bees .......... 183 E3
Bramcote Ct. Mans ............ 103 D2
Bramcote Dr W. Bees ......... 183 E4
Bramcote Dr. Bees ............ 183 F4
Bramcote Dr. Nott .............. 171 E2
Bramcote Dr. Ret ................. 39 E3
Bramcote La. Bees ............ 183 E3
Bramcote La. Nott .............. 171 E2
Bramcote Rd. Bees ............ 183 F4
Bramcote Wlk. Nott ............ 172 C3
Bramerton Rd. Nott ............ 171 E3
Bramhall Rd. Nott ............... 171 E3
Bramley Cl. South .............. 136 C4
Bramley Ct. Kim ................. 158 C3
Bramley Ct. S in A ............. 100 C2
Bramley Rd. Nott ............... 159 F1
Bramley Wlk. Mans ............ 101 E4
Bramoote St. Nott .............. 172 C3
Brampton Ave. Hean .......... 143 D1
Brampton Ct. Gam ............. 186 B4
Brampton Dr. Staple .......... 182 C3
Brancaster Cl. Nott ............ 160 A2
Brancliffe La. Shire .............. 34 C4
Brand La. S in A ................ 100 B3
Brand St. Nott .................... 173 F1
Brandish Cres. Nott ........... 184 B1
Brandon Cl. Bald ............... 140 C2
Brandreth Ave. Nott ........... 173 F4
Brandreth Ave. S in A ........ 100 B2
Brandreth Dr. Greas ........... 158 A4
Branklene Cl. Kim .............. 158 C4
Branksome Wlk. Nott .......... 173 E1
Bransdale Cl. Lo Ea ........... 193 D3
Bransdale Rd. Nott ............ 184 B1
Bransdale. Work .................. 36 A4
Branston Ave. Farns .......... 119 F3
Branston Cl. Wint ............... 125 E3
Branston Gdns. W Brid ...... 185 E2
Branston Wlk. Nott ............. 161 E2
Brantford Ave. Nott ............ 184 C1
Brassington Cl. Greas ........ 158 A4
Brassington Ct. Mans .......... 88 C2
Braunton Cl. Huck .............. 145 E3
Brayton Cres. Nott ............. 160 B3
Breach Rd. Hean ................ 157 D4
Breadsall Ct. Ilk .................. 157 F2
Breamer Rd. Coll ................ 112 A4
Brechin Cl. Arn .................. 148 A1
Brechin Ct. Mans ................. 88 A3
Brechin. Work ...................... 36 A3
Breck Bank Cres. Oll ........... 77 E3
Breck Bank. Oll .................... 77 E3
Breck Hill Rd. Arn ............... 161 F2
Breck La. Matt ...................... 20 A4
Breckbank. Mans .................. 88 C1
Brecks La. Elst ................... 154 A1
Brecks La. Stap .................. 127 F4
Brecks Rd. Ret ..................... 39 E2
Breckswood Dr. Nott ........... 195 F4
Brecon Cl. Lo Ea ................ 193 D4
Brecon Cl. Nott ................... 160 A2
Brecon Cl. Rain .................. 104 B1
Bredon Cl. Lo Ea ................ 193 D4
Breedon St. Lo Ea ............... 182 B1
Brendon Ct. Bees ................ 183 D4
Brendon Dr. Kim ................. 158 C4
Brendon Dr. Nott ................ 172 A3
Brendon Gdns. Nott ............ 172 A3
Brendon Gr. Bing ................ 177 E3
Brendon Rd. Nott ................ 172 A3
Brendon Way. Lo Ea ........... 182 A1
Brentcliffe Ave. Nott ........... 174 A4
Bretby Ct. Mans ................. 103 D3
Brett Cl. Huck ..................... 145 F3
Bretton Rd. Raven .............. 117 D2
Brewery La. Ever ................. 11 E2
Brewery La. Ret ................... 39 F3
Brewery St. Kim .................. 158 C3
Brewster Rd. Nott ................ 173 F4
Brewsters Cl. Bing .............. 177 F2
Brewsters Way. Ret .............. 29 E1
Briar Ave. Sand .................. 182 A2
Briar Cl. Bees ..................... 171 F1
Briar Cl. Huck ..................... 145 F3
Briar Cl. Keyw .................... 197 F2
Briar Cl. Rain ...................... 104 A1
Briar Cl. S in A .................. 100 B3
Briar Cl. Work ....................... 35 E1
Briar Ct. Har .......................... 8 C2
Briar Ct. Nott ...................... 173 D1
Briar Ct. Oll .......................... 77 E3
Briar Gate. Cotg ................. 188 A1
Briar Gate. Lo Ea ................ 182 A1
Briar La. Mans .................... 103 D2
Briar Lea. Ret ....................... 39 E2
Briar Lea. Work ..................... 35 E1
Briar Rd. Greas .................. 158 B4
Briar Rd. Oll .......................... 77 E3
Briarbank Ave. Carl ............ 174 A4
Briarbank Wlk. Carl ............ 174 A4
Briars The. Miss ..................... 4 B2
Briarwood Ave. Nott ........... 174 A4
Briarwood Cl. Mans .............. 89 D1
Briarwood Ct. Nott .............. 161 F2
Briber Hill. Blyth ................... 18 A1
Briber Rd. Blyth .................... 18 A1
Brick Kiln La. Mans ............ 101 E4
Brick Yard Rd. Gams ............ 50 B3
Brickcliffe Rd. E Lea ........... 205 F1
Brickenell Rd. Calv ............. 148 C3
Brickenhole La. Walker ......... 13 F3
Brickings Way. S Le S ......... 32 B3
Brickley Cres. E Lea ........... 205 F1
Brickyard Dr. Huck ............. 146 B3
Brickyard La. E Brid ........... 165 E1
Brickyard La. Farns ............ 120 A3
Brickyard La. Miss ................. 4 B2
Brickyard La. R on T .......... 176 A2
Brickyard La. S Norm ......... 113 D3
Brickyard La. Su Bo ........... 213 F4
Brickyard La. W Lea ........... 214 A4
Brickyard La. Walker ............ 13 E3
Brickyard. Huck .................. 146 B3
Bride Church La. Tick ............. 8 A4
Bridegate La. Hick .............. 209 F3
Bridge Ave. Bees ................ 183 F3
Bridge Cl. Whit ..................... 45 D3
Bridge Ct. Huck .................. 146 A3
Bridge End Ave. Sels .......... 128 C4
Bridge End Ave. Sels .......... 129 D4
Bridge Farm La. Nott .......... 184 C1
Bridge Gr. W Brid ............... 185 F4
Bridge Green Walk. Nott .... 159 F1
Bridge Pl. Sax ...................... 57 D2
Bridge Pl. Work .................... 35 F2
Bridge Rd. Gain .................... 24 B4
Bridge Rd. Nott ................... 171 E3
Bridge St. Gain ..................... 24 B4
Bridge St. Ilk ....................... 157 F2
Bridge St. La Mi .................. 143 E2
Bridge St. Lo Ea .................. 182 B1
Bridge St. Lough ................. 220 A2
Bridge St. Mans .................. 102 B4
Bridge St. N-on-T ................ 139 F4
Bridge St. Sand ................... 182 B3
Bridge St. Sax ....................... 57 D2
Bridge St. Work ..................... 35 F1
Bridgegate. Ret ..................... 39 F4
Bridgend Cl. Staple ............. 182 B3
Bridgeway Centre. Nott ....... 173 E1
Bridgeway Ct. Nott .............. 173 E1
Bridgford Rd. Kneet ............ 166 A4
Bridgford Rd. W Brid ........... 185 F4
Bridgford St. Mans .............. 102 C3
Bridgnorth Dr. Nott .............. 184 C1
Bridgnorth Way. Bees ......... 182 C2
Bridle Cl. S in A .................. 100 A3
Bridle Rd. Bees ................... 183 D4
Bridle Rd. Bu Jo .................. 163 F3
Bridle Ways. E Brid ............. 165 E1
Bridlesmith Gate. Nott ........ 173 E2
Bridleway The. Mans ............ 88 C1
Bridlington St. Nott ............. 172 C4
Bridport Ave. Nott ............... 172 B3
Brielen Rd. R on T .............. 176 A2
Brierfield Ave. Nott ............. 185 D2
Brierley Green. Carl ............ 175 D4
Brierly Cotts. S in A ............ 100 C2
Brierly Rd. S in A ................ 100 B2
Bright Sq. Mans .................... 87 E1
Bright St. Gain ...................... 24 B4
Bright St. Ilk ........................ 157 F2
Bright St. Nott ..................... 172 C3
Bright St. S Norm ................ 113 D3
Brightmoor St. Nott ............. 173 E3
Brimington Ct. Mans ............ 88 C2
Brindley Rd. Nott ................. 171 E3
Brinkhill Cres. Nott .............. 184 C2
Brinkley Hill. South ............. 137 D3
Brinsley Cl. Nott .................. 160 A1
Brinsley Hill. Brin ................ 128 B1
Brisbane Cl. Mans ................. 88 B3
Brisbane Ct. Bald ................ 140 B2
Brisbane Dr. Nott ................ 160 C4
Brisbane Dr. Staple ............. 170 C1
Bristol Rd. Ilk ...................... 157 F1
Britannia Ave. Nott ............. 160 C3
Britannia Rd. Lo Ea ............. 182 B1
Britannia Terr. Gain .............. 24 B4
British Fields. Tux ................. 65 E2
Brittania Ct. N-on-T ............ 139 F4
Britten Gdns. Nott ............... 173 F3
Brixham Rd. Huck ............... 145 E3
Brixton Rd. Nott .................. 172 C3
Brixworth Way. Ret ............... 40 A4
Broad Cl. Woodb ................. 149 E2
Broad Eadow Rd. Nott ......... 159 F4
Broad Gate. Darl ................... 66 C4
Broad Gate. E Mark ............... 66 C4
Broad Gores. Clar .................. 30 B2
Broad La. Brin ..................... 143 F4
Broad La. Cott ....................... 43 D3
Broad La. S Lev ..................... 43 D3
Broad La. Whit ...................... 45 E3
Broad La. Work ..................... 45 E3
Broad Meer. Cotg ................ 187 F2
Broad Oak Cl. Nott .............. 173 F4
Broad Oak Dr. Brin .............. 143 F4
Broad Oak Dr. Staple .......... 182 B3
Broad Pl. Whit ....................... 45 E3
Broad St. Lo Ea ................... 193 E4
Broad St. Lough .................. 220 A2
Broad St. Nott ..................... 173 E3
Broad Valley Dr. Bes Vil ..... 146 C2
Broad Wlk. Nott ................... 160 B2
Broadfields. Calv ................. 148 C4
Broadgate Ave. Bees ........... 184 A4
Broadgate La. Bees ............. 184 A4
Broadgate La. Kelh .............. 123 F3
Broadgate. Bees .................. 184 A4
Broadhill Rd. Kegw ............. 203 E1
Broadholme Rd. Sax .............. 57 D1
Broadholme St. Nott ............ 172 C2
Broadhurst Ave. Nott ........... 160 B1
Broadings La. Lane ................ 54 A3
Broadlands. S Norm ............ 113 D2
Broadlands. Sand ................. 182 A2
Broadleigh Cl. W Brid .......... 185 E2
Broadmead. Bu Jo ............... 163 F3
Broadstairs Rd. Bees ........... 182 C1
Broadstone Cl. W Brid ......... 185 E3
Broadway Ct. Nott ............... 172 C3
Broadway East. Carl ............ 174 B3
Broadway The. Mans ........... 102 B3
Broadway. Ilk ...................... 157 F2
Broadway. Nott ................... 173 E2
Broadwood Ct. Bees ............ 184 A4
Broadwood Rd. Nott ............ 161 D4
Brockdale Gdns. Keyw ........ 197 F2
Brockenhurst Rd. Mans ....... 101 E3
Brockhall Rise. Hean ........... 143 D1
Brockhurst Gdns. Nott ......... 173 F3
Brocklehurst Dr. Edwin .......... 91 E4
Brocklesby Cl. Gain ............... 24 C4
Brockley Rd. W Brid ............ 186 A4
Brockton Ave. Farn ............. 139 D3
Brockwell The. S Norm ........ 113 D2
Brockwood Cres. Keyw ....... 197 F2
Bromfield Cl. Nott ............... 174 B4
Bromley Ave. N-on-T ........... 140 A3
Bromley Cl. Nott .................. 160 A3
Bromley Pl. Nott .................. 173 D2
Bromley Rd. W Brid ............. 185 F3
Brompton Cl. Bes Vil ........... 147 D1
Brompton Way. W Brid ........ 185 E2
Bronte Ct. Nott .................... 173 D3
Brook Ave. Arn .................... 162 A4
Brook Cl. Greas ................... 144 B1
Brook Cl. Lo Ea ................... 193 F3
Brook Cl. Nott ..................... 160 A3
Brook Cotts. Ilk ................... 157 F2
Brook Ct. Hean .................... 143 D1
Brook Dr. Kinou ................... 199 F1
Brook Gdns. Arn .................. 162 A4
Brook La. Gam ..................... 186 B4
Brook Rd. Bees ................... 183 F4
Brook Side. Lough ............... 220 A2
Brook St. Huck .................... 146 A4
Brook St. Nott ..................... 173 E3
Brook St. S in A .................. 100 C1
Brook St. Tibs ........................ 99 D3
Brook Terr. Work ................... 35 F1
Brook Vale Rd. La Mi ........... 143 E1
Brook View Ct. Keyw ............ 197 F1
Brook View Dr. Keyw ........... 197 F1
Brookdale Ct. Nott ............... 161 E3
Brookdale Rd. S in A ............ 101 D2
Brooke Cl. Bald .................... 140 B3
Brooke Cl. Work ..................... 36 B2
Brooke St. Ilk ...................... 170 A3
Brooke St. Sand ................... 182 A3
Brookfield Ave. Huck ............ 146 A3
Brookfield Ave. S in A .......... 100 B2
Brookfield Cres. Shireb .......... 72 C3
Brookfield Ct. Nott ............... 173 E1
Brookfield Dr. Hover ............ 151 E2
Brookfield Gdns. Arn ............ 162 A4
Brookfield Rd. Arn ............... 161 F4
Brookfield Rd. Arn ............... 162 A4
Brookhill Ave. Pinx ............... 113 E2
Brookhill Cres. Nott ............. 171 F2
Brookhill Dr. Nott ................. 171 F2
Brookhill La. Pinx ................. 113 F3
Brookhill Leys Rd. East ........ 143 F1
Brookhill Rd. Pinx ................ 113 E1
Brookhill St. Staple .............. 182 B3
Brookland Ave. Mans ........... 101 F4
Brookland Cl. Gunt ............... 165 D3
Brookland Dr. Bees .............. 183 E3
Brooklands Cl. Coll ................ 98 A1
Brooklands Cres. Carl ........... 163 D1
Brooklands Dr. Carl .............. 163 D1
Brooklands Rd. Nott ............. 174 A4
Brooklands. Widm ................ 208 B2
Brooklyn Ave. Bu Jo ............. 163 F3
Brooklyn Cl. Nott .................. 160 B3
Brooklyn Rd. Nott ................. 160 B3
Brooksby La. Nott ................. 184 C2
Brookside Ave. E Lea ........... 205 E1
Brookside Ave. Mans .............. 88 B3
Brookside Ave. Nott ............. 171 E1
Brookside Cl. Lo Ea ............. 193 D4
Brookside Gdns. Rudd ......... 196 A4
Brookside Rd. Rudd ............. 196 A4
Brookside Wlk. Har .................. 9 D2
Brookside. E Lea ................. 214 C4
Brookside. Greas ................. 143 F2
Brookside. Huck ................... 146 A3
Brookside. Lowd ................... 150 B1
Brookthorpe Way. Nott ......... 185 D2
Brookvale Cl. Mans .............. 103 D3
Brookwood Cres. Carl .......... 174 B4
Broom Cl. Calv ..................... 148 C4
Broom Cl. Tick ........................ 8 A4
Broom Rd. Calv ..................... 148 C4
Broom Wlk. Carl ................... 174 A4
Broome Cl. Bald ................... 140 A3
Broomfield Cl. Sand .............. 182 A3
Broomfield La. Farns ............ 119 F3
Broomfield La. Matt ................ 19 F4
Broomhead St. Lough ........... 220 B2
Broomhill Ave. Ilk ................. 170 A3
Broomhill La. Mans ............... 101 F4
Broomhill Rd. Huck ............... 146 A3
Broomhill Rd. Kim ................. 159 D3
Broomhill Rd. Nott ................ 160 B3
Broomston La. Haxey ............... 2 C1
Brora Rd. Nott ...................... 160 B4
Brotts La. Nor on T ................ 81 F3
Brotts Rd. Nor on T ................ 81 F3
Brough La. Coll ..................... 112 A2
Brough La. Elk ........................ 50 A2
Brough Rd. Stap ................... 127 D4
Brough Rd. Staple ................. 112 C1
Brougham Ave. Mans .............. 87 E1
Broughton Dr. Notts ............. 172 B2
Broughton La. Lo Cl .............. 211 D1
Broughton Rd. Stap .............. 127 F4
Broughton St. Bees ............... 183 F4
Brown Ave. Mans .................... 88 A2
Brown Cres. S in A ................ 101 D2
Brown La. B in F ................... 194 C3
Brown La. Thor ....................... 70 A3
Brown St. Mans ..................... 101 F4
Brown St. Notts ..................... 172 C4
Brown's Flats. Kim ................ 158 C3
Brown's La. E Brid ................ 165 E2
Brown's Rd. Lo Ea ................ 193 F4
Brownes Rd. Bing .................. 178 A3
Brownhill Cl. Cr Bi ................ 189 D2
Browning Cl. Arn ................... 161 E4
Browning Cl. Work ................... 36 A3
Browning Rd. Bald ................. 140 C3
Browning St. Mans ................ 102 A4
Brownlow Cl. E Sto ............... 153 E4
Brownlow Dr. Nott ................. 146 C1
Brownlow Rd. Mans ................. 87 F1
Brownlow's Hill. Codd ........... 126 A1
Browns Croft. Nott ................ 160 B2
Browns La. Lough ................. 220 A2
Browns La. S-on-W ............... 198 B1
Broxholme La. Brox ................. 57 F3
Broxholme La. Sax .................. 57 E3
Broxton Rise. Nott ................. 160 A2
Broxtowe Ave. Kim ................ 158 B3
Broxtowe Ave. Nott ................ 160 B1
Broxtowe Dr. Huck ................ 131 D1
Broxtowe Dr. Mans ................ 102 B3
Broxtowe Hall Cl. Nott ........... 160 A1
Broxtowe La. Nott .................. 160 A1
Broxtowe St. Nott .................. 161 E1
Bruce Cl. Nott ....................... 173 E1
Bruce Dr. W Brid ................... 185 E4
Brunel Ave. Greas ................. 144 A2
Brunel Cl. Styr .......................... 8 C1
Brunel Dr. N-on-T .................. 125 E1
Brunnen The. S Norm ............ 113 D2
Brunner Ave. Shireb ................ 72 C2
Brunswick Dr. Staple ............. 182 C3
Brunt St. Mans ...................... 102 B3
Brunt's La. Bing ..................... 165 E1
Brushfield St. Nott ................ 172 C4
Brussels Terr. Ilk ................... 157 F1
Brusty Pl. Bu Jo .................... 163 F3
Bryans Close La. Miss ............... 3 F2
Brynsmoor Rd. Brin ............... 143 F4
Buck's La. Su Bo .................. 213 D4
Buckfast Way. W Brid ............ 186 A4
Buckingham Ave. Huck .......... 146 A4
Buckingham Cl. K-in-A ........... 114 C3
Buckingham Cl. Mans .............. 88 C3
Buckingham Ct. Sand ............ 182 A2
Buckingham Rd. Arn .............. 161 F3
Buckingham Rd. Sand ............ 182 A2
Buckingham Rise. Work ........... 35 F4
Buckland Ct. Nott .................. 172 C3
Buckland Dr. Woodb .............. 149 E2
Bucklee Dr. Calv .................... 148 C4
Bucklow Cl. Nott .................... 160 B1
Budby Ave. Mans ................... 102 C3
Budby Cres. Mar War ............... 74 C4
Budby Rd. Cuck ....................... 60 A2
Budby Rise. Huck .................. 146 A4
Bulcote Dr. Bu Jo .................. 163 E2
Bulcote Rd. Nott .................... 184 C2
Bulgrave Mews. W Brid .......... 185 E2
Bulham La. S on T .................... 81 F1
Bull Close Rd. Nott ................. 184 C4
Bull Yd. South ....................... 121 F1

Bull Yd. Work 35 F1
Bullace Ct. Mans 88 C1
Bullace Rd. Nott 173 F4
Buller Cl. Coll 98 A1
Buller St. Ilk 170 A3
Buller Terr. Nott 161 E2
Bullivant Ave. Elmt 58 B4
Bullivant St. Nott 173 E3
Bullock Cl. Mans 88 A3
Bullpit Rd. Bald 140 C3
Bulpit La. Eagle 98 C3
Bulstode Pl. Kegw 203 E1
Bulwell High Rd. Nott 160 A4
Bulwell La. Nott 160 B2
Bulwer Rd. K-in-A 114 C3
Bulwer Rd. Nott 172 C3
Bunbury St. Nott 173 E1
Bungalow La. Bils 106 A3
Bunny Hill. Bunn 206 B3
Bunny Hill. Cost 206 B3
Bunny La. E Lea 205 F3
Bunny La. Keyw 197 F1
Bunting St. Nott 172 C1
Buntings La. Carl 174 B4
Bunyan Green Rd. Sels 128 B4
Bunystone La. Co Ba 200 C4
Burbage Ct. Mans 103 D3
Burden La. Harb 202 A2
Burden La. Shel 164 B1
Burder St. Lough 220 B3
Burfield Ave. Lough 220 A2
Burford Rd. Nott 172 C4
Burford St. Arn 161 F4
Burgage La. South 121 F1
Burgage. South 121 F1
Burgass Rd. Nott 174 A4
Burge Cl. Nott 173 E1
Burgh Hall Cl. Bees 183 E1
Burhill. Cotg 188 A1
Burke St. Nott 173 D3
Burleigh Cl. Carl 174 C4
Burleigh Rd. Lough 220 A2
Burleigh Rd. W Brid 186 A3
Burleigh Sq. Bees 183 E2
Burleigh St. Ilk 157 F1
Burley Rise. Kegw 203 E1
Burlington Ave. Nott 161 D2
Burlington Ave. Shireb 72 C3
Burlington Dr. Mans 87 F1
Burlington Rd. Carl 174 C4
Burlington Rd. Nott 161 E2
Burma Rd. Blid 118 A3
Burmaston Rd. Mans 103 D3
Burn St. S in A 101 D2
Burnaby St. Nott 160 B2
Burnaston Ct. Mans 88 C2
Burnbreck Gdns. Nott 171 F2
Burndale Wlk. Nott 160 C4
Burneham Cl. E Brid 165 E1
Burnham Ave. Bees 183 F2
Burnham Ct. Mans 102 B2
Burnham St. Nott 161 E1
Burnham Way. Nott 173 E2
Burnmoor La. Egma 80 A4
Burnor Pool. Calv 148 C4
Burns Ave. Mans 88 B1
Burns Ave. Nott 173 D3
Burns La. Mar War 74 A3
Burns Rd. Work 36 A2
Burns St. Gain 15 D1
Burns St. Mans 102 A4
Burns St. Nott 173 D3
Burns The. Mar War 74 B3
Burnside Cl. K-in-A 114 C4
Burnside Dr. Bees 171 E1
Burnside Gr. Toll 186 B1
Burnside Green. Nott 171 E3
Burnside Rd. Nott 171 E3
Burnside Rd. W Brid 185 F3
Burnt Oaks Cl. Mans 88 B2
Burntleys Rd. Hayt 30 B4
Burntstump Hill. Arn 132 B1
Burnwood Ave. Mans 103 D4
Burnwood Dr. Nott 171 E3
Burr La. Ilk 157 F1
Burrows Ave. Bees 171 F1
Burrows Cres. Bees 171 F1
Burrows Ct. Nott 173 F3
Burtness Rd. Nott 184 C1
Burton Ave. Carl 174 A4
Burton Cl. Carl 175 D4
Burton Cl. Harb 202 A2
Burton Dr. Bees 183 E2
Burton La. What 179 D2
Burton Mandeville Ct. Nott 173 E1
Burton Rd. Carl 175 D4
Burton Rd. S in A 100 B2
Burton Rise. Wale 64 A1
Burton St. Gain 24 B4
Burton St. Lough 220 A1
Burton St. Nott 173 E3
Burton Wlk. E Lea 214 C4
Burton Wlks. Lough 220 A1
Burwell Ct. Mans 88 C2
Burwell St. Nott 172 C3
Bush Cl. Nott 160 C4
Bushmead Mews. Work 35 F1
Buskeyfield La. Nort 59 F2
Bute Ave. Nott 172 C2
Butler Ave. R on T 176 A2
Butler Cl. Cr Bu 189 D3
Butler Cres. Mans 87 E1
Butler Dr. Blid 117 F2
Butlers Cl. Huck 146 B3
Butt Hill. Whit 45 D3
Butt La. E Brid 165 F1
Butt La. Mans 88 B1
Butt La. N on S 213 F2
Butt Rd. Bing 178 A2
Butt St. Sand 182 A3
Buttercup Cl. Bald 140 B3
Butterhall Cl. Whit 45 D3
Buttermead Cl. Staple 170 B1
Buttermere Cl. Gam 186 B4
Buttermere Ct. Nott 161 E1
Buttermere Dr. Bees 183 E4
Butterton Cl. Ilk 170 A4
Buttery La. S in A 100 C4
Buxton Ave. Carl 162 C1
Buxton Ct. Ilk 157 E1
Buxton Rd. Mans 87 E1
Byard La. Nott 173 E2
Bycroft Rd. Mort 15 E2
Bye Pass Rd. Gunt 164 C3
Bye Path Rd. Ret 39 F4
Bye-pass Rd. Bees 183 E2
Byfield Cl. Nott 172 C3
Byford Cl. Nott 161 F1
Byley Rd. Nott 171 D3
Byrne Ct. Arn 162 A3
Byron Ave. K-in-A 115 D4
Byron Ave. Lo Ea 182 A2
Byron Ave. Mans 88 B1
Byron Ave. S in A 101 D2
Byron Cl. Darl 67 D4
Byron Cl. N-on-T 140 A3
Byron Cres. Awsw 158 B2
Byron Cres. Raven 116 C2
Byron Ct. Bald 140 C2
Byron Ct. Nott 173 F2
Byron Ct. Staple 170 C1
Byron Gdns. South 121 F1
Byron Gr. Nott 161 E2
Byron Rd. Ann Wo 130 B4
Byron Rd. W Brid 185 F4
Byron St. Arn 161 E3
Byron St. Blid 118 A3
Byron St. Huck 146 A3
Byron St. Ilk 157 F1
Byron St. Mans 102 A4
Byron St. News 130 A3
Byron St. Shireb 72 C2
Byron Way. Work 36 A2
Cabin Leas. Lough 220 A3
Cad La. Nor on T 81 F4
Caddaw Ave. Huck 146 A3
Cadlan Cl. Nott 161 D4
Cadlan Ct. Nott 161 D4
Caenby Cl. Gain 24 C4
Caernarvon Pl. Bees 183 D2
Caincross Rd. Nott 171 E4
Cairngorm Dr. Bes Vil 147 D1
Cairns Cl. Nott 161 D3
Cairns St. Nott 173 E3
Cairnsmore Cl. Lo Ea 182 A1
Cairo St. Nott 160 C1
Caister Rd. Nott 195 F4
Caithness Ct. Nott 161 D1
Calcroft Cl. Nott 160 B1
Caldbeck Cl. Gam 186 B4
Caldbeck Ct. Bees 183 D2
Caldbeck Wlk. Nott 161 D4
Calder Wlk. Nott 160 A4
Calderdale Dr. Lo Ea 193 D3
Calderdale. Nott 171 D2
Calderhall Gdns. Nott 161 E4
Caldwell St. Lough 220 A2
Caledon Rd. Nott 161 D2
Caledonian Rd. Ret 40 A3
Calf Croft. Whit 45 D3
California Rd. Farn 139 D2
Calladine La. S in A 114 B4
Callaway Cl. Nott 171 F3
Calstock Rd. Arn 161 F3
Calveley Rd. Nott 171 F4
Calver Cl. Nott 172 B2
Calver St. Mans 88 C2
Calverton Ave. Carl 162 A1
Calverton Cl. Bees 183 D1
Calverton Ct. Mans 103 D2
Calverton Rd. Arn 148 A1
Calverton Rd. Blid 118 A1
Camb's La. N Whea 31 F4
Cambell Gdns. Arn 148 B1
Camberley Rd. Nott 160 A4
Camborne Cres. Ret 29 F1
Camborne Dr. Nott 160 B1
Cambourne Gdns. Raven 116 C1
Cambrai Terr. Work 35 F2
Cambria Mews. Nott 173 E4
Cambria Rd. Mans 87 E2
Cambridge Cl. Rain 118 A4
Cambridge Cres. Staple 170 B1
Cambridge Ct. Nott 172 C3
Cambridge Gdns. Arn 162 A3
Cambridge Rd. Har 8 C2
Cambridge Rd. Nott 172 A2
Cambridge Rd. Rain 118 A4
Cambridge Rd. W Brid 186 A3
Cambridge St. Carl 174 C4
Cambridge St. Lough 220 A3
Cambridge St. Mans 102 A3
Camdale Cl. Bees 183 D3
Camden Cl. Nott 173 F2
Camelia Ave. Nott 184 B1
Camelot Ave. Nott 161 D1
Camelot Cres. Rudd 196 A4
Camelot St. Rudd 196 A4
Cameron St. Nott 161 E1
Camerons The. Mans 101 E3
Camomile Cl. Nott 160 C4
Camomile Gdns. Nott 172 C4
Campbell Cl. Work 35 F4
Campbell Dr. Carl 174 B4
Campbell Gr. Nott 173 E3
Campbell St. Gain 15 D1
Campbell St. La Mi 143 E2
Campbell St. Nott 173 E3
Campden Green. Nott 184 C1
Campion St. Arn 161 F4
Campion Way. Bing 177 E2
Camrose Cl. Nott 171 F4
Canal La. Hose 211 F4
Canal La. Lo Cl 211 E3
Canal La. Stat 202 B3
Canal La. W Sto 7 E1
Canal Rd. Work 35 F2
Canal Side. Bees 184 A2
Canal St. Ilk 158 A1
Canal St. Lo Ea 182 B1
Canal St. Nott 173 E2
Canal St. Ret 39 F3
Canal St. Sand 182 B3
Canal Terr. Work 36 A2
Canberra Cl. Staple 170 C1
Canberra Cres. W Brid 185 E2
Canberra Gdns. W Brid 185 E2
Canberra Rd. Codd 125 F1
Candle Meadow. Nott 174 B3
Candleby Cl. Cotg 187 F2
Candleby Ct. Cotg 187 F2
Candleby La. Cotg 187 F2
Candlemass Ct. Mans 88 B1
Canning Circus. Nott 173 D3
Cannock Way. Lo Ea 194 A4
Cannon Sq. Ret 39 F4
Cannon St. Nott 161 E2
Canon Cl. Ilk 157 F3
Canon's Cl. South 121 F1
Canonbie Cl. Arn 148 A1
Cantabury Ave. Nott 172 C4
Cantelupe Rd. Ilk 170 A4
Canterbury Cl. Mans 88 B3
Canterbury Cl. Work 36 A4
Canterbury Ct. Nott 173 D3
Canterbury Rd. Nott 172 B3
Canterbury Wlk. C in L 25 F4
Cantley Ave. Carl 162 C1
Cantrell Rd. Nott 160 B4
Canver Cl. Nott 171 E3
Canwick Cl. Nott 171 E3
Cape St. Mans 101 F4
Capenwray Gdns. Nott 161 E4
Capes The. What 178 C2
Capitol Ct. Nott 172 A3
Caporn Cl. Nott 160 B3
Capps Pl. Tux 66 A1
Car La. Car Co 166 B1
Carburton Ave. Mar War 74 B4
Carburton Way. K-in-A 115 E3
Cardale Rd. Mans 87 E2
Cardale Rd. Nott 174 A3
Cardiff St. Nott 173 F3
Cardinal Cl. Nott 173 F3
Cardinal Hinsley Cl. N-on-T 139 E2
Cardington Cl. Nott 146 C1
Cardle Cl. Mans 89 D1
Cardwell St. Nott 172 C4
Carew Rd. Nott 184 C1
Carey Rd. Nott 160 B4
Carisbrook Ave. Mans 103 D4
Carisbrooke Ave. Bees 184 A4
Carisbrooke Ave. Carl 163 D1
Carisbrooke Ave. Nott 161 E1
Carisbrooke Dr. Nott 161 E1
Carlile Rd. Carl 174 C4
Carlin St. Nott 160 A4
Carling Ave. Work 35 E2
Carlingford Rd. Huck 146 A4
Carlisle Ave. Nott 160 B4
Carlisle St. Gain 15 E1
Carlswark Gdns. Nott 146 C1
Carlton Ave. Work 35 F3
Carlton Cl. Hean 143 D2
Carlton Cl. Mans 89 E2
Carlton Cl. N-on-T 139 F3
Carlton Cl. Work 35 F4
Carlton Cres. E Lea 205 F1
Carlton Ferry La. Coll 97 E1
Carlton Fold. Nott 173 F2
Carlton Hall La. C in L 25 F3
Carlton Hill. Carl 174 B4
Carlton La. Brox 57 F4
Carlton La. S on T 97 D3
Carlton Mews. Carl 174 B4
Carlton Rd. Lo Ea 193 D3
Carlton Rd. N-on-T 140 A3
Carlton Rd. Nott 173 F3
Carlton Rd. Work 35 F3
Carlton Sq. Carl 174 C4
Carlton St. Mans 88 B1
Carlton St. Nott 173 E2
Carlyle Rd. W Brid 185 F4
Carman Cl. Greas 159 D4
Carmel Gdns. Arn 161 F3
Carnarvon Cl. Bing 177 F3
Carnarvon Dr. Bu Jo 164 A3
Carnarvon Gr. Carl 162 C1
Carnarvon Gr. Carl 174 B4
Carnarvon Gr. S in A 100 C3
Carnarvon Pl. Bing 177 E2
Carnarvon Rd. S in A 99 F1
Carnarvon Rd. W Brid 185 F3
Carnarvon St. Carl 175 D3
Carnarvon St. S in A 100 A4
Carnforth Cl. Staple 182 B3
Carnforth Ct. Nott 161 E4
Carnoustie Cl. K-in-A 114 C4
Carnoustie. Work 36 A3
Carnwood Rd. Nott 161 D3
Carolgate. Ret 39 F3
Caroline Cl. Raven 117 D2
Caroline Ct. Ilk 170 A3
Caroline Wlk. Nott 173 E4
Carpenter Ave. Mans 87 E1
Carpenters Cl. Cr Bu 189 D3
Carr Cl. S Norm 113 D4
Carr Farm Rd. Ann Wo 114 C1
Carr Hill Way. Ret 29 F1
Carr La. Blyt 15 E4
Carr La. E Stock 7 F1
Carr La. Gain 24 B3
Carr La. Harb 71 D2
Carr La. Mar War 74 A2
Carr La. Mist 6 C1
Carr La. S Norm 113 D4
Carr La. Swine 71 D2
Carr Rd. Bing 178 A3
Carr Rd. G on H 12 B3
Carr Rd. Ret 39 F3
Carr View. Ever 11 E2
Carradale Cl. Arn 162 B4
Carrfield Ave. Bees 182 C1
Carrfield Ave. Lo Ea 182 C1
Carrfield Cl. S in A 100 B2
Carrgate La. Elst 153 F3
Carrington La. Calv 149 D4
Carrington St. Nott 173 E2
Carroll Gdns. Nott 173 E1
Carsic La. S in A 100 C2
Carsic Rd. S in A 100 B2
Carside Ave. S in A 100 B1
Carsington Ct. Mans 88 C2
Carson Rd. Gain 15 E1
Carswell Cl. N-on-T 139 F3
Cartbridge. Cotg 187 F1
Carter Ave. R on T 176 A2
Carter Ave. Rudd 196 B3
Carter Gate. N-on-T 139 F4
Carter La E. S Norm 113 E3
Carter La W. S Norm 113 E3
Carter La W. Shireb 72 B2
Carter La. Mans 102 C3
Carter La. Mar War 73 E2
Carter La. Shireb 72 C2
Carter Rd. Bees 183 D1
Carter Rd. Bees 183 D2
Carters Wood Dr. Nuth 159 F2
Cartwright Cl. D on T 54 A1
Cartwright St. Lough 220 B3
Cartwright St. Shire 34 C4
Carver Cl. Edwin 76 A1
Carver St. Nott 172 C4
Carver's Hollow. Edin 120 A1
Carwood Rd. Bees 171 E1
Caskgate St. Gain 24 B4
Casper Ct. Nott 161 D4
Castellan Rise. Nott 161 E4
Casterton Rd. Nott 161 D4
Castle Brewery Ct. N-on-T 139 F4
Castle Bridge Rd. Nott 173 D1
Castle Bvd. Nott 173 D2
Castle Cl. Bott 181 E1
Castle Cl. Calv 148 C4
Castle Farm La. Work 46 B3
Castle Gate. N-on-T 139 F4
Castle Gate. Nott 173 E2
Castle Gate. Tick 8 A4
Castle Gdns. Nott 172 C2
Castle Gr. Nott 173 D2
Castle Hill. E Lea 205 F1
Castle Marina Rd. Nott 173 D1
Castle Meadow Rd. Nott 173 D2
Castle Meadow Ret Pk Nott 173 D2
Castle Park. Nott 173 D1
Castle Pl. Nott 173 D2
Castle Quay. Nott 173 D2
Castle Rd. Nott 173 E2
Castle Rising. N-on-T 139 F4
Castle St. East 144 A1
Castle St. Mans 88 A2
Castle St. Mans 102 A4
Castle St. Nott 173 F2
Castle St. Work 35 F1
Castle View Rd. Bott 181 E1
Castle View. Ald 143 D2
Castle View. W Brid 185 E3
Castledine St Ext. Lough 220 A1
Castledine St. Lough 220 A1
Castlefields. Nott 173 E1
Castleton Ave. Arn 161 F3
Castleton Ave. Carl 162 C1
Castleton Ave. Ilk 157 F3
Castleton Cl. Huck 145 E3
Castleton Cl. Mans 88 B2
Castleton Cl. Nott 173 D1
Castleton Cl. Raven 117 D2
Castleton Ct. Nott 159 F3
Caterham Cl. Nott 171 E4
Catfoot La. Lamb 162 C4
Catherine Ave. Mans 88 B2
Catherine Cl. K-in-A 114 C4
Catherine Cl. Nott 160 A4
Catkin Dr. Greas 158 B4
Catkin Way. Bald 140 A2
Catlow Wlk. Nott 161 E4
Caton Cl. S in A 100 B2
Cator Cl. Carl 162 B2
Cator La N. Bees 183 E3
Cator La. Bees 183 E3
Cator Rd. Mans 87 E2
Catriona Cres. Arn 148 A1
Catterley Hill Rd. Nott 174 A3
Cattle Market Rd. Nott 173 E1
Cattle Rd. Mist 6 B1
Catton Rd. Arn 162 A4
Caudwell Cl. South 121 F1
Caudwell Dr. Mans 102 B2
Cauldwell Rd. S in A 101 F1
Cauldwell Rd. S in A 102 A1
Caulton St. Nott 172 C3
Caunt's Cres. S in A 100 B2
Caunton Ave. Nott 161 F1
Caunton Cl. Mans 101 F3
Caunton Cl. Mar War 74 B4
Caunton Rd. Bath 109 F2
Caunton Rd. Hock 122 A3
Causeway La. Gams 51 D4
Causeway La. Morton 137 E2
Causeway Mews. Nott 173 D1
Causeway. Lea 24 C2
Cavan Ct. Nott 173 E1
Cave's La. Walker 13 E3
Cavell Cl. Nott 184 B1
Cavell Cl. Wood 53 D4
Cavell Ct. Nott 172 B1
Cavendish Ave. Carl 162 B1
Cavendish Ave. Edwin 75 F1
Cavendish Ave. N-on-T 140 A3
Cavendish Ave. Nott 161 E2
Cavendish Ave. S in A 100 C2
Cavendish Cl. Huck 146 B3
Cavendish Cres N. Nott 173 D2
Cavendish Cres S. Nott 173 D2
Cavendish Cres. Ann Wo 130 A4
Cavendish Cres. Carl 162 B1
Cavendish Cres. Staple 170 B1
Cavendish Dr. Carl 174 C4
Cavendish Dr. Lea 24 C1
Cavendish Pl. Bees 183 F3
Cavendish Rd E. Nott 173 D2
Cavendish Rd W. Nott 173 D2
Cavendish Rd. Carl 162 B1
Cavendish Rd. Ilk 170 A3
Cavendish Rd. Lo Ea 182 B1
Cavendish Rd. Ret 40 A2
Cavendish Rd. Work 47 D4
Cavendish St. Arn 161 F4
Cavendish St. Mans 88 A2
Cavendish St. Mans 102 B3
Cavendish St. Nott 184 C4
Cavendish St. S in A 101 D2
Cavendish St. Scarc 72 C4
Cavendish Vale. Nott 161 E2
Cawdron Wlk. Nott 184 C1
Cawston Gdns. Nott 160 A4
Cawthorne Cl. Coll 98 A1
Cawthorne Way. Mans 102 C4
Caxmere Dr. Nott 171 F3
Caythorpe Cres. Nott 161 E2
Caythorpe Ct. Mans 88 C2
Caythorpe Rd. Cayt 151 D1
Caythorpe Rd. Gunt 150 C1
Caythorpe Rise. Nott 161 E2
Cecil St. Gain 15 E1
Cecil St. Nott 172 C2
Cedar Ave. Bees 184 A4
Cedar Ave. E Lea 214 B4
Cedar Ave. K-in-A 114 C2
Cedar Ave. Lo Ea 193 E3
Cedar Ave. Mans 88 B3
Cedar Ave. N-on-T 125 D2
Cedar Ave. Nuth 159 F2
Cedar Cl. Gain 15 D2
Cedar Cl. S in A 100 B4
Cedar Cl. Sand 182 A4
Cedar Ct. Bees 184 A4
Cedar Dr. Keyw 197 F1
Cedar Dr. Sels 128 C4

Cedar Gr. Arn 162 A4
Cedar Gr. Huck 146 A3
Cedar Gr. Nott 171 F2
Cedar Gr. S Norm 113 D2
Cedar La. Oll 77 E3
Cedar Rd. Bees 183 F3
Cedar Rd. Lough 220 B1
Cedar Rd. Nott 173 D4
Cedar St. Mans 102 B3
Cedar Tree Rd. Bes Vil 147 D1
Cedar Tree Rd. Elk 50 A2
Cedarland Cres. Nuth 159 F2
Cedars The. Nott 161 E2
Celia Dr. Carl 174 B4
Cemetery Rd. Staple 182 C4
Cemetery Rd. Work 36 A1
Central Ave S. Arn 161 F4
Central Ave. Arn 161 F4
Central Ave. Arn 162 A2
Central Ave. Bees 183 E3
Central Ave. Bees 183 F4
Central Ave. Blid 118 A3
Central Ave. Elmt 58 B4
Central Ave. Huck 146 A3
Central Ave. K-in-A 115 D2
Central Ave. Mans 102 B3
Central Ave. Nott 161 D1
Central Ave. S Norm 113 D3
Central Ave. Sand 182 A3
Central Ave. Staple 182 C4
Central Ave. W Brid 185 F4
Central Ave. Wale 64 A1
Central Ave. Work 35 F2
Central Cl. Shireb 72 C2
Central Ct. Nott 172 C1
Central Dr. Baw 10 A4
Central Dr. Elst 153 F2
Central Dr. N Clip 89 F1
Central Dr. Shireb 72 C2
Central St. Nott 173 F3
Central St. S in A 101 D2
Central Wlk. Huck 146 A4
Centre Way. R on T 175 F2
Century Ave. Mans 101 F3
Century Rd. Ret 39 F3
Century St. N-on-T 140 A4
Cernan Ct. Nott 159 F3
Cerne Cl. Nott 184 C1
Chaceley Way. Nott 185 D2
Chad Gdns. Bes Vil 147 D1
Chadborn Ave. Goth 195 D1
Chadburn Rd. Mans 102 C4
Chaddesden The. Nott 173 E4
Chadwick Rd. Nott 172 C4
Chadwick Way. Wood 53 D4
Chaffinch Cl. Mans 102 C4
Chain Bridge Rd. Lound 29 E4
Chain La. N-on-T 139 F4
Chain La. Nott 172 C1
Chainbridge La. Lound 29 E4
Chalfield Cl. Nott 184 B1
Chalfont Dr. Nott 172 B3
Chalons Cl. Ilk 157 F1
Chamberlain Cl. Nott 184 B1
Chambers Ave. Ilk 170 A4
Champion Cres. Mans 101 F4
Chancery Cl. S in A 101 D3
Chancery La. Ret 39 F4
Chancery The. Bees 183 E4
Chandos Ave. Carl 175 D4
Chandos Ct. Tux 65 F2
Chandos St. Carl 175 D4
Chandos St. Nott 173 F4
Chantrey Cl. Bees 183 E2
Chantrey Rd. W Brid 185 F4
Chantry Cl. Kim 159 D3
Chantry Cl. Lo Ea 193 D2
Chantry Cl. N-on-T 139 F3
Chantry Wlk. Tux 65 F2
Chapel Bar. Nott 173 D2
Chapel Cl. Mist 6 C1
Chapel Cl. Wale 64 A1
Chapel Garth. Orst 179 F3
Chapel Gate. C in L 26 A3
Chapel La. Arn 161 F4
Chapel La. Aslo 179 D3
Chapel La. Bath 110 A2
Chapel La. Bing 177 F3
Chapel La. Caun 109 D3
Chapel La. Clayp 156 B4
Chapel La. Codd 126 A1
Chapel La. Cost 206 B1
Chapel La. Cotg 187 F2
Chapel La. Epp 150 A3
Chapel La. Ever 11 E2
Chapel La. Farn 138 C2
Chapel La. Farns 119 F3
Chapel La. Gran 191 D3
Chapel La. Hose 211 F4
Chapel La. Lamb 163 D4
Chapel La. Lax 79 E1
Chapel La. Mort 15 D2
Chapel La. N Sca 83 E2
Chapel La. Ne Br 219 E4
Chapel La. Ol Da 218 C2
Chapel La. Oxt 134 B2
Chapel La. Raven 117 D1
Chapel La. Up Br 210 A1
Chapel La. W-on-W 217 E4
Chapel La. Wale 64 A1
Chapel La. Wint 125 E3
Chapel Mews Ct. Bees 183 D4
Chapel Pl. Kim 158 C3
Chapel Rd. Sels 128 C3
Chapel St. Ann Wo 115 D1
Chapel St. B-le-V 192 A1
Chapel St. Beckin 142 B4
Chapel St. Bees 183 D4
Chapel St. Bott 181 D2
Chapel St. East 143 F1
Chapel St. Hean 157 D4
Chapel St. Huck 146 A4
Chapel St. Ilk 157 F1
Chapel St. K-in-A 114 C3
Chapel St. Kim 158 C3
Chapel St. Lo Ea 193 F4
Chapel St. Orst 179 F4
Chapel St. Plun 191 F1
Chapel St. Rudd 196 B3
Chapel St. Scarc 59 D2
Chapel St. Sels 129 D4
Chapel Staith. Gain 24 B4
Chapel Wlk. Work 35 F1
Chapelgate. Ret 39 F4
Chapman Ct. Nott 172 A4
Chapman St. Lough 220 B2
Chappel Gdns. Bils 106 A2
Chapter Dr. Kim 159 D3
Chard St. Nott 160 C1
Charlbury Ct. Bees 171 D2
Charlbury Rd. Nott 172 A3
Charlecote Dr. Nott 171 E2
Charlecote Park Dr. W Brid 185 E2
Charles Ave. Bees 183 E2
Charles Ave. East 144 A1
Charles Ave. Nott 172 A1
Charles Ave. Sand 182 A3
Charles Ave. Staple 182 C4
Charles Cl. Carl 162 C1
Charles Cl. Ilk 170 A3
Charles St. Arn 161 F4
Charles St. Gain 15 E1
Charles St. Huck 146 A4
Charles St. Lo Ea 193 E3
Charles St. Lough 220 A3
Charles St. Mans 88 A1
Charles St. Mans 88 B2
Charles St. N-on-T 140 A4
Charles St. Rudd 196 B4
Charles St. S in A 101 D2
Charlesworth Ave. Nott 172 C4
Charlesworth Ct. Mans 88 C2
Charlotte Cl. Kirton 78 A3
Charlotte Cl. N-on-T 140 A4
Charlotte Cl. Nott 147 F1
Charlotte Gr. Bees 171 E1
Charlton Ave. Lo Ea 182 C1
Charlton Gr. Bees 183 F3
Charlton Rd. C in L 26 A1
Charnock Ave. Nott 172 B2
Charnwood Ave. Bees 183 F3
Charnwood Ave. Keyw 197 F1
Charnwood Ave. Lo Ea 193 D2
Charnwood Ave. Sand 182 A2
Charnwood Ave. Su Bo 213 E3
Charnwood Cres. Newt 99 D2
Charnwood Fields. Su Bo 213 E3
Charnwood Gr. Bing 177 E2
Charnwood Gr. Huck 145 F4
Charnwood Gr. Mans 88 A3
Charnwood Gr. Mans 103 D4
Charnwood Gr. W Brid 185 F4
Charnwood La. Arn 162 A3
Charnwood Prec. Lough 220 A2
Charnwood Rd. Lough 220 A1
Charnwood St. S in A 100 B1
Charnwood Way. Woodb 149 E2
Charter Pl. Tux 66 A2
Charters Cl. K-in-A 114 C4
Chartwell Ave. Rudd 196 A4
Chartwell Gr. Carl 162 B3
Chartwell Rd. K-in-A 115 E3
Chatham Ct. N-on-T 139 F4
Chatham St. Nott 173 E3
Chatham St. South 121 F1
Chatsworth Ave. Bees 183 E1
Chatsworth Ave. Carl 162 C1
Chatsworth Ave. Lo Ea 194 A3
Chatsworth Ave. Nott 160 C1
Chatsworth Ave. R on T 176 A2
Chatsworth Ave. Sels 129 D4
Chatsworth Ave. Shireb 72 C3
Chatsworth Ave. South 121 E1
Chatsworth Cl. Mans 102 C1
Chatsworth Cl. S in A 100 C3
Chatsworth Cl. Sand 182 A2
Chatsworth Ct. Har 9 D3
Chatsworth Ct. Huck 146 A3
Chatsworth Dr. Huck 146 A3
Chatsworth Dr. Mans 102 C1
Chatsworth Rd. N-on-T 140 A3
Chatsworth Rd. W Brid 186 A4
Chatsworth Rd. Work 35 F4
Chatsworth St. S in A 101 D2
Chatsworth St. Tibs 99 D3
Chaucer Cres. S in A 101 D2
Chaucer Rd. Bald 140 C2
Chaucer St. Ilk 157 F1
Chaucer St. Mans 102 A4
Chaucer St. Nott 173 D3
Chaworth Ave. Greas 145 D1
Chaworth Rd. Bing 177 E2
Chaworth Rd. Carl 174 C3
Chaworth Rd. W Brid 185 F3
Chaworth St. Blid 118 A3
Cheadle Cl. Carl 162 A1
Cheadle Cl. Nott 171 E4
Cheapside. Nott 173 E2
Cheapside. Work 36 A1
Cheddar Cl. Rain 104 B1
Cheddar Rd. Nott 195 F4
Chedington Ave. Carl 162 B3
Chediston Vale. Nott 161 D4
Chedworth Cl. Nott 173 F3
Chelmorton Cl. Mans 88 C2
Chelmsford Rd. Nott 160 C1
Chelmsford Terr. Nott 160 C1
Chelsea St. Nott 160 C1
Cheltenham Cl. Bees 182 C1
Cheltenham Ct. Mans 102 C4
Cheltenham St. Nott 160 C2
Chennel Nook. Cotg 188 A1
Chepstow Rd. Nott 195 F4
Chepstow Wlk. Mans 102 C4
Chequers La. D on T 54 A1
Cherhill Cl. Nott 195 E4
Cheriton Cl. Mans 87 F1
Cheriton Dr. Raven 117 D1
Cheriton Dr. Ship 157 E2
Chermside Cl. Raven 117 D1
Chernside. Raven 117 D2
Cherry Ave. Huck 146 A3
Cherry Ave. K-in-A 114 B4
Cherry Cl. Arn 161 F4
Cherry Cl. S Norm 113 D4
Cherry Cl. Shireb 72 C3
Cherry Gr. Mans 101 F3
Cherry Gr. Mar War 74 B2
Cherry Hill. Keyw 197 F2
Cherry Holt. N-on-T 139 F3
Cherry Holt. Ret 29 E1
Cherry La. Mans 102 A2
Cherry Orch. Cotg 187 F2
Cherry Orchard Mnt. Nott 161 D4
Cherry St. Bing 177 F2
Cherry Tree Ave. Shire 34 C4
Cherry Tree Cl. Brin 143 F4
Cherry Tree Cl. Mans 88 A2
Cherry Tree Cl. R on T 175 F1
Cherry Tree La. W Brid 186 A2
Cherry Tree Rd. Gain 15 F1
Cherry Tree Wlk. Ran 19 E3
Cherry Wood Dr. Nott 172 A4
Cherryholt Cl. E Brid 165 E2
Cherryholt La. E Brid 165 E2
Cherrywood Gdns. Carl 174 A4
Chertsey Cl. Nott 161 F1
Cherwell Ct. Nott 159 F3
Chesham Dr. Bees 171 D1
Chesham Dr. Nott 161 D1
Cheshire Way. Sels 128 B2
Chesil Ave. Nott 172 B3
Chesil Cotts. Nott 172 B3
Cheslyn Dr. Nott 172 B4
Chess Burrow. Mans 88 B1
Chester Cl. Lough 220 A2
Chester Green. Bees 182 C1
Chester Rd. Nott 174 B3
Chester St. Mans 87 F1
Chesterfield Ave. Bing 177 F3
Chesterfield Ave. Carl 162 B1
Chesterfield Ave. Lo Ea 193 F4
Chesterfield Ct. Carl 162 B2
Chesterfield Dr. Bu Jo 164 A3
Chesterfield Dr. Ret 40 A4
Chesterfield Rd N. Mans 87 E2
Chesterfield Rd S. Mans 102 A4
Chesterfield Rd. Plea 86 C4
Chesterfield Rd. S in A 99 F2
Chesterfield Rd. Tibs 85 D1
Chesterfield St. Carl 174 B4
Chesterman Cl. Awsw 158 A2
Chesterton Dr. Work 36 A3
Chestnut Ave. Bees 183 F3
Chestnut Ave. Bing 177 F2
Chestnut Ave. Carl 162 A1
Chestnut Ave. Gain 15 E1
Chestnut Ave. K-in-A 114 C2
Chestnut Ave. N-on-T 125 D2
Chestnut Ave. Raven 117 D1
Chestnut Ave. Ret 39 F2
Chestnut Cl. Bott 181 E2
Chestnut Cl. Work 35 F1
Chestnut Dr. Baw 9 F4
Chestnut Dr. Kim 159 D3
Chestnut Dr. Mans 102 C1
Chestnut Dr. Oll 77 E3
Chestnut Dr. S Norm 113 D2
Chestnut Dr. Sels 128 C4
Chestnut Dr. Shireb 72 B2
Chestnut Gr. Arn 162 A4
Chestnut Gr. Bu Jo 163 F2
Chestnut Gr. Carl 162 C1
Chestnut Gr. Farn 139 D2
Chestnut Gr. Huck 146 A2
Chestnut Gr. K-in-A 114 C3
Chestnut Gr. Mans 88 A3
Chestnut Gr. Nott 173 E4
Chestnut Gr. R on T 175 F2
Chestnut Gr. Sand 182 A4
Chestnut Gr. W Brid 185 E4
Chestnut Hill. Mans 102 C1
Chestnut La. B in F 194 C3
Chestnut Mews. Mans 102 C1
Chestnut Rd. La Mi 143 D2
Chestnut Rd. Lan 16 C2
Chestnut St. Lough 220 A2
Chestnut Way. Tux 66 A1
Chestnuts The. Carl 163 D1
Chestnuts The. Lo Ea 193 D4
Chestnuts The. Nott 161 F1
Chestnuts The. R on T 175 F2
Chettles Ind Est. Nott 172 B3
Chetwyn Rd. Nott 171 E3
Chetwynd Rd. Bees 183 D1
Chetwynd Rd. Bees 183 E2
Cheverton Ct. Nott 173 E4
Chevin Gdns. Nott 147 D1
Cheviot Cl. Bes Vil 147 D1
Cheviot Ct. C in L 25 F4
Cheviot Dr. Nott 159 F4
Cheviot Rd. Lo Ea 182 A1
Chewton Ave. East 144 A1
Chewton St. East 144 A1
Cheyne Dr. Bils 106 A2
Cheyne Wlk. Baw 9 F4
Cheyne Wlk. Ret 39 E2
Cheyny Cl. Nott 173 E1
Chichester Cl. Ilk 170 A4
Chichester Cl. Nott 160 C4
Chichester Dr. Cotg 187 F2
Chichester Wlk. C in L 25 F4
Chidlow Rd. Nott 171 E4
Chigwell Cl. Nuth 159 F2
Childrens Highway. Bald 140 C1
Chillon Way. Huck 145 E3
Chiltern Cl. Bes Vil 147 D1
Chiltern Gdns. Lo Ea 182 A1
Chiltern Way. C in L 25 F4
Chiltern Way. Nott 161 D4
Chilton Cres. Mans 88 B3
Chilton Dr. Kim 159 D4
Chilvers Cl. Nott 161 D4
Chilwell Ct. Nott 160 B4
Chilwell La. Bees 183 E3
Chilwell Rd. Bees 183 F3
Chilwell Retail Park. Bees 183 D1
Chilwell St. Nott 172 C2
Chimes Meadow. South 136 C4
Chine Gdns. W Brid 185 E3
Chine The. S Norm 113 D2
Chingford Rd. Nott 171 F4
Chippendale St. Not 172 C2
Chippenham Rd. Nott 161 E4
Chirnside. Mans 101 E3
Chisbury Green. Nott 195 E4
Chisholm Way. Nott 161 D3
Chisworth Ct. Mans 88 C2
Christchurch Rd. Huck 145 E2
Christina Ave. Nott 160 B2
Christina Cres. Nott 160 B2
Christine Cl. Huck 131 E1
Christopher Cl. Nott 171 F3
Christopher Cres. Bald 140 B2
Chrysalis Way. East 143 E2
Church Ave. Arn 161 F4
Church Ave. Lo Ea 193 D2
Church Ave. Nott 172 C2
Church Ave. S in A 100 B1
Church Cl. Arn 161 F4
Church Cl. Bing 177 F3
Church Cl. E Lea 205 F1
Church Cl. Hose 211 F4
Church Cl. Mar War 74 A3
Church Cl. N Whea 31 F4
Church Cl. Nott 173 E3
Church Cl. Trow 170 B2
Church Cres. Arn 161 E4
Church Cres. Bees 183 D2
Church Croft. W Brid 185 F4
Church Ct. R on T 175 F2
Church Dr E. Arn 161 F4
Church Dr. Arn 161 F4
Church Dr. Huck 146 A4
Church Dr. Ilk 157 E2
Church Dr. Keyw 197 F2
Church Dr. Mist 6 C1
Church Dr. Nott 161 D1
Church Dr. Nott 161 E1
Church Dr. Raven 117 D1
Church Dr. Sand 182 A4
Church Dr. Shireb 72 C2
Church Dr. W Brid 185 F4
Church End. Ne Br 210 B1
Church Farm Gdns. Wellow 77 F1
Church Field Cl. C in L 26 A3
Church Gate. Clip 187 E1
Church Gate. Clip 198 B4
Church Gate. Co Ba 200 C4
Church Gate. Kegw 203 E1
Church Gate. Lough 220 A2
Church Gdns. S in A 100 B1
Church Gr. Nott 172 C2
Church Hill Ave. Mans 88 B2
Church Hill. Bils 106 A3
Church Hill. K-in-A 114 B2
Church Hill. Kim 158 C3
Church Hill. Mans 88 B2
Church Hill. N Whea 31 F4
Church Hill. Newt 99 D1
Church Hill. S in A 100 C1
Church La. Aver 123 F1
Church La. B in F 194 C3
Church La. Bald 140 C2
Church La. Bees 183 E1
Church La. Best 98 A3
Church La. Bing 177 F3
Church La. Both 63 F4
Church La. Boug 77 F3
Church La. Boug 78 A3
Church La. Brin 143 F4
Church La. C in L 25 F2
Church La. Car Co 166 B2
Church La. Clar 30 C2
Church La. Clay 21 E3
Church La. Coll 98 A1
Church La. Coss 158 B1
Church La. Cost 206 B1
Church La. Cotg 187 F2
Church La. Crom 110 C4
Church La. E Dray 53 D2
Church La. E Sto 138 A1
Church La. Eagle 84 B2
Church La. Eakr 92 C1
Church La. Epp 150 A3
Church La. Gams 50 C2
Church La. Halam 120 C1
Church La. Har 8 C2
Church La. Hayt 30 B3
Church La. Huck 131 D1
Church La. Let 16 A1
Church La. Linby 131 D1
Church La. Lo Cl 211 E2
Church La. Mans 102 B3
Church La. Mapl 108 A3
Church La. Mist 6 C1
Church La. Morton 137 E2
Church La. N Clift 68 B2
Church La. N Sca 83 E1
Church La. Nott 147 F1
Church La. Nott 160 B4
Church La. Ol Da 218 C2
Church La. Plea 87 D3
Church La. Plum 197 F4
Church La. Plun 191 F1
Church La. Red 192 C2
Church La. Ret 39 F2
Church La. S Clift 68 B2
Church La. S in A 100 C1
Church La. S Musk 124 C4
Church La. S Sca 98 A3
Church La. Sax 56 C3
Church La. Screv 166 C2
Church La. Sels 128 B4
Church La. Sels 129 D2
Church La. Sibt 167 F4
Church La. Staple 182 B4
Church La. Thrum 194 B2
Church La. Tibs 99 D3
Church La. Tick 8 A4
Church La. Up Br 210 A1
Church La. Upton 122 C1
Church La. W Dray 50 C1
Church La. W-on-W 217 E4
Church La. Widm 208 A3
Church Lands. Lough 220 A3
Church Mead. S in A 99 F2
Church Meadow. Calv 148 C4
Church Mews. Nott 173 E1
Church Rd. Bes Vil 146 C2
Church Rd. Bir 9 E2
Church Rd. Bu Jo 163 F2
Church Rd. Greas 144 C2
Church Rd. Harby 70 B1
Church Rd. Mar War 74 A3
Church Rd. N Clip 89 F2
Church Rd. Nott 173 E3
Church Rd. Sax 57 D2
Church Side. Farns 119 F3
Church Side. Mans 102 B3
Church Side. S in A 99 F2
Church Sq. Nott 172 C2
Church St E. Pinx 113 E2
Church St W. Pinx 113 E2
Church St. Arn 161 F4
Church St. Baw 10 A3
Church St. Beck 14 A1
Church St. Bees 183 D4
Church St. Bees 183 F3
Church St. Bing 177 F2
Church St. Bils 105 F3
Church St. Bott 181 D1
Church St. Bunn 206 C4
Church St. Carl 174 C4
Church St. Coll 111 F4
Church St. Cr Bi 189 D2
Church St. E Mark 66 A3
Church St. East 143 F1
Church St. Edwin 76 A1
Church St. Ever 11 E2

Church St. Farn 138 C2
Church St. Gain 15 E1
Church St. Goth 195 D1
Church St. Gran 191 D3
Church St. Hath 213 D1
Church St. Ilk 157 F2
Church St. K-in-A 114 B3
Church St. Lamb 163 E4
Church St. Lan 16 C1
Church St. Mans 87 D2
Church St. Mans 88 B2
Church St. Mans 102 A4
Church St. Mar War 74 A3
Church St. Mist 6 C1
Church St. N Whea 31 F4
Church St. N-on-T 139 F4
Church St. Nott 160 C1
Church St. Nott 172 C3
Church St. Oll 77 D2
Church St. Orst 179 F4
Church St. Rudd 196 B4
Church St. S in A 100 B1
Church St. S in A 100 C1
Church St. S Le S 32 B2
Church St. S Lev 42 B4
Church St. S Norm 113 D3
Church St. S on T 97 D4
Church St. Sand 182 A4
Church St. Scarc 59 D1
Church St. Shel 164 B1
Church St. South 136 C4
Church St. Staple 182 B4
Church St. What 179 D2
Church St. Wyme 216 B2
Church View Cl. Bes Vil 147 D1
Church View. Beck 14 A1
Church View. Bott 181 D2
Church View. Carl 162 C1
Church View. Glap 86 A4
Church View. Oll 77 D2
Church View. Plea 86 C4
Church View. S in A 100 B3
Church View. Scro 10 A1
Church Way. Sutt 29 D3
Church Wlk. Baw 10 A4
Church Wlk. Brin 143 F4
Church Wlk. Carl 174 C4
Church Wlk. East 143 F1
Church Wlk. Har 8 C2
Church Wlk. Staple 182 C4
Church Wlk. Upton 122 C1
Church Wlk. West 81 D3
Church Wlk. What 179 D2
Church Wlk. Work 35 F2
Churchdale Ave. Staple 170 C1
Churchfield Ct. Nott 147 D1
Churchfield Dr. Rain 103 F1
Churchfield La. Nott 172 C3
Churchfield Terr. Nott 160 C1
Churchgate. Ret 39 F4
Churchill Cl. Arn 161 F4
Churchill Dr. N-on-T 139 F3
Churchill Dr. Rudd 196 A4
Churchill Dr. Staple 182 C4
Churchill Gdns. Mans 88 B2
Churchill Park. Carl 174 C3
Churchill Way. Lea 24 C2
Churchmoor Ct. Nott 147 F1
Churchmoor La. Nott 147 F1
Churchside Gdns. Nott 172 C4
Churnet Cl. Nott 184 C2
Cinder La. Oll 77 D1
Cinderhill Gr. Carl 162 C1
Cinderhill Rd. Nott 160 A3
Cinderhill Wlk. Nott 160 A3
Circle The. Mans 88 A2
Citadel St. Nott 172 C3
City Rd. Bees 184 A3
City Rd. Nott 172 B1
City Rd. Stat 202 C2
City The. Bees 184 A3
City The. Bees 184 A4
Clandon Dr. Nott 161 D1
Clanfield Rd. Nott 171 F4
Clapham St. Nott 172 C3
Clapton La. Nott 184 C1
Clara Mount Rd. Hean 143 D1
Clarborough Dr. Arn 162 A3
Clarborough Hill. Clar 30 C2
Clare Cl. Nott 160 C2
Clare Hill. Blid 118 A2
Clare Rd. S in A 114 C4
Clare St. Nott 173 E3
Clare Valley. Nott 173 D2
Clarehaven. Staple 182 C3
Claremont Ave. Bees 183 E4
Claremont Ave. Huck 146 A3
Claremont Dr. W Brid 185 E2
Claremont Rd. Gain 24 C3
Claremont Rd. Nott 161 D1
Clarence Rd. Work 35 F2
Clarence Rd. Bees 183 E2
Clarence St. Lough 220 B3
Clarence St. Mans 87 E2
Clarence St. Mans 102 A3
Clarence St. Nott 173 F3
Clarendon Ct. Nott 173 D4
Clarendon Dr. Work 35 E3
Clarendon Rd. Mans 101 F4
Clarendon St. Nott 173 D3
Clarewood Gr. Nott 195 F4
Clarges St. Nott 160 B3
Clark La. Tux 65 F1
Clarke Ave. Arn 161 F4
Clarke Ave. N-on-T 139 F3
Clarke Cl. Cr Bi 189 D2
Clarke Dr. Lo Ea 193 D2
Clarke Rd. Nott 173 F1
Clarke's La. Bees 183 F2
Clarkson Dr. Bees 184 A3
Clater's Cl. Ret 40 A4
Claude St. Nott 172 C1
Clawson La. Hick 210 B3
Clawson La. Ne Br 210 C1
Claxton Rise. Lo Cl 211 E1
Clay Ave. Carl 162 A2
Clay St. Wyme 216 B2
Claye St. Lo Ea 193 F4
Clayfield Cl. Nott 160 A3
Claylands Ave. Work 35 E3
Claylands Cl. Work 35 E3
Claylands La. Work 35 E3
Claypit La. Fisk 137 F2
Claypole La. Dry Do 156 C1
Claypole Rd. Nott 172 C4
Claythorn Dr. Gain 24 C4
Clayton Cl. N-on-T 140 A3
Clayton Ct. Nott 172 C3
Clayton's Wharf. Nott 172 C1
Clayworth Comm. Clay 21 F2
Clayworth Ct. Mans 103 D2
Clayworth Rd. G on H 12 C1
Clegg Hill Dr. S in A 99 F2
Clement Ave. Bald 140 C2
Clensey La. Dry Do 156 C1
Clerkson St. Mans 102 A3
Clerkson's Alley. Mans 102 A4
Clether Rd. Nott 171 E3
Cleve Ave. Bees 182 C2
Cleveland Ave. Lo Ea 182 C1
Cleveland Cl. C in L 25 F4
Cleveland Cl. Nott 172 C3
Cleveland Sq. N-on-T 139 F3
Cleveland St. Gain 24 B4
Cleveleys Rd. Bees 182 C2
Clevely Way. Nott 184 C2
Cliff Bvd. Kim 158 C4
Cliff Cres. R on T 175 F2
Cliff Dr. R on T 176 A3
Cliff Gate. E Mark 65 E4
Cliff La. K in A 113 F2
Cliff Nook La. N-on-T 125 D1
Cliff Rd. Carl 174 B3
Cliff Rd. Nott 173 E2
Cliff Rd. R on T 175 F2
Cliff St. Mans 102 B4
Cliff The. Nott 160 A2
Cliff Way. R on T 175 F2
Cliffe Hill Ave. Staple 182 B4
Cliffgrove Ave. Bees 183 E3
Cliffhill La. Aslo 179 E3
Cliffhill La. Thoro 179 E3
Cliffmere Wlk. Nott 184 B1
Clifford Ave. Bees 183 F4
Clifford Cl. Keyw 197 F2
Clifford Cl. Lo Ea 193 D2
Clifford St. Lo Ea 193 F4
Clifford St. Mans 102 A2
Clifford St. Nott 172 C3
Clifton Ave. Lo Ea 194 A4
Clifton Ave. Rudd 196 B4
Clifton Bvd. Nott 184 C4
Clifton Cres. Bees 183 F2
Clifton Cres. N-on-T 125 E2
Clifton Gr. Carl 162 C1
Clifton Gr. Mans 102 C2
Clifton La. Nott 184 C2
Clifton La. Rudd 196 A4
Clifton Pl. Mans 102 A4
Clifton Rd. Rudd 196 A4
Clifton St. Bees 184 A3
Clifton Terr. Nott 173 D2
Clifton Way. Ret 39 E4
Clinthill La. Whit 45 D4
Clinton Ave. Brin 143 E3
Clinton Ave. Nott 173 D4
Clinton Ct. Nott 173 E3
Clinton Gdn La. Tux 65 F1
Clinton St E. Nott 173 E3
Clinton St W. Nott 173 E3
Clinton St. Arn 161 F4
Clinton St. Bees 183 F4
Clinton St. N-on-T 139 F4
Clinton St. Work 36 A1
Clinton Terr. Gain 24 B4
Clipston La. N-on-W 197 F4
Clipstone Ave. Arn 162 A2
Clipstone Ave. Mans 102 B4
Clipstone Ave. Nott 173 E3
Clipstone Ave. S in A 101 D2
Clipstone Dr. Mans 89 E2
Clipstone Rd E. Mans 89 E1
Clipstone Rd W. Mans 89 D1
Clive Cres. Kim 159 D3
Cliveden Green. Nott 184 B1
Cloister St. Nott 172 C1
Cloisters The. Bees 184 A4
Close Quarters. Bees 183 E4
Close The. Aver 123 F1
Close The. Bees 183 E2
Close The. Mans 103 F1
Close The. N-on-T 140 A4
Close The. Nott 161 E2
Close The. Shireb 72 C3
Close The. Upton 122 C1
Closes Side La. E Brid 165 F2
Cloud Ave. Staple 182 C4
Clouds Hill. Nott 195 F4
Cloudside Ct. Sand 182 A4
Cloudside Rd. Sand 182 A4
Clough Ct. Nott 172 A4
Clover Cl. Work 36 A4
Clover Green. Nott 160 B2
Clover Rise. Greas 158 B4
Clover St. K-in-A 115 D3
Cloverdale. Cotg 188 A1
Cloverlands Dr. Kim 159 D4
Cloverlands. W Brid 185 E2
Club Ct. Bald 140 B2
Clumber Ave. Arn 162 A2
Clumber Ave. Bees 183 E3
Clumber Ave. Brin 128 C1
Clumber Ave. Carl 175 D4
Clumber Ave. Edwin 75 F2
Clumber Ave. N-on-T 140 A3
Clumber Ave. Nott 173 D4
Clumber Ave. Rain 103 F1
Clumber Cres N. Nott 173 D2
Clumber Cres S. Nott 173 D2
Clumber Cres. S in A 100 B3
Clumber Ct. Ilk 157 F3
Clumber Ct. Mans 87 F1
Clumber Ct. Mar War 74 A2
Clumber Ct. Nott 173 D2
Clumber Dr. Mans 87 F1
Clumber Dr. R on T 176 A2
Clumber Pl. Work 35 F2
Clumber Rd E. Nott 173 D2
Clumber Rd W. Nott 173 D2
Clumber Rd. W Brid 185 F4
Clumber Rd. Work 47 D3
Clumber St. Huck 146 B3
Clumber St. K-in-A 115 E3
Clumber St. Lo Ea 193 E4
Clumber St. Mans 102 A4
Clumber St. Mar War 74 A2
Clumber St. Nott 173 E3
Clumber St. Ret 39 F3
Clumber St. S in A 100 B1
Clumber Way. Bils 106 A3
Clun Ct. Mans 88 B1
Co-operative Ave. Huck 146 A4
Co-operative St. Lo Ea 193 F3
Co-operative St. S in A 100 B3
Coach Dr. Greas 143 F2
Coach Rd. Mar War 74 B1
Coach Rd. Nott 172 A3
Coal La. Hose 211 F4
Coal Yard La. S Clift 82 C4
Coalpit La. Elk 49 F2
Coates Ave. Huck 130 C1
Coates Rd. N Le Ha 43 E4
Coatsby Rd. Kim 158 C4
Cobden Pl. Mans 87 F1
Cobden St. Gain 24 B4
Cobden St. K-in-A 115 D2
Cobden St. Lo Ea 193 F4
Cobden St. Lough 220 B2
Cobden St. Nott 172 C3
Coburn St. S in A 100 C1
Cobwell Rd. Ret 39 F3
Cochrane Terr. S in A 100 B3
Cock Hill La. Baw 10 A3
Cockayne Cl. Sand 182 A2
Cocker Beck. Lamb 163 E4
Cockerhouse Rd. East 143 F2
Cockett La. Farns 119 F4
Cockhill Cl. Baw 10 A3
Cocking Hill. Wellow 78 B2
Cocking La. Tres 42 B1
Cockington Rd. Nott 171 E3
Cockshut La. Holb 59 D2
Cockshut La. Ne La 59 D2
Coddington La. Stap 127 D3
Coddington Rd. Bald 140 C3
Codrington Gdns. Nott 161 E4
Cogenhoe Wlk. Nott 147 F1
Coggin's La. Mar War 74 B3
Coghill Ct. South 136 B4
Coging Cl. Bald 140 B2
Cogley La. Bing 178 A2
Cohen Cl. Arn 162 A3
Cokefield Ave. Nuth 159 F2
Colbeck St. Work 35 F2
Colborn St. Nott 173 F4
Colby Cl. Mans 89 D1
Coleby Ave. Nott 172 C2
Coleby Rd. Nott 159 F1
Coleby Rd. Nott 160 A1
Coleman Ave. Bald 140 A2
Coleridge Cres. Arn 161 E4
Coleridge Rd. Bald 140 C3
Coleridge Rd. Work 36 A3
Coleridge St. Nott 172 C3
Colesbourne Rd. Nott 184 C1
Colgrove Rd. Lough 220 A1
Colin Broughton Ct. Nott 160 B4
Colindale Gdns. Nuth 159 F2
Colinwood Ave. Nott 146 C1
College Dr. Nott 184 B1
College Dr. Nott 184 C2
College La. E Mark 66 A4
College La. Work 36 A1
College Rd. Bees 183 F3
College Rd. Su Bo 204 A1
College St. E Brid 165 E2
College St. Lo Ea 182 B1
College St. Nott 173 D2
Colley La. West 81 D2
Colleymoor Leys La. Nott 184 C1
Collier Ave. Mans 88 A3
Colliery Cl. Nott 173 D1
Colliery Rd. Bir 9 D2
Collin Ave. Sand 182 A2
Collin Gn. Nott 161 E2
Collin St. Bees 183 F3
Collin St. Nott 173 E2
Collingham Rd. Eagle 98 C1
Collingham Rd. Mans 87 E1
Collington St. Bees 183 F3
Collington Way. W Brid 185 E3
Collingwood Cl. Nott 184 C2
Collingwood Rd. Lo Ea 193 F3
Collins Ave. S in A 114 C4
Collins Ave. S Norm 113 D4
Collins Cl. Nott 159 F3
Collins Wlk. Ret 39 F4
Collis Cl. N-on-T 140 B4
Collison St. Nott 172 C3
Colly Gate. Kim 159 D3
Collyer Rd. Calv 148 B4
Collygate Rd. Nott 173 E1
Colmon Cl. Nott 161 D4
Colmon Wlk. Nott 161 D4
Colne Ct. Mans 88 B1
Colonel's La. Up Br 210 A1
Colonsay Cl. Staple 170 B2
Colsterdale. Work 36 A4
Colston La. Harb 202 A2
Colston Cres. W Brid 185 E2
Colston Gate. Cotg 188 A2
Colston La. Hose 201 F2
Colston Rd. Cr Bi 189 D1
Colston Rd. Mans 103 D2
Colston Rd. Nott 160 B4
Colton St. Mist 6 C1
Columbia Ave. Mans 102 C3
Columbia Ave. S in A 100 B1
Columbia Cl. Sels 129 D4
Columbia St. S in A 99 F2
Columbia St. S in A 100 A1
Colville St. Nott 173 D4
Colville Terr. Gain 24 B4
Colville Terr. Nott 173 D4
Colville Villas. Nott 173 D4
Colwick Cl. Mans 87 F1
Colwick Loop Rd. Carl 175 D4
Colwick Manor Farm. Carl 174 C3
Colwick Park Cl. Carl 174 C3
Colwick Rd. Nott 174 A2
Colwick Rd. W Brid 173 F1
Comery Ave. Nott 174 A3
Comfrey Cl. Nott 160 C4
Commerce Sq. Nott 173 E2
Commercial Ave. Bees 183 F3
Commercial Gate. Mans 102 A3
Commercial Rd. Keyw 197 F1
Commercial Rd. Nott 160 A4
Commercial St. Mans 102 A3
Commodore Gdns. Nott 160 B1
Common La. Bees 183 D3
Common La. Blyth 18 A2
Common La. Huck 145 E3
Common La. Kim 159 D4
Common La. Mans 88 A2
Common La. Plea 72 B2
Common La. Ran 19 E2
Common La. S Le S 32 B2
Common La. Scarc 72 B2
Common La. Shireb 72 B2
Common La. Tick 8 A4
Common Rd. Ret 39 F4
Common Rd. S in A 99 F1
Common Rd. S in A 113 F4
Common Rd. Th Sa 34 A3
Common Side. Sels 128 C4
Common The. Huck 145 E3
Common The. S Norm 113 D3
Commons Cl. Greas 158 A4
Compton Acres. W Brid 185 D3
Compton Rd. Nott 161 D2
Compton St. Scarc 72 C4
Comyn Gdns. Nott 173 E3
Conduit Cl. Nott 173 E1
Conery Gdns. What 179 D2
Conery La. What 178 C1
Coneygrey Spinney. Flint 152 C1
Conifer Cres. Nott 195 F4
Conifer Wlk. Carl 174 A4
Coningsby Cl. Gain 24 C4
Coningsby Gdns E. Arn 161 F2
Coningsby Rd. Arn 161 F3
Coningswath Rd. Carl 162 B1
Conisborough Terr. Nott 173 E1
Conisbrough Ave. Carl 163 D1
Coniston Ave. Nott 160 B1
Coniston Cl. Gam 186 B4
Coniston Rd. Bees 183 E4
Coniston Rd. Huck 145 F4
Coniston Rd. K-in-A 115 E3
Coniston Rd. Lo Ea 182 A1
Coniston Rd. Work 35 F4
Connaught Rd. Gain 15 E1
Connelly Cl. Arn 162 B3
Connery Mews. Bees 183 D1
Connery The. Huck 146 A4
Conrad Cl. Work 36 A2
Constance St. Nott 161 D1
Convent St. Nott 173 E3
Conway Ave. Carl 175 D4
Conway Cl. Mans 101 E4
Conway Cl. Nott 173 E4
Conway Cres. Carl 175 D4
Conway Dr. C in L 25 F3
Conway Gdns. Arn 161 F3
Conway Gdns. Ret 39 D4
Conway Rd. Carl 175 D4
Conway Rd. Huck 145 E2
Conway St. Lo Ea 193 F4
Conway Wlk. Nott 173 E4
Cook Dr. Ilk 170 A3
Cooks La. Morton 137 E1
Cooks La. South 136 A4
Cookson Ave. Carl 162 B1
Cookson St. K-in-A 114 C3
Coombe Cl. Nott 172 B2
Cooper Cl. Arn 162 B3
Cooper Cl. Cr Bi 189 D2
Cooper Cl. Nott 159 F3
Cooper Ct. Lough 220 B1
Cooper St. Carl 175 D3
Coopers Green. Bees 171 F1
Coopers Rise. Rain 104 A1
Cope St. Nott 172 C3
Copeland Ave. K-in-A 114 C3
Copeland Ave. Staple 182 C4
Copeland Gr. Bing 177 E3
Copeland Rd. Huck 146 B4
Copeland Rd. K-in-A 114 C3
Copenhagen Ct. Nott 161 E1
Copper Hill. Grass 81 F2
Coppice Ave. Ilk 157 E3
Coppice Cl. Huck 145 F3
Coppice Dr. East 143 E2
Coppice Gr. Nott 161 F1
Coppice Rd. Arn 162 A4
Coppice Rd. Mans 89 E2
Coppice Rd. Work 35 F4
Coppice The. Ba Mo 28 B3
Coppice The. Shireb 72 B2
Coppice View. S Norm 113 D2
Copplestone Dr. Carl 162 B3
Copse Cl. Bu Jo 163 F3
Copse The. Bees 183 E3
Copse The. Farn 139 D2
Copse The. Huck 146 B3
Copse The. Ilk 157 E3
Copse The. S in A 100 B3
Copseside Cl. Lo Ea 193 D4
Copsewood. S Norm 113 D2
Corben Gdns. Nott 159 F4
Corby Rd. Nott 161 F1
Cordy La. Brin 143 F4
Cordy La. Sels 143 F4
Corene Ave. S in A 100 C1
Coriander Dr. Nott 160 B2
Corinth Rd. Nott 184 C1
Corkhill La. Kirk 121 E3
Corkhill La. South 121 E3
Corn Cl. Cotg 187 F1
Corn Cl. S Norm 113 D3
Cornel Ct. Mans 88 C1
Cornell Dr. Arn 162 B4
Corner The. Lowd 150 B1
Corneries The. Lough 220 A2
Cornfield Ave. S Norm 113 D2
Cornfield Rd. Kim 158 C4
Cornhill Rd. Carl 174 A4
Cornley Rd. Mist 6 B2
Cornwall Ave. Bees 184 B2
Cornwall Ave. Mans 102 C3
Cornwall Cl. Sels 128 B2
Cornwall Dr. Oll 77 D2
Cornwall Rd. Arn 161 E4
Cornwall Rd. Ret 30 A1
Cornwall Rd. Shire 34 C4
Cornwallis Cl. Lo Ea 193 E3
Coronation Ave. Lo Cl 211 D1
Coronation Ave. Miss 4 A2
Coronation Ave. Nott 185 D4
Coronation Ave. Plea 86 C4
Coronation Ave. Sand 182 A4
Coronation Dr. Mans 103 D4
Coronation Dr. S Norm 113 D3
Coronation Dr. Shireb 72 C1
Coronation Rd. Arn 161 F2
Coronation Rd. Bes Vil 146 C2
Coronation Rd. Coss 158 A1
Coronation Rd. Huck 145 F4
Coronation Rd. Nuth 159 E3

Coronation St. Bald 140 B3
Coronation St. Mans 102 B3
Coronation St. Ret 39 F3
Coronation St. S in A 100 C1
Coronation St. Whit 45 D3
Coronation Wlk. Carl 163 D1
Corporation Oaks. Nott 173 E4
Corporation Rd. Ilk 170 A3
Corporation St. Mans 102 A4
Corringham Rd. Gain 15 F1
Corsham Gdns. Nott 174 A4
Cosby Rd. Nott 173 F2
Cosgrove Ave. S in A 101 D3
Cossall Rd. Cross 170 B3
Cossall Rd. Trow 170 B3
Costhorpe Ind Est. C in L 16 C1
Costhorpe Villas. C in L 16 C1
Costock Ave. Nott 161 D2
Costock Rd. E Le 206 A1
Costock Rd. T in G 207 E1
Costock Rd. Wys 207 E1
Cotes Rd. Lough 220 C3
Cotgrave Ave. Carl 162 C1
Cotgrave La. Toll 187 D1
Cotgrave Rd. Mans 87 F1
Cotgrave Rd. N-on-W 187 D1
Cotmanhay Rd. Ilk 157 F2
Coton Cl. Mans 88 C2
Coton Cl. Nott 185 D2
Cotswold Cl. Lo Ea 193 D4
Cotswold Ct. Bees 171 E1
Cotswold Ct. C in L 25 F4
Cotswold Gr. Mans 103 D3
Cotswold Rd. Nott 159 F1
Cottage Ave. Aslo 178 C2
Cottage Cl. Ilk 157 E2
Cottage La. Coll 111 F3
Cottage La. Mar War 74 B1
Cottage Meadow. Carl 174 C2
Cottage Pasture La. Gunt 164 C4
Cottage Terr. Nott 173 D3
Cottam Dr. Nott 161 D4
Cottam Gdns. Nott 161 D4
Cottam Gr. Mans 101 E3
Cottam Rd. S Lev 42 C4
Cottans Cl. South 136 C4
Cottesmore Rd. Nott 172 C2
Cotton Mill La. Farns 120 A3
Coulby Cl. Clayp 156 C3
Coulton's Ave. S in A 100 B2
Coulton's Cl. S in A 100 B2
County Bsns Park. Nott 173 F1
County Rd. Carl 162 B2
County Rd. Nott 173 F1
Court Cres. Nott 171 F2
Court Gdns. W Brid 185 D2
Court St. Nott 172 C4
Court Yd. Bees 183 D4
Court-Field Rd. S in A 101 D3
Courtenay Gdns. Nott 173 E4
Courtlett Way. Nott 160 A3
Courtney Cl. Nott 171 F3
Cove Rd. Haxey 2 C3
Covedale Rd. Nott 161 E3
Coventry Ct. Nott 160 B3
Coventry Dr. Work 36 A3
Coventry Rd. Bees 171 D2
Coventry Rd. Bees 184 A4
Coventry Rd. Nott 160 A3
Coverdale. Work 36 A4
Covert Cl. Bu Jo 163 F3
Covert Cl. Huck 146 B3
Covert Cl. Keyw 197 F2
Covert Rd. W Brid 186 A3
Cow La. Bees 183 E4
Cow La. N-on-T 124 C1
Cow Pasture La. K-in-A 114 B3
Cowan St. Nott 173 E3
Cowdray Cl. Lough 220 A1
Cowdrey Gdns. Arn 162 A3
Cowlairs. Nott 160 C4
Cowley St. Nott 160 C2
Cowpasture La. S in A 100 C1
Cowper Cl. Work 36 A3
Cowper Rd. Arn 161 F2
Cowper Rd. Greas 158 A4
Cowpes Cl. S in A 100 C2
Cox Dr. Bott 180 C2
Cox's Hill. Gain 15 E1
Cox's La. Mans 88 A3
Coxmoor Ct. Nott 147 D1
Coxmoor Rd. K in A 116 A3
Coxmoor Rd. S in A 101 E1
Crab La. N Musk 110 C1
Crab Nook La. Farns 119 F3
Crabtree Field. Nott 174 B2
Crabtree La. Beck 23 D4
Crabtree La. H Marn 67 E1
Crabtree Rd. Nott 160 A3
Craddock St. Lough 220 A2
Crafts Way. South 121 F1
Cragdale Rd. Nott 161 E3
Cragg La. Newt 99 D1
Cragmoor Rd. Bu Jo 163 F2
Crags Rd. Elmt 45 D1
Crags Rd. Whit 45 D1
Craig Moray. R on T 176 A2
Craig St. Lo Ea 193 F4
Craigs Green. Mans 101 F3
Craigston Rd. C in L 25 F3
Crammond Cl. Nott 173 D1
Crampton Ave. Mans 102 C4
Crampton Cl. S in A 100 A2
Crampton Ct. Nott 161 D4
Cramworth Gr. Nott 161 E2
Cranberry Cl. W Brid 185 D3
Cranbourne Cl. Staple 170 B1
Cranbourne Gr. Huck 145 F4
Cranbrook St. Nott 173 E2
Cranford Gdns. W Brid 185 E2
Cranleigh Dr. Lowd 150 B1
Cranmer Ave. Aslo 178 C2
Cranmer Gr. Mans 87 E2
Cranmer Gr. Nott 173 E4
Cranmer Rd. N-on-T 139 F3
Cranmer St. Ilk 157 F1
Cranmer St. Lo Ea 182 B1
Cranmer St. Nott 173 E4
Cranmore Cl. Arn 148 A1
Cransley Ave. Nott 171 E1
Cranston Ave. Nott 147 F1
Cranston Rd. Bees 171 E1
Cranswick Cl. Mans 89 D1
Cranthorne Dr. Nott 174 B3
Crantock Gdns. Keyw 197 F2
Cranwell Ct. Nott 159 F3
Cranwell Rd. Nott 159 E1
Craster Dr. Nott 159 F4
Craster St. S in A 100 C1
Crathie Rd. C in L 25 F3
Craven Rd. Nott 172 C4
Crawford Ave. Staple 182 B4
Crawford Cl. Nott 171 F3
Crawford Rise. Arn 162 B4
Crees La. Farn 139 D3
Cres The. N-on-T 140 A3
Crescent Ave. Carl 162 C1
Crescent Rd. Sels 128 B3
Crescent The. Arn 161 F2
Crescent The. Beck 14 A1
Crescent The. Bees 183 D1
Crescent The. Bees 183 E2
Crescent The. Bir 9 E2
Crescent The. Blid 118 A3
Crescent The. Bils 105 F3
Crescent The. E Lea 205 F1
Crescent The. East 144 A1
Crescent The. Lea 24 C1
Crescent The. Mans 102 B2
Crescent The. Ne Br 219 D3
Crescent The. Nott 173 A2
Crescent The. R on T 176 A2
Crescent The. Ret 39 E3
Crescent The. S in A 100 B4
Crescent The. Shireb 72 C3
Crescent The. Staple 170 C1
Cresswell Rd. Bees 183 D3
Cresswell Rd. Work 35 F2
Cresswell St. Work 35 F2
Cresta Gdns. Nott 161 E1
Creswell Ct. Mans 88 C2
Creswell Rd. Cuck 60 A2
Crew La. South 137 D4
Crew Rd. Coll 98 A1
Crewe Cl. Blid 118 A3
Crewe Cl. Nott 172 C3
Crewe Rd. Bir 9 D2
Cribb Cl. Nott 185 D4
Crich View. Newt 99 D2
Crich View. Nott 161 E1
Cricket Cl. Ann Wo 129 F4
Cricket Field La. Ret 39 F4
Cricketers Ct. W Brid 173 F1
Criftin Rd. Bu Jo 164 A2
Crink La. South 136 C3
Cripps Hill. Nott 172 B1
Critch's Flats. Kim 158 C3
Critchley St. Ilk 157 F1
Crocus St. K-in-A 115 D2
Crocus St. Nott 173 E1
Croft Ave. Huck 146 A3
Croft Ave. Mans 102 B1
Croft Cl. Pinx 113 E2
Croft Cres. Awsw 158 B3
Croft Ct. S in A 99 F2
Croft Dr. Tick 8 A4
Croft Farm Close. Ever 11 E2
Croft Gdns. Ol Da 218 C2
Croft Rd. Arn 161 F4
Croft Rd. Fin 1 A1
Croft Rd. Keyw 197 F2
Croft Rd. W Brid 186 A2
Croft Rise. E Brid 165 E2
Croft The. Beck 23 E4
Croft The. Kegw 203 E1
Croft The. N-on-T 140 A4
Croft The. Ret 39 F4
Croft The. S in A 100 B3
Croft The. S Norm 113 D3
Croft Way. Ever 11 E2
Croft Wlk. Whit 45 D3
Crofton Cl. Bees 183 E2
Crofton Cl. Nott 172 A3
Crofton Rd. Bees 183 E1
Crofts The. Bing 177 F2
Cromarty Cl. Mans 101 E3
Cromarty Ct. Nott 173 D1
Cromdale Cl. Arn 148 B1
Cromer Rd. Nott 173 F4
Cromford Ave. Carl 174 B4
Cromford Ave. Mans 102 A2
Cromford Cl. Ald 143 D2
Cromford Cl. Lo Ea 193 D3
Cromford Rd. Ald 143 D2
Cromford Rd. Ann Wo 115 D1
Cromford Rd. W Brid 185 F3
Cromford St. Gain 15 E1
Crompton Rd. Mans 87 E2
Crompton Rd. Bils 105 F3
Crompton Rd. Ilk 170 A2
Crompton St. Plea 86 C4
Crompton St. S in A 100 A4
Cromwell Ave. Ilk 170 A3
Cromwell Cres. Lamb 163 D4
Cromwell Dr. E Lea 205 F1
Cromwell Rd. Aslo 178 C2
Cromwell Rd. Bees 183 F3
Cromwell Rd. N-on-T 140 A4
Cromwell St. Carl 174 C4
Cromwell St. Gain 24 B3
Cromwell St. Greas 158 B4
Cromwell St. Mans 102 B3
Cromwell St. Nott 173 D3
Cromwell Way. Lea 24 C2
Crook's Ave. Mans 88 B2
Crookdole La. Calv 148 C4
Crooked Billet St. Mort 15 D2
Crookes Ave. Plea 87 D3
Croome Cl. Lough 220 B1
Cropston Cl. W Brid 185 F2
Cropton Gr. Bing 177 E2
Cropton Rd. Nott 172 A3
Cropwell Bishop Rd. Cr Bu 189 D3
Cropwell Butler Rd. Cr Bi 189 D2
Cropwell Ct. Mans 102 B4
Cropwell Gdns. R on T 176 A1
Cropwell Green. Nott 173 F3
Cropwell Rd. R on T 176 A1
Crosby Cl. Mans 89 D1
Crosby Rd. W Brid 185 F4
Cross Dr. K-in-A 115 D4
Cross Dr. Rain 104 A1
Cross Hill Cl. Wyme 216 B2
Cross Hill. G on H 12 C1
Cross La. Aust 3 E3
Cross La. Bald 140 B1
Cross La. Blid 117 E3
Cross La. Coll 112 B4
Cross La. E Brid 165 E2
Cross La. E Sto 154 A2
Cross La. Elk 49 F2
Cross La. Elst 154 A2
Cross La. Farn 138 C2
Cross La. G on H 5 D1
Cross La. Harby 70 B1
Cross La. S in A 100 A1
Cross La. S in A 100 B3
Cross St. Arn 161 F4
Cross St. B in W 141 F3
Cross St. Bees 183 F4
Cross St. Bils 105 F3
Cross St. Carl 174 B4
Cross St. Carl 175 D4
Cross St. East 144 A1
Cross St. Gain 24 B4
Cross St. Hath 213 D1
Cross St. Lan 16 C2
Cross St. Lo Ea 193 F4
Cross St. Lough 220 B3
Cross St. Mans 88 A1
Cross St. Mort 15 D2
Cross St. N-on-T 140 A4
Cross St. Ret 40 A3
Cross St. S Le S 32 B3
Cross St. Sand 182 B3
Cross The. C in L 26 A3
Cross The. Cotg 187 F2
Crossdale Dr. Keyw 197 F2
Crossdale Wlk. Nott 160 C4
Crossfield Dr. Nott 161 D4
Crossgate Dr. Nott 173 D1
Crosshill. Cotg 188 A2
Crosslands Meadow. Carl 174 C2
Crossley Ave. S in A 100 A2
Crossley Hill La. C in L 26 B2
Crossley St. Nott 161 D1
Crossman St. Nott 161 E1
Crossways Dr. E Brid 165 E2
Crossways. E Mark 66 A4
Crossways. Ret 39 F4
Crow Hill Ct. Mans 102 A4
Crow Hill Dr. Mans 102 A4
Crow Hill La. Mans 88 A1
Crow Hill Rd. Carl 174 C4
Crow Hill. Mans 87 D3
Crow La. S Musk 124 B4
Crow Park Ave. S on T 81 F1
Crow Park Dr. Bu Jo 163 F2
Crowborough Ave. Bees 171 F1
Crowley Cl. Nott 171 E3
Crown Ave. Mans 103 D4
Crown Cl. Coll 98 A1
Crown Cl. Rain 118 B4
Crown Ct. S Le S 32 B3
Crown Farm Way. Mans 103 D4
Crown St. Mans 102 C3
Crown St. N-on-T 139 F4
Crown St. Work 35 F2
Crowthorne Cl. Nott 146 C1
Crowthorne Gdns. Nott 146 C1
Croxall Cl. Nott 184 C2
Croxton Ct. Mans 88 C2
Croydon Rd. Nott 172 C3
Crummock Cl. Bees 183 E4
Cuckney Hill. Mar War 74 A4
Cuillin Cl. Lo Ea 182 A1
Cul-de-sac. Bils 105 F3
Culdrose Wlk. Nott 161 F1
Cullen's Ct. Nott 161 E1
Cullin Cl. Nott 146 C1
Cumberland Ave. Bees 183 E3
Cumberland Ave. Mar War 74 A3
Cumberland Cl. Bir 9 E2
Cumberland Cl. C in L 25 F4
Cumberland Cl. Sels 128 B2
Cumberland Dr. Mans 101 E4
Cumberland Pl. Nott 173 D2
Cumbria Rd. Work 36 A3
Cundy Hill. South 136 A3
Cunningham Cl. Matt 19 F4
Cunningham Cl. Matt 20 A4
Cupar Cl. Mar War 74 C3
Curie Ct. Nott 172 C1
Curlew Cl. Nott 174 B3
Curlew Wharf. Nott 172 C1
Currie Rd. N-on-T 125 D1
Curtis Cl. Coll 98 A1
Curtis St. Huck 146 A3
Curzon St. Nott 173 E3
Curzon Ave. Carl 174 B4
Curzon Cl. Rain 118 A4
Curzon Ct. Nott 173 E3
Curzon Dr. Work 35 F4
Curzon Gdns. Nott 173 E3
Curzon Pl. Nott 173 E3
Curzon St. Carl 175 D4
Curzon St. Gain 15 E1
Curzon St. Goth 195 D1
Curzon St. Lo Ea 182 A1
Curzon St. Lough 220 A2
Cusworth Way. Work 35 E2
Cuttings Ave. S in A 114 A4
Cuxton Cl. Nott 159 E1
Cycle Rd. Nott 172 C2
Cypress Ct. Huck 145 E3
Cyprus Ave. Bees 183 F4
Cyprus Rd. Nott 161 E1
Cyril Ave. Bees 183 F4
Cyril Ave. Nott 172 B4
Cyril Ave. Staple 182 B4
Cyril Rd. W Brid 186 A4

D'Ayncourt Wk. Farns 120 A3
Dabek Rise. Ann Wo 115 D1
Dabell Ave. Nott 159 F4
Dadley Rd. C in L 25 F4
Dadsley Rd. Tick 8 A4
Dagmar Gr. Bees 184 A3
Dagmar Gr. Nott 161 E1
Dairy La. Hose 211 F4
Daisy Cl. Cotg 187 F1
Daisy Farm Rd. Greas 158 B4
Daisy Rd. Carl 162 A1
Dakeyne St. Nott 173 F3
Dalbeattie Cl. Arn 162 A4
Dalby Sq. Nott 172 B2
Dale Ave. Carl 162 A1
Dale Ave. Carl 174 B4
Dale Ave. Lo Ea 182 B1
Dale Ave. Newt 99 D2
Dale Cl. Huck 145 E3
Dale Cl. Ret 39 F2
Dale Cl. S in A 101 D3
Dale Cl. Scarc 58 C1
Dale Cl. Scarc 72 C4
Dale Cl. W Brid 186 A4
Dale Cres. Bald 140 C1
Dale Farm Ave. Nott 174 A3
Dale Gr. Nott 173 F2
Dale La. Al Hu 86 B4
Dale La. Bees 183 F3
Dale La. Blid 118 A3
Dale Rd. Carl 174 B4
Dale Rd. Keyw 197 F2
Dale Rd. Kim 158 C3
Dale Rd. Mar War 74 B3
Dale St. Mans 88 A1
Dale St. Nott 173 F2
Dale View Rd. Nott 174 A4
Dalebrook Cres. Huck 145 E3
Dalehead Rd. Nott 184 B1
Dalemoor Gdns. Nott 172 A4
Dales Ave. S in A 100 C3
Dales La. Miss 4 C2
Daleside Rd E. Nott 174 B2
Daleside Rd. Nott 174 A2
Daleside. Cotg 187 F1
Dalestorth Ave. Mans 87 E1
Dalestorth Rd. S in A 101 D3
Dalestorth St. S in A 101 D2
Daleswood Cres. S Norm 113 D2
Dalkeith Terr. Nott 172 C4
Dallas St. Mans 102 A3
Dallas York Rd. Bees 184 A3
Dalley Cl. Staple 182 C4
Dalton Cl. Staple 182 C3
Daltons Cl. Ald 143 D2
Dam Rd. Tick 8 A3
Dame Flogan St. Mans 102 A3
Dame La. Miss 4 A1
Damson Wlk. Carl 174 A4
Danbury Mount. Nott 161 E1
Dane Cl. Nott 173 E3
Dane Ct. Nott 173 E3
Danes Cl. Arn 161 E4
Danes Rd. Gain 15 F1
Danesfield Rd. Work 35 F1
Daneshill Rd. Lound 20 A1
Daneshill Rd. Sutt 19 E1
Daneshill Rd. Torw 19 E1
Danethorpe La. Coll 126 A4
Danethorpe Vale. Nott 161 E2
Daniel Cres. Mans 101 F4
Daniels Way. Huck 145 F2
Danners Hill. Papp 131 F3
Darfield Ct. Tick 8 A4
Darfield Dr. Hean 143 D1
Dark La. B in W 142 A3
Dark La. Bing 178 A2
Dark La. W Lea 204 C1
Dark La. What 179 D2
Darkey La. Staple 182 C3
Darley Ave. Bees 182 C2
Darley Ave. Carl 162 C1
Darley Ave. K-in-A 115 E3
Darley Ave. Nott 172 C4
Darley Dale Cl. Mans 102 B2
Darley Dr. Lo Ea 193 D3
Darley Rd. Nott 172 C4
Darley Sq. Ilk 157 F3
Darlton Dr. Arn 162 A4
Darlton Rd. E Dray 53 D1
Darlton Rd. Tux 66 B2
Darlton St. Mans 101 E3
Darnal Cl. Nott 160 C4
Darnhall Cres. Nott 171 E4
Daron Gdns. Nott 161 D4
Darrel Rd. Ret 39 F3
Darricott Cl. Rain 118 A4
Darvel Cl. Nott 172 A3
Darwin Cl. Elst 153 F2
Darwin Cl. Mans 102 B2
Darwin Cl. Nott 160 C4
Darwin Dr. Wood 42 A1
Darwin Rd. Lo Ea 193 D3
Darwin St. Gain 24 B3
Davey Rd. Mans 102 A4
David Gr. Bees 171 E1
David La. Nott 160 B2
David St. K-in-A 115 D4
Davids La. Gunt 165 D3
Davidson Cl. Arn 162 B4
Davidson St. Nott 173 F2
Davies Ave. S in A 100 C2
Davies Cl. S in A 100 C2
Davies Rd. W Brid 186 A4
Davis Cl. N Clip 90 A2
Dawber St. Work 35 E4
Dawlish Cl. Huck 145 E3
Dawlish Ct. East 143 E2
Dawlish Dr. Nott 161 D3
Dawn Cl. Huck 131 E1
Dawn View. Staple 170 B1
Dawn's La. Aslo 179 D3
Dawson Cl. East 144 A1
Dawver Rd. Kim 158 C3
Day St. Mar War 74 A2
Daybell Cl. Bott 181 D2
Daybrook Ave. Nott 161 E2
Daybrook St. Nott 161 E2
De Ferrers Cl. E Lea 205 F1
De Lacy Ct. Oll 77 D2
De Morgan Cl. Sels 129 D1
De Vere Gdns. Arn 162 A3
Deabill St. Carl 175 D3
Dead La. Cross 170 B4
Deadwong La. Sibt 153 F1
Deakins Pl. Nott 172 C3
Deal Gdns. Nott 159 F4
Dean Ave. Carl 162 A2
Dean Cl. Mans 102 B2
Dean Cl. Nott 171 E3
Dean Rd. Arn 161 F3
Dean St. La Mi 143 E2
Dean St. Nott 173 E2
Dean's Cl. Caun 109 D3
Deane Cl. Coll 98 A1
Deans Cl. Mist 6 C1
Deans Croft. Bees 171 D1
Deanscourt. Cotg 188 A2
Deansgate. Plea 87 D3
Death La. Clay 21 E3
Debdale Gate. Mans 88 A1
Debdale Hill. Ol Da 218 C2
Debdale La. Keyw 197 F2
Debdale La. Mans 88 A1
Debdhill Rd. Mist 6 C1
Deddington La. Bees 171 E1
Deep Furrow Ave. Carl 174 B4
Deep La. Al Hu 85 D2

Deepdale Ave. Staple 182 B3
Deepdale Cl. Gam 186 B4
Deepdale Gdns. S in A 100 C2
Deepdale Pk. S in A 100 C2
Deepdale Rd. Lo Ea 193 D3
Deepdale Rd. Mans 88 C1
Deepdale Rd. Nott 171 E2
Deepdale St. S in A 100 C2
Deepdene Cl. Nott 160 A1
Deepdene Way. Nott 160 A1
Deeps La. Miss 4 A4
Deer Park Dr. Bes Vil 147 E1
Deer Park Dr. Bes Vil 161 E4
Deer Park Dr. Nott 147 E1
Deer Park Dr. Nott 161 E4
Deer Park. Nott 171 F2
Deerleap Dr. Arn 161 E4
Deers Acre. Lough 220 A3
Deetleton Cl. Sels 129 D4
Delamere Cl. Mans 102 B2
Delamere Dr. Mans 102 B2
Delia Ave. Huck 131 E1
Dell Lea. Mans 103 D2
Dell The. Ann Wo 129 F4
Dell Way. Nott 184 C1
Dellwood Cl. Carl 162 B1
Delta St. Nott 160 C1
Delville Ave. Keyw 197 F2
Denacre Ave. Lo Ea 182 C1
Denay Cl. Rain 104 B1
Denbigh Ct. Coll 98 A1
Denbury Rd. Raven 117 D1
Denby Dr. Mans 102 B1
Dendy Dr. Wood 53 D4
Dene Cl. Matt 20 A4
Dene The. Work 35 E1
Denehurst Ave. Nott 160 B1
Denewood Ave. Bees 171 E1
Denewood Cres. Nott 171 F4
Denholme Rd. Nott 171 E3
Denison Ave. Ret 40 A2
Denison St. Bees 183 F4
Denison St. Nott 172 C3
Denman Cl. Ret 39 E4
Denman Street C. Nott 172 C3
Denman Street E. Nott 172 C3
Denman Street W. Nott 172 C3
Denmark Gr. Hello 173 A2
Dennett Cl. Nott 173 F3
Dennis Ave. Bees 183 F4
Dennis St. Carl 175 D4
Dennis St. Work 35 F1
Dennor Dr. Mans 88 C3
Denstone Rd. Nott 173 F3
Dentdale Dr. Nott 171 D2
Denton Ave. Sand 182 A3
Denton Cl. Bald 140 B2
Denton Cl. Mans 88 C1
Denton Dr. W Brid 185 E2
Denton Green. Nott 159 F1
Denver Ct. Staple 170 C1
Deptford Cres. Nott 160 B3
Derby Gr. Nott 172 C3
Derby Rd. Ann Wo 130 A4
Derby Rd. Bees 171 E1
Derby Rd. East 143 E1
Derby Rd. East 143 E2
Derby Rd. Hath 212 C1
Derby Rd. K in A 116 A4
Derby Rd. K-in-A 115 E2
Derby Rd. Kegw 203 E1
Derby Rd. Lo Ea 193 D4
Derby Rd. Lough 220 A3
Derby Rd. Mans 102 A1
Derby Rd. Nott 172 C2
Derby Rd. S in A 102 A1
Derby Rd. Sand 182 A3
Derby Rd. Staple 182 B3
Derby Sq. Lough 220 A2
Derby St. Arn 161 F4
Derby St. Bees 183 F4
Derby St. Mans 102 B3
Derby St. Nott 173 D3
Derbyshire Ave. Trow 170 B2
Derbyshire Cres. Nott 172 A3
Derbyshire Dr. Sels 128 B2
Derbyshire La. Huck 146 A4
Dereham Dr. Arn 162 A3
Derry Dr. Nott 147 F1
Derry Hill Rd. Nott 147 F1
Derry La. Bing 178 A2
Derwent Ave. Ilk 157 E1
Derwent Ave. Mans 103 D3
Derwent Cl. Bees 183 F2
Derwent Cl. Gam 186 B4
Derwent Cl. Mans 103 D3
Derwent Cl. Mar War 74 B3
Derwent Cl. Rain 118 A4
Derwent Cl. Work 35 F3
Derwent Cres. Arn 162 A3
Derwent Ct. Bald 140 B2
Derwent Ct. Nott 173 D3
Derwent Dr. Ann Wo 130 A4
Derwent Dr. Huck 146 A2
Derwent Dr. Sels 129 D4
Derwent St. Lo Ea 193 E3
Derwent Terr. Nott 161 E1
Derwent Way. N-on-T 125 D1
Desborough Rd. Sels 128 B4
Desford Cl. Nott 161 D2
Devitt Dr. Huck 131 E1
Devon Circus. Nott 147 E1
Devon Cl. Sand 182 A3
Devon Dr. Mans 101 F4
Devon Dr. Nott 161 E1
Devon Dr. Rudd 196 B4
Devon La. Bott 181 D2
Devon Rd. N-on-T 139 F3
Devon St. Ilk 170 A3
Devon St. Nott 173 F3
Devonshire Av. Lo Ea 194 A4
Devonshire Ave. Bees 183 F3
Devonshire Cl. Ilk 157 F3
Devonshire Cl. S in A 100 A1
Devonshire Cres. Nott 161 E1
Devonshire Dr. East 143 F1
Devonshire Dr. Oll 77 D2
Devonshire Dr. Scarc 58 C1
Devonshire Dr. Scarc 72 C4
Devonshire Dr. Staple 170 B1
Devonshire Prom. Nott 172 C2
Devonshire Rd. Har 8 C2
Devonshire Rd. Nott 161 D1
Devonshire Rd. Ret 39 E3
Devonshire Rd. W Brid 185 F3
Devonshire Sq. Lough 220 A2
Devonshire St. Plea 87 D4
Devonshire St. Work 35 F1
Dewberry La. R on T 176 A1
Dial The. Cotg 187 F1
Diamond Ave. K-in-A 115 E2
Diamond Ave. Rain 118 B4
Dickens Ct. Greas 144 A2
Dickens Rd. Work 36 A2
Dickenson Terr. Gain 24 B4
Dickman's La. Harb 202 A2
Dicks La. Greas 144 B2
Dickson Dr. Rudd 196 B3
Didcot Dr. Nott 160 B1
Digby Ave. Carl 162 B2
Digby Ct. Nott 172 C2
Digby Hall Dr. Carl 162 B2
Digby St. Coss 158 A1
Digby St. Kim 158 B4
Dingley Cl. Mans 88 C3
Dingley Cl. Nott 172 A3
Dirca Cl. Nott 195 E4
Diseworth Gr. Nott 173 E1
Distillery St. Rudd 196 B3
Division Rd. Shireb 72 C2
Dixie St. Sels 128 A2
Dobbin Cl. Cr Bi 189 D2
Dock Rd. Work 35 F2
Dockholm Rd. Lo Ea 182 B1
Doddington La. Clayp 156 C3
Doddington La. Dry Do 156 A1
Dog and Duck La. Mort 15 D2
Doghill La. Syer 153 D1
Dogwood Ave. Nott 160 A4
Doles La. K-in-A 114 B3
Doles La. Whit 45 D4
Dolphin Ct. Nott 161 D4
Dominie Cross Rd. Ret 39 F3
Donbas Cl. Nott 160 A2
Doncaster Ave. Sand 182 A3
Doncaster Gr. Lo Ea 182 C1
Doncaster Rd. Baw 10 A4
Doncaster Rd. C in L 25 F4
Doncaster Rd. Haxey 2 C2
Doncaster Rd. Lan 16 C2
Doncaster Rd. Tick 8 A4
Doncaster Terr. Nott 173 E1
Donington Rd. Nott 184 C1
Donkey La. Brad 196 C2
Donner Cres. Ilk 157 F3
Dooland Dr. Nott 161 F1
Dorchester Cl. Mans 102 B1
Dorchester Dr. Mans 102 B1
Dorchester Gdns. W Brid 185 F2
Dorchester Rd. Ann Wo 115 D1
Dorchester Rd. Har 9 D3
Dorchester Rd. Kim 158 C4
Doreen Dr. S in A 100 B1
Dorewood Ct. Bald 140 C2
Doris Rd. Ilk 170 A4
Dorket Cl. Arn 148 A1
Dorket Dr. Nott 172 B2
Dorking Rd. Nott 172 C3
Dormy Cl. Bees 183 E4
Dormy Cl. Mans 88 C3
Dormy Cl. R on T 176 A2
Dormy Ct. Nott 160 B4
Dorner Ave. N-on-T 139 E4
Dornoch Ave. Nott 161 E1
Dornoch Ave. South 121 F1
Dorothy Ave. East 144 A2
Dorothy Ave. Huck 131 D1
Dorothy Ave. Mans 88 B1
Dorothy Ave. Sand 182 A3
Dorothy Dr. Mans 88 C1
Dorothy Gr. Nott 172 B3
Dorset Dr. Har 8 C2
Dorset Gdns. W Brid 185 E3
Dorset St. Nott 172 B3
Dorset Way. Mans 103 D2
Dorterry Cres. Ilk 170 A3
Dorton Ave. Gain 24 C4
Douglas Ave. Awsw 158 B3
Douglas Ave. Carl 174 C3
Douglas Cl. R on T 175 F1
Douglas Cres. Carl 174 C3
Douglas Ct. Bees 183 D1
Douglas Rd. Bing 178 A2
Douglas Rd. Lo Ea 182 A1
Douglas Rd. Mans 89 D1
Douglas Rd. Nott 172 C3
Douglas Rd. S in A 100 B1
Douro Dr. Arn 148 A1
Dove Cl. Work 35 F4
Dove Croft. Oll 77 D2
Dove Dr. Sels 129 D4
Dove La. Lo Ea 193 E4
Dove St. Nott 160 A4
Dovecoat St. Hath 213 D1
Dovecote Cl. E Brid 165 E2
Dovecote Dr. Nott 171 F2
Dovecote La. Bees 184 A3
Dovecote Rd. East 144 A1
Dovedale Ave. Lo Ea 193 D3
Dovedale Ave. S in A 100 B1
Dovedale Circ. Ilk 157 F3
Dovedale Cl. Mans 102 B2
Dovedale Ct. Lo Ea 193 D3
Dovedale Rd. Nott 174 B3
Dovedale Rd. W Brid 186 A3
Dovenby Rd. Nott 184 C1
Dover Beck Cl. Calv 149 D4
Dover Beck Cl. Raven 116 C1
Dover Beck Dr. Woodb 149 E2
Dover Bottom. Elk 50 B2
Dover St. South 121 F1
Doveridge Ave. Carl 175 D4
Doveridge Ct. Raven 117 D2
Doveridge Rd. Carl 175 D4
Downes Cl. Nott 160 A4
Downham Cl. Arn 162 A3
Downham Gdns. Raven 117 D1
Downing Cl. Nott 160 A4
Downing Gdns. Nott 160 A4
Downing St. Nott 160 A4
Downing St. S in A 100 C2
Downing St. S Norm 113 D3
Downs The. Nott 185 D2
Dowson St. Nott 173 F3
Doyne Ct. Nott 173 E1
Dragon St. Gran 191 D3
Dragwell. Kegw 203 E1
Drake St. Gain 24 B3
Draycott Ct. Ilk 157 F2
Draycott Rd. Lo Ea 193 D2
Drayton Ave. Mans 87 E1
Drayton St. Nott 161 E1
Drift Hill. Redm 192 C2
Drift The. Nott 184 C2
Drinsey Nook La. Thor 70 B4
Drive The, Park La. Ret 30 A1
Drive The. Bees 183 F2
Drive The. Gain 24 C4
Drive The. N Clip 90 A2
Drive The. Wint 125 E3
Dronfield Pl. Ilk 157 F3
Drove La. Codd 126 A2
Drove La. Langf 125 F3
Drove La. Langf 126 A2
Drovers Ct. Gain 24 C3
Droversdale Rd. Bir 9 E2
Drummond Ave. Carl 175 D4
Drummond Dr. Nuth 159 F2
Drummond Rd. Ilk 157 F1
Drury La. Tick 8 A4
Dry Pot La. Lo Wh 212 A1
Dryden Ave. Bald 140 C3
Dryden Ct. Staple 170 C1
Dryden Dale. Work 36 A2
Dryden St. Nott 173 D3
Drysdale Cl. Nott 160 A3
Duchess Gdns. Nott 160 A4
Duchess St. Elmt 58 C4
Duchess St. Nott 160 A4
Duchess St. Whit 45 D3
Ducie La. Bole 23 F2
Dudley Ct. Bees 183 D4
Duesbury The. S Norm 113 D2
Duffield Cl. Lo Ea 193 D3
Duffield Ct. Nott 160 C4
Duke Cl. Nott 160 A3
Duke Cres. Greas 144 B1
Duke Pl. Work 35 F2
Duke St. Arn 161 F4
Duke St. Huck 146 A4
Duke St. Ilk 157 F2
Duke St. Lough 220 A3
Duke St. Nott 160 A4
Duke St. Nott 160 C1
Duke St. Ret 39 F3
Duke St. S in A 100 A2
Duke St. S in A 100 C1
Duke St. S Norm 113 D3
Duke St. Whit 45 D3
Duke William Mount. Nott 173 D2
Duke's Dr. Al Hu 86 A4
Duke's Pl. Nott 173 E2
Duke's Terr. Baw 10 A4
Dukeries Cl. Work 35 E3
Dukeries Cres. Work 36 B1
Dukeries Way. Work 35 E3
Dukes Cl. S in A 101 E1
Dukes Pl. Ilk 157 F2
Dukes Rd. Ne Br 219 D3
Dulverton Vale. Nott 160 A2
Dulwich Rd. Nott 172 C3
Dumb Hall La. Shire 34 A2
Dumb Hall La. Th Sa 34 A2
Dumbles The. Lamb 163 D4
Dunbar Cl. Gain 15 F1
Dunbar Dr. Mans 101 E3
Dunblane Rd. Brad 196 B3
Duncan Ave. Raven 117 D1
Duncombe Cl. Nott 173 F4
Duncroft Ave. Carl 162 C1
Dundas Cl. Nott 173 E3
Dundee Dr. Mans 88 A3
Dunelm Cl. S in A 100 B2
Dunelm Dr. Calv 149 D4
Dungannon Rd. Nott 195 F4
Dunham Cl. Ne on T 55 D1
Dunham Cl. South 136 B4
Dunham Rd. Lane 54 A3
Dunham Rd. Ne on T 54 C1
Dunholme Ave. N-on-T 139 F4
Dunholme Cl. Gain 24 C4
Dunholme Cl. Nott 160 A4
Dunholme Rd. Gain 24 C4
Dunkery Rd. Nott 195 F4
Dunkirk Rd. Nott 172 C1
Dunlop Ave. Nott 172 C2
Dunn Brigg. Mans 88 B1
Dunnett Rd. Mans 101 F3
Dunoon Cl. Nott 146 C1
Dunoon Rd. Mans 101 F3
Dunsby Cl. Nott 184 C1
Dunsford Dr. Carl 162 B3
Dunsil Dr. Nott 185 D4
Dunsil Rd. Pinx 113 E1
Dunsmore Cl. Bees 184 A2
Dunstall Wlk. Gain 24 C4
Dunstan Cres. Work 35 F1
Dunstan St. Carl 175 D4
Dunster Rd. East 144 A1
Dunster Rd. Gain 15 F1
Dunster Rd. W Brid 186 A3
Dunston Cl. Lo Ea 193 F4
Dunvegan Dr. Nott 146 C1
Dunwoody Cl. Mans 102 C4
Durham Ave. Nott 173 F2
Durham Cl. Mans 88 B2
Durham Cl. Nott 173 F2
Durham Cl. Work 36 A4
Durham Cres. Nott 160 B3
Durham Gr. Ret 30 A1
Durham St. Ilk 157 F1
Durlston Cl. W Brid 185 D3
Durnford St. Nott 160 C1
Dursley Cl. Nott 160 A3
Dyce Cl. Nott 159 F4
Dykes End. Coll 112 A4
Dylan Thomas Rd. Nott 161 E4
Dyscarr Cl. Lan 16 C2

E Moor. Cotg 188 A1
Eagle Cl. Arn 162 A4
Eagle Cl. Bees 183 E4
Eagle Ct. Nott 160 B4
Eagle Moor. Eagle 84 C2
Eagle Pl. Ret 39 F4
Eagle Rd. N Sca 83 F2
Eagle Rd. N Sca 84 A2
Eakring Cl. Mans 102 C4
Eakring Rd. Bils 105 F4
Eakring Rd. Knee 93 F3
Eakring Rd. Mans 103 E4
Eakring Rd. Rain 104 B4
Eakring Rd. Ruff 104 B4
Eakring Rd. Wellow 92 B4
Ealing Ave. Nott 160 B2
Eardley Rd. Nott 160 C3
Earl Cres. Carl 162 C2
Earl Dr. Greas 144 B1
Earles Ct. Ret 29 E1
Earls Cl. Nott 171 E3
Earls Rd. Ne Br 219 D3
Earlsfield Dr. Nott 146 C1
Earlswood Dr. W Brid 186 A2
Earp Ave. N-on-T 140 A4
Easedale Cl. Gam 186 B4
Easegill Ct. Nott 160 C4
East Acres. Cotg 187 F2
East Circus St. Nott 173 D2
East Cl. Keyw 197 F1
East Cres. Bees 184 A3
East Dr. Nott 172 B1
East End. Lo Cl 211 E2
East Gr. Bing 177 F2
East Gr. Nott 173 D4
East Rd. Wyme 216 C2
East St. Bing 177 F2
East St. Goth 195 D1
East St. Har 9 D3
East St. Hean 157 D4
East St. Lo Ea 193 F4
East St. Nott 173 E3
East St. Ret 39 F3
East St. S in A 101 D2
East St. Saundby 23 F2
East View. Baw 10 A4
East View. E Mark 65 F3
East View. Shireb 72 C3
East View. W Brid 185 E3
East Wlk. Ret 39 E4
Eastcliffe Ave. Carl 162 B2
Eastcote Ave. Bees 171 D1
Eastcroft La. Askh 52 A1
Eastdale Rd. Nott 174 B3
Eastern Ave. Gain 15 F1
Eastern Ct. N-on-T 140 A4
Eastern Dr. Bald 140 C1
Eastern Terrace La. N-on-T 140 A4
Eastfield Cl. N Clip 89 F1
Eastfield Ct. South 136 B4
Eastfield Dr. S Norm 113 D3
Eastfield Side. S in A 101 D2
Eastfield. N Musk 110 C1
Eastfield. N Whea 31 F4
Eastgate. Nor on T 81 F4
Eastgate. Work 35 F2
Eastglade Rd. Nott 161 D3
Eastham Cl. Nott 173 F3
Eastham Rd. Arn 162 B3
Eastholme Croft. Nott 174 B3
Easthorpe La. Redm 192 C2
Easthorpe Rd. Bott 181 E1
Easthorpe St. Rudd 196 B4
Easthorpe View. Bott 181 E1
Easthorpe. South 136 C4
Eastland Terr. Mar War 74 C4
Eastlands La. Mar War 74 A3
Eastleigh Dr. Mans 88 A3
Eastmoor Dr. Carl 174 C4
Eastwell St. Huck 146 A4
Eastwold. Cotg 188 A1
Eastwood Ave. Mar War 74 A3
Eastwood Cl. Huck 145 F2
Eastwood La. Miss 4 B2
Eastwood Rd. Kim 158 C3
Eastwood Rd. R on T 176 A2
Eastwood St. Nott 160 B3
Easy Par. Whit 45 D3
Eather Ave. Mans 88 B2
Eaton Ave. Arn 162 A4
Eaton Cl. Bees 184 A3
Eaton Cl. Farns 119 F3
Eaton Ct. Mans 103 D2
Eaton Ct. Sutt 28 C3
Eaton Grange Dr. Lo Ea 193 D4
Eaton Rd. Rain 118 A4
Eaton St. Nott 161 F1
Eaton Terr. Nott 161 F1
Eatons Rd. Staple 182 B3
Ebenezer St. Ilk 157 F2
Ebenezer St. La Mi 143 D2
Ebers Gr. Nott 173 E4
Ebers Rd. Nott 173 E4
Ebony Wlk. Carl 174 A4
Ebury Rd. Nott 161 D1
Eckington Terr. Nott 173 E1
Eckington Wlk. Mans 103 D3
Eclipse Yd. Mans 102 A4
Ecton Cl. Nott 146 C1
Ecton Cl. Nott 160 C4
Edale Cl. Huck 145 E3
Edale Cl. Lo Ea 193 D3
Edale Cl. Mans 103 D2
Edale Ct. S in A 100 B2
Edale Rd. Mans 103 D3
Edale Rd. Nott 174 A3
Edale Rise. Bees 182 C2
Edale Sq. Ilk 157 F3
Eddington Cl. Cotg 188 A1
Eddison Cl. Work 36 A4
Eddleston Dr. Nott 184 C1
Edelin Rd. Lough 220 A1
Eden Cl. Arn 162 A3
Eden Low. Mans 88 C2
Edenbridge Ct. Nott 171 E1
Edenhall Gdns. Nott 184 C1
Edern Cl. Nott 161 D4
Edern Gdns. Nott 161 D4
Edgar Ave. Mans 102 B4
Edgbaston Gdns. Nott 172 B4
Edgcote Way. Nott 161 D3
Edge Hill Ct. Lo Ea 193 E2
Edge Way. Nott 159 E1
Edgehill Gr. Mans 88 B1
Edgewood Dr. Huck 145 E3
Edgewood Rd. Kim 158 C3
Edginton St. Nott 173 F4
Edgware Rd. Nott 160 B4
Edinbane Cl. Nott 146 C1
Edinburgh Dr. Bing 177 E3
Edinburgh Rd. Work 47 D4
Edinburgh Wlk. Work 47 D4
Edingdale Ct. Bees 171 D2
Edingley Ave. Mans 101 E4
Edingley Ave. Nott 161 E2
Edingley Hill. Edin 120 B2
Edingley Sq. Nott 161 D2
Edison St. Ann Wo 114 C1
Edlington Dr. Nott 171 E2
Edmond Gr. Huck 146 B4
Edmonds Cl. Bes Vil 147 D1

Edmonton Rd. Mans 89 F1
Ednaston Rd. Nott 172 B1
Edwald Rd. W Brid 186 A2
Edwaltam Ave. W Brid 185 F4
Edwalton Cl. W Brid 186 A2
Edwalton Ct. Mans 103 D2
Edwalton Ct. Nott 160 C3
Edwalton Lodge Cl. W Brid 186 A2
Edward Ave. N-on-T 139 F4
Edward Ave. Nott 172 B4
Edward Ave. S in A 100 C2
Edward Ave. Sels 128 A2
Edward Cl. Huck 145 E2
Edward Rd. East 144 A1
Edward Rd. Gain 15 E1
Edward Rd. Lo Ea 193 E4
Edward Rd. Nuth 159 E3
Edward Rd. W Brid 185 F4
Edward St. Ald 143 D2
Edward St. K-in-A 115 D3
Edward St. Lough 220 A3
Edward St. Mar War 74 A3
Edward St. Staple 182 B4
Edward St. Work 35 F2
Edwards Ct. Work 35 E2
Edwards La. Nott 161 D3
Edwards La. Nott 161 E2
Edwards La. Nott 161 E3
Edwin St. Arn 161 E3
Edwin St. S in A 100 C2
Edwinstowe Dr. Nott 161 E2
Edwinstowe Dr. Sels 129 D4
Eel La. Lax 79 E1
Eel Pool Rd. Ever 11 F1
Eel Pool Rd. Wise 11 F1
Eelwood Rd. Huck 145 E2
Egan Cl. Rain 104 B1
Egerton Cl. Mans 103 D4
Egerton Dr. Staple 170 B1
Egerton Rd. Arn 161 E2
Egerton St. Nott 173 E4
Egerton Wlk. Nott 173 E4
Egling Croft. Carl 174 C2
Egmanton Rd. Mans 103 D2
Egmanton Rd. Mar War 74 B4
Egmanton Rd. Tux 65 F1
Egmont Ct. Nott 173 E1
Egypt Rd. Nott 160 C1
Eider Cl. Shireb 72 B2
Eighth Ave. Mans 103 D4
Eisele Cl. Nott 159 F3
Ekowe St. Nott 160 C1
Eland Rd. Shireb 72 C3
Eland St. Nott 160 C1
Elder Cl. Arn 148 A1
Elder Gdns. Nott 161 D4
Elder Gr. Huck 146 A2
Elder St. K-in-A 114 C3
Elder St. S in A 100 C4
Eldon Rd. Bees 183 E1
Eldon St. N-on-T 139 F4
Eldon St. Tux 65 F2
Eleanor Ave. Ilk 170 A3
Eleanor Cres. Staple 182 C4
Elford Rise. Nott 173 F3
Elgar Dr. Lo Ea 193 D3
Elgar Gdns. Nott 173 F4
Eliot Cl. Lo Ea 193 D3
Eliot Wlk. Nott 195 E4
Elizabeth Cl. Huck 145 F3
Elizabeth Ct. Ilk 157 E1
Elizabeth Gr. Carl 162 C1
Elizabeth Rd. N-on-T 139 F3
Elkesley Rd. Mar War 74 C4
Ella Bank Rd. Hean 143 D1
Ella Rd. W Brid 173 F1
Ellastone Ave. Nott 161 E4
Ellerby Ave. Nott 184 C1
Ellerslie Cl. N-on-T 125 D1
Ellerslie Gr. Sand 182 A3
Ellesmere Cl. Arn 162 A4
Ellesmere Dr. Trow 170 B3
Ellesmere Rd. Mans 102 C4
Ellesmere Rd. W Brid 185 F2
Ellington Rd. Arn 148 A1
Elliott St. Nott 173 D3
Ellis Ave. Huck 146 A3
Ellis Cl. Lo Ea 193 E3
Ellis Ct. Nott 173 E3
Ellis Gr. Bees 183 F3
Ellis St. K-in-A 115 D3
Ellsworth Rise. Nott 160 C3
Elm Ave. Bees 183 E1
Elm Ave. Bees 183 F3
Elm Ave. Bing 178 A2
Elm Ave. Carl 174 C4
Elm Ave. E Lea 205 F2
Elm Ave. Huck 145 F3
Elm Ave. Keyw 197 F1
Elm Ave. Kim 159 D3
Elm Ave. Lo Ea 193 E4
Elm Ave. N-on-T 140 A3
Elm Ave. Sand 182 A4
Elm Bank Dr. Nott 173 E4
Elm Bank. Nott 173 E4
Elm Cl. Keyw 197 F1
Elm Cl. N-on-T 140 A3
Elm Cl. Nott 173 E4
Elm Cl. Pinx 113 E2
Elm Cl. Sax 57 D2
Elm Dr. Carl 174 C4
Elm Gr. Arn 148 A1
Elm Gr. Mar War 74 A3
Elm Tree Ave. Mans 88 A2
Elm Tree Ave. Shireb 72 B2
Elm Tree Ave. W Brid 185 E4
Elm Tree Ct. Work 35 F1
Elm Tree Dr. Baw 9 F4
Elm Tree Pl. Elk 50 A2
Elm Tree Rd. K-in-A 114 C3
Elm Tree St. Mans 102 B4
Elm Wlk. Ret 40 A3
Elma La. Holb 59 E3
Elmbridge. Nott 161 D4
Elmcroft. Oxt 134 A2
Elmdale Gdns. Nott 172 A4
Elmhurst Ave. Carl 162 B1
Elmhurst Ave. S Norm 113 D2
Elmhurst Cl. S Norm 113 D2
Elmhurst Rd. Mans 88 C1
Elmore Ct. Nott 173 D3
Elms Cl. Remp 215 E3
Elms Cl. Rudd 196 B3
Elms Gdns. Brad 196 B3
Elms Gr. Lough 220 B2
Elms Park. Rudd 196 B3
Elms Rd. Work 35 F2
Elms The. Carl 174 C3
Elms The. Kim 158 C4
Elmsfield Ave. Hean 143 D1
Elmsham Ave. Nott 146 C1
Elmsmere Dr. Old 17 D3
Elmswood Gdns. Nott 161 E2
Elmton Cl. Elmt 58 B4
Elmton Rd. Elmt 58 B4
Elmtree Ave. Sels 128 C4
Elmtree Cl. Shire 34 C4
Elmtree Rd. Calv 148 B4
Elmwood Cl. Ret 30 A1
Elnor St. La Mi 143 E2
Elsham Wlk. Gain 24 C4
Elson St. Nott 172 C4
Elston Cl. Mans 87 E1
Elston Gdns. Nott 184 C2
Elston Hall. Elst 153 E2
Elston La. Elst 153 E3
Elswick Cl. Nott 161 D4
Elswick Dr. Bees 184 B2
Elterwater Dr. Gam 186 B3
Eltham Cl. Nott 159 F2
Eltham Dr. Nott 160 A1
Eltham Rd. W Brid 186 A4
Elton Cl. Bald 140 B2
Elton Cl. Mans 103 D3
Elton Cl. Staple 182 B4
Elton Rd N. Nott 161 D1
Elton Rd. Mans 102 C3
Elton Rd. Nott 161 D1
Elvaston Ct. Mans 103 D3
Elvaston Dr. Lo Ea 193 D2
Elvaston Rd. Nott 172 A3
Ely Cl. Mans 88 B2
Emerald Cl. Mans 87 F1
Emerald Gr. K-in-A 115 E2
Emerys Rd. Carl 175 D4
Emmanuel Ave. Bes Vil 147 D1
Emmanuel Ave. Carl 162 A1
Emneth Cl. Nott 173 F4
Empingham Cl. Bees 183 D1
Empire St. Mans 102 B3
Empress Rd. Lough 220 B2
Emsworth Ave. Ret 29 F1
Emsworth Cl. Ship 157 E2
Ena Ave. Nott 173 F3
Enderby Cres. Gain 24 C4
Enderby Cres. Mans 102 C3
Enderby Gdns. Nott 147 F1
Enderby Sq. Nott 183 F4
Endsleigh Gdns. Bees 183 F4
Endsleigh Gdns. W Brid 186 A2
Enfield St. Bees 183 F4
Engine La. Greas 144 A2
England Cres. Hean 143 D1
Ennerdale Cl. Gam 186 B4
Ennerdale Rd. Lo Ea 182 A1
Ennerdale Rd. Nott 161 E3
Ennismore Mews. W Brid 185 E1
Enright Cl. N-on-T 139 F3
Enthorpe St. Nott 172 A3
Epinal Way. Lough 220 A1
Epperstone By-Ps. Lowd 150 A2
Epperstone By-Ps. Woodb 150 A2
Epperstone Ct. Mans 103 D1
Epperstone Rd. Lowd 150 B1
Epperstone Rd. Oxt 134 A1
Epperstone Rd. W Brid 185 F4
Epsom Rd. Bees 182 C2
Epsom St. Mans 102 C3
Erdington Way. Bees 182 C2
Erewash Dr. Ilk 170 A3
Erewash Gdns. Nott 161 D4
Erewash Gr. Bees 182 C1
Erewash Rd. Pinx 113 F1
Erewash Sq. Ilk 170 A3
Erewash St. Ald 128 A3
Erewash St. K-in-A 115 D3
Erewash St. Lo Ea 193 F4
Eric Ave. Huck 130 C1
Erica Dr. S Norm 113 D4
Erith Cl. Nott 159 E1
Ernest Rd. Carl 162 A1
Erskine Rd. Nott 161 D1
Esher Gr. Nott 161 E1
Eskdale Cl. Lo Ea 193 D3
Eskdale Ct. Gam 186 B4
Eskdale Dr. Bees 183 D3
Eskdale Dr. Nott 172 A4
Eskdale Dr. Work 35 F4
Essex Dr. Bir 9 E2
Essex Rd. Bir 9 E2
Essex St. East 143 F1
Essex St. Ilk 157 F1
Estefeld Cl. Tick 8 A4
Estwic Ave. East 143 F2
Ethel Ave. Carl 162 A1
Ethel Ave. Huck 131 E1
Ethel Rd. W Brid 185 F4
Ethelbert Ave. Ann Wo 115 E1
Etheldene. Cr Bi 189 D2
Etherington St. Gain 24 B4
Eton Cl. N-on-T 139 F3
Eton Gr. Nott 172 A2
Eton Rd. W Brid 185 F3
Eucalyptus Ave. Nott 184 B1
Eugene Gdns. Nott 173 E1
Eugene St. Nott 173 E2
Evans Ave. S in A 100 B2
Evans Rd. Nott 160 B2
Evedon Wlk. Nott 147 D1
Evelyn St. Bees 184 A4
Evelyn St. Nott 173 F2
Eversley Wlk. Nott 161 D4
Everton Sluice La. Ever 11 E2
Everton St. Mans 87 F1
Evesham Mews. Work 35 F1
Ewart Rd. Nott 173 D4
Ewe Lamb Cl. Bees 170 C1
Ewe Lamb La. Staple 170 C1
Ewell Rd. Nott 171 F3
Exbourne Rd. Nott 159 F1
Exbury Gdns. W Brid 185 D2
Exchange Rd. W Brid 185 F4
Exchange St. Ret 39 F4
Exchange Wlk. Nott 173 E2
Exeter Cl. Carl 162 C1
Exeter Cl. E Lea 205 E1
Exeter Rd. Nott 173 D4
Exeter Rd. W Brid 185 F3
Export Dr. S in A 113 F4
Exton Rd. Nott 161 D2
Eyam Cl. Bees 171 E1
Eyam Cl. Mans 103 D3
Eyre St. Nott 173 F2
Eyre's Gdns. Ilk 157 F1
Eyres La. Goth 205 D4

Fabis Dr. Nott 184 C2
Fackley Rd. S in A 100 A4
Fackley Rd. S in A 100 B3
Fackley Way. S in A 100 B3
Factory La. Bees 183 F3
Factory La. Ilk 157 F1
Factory Rd. K-in-A 115 D3
Factory St. Lough 220 B2
Factory Yard. S in A 101 D2
Failsworth Cl. Nott 184 C2
Fair Lea Cl. Lo Ea 193 E3
Fair Vale. Norw 110 A4
Fair View. Mans 89 D1
Fairbank Cres. Nott 161 E1
Fairburn Cl. Nott 171 E2
Faircroft Ave. Sand 182 A3
Fairdale Dr. East 144 A1
Fairfax Cl. Gain 24 C3
Fairfax Cl. Nott 160 C1
Fairfield Ave. Bald 140 B3
Fairfield Ave. Farn 139 D3
Fairfield Ave. Newt 99 E1
Fairfield Cl. Ne La 59 D1
Fairfield Cl. Nott 185 D3
Fairfield Cres. Lo Ea 193 D2
Fairfield Dr. Mans 103 D4
Fairfield Rd. S in A 101 D2
Fairfield St. Bing 177 F2
Fairfield. Ret 39 F2
Fairham Ave. Goth 195 D1
Fairham Cl. Rudd 196 A4
Fairham Dr. Nott 172 B2
Fairham Rd. Keyw 197 E2
Fairhaven. K-in-A 115 D2
Fairholme Cl. N Clip 89 F1
Fairholme Dr. Mans 87 F1
Fairisle Cl. Nott 185 D1
Fairland Cres. W Brid 185 F2
Fairlawn Pl. Nott 161 E1
Fairlawns. Mans 103 D4
Fairlie Ave. Mans 101 E3
Fairlight Way. Nott 161 D4
Fairmaid Gr. Nott 184 C1
Fairmead Cl. Nott 174 A4
Fairnley Rd. Nott 171 E4
Fairview Ave. Sels 128 C1
Fairview Ct. W Brid 185 E1
Fairview Rd. Arn 161 F2
Fairway Ave. Gain 15 D2
Fairway Cres. New 177 D4
Fairway Dr. Bees 183 E3
Fairway Dr. Nott 160 B4
Fairway. Keyw 198 A1
Fairway. N-on-T 139 E3
Fairway. Ret 39 E2
Fairways Dr. K-in-A 114 C4
Fairways The. Mans 88 B3
Fairweather Cl. Boug 77 F3
Fal Paddock. Mans 88 B1
Falcon Cl. Eagle 84 B2
Falcon Ct. Ilk 157 E1
Falcon Gr. Nott 161 D1
Falcon St. Lough 220 B3
Falcon St. Nott 161 D1
Falconers Wlk. Arn 161 E4
Falconwood Gdns. Nott 184 B1
Fallow Cl. Nott 184 C1
Fallow Cl. Ret 29 F1
Fallow Ct. Work 36 A4
Falston Rd. Nott 172 A4
Falstone Ave. N-on-T 140 A3
Far Back La. Farns 119 F3
Far Croft Ave. S in A 100 B2
Far Holme La. S on T 97 D4
Far La. N on S 213 E2
Far New Cl. Sand 182 A3
Far Pasture Cl. Keyw 197 F1
Far Rd. Fled 67 E2
Far Rye. Nott 171 F3
Far St. Brad 196 C2
Far St. Wyme 216 B2
Faraday Ave. Tux 66 A2
Faraday Ct. Staple 170 C1
Faraday Rd. Mans 102 C3
Faraday Rd. Nott 172 C2
Farfield Ave. Bees 183 F4
Farfield Gr. Bees 183 F4
Farfield Rd. Ilk 170 A4
Farley St. Nott 160 A4
Farleys La. Huck 146 A3
Farm Ave. Huck 145 E2
Farm Cl. E Brid 165 E2
Farm Cl. Ilk 170 A4
Farm Cl. Lo Ea 193 F3
Farm Cl. Nott 184 C1
Farm Croft Rd. Mans 88 B3
Farm Gr. Work 36 A4
Farm La. E Mark 65 F4
Farm Rd. Arn 162 A4
Farm Rd. Bees 183 E3
Farm View Rd. K-in-A 115 E3
Farm View. Ret 39 F2
Farmer St. Brad 196 C2
Farmhouse Cl. Bott 181 D2
Farmilo Cres. Mans 87 F1
Farmway. Mans 88 B1
Farnborough Rd. Nott 185 D1
Farndale Cl. Lo Ea 193 D3
Farndale Cl. S in A 100 C3
Farndale Dr. Nott 171 D2
Farndale Rd. S in A 100 C3
Farndale. Work 36 A4
Farndon Dr. Bees 182 C2
Farndon Gr. Work 35 E4
Farndon Green. Nott 172 B2
Farndon Rd. N-on-T 139 E3
Farndon Rd. S in A 101 E1
Farndon Way. Mans 101 F4
Farnes Ct. Work 36 A3
Farnham Rd. Lough 220 A1
Farnsfield Ave. Bu Jo 164 A3
Farnsfield Ct. Mans 103 D2
Farnsfield Rd. Bils 105 F2
Farnsworth Ave. Mans 103 F1
Farnsworth Cl. Greas 145 D1
Farr Way. Blid 118 A2
Farrar Cl. N-on-T 125 D1
Farrendale Cl. Mans 88 B1
Farringdon Cl. Nuth 159 E2
Farthingate Cl. South 136 C4
Farthingate. South 136 C4
Farthings The. Hath 213 D1
Farwells Cl. Nott 160 B2
Faulconbridge Cl. Nott 160 A3
Fawcett St. Gain 15 E1
Fearn Chase. Carl 174 C4
Fearn Cl. Lo Ea 193 D4
Fearnleigh Dr. Nott 160 B1
Featherbed La. Work 34 C1
Featherston Ave. Work 36 A1
Featherstone Cl. Mans 101 E2
Featherstone Cres. Carl 162 B2
Felen Cl. Nott 161 D4
Fell Croft. Farn 139 D3
Fell Side. Arn 162 A3
Fell Wilson St. Mar War 74 B2
Felley Ave. Ann Wo 114 C1
Felley Mill La N. Sels 129 E1
Fellows Rd. Bees 183 F4
Fellows Yd. Plum 197 F4
Felly Cl. Huck 145 F3
Felly Mill La S. Sels 129 D1
Felstead Ct. Bees 171 E1
Felton Cl. Bees 183 D3
Felton Rd. Nott 173 E1
Fen La. Bald 141 D2
Fen La. Dry Do 155 E2
Fenchurch Cl. Bes Vil 147 D1
Fenimore Ct. R on T 176 A2
Fennel St. Lough 220 A2
Fenroth Cl. Nott 159 F4
Fenton Cl. N-on-T 125 D1
Fenton Dr. Nott 146 B1
Fenton Rd. Clayp 142 B1
Fenton Rd. Nott 160 C2
Fenwick Cl. Nott 159 F1
Fenwick Rd. Nott 159 F1
Fenwick St. Mar War 74 A2
Ferguson Ave. Mans 88 A2
Fern Ave. Nott 161 F1
Fern Bank Ave. Wale 64 A1
Fern Cl. Bees 183 E4
Fern Cl. Bils 106 A3
Fern Cl. Raven 117 D1
Fern Cl. Shireb 72 C3
Fern Cl. South 121 E1
Fern Cres. East 143 E2
Fern Lea Ave. Cotg 187 F1
Fern Rd. Cr Bi 189 D2
Fern St. S in A 100 B2
Ferndale Cl. Bees 183 F1
Ferndale Cl. Boug 77 F3
Ferndale Gr. Nott 174 A3
Ferndale Rd. Nott 174 A3
Ferngill Cl. Nott 173 D1
Fernleigh Ave. Carl 162 A1
Fernleigh Rise. Mans 88 B1
Fernwood Cl. Mans 89 D1
Fernwood Cres. Nott 171 E2
Fernwood Dr. R on T 175 F2
Ferny Hollow Cl. Nott 160 C4
Ferous Cl. Nott 195 F4
Ferrers Wlk. Nott 173 F3
Ferriby Terr. Nott 173 E1
Ferry La. Ever 11 E2
Ferry La. N Musk 110 C1
Festival Ave. Har 9 D2
Festival Dr. Lough 220 A3
Festus Cl. Nott 173 E3
Festus St. Carl 175 D4
Festus St. K-in-A 115 D2
Fiat La. Eakr 92 C1
Field Ave. Huck 145 E2
Field Cl. Bees 183 D2
Field Cl. Carl 162 C1
Field Cl. Mans 88 B3
Field Cl. Work 36 A4
Field Dr. Bald 1[illegible]0 C1
Field Dr. Shireb 72 C1
Field End Cl. E Lea 205 E1
Field House Cl. Nott 171 E3
Field La. Al Hu 86 B3
Field La. Bees 183 D2
Field La. Blid 117 F2
Field La. Cr Bi 189 D2
Field La. Mort 15 D2
Field La. Woodb 149 E2
Field Pl. S in A 114 B4
Field The. Ship 157 D3
Fielden Ave. Mans 87 E1
Fields Ave. Rudd 196 B3
Fields Dr. Aslo 178 C3
Fields Farm Rd. Lo Ea 193 F3
Fieldway. Nott 185 D2
Fiennes Cres. Nott 173 D2
Fifth Ave. Edwin 75 F1
Fifth Ave. Mans 103 D4
Fifth Ave. N Clip 89 F2
Fiftyeights Rd. Fin 1 B2
Filey St. Nott 160 B4
Finch Cl. Nott 184 C4
Finchley Cl. Nott 184 B1
Findern Ct. Mans 103 D3
Findern Green. Nott 174 A3
Fingal Cl. Nott 184 C1
Fingle St. N Le Ha 32 B1
Fingleton. Work 36 A3
Finkell St. G on H 12 C2
Finningley Rd. Mans 103 D2
Finsbury Ave. Lough 220 B2
Finsbury Ave. Nott 173 F2
Finsbury Rd. Bees 171 E2
Finsbury Rd. Bes Vil 147 D1
Fir Cl. Nott 159 F4
Fir Cl. Shireb 72 B3
Fir Dale. Cotg 188 A2
Fir Tree Cl. Mans 89 E1
Fir View. Oll 77 E3
Firbank Ct. Bees 183 D3
Firbeck Ave. Mans 102 C3
Firbeck Cres. Lan 16 C2
Firbeck Rd. Arn 162 A4
Firbeck Rd. Nott 171 E2
Fircroft Ave. Nott 171 F4
Fircroft Dr. Huck 145 E3
Firemen's Row. S in A 100 C1
Firs Ave. Bees 183 F4
Firs Rd. W Brid 186 A2
Firs St. Lo Ea 193 D2
Firs The. Nott 161 E2
Firsby Rd. Nott 159 F1
First Ave. Carl 162 C1
First Ave. Carl 174 B4
First Ave. Carl 174 C3

First Ave. Edwin 76 A1
First Ave. Mans 89 D1
First Ave. Mans 103 F1
First Ave. N Clip 90 A2
First Holme La. S on T 97 D4
Firth Cl. Arn 148 B1
Firth Rd. Ret 39 E4
Fish Pond Dr. Nott 173 D2
Fisher Ave. Arn 161 F3
Fisher Cl. Coll 98 A1
Fisher Cl. E Lea 205 F1
Fisher Ct. Ilk 157 F2
Fisher Gate. Nott 173 E2
Fisher La. Bing 177 F2
Fisher La. Mans 102 B3
Fisher St. Nott 172 C4
Fishers St. Ann Wo 115 D1
Fishpool Rd. Blid 117 E2
Fiskerton Ct. Mans 103 D2
Fiskerton Rd. Roll 138 A3
Fiskerton Rd. South 137 D3
Fitzherbert St. Mar War 74 B2
Five Acres. Nott 185 D2
Five Fields Cl. Ret 40 A2
Five Fields La. Ret 40 A2
Flagholme. Cotg 187 F1
Flamingo Ct. Nott 173 D1
Flamstead Ave. Lamb 163 D4
Flamstead Rd. Ilk 157 F1
Flamsteed Rd. Nott 159 E1
Flash La. Omp 93 D4
Flat La. Fir 16 A3
Flatts La. Calv 133 F1
Flatts La. Calv 148 C4
Flatts La. Sels 128 B2
Flatts The. Bees 183 D3
Flawforth Ave. Rudd 196 B3
Flawforth La. Rudd 196 C4
Flaxendale. Cotg 188 A1
Flaxton Way. Nott 160 C4
Fleam Rd. Nott 184 C2
Fleeman Gr. W Brid 174 A1
Fleet Cl. Nott 172 B3
Fleetway Cl. East 144 A1
Fleetway. Work 35 F4
Fleming Ave. Bott 181 E2
Fleming Ave. Tux 66 A2
Fleming Cl. Greas 159 D4
Fleming Dr. Carl 174 B4
Fleming Dr. N-on-T 125 D2
Fleming Dr. Wood 53 D4
Fleming Gdns. Nott 184 B1
Fletcher Gate. Nott 173 E2
Fletcher Rd. Bees 184 A4
Fletcher St. Lo Ea 193 E4
Flewitt Gdns. Nott 173 F3
Flint Ave. Mans 88 C1
Flintham Dr. Nott 161 E2
Flintham La. Screv 166 C3
Flixton Rd. Kim 158 C4
Flood Rd The. Beck 24 A4
Floral Villas. S on T 96 C4
Florence Ave. Lo Ea 182 C1
Florence Boot Cl. Nott 184 A4
Florence Cres. Carl 175 D4
Florence Ct. Ilk 157 F1
Florence Gr. Nott 174 A4
Florence Rd. Carl 175 D4
Florence Rd. W Brid 186 A4
Florence St. Huck 146 A3
Florence Terr. Gain 24 B4
Florey Ct. Nott 172 C1
Florey Wlk. Nott 195 E4
Floss La. Cott 43 E2
Flowers Cl. Arn 162 A3
Flying Horse Wlk. Nott 173 E2
Foljambe Terr. Nott 173 E3
Folkton Gdns. Nott 161 F1
Folly Hall La. Hick 209 E2
Folly La. No Sc 98 A4
Folly La. Staple 112 C3
Folly Nook La. Ran 19 D3
Forbes Cl. Lo Ea 193 F3
Ford La. Caun 109 D3
Ford St N. Nott 161 D1
Ford St. Nott 161 D1
Fordbridge La. S Norm 113 D4
Fordham Green. Nott 195 F4
Foredrift Cl. Goth 195 D1
Forest Ave. Mans 102 B3
Forest Cl. Ann Wo 130 A4
Forest Cl. Cotg 187 F2
Forest Cl. Rain 104 B1
Forest Cl. Sels 129 D4
Forest Ct. Nott 173 D3
Forest Gr. Nott 173 D3
Forest Gr. Nott 173 D4
Forest Hill Rd. Work 36 A4
Forest Hill. Mans 102 B1
Forest La. Papp 131 F2
Forest La. Wale 63 F2
Forest La. Work 36 B1
Forest Link. Bils 106 A3
Forest Rd E. Nott 173 D4
Forest Rd W. Nott 173 D3
Forest Rd. Ann Wo 130 A4
Forest Rd. Bing 177 E2
Forest Rd. Blid 118 A3
Forest Rd. Calv 148 B4
Forest Rd. Lough 220 A2
Forest Rd. Mans 102 B3
Forest Rd. Mar War 74 B1
Forest Rd. N Clip 89 F2
Forest Rd. Oll 77 E2
Forest Rd. Oxt 134 A3
Forest Rd. S in A 101 D3
Forest Rise. Mar War 74 B1
Forest St. Ann Wo 130 A4
Forest St. K-in-A 115 D2
Forest St. S in A 100 C1
Forest View Dr. Huck 145 F4
Forest View. Oll 77 D2
Forest View. Ret 39 E2
Forester Cl. Bees 183 E2
Forester Gr. Carl 174 B4
Forester Rd. Carl 174 A4
Forester St. Carl 175 D4
Forewood La. Tres 42 A2
Forge Ave. Calv 148 C4
Forge Cl. S Musk 124 B4
Forge Cl. S on T 96 C4
Forge Hill. Bees 183 E2
Forge The. Trow 170 A3
Forman St. Nott 173 E3
Forrests Yd. Work 35 F1
Forster Ave. N-on-T 139 F3
Forster St. Gain 15 E1
Forster St. K-in-A 114 C3
Forster St. Nott 172 C3
Forsythia Gdns. Nott 172 C1
Fosbrooke Dr. Lo Ea 193 E3
Fossdyke Gdns. Sax 57 D2
Fosse Gr. Sax 57 D2
Fosse Rd. Farn 139 D2
Fosse Wlk. Cotg 188 A1
Fossett's Ave. Sels 128 C4
Foster Ave. Bees 183 F3
Foster Rd. Coll 98 A1
Foster St. Mans 102 B3
Fosters La. Bing 177 F2
Foston Cl. Mans 103 D3
Fothergill Ct. Nott 173 E4
Fountain Dale Ct. Nott 173 E4
Fountain Hill Rd. Walker 13 E4
Fountain Hill. Walker 13 E4
Fountains Cl. K-in-A 115 E3
Fountains Cl. W Brid 186 A3
Fourth Ave. Carl 174 B4
Fourth Ave. Edwin 75 F1
Fourth Ave. Edwin 76 A1
Fourth Ave. Mans 103 D4
Fourth Ave. Mans 103 F1
Fourth Ave. N Clip 89 F2
Fowler St. Hello 173 A2
Fox Cl. Lo Ea 193 E3
Fox Covert La. Mist 14 A4
Fox Covert La. Nott 184 B1
Fox Covert. Carl 174 C2
Fox Covert. Lough 220 A3
Fox Gr. Nott 160 C2
Fox Grove Ct. Nott 160 C2
Fox Hill. Cotg 187 F1
Fox Meadow. Huck 145 F3
Fox Rd. W Brid 173 F1
Fox Rd. Whit 45 D3
Fox St. Ann Wo 130 A4
Fox St. S in A 100 C2
Foxby Hill. Gain 24 C3
Foxby La. Gain 24 C3
Foxearth Ave. Nott 185 D1
Foxes Cl. Nott 173 D2
Foxglove Cl. Bald 140 B2
Foxglove Cl. Work 36 A1
Foxglove Rd. Greas 158 B4
Foxhall Rd. Nott 173 D4
Foxhill Cl. S in A 100 A2
Foxhill Ct. Carl 174 C4
Foxhill Rd Central. Carl 174 B4
Foxhill Rd E. Carl 174 B4
Foxhill Rd W. Carl 174 A4
Foxhill Rd. Bu Jo 163 F3
Foxhill Rd. Carl 174 B4
Foxhills. Kegw 203 E1
Foxhollies Gr. Nott 161 D2
Foxton Cl. Nott 159 F4
Foxwood Gr. Calv 148 C4
Foxwood La. Woodb 149 D3
Fradley Cl. Nott 146 B1
Frampton Rd. Nott 172 A4
Frances Gr. Huck 131 D1
Frances St. Sels 128 B1
Francis Chichester Wlk. Gain 24 C4
Francis Gr. Nott 160 C2
Francis Rd. Carl 174 C4
Francis St. Mans 102 C4
Francis St. Nott 173 D3
Francklin Rd. Lowd 150 B1
Frank Ave. Mans 101 F3
Franklin Cl. Nott 161 E4
Franklin Dr. Toll 186 B1
Franklin Rd. Sels 128 A2
Franklyn Gdns. Keyw 197 F2
Franklyn Gdns. Nott 172 B3
Fraser Cres. Carl 162 A1
Fraser Rd. Carl 162 A1
Fraser Rd. Nott 173 E1
Fraser Sq. Carl 162 A1
Fraser St. News 130 B3
Freckingham St. Nott 173 E2
Freda Ave. Carl 162 B1
Freda Cl. Carl 162 B2
Frederick Ave. Carl 174 A4
Frederick Ave. Ilk 170 A3
Frederick Ave. K-in-A 114 B3
Frederick Ave. Kegw 203 E2
Frederick Rd. Staple 182 B4
Frederick St. Lo Ea 193 F4
Frederick St. Lough 220 A2
Frederick St. Mans 102 B3
Frederick St. Ret 39 F3
Frederick St. S in A 100 B1
Frederick St. Work 35 F2
Freeby Ave. Mans 88 B3
Freehold St. Lough 220 B2
Freeland Cl. Bees 182 C2
Freeman's La. S Le S 32 B3
Freemans Rd. Carl 175 D4
Freemans Terr. Carl 175 D4
Freemantle Wlk. Nott 160 C4
Freeston Dr. Nott 159 F4
Freeth St. Nott 173 F1
Freiston St. Nott 172 C4
Fremount Dr. Nott 172 A4
French St. Ilk 170 A3
French Terr. Scarc 59 D1
Fretwell St. Nott 172 C4
Fria'rs Cres. N-on-T 139 F3
Friar La. Mar War 74 B1
Friar La. Nott 173 D2
Friar St. Lo Ea 193 E4
Friar St. Nott 172 C1
Friar Wlk. New 177 E4
Friars Cl. Sels 129 D4
Friars Ct. Nott 173 D2
Friary Cl. Nott 172 C1
Friary Rd. N-on-T 140 A4
Friary The. Nott 172 C1
Friday La. Carl 162 C1
Friend La. Edwin 76 A1
Friesland Dr. Sand 182 A3
Frinton Rd. Nott 159 F1
Frisby Ave. Lo Ea 193 F3
Fritchley Ct. Mans 103 D3
Frith Gr. Mans 101 F4
Frithwood La. Elmt 58 B4
Frobisher Gdns. Nott 161 E3
Frog La. Plun 202 C4
Frogmore St. Nott 173 E3
Front St. B in W 141 F3
Front St. E Stock 7 E1
Front St. Mort 15 D2
Front St. S Clift 68 C1
Frost Ave. La Mi 143 D2
Fryar Rd. Greas 143 F2
Fulford Ave. Ret 39 E4
Fulforth St. Nott 173 E3
Fuller St. Rudd 196 B3
Fullwood Ave. Ilk 157 F1
Fullwood Cl. Bees 183 E2
Fullwood St. Ilk 157 F1
Fulwood Cres. Nott 160 A1
Fulwood Rd N. S in A 114 A4
Fulwood Rd S. S in A 114 A4
Furlong Ave. Arn 161 F4
Furlong Cl. Staple 182 B4
Furlong St. Arn 161 F4
Furnace Rd. Ilk 170 A3
Furness Cl. W Brid 186 A4
Furness Rd. Nott 160 B2
Furnival St N. Work 36 A1
Furnival St. Work 36 A1
Furze Gdns. Nott 173 E4
Fylde Cl. Bees 182 C1
Fylingdale Way. Nott 171 E2

Gable's Lea. Su Bo 213 D3
Gabor Cl. Nott 195 E4
Gabrielle Cl. Nott 160 B2
Gadd St. Nott 172 C3
Gaddick View. Egma 79 F3
Gainas Ave. Gain 15 E1
Gainsborough Cl. Kinou 199 F1
Gainsborough Cl. Staple 182 C3
Gainsborough Dr. N-on-T 125 D2
Gainsborough Rd. Baw 10 A3
Gainsborough Rd. Ever 11 E1
Gainsborough Rd. Girt 82 C2
Gainsborough Rd. Lea 24 C1
Gainsborough Rd. N Whea 22 C1
Gainsborough Rd. S Le S 32 B3
Gainsborough Rd. Saundby 23 E3
Gainsborough Rd. Sax 56 C1
Gainsborough Rd. Sax 57 D2
Gainsborough Rd. Wint 125 E3
Gainsborough Rd. Wise 12 B1
Gainsford Cl. Nott 160 C3
Gainsford Cres. Nott 160 C3
Gaitskell Cres. Edwin 76 B1
Gaitskell Way. Bald 140 C2
Gale Cl. Bees 184 A3
Galen Ave. Wood 42 A1
Galen Ct. Nott 172 C1
Galena Dr. Carl 174 A4
Galley Hill Rd. Upton 122 A1
Gallows Inn Cl. Ilk 170 A3
Galway Ave. Bir 9 E3
Galway Cres. Ret 39 E4
Galway Dr. Bir 9 E3
Galway Rd. Arn 161 F4
Galway Rd. Bir 9 E3
Galway Rd. Nott 172 C2
Gamage Cl. Bald 140 C2
Gamble St. Nott 173 D3
Gamston Cres. Nott 161 E2
Gamston Lings Bar Rd. W Brid 186 B2
Gamston Rd. Mans 103 D2
Gant Ct. Tick 8 A4
Ganton Cl. Nott 161 F1
Garden Ave. Carl 174 B4
Garden Ave. Plea 86 C4
Garden Ave. Rain 104 A1
Garden Ave. Shireb 72 C2
Garden City. Carl 174 C4
Garden La. S in A 101 D2
Garden Rd. Bing 177 E2
Garden Rd. East 144 A2
Garden Rd. Huck 145 F4
Garden Rd. Mans 102 A3
Garden Row. Kegw 203 E2
Garden St. Nott 172 C3
Gardendale Ave. Nott 184 B1
Gardendale Ave. Nott 195 E4
Gardenia Cres. Carl 162 A1
Gardenia Gr. Carl 162 A1
Gardens Ct. W Brid 186 A4
Gardiner Terr. S in A 100 B3
Gardinia Cl. Bees 183 D1
Gardner Dr. Kinou 199 F2
Garfield Cl. Staple 170 C1
Garfield Rd. Nott 172 C3
Garfield St. Gain 15 E1
Garforth Cl. Nott 172 C4
Garibaldi Rd. Mans 89 E1
Garnet Ct. Nott 173 F3
Garnet St. Carl 174 C4
Garnon St. Mans 101 F3
Garratt Ave. Mans 102 B4
Garrett Gr. Nott 184 B1
Garsdale Dr. Nott 185 D2
Garside St. Work 36 A2
Garth Ave. S in A 114 C4
Garth Rd. Mans 102 A2
Garton Cl. Bees 183 D3
Garton Cl. Nott 160 A3
Garton Rd. Lough 220 A2
Garwick Cl. Mans 89 D1
Gas St. Sand 182 B3
Gas Walk. Harb 202 A2
Gatcombe Cl. R on T 176 A2
Gatcombe Gr. Sand 182 A2
Gateford Ave. Work 35 E3
Gateford Cl. Bees 171 E1
Gateford Cl. Work 35 E4
Gateford Gdns. Work 35 E3
Gateford Glade. Work 35 E3
Gateford Rd. Work 35 E3
Gateford Rise. Work 35 E4
Gateside Rd. Nott 173 D1
Gatling St. Nott 172 C3
Gattlys La. Oll 77 D2
Gaul St. Nott 160 A4
Gauntley Ct. Nott 172 C4
Gauntley St. Nott 172 C4
Gautries Cl. Nott 161 D4
Gawthorne St. Nott 161 D1
Gayhurst Green. Nott 160 C3
Gayhurst Rd. Nott 160 C3
Gaynor Ct. Nott 172 A3
Gayrigg Ct. Bees 183 D2
Gayton Cl. Nott 171 E4
Gaywood Cl. Nott 195 F4
Gedling Gr. Nott 173 D3
Gedling Rd. Arn 162 A3
Gedling Rd. Carl 174 C4
Gedling St. Mans 102 A3
Gedling St. Nott 173 E2
Gedney Ave. Nott 173 F4
Gelding Gr. Arn 161 F4
Gell Rd. Bees 183 D2
George Ave. Bees 183 F3
George Ave. Lo Ea 182 C1
George Dere Cl. Boug 77 E3
George Rd. Carl 174 C4
George Rd. W Brid 185 F4
George St. Gain 15 D1
George St. Huck 146 A4
George St. La Mi 143 D2
George St. Mans 88 B2
George St. Mans 89 D1
George St. Mans 101 F4
George St. Mar War 73 F1
George St. Mar War 74 A2
George St. N-on-T 125 D1
George St. Nott 161 F3
George St. Nott 173 E3
George St. Pinx 113 E2
George St. Ret 39 F3
George St. S in A 100 A2
George St. Scarc 59 D1
George St. Work 35 F2
George Yd. Lough 220 A2
George's La. Calv 148 B3
Georgia Dr. Nott 147 F1
Georgina Rd. Bees 183 F3
Gerrard Cl. Bes Vil 147 D1
Gerrard Cres. Kegw 203 E1
Gertrude Rd. W Brid 174 A1
Gervase Gdns. Nott 184 B1
Ghest Villas. C in L 16 C1
Ghost House La. Bees 183 D2
Ghost House La. Bees 183 D3
Gibb St. Lo Ea 193 F4
Gibbet Hill La. Scro 9 F2
Gibbons Ave. Staple 182 B3
Gibbons St. Nott 172 C1
Gibdyke. Miss 4 B2
Gibson Cres. Bald 140 B2
Gibson Rd. Nott 173 D4
Gibson's La. Ol Da 218 B1
Gifford Gdns. Nott 173 D1
Gilbert Ave. Goth 195 D1
Gilbert Ave. Tux 66 A2
Gilbert Gdns. Nott 174 A3
Gilbert Rd. Bir 9 D2
Gilcroft St. Mans 102 B3
Gilcroft St. S in A 100 C3
Gilead St. Nott 160 A4
Giles Ave. W Brid 185 E3
Gill Green Wlk. Clar 30 B2
Gill St. Nott 173 D3
Gill St. S in A 100 B1
Gill St. Sels 129 D3
Gillies The. Mans 101 F3
Gillot St. Hean 157 D4
Gillotts Cl. Bing 177 F3
Gilpet Ave. Nott 173 F4
Gilstrap Cl. N-on-T 140 B4
Gilt Hill. Kim 158 B4
Giltbrook Cres. Greas 158 B4
Giltway. Greas 158 B4
Gin Close Way. Awsw 158 B3
Gin Close Way. Kim 158 B3
Gipsy La. Bleas 152 A4
Girton La. N Sca 83 D1
Girton Rd. Nott 161 D2
Gisburn Cl. Nott 185 D2
Glade Ave. Nott 172 B3
Glade The. Nott 195 F4
Gladehill Rd. Arn 161 E4
Gladstone Ave. Goth 195 D1
Gladstone Ave. Lough 220 A3
Gladstone Dr. Brin 143 F4
Gladstone Rd. N-on-T 139 F3
Gladstone St. Bees 183 F3
Gladstone St. Carl 174 B4
Gladstone St. Gain 15 E1
Gladstone St. Hath 213 D1
Gladstone St. K-in-A 115 D3
Gladstone St. La Mi 143 E2
Gladstone St. Lo Ea 193 E3
Gladstone St. Lough 220 A3
Gladstone St. Mans 88 B1
Gladstone St. Mans 102 B4
Gladstone St. Nott 172 C4
Gladstone St. Nott 173 D4
Gladstone St. S Norm 113 D3
Gladstone St. Work 35 F2
Gladstone Terr. K-in-A 114 C3
Gladstone Terr. Mans 88 B1
Gladys St. Nott 161 D1
Glaisdale Dr E. Nott 171 F3
Glaisdale Dr W. Nott 171 E3
Glaisdale Parkway. Nott 171 E3
Glaisdale. Work 36 A4
Glamis Rd. C in L 25 F3
Glamis Rd. Nott 161 D1
Glannis Sq. Mar War 74 B3
Glapton Rd. Nott 173 E1
Glaramara Cl. Nott 173 D1
Glasby Cl. Oll 77 D2
Glasshouse St. Nott 173 E3
Glastonbury Cl. Mans 88 B2
Glaven Cl. Mans 88 B1
Glebe Ave. Mar War 74 B2
Glebe Ave. Pinx 113 E2
Glebe Cl. N Whea 31 F4
Glebe Cl. Work 35 E2
Glebe Cres. Ilk 170 A4
Glebe Dr. Bu Jo 163 F2
Glebe Farm Cl. W Brid 185 E2
Glebe Farm View. Carl 162 C2
Glebe Rd. Carl 162 B1
Glebe Rd. Nuth 159 E3
Glebe Rd. W Brid 185 F4
Glebe St. Ann Wo 129 F4
Glebe St. Bees 183 F3
Glebe St. Huck 146 A4
Glebe St. Lough 220 B3
Glebe The. Awsw 158 A2
Glebe The. Ret 39 E4
Glebe View. Mans 102 C4
Glen Ave. East 144 A1
Glen Cl. Newt 99 D2
Glen Eagles Way. Ret 39 E2
Glen Helen. Carl 174 C3
Glen Mooar Cl. Mans 89 D1
Glen Parva Ave. Nott 147 F1
Glen Rd. Bu Jo 163 F3
Glen St. S in A 100 C2

Glen The. Nott 184 C1
Glenbrook Cres. Nott 172 A4
Glenbrook. Cotg 188 A2
Glencairn Dr. Nott 172 A4
Glencoe Rd. Nott 184 C1
Glencoe Rd. Nott 185 D1
Glencoyne Rd. Nott 195 F4
Glendale Cl. Carl 162 B1
Glendale Ct. Bees 183 F2
Glendale Gdns. Arn 161 F4
Glendoe Gr. Bing 177 E2
Glendon Dr. Huck 146 A3
Glendon Dr. Nott 161 D2
Gleneagles Ct. W Brid 186 B2
Gleneagles Dr. Arn 148 A1
Gleneagles Dr. K-in-A 114 C4
Glenfield Ave. Kim 158 B4
Glenfield Rd. Lo Ea 193 E3
Glenlivet Gdns. Nott 184 C1
Glenloch Dr. Nott 195 F4
Glenmore Rd. W Brid 186 A3
Glenorchy Cres. Nott 160 C4
Glensford Gdns. Nott 146 C1
Glenside Rd. Bees 171 E1
Glenside. Arn 162 A3
Glenside. K-in-A 115 E3
Glenstone Ct. Nott 172 C4
Glenthorn Cl. Shire 34 C4
Glentworth Rd. Nott 172 C3
Glenwood Ave. Nott 171 E2
Glinis Rd. Nott 160 C4
Glossop Ave. Mans 103 D3
Gloucester Ave. Bees 183 F3
Gloucester Ave. Nott 172 C2
Gloucester Ave. Nuth 159 F2
Gloucester Ave. Sand 182 A2
Gloucester Rd. Work 36 A4
Glover Ave. Nott 171 E2
Glover Cl. S Lev 42 B3
Glovers Cl. Cuck 60 A2
Glovers La. Bald 140 B2
Goatchurch Ct. Nott 147 D1
Goathland Cl. Nott 161 D4
Godber Rd. Huck 145 F3
Godfrey St. Carl 175 D3
Godfrey's Ct. Work 35 F2
Godkin Dr. Ald 143 D2
Goldenholme La. Ramp 43 D1
Goldfinch Cl. Mans 102 C4
Goldham Rd. Nott 171 E4
Goldsmith Rd. Bald 140 B3
Goldsmith Rd. Work 36 A3
Goldsmith St. Mans 102 A4
Goldsmith St. Nott 173 D3
Goldswong Terr. Nott 173 E4
Goldthorpe Ave. Lan 16 C2
Goldthorpe Cl. Lan 16 C2
Golf Club Rd. S-by-D 170 A1
Golf Course Rd. S-on-W 198 A1
Golf Rd. R on T 176 A2
Gomersall Cl. Ret 40 A3
Gonalston La. Epp 150 B2
Gonalston La. Gona 150 B2
Gonalston La. Hover 151 E1
Goodacre St. Mans 102 B4
Goodall Cres. Huck 146 B3
Goodall St. Nott 172 C4
Goodhand Cres. Mans 101 F3
Goodliffe St. Nott 172 C4
Goodman Cl. Greas 158 B4
Goodwin Cl. N-on-T 140 B4
Goodwin Ct. Farns 119 F4
Goodwin Dr. Kim 158 C3
Goodwin St. Nott 173 D3
Goodwood Ave. Arn 161 F4
Goodwood Dr. Bees 182 C1
Goodwood Rd. Nott 171 E2
Goodwood Way. Mans 102 C4
Goose Gate. Nott 173 E2
Goosedale La. Bes Vil 147 D4
Goosemoor La. Ret 39 F2
Gopher Rd. N-on-T 139 F3
Gordon Ave. Mans 102 C3
Gordon Cl. Bees 183 E1
Gordon Cl. Farns 119 F3
Gordon Cl. Work 36 A2
Gordon Cres. S Norm 113 D2
Gordon Rd. Bu Jo 164 A3
Gordon Rd. Lough 220 A3
Gordon Rd. Nott 173 F3
Gordon Rd. W Brid 185 F4
Gordon Rise. Nott 161 F1
Gordon Sq. W Brid 185 F4
Gordon St. Gain 24 B3
Gordon St. Ilk 158 A1
Gordon St. Nott 160 B2
Gordonbrae. Mans 102 B2
Gordondale Rd. Mans 88 A1
Gorman Ct. Arn 162 A4
Gorse Ave. Mans 103 D3
Gorse Cl. Calv 148 B4
Gorse Cl. Greas 158 B4
Gorse Ct. Nott 160 C3
Gorse Hill. Raven 117 D1
Gorse Rd. Keyw 197 E2
Gorse Rd. N-on-T 139 F3
Gorselands Ave. Work 36 B1
Gorseway. N Clip 90 A2
Gorsey Rd. Hello 173 A2
Gorsy La. Morton 137 E1
Gosforth Ct. Nott 173 E1
Gotham La. Bunn 206 B4
Gotham Rd. E Lea 205 F2
Gotham Rd. K on S 204 B3
Gothic Cl. Nott 160 C2
Goverton Hill. Bleas 136 C1
Goverton Sq. Nott 160 B3
Goyden Cl. Nott 161 D4
Grace Ave. Bees 184 A3
Grace Dr. Nott 172 B4
Gracefield La. L Marn 81 F4
Grafton Ave. Arn 161 F3
Grafton Ct. K-in-A 114 C4
Grafton Ct. Nott 173 D3
Grafton St. Work 35 F2
Graham Cl. Bald 140 A2
Graham St. Nott 172 C3
Grainger Ave. Ann Wo 115 D1
Grainger Ave. W Brid 185 F2
Grainger St. Nott 173 F1
Graingers Terr. Huck 146 A3
Grampian Dr. Bes Vil 147 D1
Grampian Way. Lo Ea 193 D4
Granby Ave. Mans 102 A4
Granby Ave. N-on-T 140 A3
Granby Ct. Bing 177 E2
Granby Dr. Bald 140 B2
Granby Dr. Bott 181 D1
Granby Hill. Gran 191 D3
Granby La. Aslo 178 B1
Granby La. Plun 191 F1
Granby La. What 178 B1
Granby St. Ilk 157 F1
Granby St. Lough 220 A2
Grandfield Ave. R on T 175 F2
Grandfield Cres. R on T 175 F2
Grange Ave. Baw 9 F4
Grange Ave. Bees 183 F3
Grange Ave. Mans 101 F3
Grange Ave. Mist 14 A4
Grange Ave. N-on-T 139 F2
Grange Ave. Oll 77 D2
Grange Ave. Rudd 196 B4
Grange Cl. C in L 26 A3
Grange Cl. Lamb 163 E4
Grange Cl. Mist 14 A4
Grange Cl. Nott 185 D4
Grange Cres. Carl 162 C2
Grange Ct. K-in-A 115 E3
Grange Dr. Har 9 D3
Grange Dr. Lo Ea 193 F4
Grange Dr. Mist 14 A4
Grange La. Bald 155 D2
Grange La. Coth 155 D2
Grange Park. W Brid 186 B3
Grange Rd. Arn 161 F2
Grange Rd. Blid 118 A3
Grange Rd. Lo Ea 193 F4
Grange Rd. Nott 160 B2
Grange Rd. Ret 39 F2
Grange Rd. W Brid 186 A2
Grange St. Lough 220 A3
Grange The. N Musk 110 C2
Grange The. Ret 39 F2
Grange The. S Norm 113 D2
Grange View Rd. Carl 163 D1
Grange View. East 143 F2
Grange View. Har 9 D3
Grange Wlk. Mist 7 D1
Grangelea Gdns. Bees 183 E4
Granger Ct. Lough 220 A2
Grangewood Ct. Nott 171 E2
Grangewood Rd. K-in-A 114 C4
Grangewood Rd. Nott 171 E2
Grannis Dr. Nott 172 A4
Grant St. Nott 172 C3
Grantham Cl. Greas 158 B4
Grantham Rd. Bing 178 B2
Grantham Rd. Bott 181 E1
Grantham Rd. R on T 175 F1
Grantham Rd. R on T 176 B2
Grantleigh Cl. Nott 171 F3
Granton Ave. Nott 195 F4
Granton Rise. Mans 101 E3
Granville Ave. Lo Ea 182 B1
Granville Cres. R on T 175 F1
Granville Ct. Nott 173 F3
Granville Gr. Nott 173 F3
Granville St. Lough 220 A2
Grasmere Cl. Gain 15 F1
Grasmere Cl. Huck 145 F4
Grasmere Rd. Bees 183 E4
Grasmere Rd. Lo Ea 182 A1
Grasmere Rd. Work 35 F4
Grasmere St. Sand 182 A3
Grass St. Ilk 157 F2
Grassingdale Cl. Carl 162 B1
Grassington Rd. Nott 172 B4
Grassmere. Cotg 188 A2
Grassthorpe Rd. S on T 81 F1
Gravel La. Egma 79 E4
Gravel Pit La. W Dray 50 C1
Gravelholes La. Mist 6 C1
Gravelly Hollow. Calv 133 D1
Gravelly La. Fisk 137 F2
Gravelly La. Morton 137 F2
Graveney Gdns. Arn 162 B3
Graves Moor La. Blyth 18 C1
Graves Moor La. Torw 18 C1
Gray La. Halam 120 C1
Gray St. Lough 220 A1
Graylands Rd. Nott 171 F3
Grazingfield. Nott 185 D2
Greasley Ave. East 144 B1
Greasley Ct. Mans 103 D2
Greasley St. Nott 160 A4
Great Central Rd. Lough 220 B2
Great Central Rd. Mans 102 B3
Great Freeman St. Nott 173 E3
Great Hoggett Dr. Bees 183 D3
Great La. E Mark 65 F4
Great North Rd. Ba Mo 28 B3
Great North Rd. Bald 155 F3
Great North Rd. C on T 96 C3
Great North Rd. Crom 110 C3
Great North Rd. Dry Do 155 F3
Great North Rd. E Mark 65 E3
Great North Rd. Eaton 40 A1
Great North Rd. Gams 51 D2
Great North Rd. Kelh 124 B3
Great North Rd. N Musk 110 C3
Great North Rd. N-on-T 124 B3
Great North Rd. Ran 19 D2
Great North Rd. S Musk 124 B3
Great North Rd. S on T 96 C3
Great North Rd. Scro 10 A1
Great North Rd. Sutt 28 B3
Great North Rd. Torw 19 D2
Great North Rd. Tux 65 E3
Great North Rd. W Dray 51 D2
Great North Rd. West 81 E2
Great Northern Cl The. Nott 173 E2
Great Northern Rd. East 143 E1
Great Northern Way. Carl 175 D4
Greaves Ave. Ne Br 219 E3
Greaves Cl. Arn 162 A3
Greaves Cl. N-on-T 140 B4
Greaves Cl. Nott 159 E1
Greaves La. Edin 120 A2
Greaves La. Oxt 119 F1
Grebe Cl. Bald 140 B3
Greek St. Nott 173 D3
Green Acre. Nott 171 D3
Green Acre. W Brid 186 A2
Green Ave. Carl 175 D4
Green Bank. Rain 118 B4
Green Cl. Blid 118 A2
Green Cl. Huck 146 B3
Green Cl. Keyw 197 F2
Green Cl. Newt 99 D2
Green Cres. Sels 128 C3
Green Farm Rd. Sels 128 B3
Green Hill Rise. Hath 213 D1
Green Hill. Hath 213 D1
Green La. Babw 38 C3
Green La. Bath 110 A1
Green La. Bott 181 E1
Green La. Coll 112 A4
Green La. Darl 67 E2
Green La. Dry Do 156 C1
Green La. Eagle 84 C2
Green La. Gran 191 D3
Green La. Harb 202 B1
Green La. Hick 210 A2
Green La. Ilk 170 A4
Green La. Lamb 149 D1
Green La. Lax 79 E1
Green La. Lax 80 A1
Green La. Lea 24 C2
Green La. Mans 87 D1
Green La. Mans 102 B2
Green La. Nott 184 C1
Green La. Plea 86 B4
Green La. S Lev 42 B3
Green La. Scro 18 C4
Green La. Tres 42 B2
Green La. Wale 64 A1
Green La. Whit 45 E3
Green Leys. W Brid 185 E2
Green Mile La. Babw 28 A1
Green Mile La. Babw 38 C4
Green Platt. Cotg 187 F2
Green Rd. G on H 13 D1
Green St. B in F 195 D4
Green St. Nott 173 E1
Green The. Al Hu 85 D2
Green The. B-le-V 192 A1
Green The. Bees 183 F2
Green The. Bils 105 F4
Green The. C in L 26 A3
Green The. Codd 126 A1
Green The. Coll 111 F4
Green The. E Lea 205 F1
Green The. Elst 153 E2
Green The. Gain 24 C4
Green The. Glap 86 A4
Green The. Har 8 C2
Green The. Hath 213 D1
Green The. Hose 211 F4
Green The. K on S 204 A2
Green The. Kirk 120 C4
Green The. Lo Wh 212 B2
Green The. Lowd 149 F1
Green The. Mans 88 A3
Green The. Orst 179 F4
Green The. R on T 175 F2
Green The. S in A 99 F1
Green Wlk. Aslo 178 C2
Green's Farm La. Carl 163 D1
Greenacre Ave. Hean 143 D2
Greenacre Rd. Work 36 A3
Greenacre. Lamb 163 F3
Greenacre. Mans 102 C3
Greenacre. S in A 100 B3
Greenacres Cl. Greas 144 B1
Greenacres Dr. S Norm 113 D3
Greenacres. K-in-A 115 D1
Greenbank Dr. S in A 100 C3
Greenbank. Carl 174 B3
Greenclose La. Lough 220 A2
Greencroft. Nott 184 C2
Greendale Ave. Edwin 76 A2
Greendale Cl. Mar War 74 A2
Greendale Cres. N Clip 90 A2
Greendale Gdns. Nott 172 A4
Greendale Rd. Arn 161 F3
Greendale Rd. Nott 174 B3
Greenfield Ave. Whit 45 E3
Greenfield Cl. Mans 89 D1
Greenfield Gr. Carl 174 B4
Greenfield St. Nott 172 B1
Greenfields Cres. Oll 77 E2
Greenfields Dr. Cotg 187 F1
Greenfields. Ald 143 D2
Greenfields. S in A 101 D3
Greengate Rd. E Dray 53 D2
Greengate. Syer 153 D2
Greengates Ave. Arn 161 F2
Greenhill Cres. Carl 174 C3
Greenhill La. Ann Wo 129 F4
Greenhill Rd. Carl 174 C3
Greenhill Rise. Carl 174 C4
Greenhills Rd. East 143 F2
Greenhills Ave. East 144 A2
Greenhills Rd. East 144 A2
Greenholme Cl. K-in-A 115 D2
Greenland Cres. Bees 183 E2
Greenland Rd. S in A 100 C4
Greens Ct. Ilk 157 E1
Greens La. Kim 159 D3
Greenside Ave. Ramp 42 C1
Greenside Cl. Lo Ea 193 F4
Greensquare Rd. K in A 113 F1
Greenvale. Farns 120 A3
Greenview Cl. Mans 89 D1
Greenway Cl. R on T 175 F2
Greenway The. Sand 182 A3
Greenway. C in L 26 A3
Greenway. Mans 89 E2
Greenway. N-on-T 139 F3
Greenway. Ret 39 E2
Greenwich Ave. Nott 160 B2
Greenwood Ave. Edwin 76 A1
Greenwood Ave. Har 8 C3
Greenwood Ave. Huck 145 F4
Greenwood Ave. Ilk 170 A4
Greenwood Ave. Mans 88 A2
Greenwood Ave. Nott 174 B3
Greenwood Ave. S in A 99 F1
Greenwood Cl. Farns 120 A3
Greenwood Cotts. Mans 102 C4
Greenwood Cres. Boug 77 F3
Greenwood Cres. Carl 174 C3
Greenwood Dr. K-in-A 114 C3
Greenwood Gdns. Hudd 196 B3
Greenwood Rd. Carl 174 B3
Greenwood Rd. Nott 174 B3
Greenwood Vale. Huck 145 F4
Greet Farm Cl. South 121 F1
Greetwell Cl. Nott 172 A3
Gregory Bvd. Nott 173 D4
Gregory Ave. Ald 143 D2
Gregory Ave. Carl 162 A1
Gregory Ave. La Mi 143 D2
Gregory Ave. Nott 172 C2
Gregory Cl. Staple 182 C4
Gregory Cres. Har 8 C2
Gregory Ct. Bees 183 D2
Gregory Ct. Nott 172 C2
Gregory Gdns. Farns 119 F3
Gregory St. Ilk 157 F1
Gregory St. Lough 220 A2
Gregory St. Nott 172 C1
Grenville Dr. Ilk 157 F2
Grenville Dr. Staple 182 C4
Grenville Rd. Bees 184 A2
Grenville Rise. Nott 147 F1
Gresham Cl. N-on-T 140 C4
Gresham Cl. W Brid 185 E4
Gresham Gdns. Arn 162 A3
Gresham Gdns. W Brid 185 E4
Gresley Ave. Baw 10 A4
Gresley Rd. Ilk 157 F1
Gresley Rd. Ret 39 E3
Gressy Rd. Nott 184 C1
Gretton Cl. Clayp 156 B3
Gretton Rd. Arn 162 A2
Grey St. East 144 A1
Grey St. Gain 15 D1
Grey St. K-in-A 114 B3
Greyfriar Gate. Nott 173 E2
Greys Rd. Arn 161 F2
Greystoke Dr. Nott 171 E4
Greystones Rd. Gain 15 D2
Greythorn Dr. W Brid 185 E2
Griceson Cl. Oll 77 D1
Grierson Ave. Nott 161 D4
Griffs Hollow. Carl 174 C4
Grimesmoor Rd. Calv 149 D4
Grimsby Terr. Nott 173 E3
Grimston Rd. Nott 172 C4
Grindon Cres. Nott 146 B1
Gringley Rd. Clay 21 F3
Gringley Rd. G on H 21 F3
Gringley Rd. Mist 6 C1
Gringley Rd. Walker 13 F2
Gripps Comm. Cotg 187 F1
Grisedale Ct. Bees 183 D2
Gritley Mews. Nott 173 D1
Grives La. K-in-A 115 D1
Grizedale Gr. Bing 177 D2
Grosvenor Ave. Lo Ea 193 D2
Grosvenor Ave. Nott 161 E1
Grosvenor Ave. S in A 100 B1
Grosvenor Rd. Bald 140 A2
Grosvenor Rd. East 143 F1
Grosvenor Rd. Har 9 D2
Grouville Dr. Arn 162 A3
Grove Ave. Bees 183 F3
Grove Ave. Nott 173 D3
Grove Cl. Bu Jo 163 F3
Grove Coach Rd. Ret 40 A2
Grove La. Ret 40 A3
Grove Mews. East 143 F1
Grove Park. Mist 6 C1
Grove Rd. Grove 41 E3
Grove Rd. Mar War 74 A3
Grove Rd. Nott 172 C2
Grove Rd. Ret 40 B2
Grove Rd. S in A 101 D2
Grove Rd. S Lev 41 E3
Grove St. Bald 140 B3
Grove St. Bees 184 A3
Grove St. Mans 88 A2
Grove St. Mans 102 A3
Grove St. Ret 39 F4
Grove The. Beck 14 A1
Grove The. Calv 149 D4
Grove The. Ne on T 55 D1
Grove The. Nott 161 D1
Grove The. Nott 172 C3
Grove Way. Mans 88 A2
Grove Wood Rd. Mist 6 C1
Grove Wood Terr. Mist 6 C1
Grover Ave. Carl 162 A2
Groveside Cres. Bees 184 B2
Groveview Rd. Bald 140 B3
Grundy Ave. Sels 128 B4
Grundy Nook. Whit 45 D3
Grundy St. Nott 172 C4
Guildford Ave. Mans 88 B3
Guildhall St. N-on-T 140 A4
Gunn Cl. Nott 160 A4
Gunnersbury Way. Nuth 159 F2
Gunthorpe Cl. Nott 161 D2
Gunthorpe Dr. Nott 161 E2
Gunthorpe Rd. Carl 162 B2
Gunthorpe Rd. Gain 164 C4
Gunthorpe Rd. Haxey 7 F4
Gutersloh Ct. Staple 182 C4
Gwenbrook Ave. Bees 183 F3
Gwenbrook Rd. Bees 183 E3
Gwndy Gdns. Nott 161 D4

Habblesthorpe Cl. N Le Ha 32 C1
Habblesthorpe Rd. N Le Ha 32 C1
Hackers Cl. E Brid 165 E2
Hackworth Cl. Greas 144 A2
Hadbury Rd. Nott 160 C2
Hadden Ct. Nott 171 E3
Haddon Cl. Carl 162 B1
Haddon Cl. Huck 146 A3
Haddon Cl. Sels 129 D4
Haddon Cres. Bees 183 E1
Haddon Dr. Bald 140 B2
Haddon Nurseries. Ilk 157 F2
Haddon Pl. Shireb 72 B3
Haddon Rd. Mans 102 A4
Haddon Rd. Raven 117 D2
Haddon Rd. Ret 40 A2
Haddon Rd. W Brid 185 F3
Haddon St. Ilk 157 F2
Haddon St. Nott 161 D1
Haddon St. S in A 100 C2
Haddon St. Tibs 99 D3
Haddon Way. R on T 176 A2
Hades La. W-on-W 217 E3
Hades La. Wyme 217 F2
Hadfield Wlk. Mans 103 D3
Hadleigh Cl. Bees 182 C1
Hadley St. Ilk 170 A3
Hadrian Gdns. Bes Vil 147 D1
Hadstock Cl. Sand 182 A2
Hagg La. Egma 80 A3
Hagg La. Miss 10 C4
Hagley Cl. Nott 174 A3
Haileybury Cres. W Brid 185 F3
Haileybury Rd. W Brid 185 F3
Hainton Cl. Gain 24 C4
Haise Ct. Nott 159 F3

Halam Cl. Mans 101 E4
Halam Hill. Halam 121 D1
Halberton Dr. W Brid 185 E2
Haldane St. Gain 15 D1
Hales Cl. Cotg 187 F2
Haley Cl. Kim 158 B3
Halfmoon Dr. K-in-A 115 D2
Halifax Ct. Nott 159 E1
Halifax Pl. Nott 173 E2
Hall Barn La. Mans 101 E4
Hall Cl The. E Mark 66 A4
Hall Cl. R on T 175 F2
Hall Cl. Rain 118 A4
Hall Croft. Bees 183 F3
Hall Dr. Bees 183 E3
Hall Dr. Clay 21 E3
Hall Dr. Cr Bi 189 D2
Hall Dr. Goth 195 D1
Hall Dr. Nott 171 F2
Hall Dr. Sand 182 A3
Hall Gdns. Bees 183 D4
Hall Gdns. E Lea 214 C4
Hall La. Brin 143 E3
Hall La. Co Ba 200 B4
Hall La. E Mark 66 A4
Hall La. Kinou 200 A2
Hall La. Newt 99 D2
Hall Rd. Ald 143 E2
Hall St. Mans 102 C3
Hall St. Nott 161 E2
Hall St. S in A 100 C3
Hall View Dr. Nott 171 E3
Hall View. Matt 20 A4
Hall's Rd. G on H 13 D2
Hallam Fields Rd. Ilk 170 A2
Hallam Rd. Bees 183 F3
Hallam Rd. Carl 162 A1
Hallam's La. Arn 161 F4
Hallams La. Bees 183 E3
Hallamway. Mans 88 B1
Hallcroft Ave. Ret 39 F4
Hallcroft Rd. Ret 29 E1
Hallfield Rd. Newt 99 D2
Hallfields. W Brid 186 A2
Hallifax Ave. Mar War 74 A4
Halloughton Rd. South 136 B4
Hallowell Dr. Nott 171 F2
Halls La. Greas 158 A4
Halls Rd. Staple 182 B3
Hallum Ct. Ilk 157 F2
Halstead Cl. Bees 183 E2
Halstead Cl. Nott 160 A2
Haltham Green. Gain 24 C4
Haltham Wlk. Nott 195 E4
Hambledon Dr. Nott 172 A3
Hambleton Cl. Lo Ea 182 A1
Hambleton Ct. C in L 25 F4
Hambling Cl. Nott 160 A4
Hamilton Cl. Arn 148 B1
Hamilton Cl. Bees 182 C1
Hamilton Dr. Mar War 74 A2
Hamilton Dr. Nott 173 D2
Hamilton Dr. R on T 175 F2
Hamilton Gdns. Nott 161 D1
Hamilton Rd. Lo Ea 182 B1
Hamilton Rd. Nott 173 D4
Hamilton Rd. S in A 101 E1
Hamilton St. Mans 102 C3
Hamilton St. Work 35 F3
Hamlet La. S Norm 113 D3
Hamlet The. S Norm 113 D3
Hammerwater Dr. Mar War 74 A2
Hammond Gr. K-in-A 115 D1
Hampden St. Nott 173 D3
Hampden Gr. Bees 183 F3
Hampden St. Greas 158 B4
Hampden St. K-in-A 114 C3
Hampshire Ct. Sels 128 A2
Hampshire Dr. Sand 182 A3
Hampstead Rd. Nott 161 F1
Hampton Cl. Bees 182 C2
Hampton Rd. W Brid 185 F3
Hanbury Ct. Mans 103 D3
Hand's Rd. Hean 143 D1
Hand's Wlk. Bott 181 D1
Handel St. Nott 173 F3
Handley Ct. N-on-T 124 C1
Hanford Way. Lough 220 A3
Hangar Hill. Whit 45 D3
Hankin St. Huck 146 B3
Hanley Ave. Bees 183 D4
Hanley St. Nott 173 D3
Hannah Cres. Nott 185 D4
Hanover Ct. Nott 171 E3
Hanslope Cres. Nott 171 E4
Hanson Cres. Huck 146 A4
Hanstubbin Rd. Sels 128 C3
Hanton Ave. Sels 129 D1
Hanworth Gdns. Arn 161 E4
Harberton Cl. Nott 147 F1
Harby Ave. Mans 88 B3
Harby Ave. S in A 101 E1
Harby Cl. Bald 140 B2
Harby Dr. Nott 172 B2
Harby La. Co Ba 200 C3
Harby La. Hose 211 F4
Harby La. Lang 201 D3
Harby La. Plun 202 C3
Harby La. Stat 202 C2
Harby La. Stat 202 C3
Harcourt Cres. Nuth 159 F2
Harcourt Pl. Ret 40 A2
Harcourt Rd. Nott 173 D4
Harcourt St. Bees 183 F3
Harcourt St. K-in-A 115 D3
Harcourt St. Mans 102 B3
Harcourt St. N-on-T 140 A4
Harcourt Terr. Nott 173 E3
Harden Ct. Nott 195 E4
Hardie Ave. S Norm 113 D3
Hardigate Rd. Cr Bu 189 D4
Hardstaff Cl. Ann Wo 114 C1
Hardstaff Cl. Ret 29 E1
Hardstaff Rd. Nott 174 A2
Hardwick Ave. N-on-T 139 F4
Hardwick Ave. Rain 103 F1
Hardwick Ave. S in A 101 D3
Hardwick Ave. Shireb 72 C2
Hardwick Cl. S in A 101 D3
Hardwick Cres. Work 36 A1
Hardwick Ct. Har 9 D3
Hardwick Dr. Oll 77 D2
Hardwick Dr. Sels 129 D4
Hardwick Gr. Nott 172 C2
Hardwick Gr. W Brid 173 F1
Hardwick La. S in A 100 C1
Hardwick Rd E. Work 36 A1
Hardwick Rd W. Work 36 A1
Hardwick Rd. Nott 161 E2
Hardwick Rd. Nott 173 D2
Hardwick St. Mans 102 B4
Hardwick St. S in A 100 C1
Hardwick St. Scarc 72 C4
Hardwick St. Shireb 73 D2
Hardwick St. Tibs 99 D4
Hardwick View. S in A 101 D3
Hardwicke Rd. Bees 183 E2
Hardwood Cl. Nott 159 F4
Hardy Barn. Ship 157 D4
Hardy Cl. Lo Ea 193 E3
Hardy Pl. Mans 101 F4
Hardy St. Kim 158 C4
Hardy St. Nott 173 D3
Hardy St. Work 35 F1
Hardy's Dr. Carl 162 C1
Hardys Cl. Cr Bi 189 D2
Hareholme St. Mans 102 A4
Harewood Ave. N-on-T 139 F4
Harewood Ave. Nott 160 B3
Harewood Ave. Ret 39 E3
Harewood Cl. R on T 176 A2
Harewood Ct. Har 9 D3
Harewood Cl. Sand 182 A2
Harewood Rd. Work 35 F4
Hargon La. Wint 125 E3
Harkstead Rd. Nott 147 D1
Harlaxton Dr. Lo Ea 194 A4
Harlaxton Dr. Nott 172 C2
Harlaxton Wlk. Nott 173 E3
Harlech Rise. Bees 183 D2
Harlequin Cl. R on T 176 A2
Harlequin Ct. East 143 E2
Harles Acres. Hick 210 B3
Harley St. Nott 172 C2
Harlow Ave. Mans 102 B2
Harlow Cl. Mans 88 B3
Harlow Cl. S in A 100 C3
Harlow Gr. Carl 162 C1
Harlow St. Blid 118 A3
Harmston Rise. Nott 160 C2
Harold Ave. Ald 143 D2
Harold St. Nott 173 F2
Harpenden Sq. Nott 160 A2
Harpole Wlk. Nott 147 F1
Harriett St. Staple 182 B4
Harrimans La. Nott 184 C4
Harrington Dr. Nott 172 C2
Harrington St. Lo Ea 193 D3
Harrington St. Mans 102 A3
Harrington St. Work 35 E1
Harris Cl. Nott 171 F3
Harris Rd. Bees 183 E3
Harrison Ct. Bing 177 E2
Harrison Dr. Lan 16 C2
Harrison Rd. Mans 101 F3
Harrison Rd. Staple 182 B4
Harrison Way. South 121 F1
Harrogate Rd. Nott 174 B3
Harrogate St. Carl 174 C4
Harrop White Rd. Mans 101 F4
Harrow Cl. Gain 15 F1
Harrow Cl. Rain 118 A4
Harrow Gdns. Nott 172 B2
Harrow La. Boug 77 F3
Harrow La. Boug 77 F3
Harrow Rd. Huck 145 E3
Harrow Rd. Nott 172 A2
Harrow Rd. W Brid 185 F3
Harrowby Rd. Nott 172 C2
Harstoft Ave. Work 35 F3
Hart Ave. Sand 182 A3
Hart St. Nott 172 C2
Hartcroft Rd. Nott 161 D3
Hartford Cl. Nott 173 E1
Hartill Dr. Mans 101 E3
Hartington Ave. Carl 162 B1
Hartington Ave. Huck 145 E3
Hartington Cl. Carl 163 D1
Hartington Ct. Mans 103 D3
Hartington Dr. S in A 101 D2
Hartington Dr. Sels 129 D4
Hartington Pl. Ilk 157 F3
Hartington Rd. Nott 161 E2
Hartington St. Scarc 72 C4
Hartland Rd. Work 35 F1
Hartley Ct. Nott 172 C3
Hartley Dr. Bees 184 A3
Hartley Rd. K-in-A 114 C3
Hartley Rd. Nott 172 C3
Hartness Rd. Nott 184 B1
Hartside Cl. Gam 186 B4
Hartside Gdns. Lo Ea 193 D4
Hartwell St. Nott 173 E3
Hartwood Dr. Staple 170 B1
Harvest Cl. Nott 160 C4
Harvest Cl. Work 36 A4
Harvey Ave. Codd 125 F1
Harvey Cl. Rudd 196 B3
Harvey Croft. Trow 170 B2
Harvey Ct. Nott 172 C1
Harvey Rd. Mans 102 C3
Harvey Rd. Nott 171 F4
Harvey's Field. South 136 C4
Harwell La. Ever 11 D2
Harwell Sluice La. Ever 11 D3
Harwich Cl. Nott 160 A4
Harwill Cres. Nott 160 A1
Harwood Cl. Arn 162 A4
Harwood Cl. S in A 101 D2
Harwood Pl. S in A 101 D2
Harworth Ave. Blyth 18 A3
Harworth Cl. Mans 101 E3
Haslam St. Nott 173 D2
Haslemere Gdns. Raven 116 C1
Haslemere Rd. Lo Ea 193 D4
Haslemere Rd. Nott 172 B4
Hassock La N. Ship 157 D4
Hassock La S. Ship 157 E3
Hassocks La. Bees 184 A4
Hassop Wlk. Mans 103 D3
Hastings St. Carl 174 B4
Hastings St. Lough 220 A2
Haswell Rd. Nott 160 A3
Hatchet's La. N-on-T 125 D2
Hatfield Ave. Mar War 74 C4
Hatfield Ave. Sand 182 A2
Hatfield Cl. Rain 104 A1
Hatfield Dr. W Brid 185 E2
Hatfield Rd. Nott 161 E1
Hatfield St. Ret 40 A3
Hather Cl. Gams 51 D3
Hatherleigh Cl. Carl 162 B3
Hathern Cl. Lo Ea 193 E3
Hathern Green. Nott 184 A4
Hathern Rd. Lo Wh 212 B1
Hathersage Ave. Lo Ea 193 D3
Hathersage Way. S in A 100 C2
Hathersage Wlk. Mans 103 D3
Hatley Cl. Nott 173 D1
Hatton Cl. Bes Vil 147 D1
Hatton Ct. Mans 103 D3
Hatton Gdns. N-on-T 140 A4
Hatton Gdns. Nuth 159 F2
Haughgate Hill. N Whea 22 A1
Haven Cl. N Clip 89 F2
Haven Cl. S in A 100 B2
Haven Cl. W Brid 185 E3
Haven Hill. Fir 16 B3
Haven Hill. Malt 16 B3
Havenden Gdns. Nott 172 C4
Havenwood Rise. Nott 195 E4
Haverhill Cres. Nott 146 B1
Haversham Cl. Nott 160 B1
Hawarden Terr. Nott 172 C4
Hawbush Rd. West 81 D3
Hawkesworth Ave. Mans 89 D1
Hawkhill Cl. Oll 77 D2
Hawkhurst Dr. Nott 171 E1
Hawking La. Al Hu 85 D4
Hawkins Ct. Ilk 157 F2
Hawkridge St. Nott 173 E3
Hawksley Gdns. Nott 184 B1
Hawksley Rd. Nott 172 C4
Hawkswood Cl. Bees 183 D2
Hawksworth Ave. Nott 161 E2
Hawksworth Rd. Scarr 178 C4
Hawksworth Rd. Screv 167 D2
Hawksworth Rd. Syer 153 D2
Hawksworth Rd. W Brid 173 F1
Hawksworth St. Gain 24 B4
Hawksworth St. Nott 173 F3
Hawley Cl. E Lea 205 F1
Hawson Way. Work 35 E4
Hawthorn Ave. Gain 15 E1
Hawthorn Ave. Glap 86 A4
Hawthorn Ave. Huck 145 F4
Hawthorn Ave. Staple 182 B3
Hawthorn Cl. Beck 23 D4
Hawthorn Cl. Boug 77 E3
Hawthorn Cl. Keyw 197 F1
Hawthorn Cl. Nott 173 D1
Hawthorn Cl. Ol Da 218 C2
Hawthorn Cl. W Brid 186 A2
Hawthorn Cres. Arn 148 A1
Hawthorn Cres. K-in-A 115 D3
Hawthorn Ct. Nott 173 D1
Hawthorn Dr. Boug 77 E3
Hawthorn Gr. Gain 15 E1
Hawthorn Way. C in L 25 F4
Hawthorne Ave. Hath 213 D1
Hawthorne Ave. Lo Ea 193 E3
Hawthorne Ave. Shireb 72 B2
Hawthorne Ave. Tibs 99 D4
Hawthorne Cl. S in A 100 A3
Hawthorne Cl. Woodb 149 E2
Hawthorne Cres. Farn 139 D2
Hawthorne Gr. Bees 184 A3
Hawthorne Rd. Pinx 113 E2
Hawthorne Rise. Awsw 158 A2
Hawthorne Way. Edwin 91 E4
Hawthorns The. Mar War 74 A2
Hawthorns The. Wale 64 A1
Hawton Cl. Gain 15 F1
Hawton Cl. Mans 87 F1
Hawton Cres. Nott 172 B2
Hawton La. Bald 140 A2
Hawton Rd. N-on-T 139 F3
Hawton Spinney. Nott 172 B2
Haxey Gate Rd. Haxey 6 C3
Haxey Gate Rd. Mist 6 C3
Haxey Rd. Mist 6 C2
Haycroft Cl. Mans 88 C3
Haycroft Way. E Brid 165 E1
Hayden La. Huck 131 D1
Hayden La. Linby 131 D1
Haydn Ave. Nott 161 D1
Haydn Rd. Nott 161 D1
Haydock Cl. Kim 158 C4
Hayes Cl. Pinx 113 E2
Hayes Rd. Keyw 197 F2
Hayland Dr. Nott 160 B1
Hayles Cl. Nott 161 D3
Hayling Cl. Ship 157 E2
Haynes Ave. Trow 170 B3
Haynes Cl. Nott 184 C2
Haynes Cl. Tux 66 A2
Hayward Ave. Lough 220 B1
Haywood Ave. Blid 118 A3
Haywood Ct. Nott 173 F2
Haywood Oaks La. Blid 118 B2
Haywood Rd. Carl 162 A2
Haywood St. Nott 173 F2
Hayworth Rd. Sand 182 A3
Hazel Bank. Mans 102 C4
Hazel Cl. Bing 178 A2
Hazel Cres. Shireb 72 B2
Hazel Dr. Nuth 159 D3
Hazel Gr. Arn 162 A2
Hazel Gr. Bald 140 B3
Hazel Gr. Huck 146 A3
Hazel Gr. K-in-A 115 E3
Hazel Gr. Mans 88 A3
Hazel Gr. S Norm 113 D3
Hazel Hill Cres. Nott 161 D4
Hazel Meadows. Huck 146 A3
Hazel St. Nott 160 A4
Hazel St. S in A 100 B4
Hazelbank Ave. Nott 161 F1
Hazelby Rd. Elmt 58 C4
Hazelhurst Gdns. Nott 160 A4
Hazelwood Cl. East 144 A1
Hazelwood Cl. Mans 89 D1
Hazelwood Dr. Huck 145 E3
Hazelwood La. Head 41 F1
Hazelwood Rd. Nott 172 C4
Hazelwood. Cotg 188 A2
Headingley Gdns. Nott 172 B4
Headland Ave. Elk 50 A2
Headstead Bank. Cott 43 E3
Heafield Dr. Kegw 203 E1
Healdswood St. S in A 100 B4
Healey Cl. Coll 112 A4
Healey Cl. Nott 173 E1
Heanor Rd. Ilk 157 E2
Heanor Wlk. Mans 103 D3
Heapham Cres. Gain 24 C4
Heapham Rd. Gain 24 C4
Heard Cres. Bees 183 F4
Heath Ave. Mans 103 D4
Heath Gdns. Lo Ea 193 D4
Heath The. Gain 158 A4
Heathcoat St. Lough 220 A2
Heathcoat St. Nott 173 E3
Heathcote Pl. S in A 101 D1
Heather Cl. Greas 144 B1
Heather Cl. K-in-A 114 C4
Heather Cl. Nott 173 E4
Heather Cl. S Norm 113 D2
Heather Cl. Tick 8 A4
Heather Croft. W Brid 185 E2
Heather Rd. Carl 162 B1
Heather Rise. Bees 171 F1
Heather Way. Mans 103 D3
Heatherley Dr. Mans 88 C1
Heatherley Dr. Nott 160 C2
Heathers The. Boug 77 F3
Heathervale. W Brid 185 D3
Heathfield Ave. Ilk 170 A4
Heathfield Ct. K-in-A 114 C4
Heathfield Gdns. Ret 39 F4
Heathfield Gdns. Tibs 99 D4
Heathfield Gr. Bees 183 E2
Heathfield Rd. Nott 160 C2
Heathing Gdns. Nott 147 D1
Heathland Cl. Mans 103 D3
Heaton Cl. N-on-T 140 B4
Heaton Cl. Nott 161 F1
Heaton St. Gain 24 B4
Heavytrees Ave. Raven 117 D1
Hecadeck La. Ne Br 219 E4
Heckdyke La. Haxey 7 F3
Heckington Dr. Nott 172 A3
Heddington Gdns. Arn 161 E4
Heddon Bar. Mans 88 C2
Hedley St. Nott 173 D4
Hedley Villas. Nott 161 D1
Helen Cl. Bees 183 E3
Helenship La. Lane 54 A4
Hellebore Cl. Nott 160 C4
Helm Cl. Nott 159 F4
Helmsdale Cl. Arn 148 A1
Helmsdale Cl. Mans 101 F3
Helmsdale Gdns. Nott 146 C1
Helmsley Rd. Mans 103 F2
Helston Dr. Nott 159 F1
Helvellyn Cl. Nott 173 E1
Hemingway Cl. Carl 174 B4
Hemingway Cl. Greas 144 B1
Hemlock Ave. Lo Ea 182 B1
Hemlock Ave. Staple 182 C4
Hemlock Gdns. Nott 159 F3
Hemmingfield Cl. Work 35 F4
Hemmingfield Cres. Work 35 F4
Hemmingfield Rd. Work 36 A4
Hemmingfield Way. Work 36 A4
Hemplands La. S on T 96 C4
Hemplands The. Coll 98 A1
Hempshill La. Nott 160 A3
Hemsby Gdns. Nott 160 A4
Hemscott Cl. Nott 159 F4
Hemsley Dr. East 143 E2
Hemswell Cl. Nott 174 A3
Hendon Rise. Nott 173 F4
Hendre Gdns. Nott 161 D4
Henley Cl. Carl 175 D4
Henley Ct. Gain 15 E1
Henley Gdns. Staple 170 C1
Henley Rise. Nott 161 D2
Henning Gdns. Nott 161 D4
Henning La. S in A 100 A1
Hennymoor Cl. Whit 45 D3
Hennymoor La. Whit 45 E1
Henrietta St. Nott 160 B3
Henry Ave. Mans 88 A3
Henry Ct. Nott 173 E1
Henry Rd. Bees 184 A3
Henry Rd. Nott 172 C2
Henry Rd. W Brid 185 F4
Henry St. Huck 146 A3
Henry St. Nott 147 F1
Henry St. Nott 173 F2
Henry St. S in A 100 C1
Henshaw Pl. Ilk 157 F2
Henson Cl. Cr Bu 176 C2
Henson La. Cr Bu 176 C1
Henson's Sq. Bees 183 D4
Henton Rd. Edwin 76 B1
Hepple Dr. Nott 159 F4
Herald Cl. Bees 184 A4
Herbert Rd. Ann Wo 115 D1
Herbert Rd. Nott 161 D1
Herbert St. Lough 220 A3
Herbert St. Mans 102 A3
Hereford Ave. Mans 88 B3
Hereford Ave. Oll 77 D2
Hereford Cl. Work 36 A3
Hereford Rd. Arn 161 F3
Hereford Rd. Carl 162 C1
Hereford Rd. Nott 174 A3
Hereford Rd. Raven 117 D2
Herewood Cl. Shireb 72 C2
Hermes Cl. Baw 9 F4
Hermitage Ave. Mans 101 F3
Hermitage La. Mans 101 F2
Hermitage Sq. Nott 173 F2
Hermitage Way. Mans 101 F2
Hermitage Wlk. Nott 173 D2
Hermon St. Nott 173 D3
Herne St. S in A 101 D2
Heron Dr. Nott 172 C2
Heron Way. Bald 140 B3
Heron Wharf. Nott 172 C1
Herons Ct. W Brid 186 B2
Herrick Rd. Lough 220 A1
Herril Ings. Tick 8 A4
Hervey Green. Nott 184 C1
Heskey Cl. Nott 173 E3
Heskey Wlk. Nott 173 E3
Heslington Ave. Nott 172 C4
Hethbeth Ct. Nott 173 E1
Hethersett Gdns. Nott 160 A4
Hetley Rd. Bees 183 F4
Hett's La. Mar War 74 A3
Hewett St. Mar War 73 E3
Hewson's La. Coll 112 A3
Hexham Ave. Ilk 170 A2
Hexham Cl. W Brid 186 A3
Hexham Gdns. Bes Vil 147 D1
Hey St. Lo Ea 193 E2
Heyward St. Mans 102 B4

Heywood Cl. South 121 F1
Heywood St. Mans 102 B4
Hibbert Cres. S in A 101 D2
Hibbert Rd. Mans 102 B4
Hickings La. Staple 182 C4
Hickling Ct. Mans 102 B4
Hickling La. Lo Cl 211 D2
Hickling Rd. Carl 162 A1
Hickling Rd. Kinou 200 A1
Hickling Way. Cotg 188 A1
Hickman Cres. Mort 15 E2
Hickman Ct. Gain 24 C4
Hickman St. Gain 24 B4
Hickory Cl. K-in-A 114 C4
Hide Hill View. Toll 186 B1
High Church St. Nott 161 D1
High Cl. Ann Wo 115 D1
High Common La. Aust 3 D3
High Common La. Tick 9 D4
High Cres. Ann Wo 115 D1
High Cross St. Nott 173 E3
High Cross. Bleas 136 C1
High Field La. Aust 3 D2
High Hoe Ct. Work 36 A2
High Hoe Dr. Work 36 A2
High Hoe Rd. Work 36 A2
High Holborn. Ilk 157 F2
High Hurst. Calv 148 C4
High La Central. WeHa 157 D1
High La E. WeHa 157 D1
High Leys Rd. Huck 145 F3
High Meadow. Baw 9 F4
High Meadow. Hath 213 D1
High Meadow. Toll 186 B1
High Oakham Dr. Mans 102 A2
High Oakham Hill. Mans 102 A2
High Oakham Rd. Mans 102 A2
High Park Cotts. Greas 144 B3
High Pavement. Nott 173 E2
High Pavement. S in A 100 C1
High Rd. Bees 183 D1
High Rd. Bees 183 E2
High Rd. Bees 184 A4
High Rd. C in L 26 A3
High Ridge. Mans 88 C1
High Spania. Kim 158 C4
High St. Arn 161 F4
High St. Baw 10 A4
High St. Beck 23 D4
High St. Blyth 18 A1
High St. Bott 181 D1
High St. Brin 128 B1
High St. Coll 98 A1
High St. Coll 112 A4
High St. E Mark 65 F4
High St. Eagle 84 B2
High St. Edwin 76 A1
High St. Elk 50 A2
High St. Ever 11 E2
High St. G on H 12 C1
High St. Gain 24 B4
High St. Girt 82 C1
High St. Harby 70 C1
High St. Huck 146 A4
High St. Kegw 203 E1
High St. Kim 158 C3
High St. Lo Ea 193 F4
High St. Lough 220 A2
High St. Mans 87 D3
High St. Mans 88 B2
High St. Mans 102 A3
High St. Mar War 74 A2
High St. Mart 44 B4
High St. Miss 4 B1
High St. Mist 6 C1
High St. N Sca 83 E1
High St. Ne on T 55 D1
High St. Nott 173 E2
High St. Orst 179 F4
High St. Ret 39 F2
High St. Rudd 196 B4
High St. S in A 100 A2
High St. S in A 100 B1
High St. S in A 100 B3
High St. S in V 169 D2
High St. S Lev 42 B3
High St. S Norm 113 D3
High St. S on T 96 C4
High St. Sax 57 D2
High St. Staple 182 C4
High St. Tibs 99 D4
High St. Walker 13 F3
High Street Ave. Arn 161 F4
High Street Pl. Nott 173 E2
High Tor. S in A 100 C4
High View Ave. Keyw 198 A2
High View Rd. S Norm 113 E4
Highbank Dr. Nott 195 F4
Highbury Ave. Nott 160 B3
Highbury Cl. Nuth 159 F2
Highbury Rd. Keyw 197 F2
Highbury Rd. Nott 160 B3
Highbury Wlk. Nott 160 B3
Highclere Dr. Carl 174 C4
Highcliffe Ave. Shireb 72 B2
Highcliffe Rd. Nott 174 A2
Highcroft Cl. Lo Ea 193 F3
Highcroft Dr. Nott 171 D3
Highcroft. Arn 161 F2
Highcross Ct. Nott 172 C3
Highcross Hill. South 136 B2
Highfield Ave. K-in-A 114 C3
Highfield Ave. Mans 88 A1
Highfield Ave. Shireb 72 B3
Highfield Cl. Gain 15 F1
Highfield Cl. Mans 88 A1
Highfield Cl. Raven 117 D1
Highfield Ct. Bees 183 F3
Highfield Dr. Bils 105 F2
Highfield Dr. Carl 174 A4
Highfield Dr. Nuth 159 F2
Highfield Dr. S Norm 113 D3
Highfield Dr. Stap 127 D2
Highfield Gr. W Brid 185 F4
Highfield Grove. C in L 26 A3
Highfield La. Work 36 B1
Highfield Rd. Baw 10 A4
Highfield Rd. Bees 183 D2
Highfield Rd. Keyw 197 F2
Highfield Rd. N Clip 90 A2
Highfield Rd. Nott 172 B1
Highfield Rd. Nuth 159 F2
Highfield Rd. S in A 100 B2
Highfield Rd. Sax 57 D2
Highfield Rd. W Brid 185 F4
Highfield St. Lo Ea 182 B1
Highfield Terr. Mans 102 A3
Highfield Villas. C in L 25 F4
Highfield Way. Mans 102 A3
Highfield. Ret 29 E1
Highfields Science Pk. Nott 172 B1
Highgate Cl. Carl 162 B1
Highgate Dr. Ship 157 E2
Highgate La. Plun 202 C4
Highgrove Ave. Bees 183 E3
Highgrove Gdns. W Brid 186 A2
Highland Cl. Mans 88 B2
Highland Gr. Work 36 A3
Highland Rd. Mans 102 C1
Highurst St. Nott 173 D3
Highwood Ave. Nott 171 F4
Highwray Gr. Nott 184 B1
Hilary Cl. Nott 171 E2
Hilcot Dr. Nott 160 B1
Hilcote La. Newt 99 D1
Hilcote St. S Norm 113 D3
Hill Cl. East 144 B1
Hill Cl. W Brid 186 A3
Hill Cres. Gain 15 F1
Hill Cres. S in A 101 D2
Hill Crest Gr. Nott 161 D2
Hill Crest. Shireb 72 B2
Hill Dr. Bing 177 E3
Hill Farm Cl. Toll 186 B1
Hill Farm Ct. W Brid 186 A1
Hill Fields. S Norm 113 D2
Hill Rd. Bes Vil 146 C2
Hill Rd. Goth 205 D4
Hill Rd. Har 8 C2
Hill Rd. Orst 180 A3
Hill Rise. Trow 170 B2
Hill Side. Nott 172 B2
Hill St. Mans 87 D3
Hill St. Ret 39 F2
Hill St. Work 35 F1
Hill Syke. Lowd 150 A1
Hill The. K-in-A 114 C3
Hill Top Ave. Shireb 72 C2
Hill Top Ct. Har 9 D2
Hill Top. Orst 180 A3
Hill View Rd. Bees 183 D1
Hill View Rd. K-in-A 115 E3
Hill Vue Ave. N-on-T 140 A4
Hill Vue Gdns. N-on-T 140 A4
Hillary Way. Bald 140 C2
Hillbeck Cres. Nott 171 E2
Hillcrest Ave. S Norm 113 D2
Hillcrest Cl. Kim 159 D4
Hillcrest Dr. Huck 145 E3
Hillcrest Gdns. Bu Jo 163 F3
Hillcrest Mews. Ret 40 A4
Hillcrest Rd. Keyw 197 F2
Hillcrest View. Carl 162 A1
Hillcrest. South 136 B4
Hillfield Gdns. Nott 146 C1
Hillfield Rd. Staple 170 C1
Hillgrove Gdns. Nott 161 D4
Hilliers Ct. Nott 160 C4
Hillington Rise. Nott 161 E4
Hillmoor St. Mans 87 E2
Hills Rd. Arn 161 F2
Hillsborough Ave. S in A 114 B4
Hillsborough Way. S in A 114 B4
Hillsford Cl. Nott 172 A3
Hillside Ave. Arn 162 A2
Hillside Ave. Mist 7 D1
Hillside Cres. Bees 183 F4
Hillside Cres. Work 35 F3
Hillside Dr. Bu Jo 163 F3
Hillside Dr. Lo Ea 193 D4
Hillside Dr. South 136 B4
Hillside Gr. Sand 182 A3
Hillside Rd. Bees 183 D2
Hillside Rd. Bees 183 E4
Hillside Rd. Blid 118 A2
Hillside Rd. R on T 176 A2
Hillside Wlk. Blid 118 A2
Hillside. Beckin 142 B4
Hillside. Kegw 203 E1
Hillside. La Mi 143 D2
Hillside. Tux 66 A2
Hillsway Cres. Mans 102 A2
Hillsway. Shireb 72 B2
Hilltop Cl. Eagle 84 B2
Hilltop Rd. Pinx 113 E2
Hillview Ave. Nott 161 E1
Hillview Cres. Clar 30 C2
Hillview Ct. Mans 88 B2
Hillview Rd. Carl 162 A1
Hillview Rd. Ret 39 F2
Hilton Cres. W Brid 186 A3
Hilton Ct. W Brid 186 A3
Hilton Rd. Carl 162 A2
Hind St. Ret 40 A3
Hindlow Ct. Mans 103 D3
Hine Ave. N-on-T 140 C4
Hinsley Cl. Arn 162 A4
Hirst Cres. Nott 171 F2
Hirst Rd. Ret 40 A4
Hives La. N Sca 83 E2
Hobart Cl. Nott 173 E1
Hobart Dr. Staple 170 C1
Hobhouse Rd. Mans 87 E1
Hobsic Cl. Brin 143 E4
Hobsic La. Sels 128 C4
Hobson's Acre. Gunt 165 D3
Hockerton Hts. Hock 122 A3
Hockerton Rd. South 122 A2
Hockerton Rd. Upton 122 C1
Hockerwood La. Upton 122 B1
Hockerwood. Nott 184 C2
Hockley Pl. K-in-A 114 C2
Hockley. Nott 173 E2
Hodgkin Cl. Nott 184 B1
Hodgkinson Rd. K-in-A 115 D2
Hodgkinson St. Carl 175 D3
Hodmire La. Al Hu 85 F4
Hodsock La. C in L 26 A3
Hoe La. Cr Bu 189 D3
Hoe Nook. Cr Bi 189 D2
Hoe View Rd. Cr Bi 189 D2
Hoefield Cres. Nott 160 A3
Hoewood Rd. Nott 160 A4
Hogan Gdns. Nott 147 D1
Hogarth Cl. Staple 182 C3
Hogarth St. Nott 173 F3
Hogg La. R on T 175 F2
Hoggetts Cl. Bees 183 D3
Hoggs Field. East 143 F1
Holbeck La. Holb 59 E4
Holbeck Rd. Huck 131 D1
Holbeck Rd. Nott 172 B3
Holbeck Way. Rain 104 A1
Holbein Cl. Lough 220 B2
Holborn Ave. Nott 173 F2
Holborn Cl. Nuth 159 E2
Holborn Pl. Nott 160 B4
Holbrook Cl. Plea 87 D3
Holbrook Ct. Mans 103 D3
Holbrook Ct. Nott 195 F4
Holbrook St. Hean 143 D1
Holby Cl. Nott 160 C4
Holcombe Cl. Nott 160 A1
Holdale Rd. Nott 174 A3
Holden Cres. N-on-T 139 F3
Holden Cres. Nuth 159 E3
Holden Rd. Bees 183 F4
Holden St. Mans 102 A3
Holden St. Nott 173 D3
Holdenby Cl. Ret 40 A4
Holderness Cl. Har 9 D2
Holding. Work 36 A3
Holds La. Torw 19 D1
Holgate Rd. Nott 173 E1
Holgate Wlk. Huck 145 F3
Holgate. Nott 184 B1
Holkham Ave. Bees 183 E3
Holkham Cl. Arn 162 A3
Holkham Cl. Ship 157 E2
Holland Cl. Goth 195 D1
Holland Cres. Sels 129 D4
Holland Meadow. Lo Ea 193 E3
Holland St. Nott 172 C4
Holles St. Work 35 F1
Hollies Ave. Codd 125 D2
Hollies Cres. Nott 173 D2
Hollies Dr. W Brid 186 A2
Hollies The. Boug 77 F3
Hollies The. East 143 F1
Hollies The. Rain 104 A1
Hollies The. Sand 182 A3
Hollington Rd. Nott 172 A3
Hollington Way. Mans 103 D4
Hollingwood La. Calv 133 E1
Hollingworth Ave. Sand 182 A2
Hollins The. Calv 149 D4
Hollinwell Ave. Nott 172 B3
Hollinwell Cl. K-in-A 114 C4
Hollinwell Ct. W Brid 186 A2
Hollis St. Nott 161 D1
Hollow Stone. Nott 173 E2
Holloway Cl. E Brid 165 E2
Hollowdyke La. Bald 140 C1
Hollowdyke La. Bald 140 C2
Hollowgate La. H Marn 68 A1
Hollows The. Lo Ea 194 A4
Hollows The. Mapl 108 A4
Hollows The. Nott 185 D2
Hollows The. Thur 151 E4
Holly Ave. Carl 174 B4
Holly Ave. Nott 174 A4
Holly Ave. Nott 185 D4
Holly Bush Cl. Elk 50 A2
Holly Cl. Bing 178 A2
Holly Cl. Huck 146 A3
Holly Ct. Bees 183 E4
Holly Ct. Har 8 C2
Holly Ct. Mans 88 C1
Holly Ct. Ret 39 F3
Holly Dr. Mans 89 D1
Holly Farm Ct. Greas 144 B1
Holly Gdns. Nott 173 F4
Holly Gr. K-in-A 114 C3
Holly Hill Rd. Sels 128 C3
Holly Hill Rd. Sels 129 D3
Holly La. Bees 183 F3
Holly Rd. Kim 159 D4
Holly Rd. Mans 89 D1
Holly Rd. Ret 40 A3
Holly Rise. Oll 77 E3
Hollycroft. W Brid 186 A2
Hollydale Rd. Nott 174 A3
Hollydene Cl. Huck 145 E3
Hollydene Cres. Nott 160 A2
Hollygate La. Cotg 188 A3
Hollyhouse Dr. S Norm 113 D3
Hollythorpe Pl. Huck 145 E3
Hollytree Cl. Hoton 215 E1
Holme Ave. E Lea 205 F2
Holme Cl. Woodb 149 E2
Holme Gr. W Brid 174 A1
Holme La. E Mark 51 E1
Holme La. Edin 120 C2
Holme La. Egma 79 F3
Holme La. Halam 120 C2
Holme La. Ho Pi 175 E2
Holme La. Holm 125 E4
Holme La. L Marn 82 A4
Holme La. Langf 111 F2
Holme La. Nor on T 82 A3
Holme La. R on T 175 E2
Holme La. W Dray 51 E1
Holme La. Wint 125 E4
Holme Rd. Bing 178 A2
Holme Rd. W Brid 174 A1
Holme St. Nott 173 F1
Holme The. South 136 A4
Holmecroft Ave. S in A 100 C3
Holmefield Cres. Ilk 170 A4
Holmefield Rd. Whit 45 D3
Holmefield Wlk. Mans 103 D3
Holmes Cl. La Mi 143 D2
Holmes Rd. Ret 39 F4
Holmesfield Dr. Ship 157 D4
Holmewood Cres. Nott 161 D3
Holmewood Dr. Greas 158 A4
Holmfield Cl. Work 36 A3
Holmfield Rd. Bees 183 E2
Holmhurst Cl. Work 35 F3
Holmsfield. Keyw 197 F1
Holmwood Rd. Rain 104 B1
Holroyd Ave. Nott 173 F2
Holt Dr. Lough 220 A1
Holt Gr. Calv 148 C4
Holt The. N-on-T 139 E3
Holwood Ct. Nott 160 A3
Holyoake Rd. Carl 162 B2
Holyrood Ct. Bees 171 E1
Holywell Rd. Ship 157 E2
Home Cl. Arn 161 E4
Home Croft The. Bees 183 D4
Home Farm Cl. Goth 195 D1
Home Fm Ct. Sels 128 B3
Home Meadows. Tick 8 A3
Home Pastures. Hose 211 F4
Homecroft Dr. Sels 128 C4
Homefarm La. Thor 70 A3
Homefield Ave. Arn 148 A1
Homefield Rd. Nott 172 B4
Homelands The. S in A 100 C1
Homestead. Ald 143 D2
Homesteads The. Mar War 74 A2
Homewood Dr. K-in-A 114 C4
Honeyknab La. Oxt 134 B3
Honeys La. Farn 139 D1
Honeysuckle Cl. Bald 140 B2
Honeysuckle Cl. Nott 159 F1
Honeywood Dr. Carl 174 A4
Honeywood Wlk. Carl 174 A4
Honing Dr. South 136 B4
Honingham Cl. Arn 162 A3
Honister Cl. Gam 186 B4
Honister Cl. Mans 102 B2
Honister Cl. Nott 195 E4
Honister Ct. Mans 102 B2
Honiton Cl. Bees 183 D1
Honiton Rd. Nott 159 F1
Hood St. Nott 161 E1
Hooley Cl. Lo Ea 193 D3
Hooley Pl. Nott 161 E2
Hooley St. Sels 128 C3
Hoopers Wlk. Nott 173 E1
Hooton Rd. Carl 174 B4
Hooton St. Nott 173 F3
Hope Cl. Nott 173 D1
Hope Dr. Nott 173 D2
Hope St. Bees 183 F4
Hope St. Mans 102 B3
Hopedale Cl. Nott 172 C3
Hopewell Cl. R on T 176 A2
Hopewell Wlk. Ilk 157 F3
Hopkiln La. South 121 E1
Hopkins Ct. East 143 F2
Hopyard La. Egma 79 F4
Hopyard La. Nor on T 82 A3
Horace Ave. Staple 182 B3
Hornbeam Cl. Ilk 170 A4
Hornbeam Gdns. Nott 159 F4
Hornbuckle Ct. Nott 172 C3
Hornchurch Rd. Nott 171 E4
Hornsby Wlk. Nott 160 C4
Horridge St. Ilk 157 F2
Horsendale Ave. Nuth 159 F2
Horsewells St. G on H 12 C1
Horsham Dr. Nott 160 C4
Horsley Cres. La Mi 143 D2
Hose La. Hose 201 D2
Hose La. Hose 202 A1
Hose La. Hose 211 F3
Hose La. Lo Cl 211 F3
Hoselett Field Rd. Lo Ea 193 F3
Hosiery St. K-in-A 115 D3
Hospital Dr. R on T 176 B2
Hospital Rd. Ret 39 F4
Hoten Rd. Nott 173 F2
Hoton Rd. Wyme 216 A2
Hotspur Cl. Nott 160 C3
Hotspur Rd. Gain 15 E1
Houfton Rd. Mans 102 C4
Hougham Rd. Dry Do 156 C1
Houghton Cl. Nuth 159 F2
Houldsworth Rise. Nott 147 F1
Hound Rd. W Brid 185 F4
Hounds Gate. Nott 173 D2
Hounsfield Cl. N-on-T 140 C4
Hounsfield Way. S on T 96 C4
Houseman Gdns. Nott 173 E1
Houston Cl. Nott 146 C1
Hove Rd. Nott 160 C3
Hoveringham Rd. Cayt 165 E4
Hoveringham Rd. Hover 165 E4
Howard Cl. Lo Ea 182 C1
Howard Rd. Bir 9 E2
Howard Rd. Mans 101 F4
Howard St. Lough 220 A3
Howard St. Nott 173 E3
Howard St. S in A 100 C2
Howard St. Work 36 A1
Howbeck La. Clar 30 C2
Howbeck Rd. Arn 162 A4
Howden Rd. Nott 146 B1
Howe Rd. Lough 220 A1
Howells Cl. Nott 161 E4
Howes Ct. N-on-T 140 A4
Howick Dr. Nott 159 F4
Howitt St. Hean 143 D1
Howitt St. Lo Ea 193 F4
Hoylake Cres. Nott 171 E4
Hoyland Ave. Nott 172 C1
Hubert St. Nott 172 C3
Hucklow Ct. Mans 103 D3
Hucknall Cres. Carl 162 C1
Hucknall La. Nott 146 B1
Hucknall Rd. Ann Wo 130 B3
Hucknall Rd. News 130 B3
Hucknall Rd. Nott 160 C3
Huddlestones Whrf. N-on-T 139 F4
Hudson St. Lough 220 B2
Hudson St. Nott 173 F3
Hufton's Ct. Ship 157 D4
Hufton's Dr. Ship 157 D4
Hugessen Ave. Huck 146 B4
Hugget Gdns. Nott 161 D4
Humber Cl. Nott 173 E1
Humber La. E Sto 153 D4
Humber Rd S. Bees 184 A3
Humber Rd. Bees 184 A4
Humber Rd. Lo Ea 182 B1
Humber St. Ret 40 A3
Humber St. Work 35 F2
Humberston Rd. Nott 171 E2
Hume St. Lough 220 B2
Hundred Acre La. C in L 26 B2
Hundred Acres La. Bald 140 B1
Hundreds La. G on H 5 D2
Hungary La. Su Bo 213 E4
Hungerhill Rd. Nott 173 E4
Hungerton St. Nott 172 C2
Hunston Cl. Nott 172 A4
Hunt's Hill. Greas 144 A4
Hunter Rd. Arn 162 B3
Hunter's Dr. G on H 12 C1
Hunters Cl. Nott 185 D3
Hunters Ct. K-in-A 114 C3
Huntingdon Dr. Nott 173 D2
Huntingdon St. Nott 173 E3
Huntingdon Way. Bees 182 C1
Huntingdon Wlk. Sand 182 A3
Huntly Cl. Mans 101 E3
Huntly Cl. Nott 184 C1

Huntsman Pl. Torw 19 D1
Hurcomb St. Nott 173 F4
Hurst Cl. Mans 103 F1
Hurt's Yd. Nott 173 E2
Hurts Croft. Bees 183 E2
Huss's La. Lo Ea 193 F4
Hutchinson Green. Nott 173 E3
Huthwaite La. Newt 99 E1
Huthwaite Rd. S in A 100 B1
Hutton Cl. Bees 171 E1
Hutton St. Nott 173 F2
Huxley Cl. Nott 171 E4
Hyde Cl. Nott 184 C2
Hyson Cl. Nott 172 C4
Hyson St. Nott 172 C4

Ian Gr. Carl 174 C4
Icle View. Ret 29 F1
Idle Bank. Haxey 2 B2
Idle Bank. Miss 5 E4
Idle Bank. Wroot 2 B2
Idlewells Shpg Cntr. S in A 100 C1
Ilam Sq. Ilk 157 F3
Ilford Cl. Ship 157 E2
Ilion St. Mans 87 F1
Ilkeston Rd. Bees 171 D1
Ilkeston Rd. Hean 157 D4
Ilkeston Rd. S-by-D 182 B4
Ilkeston Rd. Sand 182 B4
Ilkeston Rd. Staple 170 C1
Ilkeston Rd. Trow 170 B3
Imperial Ave. Bees 183 F3
Imperial Ave. Carl 162 C1
Imperial Rd. Bees 183 F3
Imperial Rd. Nott 160 B3
Inchwood Cl. Bees 182 C1
Incinerator Rd. Nott 173 F1
Independent St. Nott 172 C3
Infield La. N Le Ha 32 C1
Infield La. Nort 60 A3
Infield La. West 81 D2
Ingham Gr. Nott 172 C2
Ingham Rd. Baw 9 F4
Ingham Rd. Lo Ea 182 B1
Ingleborough Gdns. Lo Ea 193 D4
Ingleby Cl. Cotg 187 F1
Ingleby Cl. Nott 171 D2
Inglefield Rd. Ilk 170 A3
Inglemere Cl. Work 36 A3
Inglewood Rd. Nott 184 C1
Ingram La. Grass 82 A2
Ingram La. S on T 82 A2
Ingram Rd. Nott 160 B3
Ingram Terr. Nott 160 B3
Ings Rd. G on H 12 C3
Inham Circus. Bees 183 E3
Inham Cl. Bees 183 D3
Inham Fields Cl. Gunt 165 D3
Inham Rd. Bees 183 D3
Inholms Gdns. Flint 152 C1
Inholms Rd. Flint 152 C1
Inkerman Rd. Sels 128 C3
Inkerman St. Sels 128 C3
Innes Rd. Carl 174 B4
Institute St. S in A 100 B3
Instow Rise. Nott 173 E3
Intake Ave. Mans 101 F3
Intake Rd. Keyw 197 E2
Intake Rd. N Clip 90 A2
Iona Cl. Gain 15 F1
Iona Dr. Staple 170 B1
Iona Gdns. Bes Vil 147 D1
Ipswich Circus. Nott 174 A3
Ireland Ave. Bees 184 A3
Ireland Cl. Bees 184 A3
Iremonger Rd. Nott 173 E1
Irene Terr. Nott 160 C1
Ireton Gr. Bees 183 E1
Ireton St. Bees 183 F3
Ireton St. Nott 173 D3
Irwin Dr. Nott 160 A3
Isaac's La. Staple 182 B4
Isabella St. Nott 173 E2
Island St. Nott 173 E2
Islay Cl. Nott 147 F1
Islay Cl. Staple 170 B2
Ivatt Cl. Baw 10 A4
Iveagh Cl. Mar War 74 B3
Ives Cl. W Brid 185 E2
Ivy Cl. Greas 144 C1
Ivy Gr. Carl 174 B4
Ivy Gr. K-in-A 114 C3
Ivy Gr. Nott 173 D4
Ivy La. East 143 F1
Ivy Lodge La. Let 16 A2
Ivy Row. What 179 D2

Jacklin Gdns. Nott 147 D1
Jackson Ave. Ilk 157 F1
Jackson Ave. Sand 182 A3
Jackson Terr. Mar War 74 C4
James St. Ann Wo 115 D1
James St. Arn 161 F4
James St. Kim 158 C3
James St. Work 35 F3
James William Turner Ave. S in A 100 C1
James' Yd. Mans 102 B4
Japan Rd. Gain 15 D1
Jardine. Work 36 A3
Jardines The. Bees 171 E1
Jarrow Gdns. Nott 146 C1
Jarvis Ave. Nott 174 A3
Jasmin Cl. Shireb 72 B3
Jasmine Cl. Bees 171 E1
Jasmine Cl. Nott 159 F1
Jasmine Cl. Nott 184 B1
Jasmine Rd. Nott 160 C2
Jasper Cl. R on T 175 F1
Jayne Cl. Carl 163 D1
Jayne Cl. Nott 171 F3
Jedburgh Cl. Nott 173 E3
Jedburgh Wlk. Nott 173 E3
Jeffares Cl. Kegw 203 E2
Jellicoe St. Scarc 59 D1
Jenford St. Mans 101 F3
Jenkins Ave. Mans 101 E4
Jenned Rd. Arn 148 A1
Jenner St. Nott 161 D1
Jenness Ave. Nott 146 C1
Jennison St. Mans 88 A1
Jenny Beckett's La. Mans 102 C2
Jephson Rd. S in A 114 C4
Jericho La. B-le-V 192 A2
Jermyn Dr. Bes Vil 147 D1
Jersey Gdns. Nott 173 F3
Jersey St. N-on-T 139 F3
Jerusalem Rd. Skel 71 F2
Jerusalem. Skel 71 F1
Jervis Ct. Ilk 157 F2
Jesmond Rd. Nott 160 B3
Jessop Cl. N-on-T 125 E1
Jessop Way. N-on-T 125 E1
Jessop's La. Carl 162 C1
Job La. Matt 20 A4
Job's La. Eagle 84 C1
Jockey La. Elk 50 A3
John Carroll Ct. Nott 173 F3
John St. Ilk 157 F1
John St. Nott 160 C1
John St. S in A 100 C2
John St. Work 35 F2
Johns Rd. R on T 176 A2
Johnson Ave. Huck 146 A3
Johnson Dr. Mans 102 B2
Joyce Ave. Bees 182 C2
Joyce Ave. Nott 161 E3
Joyce Cl. Nott 161 E2
Jubilee Cl. Miss 4 A2
Jubilee Dr. Lough 220 A3
Jubilee Rd. Arn 161 F3
Jubilee Rd. Ret 39 E3
Jubilee Rd. S in A 100 B2
Jubilee St. Kim 158 C4
Jubilee St. N-on-T 140 A4
Jubilee St. Nott 173 F2
Jubilee Way N. Mans 103 E3
Jubilee Way S. Mans 103 D2
Judges St. Lough 220 B2
Julian Cl. Ilk 170 A3
Julian La. Shel 164 B1
Julian Rd. W Brid 174 A1
Julie Ave. Hean 143 D1
Jumelles Dr. Calv 148 B4
Junction Rd. Lo Ea 194 A3
Juniper Cl. Nott 184 B1
Juniper Ct. Greas 158 B4
Juniper Gdns. Bing 178 A2

Karen Rise. Arn 148 A1
Katherine Dr. Bees 182 C2
Kaye Rd. Mans 101 E4
Kayes Wlk. Nott 173 E2
Keats Ave. S in A 100 A2
Keats Cl. Arn 161 E4
Keats Cl. Kim 159 D3
Keats Cl. Lo Ea 193 D3
Keats Cres. Work 36 A2
Keats Dr. Huck 145 E3
Keats Rd. Bald 140 B3
Kedleston Cl. Bees 183 E3
Kedleston Cl. Lo Ea 193 D3
Kedleston Dr. Ilk 157 E2
Kedleston Rd. Work 35 F3
Keel Dr. Bott 181 D1
Keeling Cl. East 144 A1
Keep The. E Lea 205 F1
Keepers Cl. Bes Vil 146 C2
Kegworth La. Lo Wh 212 B3
Kegworth Rd. Goth 204 C4
Kegworth Rd. K on S 203 F3
Kegworth Rd. R on S 203 F3
Keighton Hill. Nott 172 B1
Keilder Dr. Bing 177 E2
Kelfield Cl. Nott 160 C3
Kelham Green. Nott 173 F3
Kelham La. N-on-T 124 B2
Kelham La. S Musk 124 B3
Kelham Rd. Mans 101 F4
Kelham Rd. N-on-T 124 C1
Keller Ct. Wood 53 D4
Kelling Cl. Nott 161 D3
Kelsey Cl. Bees 183 F2
Kelso Gdns. Nott 173 D1
Kelstedge Dr. Mans 103 D3
Kelstern Cl. Mans 103 D4
Kelstern Cl. Nott 160 B2
Kelvedon Gdns. Nott 173 F3
Kelvin Cl. Staple 182 B3
Kelvin Rd. Mans 89 E2
Kelvin Rd. Nott 174 A4
Kemmel Rd. Nott 160 B3
Kempsey Cl. Nott 160 C4
Kempson St. Rudd 196 B3
Kempton Cl. Kim 158 C4
Kempton Dr. Arn 148 A1
Kempton Rd. Mans 102 C4
Kendal Cl. Ann Wo 130 A4
Kendal Cl. Huck 145 F4
Kendal Cl. Work 35 F4
Kendal Ct. W Brid 186 A4
Kendal Dr. Bees 183 E4
Kendal Rd. Cr Bi 189 D2
Kendal Rd. Lo Ea 182 A1
Kendale Ct. Nott 161 F1
Kenia Cl. Carl 174 B4
Kenilworth Ave. S in A 101 D2
Kenilworth Ct. Bees 184 A4
Kenilworth Ct. Nott 173 D2
Kenilworth Dr. C in L 25 F3
Kenilworth Rd. Bees 184 A4
Kenilworth Rd. Nott 173 D2
Kenmare Cres. Gain 24 C3
Kenmore Cl. Mans 101 F3
Kenmore Gdns. Nott 173 E3
Kennedy Ct. Wale 64 A1
Kennedy Ave. Lo Ea 193 E3
Kennedy Ave. Mans 88 B2
Kennedy Cl. Arn 161 F4
Kennedy Ct. Work 36 A2
Kennedy Dr. Staple 170 C1
Kennedy Rise. Wale 64 A1
Kennedy Wlk. Bald 140 C2
Kennel Dr. Ba Mo 28 B3
Kennel La. Ann Wo 130 A1
Kennel La. Swine 71 E1
Kennet Paddock. Mans 88 B2
Kenneth Rd. Nott 147 F1
Kennington Rd. Nott 172 B3
Kenrick Rd. Carl 162 A1
Kenrick St. Carl 175 D4
Kensington Cl. Bees 183 D1
Kensington Cl. Mans 88 C3
Kensington Cl. S in A 100 C1
Kensington Ct. Nott 161 E2
Kensington Gdns. Carl 174 C4
Kensington Gdns. Ilk 170 A4
Kensington Rd. Sand 182 A2
Kenslow Ave. Nott 172 C4
Kent Ave. Bees 183 F2
Kent Ave. Sels 128 A2
Kent Cl. Work 36 A3
Kent Rd. Carl 162 A1
Kent Rd. Greas 158 B4
Kent St. Nott 173 E3
Kentmere Cl. Gam 186 B4
Kenton Ct. Nott 173 E1
Kentwood Rd. Nott 173 F2
Kenyon Rd. Nott 172 B2
Keppel Ct. Ilk 157 F2
Kersall Ct. Nott 160 B3
Kersall Dr. Nott 160 B3
Kersall Gdns. Huck 146 A4
Kestral Rd. Mans 101 F2
Kestrel Ct. Carl 162 A1
Kestrel Mews. Work 35 E4
Kestrel Rise. Eagle 84 B1
Keswick Cl. Bees 183 E4
Keswick Ct. Lo Ea 182 A1
Keswick Ct. Nott 173 F2
Keswick Rd. Work 35 F4
Keswick St. Nott 173 F2
Ketlock Hill La. N Le Ha 32 B1
Kett St. Nott 160 A3
Kettlethorpe Rd. Kettl 55 E3
Keverne Cl. Nott 160 B1
Kevin Rd. Nott 171 E1
Kew Cl. W Brid 185 E2
Kew Cres. Hean 143 D1
Kew Gdns. Bald 140 A2
Kexby Wlk. Gain 24 C4
Key St. Nott 173 F3
Keyes Cl. Matt 19 F4
Keyes Ct. Matt 19 F4
Keyes Rise. Matt 19 F4
Keys Cl. Nott 160 A4
Keyworth Cl. Mans 101 F4
Keyworth Ct. Mans 101 F4
Keyworth Dr. Mans 89 E1
Keyworth Rd. Carl 162 B2
Keyworth Rd. Widm 208 B3
Keyworth Rd. Wys 207 E3
Kibworth Cl. Nott 160 C2
Kid La. Fir 16 A3
Kiddier Ave. Arn 162 A4
Kighill La. Raven 132 A4
Kilbourn St. Nott 173 E3
Kilbourne Rd. Arn 148 A1
Kilburn Cl. Bees 171 D1
Kilby Ave. Nott 174 A3
Kildare Rd. Nott 173 F4
Kildonan Cl. Nott 159 E1
Killerton Green. Nott 195 F4
Killerton Park Dr. W Brid 185 D2
Killisick Rd. Arn 162 A4
Kilnbrook Ave. Arn 148 A1
Kilnwood Cl. Nott 174 A4
Kilsby Rd. Nott 184 C1
Kilton Cl. Work 36 A2
Kilton Cres. Work 36 A2
Kilton Glade. Work 36 A2
Kilton Hill. Work 36 A3
Kilton Rd. Work 36 A2
Kilton Terr. Work 36 A2
Kilverton Cl. Nott 172 B2
Kilvington Rd. Arn 162 A4
Kimber Cl. Nott 171 E3
Kimberley Cl. Kim 158 C3
Kimberley Rd. Nott 174 A2
Kimberley Rd. Nuth 159 E3
Kimbolton Ave. Nott 172 C2
King Charles St. Nott 173 D2
King Edward Ave. Mans 102 A2
King Edward Rd. Lough 220 B2
King Edward St. Huck 146 A3
King Edward St. Nott 173 E3
King Edward St. Sand 182 A3
King Edward St. Shireb 72 C2
King Edward's Terr. Ret 39 F3
King George Ave. Lough 220 B1
King George Rd. Lough 220 B1
King George V Ave. Mans 102 C3
King John's Rd. N Clip 90 A2
King Rd. Mar War 74 A2
King St E. Gain 24 B4
King St. Bees 184 A3
King St. East 143 F1
King St. Gain 24 B4
King St. Ilk 157 F1
King St. K-in-A 115 D2
King St. Lo Ea 193 E4
King St. Lough 220 B2
King St. Mans 88 B1
King St. Mans 102 B4
King St. Mar War 73 E3
King St. N-on-T 139 F4
King St. Ne Br 219 E4
King St. Nott 173 E3
King St. Pinx 113 E2
King St. S in A 100 A2
King St. S in A 100 C1
King St. S Norm 113 D3
King St. South 121 F1
King St. Tibs 99 D4
King St. Whit 45 E3
King St. Work 35 F1
King's Meadow Rd. Nott 173 D1
King's Pl. Nott 173 E2
King's Rd. N-on-T 124 C1
King's Wlk. Nott 173 E3
Kingerby Cl. Gain 24 C4
Kingfield Cl. Rain 118 A4
Kingfisher Cl. Bald 140 B3
Kingfisher Cl. Nott 160 B2
Kingfisher Ct. Bees 184 A3
Kingfisher Ct. Lough 220 A1
Kingfisher Way. Lough 220 A1
Kingfisher Wharf. Nott 172 C1
Kingfisher Wlk. Work 35 E4
Kingfishers Ct. W Brid 186 B2
Kinglake Pl. Nott 173 E1
Kingrove Ave. Bees 183 E3
Kings Ave. Carl 162 C1
Kings Ct. South 121 F1
Kings Dr. Brin 143 F4
Kings Lodge Dr. Mans 101 F2
Kings Mill La. Mans 101 E2
Kings Mill Rd E. S in A 101 D3
Kings Mill Rd E. S in A 114 C4
Kings Mill Way. Mans 101 F2
Kings Moor. Nott 160 C4
Kings Rd. Lo Cl 211 E1
Kings Rd. Lo Cl 211 E2
Kings Rd. Sand 182 A3
Kings Wood Cl. Baw 10 A4
Kingsbridge Ave. Carl 162 B3
Kingsbridge Way. Bees 183 E3
Kingsbury Dr. Nott 172 A4
Kingsdale Cl. Lo Ea 193 D3
Kingsdale. Work 36 A4
Kingsdown Mount. Nott 171 F1
Kingsford Ave. Nott 172 C3
Kingsley Ave. Mans 88 B3
Kingsley Cl. Mans 88 B2
Kingsley Cres. Lo Ea 193 D2
Kingsley Ct. Mans 88 B3
Kingsley Dr. Carl 175 D4
Kingsley Rd. Nott 174 A2
Kingsley St. K-in-A 115 D2
Kingsmead Ave. Staple 170 B1
Kingsmead. Ret 39 E2
Kingsmeadow. Rain 118 B4
Kingsnorth Cl. N-on-T 140 A4
Kingsthorpe Cl. Mans 88 C1
Kingsthorpe Cl. Nott 161 F1
Kingston Ave. Ilk 170 A2
Kingston Cl. Work 47 E4
Kingston Ct. Nott 173 F2
Kingston Dr. Cotg 187 F1
Kingston Dr. Oll 77 D2
Kingston Rd. C in L 25 F3
Kingston Rd. Mans 102 B4
Kingston Rd. W Brid 185 F3
Kingston Rd. Work 47 E4
Kingsway Ave. Boug 77 E3
Kingsway Gdns. Huck 145 F2
Kingsway. Bald 140 B2
Kingsway. Ilk 170 A3
Kingsway. K-in-A 115 D2
Kingsway. Mans 89 D1
Kingsway. R on T 175 F1
Kingsway. Work 36 A2
Kingswell Rd. Arn 161 F3
Kingswood Cl. Fir 16 A3
Kingswood Cl. W Brid 185 E3
Kingswood Dr. K-in-A 114 C3
Kingswood Rd. Nott 172 A3
Kinlet Rd. Nott 161 D3
Kinoulton La. Kinou 209 D4
Kinoulton La. Owth 199 F2
Kinoulton Rd. Cr Bi 188 C1
Kinsdale Wlk. Nott 184 C2
Kipling Cl. Nott 195 E4
Kipling Cl. Work 36 A3
Kipling St. Mans 102 A4
Kippis St. Nott 173 E3
Kirby Cl. Blid 118 A2
Kirby Cl. East 144 A2
Kirby Dr. Kegw 203 E1
Kirby Rd. East 144 A2
Kirk Ave. Kegw 203 E1
Kirk Cl. Bees 183 E2
Kirk Dr. Boug 77 F3
Kirk Gate. N-on-T 124 C1
Kirk Hill. E Brid 165 D1
Kirk La. Rudd 196 B4
Kirk Ley Rd. E Lea 214 B4
Kirk Rd. Carl 162 A1
Kirk White Ct. Nott 173 E1
Kirk's Bldgs. Carl 174 B4
Kirkbride Ct. Bees 183 D2
Kirkby Cl. South 121 F1
Kirkby Folly Rd. S in A 101 D1
Kirkby Gdns. Nott 173 E1
Kirkby House Dr. K-in-A 114 C3
Kirkby La. K-in-A 114 A2
Kirkby Rd. Raven 116 B2
Kirkby Rd. S in A 100 C1
Kirkdale Cl. Nott 171 D2
Kirkdale Gdns. Lo Ea 193 D3
Kirkdale Rd. Lo Ea 193 D3
Kirkdale Rd. Nott 174 A3
Kirke Cl. E Mark 66 A4
Kirke St. Ret 39 F4
Kirkewhite Ave. Lo Ea 193 E4
Kirkham Dr. Bees 182 C1
Kirkhill. Bing 177 F3
Kirkland Ave. Mans 101 F3
Kirkland Dr. Bees 183 E1
Kirkley Gdns. Arn 162 A4
Kirklington Rd. Bils 105 E1
Kirklington Rd. Bils 106 B1
Kirklington Rd. Eakr 106 C4
Kirklington Rd. Kirk 106 B1
Kirklington Rd. Rain 104 B1
Kirklington Rd. Ruff 104 B1
Kirklington Rd. South 121 E1
Kirkpatrick Dr. Work 35 E4
Kirkstead Cl. Pinx 113 E2
Kirkstead Gdns. Nott 172 C4
Kirkstead Rd. Pinx 113 E2
Kirkstead St. Nott 172 C4
Kirkstone Ct. Lo Ea 182 A1
Kirkstone Dr. Gam 186 B4
Kirtle Cl. Nott 172 A4
Kirton Ave. Lo Ea 193 E4
Kirton Cl. Mans 101 E4
Kirton Ct. Kirton 78 A3
Kirton Park. Kirton 78 B3
Kirton Rd. Egma 79 E3
Kitchener Dr. Mans 102 B3
Kitchener Terr. Scarc 59 D1
Kitson Ave. Sels 128 B2
Kiwi Cl. Huck 145 E3
Knapp Ave. East 143 F1
Knaton Rd. C in L 25 F4
Kneesall Cl. Mar War 74 B4
Kneesall Gr. Huck 146 A4
Kneeton Cl. Carl 162 B2
Kneeton Cl. Nott 161 E2
Kneeton Rd. E Brid 165 F3
Kneeton Vale. Nott 161 E2
Knight St. Carl 174 C3
Knight St. Carl 175 D3
Knight's Cl. Screv 166 C2
Knight's Ct. N-on-T 140 A4
Knighton Ave. Nott 172 C3
Knighton Rd. Arn 161 E3
Knights Cl. Nott 160 C4
Knights Cl. W Brid 185 E2
Knightsbridge Dr. Nuth 159 F2
Knightsbridge Dr. W Brid 185 E2
Knightsbridge Gdns. Huck 130 C1
Knipton Cl. Bald 140 B2
Knole Rd. Nott 171 F3
Knoll Ave. Huck 145 E3
Knoll The. Mans 101 F3
Knoll The. Shireb 72 B2
Knott End. Lan 16 C2
Knott's Ct. Bald 140 B2

Knowle Hill. Kim 159 D3
Knowle La. Kim 159 D3
Knowle Park. Kim 159 D3
Knowles Wlk. Arn 161 E4
Krebs Cl. Nott 184 B1
Kyle View. Nott 147 D1
Kyme St. Nott 172 C3
Kynance Gdns. Nott 185 D3

Labray Rd. Calv 148 C4
Laburnium Cl. Bald 140 B3
Laburnum Ave. Gain 15 E1
Laburnum Ave. K-in-A 114 B2
Laburnum Ave. Keyw 198 A1
Laburnum Avenue. Shireb 72 C3
Laburnum Cl. Hath 213 D1
Laburnum Cl. S Norm 113 D4
Laburnum Cl. Sand 182 A4
Laburnum Cl. Work 35 E1
Laburnum Gr. Bees 184 A3
Laburnum Gr. Huck 146 A3
Laburnum Gr. Mans 88 A2
Laburnum Rd. Lan 16 C2
Laburnum St. Nott 173 E4
Lace Rd. Bees 183 F4
Lace St. Nott 172 B1
Laceby Ct. Mans 88 C2
Lacey Ave. Huck 146 A3
Lacey Fields Rd. Hean 143 D1
Lacey Gn. Bald 140 C2
Ladbrooke Cres. Nott 160 B2
Lady Bay Ave. W Brid 173 F1
Lady Bay Bridge. Nott 173 F1
Lady Bay Bridge. W Brid 173 F1
Lady Bay Rd. W Brid 174 A1
Lady Well La. Head 52 A4
Lady Wlk. Work 35 E4
Ladybank Rise. Arn 162 B4
Ladybridge Cl. Bees 183 F2
Ladybrook La. Mans 101 F4
Ladybrook Pl. Mans 101 F4
Ladycroft Ave. Huck 146 A4
Ladylea Rd. Lo Ea 193 D2
Ladysmith Rd. Nott 174 A2
Ladysmock Gdns. Nott 173 E1
Ladywood La. West 80 C3
Lake Ave. Mans 101 F4
Lake Farm Rd. Mans 103 F1
Lake St. Nott 172 C3
Lakeland Ave. Huck 146 B3
Lakeside Ave. Lo Ea 193 E3
Lakeside Cres. Lo Ea 193 E3
Lamartine St. Nott 173 E3
Lamb Cl. N-on-T 139 E4
Lamb Close Dr. Greas 144 A2
Lamb La. Fir 16 B3
Lambcroft Rd. Pinx 113 E2
Lambert Ct. Bees 184 A4
Lambert Gdns. Nott 172 B4
Lambert St. Nott 172 C4
Lambeth Rd. Bes Vil 147 D1
Lambie Cl. Nott 172 B3
Lambley Ave. Carl 162 A2
Lambley Ave. Mans 102 C3
Lambley Bridle Rd. Bu Jo 163 E3
Lambley La. Bu Jo 163 F3
Lambley La. Carl 162 C2
Lambley Rd. Lowd 150 A1
Lambourne Cres. Lowd 150 C1
Lambourne Gdns. Arn 162 A3
Lambton Cl. Ilk 157 F2
Lamcote Gdns. R on T 175 F2
Lamcote Gr. Nott 173 E1
Lamcote Mews. R on T 175 F2
Lamcote St. Nott 173 E1
Laming Gap La. N-on-W 198 C3
Lamins La. Bes Vil 147 E2
Lammas Cl. S in A 100 C1
Lammas Gdns. E Brid 165 E2
Lammas Gdns. Nott 173 E1
Lammas La. E Brid 165 E2
Lammas Rd. S in A 100 C1
Lamond Cl. Mans 101 F3
Lamorna Gr. Nott 185 D3
Lamp Wood Cl. Calv 148 C4
Lamplands. Cotg 187 F2
Lanark Cl. Nott 172 B2
Lancaster Ave. Sand 182 A2
Lancaster Ave. Staple 182 C4
Lancaster Cl. Tick 8 A4
Lancaster Dr. Baw 9 F4
Lancaster Rd. Bes Vil 146 C2
Lancaster Rd. G on H 22 A4
Lancaster Rd. Huck 145 E2
Lancaster Rd. Nott 174 A4
Lancaster Way. Nott 159 E1
Lancastrian Way. Work 36 A3
Lancelot Dr. Greas 145 D1
Lancelyn Gdns. W Brid 185 F2
Lancster Cres. Tick 8 A4
Landa Gr. Tux 66 A2
Landcroft Cres. Nott 161 D3
Landcroft La. Su Bo 204 B1
Landmere Cl. Ship 157 E2
Landmere Gdns. Nott 161 F1
Landmere La. Rudd 185 F1
Landmere La. W Brid 185 E2
Landmere La. W Brid 186 A1
Landsdown Gr. Lo Ea 182 C1
Landsdowne Rd. Nott 160 C2
Landseer Cl. Nott 172 C3
Landseer Cl. South 136 B4
Landseer Rd. South 136 B4
Lane End. K-in-A 115 D3
Lane The. Awsw 158 B2
Lane The. Coth 154 C2
Laneham Ave. Arn 162 A4
Laneham Rd. D on T 54 A1
Laneham St. Ramp 43 D1
Lanercost Mews. Work 35 F1
Lanesborough Ct. Lough 220 A1
Laneside Ave. Bees 182 C1
Langar Cl. Nott 161 E2
Langar La. Co Ba 200 C4
Langar La. Harb 202 A2
Langar Pl. Mans 103 D4
Langar Rd. Bing 177 F2
Langdale Cl. N-on-T 139 F2
Langdale Dr. Lo Ea 193 D3
Langdale Dr. Tick 8 A4
Langdale Gr. Bing 177 D2
Langdale Rd. Nott 174 B3
Langdale Rd. Work 35 F4
Langdon Cl. Lo Ea 182 A1
Langdown Cl. Nott 160 A4
Langford La. Holme 111 D2
Langford Rd. Arn 162 A4
Langford Rd. Mans 101 F3
Langford St. Mans 101 E3
Langford St. S in A 100 C2
Langham Ave. Nott 174 A3
Langham Dr. Bu Jo 163 F3
Langham Pl. Mans 101 F4
Langley Ave. Arn 161 F3
Langley Ave. Ilk 157 E3
Langley Cl. Mans 87 F1
Langley Dr. Kegw 203 E1
Langley Park. La Mi 143 D2
Langley St. Work 35 F1
Langstrath Rd. Nott 184 C1
Langton Ave. K-in-A 114 B3
Langton Hollow. Sels 128 B3
Langton Rd. S in A 100 C1
Langtree Gdns. Bing 177 F3
Langtry Gr. Nott 161 D1
Langwell Dr. Mans 89 E1
Langwith Dr. Scarc 58 C1
Langwith Maltings. Scarc 72 C4
Langwith Rd. Cuck 60 A1
Langwith Rd. Shireb 72 C3
Lansbury Ave. Oll 77 E3
Lansbury Dr. Bils 105 F4
Lansbury Dr. S Norm 113 D3
Lansbury Gdns. Mans 102 C4
Lansbury Rd. Bald 140 B2
Lansbury Rd. Bils 105 F4
Lansbury Rd. Edwin 76 A1
Lansbury Rd. S in A 100 C1
Lansdall Ave. Lea 24 C2
Lansdown Cl. Bees 183 D2
Lansdowne Ave. Mans 102 B1
Lansdowne Dr. Lough 220 A1
Lansdowne Dr. W Brid 185 E2
Lansic La. Hover 151 E1
Lansing Cl. Nott 195 F4
Lantern La. E Lea 205 F1
Lanthwaite Cl. Nott 184 C1
Lanthwaite Rd. Nott 184 C1
Lapford Cl. Carl 162 B3
Larch Ave. Mans 88 A3
Larch Ave. Shireb 72 B2
Larch Cl. Bes Vil 161 E4
Larch Cl. Bing 178 A2
Larch Cl. Huck 146 A3
Larch Cres. Bees 183 E4
Larch Cres. East 143 F1
Larch Gdns. Nott 160 A4
Larch Rd. Oll 77 E3
Larch Way. Keyw 198 A1
Larchdale Cl. S Norm 113 D2
Larchdene Ave. Nott 171 E2
Largs Cl. Nott 146 C1
Lark Cl. Bees 183 D3
Larkdale St. Nott 173 D3
Larkfield Ave. Ann Wo 114 C1
Larkfield Rd. Kim 159 D3
Larkhall Pl. Mans 101 F3
Larklands Ave. Ilk 170 A4
Larkspur Ave. Nott 147 F1
Larkspur Cl. Mans 88 B1
Larkspur Cl. S Norm 113 D2
Larpit Green. Whit 45 D3
Larwood Cres. Ann Wo 114 C1
Larwood Gr. Nott 161 E2
Larwood. Work 36 A3
Lascelles Ave. Carl 162 B1
Latham St. Nott 160 A4
Lathkill Ave. Ilk 157 F3
Lathkill Cl. Nott 160 A4
Lathkill Dr. Sels 128 C4
Lathkilldale Cres. Lo Ea 193 D3
Latimer Cl. Nott 160 B3
Latimer Dr. Bees 171 D2
Laughton Ave. W Brid 185 E2
Laughton Cres. Huck 145 F2
Laughton Rd. Blyt 15 E4
Laughton Rd. Mort 15 E4
Launceston Cres. Nott 185 D2
Launder St. Nott 173 E1
Launder St. Orst 179 F4
Launds Ave. Sels 128 B4
Laurel Ave. Keyw 197 F1
Laurel Ave. Mans 89 D1
Laurel Ave. Mans 102 B3
Laurel Ave. Mar War 74 A4
Laurel Ave. Mist 6 C2
Laurel Cl. Gain 15 F1
Laurel Cl. Shireb 72 B3
Laurel Cl. Wys 207 E2
Laurel Cres. Kim 159 D3
Laurel Cres. Lo Ea 193 E3
Laurel Gr. K-in-A 115 E3
Laurel Gr. S Norm 113 D2
Laurel Rd. Carl 174 B4
Laurie Ave. Nott 173 D4
Laurie Cl. Nott 173 D4
Lauriston Dr. Nott 160 B2
Lavender Cl. Nott 159 F1
Lavender Cres. Carl 162 B1
Lavender Gr. Bees 184 A3
Lavender Wlk. Nott 173 E4
Lavenham Mews. Work 35 F1
Laver Cl. Arn 162 A4
Laverick Rd. Sels 128 A2
Lawdon Rd. Arn 148 A1
Lawley Ave. Nott 172 A1
Lawn Ave. S in A 100 C1
Lawn La. Grim 218 C1
Lawn La. S in A 100 C1
Lawn Mill Rd. Kim 158 C4
Lawn Rd. C in L 25 F4
Lawn Rd. S in A 101 D2
Lawns Rd. Ann Wo 129 F4
Lawns The. Coll 98 A1
Lawns The. What 179 D2
Lawnwood Ave. Elk 50 A2
Lawnwood La. Elk 50 A2
Lawrence Ave. Awsw 158 B2
Lawrence Ave. East 143 F1
Lawrence Ave. K-in-A 114 C3
Lawrence Ave. Mans 88 A2
Lawrence Cl. Cotg 187 F2
Lawrence Cres. S in A 101 D2
Lawrence Dr. Brin 143 E4
Lawrence Pl. N-on-T 125 D1
Lawrence St. Lo Ea 193 E4
Lawrence St. N-on-T 125 D1
Lawrence St. Sand 182 A4
Lawrence St. Staple 182 B3
Lawrence Way. Nott 173 D1
Lawson Ave. Lo Ea 193 F4
Lawson Cl. W Dray 50 C1
Lawson St. Nott 173 D3
Lawton Dr. Nott 146 B1
Laxton Ave. Nott 160 B3
Laxton Ave. S in A 101 E1
Laxton Dr. Huck 145 F3
Laxton Dr. Mar War 74 B4
Laxton Rd. Egma 79 E2
Laxton Rd. Lax 79 E2
Laycock Ave. G on H 12 C1
Layton Ave. Mans 102 A4
Layton Burroughs. Mans 102 A4
Le Brun Sq. C in L 25 F4
Le Page Ct. Nott 172 A4
Lea Cl. Raven 117 D1
Lea Ct. Work 35 E1
Lea La. Sels 128 C3
Lea Rd W. Gain 24 B3
Lea Rd. Gain 24 C3
Lea Rd. Mar War 74 B2
Lea Rd. Raven 117 D1
Lea Vale. S Norm 113 D2
Leabrook Cl. Nott 184 B2
Leabrook Gdns. Huck 146 B4
Leabrooks Ave. Mans 88 B3
Leabrooks Ave. S in A 101 E1
Leach Cl. D on T 54 B1
Leachcroft Hill. South 136 A4
Leacroft Rd. Nott 172 B4
Lead Hill. Work 35 F1
Leadale Ave. Huck 146 B4
Leadale Cres. Mans 88 C3
Leafield Green. Nott 184 C1
Leafield. Ret 29 E1
Leafield. Ret 39 E4
Leahurst Gdns. W Brid 186 A3
Leahurst Rd. W Brid 186 A3
Leake La. S on S 214 B2
Leake Rd. Cost 206 A1
Leake Rd. Goth 205 E3
Leam Glen. Mans 88 B1
Leamington Dr. Bees 183 E2
Leamington Dr. S in A 114 C4
Leamington Dr. S Norm 113 D3
Leamington Hall. S in A 100 C1
Leander Cl. Nott 185 D3
Leas Ave. Plea 87 D3
Leas Rd. Mans 88 B2
Leas The. Bulc 164 A3
Leaway The. Shireb 72 B2
Lechlade Rd. Nott 161 D3
Ledbury Vale. Nott 172 A4
Lee Cres. Ilk 170 A4
Lee La. Hean 143 D1
Lee Rd. Bu Jo 164 A3
Lee Rd. Calv 148 B4
Leech Ct. Greas 158 A4
Leeds Rd. Shire 34 C4
Leeks Rd. South 121 F1
Leeming Cl. Mar War 74 B3
Leeming La N. Mans 88 C3
Leeming La S. Mans 88 B1
Leeming La. Mar War 88 C4
Leeming Park. Mans 88 B2
Leeming St. Mans 102 A4
Leen Cl. Bes Vil 146 C2
Leen Cl. Huck 146 B4
Leen Dr. Huck 131 D1
Leen Gate. Nott 172 C1
Leen Mills La. Huck 131 D1
Leen Pl. Nott 172 C3
Leen Valley Dr. Shireb 72 C2
Lees Ave. Mans 101 E4
Lees Barn Rd. R on T 175 E1
Lees Hill St. Nott 173 F2
Lees La. S Norm 113 D3
Lees Rd. Carl 162 A1
Leeway Cl. Mans 103 F1
Leeway Rd. Mans 103 F1
Leeway Rd. South 121 E1
Legion Dr. S in A 100 B3
Leicester Rd. Lough 220 B1
Leicester St. Lo Ea 193 F3
Leigh Cl. W Brid 185 E3
Leigh Rd. Bees 182 C2
Leighton St. Nott 173 F3
Leiston Gdns. Nott 161 D4
Leivers Ave. Arn 161 F4
Lema Cl. Nott 160 B4
Lemont Rd. Mans 89 D1
Lemynton St. Lough 220 A2
Lendrum Ct. Bu Jo 163 F2
Lennox St. Nott 173 E3
Lenton Ave. Nott 173 D2
Lenton Ave. Toll 186 B1
Lenton Boulevard. Nott 172 C2
Lenton Cir. Toll 186 B1
Lenton Ct. Nott 172 C2
Lenton Hall Dr. Nott 172 B1
Lenton La. Nott 184 C4
Lenton La. Nott 185 D3
Lenton Manor. Nott 172 C2
Lenton Rd. Nott 173 D2
Lenton St. Sand 182 B4
Leonard Ave. Nott 161 D1
Leonard St. Nott 160 B3
Leopold St. Lo Ea 193 E4
Leopold St. Lough 220 A3
Leopold St. S in A 100 C1
Leroy Wallace Ave. Nott 172 C3
Lerwick Cl. Nott 185 D1
Leslie Ave. Bees 183 F3
Leslie Ave. Kim 158 C3
Leslie Ave. Nott 173 D4
Leslie Gr. Calv 148 C4
Leslie Rd. Nott 173 D4
Letchworth Cres. Bees 183 E2
Letcombe Rd. Nott 184 C2
Letwell Ave. Let 16 A1
Levels La. Blax 1 A4
Levels La. Miss 4 C4
Leverton Green. Nott 184 C1
Leverton Rd. Mans 101 F4
Leverton Rd. Ret 40 B4
Leverton Rd. S Le S 32 B2
Leverton Wlk. Arn 162 A4
Levick Ct. Nott 173 E1
Lewcote La. WeHa 157 D1
Lewindon Ct. Arn 161 F2
Lewis Cl. Nott 173 E3
Lewis St. Gain 24 B4
Lexington Ct. Tux 65 F1
Lexington Gdns. Nott 161 E2
Lexington Gdns. Tux 65 F1
Ley Croft. Mans 88 B3
Ley La. E Dray 53 E2
Ley La. Mans 88 B2
Ley St. Carl 175 D4
Leybourne Dr. Nott 160 C3
Leyland Cl. Bees 182 C1
Leys La. G on H 12 C1
Leys Rd. Rudd 196 B3
Leys The. Lowd 150 B1
Leys The. N-on-W 197 F4
Leys The. Nott 184 B1
Leyton Ave. S in A 101 D3
Leyton Cres. Bees 184 A3
Liber Cl. Mans 102 C4
Library Rd. Nott 172 B1
Lichfield Ave. Mans 102 B1
Lichfield Cl. Bees 182 C2
Lichfield Cl. Mans 102 B1
Lichfield Cl. Work 36 A4
Lichfield La. Mans 102 B2
Lichfield Rd. Nott 174 A2
Lichfield Wlk. C in L 25 F4
Liddell Gr. Nott 171 F2
Liddington St. Nott 160 C1
Lidget La. Ret 40 A4
Lifton Ave. Ret 29 F1
Lightfoot Cl. N-on-T 140 C4
Lilac Ave. Carl 174 B4
Lilac Cl. Keyw 198 A1
Lilac Cl. N-on-T 139 F2
Lilac Cl. Nott 159 F1
Lilac Cres. Bees 184 A3
Lilac Gr. Baw 9 F4
Lilac Gr. Bees 184 A3
Lilac Gr. C in L 25 F4
Lilac Gr. Glap 86 A4
Lilac Gr. Mans 89 E1
Lilac Gr. Mar War 73 F4
Lilac Gr. S Norm 113 D2
Lilac Gr. Shireb 72 C3
Lilac Mews. Ilk 157 E2
Lilac Rd. Huck 146 A3
Lillee Ct. Work 36 A3
Lilleker Rise. Nott 147 F1
Lillington Rd. Nott 160 A4
Lily Ave. Carl 175 D4
Lily Gr. Bees 184 A3
Limb Cres. S in A 100 C1
Lime Ave. Fir 16 A3
Lime Ave. La Mi 143 E1
Lime Ave. Lough 220 B2
Lime Ave. S in A 100 A2
Lime Ave. S in A 100 C2
Lime Cl. Kim 159 D3
Lime Cl. Pinx 113 E2
Lime Cl. R on T 175 F2
Lime Cres. Mar War 73 F4
Lime Gr Ave. Bees 183 F3
Lime Gr. Lo Ea 193 E4
Lime Gr. Mans 89 E1
Lime Gr. N-on-T 139 F4
Lime Gr. Ret 39 E4
Lime Gr. S Norm 113 D3
Lime Gr. Sand 182 A3
Lime Gr. Staple 182 B3
Lime La. Arn 147 F2
Lime St. K-in-A 115 D3
Lime St. Mans 102 B4
Lime St. Nott 160 A4
Lime St. S in A 101 D2
Lime Terr. Lo Ea 193 E4
Lime Tree Ave. C in L 25 F4
Lime Tree Ave. Gain 15 E1
Lime Tree Ave. Glap 86 A4
Lime Tree Ave. K-in-A 114 C3
Lime Tree Ave. Mans 88 A3
Lime Tree Ave. Nott 160 B2
Lime Tree Ave. Ret 39 E4
Lime Tree Ave. S in A 100 B3
Lime Tree Cres. Baw 9 F4
Lime Tree Ct. Nott 172 A1
Lime Tree Gdns. Lowd 150 C1
Lime Tree Pl. Mans 102 B3
Lime Tree Pl. Rain 104 B1
Lime Tree Rd. Elk 50 A2
Lime Tree Rd. Huck 146 A2
Lime Tree Rd. Oll 77 E3
Limehurst Ave. Lough 220 A3
Limes Ave. Ne La 59 D1
Limes Cres. Shireb 72 B3
Limes Ct. S in A 101 E1
Limes The. Beck 14 A1
Limestone Terr. Mans 88 A2
Limetree Ave. Work 48 B3
Limetree Cl. Keyw 197 F1
Limmen Gdns. Nott 173 F3
Limpenny St. Nott 173 D3
Linby Ave. Huck 146 A4
Linby Ave. Mans 101 E3
Linby Cl. Carl 162 C1
Linby Cl. Nott 161 E3
Linby Gr. Huck 146 A4
Linby La. Linby 131 E2
Linby La. Papp 131 E2
Linby Rd. Huck 146 A4
Linby St. Nott 160 B4
Linby Wlk. Huck 146 A4
Lincoln Rd. Tux 66 A2
Lincoln Ave. Sand 182 A2
Lincoln Cir. Nott 173 D2
Lincoln Cl. Staple 170 C1
Lincoln Cl. Tibs 99 D3
Lincoln Ct. Nott 171 F4
Lincoln Dr. Mans 88 B2
Lincoln Gr. R on T 175 F2
Lincoln Rd. Brox 57 E2
Lincoln Rd. E Mark 66 A4
Lincoln Rd. Fent 55 E3
Lincoln Rd. N-on-T 125 D2
Lincoln Rd. Sax 57 E2
Lincoln Rd Bridge. N-on-T 125 D1
Lincoln St. Gain 15 E1
Lincoln St. N-on-T 125 D1
Lincoln St. Nott 160 C2
Lincoln St. Nott 173 E3
Lincoln St. Tibs 99 D3
Lincoln St. Work 36 A1
Lincoln View. Work 36 A1
Lind Cl. Mans 103 F1
Lindale Cl. Gam 186 B3
Lindbridge Rd. Nott 159 F1
Linden Gr. Bees 184 A3
Linden Ave. Bald 140 A3
Linden Ave. Nott 184 B1
Linden Ave. Tux 66 A1

Linden Gr. Carl .................. 163 D1
Linden Gr. K-in-A .............. 114 B3
Linden Gr. Sand ................. 182 A4
Linden Gr. Shireb .................. 72 C2
Linden Gr. Staple ............... 182 C3
Linden Rd. Lough ............... 220 A3
Linden Rd. Mans ................ 102 C4
Linden St. Mans .................... 88 A1
Linden St. Nott .................. 173 E4
Linden St. Shireb .................. 72 C2
Linden Terr. Gain ................. 24 B4
Lindfield Cl. Nott ................ 160 A1
Lindfield Rd. Nott ............... 159 F1
Lindholme Way. S in A ....... 100 C3
Lindhurst La. Mans ............. 102 C2
Lindisfarne Gdns. Bes Vil ... 147 D1
Lindley St. Greas ............... 144 A2
Lindley St. Mans ................ 102 A4
Lindley St. Sels .................. 128 B3
Lindley Terr. Nott ................ 172 C4
Lindley's La. K-in-A ........... 115 D2
Lindrick Cl. C in L ................. 25 F4
Lindrick Cl. Work .................. 36 A3
Lindrick Ct. Ret ..................... 39 E1
Lindrick La. Tick ...................... 8 A3
Lindrick Rd. K-in-A ............ 114 C4
Lindrick. Tick ........................... 8 A3
Lindsay Ave. Ann Wo .......... 115 D1
Lindsay Ave. N-on-T ......... 139 F2
Lindsay Cl. Mans ............... 102 A3
Lindsey Dr. Mans ............... 103 D2
Lindsey Rd. Har ....................... 9 D3
Lindum Gr. Nott .................. 173 F2
Lindum Mews. N-on-T ........ 140 A4
Lindum Rd. Nott ................. 160 B2
Lindum St. N-on-T .............. 140 A4
Lindwall Ct. Work ................. 36 A3
Lindy Cl. Kinou ................... 199 F1
Linecroft La. Walker ............. 14 B4
Linette Cl. Nott ................... 161 D1
Linford. Bees ...................... 171 D2
Ling Cres. Rudd ................. 196 B4
Ling Rd. Lough ................... 220 A1
Lingdale Cl. Lough ............. 220 A1
Lingfield Cl. Mans .............. 102 C3
Lingfield Ct. Nott ................ 171 E2
Lingford St. Huck ............... 146 A3
Lingford. Cotg .................... 188 A2
Lingforest Cl. Mans ............ 103 D3
Lingforest Rd. Mans ........... 103 D3
Lings La. Keyw ................... 207 F4
Lings View. Mar War ............ 74 B2
Lingwood Gr. Mans ............ 103 D4
Lingwood La. Lamb ............ 149 D2
Lingwood La. Woodb .......... 149 D2
Linkin Rd. Bees .................. 183 E3
Linkmel Rd. East ................ 143 E2
Links The. Mans .................. 103 D3
Linksfield Ct. W Brid ........... 185 E1
Linley Cl. Coll ..................... 112 A4
Linmell St. Nott .................. 173 F3
Linnets Dr. Mans ................ 102 C4
Linnets The. Work ................ 35 E4
Linsdale Cl. Nott ................. 171 D3
Linsdale Gdns. Carl ........... 162 B2
Lintin Ave. Edwin ................. 75 F1
Linton Cl. Farn ................... 139 D3
Linton Cl. Mans .................. 103 D3
Linton Dr. Boug .................... 77 F3
Linton Rise. Nott ................ 174 A3
Linwood Cl. Gain .................. 24 C4
Linwood Cres. East ............ 144 A1
Linwood Cres. Raven ......... 116 C2
Linwood Ct. Mans ................ 88 C2
Lion Cl. Nott ....................... 160 B1
Liquorice La. C in L .............. 26 A2
Lisle St. Lough ................... 220 A3
Lismore Cl. Nott ................. 172 C3
Lismore Ct. Mans ............... 101 E3
Lissington Rd. Gain .............. 24 C4
Lister Ct. Nott ..................... 172 C1
Lister Gate. Nott ................. 173 E2
Listowel Cres. Nott ............. 195 F4
Litchen Cl. Ilk ..................... 157 F1
Litchfield Cl. Lo Ea ............ 194 A4
Litchfield Rise. Nott ............ 147 F1
Little Acre. Mans .................. 88 C3
Little Barn Ct. Mans .......... 102 C3
Little Barn Gdns. Mans ...... 102 C3
Little Barn La. Mans .......... 102 C3
Little Belt The. Gain ............. 15 E2
Little Breck. S Norm ........... 113 D2
Little Carter La. Mans ......... 102 C4
Little Debdale La. Mans ........ 87 F1
Little Hallam La. Ilk ............ 170 A3
Little Hayes. W Brid ........... 185 E2
Little Hollies. Mans .............. 89 D1
Little John Ave. Mar War ...... 74 B1
Little John Cl. Boug .............. 77 E3
Little John Dr. Rain ............. 104 A1
Little John Wlk. Nott ........... 173 E4
Little La. Blyth ...................... 18 A2
Little La. Calv ..................... 148 B4
Little La. Coll ...................... 111 F4
Little La. Edin ..................... 120 B2
Little La. G on H .................... 12 C1
Little La. Kim ...................... 158 C3
Little La. Mans ...................... 87 D3
Little La. S in A ..................... 99 F1
Little La. Shireb ..................... 72 B2
Little La. Th Sa ...................... 34 A3
Little La. Toll ...................... 186 C2
Little Lunnon. B in F ........... 194 C3
Little Meadow. Cotg ........... 188 A1
Little Moor La. Lough ......... 220 B2
Little Oak Ave. Ann Wo ...... 130 A4
Little Oakwood Dr. Nott ...... 146 B1
Little Ox. Carl ..................... 174 C2
Little Ricket La. Raven ....... 116 B2
Little Tennis St S. Nott ....... 174 A1
Little Tennis St. Nott .......... 174 A2
Little Top La. Lound ............. 20 B1
Little Wlk. E Stock .................. 7 E1
Littleborough Rd. S Le S ...... 33 D2
Littlegreen Rd. Arn ............. 161 F3
Littleover Ave. Mans .......... 103 D3
Littlewood Gdns. Nott ......... 171 E3
Littlewood La. Mans ............ 88 A3
Littleworth. Mans ................ 102 B3
Litton Ave. S in A ............... 101 D3
Litton Cl. Arn ...................... 161 F2
Litton Cl. Ilk ........................ 157 F2
Litton Cl. Raven ................. 117 D2
Litton Rd. Mans .................... 88 C2
Littondale. Work ................... 36 A4
Liverpool St. Nott ............... 173 F3
Livingstone St. News ......... 130 C3
Llanberis Gr. Nott ............... 160 B1
Lloyd St. Nott ..................... 161 E1
Loach Ct. Nott .................... 172 B3
Lobelia Cl. Nott .................. 173 E4
Lock La. Lo Ea ................... 193 E2
Lock La. Sand .................... 182 B2
Lockerbie St. Carl .............. 174 C3
Locksley La. Nott ................ 184 C2
Lockwood Cl. Bees ............ 184 B2
Lockwood Ct. Nott .............. 147 D1
Lodge Cl. Nott .................... 147 F1
Lodge Cl. Nott .................... 172 B4
Lodge Farm La. Nott ........... 147 F1
Lodge La. Elst .................... 153 E3
Lodge La. K-in-A ................ 115 E2
Lodge La. Screv ................. 166 B3
Lodge La. Tux ....................... 66 A1
Lodge Rd. Greas ................ 158 A4
Lodge Rd. Lo Ea ................ 193 E3
Lodgefield La. Hover .......... 151 F1
Lodgewood Cl. Nott ............ 160 A3
Lodore Rd. Work ................... 35 F4
Logan St. Nott .................... 160 B3
Lois Ave. Nott .................... 172 C2
Lombard Cl. Nott ................ 172 C2
Lombard St. N-on-T ............ 139 F4
Lombard St. Orst ................ 180 A3
Lonan Cl. Mans .................... 89 D1
London La. W-on-W ........... 217 E4
London La. Wyme ............... 216 A2
London Rd. Bald ................ 140 B3
London Rd. Kegw ............... 203 E1
London Rd. Lo Wh .............. 212 C3
London Rd. N-on-T ............. 140 B3
London Rd. Nott ................. 173 E1
London Rd. Ret ..................... 39 F3
London Rd. Ret ..................... 40 A2
Long Acre. Huck ................. 145 E4
Long Brecks La. Blyth .......... 18 B1
Long Hill Rise. Huck ........... 145 F3
Long La. B in W .................. 141 F4
Long La. B-le-V ................... 192 C1
Long La. Bees ..................... 183 F2
Long La. C in L ...................... 25 F3
Long La. E Dray .................... 53 E2
Long La. Farn ..................... 139 D3
Long La. Greas ................... 145 D1
Long La. Hick ...................... 210 B3
Long La. Kegw .................... 203 E3
Long La. Redm .................... 192 C1
Long La. Ship ...................... 157 E3
Long La. Ship ...................... 157 F4
Long La. Shireb ..................... 72 C2
Long La. Stat ...................... 202 C2
Long Meadow Hill. Lowd .... 149 F1
Long Meadow Hill. Lowd .... 150 A1
Long Meadow. Farns .......... 120 A3
Long Meadow. Mans ............ 88 B3
Long Meadows. Ever ............ 11 D2
Long Row W. Nott ............... 173 E2
Long Row. K on S ................ 204 A2
Long Row. N-on-T ............... 140 A4
Long Row. Nott ................... 173 E2
Longacre. Arn ..................... 161 F2
Longbeck Ave. Nott ............. 162 A1
Longcliff Hill. Ol Da ............ 218 C2
Longcroft View. Whit ............ 45 D3
Longdale Ave. Raven .......... 117 D1
Longdale La. Raven ............ 132 B4
Longdale Rd. Nott ............... 161 E3
Longdale. Mans .................... 88 C1
Longden Cl. Staple ............. 170 C1
Longden St. Nott ................. 173 F3
Longden Terr. Mar War ......... 74 A2
Longden Terr. S in A ........... 100 B3
Longfellow Dr. Bald ............ 140 B3
Longfellow Dr. Work .............. 36 A2
Longfellows Cl. Nott ............ 161 D4
Longfield La. Ilk ................. 170 A3
Longford Cres. Nott ............ 146 B1
Longford Wlk. Mans ........... 103 D3
Longhedge La. Alv .............. 180 C4
Longhedge La. Bott ............. 180 C2
Longhedge La. Bott ............. 180 C4
Longhedge La. Hawk ........... 167 F3
Longhedge La. Orst ............. 168 A1
Longhedge La. Plea .............. 86 C3
Longhill Rise. Ann Wo ......... 114 C1
Longholme Rd. Ret ................ 40 A4
Longhurst View. Whit ............ 45 D3
Longhurst. Work .................... 36 A3
Longland La. Farns ............. 119 E2
Longlands Cl. Bees ............. 184 A2
Longlands Rd. Bees ............ 184 A2
Longleat Cres. Bees ........... 183 E3
Longmead Cl. Nott .............. 161 E3
Longmead Dr. Fisk .............. 137 F2
Longmead Dr. Nott .............. 161 E3
Longmoor Ave. Lowd .......... 164 C4
Longmoor Gdns. Lo Ea ....... 182 A1
Longmoor La. Aslo .............. 179 D4
Longmoor La. Lo Ea ............ 182 A1
Longmoor La. Sand ............. 182 A2
Longmoor La. Scarr ............ 179 D4
Longmoor Rd. Lo Ea ........... 182 A1
Longnor Wlk. Mans ............. 103 D3
Longore Sq. Nott ................ 172 B2
Longridge Rd. Arn ............... 161 F3
Longshaw Rd. Mans ............ 103 D3
Longster La. Mar War ............ 73 E2
Longstone Way. Mans ......... 101 E3
Longue Dr. Calv .................. 148 B4
Longwall Ave. Nott .............. 173 D1
Longwood Ct. Nott ............... 160 C4
Longwood Rd. Pinx .............. 113 F1
Lonsdale Dr. Bees .............. 182 C1
Lonsdale La. Calv ............... 133 D3
Lonsdale Rd. Nott ............... 172 C3
Lord Haddon Rd. Ilk ............ 157 F1
Lord Nelson St. Nott ........... 173 F2
Lord St. Gain ......................... 24 B4
Lord St. Mans ..................... 102 A3
Lord St. Nott ....................... 173 F2
Lordship La. Orst ................ 180 A3
Lorimer Ave. Carl ................ 162 C1
Lorne Cl. Nott ..................... 173 E4
Lorne Gr. R on T ................. 175 F2
Lorne Wlk. Nott ................... 173 E4
Lortas Rd. Nott .................... 160 C1
Loscoe Gdns. Nott .............. 161 D1
Loscoe Mount Rd. Nott ........ 161 E1
Loscoe Rd. Nott .................. 161 E1
Lothian Rd. Toll ................... 186 B1
Lothmore Ct. Nott ................ 173 D1
Lotus Cl. Nott ...................... 173 F4
Loughbon. Orst .................... 180 A4
Loughborough Ave. Nott ...... 173 F2
Loughborough Rd. Brad ...... 196 C3
Loughborough Rd. Bunn .... 206 C4
Loughborough Rd. Cost ...... 215 E3
Loughborough Rd. E Lea .... 214 C4
Loughborough Rd. Hath ..... 213 D1
Loughborough Rd. Hoton .... 215 E1
Loughborough Rd. Lough .. 220 B1
Loughborough Rd. Remp .. 215 E3
Loughborough Rd. Rudd .... 196 C3
Loughborough Rd. W Brid . 185 F3
Loughborough Rd. Cotes ..... 220 C3
Loughrigg Cl. Nott ............... 173 D1
Louis Ave. Bees .................. 183 F4
Louise Ave. Carl .................. 175 D4
Lound House Cl. S in A ...... 100 C3
Lound House Rd. S in A ..... 100 C3
Lound Low Rd. Lound .......... 29 E4
Louwil Ave. Mans .................. 88 C3
Love La. Gain ........................ 15 E1
Loveden Cl. Bald ................. 140 B2
Lovell Cl. Nott ..................... 159 F3
Lover's La. N-on-T .............. 125 D1
Low Field La. Aust .................. 3 E1
Low Holland La. S Le S ........ 32 C2
Low Moor Rd. K-in-A ........... 115 D3
Low Pavement. Nott ............ 173 E2
Low Rd. Best ......................... 97 F3
Low Rd. S in A .................... 100 C4
Low St. Beck ......................... 14 B1
Low St. C in L ........................ 26 A3
Low St. Coll ......................... 111 F4
Low St. E Dray ....................... 53 D2
Low St. E Mark ...................... 66 A4
Low st. Elst ......................... 153 E3
Low St. G on H ...................... 12 C1
Low St. Harby ........................ 70 B1
Low St. N Whea ..................... 31 E4
Low St. S in A ..................... 100 C1
Low St. Torw ......................... 19 D1
Low Wood La. Eagle .............. 98 C4
Low Wood Rd. Nott .............. 159 F3
Low Wood Rd. Nuth ............. 159 F3
Low's La. S-by-D ................. 170 A1
Lowater St. Carl .................. 174 A4
Lowcroft. Arn ....................... 161 F2
Lowdam Rd. Epp ................. 150 A3
Lowdham La. Woodb .......... 149 F2
Lowdham Rd. Carl ............... 162 B2
Lowdham Rd. Gunt .............. 164 C4
Lowdham St. Nott ................ 173 F3
Lower Bagthorpe. Sels ....... 128 C2
Lower Beauvale. Greas ..... 144 A2
Lower Bloomsgrove Rd. Ilk 157 F1
Lower Brook St. Lo Ea ....... 193 F4
Lower Cambridge St. Lough220 A3
Lower Canaan. Rudd ......... 196 B4
Lower Chapel St. Ilk ........... 157 F1
Lower Clara Mount Rd. Hean143 D1
Lower Ct. Bees .................. 184 A4
Lower Dunstead Rd. Ald .... 143 D2
Lower Dunstead Rd. La Mi 143 D2
Lower Eldon St. Nott .......... 173 F2
Lower Gladstone St. Lough 220 A3
Lower Granby St. Ilk .......... 157 F1
Lower Kirklington Rd. South121 E1
Lower Middleton St. Coss .. 158 A1
Lower Orchard St. Staple ... 182 B4
Lower Park St. Staple ........ 182 B3
Lower Parliament St. Nott .. 173 E2
Lower Pasture La. N Whea .. 31 F4
Lower Regent St. Bees ...... 184 A3
Lower St. Bees ................... 184 A4
Lowes Wong. South ........... 136 B4
Loweswater Ct. Gam .......... 186 B4
Lowfield La. Bald ............... 140 B1
Lowfield. Ret ......................... 29 E1
Lowlands Dr. Keyw ............ 197 F2
Lowther Sq. C in L ................ 25 F4
Lowther Way. Lough .......... 220 A1
Lowtown Cl. Work ................ 36 A1
Lowtown St. Work ................ 36 A1
Lowtown View. Work ............ 36 A1
Lucerne Cl. Nott ................. 185 D3
Lucknow Ave. Nott ............. 161 E1
Lucknow Ct. Nott ................ 173 A2
Lucknow Dr. Mans ............. 101 F3
Lucknow Dr. Nott ............... 161 E1
Lucknow Dr. S in A ............ 101 D2
Lucknow Rd. Nott ............... 173 A2
Ludborough Wlk. Mans ........ 88 C2
Ludford Cres. Gain ............... 24 C4
Ludford Rd. Nott ................. 160 B4
Ludgate Cl. Bes Vil ............. 147 D1
Ludgate Dr. E Brid .............. 165 E1
Ludham Ave. Nott ............... 160 A4
Ludlam Ave. Greas ............. 158 A4
Ludlow Cl. Bees ................. 171 E1
Ludlow Hill Rd. W Brid ....... 185 F3
Lulworth Cl. W Brid ............ 185 E3
Lulworth Ct. Kim ................. 158 C4
Lumley Dr. Tick ...................... 8 A4
Lune Cl. Bees ..................... 183 F2
Lune Meadow. Mans ............ 88 C2
Lunn La. Coll ...................... 111 F4
Lupin Cl. Nott ..................... 173 E4
Luther Ave. S in A .............. 100 C1
Luther Cl. Nott .................... 173 F4
Luton Cl. Nott ..................... 160 B1
Lutterell Way. W Brid ......... 186 B3
Lybster Mews. Nott ............ 173 D1
Lydney Park. W Brid ........... 185 E3
Lyle Cl. Kim ........................ 158 C4
Lyme Park. W Brid .............. 185 D3
Lymington Gdns. Nott ......... 174 A3
Lymington Rd. Mans ........... 101 E3
Lymn Ave. Carl ................... 162 C1
Lyncombe Ct. Ret ................. 39 E2
Lyncombe Gdns. Keyw ...... 197 F2
Lynd Cl. Sels ...................... 129 D4
Lyndale Rd. Bees ............... 183 D4
Lynden Ave. Lo Ea ............. 193 E3
Lyndhurst Ave. Blid ............. 118 A3
Lyndhurst Gdns. W Brid ...... 185 E2
Lyndhurst Rd. Nott .............. 173 F2
Lynds Cl. Edwin .................... 76 A1
Lyngs The. E Brid ............... 165 E1
Lynmouth Cres. Nott ........... 172 C4
Lynmouth Dr. Ship .............. 157 E2
Lynncroft. East ................... 144 A2
Lynnes Cl. Blid ................... 118 A2
Lynstead Dr. Huck .............. 145 E3
Lynton Gdns. Arn ................ 162 A4
Lynton Rd. Bees ................. 183 E3
Lyons Cl. Rudd ................... 196 A4
Lytham Dr. W Brid ............... 186 B2
Lytham Gdns. Nott .............. 147 D1
Lytham Rd. K-in-A ............... 114 C4
Lythe Cl. Nott ..................... 185 D3
Lytton Cl. Nott .................... 173 F3

Mabel Ave. S in A ............... 101 D1
Mabel Gr. W Brid ................ 186 A4
Mabel St. Nott ..................... 173 E1
Mable St. Rhod ..................... 35 D2
Macaulay Cl. Bald ............... 140 B3
Macaulay Cl. Work ................ 36 B2
Macaulay Dr. Bald ............... 140 B3
Macaulay Gr. Kim ................ 159 D3
Mackinley Ave. Staple ......... 170 C1
Mackleys La. N Musk .......... 110 C1
Mackworth Ct. Mans ........... 103 D3
Maclaren Gdns. Rudd ......... 196 B3
Maclean Rd. Carl ................ 174 B4
Macmillan Cl. Nott ............... 161 F1
Madryn Wlk. Nott ................ 161 D4
Mafeking St. Nott ................ 174 A2
Mag La. Elmt ......................... 58 A3
Magdala Rd. Nott ................ 173 E4
Magdalen Dr. E Brid ........... 165 E2
Magdalene View. N-on-T ... 140 A4
Magdalene Way. Huck ....... 146 A4
Magna Cl. Lowd ................. 150 C1
Magnolia Cl. Nott ............... 159 F1
Magnolia Ct. Bees .............. 171 E1
Magnolia Gr. Huck .............. 146 A2
Magnus Rd. Nott ................ 161 E2
Magnus St. N-on-T .............. 140 A4
Magpie Cl. Work ................... 35 E4
Magpie La. N Le Ha ............. 32 C1
Magson St. Nott .................. 173 F3
Maid Marian Ave. Sels ........ 129 D4
Maid Marian Way. Nott ....... 173 E2
Maid Marion Ave. Bils ......... 106 A2
Maid Marion Way. Boug ....... 77 E3
Maid Marrion Dr. Edwin ........ 76 B1
Maida La. Oll ........................ 77 D2
Maiden La. Nott .................. 173 E2
Maidens Dale. Arn .............. 161 E4
Maidstone Dr. Nott .............. 171 E1
Main Ave. Mans .................. 103 D4
Main La. Shel ..................... 164 B1
Main Rd. Ald ....................... 128 A3
Main Rd. Ann Wo ................ 114 C1
Main Rd. Carl ...................... 162 C1
Main Rd. Carl ...................... 163 D1
Main Rd. Cotg ..................... 187 F2
Main Rd. Kelh ...................... 124 A2
Main Rd. Kim ....................... 159 D4
Main Rd. Ne La ...................... 59 D1
Main Rd. Nott ...................... 185 D4
Main Rd. Ol Da .................... 218 C2
Main Rd. Plum ..................... 197 F4
Main Rd. R on T .................. 175 F2
Main Rd. Raven ................... 116 C2
Main Rd. Raven ................... 117 D2
Main Rd. Sels ...................... 128 A2
Main Rd. Sels ...................... 128 C1
Main Rd. Shel ...................... 176 B4
Main Rd. Upton ................... 122 C1
Main St. Ann Wo ................. 129 F4
Main St. Aslo ...................... 179 D3
Main St. Awsw ..................... 158 B3
Main St. Bald ....................... 140 C2
Main St. Bath ....................... 110 A2
Main St. Bleas ..................... 152 A4
Main St. Blid ........................ 117 F2
Main St. Blid ........................ 118 A2
Main St. Both ......................... 63 F4
Main St. Brad ....................... 196 C2
Main St. Brin ........................ 128 B1
Main St. Bu Jo ..................... 163 F2
Main St. Bunn ...................... 206 C4
Main St. Calv ....................... 148 B4
Main St. Caun ...................... 109 D3
Main St. Clar .......................... 30 B3
Main St. Codd ...................... 126 A1
Main St. Cost ....................... 206 B1
Main St. Cr Bu ..................... 189 D4
Main St. Crom ...................... 110 C4
Main St. Dry Do .................... 156 C1
Main St. E Brid ..................... 165 E1
Main St. E Lea ..................... 205 F1
Main St. Eakr ......................... 92 C1
Main St. East ....................... 143 F1
Main St. East ....................... 144 B1
Main St. Edin ....................... 120 B2
Main St. Egma ....................... 79 F3
Main St. Farn ....................... 139 D2
Main St. Farns ..................... 119 F3
Main St. Fenton ................... 142 B1
Main St. Fisk ........................ 137 F2
Main St. Flint ........................ 167 D4
Main St. Gam ....................... 186 B4
Main St. Gran ....................... 191 E2
Main St. Greas ..................... 144 B1
Main St. Gunt ....................... 165 D3
Main St. Har ............................. 8 C2
Main St. Harb ....................... 202 A2
Main St. Hayt ......................... 30 B3
Main St. Hick ....................... 210 B3
Main St. Hover ..................... 151 E1
Main St. Keyw ...................... 197 F1
Main St. Kim ........................ 158 C3
Main St. Kinou ..................... 199 F1
Main St. Kirton ....................... 78 A3
Main St. Lamb ...................... 163 E4
Main St. Lane ......................... 54 A3
Main St. Lax ........................... 79 E2
Main St. Linby ...................... 131 D2
Main St. Lo Ea ..................... 193 F4
Main St. Lo Wh .................... 212 A2
Main St. Lowd ...................... 150 B1
Main St. Matt .......................... 20 A4
Main St. Morton .................... 137 E2
Main St. N Le Ha ................... 32 B1
Main St. N Musk ................... 110 C1
Main St. N on S .................... 213 E2
Main St. Newt ......................... 99 D2
Main St. Nott ........................ 160 B4
Main St. Old ............................ 16 C3
Main St. Oll ............................ 77 D2
Main St. Oss ........................... 95 E3
Main St. Oxt ......................... 134 A2
Main St. Papp ...................... 131 E2
Main St. Papp ...................... 131 F3
Main St. Redm ..................... 192 C2

Main St. S in A 99 F2
Main St. S Musk 124 B4
Main St. S Norm 113 D3
Main St. S on S 214 B1
Main St. S on T 96 C4
Main St. Scarc 59 D1
Main St. Scarr 178 C4
Main St. Shireb 72 B2
Main St. Sibt 167 F4
Main St. Stre 159 D1
Main St. Su Bo 213 D2
Main St. Su Bo 213 D4
Main St. Swine 71 E1
Main St. Tork 44 A1
Main St. W Lea 204 C1
Main St. W Sto 7 F1
Main St. W-on-W 217 E4
Main St. Wale 64 A1
Main St. West 81 D2
Main St. What 179 D2
Main St. Woodb 149 E2
Main St. Wys 207 E2
Mainside Cres. Sels 129 D1
Maitland Ave. Arn 161 F2
Maitland Rd. Arn 161 F2
Major St. Nott 173 E3
Malbon Cl. Nott 173 F4
Malcolm Cl. Nott 173 E4
Maldon Cl. Bees 183 E2
Malham Cl. Baw 9 F4
Malin Hill. Nott 173 E2
Malkin Ave. R on T 176 A2
Mallam Rd. Boug 77 E3
Mallard Cl. Nott 160 C2
Mallard Cl. Shireb 72 C2
Mallard Ct. Bees 184 A3
Mallard Gn. Bald 140 A3
Mallatratt Pl. Mans 88 A3
Malling Wlk. Nott 161 F1
Malmesbury Rd. Arn 162 A2
Malt Cotts. Nott 160 C1
Malt St. Goth 195 D1
Maltby Cl. Nott 160 A1
Maltby Rd. Arn 162 A2
Maltby Rd. Mans 102 C3
Maltby Rd. Old 16 C3
Malthouse Cl. East 143 F1
Malthouse Cotts. Scarc 72 C4
Malthouse Rd. Whit 45 D3
Malting Cl. Rudd 196 B3
Maltings The. Blyth 18 A2
Maltings The. Cr Bi 189 D2
Maltkiln Cl. Oll 77 E1
Maltkiln La. N-on-T 125 D1
Maltkiln Rd. Fent 55 E3
Maltmill La. Nott 173 E2
Malton Rd. Nott 160 C1
Maltsters The. N-on-T 139 E3
Malvern Cl. Nott 161 F1
Malvern Cres. W Brid 185 F3
Malvern Gdns. Lo Ea 193 D4
Malvern Rd. Nott 161 F1
Malvern Rd. W Brid 185 F3
Manby Ct. Mar War 74 B4
Manchester St. Lo Ea 193 E3
Mandalay St. Nott 160 B2
Mandeen Gr. Mans 103 D2
Manesty Cres. Nott 195 F4
Mangham La. Tick 8 A4
Manifold Dr. Sels 128 C4
Manifold Dr. Sels 129 D4
Manifold Gdns. Nott 173 E1
Manitoba Way. Sels 128 C4
Manly Cl. Nott 160 C4
Mann St. Nott 172 C4
Manners Ave. Ilk 157 E1
Manners Rd. Bald 140 B2
Manners Rd. Ilk 157 F1
Manners Rd. N-on-T 124 C1
Manners St. Ilk 170 A3
Manning St. Nott 173 E4
Manning View. Ilk 157 F1
Mannion Cres. Lo Ea 193 D3
Manns Leys. Cotg 187 F1
Manor Ave. Bees 183 F2
Manor Ave. Bees 183 F3
Manor Ave. Staple 182 B4
Manor Cl. Bleas 152 A4
Manor Cl. Boug 77 F3
Manor Cl. Cost 206 B1
Manor Cl. Gams 50 C3
Manor Cl. Lo Wh 212 A2
Manor Cl. Miss 4 B2
Manor Cl. Newt 99 D2
Manor Cl. South 121 F1
Manor Cl. W Brid 186 A2
Manor Cl. Wale 64 A1
Manor Cl. Work 35 E1
Manor Cres. Carl 174 C4
Manor Cres. K-in-A 115 D2
Manor Croft. Nott 160 C2
Manor Ct. Bees 183 D4
Manor Ct. Carl 174 C4
Manor Ct. Mar War 74 B3
Manor Dr. Morton 137 E2
Manor Farm Cl. Brad 196 C2
Manor Farm La. Nott 184 C1
Manor Fm Meadow. E Lea 205 F1
Manor Fm Rise. N Le Ha 32 B1
Manor Gr. Work 35 E1
Manor Green Wlk. Carl 174 C4
Manor House Cl. Lowd 150 B1
Manor House Ct. K-in-A 114 B2
Manor House La. Dry Do 156 B1
Manor House Rd. Lo Ea 193 F3
Manor La. Broad 71 D4
Manor La. Shel 164 B1
Manor La. What 179 D1
Manor Park. Rudd 196 B4
Manor Rd. B in F 194 C3
Manor Rd. Bing 177 F2
Manor Rd. Bott 181 E1
Manor Rd. Calv 148 C4
Manor Rd. Carl 174 C4
Manor Rd. Caun 109 D2
Manor Rd. Coll 112 A4
Manor Rd. E Lea 205 F2
Manor Rd. East 143 F1
Manor Rd. Ilk 157 F1
Manor Rd. Keyw 197 F2
Manor Rd. Mans 88 A2
Manor Rd. Mar War 74 B3
Manor Rd. Mort 15 D2
Manor Rd. S in A 100 C4
Manor Rd. Sax 57 D2
Manor Rise. E Brid 165 E2
Manor St. Nott 173 F2
Manor St. S in A 100 C1
Manorwood Rd. Cotg 187 F1
Manse Ave. Elmt 58 B4
Manse Cl. Elmt 58 B4
Mansell Cl. East 144 A1
Mansfield Gr. Nott 173 D3
Mansfield Ct. Nott 173 D4
Mansfield La. Calv 148 C4
Mansfield La. S in A 101 D3
Mansfield Rd. Ann Wo 130 A3
Mansfield Rd. Arn 132 A2
Mansfield Rd. Arn 161 E2
Mansfield Rd. Babw 38 B2
Mansfield Rd. Bes Vil 147 E3
Mansfield Rd. Blid 118 A3
Mansfield Rd. Blid 118 C4
Mansfield Rd. Brin 143 F2
Mansfield Rd. Cuck 60 A2
Mansfield Rd. East 143 F2
Mansfield Rd. Edin 120 B3
Mansfield Rd. Edwin 75 F1
Mansfield Rd. Edwin 76 A1
Mansfield Rd. Farns 119 E4
Mansfield Rd. Glap 86 B4
Mansfield Rd. Hean 143 D1
Mansfield Rd. Mans 88 B1
Mansfield Rd. Mar War 73 F1
Mansfield Rd. N Clip 90 A3
Mansfield Rd. Nott 161 E2
Mansfield Rd. Oll 76 C2
Mansfield Rd. Papp 132 A2
Mansfield Rd. Raven 116 C1
Mansfield Rd. Raven 116 C2
Mansfield Rd. Raven 132 A2
Mansfield Rd. S in A 100 C3
Mansfield Rd. S in A 101 D2
Mansfield Rd. S Norm 113 E3
Mansfield Rd. Sels 128 C4
Mansfield Rd. Sels 129 D2
Mansfield Rd. Tibs 99 D4
Mansfield Rd. Work 46 A4
Mansfield St. Nott 161 E1
Manthorpe Cres. Nott 161 F2
Manthorpe House. Bald 140 C2
Manthorpe Way. Bald 140 C2
Manton Cl. Rain 118 A4
Manton Cres. Nott 184 A4
Manton Cres. Work 36 A1
Manton Dale. Work 36 A1
Manton Villas. Work 36 B1
Manvers Cres. Edwin 75 F1
Manvers Ct. Nott 173 F2
Manvers Gr. R on T 175 F2
Manvers Rd. Ret 39 E3
Manvers Rd. W Brid 185 F3
Manvers St. Carl 175 D3
Manvers St. Mans 88 A2
Manvers St. Mans 102 A4
Manvers St. Mar War 73 D2
Manvers St. Mar War 74 A2
Manvers St. Nott 173 F2
Manvers St. Work 35 F2
Manvers View. Boug 77 F3
Manville Cl. Bees 171 D2
Manville Cl. Nott 172 B3
Maori Ave. Huck 145 E3
Maple Ave. Bees 184 A3
Maple Ave. Sand 182 A4
Maple Cl. E Lea 214 B4
Maple Cl. Gain 15 D2
Maple Cl. Keyw 198 A1
Maple Cl. Mans 88 C1
Maple Cl. R on T 175 F1
Maple Cl. Tux 66 A1
Maple Cres. K-in-A 114 C3
Maple Dr. Carl 163 D1
Maple Dr. Elk 50 A2
Maple Dr. Huck 145 F3
Maple Dr. Nuth 159 E3
Maple Dr. S Norm 113 D2
Maple Dr. Work 36 A4
Maple Gr. Baw 9 F4
Maple Gr. Glap 86 A4
Maple Gr. N-on-T 139 F2
Maplebeck Ave. Mar War 74 B4
Maplebeck Rd. Arn 162 A4
Maplebeck Rd. Caun 108 C3
Mapledene Cres. Nott 171 E2
Maples St. Nott 172 C4
Maplestead Ave. Nott 185 D3
Mapletoft Ave. Mans 88 A3
Mapleton Way. S in A 101 D2
Mapperley Cres. Nott 161 F1
Mapperley Hall Dr. Nott 161 E1
Mapperley Orch. Arn 162 B4
Mapperley Park Dr. Nott 173 E4
Mapperley Plains. Arn 162 B3
Mapperley Rd. Nott 173 E4
Mapperley Rise. Nott 161 F1
Mapperley Rise. Nott 161 F2
Mapperley St. Nott 161 E1
Mappleton Dr. Mans 103 D3
Mapplewells Cres. S in A 100 A1
Mapplewells Rd. S in A 100 B1
March Cl. Nott 160 C4
Marches Cl. Huck 145 F2
Marchwood Cl. Nott 172 B3
Margaret Ave. Lo Ea 182 C1
Margaret Ave. Sand 182 A2
Margaret Cres. Carl 162 C1
Margaret Pl. Bing 177 E3
Margaret's Ct. Bees 183 D4
Marhill Rd. Carl 174 C4
Marie Gdns. Huck 146 A3
Marina Ave. Bees 183 F3
Mariner Ct. Nott 160 A3
Marion Ave. Huck 131 E1
Marion Ave. K-in-A 115 D1
Marion Murdoch Ct. Carl 162 C1
Maris Cl. Nott 184 B1
Maris Dr. Bu Jo 163 F2
Marjorie St. Rhod 35 D2
Mark La. E Mark 65 F3
Mark St. Sand 182 B3
Market Cl. S Norm 113 D3
Market Cl. Shireb 72 C2
Market Pl. Bing 177 F2
Market Pl. Gain 24 B4
Market Pl. Huck 146 A4
Market Pl. Lo Ea 193 F4
Market Pl. Lough 220 A2
Market Pl. Mans 88 B2
Market Pl. Mans 102 A4
Market Pl. Nott 160 A4
Market Pl. Nott 160 B4
Market Pl. Oll 77 D2
Market Pl. Ret 39 F4
Market Pl. S in A 99 F2
Market Pl. S in A 100 C1
Market Pl. S Norm 113 D3
Market Pl. South 136 C4
Market Pl. Tick 8 A4
Market Pl. Tux 65 F2
Market Pl. Work 35 F1
Market Place. Kegw 203 E1
Market Side. Nott 160 A4
Market St. Bing 177 F2
Market St. Bott 181 D1
Market St. Gain 24 B4
Market St. Lough 220 A2
Market St. Mans 102 A4
Market St. Nott 173 E2
Market St. S in A 99 F2
Market St. S in A 100 C1
Market St. S Norm 113 D3
Market St. Shireb 72 C2
Market St. Work 35 F2
Markham Ave. N-on-T 125 D2
Markham Cres. Nott 161 E2
Markham Pl. Mans 101 E4
Markham Rd. Bees 171 E1
Markham Rd. Lan 16 C2
Markham Rd. Tux 65 F2
Markham St. News 130 B3
Markhams The. Oll 77 D2
Markland La. Elmt 58 A4
Marklew Cl. Blid 118 A3
Markwick Cl. N-on-T 140 B4
Marl Rd. R on T 176 A2
Marlborough Cl. N-on-T 139 E3
Marlborough Rd. Arn 161 F3
Marlborough Rd. Bees 183 F4
Marlborough Rd. K-in-A 115 D3
Marlborough Rd. Lo Ea 182 C1
Marlborough Rd. Mans 87 F1
Marlborough St. Gain 24 B4
Marldon Cl. Nott 171 E3
Marle Pit Hill. Su Bo 213 D4
Marlock Cl. Fisk 137 F2
Marlow Ave. Nott 160 C1
Marlow Rd. Gain 15 F1
Marlowe Dr. Bald 140 B2
Marlowe Gdns. Work 36 A2
Marlwood. Cotg 188 A1
Marmion Rd. Nott 174 A3
Marnham Dr. Nott 161 F1
Marnham Rd. Tux 66 B1
Marple Sq. Nott 173 E3
Marples Ave. Mans 88 C3
Marquis Ave. Bald 140 B2
Marquis Gdns. Ret 40 A2
Marquis Rd. Ne Br 219 D3
Marriots La. Blid 117 F2
Marriott Ave. Bees 183 D3
Marriott Ave. Mans 101 F4
Marriott Cl. Bees 183 D3
Marsh La. Farn 139 D3
Marsh La. Mist 7 E1
Marsh La. N Musk 110 C1
Marsh La. Saundby 23 E3
Marsh Rd. Walker 14 B3
Marsh's Paddock. Hick 210 B3
Marshall Ave. K-in-A 115 E2
Marshall Ct. Bald 140 C2
Marshall Dr. Bees 183 D4
Marshall Hill Dr. Carl 162 A1
Marshall Rd. Carl 162 A1
Marshall Rd. Cr Bi 189 D2
Marshall St. Hean 143 D1
Marshall St. Nott 161 E1
Marshall Terr. S in A 100 B3
Marston Ave. Mar War 74 B4
Marston Cl. Bald 140 B2
Marston Rd. Nott 174 A4
Martin Cl. Nott 160 A4
Martin Ct. Nott 160 A4
Martin La. Baw 9 F4
Martindale Cl. Gam 186 B4
Martins Hill. Carl 174 C4
Martlet Way. Work 47 D4
Marton Rd. Bees 183 E2
Marton Rd. N-on-T 140 A3
Marton Rd. Nott 146 B1
Martyn Ave. S in A 100 C1
Marvin Rd. Bees 183 F3
Marwood Cres. Carl 162 B1
Marwood Rd. Carl 162 B1
Mary Rd. East 144 A1
Mary St. K-in-A 115 D3
Mary St. Rhod 35 D2
Mary St. Scarc 59 D1
Maryfield Cl. Ret 29 F1
Maryland Ct. Staple 170 C1
Masefield Cres. Bald 140 B2
Masefield Pl. Work 36 A2
Mason St. S in A 101 D2
Masonic Pl. Nott 173 D3
Massey Cl. Bu Jo 163 F2
Massey Gdns. Nott 173 F3
Massey St. N-on-T 140 A4
Masson Ct. Nott 147 D1
Matlock Ave. Mans 102 A3
Matlock Ct. Nott 173 E3
Matlock St. Carl 174 C4
Mattersey Ct. Mans 88 A1
Mattersey Rd. Ever 11 E1
Mattersey Rd. Lound 20 A1
Mattersey Rd. Ran 19 E3
Mattersey Rd. Sutt 29 D4
Matthews Ct. Staple 170 C1
Mattingly Rd. Nott 160 A3
Mattley Ave. Ann Wo 115 D1
Maud St. Nott 161 D1
Maun Ave. K-in-A 115 D4
Maun Ave. Nott 172 B3
Maun Cl. Mans 101 F2
Maun Gn. N-on-T 125 D1
Maun Way. Mans 101 F2
Maundale Ave. S in A 101 D2
Maunleigh. Mans 88 C1
Maunside Ave. S in A 101 D1
Maunside. Mans 101 F2
Maurice Dr. Nott 161 F2
Mavis Ave. Raven 117 D1
Maws La. Kim 158 C4
Maxtoke Rd. Nott 173 D2
Maxwell Cl. Nott 172 C2
May Ave. Nott 171 F2
May Ct. Nott 161 D1
May Fair Pl. Tux 66 A1
May Lodge Dr. Ruff 91 F3
May St. Ilk 157 F2
Maycroft Gdns. Carl 174 A4
Mayes Rise. Bes Vil 146 C2
Mayfair Ave. Mans 102 B3
Mayfair Cl. Har 8 C2
Mayfair Ct. Nott 160 C1
Mayfair Gdns. Nott 160 C3
Mayfield Ave. Bu Jo 163 F3
Mayfield Ave. Gain 15 D2
Mayfield Cl. Mans 103 D3
Mayfield Ct. Nott 173 E1
Mayfield Dr. Lough 220 A1
Mayfield Dr. Staple 170 C1
Mayfield Gr. Lo Ea 182 C1
Mayfield Pl. S in A 100 B1
Mayfield Rd. Carl 174 A4
Mayfield St. K-in-A 114 B2
Mayfield Terr. Mar War 74 A2
Mayflower Ave. Scro 10 A1
Mayflower Cl. Baw 10 A4
Mayflower Cl. Lea 24 C2
Mayflower Cl. W Brid 186 A4
Mayflower Ct. Shireb 72 C2
Mayflower Rd. Greas 158 B4
Mayhall Ave. Mans 88 A2
Mayland Cl. Nott 171 E3
Mayo Rd. Nott 161 D1
Maypole Ct. Wellow 92 C4
Maypole Rd. Wellow 92 C4
Maypole Yd. Nott 173 E3
Maypole. Nott 184 C2
Mays Ave. Carl 174 B3
Mays Cl. Carl 174 B3
Mays La. Sax 57 E2
Maythorn Cl. W Brid 185 E2
Maythorn Gr. Edwin 76 A2
Maythorne Cl. Bald 140 B3
Maythorne Wlk. Nott 161 E4
Mcintosh Rd. Carl 162 B2
Meade Dr. Work 36 A4
Meadow Ave. Lough 220 A3
Meadow Ave. Mans 102 B3
Meadow Bank. Mans 88 C3
Meadow Cl. Aslo 179 D3
Meadow Cl. Farns 120 A3
Meadow Cl. Greas 143 F2
Meadow Cl. Huck 145 E3
Meadow Cl. K-in-A 114 C3
Meadow Cl. N Musk 110 C1
Meadow Cl. Nott 173 F1
Meadow Cl. Ret 29 F1
Meadow Cl. Tibs 99 D4
Meadow Cotts. Carl 174 C4
Meadow Cotts. Mans 88 B2
Meadow Ct. Nott 173 F1
Meadow Ct. S Norm 113 D2
Meadow Dr. Keyw 198 A2
Meadow Dr. Mist 6 C1
Meadow Dr. S in A 100 B2
Meadow Dr. Tick 8 B4
Meadow Dr. Work 35 E1
Meadow End. Goth 195 D1
Meadow End. R on T 176 B2
Meadow Gdns. Bees 183 F2
Meadow Gr. Newt 99 D2
Meadow Gr. Nott 173 F1
Meadow La Ind Est. Lough 220 A3
Meadow La. Bees 183 F2
Meadow La. Both 63 F4
Meadow La. Bu Jo 163 F2
Meadow La. Girt 82 C2
Meadow La. Lo Ea 193 F4
Meadow La. Lough 220 A4
Meadow La. N Sca 83 F1
Meadow La. Nott 173 F1
Meadow La. S Norm 113 D4
Meadow La. Sons 220 A4
Meadow La. West 81 D2
Meadow Pl. Mar War 74 A2
Meadow Rd. Awsw 158 B3
Meadow Rd. Bald 140 B2
Meadow Rd. Bees 184 A2
Meadow Rd. Blid 118 A3
Meadow Rd. Carl 174 C4
Meadow Rd. Ran 19 E3
Meadow Rd. Work 35 E1
Meadow Rise. Nott 159 F3
Meadow Rise. Sax 57 D2
Meadow St. Ilk 157 F1
Meadow The. Ret 39 F3
Meadow View. South 121 F1
Meadow Way. Har 8 C3
Meadow Way. Kinou 199 F1
Meadowbank Way. East 143 E2
Meadows La. Hose 201 E1
Meadows The. Beck 23 D4
Meadows The. Farn 139 D3
Meadows The. S Whea 31 F4
Meadows The. Woodb 149 D2
Meadows Way. Nott 173 E1
Meadowsweet Hill. Bing 177 E2
Meadowvale Cres. Nott 184 C1
Medawar Cl. Nott 184 B1
Meden Ave. Mar War 74 B3
Meden Ave. Plea 86 C4
Meden Bank. Both 63 F4
Meden Bank. Mans 87 D3
Meden Bank. S in A 100 B3
Meden Cl. Mans 87 D3
Meden Cl. Nott 184 C2
Meden Cres. S in A 100 B2
Meden Gdns. Nott 172 B4
Meden Glen. Mar War 74 B3
Meden Rd. Mans 88 B2
Meden Sq. Mans 87 D3
Medina Dr. Toll 186 C1
Medway Cl. Bees 183 E3
Medway. Ret 29 E1
Meeks Rd. Arn 162 A4
Meer Rd. Bees 183 D3
Meering Ave. N-on-T 125 D2
Meering Cl. Coll 98 A1
Meerings The. S on T 81 F1
Meeting House Cl. E Lea 205 F1
Meetinghouse La. S Lev 42 A3
Melbourne Ct. Mans 103 D3
Melbourne Ct. Nott 160 B1
Melbourne Gr. Har 8 C2
Melbourne Rd. Nott 160 B1
Melbourne Rd. Staple 170 C1
Melbourne Rd. W Brid 174 A1
Melbourne St. Mans 88 B3
Melbourne St. Sels 129 D3

Melbury Rd. Arn 162 A3
Melbury Rd. Nott 171 E4
Meldreth Rd. Nott 171 F4
Meldrum Cres. N-on-T 139 F3
Melford Hall Dr. W Brid 185 E2
Melford Rd. Nott 171 E4
Melksham Rd. Nott 161 E4
Mellish Rd. Lan 16 C1
Mellors Rd. Mans 101 E4
Mellors Rd. Nott 147 F1
Mellors Rd. W Brid 185 F3
Melrose Ave. Bees 184 A3
Melrose Ave. Mans 102 B3
Melrose Ave. Nott 161 E2
Melrose Gdns. W Brid 185 E2
Melrose Rd. Gain 15 E1
Melrose St. Nott 161 E2
Melrose Wlk. Work 35 F1
Melton Ave. Plum 197 F4
Melton Ct. Sand 182 A3
Melton Gdns. W Brid 186 A2
Melton Gr. W Brid 185 F4
Melton La. Su Bo 204 B1
Melton Rd. E Lea 214 C3
Melton Rd. Hick 209 E2
Melton Rd. Lo Cl 211 D1
Melton Rd. N-on-W 198 B2
Melton Rd. Remp 215 E3
Melton Rd. S on S 214 C3
Melton Rd. S-on-W 198 B2
Melton Rd. Toll 197 F4
Melton Rd. Up Br 210 A1
Melton Rd. W Brid 186 A2
Melton Rd. Widm 208 C4
Melton Way. Mans 101 F2
Melville Ct. Nott 173 E4
Melville Gdns. Nott 173 F3
Melville St. Nott 173 E2
Melvyn Dr. Bing 177 F2
Memorial Ave. Work 35 F1
Mendip Cl. Lo Ea 182 A1
Mendip Ct. C in L 25 F4
Mendip Ct. Nott 160 C4
Mensing Ave. Cotg 187 F2
Mercer Rd. Gain 15 D1
Merchant St. Nott 160 A4
Merchant St. Shireb 73 D2
Mercia Ave. Cr Bi 189 D2
Mercia Cl. Work 36 A4
Mercia Rd. N-on-T 139 F3
Mercury Cl. Nott 160 C3
Mere Ave. Calv 148 C4
Mere Cl. Calv 148 C4
Meredith Cl. Nott 173 D1
Meredith Ct. Staple 170 C1
Meregill Cl. Nott 146 C1
Merevale Ave. Nott 184 C2
Merevale Cl. Lowd 150 C1
Meriac Cl. Nott 160 C4
Meriden Ave. Nott 184 A4
Merlin Cl. Nott 184 C1
Merlin Dr. Huck 145 F2
Merrick Dr. Work 36 B2
Merrivale Ct. Nott 173 E4
Merryvale Dr. Mans 101 E3
Merryweather Cl. Edwin 91 E4
Merryweather Cl. South 121 F1
Mersey St. Nott 160 A4
Merton Ave. Ret 29 F1
Merton Cl. Arn 148 A1
Merton Ct. Staple 170 C1
Metcalf Cl. Bils 105 F4
Metcalf Rd. Greas 144 A2
Metcalfe Cl. South 136 C4
Methuen St. Mans 102 C3
Metro Ave. Newt 99 D2
Mettham St. Nott 172 C2
Mews La. Calv 148 C4
Meynell Gr. Nott 161 D1
Meynell Rd. Lo Ea 193 E3
Meyrick Rd. N-on-T 125 D1
Miall Ct. Nott 172 C3
Micklebarrow Cl. South 136 B4
Mickleborough Ave. Nott 174 A4
Mickleborough Way. W Brid 185 E2
Mickledale Cl. Bils 105 F4
Mickledale La. Bils 105 F4
Mickleden Cl. Nott 173 D1
Mickledon Cl. Lo Ea 193 D4
Middle Ave. Carl 174 B4
Middle Furlong Gdns. Nott 173 D1
Middle Furlong Mews. Nott 173 D1
Middle Gate. N-on-T 139 F4
Middle Hill. Nott 173 E4
Middle Holme La. S on T 97 D4
Middle La. Bees 183 F3
Middle La. Morton 137 E2
Middle La. Ne Br 219 E4
Middle Pavement. Nott 173 E2
Middle St. B-le-V 192 B1
Middle St. Bees 183 F3
Middle St. Bees 184 A3
Middle St. Hose 211 F4
Middle St. Miss 4 B1
Middle Wood La. Miss 4 B3
Middlebeck Ave. Arn 162 B4
Middlebeck Dr. Arn 162 B4
Middlebridge Rd. G on H 12 C2
Middlebrook Rd. Sels 129 D2
Middledale Rd. Carl 174 B3
Middlefell Way. Nott 184 B1
Middlefield La. Gain 24 C4
Middlefield Rd. N Whea 31 F4
Middlegate Field Dr. Whit 45 D3
Middleton Bvd. Nott 172 B2
Middleton Cl. Nuth 159 E3
Middleton Cres. Bees 171 F1
Middleton Ct. Mans 103 D3
Middleton Ct. Oll 77 E3
Middleton Pl. Lough 220 A1
Middleton Rd. Ilk 170 A3
Middleton Rd. Mans 88 B3
Middleton Rd. N-on-T 125 E2
Middleton St. Awsw 158 A2
Middleton St. Bees 183 F4
Middleton St. Coss 158 A1
Middleton St. Nott 172 C3
Midfield Rd. Ann Wo 115 D1
Midhurst Cl. Bees 183 D2
Midhurst Way. Nott 184 C1
Midlame Gdns. Nott 159 F4
Midland Ave. Carl 175 D4
Midland Ave. Nott 172 C2
Midland Ave. Staple 182 B3
Midland Cres. Carl 174 C4
Midland Gr. Carl 175 D4
Midland Rd. Carl 174 C4
Midland Rd. East 143 F1
Midland St. Lo Ea 193 F4
Midway The. Nott 184 C4
Midworth St. Mans 102 A3
Mikado Rd. Lo Ea 193 E3
Milburn Gr. Bing 177 E2
Mildenhall Cres. Nott 161 E4
Mile End Rd. Carl 174 C3
Miles Yd. Lough 220 A2
Milford Ave. Lo Ea 182 A2
Milford Cl. Nott 160 A4
Milford Cres. Mans 101 E4
Milford Ct. Arn 161 E3
Milford Dr. Ilk 157 E2
Milford Dr. Nott 174 B3
Milford Dr. Nott 174 B4
Mill Baulk Rd. Walker 14 A3
Mill Cl. N Le Ha 32 B1
Mill Cl. S in A 100 A2
Mill Cl. S on T 96 C4
Mill Cres. Arn 161 F4
Mill Cres. Whit 45 D3
Mill Croft. S in A 100 C1
Mill Field Cl. Bu Jo 163 F2
Mill Field Cl. Harby 70 B1
Mill Gate. E Brid 165 E2
Mill Gate. N-on-T 139 F4
Mill Gdns. Work 35 E1
Mill Green. N-on-T 140 A4
Mill Heyes. E Brid 165 E2
Mill Hill. G on H 12 B1
Mill La. Al Hu 85 E4
Mill La. Ann Wo 114 C1
Mill La. Arn 161 F4
Mill La. Aslo 178 C4
Mill La. Caun 109 D3
Mill La. Coss 158 B1
Mill La. Cotg 187 F2
Mill La. E Lea 214 C4
Mill La. Eagle 84 C2
Mill La. Edwin 76 A1
Mill La. K-in-A 114 C1
Mill La. Kegw 203 E1
Mill La. Lamb 163 D4
Mill La. Lo Cl 211 E2
Mill La. Lo Wh 212 B2
Mill La. Lough 220 B3
Mill La. Mort 15 E3
Mill La. N Clift 68 C3
Mill La. N Le Ha 42 A4
Mill La. N Musk 110 C1
Mill La. N-on-T 139 F4
Mill La. Nor on T 81 E4
Mill La. Orst 180 A4
Mill La. Pinx 113 E1
Mill La. S in A 100 A1
Mill La. S Lev 42 B4
Mill La. Sand 182 B3
Mill La. Sax 57 D2
Mill La. Scarr 178 C4
Mill La. Scro 10 A2
Mill La. Upton 137 F4
Mill La. W Dray 51 D1
Mill La. W-on-W 217 E4
Mill La. Wale 63 F1
Mill La. Walker 13 F2
Mill La. Whit 45 D3
Mill Meadow View. Blyth 18 A2
Mill Rd. East 144 A2
Mill Rd. Elst 153 F2
Mill Rd. Hean 157 D4
Mill Rd. Staple 182 B4
Mill St. Ilk 157 F1
Mill St. Mans 102 B3
Mill St. Nott 160 B2
Mill St. S in A 100 C1
Mill St. Work 35 F2
Mill Wlk. Whit 45 D3
Mill Yd. Bees 183 F3
Mill Yd. Huck 146 A4
Millash La. Whit 45 D2
Millbank Cl. Ship 157 E2
Millbank. Hean 157 D4
Millbaulk La. Knee 93 F4
Millbeck Ave. Nott 171 E2
Millbeck Cl. Gam 186 B3
Milldale Cl. Nott 184 B1
Milldale Rd. Farns 120 A3
Milldale Rd. Lo Ea 193 D3
Milldale Wlk. S in A 100 B2
Miller Hives Cl. Cotg 187 F2
Miller's La. Cost 206 B1
Millers Bridge. Cotg 187 F1
Millers Cl. Shel 164 B1
Millers Ct. Nott 172 C3
Millers Way. Ret 39 E4
Millersdale Ave. Ilk 157 F3
Millersdale Ave. Mans 101 F2
Millfield Ave. Sax 57 D2
Millfield Cl. Ret 39 F2
Millfield Rd. Ilk 170 A4
Millfield Rd. Kim 158 C4
Millfield Rd. S Lev 42 A3
Millfield View. Work 35 E1
Millicent Gr. W Brid 185 F4
Millicent Rd. W Brid 185 F4
Millingdon Ave. Nuth 159 E2
Millman Way. Ret 29 E1
Mills Dr. N-on-T 139 E3
Millview Cl. Nott 173 F2
Millview Ct. Nott 173 F2
Millway. Mans 88 B1
Milne Ave. Bir 9 E2
Milne Dr. Bir 9 E2
Milne Gr. Bir 9 E2
Milne Rd. Bir 9 E2
Milner Rd. Lo Ea 193 E4
Milner Rd. Nott 161 E1
Milner St. N-on-T 140 A4
Milner St. S in A 101 D3
Milnercroft Green. Ret 29 E1
Milnercroft. Ret 29 E1
Milnhay Rd. Hean 143 E1
Milnhay Rd. La Mi 143 E1
Milton Ave. Ilk 157 F2
Milton Cl. S in A 101 D2
Milton Cres. Bees 183 E1
Milton Cres. Raven 117 D1
Milton Ct. Arn 162 A4
Milton Dr. Raven 117 D1
Milton Dr. Work 36 A2
Milton Rd. Gain 15 F1
Milton Rd. Ilk 157 F2
Milton Rd. W Mark 65 D3
Milton Rise. Huck 145 E3
Milton St. Bald 140 B3
Milton St. Ilk 157 F2
Milton St. K-in-A 115 D3
Milton St. Lo Ea 193 E4
Milton St. Mans 102 A4
Milton St. Nott 173 E3
Milton Wlk. Work 36 A2
Milverton Rd. Nott 161 E4
Mimosa Cl. Nott 184 B1
Minerva St. Nott 160 A4
Minster Cl. Huck 146 A4
Minster Cl. K-in-A 114 C3
Minster Gdns. East 144 A1
Minster Rd. Mist 6 C1
Minver Cres. Nott 160 A1
Mirberry Mews. Nott 172 C2
Mire La. Sutt 28 C3
Misk Hollows. Huck 145 F4
Misk View. East 144 A1
Mission St. Nott 161 F1
Misterton Ct. Mans 88 A1
Mitchel Ave. Codd 125 F1
Mitchell Ave. La Mi 143 D2
Mitchell Cl. Nott 160 A3
Mitchell St. Lo Ea 193 F4
Mitchell Terr. Ilk 170 A3
Mob La. W-on-W 217 E4
Model Village. Elmt 58 C4
Moffat Cl. Nott 173 F4
Moira St. Lough 220 A2
Mollington Sq. Nott 160 A2
Mona Rd. W Brid 174 A1
Mona St. Bees 184 A3
Monarch Way. Lough 220 A3
Monckton Rd. Bir 9 E2
Monckton Rd. Ret 39 E4
Monk's La. Goth 195 D1
Monks Cl. Ilk 170 A4
Monks Meadow. E Lea 205 F1
Monksway. Nott 185 D2
Monkton Cl. Ship 157 E2
Monkton Dr. Nott 171 F4
Monkton Dr. South 121 F1
Monkwood Cl. Coll 98 A1
Monmouth Cl. Nott 171 D2
Monmouth Rd. Work 36 A3
Monroe Wlk. Nott 161 D4
Monsaldale Cl. Lo Ea 193 D3
Monsall Ave. Ilk 157 F3
Monsall St. Nott 160 C1
Monsall St. Nott 161 D1
Monsell Dr. Nott 147 F1
Montague Rd. Huck 146 A4
Montague St. Bees 183 F4
Montague St. Mans 102 C3
Montague St. Nott 160 B4
Montfort Cres. Nott 161 E2
Montfort St. Nott 173 D3
Montgomery Rd. N-on-T 140 A3
Montgomery St. Nott 173 D3
Montpelier Rd. Nott 172 C1
Montrose Ct. Staple 170 C1
Montrose Sq. Mans 88 A3
Montrose. Work 36 A3
Monyash Cl. Ilk 157 F2
Moor Bridge. Nott 146 B1
Moor Farm Inn La. Bees 171 D1
Moor La. Aslo 178 B3
Moor La. Bees 171 D2
Moor La. Best 98 B3
Moor La. Bing 177 F3
Moor La. Blyth 18 B1
Moor La. Bunn 206 B4
Moor La. Dry Do 169 F3
Moor La. E Sto 154 A3
Moor La. Epp 149 E3
Moor La. Goth 205 E4
Moor La. Lough 220 B2
Moor La. Mans 101 F3
Moor La. Morton 137 E2
Moor La. N on S 213 E2
Moor La. Rudd 196 B3
Moor La. S Clift 68 C1
Moor La. S Clift 69 E2
Moor La. Scarc 72 A4
Moor La. Scarr 178 B3
Moor La. Stat 202 C3
Moor La. Syer 153 E2
Moor La. Thor 69 E2
Moor La. Torw 18 B1
Moor La. Woodb 149 E3
Moor Rd. Brin 143 F4
Moor Rd. Calv 149 D4
Moor Rd. Coll 98 A1
Moor Rd. Huck 146 C3
Moor Rd. Nott 159 E1
Moor St. Carl 174 C4
Moor St. Carl 175 D4
Moor St. Mans 102 A3
Moor Top Rd. Har 8 C3
Moorbridge Cotts. Nott 146 B1
Moorbridge La. Staple 170 B1
Moorbridge Rd. Bing 177 F3
Moore Ave. Kegw 203 E2
Moore Cl. E Lea 205 F1
Moore Cl. W Brid 174 A1
Moore Gate. Bees 184 A3
Moore Rd. Carl 162 A1
Moores Ave. Sand 182 B4
Moorfield Cres. Sand 182 A3
Moorfield Ct. Staple 170 C1
Moorfield La. Scarc 58 C2
Moorfield Pl. Mar War 74 B3
Moorfields Ave. East 143 F2
Moorgate Ave. Plea 86 C4
Moorgate Park. Ret 39 F4
Moorgate St. Nott 173 D3
Moorgreen. Greas 144 B2
Moorhaigh La. Mans 87 D2
Moorhouse Rd. Lax 80 B2
Moorhouse Rd. Nott 171 F3
Moorhouse Rd. West 80 B2
Moorings The. Nott 172 C1
Moorland Ave. Staple 182 B3
Moorland Ave. Walker 13 F3
Moorland Cl. Mans 101 F4
Moorland Cl. Walker 13 F3
Moorland La. Mans 101 F4
Moorland Way. Mans 103 D3
Moorland Wlk. Walker 13 F3
Moorsholm Dr. Nott 171 E2
Moray Ct. Kim 158 C4
Moray Sq. Mans 101 E3
Morden Cl. Nott 171 E4
Morden Rd. Greas 158 B4
Moreland Ct. Carl 174 B4
Moreland St. Nott 173 F2
Moreland Terr. Nott 173 F2
Morello Ave. Carl 174 C4
Moreton Rd. Nott 195 F4
Morgan Mews. Nott 184 C1
Morgans Cl. Codd 126 A1
Morkinshire Cres. Cotg 187 F2
Morley Ave. Nott 161 F1
Morley Ave. Ret 29 E1
Morley Cl. Mans 103 D3
Morley Ct. Nott 173 F3
Morley Dr. Ilk 157 E2
Morley Rd. Carl 162 A1
Morley St. Arn 161 F3
Morley St. Gain 24 B4
Morley St. K-in-A 115 D2
Morley St. Lough 220 B3
Morley St. S in A 100 B3
Morley St. S in A 100 C2
Mornington Cl. Sand 182 B3
Mornington Cres. Nuth 159 E2
Morrell Bank. Nott 160 C3
Morris Cl. Lough 220 B2
Morris Rd. Nott 159 E1
Morris St. Carl 175 D4
Morton Cl. Mans 103 D3
Morton Cl. Mort 15 D2
Morton Gdns. R on T 176 B2
Morton Rd. Gain 15 E2
Morton St. Mans 87 F1
Morton Terr. Gain 15 E1
Morval Rd. Nott 171 F4
Morven Ave. Huck 146 A3
Morven Ave. Mans 88 A1
Morven Ave. S in A 100 C1
Morven Rd. K-in-A 115 D3
Morven St. Elmt 58 C4
Morven Terr. Mar War 74 A2
Mosborough Rd. S in A 100 A1
Moseley Rd. Ann Wo 130 B4
Mosley St. Huck 146 A3
Mosley St. Nott 172 C4
Moss Cl. Bes Vil 147 E1
Moss Cl. E Brid 165 E2
Moss Rd. Huck 145 F4
Moss Rise. Carl 162 A1
Moss Side. Nott 185 D2
Mosscroft Ave. Nott 184 B1
Mossdale Rd. Mans 102 C4
Mossdale Rd. Nott 161 E3
Mosswood Cres. Nott 161 D4
Mottram Rd. Bees 183 E3
Moulton Cres. Bald 140 B2
Mount Ave. Work 35 F3
Mount Cl. Har 8 C3
Mount Cres. Mar War 74 B2
Mount Cres. S Norm 113 D2
Mount Ct. Bald 140 B2
Mount Hooton Rd. Nott 173 D3
Mount La. N-on-T 140 A4
Mount Milner. Mans 102 B3
Mount Pleasant Cl. Mart 44 B4
Mount Pleasant. Carl 174 C4
Mount Pleasant. Ilk 157 F2
Mount Pleasant. Keyw 198 A1
Mount Pleasant. Keyw 198 A2
Mount Pleasant. Lowd 150 B1
Mount Pleasant. Mans 102 A4
Mount Pleasant. Nott 160 C1
Mount Pleasant. R on T 175 F2
Mount Pleasant. Ret 39 F4
Mount Pleasant. S in A 100 C2
Mount Rd. Bald 140 B2
Mount St. Mans 88 A1
Mount St. Nott 160 C1
Mount St. Nott 173 D2
Mount St. Staple 182 C4
Mount The. Bes Vil 146 C2
Mount The. Carl 162 B1
Mount The. Mans 89 E2
Mount The. Nott 147 E1
Mount The. Nott 159 F1
Mount The. Staple 182 B3
Mount View Cl. Mans 102 B3
Mountbatten Ct. Ilk 157 F2
Mountbatten Gr. Carl 162 C1
Mountfield Ave. Sand 182 A2
Mountfield Dr. Nott 161 D4
Mountsorrel Dr. W Brid 186 A3
Mowbray Ct. Nott 173 E3
Mowbray Gdns. W Brid 185 F3
Mowbray Rise. Arn 161 F4
Mowbray Str. Gain 15 E1
Mowlands Cl. S in A 101 D1
Moyra Dr. Arn 161 E4
Mozart Cl. Nott 172 C3
Muir Ave. Toll 197 E4
Muirfield Cl. K-in-A 114 C4
Muirfield Rd. Bes Vil 147 D1
Muirfield Way. Mans 88 C3
Muirfield. Work 36 A3
Mulberry Cl. W Brid 185 D3
Mulberry Cres. C in L 25 F4
Mulberry Gdns. Nott 160 A4
Mulberry Gr. Huck 146 A2
Mumby Cl. N-on-T 125 D1
Mundella Rd. Nott 173 E1
Mundy St. Ilk 157 F1
Munford Circ. Nott 160 A2
Munks Ave. Huck 145 F4
Munt's Hill. Greas 144 A4
Murby Cres. Nott 160 A4
Murden Way. Bees 184 A3
Muriel Rd. Bees 183 F4
Muriel St. Nott 160 A4
Murray St. Mans 102 A3
Muschamp Terr. Mar War 74 A2
Mushill La. Wyme 216 B3
Muskham Ave. Ilk 157 F2
Muskham Ct. Mans 88 A1
Muskham La. Bath 110 B1
Muskham St. Nott 173 E1
Musters Cres. W Brid 185 F3
Musters Croft. Carl 174 C2
Musters Rd. Bing 177 E2
Musters Rd. News 130 B3
Musters Rd. Rudd 196 B3
Musters Rd. W Brid 185 F3
Musters Rd. W Brid 185 F4
Musters St. Shireb 73 D2
Musters Wlk. Nott 160 A4
Muston Cl. Nott 161 F1

Muston La. Bott 181 E1
Mutton La. Beck 23 D4
Muttonshire Hill. Gams 50 C3
Mynd The. Mans 88 C3
Myrtle Ave. Lo Ea 193 E3
Myrtle Ave. Nott 173 D4
Myrtle Ave. Staple 182 C3
Myrtle Cl. Shireb 72 B3
Myrtle Gr. Bees 184 A4
Myrtle Rd. Carl 174 B4
Myrtle St. Ret 39 E3
Myrtus Cl. Nott 184 B1

Nabbs La. Huck 145 F3
Nairn Cl. Arn 148 A1
Nairn Cl. Farns 119 F3
Nairn Mews. Carl 174 C4
Nan Sampson Bank. Blax 1 B4
Nansen St. Nott 160 B3
Naomi Cres. Nott 146 B1
Naomi Ct. Nott 146 B1
Narrow La. Baw 10 A4
Narrow La. Greas 145 D2
Narrow La. Hath 213 D1
Narrow La. Wyme 217 D1
Naseby Cl. Nott 160 C2
Naseby Dr. Lo Ea 193 F2
Nash Cl. Work 36 B2
Nathaniel Rd. Lo Ea 193 F3
Nathans La. Ho Pi 187 D4
Navenby Wlk. Nott 184 C1
Navigation Way. Lough 220 A3
Navigation Yd. N-on-T 139 F4
Naworth Cl. Nott 160 C3
Naylor Ave. Goth 195 D1
Naylor Ave. Lough 220 B1
Neal Ct. La Mi 143 D2
Neale St. Lo Ea 193 F4
Near Meadow. Lo Ea 193 F3
Nearsby Dr. W Brid 186 A3
Neburn Ct. Nott 172 B4
Needham Rd. Arn 162 A4
Needham St. Bing 177 F2
Needwood Ave. Staple 170 B1
Neeps Croft. Epp 150 A3
Neighwood Cl. Bees 182 C1
Nell Gwyn Cres. Bes Vil 147 E1
Nelper Cres. Ilk 170 A3
Nelson La. N Musk 110 C1
Nelson Rd. Arn 161 F4
Nelson Rd. Bald 140 A2
Nelson Rd. Bees 184 A2
Nelson Rd. Nott 160 B4
Nelson St. Gain 15 E1
Nelson St. Ilk 157 F2
Nelson St. Lo Ea 193 E3
Nelson St. Nott 173 E2
Nelson St. Ret 39 F3
Nene Cl. Huck 145 F2
Nene Wlk. Work 35 F4
Nesbitt St. S in A 100 C1
Nesfield Ct. Ilk 157 F1
Nesfield Rd. Ilk 157 F1
Neston Dr. Nott 160 B2
Nether Cl. Greas 143 F2
Nether Cl. Nott 174 A3
Nether Ct. Farns 120 A3
Nether St. Bees 184 A3
Nether St. Harb 202 A2
Nether Thorpe Rd. Th Sa 34 A3
Nethercross Dr. Mar War 74 B3
Netherfield La. Budby 61 E1
Netherfield La. Carl 175 D3
Netherfield La. Mar War 74 B4
Netherfield Rd. Lo Ea 193 E2
Netherfield Rd. Sand 182 A2
Nethergate. Nott 184 B1
Netherholme Shop Cntre. Work 35 F2
Netherton Pl. Work 36 A1
Netherton Rd. Work 47 D4
Nettle Croft. Tick 8 B4
Nettlecliff Wlk. Nott 160 C4
Nevile Dr. Kinou 200 A1
Neville Rd. Calv 148 C3
Neville Sadler Ct. Bees 184 A4
New Hill. Wale 64 A1
New Brickyard La. Kegw 203 E1
New Causeway. B-le-V 192 B1
New Cl. Blid 118 A3
New Cl. K-in-A 115 D3
New Cottages. Cuck 59 F2
New Cross St. S in A 100 C2
New Derby Rd. East 143 E1
New Eaton Rd. Staple 182 C3
New England Way. Mans 87 E2
New Fall St. S in A 99 F2
New Farm La. Nuth 159 E3
New Hill. Farns 119 F3
New Holles Ct. Work 35 F1
New Inn Wlk. Ret 39 F3
New King St. Lough 220 B2
New La. Blid 117 F3
New La. Blid 118 A3
New La. Girt 83 D2
New La. Newt 99 E1
New La. S in A 100 B3
New La. Scarr 178 C3
New Linden St. Shireb 73 D2
New Mill La. Mans 88 C2
New Pl. Ret 40 A4
New Rd. B in F 194 C3
New Rd. Blid 118 A3
New Rd. Bils 105 F3
New Rd. Co Ba 189 E1
New Rd. Fir 16 A3
New Rd. Greas 144 C3
New Rd. Hawk 167 E2
New Rd. Morton 137 E3
New Rd. Oxt 134 A2
New Rd. R on T 175 F2
New Rd. S in V 169 E2
New Rd. Staple 170 B1
New Rd. Tick 8 A4
New Rd. Tith 189 E1
New Rd. Tres 42 B2
New Row. Carl 174 B4
New Row. Sels 128 A3
New St. Gain 15 E1
New St. K-in-A 115 D2
New St. Kegw 203 F2
New St. Lo Ea 193 F4
New St. Lough 220 A2
New St. N-on-T 140 A4
New St. Newt 99 D2
New St. Nott 173 D4
New St. Ret 39 F3
New St. S in A 99 F2
New St. S in A 100 C1
New St. S Norm 113 D3
New St. S Norm 113 E4
New Terr. Plea 86 C3
New Terr. Sand 182 A3
New Tythe St. Lo Ea 193 F4
New Vale Rd. Carl 174 C3
Newall Dr. Matt 11 D1
Newark Cl. Mans 102 C1
Newark Cres. Nott 173 F2
Newark Dr. Mans 102 C1
Newark Rd. B in W 141 E3
Newark Rd. Boug 77 E1
Newark Rd. Caun 109 D2
Newark Rd. Codd 125 F1
Newark Rd. Eakr 92 C1
Newark Rd. Fent 55 D4
Newark Rd. Kirk 120 C4
Newark Rd. Oll 77 D2
Newark Rd. S in A 101 E1
Newark Rd. South 121 F1
Newark Rd. Stap 127 E4
Newark Rd. Staple 112 C2
Newark Rd. Tux 65 F1
Newark Rd. Wellow 77 E1
Newark St. Nott 173 F2
Newark Way. Mans 103 D1
Newbarn Cl. Shireb 72 B1
Newberry Cl. Cr Bi 189 D2
Newbery Ave. Lo Ea 193 F3
Newbery Cl. Edwin 76 A1
Newbold Way. Kinou 199 F1
Newbound La. S in A 86 B1
Newboundmill La. Plea 87 D3
Newbury Cl. Arn 162 A2
Newbury Ct. Nott 173 D4
Newbury Mews. Work 35 F1
Newcastle Ave. Bees 183 F3
Newcastle Ave. Carl 162 C1
Newcastle Ave. N-on-T 140 A3
Newcastle Ave. Work 35 F1
Newcastle Cir. Nott 173 D2
Newcastle Dr. Nott 173 D3
Newcastle St. Mans 88 A2
Newcastle St. Mans 102 A4
Newcastle St. Mar War 74 A2
Newcastle St. Nott 160 B4
Newcastle St. Nott 173 E3
Newcastle St. S in A 100 A2
Newcastle St. Tux 65 F1
Newcastle St. Work 35 F1
Newcombe Dr. Arn 162 B4
Newdigate Rd. Kim 159 D4
Newdigate St. Ilk 170 A3
Newdigate St. Kim 159 D3
Newdigate St. Nott 173 D3
Newdigate Villas. Nott 173 D3
Newfield La. Sibt 167 F3
Newfield Rd. Nott 161 D2
Newgate Cl. Carl 174 C4
Newgate Ct. Nott 172 C2
Newgate La. Mans 102 B4
Newgate St. Bing 177 F3
Newgate St. Work 35 F1
Newgates La. S in A 86 C1
Newhall Gr. W Brid 173 F1
Newhall La. Edin 120 B1
Newhall La. Halam 120 B1
Newhaven Ave. Mans 88 A2
Newholm Dr. Nott 185 D2
Newings La. S Lev 42 C4
Newington Rd. Aust 10 B4
Newland Cl. Bees 183 D1
Newland Cl. Nott 172 B3
Newlands Ave. Boug 77 F3
Newlands Cres. Newt 99 D2
Newlands Dr. Carl 162 C1
Newlands Dr. Mans 89 E1
Newlands Rd. Mans 103 D4
Newlands. Gain 15 F1
Newlands. Ret 39 E2
Newlyn Dr. Nott 172 B4
Newlyn Gdns. Nott 172 B4
Newman Rd. Calv 148 C4
Newmanleys Rd S. East 157 F4
Newmanleys Rd. East 157 F4
Newmarket Rd. Nott 160 A3
Newmarket St. Mans 102 C3
Newmarket Way. Bees 182 C1
Newnham Rd. N-on-T 125 D1
Newport Cres. Mans 87 F1
Newport Dr. Nott 160 B1
Newquay Ave. Nott 172 C4
Newstead Ave. Carl 162 B1
Newstead Ave. N-on-T 125 D1
Newstead Ave. R on T 176 A2
Newstead Cl. K-in-A 115 E3
Newstead Cl. Sels 129 D4
Newstead Dr. W Brid 186 A4
Newstead Gr. Bing 177 E2
Newstead Gr. Nott 173 D3
Newstead Rd S. Ilk 157 E2
Newstead Rd. Lo Ea 182 B2
Newstead St. Mans 101 E4
Newstead St. Nott 161 E2
Newstead Terr. Huck 146 A4
Newthorpe Comm. East 144 A1
Newthorpe St. Nott 173 E1
Newton Ave. Bing 177 E2
Newton Ave. Bing 177 E3
Newton Ave. R on T 176 A2
Newton Cl. Arn 162 A3
Newton Cl. Gain 24 C4
Newton Cl. Lowd 150 C1
Newton Cl. Work 35 E4
Newton Dr. Staple 182 C3
Newton Dr. W Brid 185 E2
Newton Gdns. Bing 177 E3
Newton Rd. Carl 162 C2
Newton Rd. Newt 99 D2
Newton St. Bees 183 F3
Newton St. Mans 102 B3
Newton St. N-on-T 140 A4
Newton St. Nott 172 C1
Newton St. Ret 39 F2
Newton's La. Awsw 158 A2
Newtondale Ave. Mans 88 C1
Newtondale Cl. Nott 160 B1
Newtonwood La. Tibs 99 D3
Nicholas Pl. Tux 66 A2
Nicholas Rd. Bees 171 E1
Nicholson St. N-on-T 140 A4
Nicholson's Row. Shireb 72 C2
Nicker Hill. Keyw 198 A2
Nicklaus Ct. Nott 161 D4
Nidderdale. Nott 171 E2
Nightingale Ave. Hath 213 D1
Nightingale Ave. Plea 87 D2
Nightingale Cl. Bald 140 C2
Nightingale Cl. Nuth 159 E3
Nightingale Cres. Sels 129 D3
Nightingale Dr. Mans 87 F1
Nightingale Gr. Work 35 E4
Nightingale Way. Wood 53 D4
Nine Acre Gdns. Nott 159 F4
Nine Acres. Kegw 203 E1
Nine Scores La. Fin 1 C4
Ninth Ave. Mans 103 D4
Nixon Rise. Huck 145 E3
Noble La. Aslo 179 D3
Noburn Cres. Nott 160 C2
Noel St. Gain 15 E1
Noel St. Kim 159 D3
Noel St. Mans 102 A4
Noel St. Nott 172 C4
Nook The. Bees 183 F2
Nook The. Bees 184 A4
Nook The. Calv 148 C4
Nook The. E Lea 205 F1
Nook The. Nott 171 F2
Nook The. Shireb 72 B2
Nookin. E Mark 66 A3
Norbett Cl. Bees 183 E2
Norbett Ct. Arn 148 A1
Norbett Rd. Arn 148 A1
Norbreck Cl. Nott 160 A2
Norbury Dr. Mans 102 C2
Nordean Rd. Arn 162 A3
Norfolk Ave. Bees 183 D1
Norfolk Ave. Bir 9 E2
Norfolk Cl. Huck 145 E3
Norfolk Cl. Mar War 74 A2
Norfolk Ct. Mans 88 C3
Norfolk Dr. Bir 9 E2
Norfolk Dr. Mans 102 A4
Norfolk Gr. Bir 9 E2
Norfolk Pl. Arn 162 A3
Norfolk Pl. Nott 173 E3
Norfolk Rd. Bir 9 E2
Norfolk Rd. Lo Ea 182 C1
Norfolk St. Work 35 F1
Norfolk Wlk. Sand 182 A3
Norland Cl. Nott 173 F4
Norman Ave. N-on-T 125 D2
Norman Ave. S in A 101 D1
Norman Cl. Bees 183 E3
Norman Cl. Nott 173 E3
Norman Cres. Ilk 157 F2
Norman Dr. East 144 A1
Norman Dr. Huck 145 F2
Norman Rd. Carl 174 A4
Norman St. Carl 175 D3
Norman St. Ilk 157 F2
Norman St. Kim 158 C4
Normanby Rd. Nott 171 E2
Normanton Cl. Edwin 75 F2
Normanton Dr. Mans 102 C4
Normanton La. Bott 181 D3
Normanton La. Keyw 197 F2
Normanton La. S on S 214 A1
Normanton Rd. South 121 F1
Normanton Rd. South 122 A1
Normanton Rd. Upton 122 A1
Nornay Cl. Blyth 18 A2
North Ave. Baw 10 A4
North Ave. Rain 104 A1
North Ave. Sand 182 A3
North Carr Rd. Mist 7 E2
North Carr Rd. W Sto 7 E2
North Church St. Nott 173 E3
North Circus St. Nott 173 D3
North Cr. N Clip 90 A2
North Cres. Bott 181 D1
North Dr. Bald 140 C1
North Dr. Bees 183 F3
North Dr. Bils 105 F4
North End. Farn 138 C3
North Gate Pl. Nott 160 C1
North Gate. N-on-T 124 C1
North Gate. N-on-T 125 D1
North Gate. Nott 160 C1
North Gate. Tick 8 A4
North Green. Calv 133 E1
North Green. E Dray 53 D2
North Hill Ave. Huck 145 F4
North Hill Cres. Huck 145 F4
North Leys Rd. N LeHa 43 E4
North Marsh Rd. Gain 15 E1
North Moor Dr. Walker 13 F3
North Moor Rd. Walker 13 F3
North Par. Gain 24 C4
North Park. Mans 102 C2
North Rd. Lo Ea 193 E3
North Rd. Lough 220 A3
North Rd. Nott 173 D2
North Rd. Ret 29 D1
North Rd. Rudd 196 A4
North Rd. W Brid 185 F4
North Scarle Rd. S Sca 98 C4
North Sherwood St. Nott 173 E3
North St. Ann Wo 115 D1
North St. Bees 183 F3
North St. East 144 B1
North St. Gain 15 E1
North St. Ilk 157 F1
North St. Kim 159 D3
North St. La Mi 143 D2
North St. Mar War 73 E2
North St. Mort 15 D2
North St. Nott 173 F2
North St. Pinx 113 E2
North St. S in A 100 A2
North St. S in A 100 C2
North St. S Le S 32 B3
North St. S Norm 113 D3
North St. Scarc 59 D1
North Warren Rd. Gain 15 D1
North Way. C in L 25 F4
North Wlk. Ret 39 E4
Northall Ave. Nott 160 A3
Northampton St. Nott 173 F3
Northcliffe Ave. Carl 162 A1
Northcote St. Lo Ea 193 F4
Northcote Way. Nott 160 B3
Northdale Rd. Nott 174 A4
Northdown Dr. Bees 183 E2
Northdown Rd. Nott 172 B3
Northern Ct. Nott 160 B2
Northern Dr. Staple 170 B2
Northern Rd. N-on-T 125 D1
Northern View. S in A 100 C2
Northfield Ave. Ilk 157 F1
Northfield Ave. Lo Ea 193 D2
Northfield Ave. Mans 87 F2
Northfield Ave. Mans 88 A2
Northfield Ave. R on T 176 B2
Northfield Cres. Bees 183 D2
Northfield Dr. Mans 102 C3
Northfield La. Mans 87 F2
Northfield La. Mans 88 A3
Northfield La. Tres 42 A2
Northfield Park. Mans 88 A3
Northfield Rd. Bees 183 D2
Northfield Rd. N Le Ha 33 D1
Northfield Way. Ret 39 E4
Northfields Cl. S in A 100 C2
Northfields. Lo Ea 193 D2
Northgate St. Ilk 157 F1
Northolme Ave. Nott 160 B4
Northolme. Gain 15 E1
Northolt Dr. Nuth 159 E2
Northrowe. Ann Wo 129 F4
Northside La. N Le Ha 32 C1
Northside Wlk. Nott 147 F1
Northumberland Ave. C in L 25 F4
Northumberland Cl. Nott 173 E3
Northumbria Cl. Work 36 A3
Northumbria Dr. Ret 39 E3
Northwold Ave. W Brid 185 E3
Northwood Ave. S in A 100 B2
Northwood Cres. Nott 161 E3
Northwood Rd. Nott 161 E3
Northwood St. Staple 182 B4
Northwood. Work 36 A3
Norton La. Cuck 60 A2
Norton Rd. Stap 127 F4
Norton St. Nott 172 C3
Norwell Ct. Mans 88 A1
Norwell La. Crom 110 B4
Norwell Rd. Caun 109 E3
Norwich Cl. Mans 88 B3
Norwich Gdns. Nott 146 A1
Norwood Cl. S in A 100 A2
Norwood Gdns. South 121 F1
Norwood Rd. Nott 172 C3
Nostell Mews. Work 35 F1
Notintone St. Nott 173 F2
Nottingham La. Ol Da 218 B3
Nottingham Rd E. East 144 A1
Nottingham Rd. Ann Wo 115 D1
Nottingham Rd. Arn 161 F3
Nottingham Rd. B in F 195 D2
Nottingham Rd. Bees 183 D1
Nottingham Rd. Bing 177 E2
Nottingham Rd. Bott 180 C1
Nottingham Rd. Bu Jo 163 E2
Nottingham Rd. Bulc 164 A4
Nottingham Rd. Cost 206 B1
Nottingham Rd. Cr Bi 188 C2
Nottingham Rd. East 144 A1
Nottingham Rd. Goth 195 D1
Nottingham Rd. Greas 158 B4
Nottingham Rd. Huck 146 B2
Nottingham Rd. Ilk 170 A3
Nottingham Rd. K in A 116 B4
Nottingham Rd. Kegw 203 E1
Nottingham Rd. Keyw 197 F2
Nottingham Rd. Kim 159 D3
Nottingham Rd. Lamb 148 C1
Nottingham Rd. Lo Ea 193 F4
Nottingham Rd. Lough 220 B3
Nottingham Rd. Lowd 164 A4
Nottingham Rd. Mans 102 B2
Nottingham Rd. Ne Br 219 F4
Nottingham Rd. Nott 160 C1
Nottingham Rd. Nott 160 C2
Nottingham Rd. Nuth 159 F2
Nottingham Rd. Oxt 134 A1
Nottingham Rd. R on T 175 E1
Nottingham Rd. Raven 116 C2
Nottingham Rd. Sels 129 D3
Nottingham Rd. South 136 B3
Nottingham Rd. Staple 170 C3
Nottingham Rd. Staple 182 C4
Nottingham Rd. Thur 151 E3
Nottingham Rd. Trow 170 C3
Nuart Rd. Bees 183 F4
Nugent Gdns. Nott 173 F3
Nuncar Ct. Ann Wo 115 D1
Nuncargate Rd. Ann Wo 115 D1
Nunn Brook Rd. S in A 99 F1
Nunn Brook Rise. S in A 99 F1
Nunn Cl. S in A 99 F1
Nurseries The. East 144 A1
Nursery Ave. Bees 183 E3
Nursery Ave. Farn 139 D3
Nursery Ave. S in A 100 B1
Nursery Cl. Huck 146 A2
Nursery Cl. R on T 176 A2
Nursery Cl. Sax 57 D2
Nursery Ct. Mans 102 B4
Nursery Ct. N-on-T 125 D1
Nursery Dr. Carl 174 B4
Nursery End. South 121 E1
Nursery Gdns. S Norm 113 E2
Nursery La. Nott 160 C2
Nursery La. S on T 96 C4
Nursery Rd. Arn 162 A4
Nursery Rd. Bing 178 A3
Nursery Rd. R on T 176 A2
Nursery St. Mans 102 B4
Nursury Gdns. Lowd 150 B1
Nuthall Gdns. Nott 172 B4
Nuthall Rd. Nott 160 B1

Oak Acres. Bees 183 D3
Oak Ave. Ald 143 D3
Oak Ave. Bing 178 A2
Oak Ave. Blid 118 A2
Oak Ave. Farn 139 D2
Oak Ave. Mans 102 B4
Oak Ave. Oll 77 E2
Oak Ave. R on T 175 F2
Oak Ave. Rain 104 B1
Oak Ave. Sand 182 A4
Oak Ave. Shireb 72 B2
Oak Bank Cl. Mans 102 A4
Oak Cl. Pinx 113 E2
Oak Cl. Work 35 F1
Oak Cres. E Lea 214 B4
Oak Dr. Bald 140 B2
Oak Dr. East 143 F1

Oak Dr. Kim 159 D3
Oak Flatt. Bees 183 D3
Oak Gr. Huck 146 A2
Oak Lodge Dr. Kim 158 C4
Oak Rise. Bils 105 F4
Oak St. K-in-A 115 D3
Oak St. Nott 161 D1
Oak St. S in A 100 B4
Oak Tree Ave. Edwin 76 A1
Oak Tree Ave. Glap 86 A4
Oak Tree Ave. R on T 175 F2
Oak Tree Cl. Huck 145 E2
Oak Tree Cl. Mans 103 D4
Oak Tree Cl. W Brid 186 A4
Oak Tree Cres. Mans 88 A2
Oak Tree Dr. Carl 163 D1
Oak Tree La. Mans 103 D3
Oak Tree Rd. Baw 9 F4
Oak Tree Rd. S in A 101 D2
Oakdale Dr. Bees 183 E2
Oakdale Rd. Arn 162 A4
Oakdale Rd. Carl 174 B3
Oakdale Rd. Nott 174 B3
Oakdale Rd. S Norm 113 D2
Oakenhall Ave. Huck 146 B4
Oakfield Ave. Mar War 74 A2
Oakfield Ave. S in A 114 C4
Oakfield Cl. Mans 102 C1
Oakfield Cl. Nott 171 E2
Oakfield Dr. Sand 182 A2
Oakfield La. Mar War 74 A1
Oakfield Rd. Huck 146 A3
Oakfield Rd. Nott 171 E2
Oakfield Rd. Staple 182 B4
Oakfield. Sax 57 D2
Oakfields Rd. W Brid 174 A1
Oakford Cl. Nott 160 A1
Oakham Cl. Mans 102 A2
Oakham Cl. Nott 160 C4
Oakham Rd. W Brid 185 E1
Oakham Way. Ilk 157 F2
Oakhampton Cres. Carl 162 B3
Oakholme Ave. Work 35 F3
Oakholme Rise. Work 35 F3
Oakington Cl. Nott 161 D3
Oakland Ave. Lo Ea 193 E3
Oakland Ave. S in A 99 F1
Oakland Gr. Calv 148 C4
Oakland Rd. Mans 102 C4
Oakland St. Nott 172 C4
Oakland Terr. Lo Ea 193 E3
Oaklands Ave. Hean 143 D1
Oaklands Dr. Styr 8 B1
Oaklands La. Ret 40 A3
Oaklands The. S Norm 113 D2
Oaklands. Coll 112 A4
Oakleigh Ave. Carl 162 B1
Oakleigh St. Nott 160 B2
Oakley Dr. Lo Wh 212 B1
Oakley Mews. Nott 159 F3
Oakley's Rd W. Lo Ea 193 E3
Oakley's Rd. Lo Ea 193 F4
Oakmead Ave. Nott 171 F4
Oakridge Cl. Mans 88 C1
Oaks Ave. Elmt 58 B4
Oaks Cl. Ran 19 D3
Oaks Ind Est. Lough 220 A3
Oaks La. Oxt 133 F4
Oaks La. Walker 13 F2
Oaktree Dr. Bils 106 A2
Oaktree Rd. Newt 99 E1
Oakwood Dr. Nott 172 B4
Oakwood Dr. Raven 117 D1
Oakwood Gr. Edwin 91 E4
Oakwood Rd. Mans 103 D2
Oardale Rd. Mans 101 F4
Oatfield La. New 176 B3
Oban Rd. Bees 183 E3
Occupation La. Fisk 137 F3
Occupation La. K-in-A 114 C3
Occupation La. W-on-W 217 F3
Occupation Rd. Huck 146 A3
Occupation Rd. Nott 160 A3
Occupation Rd. Plea 86 C4
Ochbrook Ct. Ilk 157 F2
Ockerby St. Nott 160 B3
Oddicroft La. S in A 101 D1
Odesa Dr. Nott 160 A2
Ogdon Ct. Nott 173 F3
Ogle Dr. Nott 173 D2
Ogle St. Huck 146 A4
Old Bell La. C on T 96 C2
Old Blyth Rd. Babw 37 F4
Old Blyth Rd. Babw 38 A3
Old Brickyard. Carl 174 A4
Old Chapel Cl. K-in-A 114 C3
Old Chapel La. Elst 153 F3
Old Chapel La. Sels 129 D2
Old Church St. Nott 172 C1
Old Coach Rd. Nott 171 F3
Old Coach Rd. Work 47 F4
Old Dalby La. Ne Br 219 E3
Old Derby Rd. East 143 E2
Old Dr. Bees 183 F4
Old Engine Yd The. Remp 215 F3
Old Epperstone Rd. Lowd 150 A2
Old Farm Rd. Nott 160 C4
Old Forge Cl. Hath 213 D1
Old Forge La. Gran 191 E3
Old Forge Rd. Mist 6 C1
Old Great North Rd. S on T 96 C4
Old Hall Cl. Farn 138 C2
Old Hall Cl. Mar War 74 B3
Old Hall Dr. Nott 161 E1
Old Hall Dr. Widm 208 B3
Old Hall Gdns. Codd 125 F1
Old Hall La. E Mark 65 F4
Old Hall La. Norw 110 A4
Old La. Rudd 185 E1
Old Lenton Cl. Cr Bi 189 D2
Old Lenton St. Nott 173 E3
Old London Rd. Ba Mo 28 B2
Old London Rd. Babw 28 B2
Old London Rd. Babw 38 C2
Old London Rd. Babw 49 F4
Old London Rd. W Dray 50 C1
Old Main Rd. Bulc 164 A3
Old Main Rd. Cost 206 B1
Old Manor Cl. Woodb 149 E2
Old Manor Rd. Mans 88 B2
Old Market Pl. Mans 102 A4
Old Market Pl. S Norm 113 D3
Old Market Sq. Nott 173 E2
Old Melton Rd. Plum 197 F4
Old Mill Cl. Bees 183 D1
Old Mill Cl. Huck 146 B2
Old Mill Cl. Nott 172 C3
Old Mill Cres. N-on-T 140 A4
Old Mill Ct. Bing 177 F3
Old Mill La. Cuck 60 A2
Old Mill La. Mans 88 C1
Old Newark Rd. Mans 102 C1
Old Park Cl. R on S 203 F3
Old Parsonage La. Hoton 215 E1
Old Post Office St. Ever 11 E2
Old Rd. S in A 100 C3
Old Rectory Cl. E Lea 205 F1
Old Rufford Rd. Calv 133 E3
Old Rufford Rd. Edwin 76 C1
Old Rufford Rd. Farns 119 D3
Old Rufford Rd. Oll 77 D2
Old Rufford Rd. Ruff 91 E2
Old Rufford Rd. Ruff 105 E2
Old School La. Plea 87 D3
Old Sookholme La. Mar War 74 A2
Old St. Nott 173 E3
Old Storth La. S Norm 113 D2
Old Terr. Plea 86 C2
Old Tollerton Rd. Gam 186 B4
Old Trent Rd. Beck 14 C1
Old Way. Hath 213 D1
Oldacres. Woodb 149 E2
Oldbury Cl. Nott 195 E4
Oldershaw Ave. Kegw 203 E1
Oldershaw Rd. E Lea 205 F1
Oldershaw Rd. E Lea 214 C4
Oldknow St. Nott 172 C4
Oldoak Rd. Nott 185 D1
Olga Rd. Nott 173 F3
Olive Ave. Lo Ea 182 C1
Olive Ave. Shireb 72 B3
Olive Gr. Bu Jo 163 F3
Olive Gr. Mans 103 D4
Oliver Cl. Hean 143 D1
Oliver Cl. Nott 173 D3
Oliver Ct. N-on-T 140 A4
Oliver Rd. Lough 220 A1
Oliver St. Nott 173 D3
Ollerton Rd. Arn 147 F3
Ollerton Rd. Budby 61 E3
Ollerton Rd. Calv 132 C1
Ollerton Rd. Edwin 76 B2
Ollerton Rd. Gams 50 C3
Ollerton Rd. Kelh 124 A3
Ollerton Rd. Oll 77 D2
Ollerton Rd. Oxt 119 D1
Ollerton Rd. Ret 39 F2
Ollerton Rd. S Musk 124 A4
Ollerton Rd. Tux 65 E1
Ollerton Rd. Tux 78 C4
Ollerton Rd. Work 47 D2
Olton Ave. Nott 171 F1
Olympus Ct. Huck 145 E2
Omberley Ave. S in A 101 D3
Onchan Ave. Carl 174 C3
Ontario Dr. Sels 129 D4
Orange Cl. Shireb 72 C3
Orange Croft. Tick 8 A4
Orange Gdns. Nott 173 E1
Orby Cl. Nott 173 F3
Orby Wlk. Nott 173 F3
Orchard Ave. Bing 177 E2
Orchard Ave. Carl 174 C4
Orchard Ave. N Le Ha 42 B4
Orchard Bsns Park. Ilk 157 E1
Orchard Bsns Park. Sand 182 B3
Orchard Cl. Bleas 152 A4
Orchard Cl. Bu Jo 163 F3
Orchard Cl. E Brid 165 E2
Orchard Cl. E Lea 214 B4
Orchard Cl. Gunt 165 D3
Orchard Cl. Mort 15 D3
Orchard Cl. N Le Ha 42 B4
Orchard Cl. R on T 175 F2
Orchard Cl. Ramp 43 D1
Orchard Cl. Shireb 72 C3
Orchard Cl. South 121 E1
Orchard Cl. Su Bo 213 E3
Orchard Cl. Toll 186 B1
Orchard Cres. Bees 183 E3
Orchard Cres. Glap 86 A4
Orchard Cres. Tux 65 F1
Orchard Ct. Carl 162 B1
Orchard Ct. Huck 146 A3
Orchard Ct. La Mi 143 D2
Orchard Ct. Nott 172 C4
Orchard Dr. Calv 149 D4
Orchard Gr. Arn 161 E3
Orchard La. Sax 57 D2
Orchard Leigh. Ret 39 E2
Orchard Rd. K-in-A 114 C3
Orchard Rise. Lamb 163 E4
Orchard St. East 144 A1
Orchard St. Goth 195 D1
Orchard St. Huck 146 A3
Orchard St. Kim 158 C3
Orchard St. La Mi 143 D2
Orchard St. Lo Ea 193 F4
Orchard St. Lough 220 A2
Orchard St. Mans 88 A1
Orchard St. Staple 182 B4
Orchard The. S in A 101 D2
Orchard View. Mans 88 A2
Orchard Way. Bald 140 B2
Orchard Way. Sand 182 A2
Orchard Way. Wyme 216 B2
Orchards The. Carl 163 D1
Orchards The. Lowd 164 C4
Orchards The. Oxt 134 B2
Orchid Cl. Bald 140 A3
Orchid Cl. K-in-A 114 C4
Orchid Cl. W Brid 185 E2
Orchid Dr. Farn 139 D3
Ordsall Park Cl. Ret 39 E3
Ordsall Park Dr. Ret 39 E3
Ordsall Park Rd. Ret 39 E3
Ordsall Rd. Ret 39 E3
Orford Ave. Nott 184 C2
Orford Ave. R on T 175 F1
Orion Cl. Nott 171 F4
Orion Dr. Nott 171 F4
Orlando Dr. Carl 174 C4
Orlock Wlk. Nott 161 D3
Ormonde St. Ald 143 D2
Ormonde Terr. Ald 143 D2
Ormonde Terr. Nott 161 E1
Ornsay Cl. Nott 146 C1
Orpean Way. Bees 182 C1
Orston Ave. Arn 162 A4
Orston Ave. N-on-T 139 F3
Orston Dr. Nott 172 B2
Orston Green. Nott 172 B2
Orston La. Bott 180 C2
Orston Rd E. W Brid 173 F1
Orston Rd W. W Brid 173 F1
Orton Ave. Bees 183 E3
Ortzen St. Nott 172 C3
Orville Rd. Nott 160 C3
Osberton Rd. Ret 39 F3
Osberton View. Work 36 A3
Osborne Ave. Nott 161 E2
Osborne Cl. Sand 182 A2
Osborne Gr. Nott 161 E2
Osborne St. Nott 172 C3
Osbourne St. Ann Wo 129 F4
Osgood Rd. Arn 162 B3
Osier Cl. Nott 173 E1
Osman Cl. Nott 173 D1
Osmaston St. Nott 172 C2
Osmaston St. Sand 182 B3
Osprey Cl. Nott 184 B1
Ossington Cl. Mar War 74 B4
Ossington Cl. Nott 173 E3
Ossington Rd. Knee 93 F3
Ossington St. Nott 172 C3
Osterley Gr. Nott 159 E1
Otter Ave. Sax 57 D2
Oulton Cl. Arn 161 F3
Oundle Dr. Ilk 170 A4
Oundle Dr. Mans 87 E1
Oundle Dr. Nott 172 B2
Oursham St. S in A 100 C1
Ouse Bridge Dr. Carl 175 D4
Ousebridge Cres. Carl 175 D4
Outgang La. Mans 88 B2
Outgang La. Plea 87 D3
Outgang La. Tres 42 C2
Outgang Rd. Cott 43 E2
Outram St. S in A 100 C2
Oval Gdns. Nott 172 B4
Oval The. Ret 39 E2
Oval The. S in A 100 B2
Oval The. Tick 8 A4
Overdale Ave. S in A 100 C4
Overdale Cl. Lo Ea 193 D3
Overdale Rd. Nott 160 B2
Overend Rd. Work 35 F2
Overstone Cl. S in A 100 C3
Overstrand Cl. Arn 161 F3
Owday La. C in L 25 E2
Owday La. Work 25 E2
Owen Ave. Lo Ea 194 A3
Owlston Cl. East 143 F2
Owsthorpe Cl. Nott 161 D4
Owston Ferry Rd. Haxey 7 E4
Owston Rd. W Sto 7 E2
Owthorpe Gr. Nott 161 D1
Owthorpe La. Kinou 199 F2
Owthorpe Rd. Co Ba 200 A4
Owthorpe Rd. Cotg 187 F1
Oxborough Rd. Arn 161 E4
Oxbow Cl. Nott 173 E1
Oxbury Rd. Greas 158 C4
Oxclose La. Arn 161 E4
Oxclose La. Mans 87 E2
Oxclose La. Mans 88 A2
Oxcroft La. Elmt 58 A4
Oxengate. Arn 161 E3
Oxford Cl. Rain 118 A4
Oxford Dr. Har 8 C3
Oxford Rd. C in L 25 F3
Oxford Rd. W Brid 186 A4
Oxford St. Carl 174 C4
Oxford St. East 143 F1
Oxford St. K-in-A 115 D2
Oxford St. Lo Ea 193 E4
Oxford St. Lough 220 A2
Oxford St. Mans 88 B1
Oxford St. Nott 173 D2
Oxford St. S in A 100 B1
Oxpasture La. Elmt 58 A3
Oxton Ave. Nott 161 E2
Oxton By Pass. Oxt 134 A2
Oxton Cl. Mans 101 F4
Oxton Hill. Oxt 134 C2
Oxton Rd. Arn 148 A4
Oxton Rd. Calv 133 E1
Oxton Rd. South 135 E3
Ozier Holt. Carl 174 C2
Pack Horse La. Lough 220 A2
Packe St. Lough 220 A2
Packington Hill. Kegw 203 E1
Packman Dr. Rudd 196 B4
Paddock Cl. Calv 148 C4
Paddock Cl. Edwin 76 A2
Paddock Cl. R on T 175 F1
Paddock The. Bees 183 E1
Paddock The. Bing 177 F2
Paddock The. Coll 112 A4
Paddock The. Gunt 164 C3
Paddock The. K-in-A 114 C2
Paddock The. Ret 40 A2
Paddock The. S in A 100 B3
Paddock The. Tick 8 A4
Paddocks Cl. Elst 153 F2
Paddocks Cl. Pinx 113 E2
Paddocks The. Beck 14 A1
Paddocks The. Bott 181 D1
Paddocks The. Elst 153 F2
Paddocks The. Hock 122 A3
Paddocks The. Lound 20 B1
Paddocks The. Mans 88 C3
Paddocks The. N-on-T 140 A4
Paddocks The. Sand 182 A3
Paddocks The. Stap 127 F4
Paddocks The. Su Bo 213 D3
Paddocks The. W Brid 186 A2
Paddocks The. Work 36 A4
Paddocks View. Lo Ea 193 D4
Paddy's La. Ol Da 218 A1
Padge Rd. Bees 184 A3
Padgham Ct. Nott 161 D4
Padley Hill. Mans 102 A3
Padleys La. Bu Jo 163 F3
Padstow Rd. Nott 160 C3
Pagdin Dr. Styr 8 C1
Paget Cres. Rudd 196 B4
Paget St. Lough 220 A3
Paignton Cl. Nott 160 A1
Palace View. South 136 C4
Palatine St. Nott 173 D2
Palin Gdns. R on T 176 A2
Palin St. Nott 172 C3
Paling Cres. S in A 100 C2
Palm Court Ind Cntre. Nott 160 C1
Palm St. Nott 160 C1
Palm Wood Ct. Nott 160 B3
Palmer Ave. Huck 146 A4
Palmer Cres. Carl 174 B4
Palmer Dr. Staple 182 B3
Palmer Rd. Ret 30 A1
Palmer Rd. S on T 96 C4
Palmerston Gdns. Nott 173 E3
Palmerston St. Sels 128 B2
Palmwood Ct. Nott 160 B3
Paper Mill La. Tick 8 B4
Papplewick La. Huck 146 B4
Paradise La. Ol Da 218 C2
Park Ave E. Keyw 197 E1
Park Ave E. Keyw 197 F2
Park Ave W. Keyw 197 E2
Park Ave. Ann Wo 130 A4
Park Ave. Arn 161 F3
Park Ave. Awsw 158 A3
Park Ave. Blid 118 A3
Park Ave. Bu Jo 163 F2
Park Ave. Carl 174 C4
Park Ave. East 143 F2
Park Ave. Huck 145 F4
Park Ave. Keyw 197 F2
Park Ave. Kim 159 D2
Park Ave. Lough 220 A1
Park Ave. Mans 88 B2
Park Ave. Mans 102 B4
Park Ave. Mist 6 C2
Park Ave. Nott 173 A2
Park Ave. Shireb 72 C2
Park Ave. W Brid 185 F4
Park Ave. Woodb 149 D2
Park Cl. Lea 24 C1
Park Cl. Nott 161 F1
Park Cl. Pinx 113 E1
Park Cres. Greas 143 F2
Park Cres. Ilk 170 A4
Park Cres. N-on-T 125 D2
Park Cres. Nott 171 E2
Park Cres. Ret 40 A4
Park Ct. Lough 220 A1
Park Ct. Mans 102 B4
Park Dr. Blyth 18 A2
Park Dr. Huck 146 A3
Park Dr. Nott 173 D2
Park Dr. Sand 182 A2
Park Farm Cotts. Kettl 55 F1
Park Hall Gdns. Mans 88 B3
Park Hall Rd. Mans 88 B3
Park Hill Dr. Fir 16 A3
Park Hill. Awsw 158 A3
Park House Gates. Nott 161 E1
Park La. Elk 50 B2
Park La. Holb 59 E3
Park La. K-in-A 114 B1
Park La. Lamb 163 F4
Park La. Nott 160 C2
Park La. Owth 199 F4
Park La. Pinx 113 E1
Park La. Ret 40 A4
Park La. South 136 B3
Park La. Su Bo 213 E3
Park Mews. Mans 88 B2
Park Mews. Nott 173 E4
Park Pl. Work 35 F1
Park Ravine. Nott 173 D2
Park Rd E. Calv 149 D4
Park Rd N. Bees 183 F3
Park Rd. Arn 161 F3
Park Rd. Baw 9 F4
Park Rd. Bees 183 D4
Park Rd. Bees 183 F3
Park Rd. Bes Vil 146 C2
Park Rd. Calv 148 C4
Park Rd. Carl 174 C4
Park Rd. Huck 145 F4
Park Rd. Ilk 170 A4
Park Rd. Keyw 197 F3
Park Rd. Lough 220 A1
Park Rd. Mans 88 A2
Park Rd. Nott 172 C2
Park Rd. R on T 175 F2
Park Rd. Shireb 72 C3
Park Row. Nott 173 D2
Park Springs Rd. Gain 24 C3
Park St. Bees 183 F3
Park St. K-in-A 114 C3
Park St. Lo Ea 182 B1
Park St. Lough 220 A2
Park St. Mans 88 A2
Park St. Nott 172 C2
Park St. S in A 100 C2
Park St. Staple 182 B3
Park Terr. Keyw 197 F3
Park Terr. Nott 173 D2
Park The. Cotg 187 F2
Park The. Mans 102 B4
Park The. N Musk 110 C2
Park The. N-on-T 140 A4
Park Valley. Nott 173 D2
Park View Way. Mans 102 B3
Park View. Bees 183 E3
Park View. Nott 161 F1
Parkcroft Rd. W Brid 185 F3
Parkdale Rd. Carl 174 B3
Parkdale Rd. Nott 174 B3
Parker Cl. Arn 162 B4
Parker St. Huck 146 A4
Parker St. N-on-T 140 A4
Parker's La. Mans 88 B2
Parkes Cl. Codd 126 A1
Parkham Rd. Kim 158 C4
Parkin Cl. Cr Bi 189 D2
Parkland Cl. Mans 102 C1
Parkland Cl. Nott 184 B2
Parklands Cl. Codd 125 F1
Parklands Dr. Lough 220 A1
Parkside Ave. Lo Ea 193 D4
Parkside Dr. Lo Ea 193 D4
Parkside Gdns. Nott 171 F1
Parkside Rd. Edwin 75 F1
Parkside Rise. Nott 171 F1
Parkside. Keyw 197 F2
Parkside. Nott 171 F1
Parkside. S in A 100 A2
Parkstone Ave. Mans 103 F1
Parkstone Cl. W Brid 185 E3
Parkview Rd. Nott 161 D4
Parkway Ct. Nott 171 E3
Parkway. Mans 89 E2
Parkway. N-on-T 139 F3
Parkway. S in A 100 A2

Parkway. Whit 45 D3
Parkwood Cres. Nott 161 F2
Parkwood Ct. Nott 160 C3
Parkyn Rd. Arn 161 E3
Parkyns St. Rudd 196 B3
Parliament Ct. N-on-T 139 F4
Parliament Rd. Mans 101 F4
Parliament St. N-on-T 139 F4
Parliament St. S in A 100 C1
Parliament Terr. Nott 173 D3
Parliament Wlk. N-on-T 139 F4
Parnell St. Gain 24 B4
Parnham's Cl. Ne Br 219 E4
Parr Gate. Bees 183 D3
Parr La. Epp 150 A3
Parry Way. Arn 162 A4
Parsons Meadow. Carl 174 C2
Paschall Rd. Ann Wo 115 D1
Pasteur Ct. Nott 172 C1
Pasture Cl. Carl 174 C2
Pasture Cl. S in A 100 B3
Pasture Cl. Work 35 E1
Pasture La. Hath 213 D1
Pasture La. Hose 211 F3
Pasture La. Lo Ea 194 A3
Pasture La. Newt 99 E1
Pasture La. Rudd 196 A4
Pasture La. Su Bo 213 D3
Pasture Rd. Gain 24 C4
Pasture Rd. Staple 170 B1
Pasture View. Gunt 165 D3
Pastures Ave. Nott 195 E4
Pastures The. Baw 10 A3
Pastures The. Calv 148 B4
Pastures The. Greas 158 B4
Pastures The. Mans 88 C3
Pastures The. Ramp 43 D1
Pastures The. Tux 65 F1
Patchills The. Mans 102 C4
Pateley Rd. Arn 162 A2
Paton Rd. Nott 160 C3
Patricia Dr. Arn 148 A1
Patrick Rd. W Brid 185 F4
Patterdale Rd. Arn 161 F3
Patterson Pl. Mans 102 B4
Patterson Rd. Nott 172 C4
Paul Ave. Mans 103 D3
Paulson's Dr. Mans 102 A4
Pavilion Cl. Nott 173 E1
Pavilion Ct. Gunt 164 C4
Pavilion Gdns. Plea 86 C4
Pavilion Rd. Bes Vil 147 D1
Pavilion Rd. Ilk 157 F3
Pavilion Rd. W Brid 173 F1
Paxton Gdns. Nott 173 F3
Paxtons Court. N-on-T 124 C1
Peach Ave. S Norm 113 D4
Peach Ave. Sels 128 C3
Peache Way. Bees 183 E4
Peachey St. Nott 173 E3
Peacock Cl. Gunt 165 D2
Peacock Cl. Rudd 196 A3
Peacock Cres. Nott 184 C1
Peacock Dr. Rain 118 B4
Peacock Pl. Ilk 157 E2
Peacock St. Mans 102 A3
Peafield La. Mans 88 C2
Peafield La. Mar War 89 D4
Peak The. Shireb 72 C2
Peakdale Cl. Lo Ea 193 D3
Peake's Croft. Baw 10 A4
Pear Tree Cl. Clar 30 B2
Pear Tree Ct. Nott 160 C2
Pear Tree Dr. Shireb 72 C3
Pearce Dr. Nott 172 A4
Pearl Ave. K-in-A 115 D2
Pearmain Dr. Nott 173 F4
Pearson Ave. Bees 183 D3
Pearson Cl. Bees 183 D3
Pearson St. Carl 175 D3
Pearson St. Nott 160 C1
Peartree La. S in A 86 A1
Peartree Orch. Rudd 196 B4
Peary Cl. Nott 160 C3
Peas Hill Rd. Nott 173 E3
Peatfield Rd. Staple 170 B1
Peck La. Nott 173 E2
Pecks Hill. Mans 102 C4
Pedmore Valley. Nott 161 D4
Peebles Rd. N-on-T 139 E3
Peel Ave. Ret 40 A2
Peel Ave. Tux 65 F1
Peel Cres. Mans 87 E1
Peel Dr. Lough 220 B2
Peel Rd. Mans 101 F4
Peel St. La Mi 143 D2
Peel St. Lo Ea 193 F4
Peel St. Nott 173 D3
Peel St. S in A 101 D2
Peel St. S Norm 113 D3
Peets Dr. N Musk 110 C1
Pelham Ave. Ilk 157 F1
Pelham Ave. Nott 173 D4
Pelham Cl. N-on-T 139 F4
Pelham Cres. Bees 184 A4
Pelham Cres. Nott 172 C2
Pelham Ct. Nott 173 D4
Pelham Gdns. N-on-T 139 F4
Pelham Rd. K-in-A 115 D3
Pelham Rd. Nott 173 D4
Pelham Rd. Ret 39 E3
Pelham St. Mans 102 B4
Pelham St. N-on-T 139 F4
Pelham St. Nott 173 E2
Pelham St. S in A 100 B1
Pelham St. Work 36 A1
Pelham Way. Mans 89 E2
Pemberton St. Nott 173 E2
Pemberton The. S Norm 113 D2
Pembleton Dr. Mans 87 E1
Pembrey Cl. Staple 170 B1
Pembridge Cl. Nott 160 B1
Pembroke Cres. Codd 125 E2
Pembroke Dr. C in L 25 F3
Pembroke Dr. Nott 161 E1
Pembroke Rd. Shire 34 C4
Pembury Rd. Nott 171 F3
Pen La. Widm 208 B2
Penarth Gdns. Nott 161 F2
Penarth Rise. Nott 161 F2
Pendeen Cl. Gain 15 F1
Pendennis Cl. Carl 163 D1
Pendine Cl. Nott 147 E1
Pendle Cres. Nott 161 F1
Pendock La. Brad 197 D1
Penfold Cl. Hath 213 D1
Penhale Dr. Huck 145 E3
Penhurst Cl. Nott 185 D2
Penllech Cl. Nott 161 D4
Penllech Wlk. Nott 161 D4
Penn Ave. Nott 172 C2
Penn La. Stat 202 C2
Penn St. S in A 100 C2
Pennant Rd. Nott 160 B1
Pennard Wlk. Nott 195 E4
Pennhome Ave. Nott 161 E1
Penniment La. Mans 87 D1
Pennine Cl. Bes Vil 147 D1
Pennine Cl. Lo Ea 182 A1
Pennine Cl. Lo Ea 193 E2
Pennine Cl. Newt 99 D2
Pennine Cl. S in A 99 F2
Pennine Dr. K-in-A 114 B2
Pennine Dr. Sels 128 C4
Pennington Wlk. Ret 40 A3
Penny Green. Whit 45 D3
Pennyfoot St. Nott 173 F2
Penrhyn Cl. Nott 173 E3
Penrhyn Cres. Bees 183 D2
Penrith Ave. R on T 176 A2
Penrith Cres. Nott 160 B1
Penrith Pl. Mans 101 E4
Penshore Cl. Nott 184 B1
Penswick Gr. Codd 125 F1
Pentland Ct. Mans 101 E3
Pentland Dr. Bes Vil 147 D1
Pentland Dr. C in L 25 F4
Pentland Gdns. Lo Ea 182 A1
Pentrich Wlk. Mans 103 D3
Pentwood Ave. Nott 147 F1
Penzance Pl. Mans 103 D4
Pepper Rd. Calv 148 C4
Pepper St. Nott 173 E2
Pepper St. S in A 101 D1
Peppercorn Gdns. Nott 172 B3
Peppers Dr. Kegw 203 D1
Percival Cl. S in A 100 C2
Percival Cres. S in A 100 C2
Percival Rd. Nott 161 E1
Percival St. Work 35 F3
Percy St. East 144 A1
Percy St. Nott 160 B2
Percy St. S in A 100 B1
Peregrine Ct. Work 35 E4
Perivale Cl. Nuth 159 E2
Perkin's La. Grim 219 D1
Perlethorpe Ave. Carl 162 C1
Perlethorpe Ave. Mans 88 A1
Perlethorpe Ave. Nott 173 F2
Perlethorpe Cl. Carl 162 C1
Perlethorpe Cl. Edwin 75 F2
Perlethorpe Cres. Carl 162 C1
Perlethorpe Dr. Carl 162 C1
Perlethorpe Dr. Huck 146 A4
Perlthorpe Ave. Mar War 74 B4
Perry Gdns. Nott 161 D2
Perry Gr. Bing 177 F2
Perry Rd. Nott 161 D2
Perth Cl. Mans 88 B3
Perth Dr. Staple 170 C1
Perth St. Nott 173 E3
Peterborough Rd. Coll 98 A1
Peters Cl. Arn 162 B3
Peters Cl. Greas 144 B1
Petersfield Cl. Mans 101 E4
Petersfield Cl. Nott 160 C4
Petersgate Cl. Lo Ea 182 A1
Petersgate. Lo Ea 182 A1
Petersham Mews. Nott 172 C2
Petersham Rd. Lo Ea 182 A1
Petersmiths Cres. Oll 77 E3
Petersmiths Dr. Oll 77 E3
Petworth Ave. Bees 182 C2
Petworth Dr. Nott 160 C2
Peveril Cres. Lo Ea 193 D3
Peveril Dr. Ilk 157 E1
Peveril Dr. Nott 173 D2
Peveril Dr. S in A 100 B1
Peveril Dr. W Brid 185 F2
Peveril Rd. Bees 184 A4
Peveril St. Huck 146 A4
Peveril St. Nott 172 C3
Pheasant Hill. Mans 88 A1
Philip Ave. East 144 A1
Philip Ave. K-in-A 115 D1
Philip Ave. Nuth 159 E3
Philip Gr. Carl 162 C1
Philip Rd. N-on-T 139 F3
Phoenix Ave. Carl 162 C1
Phoenix Cl. Nott 173 D1
Phoenix Ct. East 144 A1
Phoenix Ct. Nott 184 C4
Phoenix St. S in A 101 D2
Phyllis Cl. Huck 130 C1
Phyllis Gr. Lo Ea 193 F4
Piccadilly. Nott 160 B3
Pickard St. Mans 102 C4
Pickering Ave. East 143 F1
Pieris Dr. Nott 184 B1
Pierrepont Ave. Carl 162 C1
Pierrepont Rd. W Brid 174 A1
Pierson St. N-on-T 139 F3
Pilcher Gate. Nott 173 E2
Pilgrim Cl. Babw 38 C3
Pilgrim Cl. Raven 116 C1
Pilgrim Rise. Aust 3 E1
Pilgrim Way. Work 35 F1
Pilkington Rd. Carl 162 A1
Pilkington St. Nott 160 A4
Pillared House La. Gain 24 B4
Pimlico Ave. Bees 171 D2
Pinder St. Nott 173 E2
Pine Ave. La Mi 143 D2
Pine Ave. Oll 77 E2
Pine Cl. E Lea 214 B4
Pine Cl. Ever 11 E2
Pine Cl. K-in-A 114 C3
Pine Cl. Mans 88 B3
Pine Cl. N-on-T 125 D2
Pine Cl. Rain 103 F1
Pine Cl. Shireb 72 C3
Pine Hill Cl. Nott 146 C1
Pine Tree Cl. Work 35 F1
Pine Tree Wlk. East 143 E1
Pinehurst Ave. Huck 145 E3
Pines The. Gain 24 C3
Pineview Cl. Mans 102 C1
Pinewood Ave. Arn 148 A1
Pinewood Ave. Edwin 91 E4
Pinewood Cl. K-in-A 115 E3
Pinewood Cl. South 121 E1
Pinewood Dr. Mans 102 C2
Pinewood Gdns. Nott 195 E4
Pinfold Cl. Bott 181 D2
Pinfold Cl. Coll 98 A1
Pinfold Cl. Cotg 187 F2
Pinfold Cl. Kinou 199 F1
Pinfold Cl. Lound 20 B1
Pinfold Cl. Tick 8 A4
Pinfold Cl. Woodb 149 E2
Pinfold Cres. Woodb 149 E2
Pinfold Gate. Lough 220 A2
Pinfold Gdns. Lough 220 A2
Pinfold Jetty. Lough 220 B2
Pinfold La. Aver 123 F1
Pinfold La. Bald 140 B2
Pinfold La. Bott 181 D2
Pinfold La. Clar 40 C4
Pinfold La. Elst 153 E3
Pinfold La. Harb 202 B2
Pinfold La. Kinou 199 F1
Pinfold La. Shel 164 B1
Pinfold La. Staple 182 C4
Pinfold La. Styr 8 B1
Pinfold La. Tick 8 A4
Pinfold Place. Harb 202 B2
Pinfold Rd. Greas 144 B1
Pinfold The. Miss 4 A1
Pinfold. Bing 177 F2
Pingle Cl. Gain 24 C4
Pingle Cres. Nott 160 C4
Pingle The. Lo Ea 193 E4
Pingley Cl. Stay 138 B4
Pingley La. Stay 123 E1
Pingley La. Stay 138 B4
Pinxton Ct. Mans 103 D3
Pinxton Green. K in A 113 F2
Pinxton La. K-in-A 114 B2
Pinxton La. S in A 114 A4
Pinxton La. S Norm 113 E3
Pinxton Rd. K-in-A 114 B2
Piper Cl. Lo Wh 212 B1
Piper Dr. Lo Wh 212 B1
Piper La. Work 61 E4
Pippin Cl. Nott 173 F4
Pit La. Ship 157 D3
Pitcairn Cl. Nott 173 E1
Pithouse La. W Lea 204 C1
Pitt Hill. Scarc 58 C1
Pitt La. G on H 12 C2
Pl. South 136 B4
Pl. South 136 B4
Plains Farm Cl. Arn 162 B3
Plains Gr. Arn 162 A2
Plains Rd. Arn 162 A2
Plainspot Rd. Sels 128 C1
Plane Cl. Nott 159 F4
Plant La. Lo Ea 193 D2
Plantagenet Ct. Nott 173 E3
Plantagenet St. Nott 173 E3
Plantation Ave. E Mark 66 A4
Plantation Cl. Bes Vil 147 D1
Plantation Hill. Work 36 A2
Plantation La. Hod 27 D4
Plantation Rd. E Mark 66 A3
Plantation Rd. Keyw 197 E2
Plantation Rd. Nott 171 E2
Plantation Side. Nott 172 C4
Plantations The. Lo Ea 193 D4
Plants Yd. Work 35 F1
Platt La. Keyw 198 A3
Platt La. N-on-W 198 A3
Platt St. Pinx 113 E1
Platts The. N-on-T 139 F3
Player St. Nott 172 C3
Plaza Gdns. Nott 160 C2
Pleasant Pl. Kegw 203 E1
Pleasant Row. Nott 172 C4
Pleasley Rd. S in A 101 D3
Plot La. S Sca 98 C2
Plough La. Lowd 150 B1
Plough La. Nott 173 F2
Ploughman Ave. Woodb 149 E2
Plowman Ct. Staple 182 B3
Plowright Ct. Nott 173 E4
Plowright St. Nott 173 E4
Plum Tree Ave. Mans 89 D1
Plumb Rd. Huck 145 F4
Plummer La. Kegw 203 E1
Plumptre Cl. East 143 F1
Plumptre Pl. Nott 173 E2
Plumptre Sq. Nott 173 E2
Plumptre St. Nott 173 E2
Plumptre Way. East 143 F1
Plumptre. Ald 143 D3
Plumtree Gdns. Calv 148 C4
Plumtree Rd. Bir 9 E3
Plumtree Rd. Cotg 187 F2
Plungar Cl. Nott 172 A3
Plungar La. B-le-V 192 A1
Plungar Rd. Gran 191 E3
Plymouth Ave. Pinx 113 F1
Poacher's La. N Whea 31 E4
Pocklington Cres. Wint 125 E3
Pocklington Rd. Coll 98 A1
Podder La. Carl 162 B3
Point The. Nott 173 A2
Pollard Dr. Mans 102 B4
Pollard's La. South 136 C4
Polly Taylor' S Rd. H Marn 67 F1
Polperro Way. Huck 145 E3
Pond Hills La. Nott 147 F1
Pond St. K-in-A 115 D3
Pool Cl. Pinx 113 E1
Poole Meadow. Carl 174 C2
Popham Ct. Nott 173 E2
Popham St. Nott 173 E2
Poplar Ave. E Lea 214 B4
Poplar Ave. K-in-A 115 E3
Poplar Ave. Nott 161 D1
Poplar Ave. Sand 182 A4
Poplar Cl. Bing 178 A2
Poplar Cl. S on T 96 C4
Poplar Cl. Work 35 E1
Poplar Cres. Kim 159 D3
Poplar Dr. Glap 86 A4
Poplar Dr. Mans 87 D2
Poplar Gr. Mans 89 E1
Poplar Gr. Mar War 74 A3
Poplar Rd. S Norm 113 D4
Poplar St. Mans 88 B2
Poplar St. Nott 173 F2
Poplar St. Oll 77 E2
Poplar St. Ret 39 F3
Poplars Ave. Bu Jo 164 A3
Poplars Cl. Keyw 197 F2
Poplars The. Bees 183 F4
Poplars The. S in A 101 D2
Poplars The. W Brid 185 F4
Poplars The. Whit 45 D3
Porchester Cl. Huck 146 B4
Porchester Rd. Bing 177 E2
Porchester Rd. Carl 162 A1
Porlock Cl. Lo Ea 193 D4
Port Arthur Rd. Nott 174 A2
Portage Cl. R on T 175 F1
Porter Cl. Nott 195 E4
Portinscale Cl. W Brid 186 B3
Portland Cres. Mans 88 B2
Portland Cres. Staple 182 C3
Portland Ct Mews. Mans 88 B2
Portland Ct. Nott 161 D3
Portland Gdns. Huck 145 F4
Portland Grange. Huck 145 F4
Portland Hill. Nott 172 B1
Portland Meadows. Sutt 29 D3
Portland Park Cl. Huck 145 F4
Portland Pl. Sutt 29 D3
Portland Pl. Work 35 F2
Portland Rd. Bees 183 D1
Portland Rd. Carl 162 B1
Portland Rd. Greas 158 B4
Portland Rd. Huck 146 A3
Portland Rd. Ilk 157 F2
Portland Rd. Lo Ea 193 D2
Portland Rd. Nott 173 D3
Portland Rd. Ret 39 E3
Portland Rd. Scarc 59 D1
Portland Rd. Sels 129 D4
Portland Rd. Shireb 72 C2
Portland Rd. W Brid 185 F3
Portland St. Arn 161 F3
Portland St. Bees 184 A4
Portland St. K-in-A 115 D3
Portland St. Mans 88 B2
Portland St. Mans 102 A3
Portland St. Mar War 74 A2
Portland St. N-on-T 139 F4
Portland St. Plea 87 D4
Portland St. S in A 100 C1
Portland St. S in A 100 C1
Portland St. Work 35 F2
Portland Terr. Gain 24 B4
Portland Terr. Mar War 60 C1
Portland Terr. Scarc 59 D1
Portree Dr. Nott 146 C1
Post Office La. Plun 191 F1
Post Office La. Redm 192 C2
Post Office Rd. K-in-A 115 D3
Post Office Yd. Hover 151 E1
Postern St. Nott 173 D2
Posts The. Cr Bu 189 D3
Potter La. Wellow 92 B4
Potter St. S in A 101 D2
Potter St. Work 35 F1
Potters Ct. Bees 171 E1
Potters La. E Lea 214 C4
Potters Way. Ilk 170 A4
Poulter Cl. Nott 172 B4
Poulter St. Scarc 58 C1
Poulton Dr. Nott 173 F1
Poultry. Nott 173 E2
Powtrell Pl. Ilk 170 A3
Poynton St. Nott 173 D3
Poyser Cl. Nott 161 D1
Pratt Cl. Mans 87 E1
Prebends Cl. Farn 138 C2
Precinct Rd. K-in-A 115 D3
Precinct The. Cotg 187 F2
Premier Rd. Nott 173 D4
Prendwick Gdns. Nott 161 D4
Prest Ave. Mar War 74 C4
Preston Rd. Rain 118 A4
Prestwick Cl. Nott 159 E1
Prestwold Ave. Mans 89 D1
Prestwold Ave. Mans 103 D4
Prestwold La. Hoton 215 E1
Prestwood Dr. Nott 172 A4
Previn Gdns. Nott 173 F3
Priestgate. E Mark 65 F3
Priestsic Rd. S in A 100 C2
Primrose Ave. Farn 139 D3
Primrose Ave. N-on-T 125 D2
Primrose Ave. Sels 128 C1
Primrose Cl. K-in-A 114 C4
Primrose Cl. Nott 173 E4
Primrose Cres. Carl 174 C4
Primrose La. Kirton 78 B3
Primrose Rise. Greas 158 B4
Primrose St. Carl 174 C4
Primrose St. Gain 24 B4
Primrose St. Ilk 157 F2
Primrose Way. Work 36 A3
Primula Cl. Nott 184 B1
Prince Charles Rd. Work 35 E3
Prince Edward Cres. R on T 175 F1
Prince Of Wales St. Ret 39 F3
Prince St. Ilk 157 F2
Prince St. Lo Ea 193 E4
Prince William Rd. Lough 220 A3
Prince's St. N-on-T 139 F4
Princes Rd. Ne Br 219 D3
Princes St. Mans 102 A3
Princess Anne Rd. Work 35 F3
Princess Ave. Bees 184 A3
Princess Ave. Mans 103 D4
Princess Ave. Mar War 74 B2
Princess Ave. S Norm 113 D3
Princess Cl. Carl 162 C1
Princess Dr. Sand 182 A2
Princess St. East 143 F2
Princess St. K-in-A 114 B2
Princess St. Lo Ea 193 E4
Princess St. Lough 220 A2
Princess Wlk. Gain 15 F1
Prior Cl. S in A 101 D2
Prior Rd. Arn 161 E3
Priors Cl. Bing 178 A3
Priors The. Lowd 150 B1
Priorswell Rd. Work 35 F1
Priory Ave. Ann Wo 130 A4
Priory Ave. Raven 117 D1
Priory Ave. Toll 186 B1
Priory Cir. Toll 186 B1
Priory Cl. Bald 140 C2
Priory Cl. Blyth 18 A2
Priory Cl. Gain 24 C4
Priory Cl. Matt 20 A4
Priory Cres. Carl 162 C1
Priory Ct. Carl 162 C1

Priory La. Thur 151 E4
Priory Mews. Nott 172 C1
Priory Park. Thur 151 E4
Priory Rd. Blid 118 A3
Priory Rd. Carl 162 C1
Priory Rd. East 143 F1
Priory Rd. Huck 145 F4
Priory Rd. Mans 88 A2
Priory Rd. W Brid 186 A4
Priory Sq. Mans 88 A2
Priory St. Nott 172 C1
Private Rd. Huck 145 F4
Private Rd. Nott 161 E1
Private Rd. South 121 F1
Private Rd. Woodb 149 E3
Private St. N-on-T 140 A4
Privet Ave. K-in-A 115 D3
Prize Cl. Nott 184 B1
Procters Dr. Girt 82 C1
Promenade The. K-in-A 115 E3
Promenade. Nott 173 E3
Prospect Cl. K-in-A 115 D4
Prospect Ct. S in A 99 F1
Prospect Dr. Shireb 72 C2
Prospect Dr. Work 35 F3
Prospect Pl. Nott 172 C2
Prospect Pl. S in A 100 C1
Prospect Prec. Work 36 A3
Prospect Rd. Carl 162 A1
Prospect Rd. Hean 157 D4
Prospect St. Mans 102 B3
Prospect St. Nott 172 C3
Prospect Terr. Gain 24 B4
Prospect Terr. Nott 172 C3
Providence Pl. Ilk 157 F1
Providence Rd. Sels 128 A2
Prudhoe Ct. Nott 173 E1
Pudding La. Hick 210 B3
Pulborough Cl. Nott 160 C2
Pullman Rd. Nott 173 F2
Pump Hollow La. Mans 103 D4
Pump Hollow Rd. Mans 103 D4
Pump La. Fenton 142 C1
Pump La. Wale 64 A1
Purbeck Cl. Lo Ea 193 D4
Purbeck Dr. W Brid 185 E3
Purdy Meadow. Lo Ea 193 D3
Pyatt St. Nott 173 E1
Pye Ave. Mans 101 E4
Pye Hill Rd. Sels 128 A2
Pygall Ave. Goth 195 D1
Pym St. Nott 173 F3
Pym Wlk. Nott 173 F3
Python Hill Rd. Rain 104 A1

Quadrangle The. Blid 118 A3
Quadrangle The. News 130 B3
Quakefield Rd. E Mark 66 A3
Quaker La. Farns 119 F3
Quaker La. Mans 102 A3
Quaker Way. Mans 102 A4
Quantock Cl. Bes Vil 147 D1
Quantock Gr. Bing 177 E2
Quantock Rd. Lo Ea 182 A1
Quarry Ave. Nott 160 A3
Quarry Cl. Raven 132 A4
Quarry Dr. K-in-A 115 D2
Quarry Hill. S-by-D 182 A4
Quarry La. Linby 131 D2
Quarry La. Mans 102 A3
Quarry Rd. Raven 117 D1
Quarry Rd. Raven 132 A4
Quarry Yard. S in A 100 C1
Quarrydale Ave. S in A 100 C3
Quarrydale Dr. S in A 100 C3
Quarrydale Rd. S in A 100 C2
Quayside Cl. Nott 173 F1
Queen Elizabeth Cres. Rhod 35 D2
Queen Elizabeth Rd. Bees 183 D2
Queen St. Arn 148 A1
Queen St. Bald 140 C2
Queen St. Bott 181 D1
Queen St. Coll 98 A1
Queen St. Gain 24 B4
Queen St. Huck 145 F4
Queen St. K-in-A 115 D2
Queen St. La Mi 143 E2
Queen St. Lo Ea 193 F4
Queen St. Lough 220 B2
Queen St. Mans 102 A4
Queen St. Mar War 74 A3
Queen St. N-on-T 139 F4
Queen St. Nott 173 E3
Queen St. Pinx 113 E2
Queen St. Ret 39 E3
Queen St. S in A 100 C2
Queen St. S Norm 113 D3
Queen St. South 121 E1
Queen St. Work 35 F1
Queen's Ave. Carl 162 C1
Queen's Bridge Rd. Nott 173 E2
Queen's Cres. Baw 10 A4
Queen's Ct. Bing 177 E3
Queen's Ct. Mans 89 E2
Queen's Ct. N-on-T 125 D1
Queen's Dr. Nuth 159 E3
Queen's Head Ct. N-on-T 139 F4
Queen's Rd. Lough 220 B2
Queen's Rd. N-on-T 125 D1
Queen's Rd. Nott 173 E2
Queen's Rd. R on T 176 A2
Queen's Sq. East 143 F1
Queen's Wlk. Ne La 59 D1
Queen's Wlk. Nott 173 D1
Queens Dr. Bees 184 A3
Queens Ave. Ilk 170 A3
Queens Bower Rd. Arn 161 E4
Queens Bower Rd. Nott 161 E4
Queens Cl. Whit 45 E3
Queens Dr. Brin 143 F4
Queens Dr. Nott 185 D4
Queens Dr. Sand 182 A2
Queens Rd E. Bees 184 A4
Queens Rd N. East 143 F1
Queens Rd S. East 143 F1
Queens Rd W. Bees 183 F2
Queens Rd. Bees 184 A3
Queens Rd. C in L 25 F4
Queens Rd. Kegw 203 E1
Queens Rd. Whit 45 E3
Queensberry St. Nott 160 C2
Queensbury Ave. W Brid 185 E2
Queensway. Gain 24 C4
Queensway. K-in-A 115 D1
Queensway. Mans 89 D1
Queensway. Ne Br 219 E3
Queensway. Sax 57 D2
Queensway. Skel 71 F2
Queensway. Work 35 F2
Querneby Ave. Nott 161 F1
Querneby Rd. Nott 161 F1
Quibell Rd. N-on-T 140 A3
Quibell's La. N-on-T 125 D2
Quines Hill Rd. Mans 89 D1
Quinton Cl. Nott 185 D3
Quorn Cl. Bees 183 F2
Quorn Cl. Lough 220 B1
Quorn Gr. Nott 161 D2
Quorn Rd. Nott 161 D1
Quorndon Cres. Lo Ea 193 E3

Rabbithill La. Spal 83 D3
Racecourse Rd. Mans 102 C3
Rachel Cl. Gain 15 E2
Radbourne Rd. Nott 173 F2
Radbourne St. Mans 88 C2
Radburn Ct. Staple 170 C1
Radcliffe Gdns. Carl 174 B4
Radcliffe Mount. W Brid 173 F1
Radcliffe Rd. Cr Bu 189 D4
Radcliffe Rd. Gam 186 B4
Radcliffe Rd. Ho Pi 175 D1
Radcliffe Rd. W Brid 186 A4
Radcliffe St. Nott 173 E1
Radford Bridge Rd. Nott 172 B3
Radford Bvd. Nott 172 C3
Radford Cres. Carl 162 C1
Radford Ct. Nott 172 C3
Radford Grove La. Nott 172 C3
Radford Rd. Nott 172 C4
Radford St. Mans 102 A3
Radford St. Work 36 A1
Radley La. Halam 135 E4
Radley Sq. Nott 160 B3
Radmanthwaite Rd. Mans 87 E2
Radmoor Rd. Lough 220 A2
Radnor Gr. Bing 177 E2
Radnor Pl. Mans 87 E2
Radstock Rd. Nott 174 A4
Radway Dr. Nott 185 D3
Raeburn Dr. Bees 182 C1
Ragdale Rd. Nott 160 B4
Raglan Cl. Nott 173 E4
Raglan Ct. N-on-T 140 A4
Raglan Ct. Nott 172 A1
Raglan Dr. Carl 163 D1
Raglan Gdns. N-on-T 140 A4
Raglan Rd. Ret 40 A4
Raglan St. East 144 A1
Raibank Gdns. Arn 161 F3
Railway Ave. Elmt 58 B4
Railway Cotts. Kim 158 C3
Railway Terr. Lough 220 B3
Raines Ave. Work 35 F3
Raines Park Rd. Work 35 F4
Rainham Gdns. Rudd 196 B3
Rainworth Water Rd. Rain 103 F1
Raithby Cl. Nott 161 D3
Raleigh Cl. Ilk 157 F2
Raleigh Cl. Nott 184 B1
Raleigh Rd. Mans 101 F4
Raleigh St. Nott 173 D3
Ralf Cl. W Brid 185 F2
Ramblers Cl. Carl 174 C3
Ramper Rd. Beck 23 E4
Ramper Rd. Let 16 A2
Rampton Green Rd. Ramp 42 C1
Rampton La. S Lev 42 B3
Rampton Rd. Lane 54 A3
Rampton Rd. Tres 42 C2
Ramsdale Ave. Calv 148 B4
Ramsdale Cres. Nott 161 E2
Ramsdale Rd. Carl 162 C1
Ramsden Ave. Lan 16 C1
Ramsden Cft. Rain 104 A1
Ramsden Cres. C in L 25 F4
Ramsey Cl. Mans 89 D1
Ramsey Cl. Staple 170 C1
Ramsey Ct. Nott 161 D1
Ramsey Dr. Arn 162 B3
Ranby Wlk. Nott 173 F3
Rancliffe Ave. Keyw 197 E2
Randal Gdns. Nott 172 C4
Randal St. Nott 172 C4
Randall Cl. N-on-T 140 B4
Randall Way. Ret 29 E1
Randol Cl. Mans 101 E2
Ranelagh Gr. Nott 172 A3
Ranmere Rd. Nott 172 A4
Ranmoor Rd. Carl 162 C1
Ranmore Cl. Bees 171 D1
Rannoch Dr. Mans 101 F3
Rannoch Rise. Nott 147 F1
Rannock Gdns. Keyw 197 F2
Ranskill Gdns. Nott 161 D4
Ranskill Rd. Matt 19 F3
Ransom Dr. Nott 161 F1
Ransom Rd. Mans 103 E2
Ransom Rd. Nott 173 F4
Ransome Cl. N-on-T 140 B4
Ratcliffe Gate. Mans 102 B3
Ratcliffe La. Kegw 203 E4
Ratcliffe Rd. Lough 220 B3
Ratcliffe St. East 143 F1
Rathgar Cl. Nott 171 E2
Rathmines Cl. Nott 172 C2
Rathvale Ct. Bees 183 D2
Raven Ave. Nott 161 D2
Ravencroft La. Beck 14 A1
Ravendale Rd. Gain 24 C4
Ravendale Rd. Gain 24 C4
Ravenhill Cl. Bees 183 D2
Ravens Ct. Nott 161 D3
Ravenscourt. Work 36 A3
Ravensdale Ave. Lo Ea 182 A1
Ravensdale Ave. Mans 102 B4
Ravensdale Dr. Nott 171 E2
Ravensdale Rd. Mans 102 C4
Ravensdene Ct. Nott 173 A2
Ravensfleet Rd. E Stock 7 F2
Ravenshill Cl. Ran 19 D2
Ravensmore Rd. Nott 161 D1
Ravenswood Rd. Arn 162 A4
Ravensworth Rd. Nott 160 A4
Rawson St. Nott 160 C1
Rawson St. Sels 129 D3
Raylawn St. Mans 103 D3
Raymede Cl. Nott 160 C3
Raymede Dr. Nott 160 C3
Raymond Cl. K-in-A 114 C4
Raymond Dr. Bing 178 A2
Raymoth La. Work 35 F4
Rayner Ct. Nott 172 C3
Raynford Ave. Bees 183 E2
Raysmith Cl. South 121 F1
Rayton La. Work 36 B2
Rayton Spur. Work 36 A2
Read Ave. Bees 184 A3
Readman Rd. Bees 183 D2
Rearsby Cl. Nott 171 E3
Recreation Dr. Shireb 72 C1
Recreation Rd. Ann Wo 130 B4
Recreation Rd. Plea 86 C4
Recreation Rd. Sand 182 A3
Recreation Rd. Shireb 72 C2
Recreation St. Lo Ea 193 F4
Recreation St. Mans 102 B4
Recreation St. Sels 129 D3
Recreation Terr. Staple 182 B3
Recreation View. Shireb 72 C3
Rectory Ave. Gain 15 E1
Rectory Ave. Nott 171 F2
Rectory Dr The. Carl 162 C1
Rectory Gdns. Beck 14 A1
Rectory Gdns. Kirton 78 A3
Rectory Gdns. Nott 171 F2
Rectory La. Bott 181 D2
Rectory La. Clayp 156 C4
Rectory La. Cotg 187 F2
Rectory La. Gams 50 C3
Rectory La. Lea 24 C1
Rectory Pl. B in F 194 C3
Rectory Pl. Lough 220 A2
Rectory Rd. Carl 174 C3
Rectory Rd. Lough 220 A3
Rectory Rd. Mar War 74 B4
Rectory Rd. Ret 39 F4
Rectory Rd. Tres 42 A2
Rectory Rd. W Brid 185 F4
Rectory St. Beckin 142 B4
Red Barn Cl. Newt 99 D2
Red Causeway The. Harb 202 A1
Red La. Brin 128 C1
Red La. C in L 26 A1
Red La. Lowd 150 B1
Red Lodge La. Kneet 166 A4
Redbarn La. Newt 99 D2
Redbourne Dr. Nott 172 B3
Redbridge Dr. Nuth 159 E2
Redcar Cl. Carl 162 C1
Redcliffe Gdns. Nott 173 E4
Redcliffe Rd. Mans 102 B3
Redcliffe Rd. Nott 173 E4
Redcliffe St. S in A 101 D2
Redfield Rd. Nott 184 C4
Redfield Way. Nott 184 C4
Redforde Park Ave. Ret 29 E1
Redforde Park Dr. Ret 29 E1
Redforde Park Rd. Ret 29 E1
Redgate Cl. Mans 101 F4
Redgate St. Mans 101 F4
Redgate St. Pinx 113 E1
Redgates Ct. Calv 148 B4
Redhill La. Both 63 F4
Redhill Lodge Dr. Nott 147 E1
Redhill Rd. Arn 161 F4
Redhill Rd. Nott 147 F1
Redland Ave. Carl 174 C4
Redland Cl. Bees 183 E2
Redland Cl. Ilk 157 F2
Redland Dr. Bees 183 E2
Redland Gr. Carl 174 C4
Redman Cl. Gain 15 F1
Redmays Dr. Bulc 164 A3
Redmile La. B-le-V 192 B2
Redmile La. Redm 192 B2
Redmile Rd. Nott 160 B1
Redoubt St. Nott 172 C3
Redruth Cl. Nott 171 E3
Redruth Dr. Mans 103 D1
Redthorn Way. Clayp 156 C3
Redwood Ave. Nott 171 E2
Redwood Cres. Bees 184 A3
Redwood Ct. Huck 145 F4
Redwood. W Brid 185 E3
Reedham Wlk. Nott 161 D4
Reedman Rd. Lo Ea 193 D2
Rees Gdns. Nott 147 D1
Rees Row. Wood 42 A1
Reform St. Ann Wo 129 F4
Reform St. S in A 100 C1
Regatta Way. Gam 186 B4
Regency Ct. Bees 184 A4
Regent St. Bees 184 A4
Regent St. K-in-A 114 C2
Regent St. Kim 158 C3
Regent St. La Mi 143 D2
Regent St. Lo Ea 193 E4
Regent St. Lough 220 A2
Regent St. Mans 102 A4
Regent St. Nott 161 D1
Regent St. Nott 173 D2
Regent St. S in A 100 B1
Regent St. Staple 182 B3
Regents Cl. Coll 112 A4
Regina Cl. R on T 175 F1
Regina Cres. Raven 116 C1
Reigate Cl. Bees 183 F1
Reigate Dr. Bees 183 F1
Reigate Rd. Nott 160 C1
Reindeer St. Mans 102 C3
Rempstone Dr. Nott 160 B3
Rempstone Rd. E Lea 214 C4
Rempstone Rd. Hoton 215 E1
Rempstone Rd. N on S 214 A3
Rempstone Rd. Wyme 216 A2
Renals Way. Calv 148 C4
Renfrew Ct. Mans 101 F3
Renfrew Dr. Nott 171 F2
Repton Ct. Mans 88 C2
Repton Dr. Ilk 170 A4
Repton Rd. Nott 160 B3
Repton Rd. W Brid 185 F3
Reston Cl. Mans 103 D3
Retford Gate. N Le Ha 41 F4
Retford Rd. Babw 37 E2
Retford Rd. Blyth 18 A1
Retford Rd. Boug 77 F4
Retford Rd. E Dray 52 C2
Retford Rd. Matt 20 B3
Retford Rd. N Le Ha 41 F4
Retford Rd. N Le Ha 42 A4
Retford Rd. N Whea 31 E4
Retford Rd. Nott 161 D2
Retford Rd. Ramp 42 B1
Retford Rd. S Lev 42 A4
Retford Rd. Wood 42 B1
Retford Rd. Work 36 B1
Retford Rd. Work 37 E2
Revelstoke Ave. Nott 146 B1
Revelstoke Way. Nott 146 C1
Revesby Gdns. Nott 172 B4
Revesby Rd. Arn 161 F3
Revill Cres. Staple 182 C4
Revill Ct. K-in-A 114 C4
Reydon Dr. Nott 160 B1
Reynolds Dr. Nott 171 F3
Rhodes Wlk. Mans 101 F3
Rhyl Cres. Carl 162 C1
Ribble St. Nott 172 B3
Ribblesdale Ct. Bees 183 D2
Ribblesdale Rd. Lo Ea 193 D3
Ribblesdale Rd. Nott 161 E3
Ribblesdale. Work 36 A4
Riber Cl. Ann Wo 115 D1
Riber Cl. Lo Ea 193 E3
Richard St. Ret 40 A3
Richards Cl. Cr Bi 189 D2
Richardson Cl. Nott 184 B1
Richborough Pl. Nott 171 F1
Richey Cl. Arn 162 A4
Richmond Ave. Calv 149 D4
Richmond Ave. East 144 A1
Richmond Ave. Ilk 157 F2
Richmond Ave. Lo Ea 193 D4
Richmond Ave. Nott 173 F4
Richmond Ave. Sand 182 A2
Richmond Cl. Bald 140 A2
Richmond Dr. Bees 183 F3
Richmond Dr. Mans 88 B1
Richmond Dr. Nott 161 E1
Richmond Dr. R on T 175 F2
Richmond Gdns. Nott 147 F1
Richmond Rd. C in L 25 F3
Richmond Rd. Gain 24 C4
Richmond Rd. K-in-A 115 E3
Richmond Rd. Ret 30 A1
Richmond Rd. W Brid 173 F1
Richmond Rd. Work 36 A1
Richmond St. Mans 102 C3
Richmond Terr. R on T 175 F2
Rick St. Nott 173 E3
Ricket La. Blid 117 E3
Ricket La. Raven 116 C2
Ricket La. Raven 117 E3
Ricklow Ct. Nott 161 D4
Riddell Ave. Lan 16 C2
Ridding Terr. Nott 173 E3
Ridge Cl. S in A 100 B2
Ridge Hill. Lowd 150 B1
Ridge La. R on T 176 A3
Ridgeway Cl. Farns 119 F3
Ridgeway La. Mar War 74 A2
Ridgeway St. Nott 173 F3
Ridgeway Terr. Mar War 74 A2
Ridgeway The. Farns 120 A3
Ridgeway Wlk. Nott 161 D4
Ridgeway. Hean 157 D4
Ridgeway. Nott 161 D4
Ridgeway. South 121 E1
Ridgeway. Work 36 A3
Ridgewood Dr. Bees 183 E2
Ridgewood Gr. Raven 117 D1
Ridgmont Walk. Nott 195 E4
Ridgway Cl. W Brid 186 B3
Riding or Ridding La. Aust 3 D2
Ridings The. Bulc 164 A3
Ridings The. E Brid 165 E2
Ridings The. Keyw 198 A2
Ridings The. Mans 88 C1
Ridsdale Rd. Nott 161 E3
Rifle St. Nott 172 C3
Rigg La. Raven 132 C4
Rigley Ave. Ilk 157 F1
Rigley Dr. Nott 160 C4
Riley Ave. S in A 100 B2
Riley Cl. S in A 100 B2
Ring Leas. Cotg 188 A1
Ringrose Cl. N-on-T 140 B4
Ringstead Cl. W Brid 185 E3
Ringstead Wlk. Nott 161 D4
Ringwood Ave. Mans 102 B2
Ringwood Cres. Nott 172 B3
Ringwood Rd. Bing 177 E2
Ringwood. Work 36 A3
Ripon Rd. Nott 174 A3
Rise Park Rd. Nott 146 C1
Rise The. Nott 161 E2
Riseborough Wlk. Nott 146 B1
Risegate. Cotg 187 F2
Riseholme Ave. Nott 171 E2
Riseholme Rd. Gain 24 C4
Risley Ct. Ilk 157 F2
Risley Dr. Nott 173 D1
Riste's Pl. Nott 173 E2
Ritson Cl. Nott 173 E3
River Cl. Ret 29 F1
River La. Miss 4 B1
River La. Ret 39 F4
River Rd. Carl 174 C2
River View. Ald 128 A3
River View. Mar War 74 A3
River View. Nott 173 E1
River View. Ret 39 F2
Riverdale Rd. Bees 183 E1
Rivergreen Cl. Bees 171 E1
Rivergreen Cres. Bees 171 E1
Rivergreen. Nott 184 C2
Rivermead. Cotg 188 A2
Rivermead. N-on-T 139 F3
Riverside Cl. Bott 181 D2
Riverside Cl. Cuck 60 A2
Riverside Rd. Bees 184 A2
Riverside Rd. N-on-T 139 E3
Riverside Way. Mans 88 B3
Riverside Way. Nott 173 D1
Riverside. South 121 F1
Riverside. What 179 D2
Riverview Cotts. Miss 4 B1
Riverway Gdns. Nott 173 E1
Rivington Rd. Bees 182 C1
Road No 1. Carl 174 C3
Road No 2. Carl 174 C3
Road No 3. Carl 175 D3
Road No 4. Carl 175 E3
Road No 5. Carl 175 D3
Road No 7. Carl 174 C3
Road No 8. Carl 174 C3
Robbie Burns Rd. Nott 161 E4
Robert Ave. Mans 101 F3

Robert's La. Huck 145 F4
Roberts Ave. S in A 99 F1
Roberts Cl. D on T 54 A1
Roberts Cl. Kegw 203 E1
Roberts St. Ilk 170 A3
Roberts St. Nott 173 F2
Roberts Yd. Bees 184 A4
Robey Cl. Mans 89 D1
Robey Dr. East 143 F2
Robin Down Cl. Mans 102 B1
Robin Down La. Mans 102 B1
Robin Gr. Raven 117 D1
Robin Hood Ave. Edwin 91 E4
Robin Hood Ave. Mar War 74 B1
Robin Hood Cl. East 143 F1
Robin Hood Dr. Huck 145 F3
Robin Hood Ind Est. Nott 173 F3
Robin Hood Rd. Ann Wo 130 A4
Robin Hood Rd. Bes Vil 147 E1
Robin Hood Rd. Blid 118 A3
Robin Hood St. Nott 173 F3
Robin Hood Terr. Nott 173 E3
Robin Hood Terr. Raven 117 D2
Robin Hood Way. Nott 173 D1
Robin's Wood Rd. Nott 172 A4
Robina Dr. Greas 158 B4
Robinet Rd. Bees 183 F3
Robinettes La. Coss 158 B1
Robinia Ct. W Brid 186 A3
Robins Ct. N-on-T 140 A4
Robinson Cl. N-on-T 140 C4
Robinson Dr. Work 35 F1
Robinson Gdns. Nott 184 B1
Robinson Rd. Carl 162 A1
Roche Cl. Arn 162 B4
Rochester Ave. Carl 175 D4
Rochester Cl. Work 36 A4
Rochester Ct. Nott 159 F3
Rochester Rd. Rain 118 A4
Rochester Wlk. Nott 184 C1
Rochford Ct. W Brid 186 B2
Rock Ct. Mans 102 B4
Rock Ct. Nott 160 B2
Rock Dr. Nott 173 D2
Rock Hill. Mans 102 B3
Rock St. Mans 102 B3
Rock St. Nott 160 A4
Rock Valley. Mans 102 B4
Rockford Ct. Staple 170 C1
Rockford Rd. Nott 160 C2
Rockingham Gr. Bing 177 E2
Rocklands The. Shireb 72 C2
Rockley Ave. East 144 A1
Rockley Ave. R on T 175 F2
Rockley Cl. Huck 145 E3
Rockley Way. Shireb 72 C2
Rockleys View. Lowd 150 A1
Rockwood Cl. Blid 118 A3
Rockwood Wlk. Huck 145 F3
Rodel Ct. Nott 173 E3
Roden St. Nott 173 F3
Roderick Ave. Ann Wo 115 D1
Roderick St. Nott 160 B2
Rodney Rd. W Brid 186 A3
Rodney Way. Ilk 157 F2
Rodwell Cl. Nott 172 B3
Roe Hill. Woodb 149 E3
Roebuck Dr. Mans 102 A2
Roecliffe. W Brid 185 F2
Roehampton Dr. Staple 170 B1
Roes La. Calv 149 D4
Roewood La. Wink 107 F1
Roger Cl. S in A 100 C3
Roker Cl. Nott 160 A1
Rolaine Cl. Mans 88 B2
Roland Ave. Nott 185 D4
Roland Ave. Nuth 159 F2
Rolleston Cl. Huck 145 E3
Rolleston Cres. Greas 144 C1
Rolleston Cres. Greas 158 C4
Rolleston Dr. Arn 162 A4
Rolleston Dr. Greas 158 B4
Rolleston Dr. Nott 172 C2
Roman Bank La. Ran 18 C3
Roman Bank. Mans 88 B2
Roman Dr. Nott 160 C2
Romans Ct. Nott 160 C1
Romilay Cl. Nott 172 A1
Romney Ave. Nott 171 E1
Rona Cl. Mans 101 F3
Rona Ct. Nott 160 C3
Ronald St. Nott 172 C3
Rook's La. Mist 6 C1
Rookery Gdns. Arn 161 F4
Rookery La. S in A 114 A4
Rookery The. Mans 102 A4
Rookwood Cl. Bees 183 F3
Rookwood Cres. Huck 145 E3
Rooley Ave. S in A 100 B2
Rooley Dr. S in A 100 B2
Roosa Cl. Nott 159 F3
Roosevelt Ave. Lo Ea 193 E3
Roosevelt Rd. S in A 101 D2
Rooth St. Mans 102 A3
Rope Wlk. E Lea 205 E1
Ropery Rd. Gain 15 E1
Ropewalk The. Ilk 158 A1
Ropewalk The. N-on-T 140 A4
Ropewalk The. Nott 173 D2
Ropewalk The. South 121 F1
Ropewalk. Kegw 203 E1
Ropework Seedbed Cntr. Ilk 158 A1
Ropsley Cres. W Brid 186 A4
Roscoe Ave. Nott 147 F1
Rose Ash La. Nott 161 D4
Rose Ave. Ilk 157 F1
Rose Ave. Ret 40 A2
Rose Cl. Nott 173 E4
Rose Cottage Dr. S in A 99 F1
Rose Cotts. Bu Jo 163 F3
Rose Ct. Lo Ea 182 A1
Rose Farm Dr. S on T 96 C4
Rose Gr. Bees 184 A3
Rose Gr. Keyw 197 F2
Rose Hill. Keyw 197 F2
Rose La. Mans 88 B2
Rose Lea. Ret 39 E2
Rosebank Dr. Arn 148 A1
Roseberry Ave. W Brid 173 F1
Roseberry Gdns. Huck 146 B3
Roseberry St. K-in-A 115 E2
Rosebery Hill. Mans 102 B3
Rosebery St. Nott 160 C2
Rosecroft Dr. Nott 161 E3
Rosedale Cl. Lo Ea 193 D3
Rosedale Dr. Nott 171 D2
Rosedale La. Raven 116 C2
Rosedale Rd. Nott 174 B3
Rosedale. Work 36 A4
Rosegarth Wlk. Nott 160 B2
Rosegrove Ave. Nott 147 F1
Rosehill Cl. Sax 57 D2
Roseleigh Ave. Carl 162 A1
Rosemary Ave. Mans 102 A4
Rosemary Cl. Nott 159 F1
Rosemary St. Mans 102 A4
Rosemont Cl. S in A 100 C3
Roseneath Ave. Nott 146 C1
Rosetta Rd. Nott 160 C1
Rosewall Ct. Arn 162 A4
Roseway. Gain 15 E1
Rosewood Cl. N-on-T 125 D1
Rosewood Cl. S Norm 113 D4
Rosewood Cres. Hean 143 D1
Rosewood Dr. K-in-A 115 E3
Rosewood Gdns. Nott 159 F4
Rosewood Gdns. W Brid 185 E2
Roslyn Ave. Carl 162 C1
Ross Cl. Codd 126 A1
Ross Cl. Lowd 150 C1
Ross La. Lamb 163 E4
Rossell Dr. Staple 182 C3
Rossendale. Ilk 157 F2
Rossetti Gdns. Work 36 B2
Rossington Rd. Nott 173 F3
Rosslyn Dr. Huck 146 B4
Rosslyn Dr. Nott 160 A1
Rosthwaite Cl. W Brid 186 B3
Rothbury Ave. Staple 170 B1
Rothbury Gr. Bing 177 E3
Rotherham Baulk. Cl in L 25 E4
Rotherham Baulk. Let 25 E4
Rotherham Rd. Plea 86 C4
Rothley Ave. Nott 173 F3
Rothwell Cl. Gain 24 C4
Rothwell Cl. Nott 185 D2
Roughs Wood La. Huck 145 E2
Roulstone Cres. E Lea 205 F2
Roundhill Cl. S in A 101 E1
Roundwood Rd. Arn 161 E4
Row The. Orst 179 F3
Rowan Ave. Hath 213 D1
Rowan Ave. Raven 117 D1
Rowan Ave. Staple 170 C1
Rowan Cl. Calv 148 B4
Rowan Cl. Mans 88 B1
Rowan Cres. Work 35 F1
Rowan Croft. S in A 99 F2
Rowan Ct. Kim 159 D3
Rowan Dr. K-in-A 114 C3
Rowan Dr. Keyw 198 A1
Rowan Dr. Nott 185 D2
Rowan Dr. Sels 128 B4
Rowan Dr. Shireb 72 B3
Rowan Gdns. Nott 159 F4
Rowan Way. Bald 140 A3
Rowan Wlk. Carl 174 A4
Rowe Gdns. Nott 160 B3
Rowland Ave. Carl 162 A1
Rowland Mews. Nott 173 F4
Rowsley Ave. Lo Ea 193 D3
Rowston Cl. Gain 15 E1
Rowthorne La. Al Hu 86 A4
Rowthorne La. Glap 86 A4
Roxton Ct. Kim 158 C4
Roy Ave. Bees 184 A2
Royal Ave. Lo Ea 182 B1
Royal Cres. Work 35 F3
Royal Mews. Bees 183 E2
Royal Oak Ct. Edwin 76 A1
Royal Oak Dr. Sels 129 D4
Royal Way. Lough 220 A3
Royce Ave. Huck 145 F2
Royds Cres. Rhod 35 D3
Royland Rd. Lough 220 A2
Royston Cl. Nott 173 D1
Ruddington Ct. Mans 103 D1
Ruddington La. Nott 185 D3
Ruddington Rd. Mans 103 D1
Rudge Cl. Nott 171 F3
Ruffles Ave. Arn 162 A3
Rufford Ave. Bees 183 D4
Rufford Ave. Carl 162 B1
Rufford Ave. Mans 102 B4
Rufford Ave. Mar War 74 C4
Rufford Ave. N-on-T 139 F4
Rufford Ave. Oll 77 E2
Rufford Ave. Rain 104 B1
Rufford Ave. Ret 39 E2
Rufford Cl. Bils 106 A2
Rufford Cl. Huck 146 B3
Rufford Cl. S in A 100 C3
Rufford Dr. Mans 88 C2
Rufford Gr. Bing 177 E2
Rufford La. Oll 92 A4
Rufford La. Ruff 91 F4
Rufford Rd. Edwin 91 E4
Rufford Rd. Lo Ea 193 D2
Rufford Rd. Nott 161 E2
Rufford Rd. Rudd 196 B4
Rufford St. Work 47 D4
Rufford Way. W Brid 186 A3
Rufford Wlk. Nott 160 A4
Ruffs Dr. Huck 145 F3
Rugby Cl. Nott 160 C4
Rugby Rd. Rain 118 A4
Rugeley Ave. Lo Ea 194 A4
Ruislip Cl. Kim 158 C4
Runcie Cl. Cotg 187 F1
Runnymede Ct. Nott 173 D3
Runswick Dr. Arn 161 F4
Runswick Dr. Nott 172 A3
Runton Dr. Nott 160 C2
Rupert Cres. N-on-T 139 F4
Rupert Rd. Bing 177 E2
Rupert St. Ilk 158 A1
Rush Leys. Lo Ea 193 E3
Rushcliffe Ave. Carl 174 B4
Rushcliffe Ave. R on T 175 F2
Rushcliffe Ct. Nott 160 B3
Rushcliffe Gr. E Lea 205 F2
Rushcliffe Rd. Huck 145 F3
Rushcliffe Rise. Nott 161 E3
Rushes The. Goth 195 D1
Rushes The. Lough 220 A2
Rushes The. Mans 88 B3
Rushey Cl. Work 36 A1
Rushford Dr. Nott 171 F2
Rushmere Wlk. Arn 161 F3
Rushpool Ave. Mans 88 B2
Rushton Gdns. Nott 173 F4
Rushworth Ave. W Brid 185 F4
Rushworth Cl. Nott 173 F4
Rushy Cl. Nott 171 E3
Ruskin Ave. Bees 183 E2
Ruskin Ave. Lo Ea 193 D3
Ruskin Rd. Mans 87 E1
Ruskin St. Gain 24 B3
Russell Ave. Bald 140 A2
Russell Ave. Har 8 C2
Russell Ave. Nott 171 F2
Russell Cres. Nott 171 F2
Russell Dr. Nott 171 F2
Russell Pl. Nott 173 D3
Russell Rd. Nott 172 C4
Russell St. Lo Ea 182 B1
Russell St. Lough 220 B2
Russell St. Nott 173 D3
Russell St. S in A 100 C2
Russet Ave. Carl 174 C4
Russet Gr. Baw 10 A4
Russey Cl. Lowd 150 C1
Russley Rd. Bees 183 D4
Ruth Dr. Arn 148 A1
Rutherford Ave. Mans 102 C2
Ruthwell Gdns. Bes Vil 147 D1
Rutland Ave. Bees 183 D1
Rutland Ave. N-on-T 140 A3
Rutland Cl. Mar War 74 A2
Rutland Cres. Har 8 C3
Rutland Dr. Har 8 B2
Rutland Dr. Har 8 C3
Rutland Gr. Staple 182 B3
Rutland La. Bott 181 D1
Rutland Rd. Bing 177 F3
Rutland Rd. Carl 162 B2
Rutland Rd. Ret 40 A2
Rutland Rd. Sels 128 B2
Rutland Rd. W Brid 186 A4
Rutland St. Ilk 157 F1
Rutland St. Lough 220 B2
Rutland St. Mans 102 B3
Rutland St. Nott 173 D2
Rutland Terr. Ilk 157 F1
Rutland. K-in-A 115 E3
Rydal Dr. Huck 145 F4
Rydal Ave. Lo Ea 182 A1
Rydal Dr. Bees 183 E4
Rydal Dr. Work 35 F4
Rydal Gdns. W Brid 186 A3
Rydal Gr. Nott 160 C2
Rydale Rd. Nott 161 E3
Ryder St. Nott 160 B2
Rye Croft. Tick 8 A4
Rye St. Nott 160 C1
Ryecroft St. Staple 182 C4
Ryehill Cl. Nott 173 E1
Ryehill St. Nott 173 E1
Ryeholme Cl. E Lea 205 F2
Ryeland Gdns. Nott 173 E1
Ryemere Cl. East 143 F1
Rylands Cl. Bees 184 A2
Ryton Cl. Blyth 18 A1
Ryton Ct. Nott 173 E1
Ryton Fields. Blyth 18 A1
Ryton Pl. Work 35 F2
Ryton Sq. Nott 160 A1
Ryton St. Work 35 F2

Sacheverall Ave. Pinx 113 E2
Saddlers Cl. Mans 88 C1
Saddleworth Ct. Nott 173 E3
Sadler St. Mans 101 F4
Saffron Gdns. Nott 173 D1
St Agnes Cl. Nott 171 E4
St Aidan's Ct. Nott 160 C2
St Albans Ct. Bes Vil 147 D1
St Albans Mews. Nott 160 B3
St Albans Rd. Arn 161 F4
St Albans Rd. Bes Vil 146 C2
St Albans Rd. Nott 160 B4
St Albans St. Nott 161 E2
St Andrew Cl. Goth 195 D1
St Andrew St. Mans 102 B3
St Andrew's Cl. Huck 146 A4
St Andrew's Rd. Nott 173 E4
St Andrew's Rise. Kegw 203 E1
St Andrews Cl. Nott 160 B4
St Andrews Cres. S in A 100 C3
St Andrews Ct. Nott 160 B4
St Andrews Dr. Sax 56 C2
St Andrews St. K-in-A 115 D3
St Andrews St. S in A 100 C3
St Ann's Gdns. Nott 173 F4
St Ann's Hill Rd. Nott 173 E4
St Ann's Hill. Nott 173 E4
St Ann's St. Nott 173 E3
St Ann's Valley. Nott 173 F4
St Ann's Way. Nott 173 E3
St Ann's Way. Shelt 168 B3
St Ann's Well Rd. Nott 173 F3
St Anne's La. Su Bo 213 D3
St Annes Cl. Work 35 E2
St Annes Dr. Work 35 E1
St Annes Mews. Work 35 E2
St Annes View. Work 35 E2
St Annes Way. Work 35 E2
St Anthony Ct. Nott 172 C1
St Augustines Cl. Nott 161 D1
St Austell Dr. Nott 185 D3
St Austins Ct. Carl 174 C4
St Austins Dr. Carl 174 C4
St Bartholomew's Rd. Nott 173 F4
St Botolphs Cl. Sax 57 D3
St Catherine St. Mans 102 B3
St Catherines Cl. N-on-T 139 F4
St Catherines St. R on T 175 F1
St Cecilia Gdns. Nott 173 E3
St Chad's Rd. Nott 173 F3
St Christopher St. Nott 173 F2
St Clare's Gate. N-on-T 140 A3
St Cuthbert St. Work 35 F1
St Cuthbert's Rd. Nott 173 F3
St David's Cl. Work 36 A3
St Edmund's Ave. Mans 88 B2
St Edwin's Dr. Edwin 76 A1
St Ervan Rd. Nott 185 D3
St George's Ct. Huck 146 A4
St George's Dr. Nott 173 E1
St Giles Way. Cr Bi 189 D2
St Giles' Way. Bald 140 C2
St Helen's Cres. Bu Jo 163 F2
St Helen's Cres. Trow 170 B2
St Helen's Dr. Sels 128 B4
St Helen's Gr. Bu Jo 163 F2
St Helen's La. Halam 120 C1
St Helen's Rd. Ret 40 A2
St Helen's Rd. W Brid 185 F3
St Helen's St. Nott 173 D3
St Helens Ave. Pinx 113 E2
St Jame's Terr. Nott 173 D2
St James Ave. Ilk 170 A4
St James Ct. Sand 182 A2
St James' Dr. Brin 143 E4
St James's Ct. Huck 146 A4
St James's St. Staple 182 B3
St James's Terr. Staple 182 B3
St John St. Mans 102 A4
St John St. Ret 39 F4
St John's Ave. K-in-A 115 D2
St John's Cl. Brin 128 B1
St John's Cres. Huck 146 B3
St John's Dr. Clar 30 B2
St John's Pl. Mans 102 A4
St John's Rd. Ilk 170 A4
St John's Rd. Rudd 196 B4
St John's St. Lo Ea 193 E4
St John's Terr. Gain 24 B4
St Johns Ct. Carl 174 B4
St Jude's Ave. Nott 161 F1
St Judes Way. Rain 104 A1
St Lawrence Bvd. R on T 175 F1
St Leonard's Ct. N-on-T 124 C1
St Leonard's Dr. Nott 171 F2
St Leonard's. Tick 8 A4
St Leven Cl. Nott 171 E4
St Luke's Cl. W Brid 186 A3
St Luke's St. Nott 173 F3
St Luke's Way. St Ba 175 F4
St Lukes Way. Wood 53 D4
St Margaret St. Mans 102 B3
St Margarets Ave. Nott 172 B4
St Mark's La. N-on-T 139 F4
St Mark's Pl. N-on-T 139 F4
St Marks St. Nott 173 E3
St Martin's Ave. Baw 9 F4
St Martin's Cl. Fir 16 A3
St Martin's Cl. Nott 171 F4
St Martin's Rd. Nott 171 F4
St Martin's Wlk. Whit 45 E3
St Martins Cl. Blyth 18 A1
St Martins Rd. N Le Ha 42 B4
St Mary's Rd. S in A 100 B2
St Mary's Ave. Carl 162 C1
St Mary's Cl. Bott 181 D2
St Mary's Cl. Lough 220 A2
St Mary's Cl. Lowd 150 B1
St Mary's Cl. Nott 147 F1
St Mary's Cres. E Lea 205 F2
St Mary's Cres. Rudd 196 B4
St Mary's Cres. Tick 8 A4
St Mary's Ct. S in A 100 B2
St Mary's Dr. Edwin 76 A1
St Mary's Gate. Nott 173 E2
St Mary's Gate. Tick 8 A4
St Mary's Gdns. N-on-T 139 F3
St Mary's La. Bott 181 D1
St Mary's Mews. Tick 8 A4
St Mary's Pl. Nott 173 E2
St Mary's Rd. Tick 8 A4
St Mary's Way. Huck 146 A4
St Mary's Wlk. Sels 128 A2
St Marys Cl. Bees 183 E1
St Marys Rd. Bing 177 F3
St Matthias Rd. Nott 173 F3
St Mawes Ave. Nott 185 D3
St Mellion Way. K-in-A 114 C4
St Michael's Ave. Carl 162 C1
St Michael's Cl. Halam 120 C1
St Michael's Dr. S Norm 113 D4
St Michael's Green. Ret 39 E4
St Michael's Sq. Bees 183 D4
St Michael's St. S in A 101 D2
St Michaels Ave. Nott 171 E4
St Nicholas Cl. Arn 161 F4
St Nicholas St. Nott 173 E2
St Patrick's Rd. Huck 145 F4
St Patrick's Rd. Nuth 159 E3
St Patrick's Rd. Nuth 159 E3
St Paul's Ave. Nott 172 C4
St Paul's Rd. Gain 15 D2
St Paul's St. Nott 172 B3
St Peter's Ave. Mar War 74 A3
St Peter's Church Wlk. Nott 173 E2
St Peter's Cres. Rudd 196 B4
St Peter's Gate. Nott 173 E2
St Peter's La. Clay 21 E3
St Peter's St. Nott 172 C3
St Peter's Way. Mans 102 B3
St Peters Ave. Hath 213 D1
St Peters Cl. E Stock 7 F1
St Peters Cl. Farn 138 C2
St Peters Cl. Oll 77 D2
St Peters Dr. Rain 104 A1
St Saviour's Cl. Ret 40 A4
St Saviour's Gdns. Nott 173 E1
St Stephen's Ave. Nott 173 F2
St Stephen's Rd. Nott 173 F2
St Stephen's Rd. Ret 40 A2
St Thomas' Ave. K-in-A 115 D2
St Vincent Cl. Lo Ea 193 F3
St Wilfreds Cl. N Musk 110 C1
St Wilfrid's Sq. Calv 148 C4
St Wilfrids Dr. K-in-A 114 B3
Salamander Cl. Carl 162 B1
Salcey Dr. Staple 170 B1
Salcombe Circus. Nott 147 E1
Salcombe Cres. Rudd 196 B4
Salcombe Dr. Nott 147 E1
Salcombe Gr. Baw 9 F4
Salcombe Rd. Nott 160 C2
Salford Gdns. Nott 173 E3
Saliisbury St. Lough 220 B2
Salisbury Ave. E Lea 205 F1
Salisbury Cl. Mans 88 B2
Salisbury Rd. Gain 15 E1
Salisbury Rd. Mans 101 F4
Salisbury Rd. N-on-T 139 F3
Salisbury Sq. Nott 172 C2
Salisbury St. Bees 184 A4
Salisbury St. Lo Ea 193 F4
Salisbury St. Nott 172 C2
Sallie Bank La. Kettl 55 D2
Salmon Cl. Nott 159 F4
Salmon La. Ann Wo 129 E4
Salop St. Arn 161 E4
Salt Hill. Fir 16 A3
Saltburn Rd. Nott 172 A3
Salterford Ave. Calv 148 C4
Salterford La. Calv 133 E3

Salterford Rd. Huck 145 F3
Saltford Cl. Carl 162 C1
Salthouse Ct. Bees 184 A4
Salthouse La. Bees 184 A4
Saltney Way. Nott 185 D2
Salvin Cl. Cr Bi 189 D2
Sampson St. Ann Wo 130 A4
Sampson's La. Mans 87 D2
Samson Ct. Rudd 196 A4
Samuel Cl. Mans 101 F4
Sand La. Best 97 F4
Sand La. Sax 70 C4
Sand La. Spal 83 D4
Sand La. Tork 44 B1
Sand Pit La. Lo Cl 211 E2
Sandalwood Cl. Mans 103 D2
Sandalwood Dr. K-in-A 115 E3
Sandays Cl. Nott 173 E1
Sandby Ct. Bees 183 E3
Sanders Ave. Mans 102 C4
Sanderson's Bank. Miss 2 A2
Sanderson's Bank. Wroot 2 A2
Sandfield Ave. Raven 132 A4
Sandfield La. Kirton 78 A3
Sandfield Rd. Ann Wo 129 F4
Sandfield Rd. Arn 161 F3
Sandfield Rd. Bees 182 C1
Sandfield Way. N-on-T 139 E3
Sandford Ave. Lo Ea 193 F4
Sandford Rd. Carl 162 A2
Sandford Rd. Nott 172 C2
Sandgate Ave. Mans 88 B2
Sandgate Rd. Mans 88 B2
Sandgate. Bees 171 E1
Sandhill Rd. Farn 139 D3
Sandhill Rd. Sels 129 D2
Sandhill St. Work 35 F2
Sandhurst Ave. Mans 102 B2
Sandhurst Dr. Rudd 196 A3
Sandhurst Rd. Nott 146 B1
Sandiacre Rd. Staple 182 B3
Sandmartins. Work 35 E4
Sandon St. Nott 161 D1
Sandown Rd. Bees 182 C1
Sandown Rd. Mans 103 D2
Sandown Rd. S in A 101 D2
Sandringham Ave. W Brid 185 F4
Sandringham Cres. Nott 171 E3
Sandringham Cres. Work 35 F3
Sandringham Ct. Har 9 D3
Sandringham Ct. Mans 88 A3
Sandringham Dr. Bees 171 E1
Sandringham Dr. Mans 88 A3
Sandringham Pl. Huck 146 A4
Sandringham Rd. Mans 88 C3
Sandringham Rd. Nott 173 F2
Sandringham Rd. Ret 29 E1
Sandringham Rd. Sand 182 A2
Sandrock Rd. Har 8 C3
Sands The. Lo Cl 211 E2
Sandsfield La. Gain 24 B3
Sandsfield La. Gain 24 B4
Sandside. Cotg 187 F1
Sandwich Cl. K-in-A 114 C4
Sandwood Cl. Newt 99 D2
Sandy La. Bees 171 E1
Sandy La. Edwin 91 D4
Sandy La. Gams 50 C2
Sandy La. Ho Pi 175 D1
Sandy La. Huck 146 A4
Sandy La. Mans 102 B4
Sandy La. Mar War 74 A3
Sandy La. Oxt 134 B2
Sandy La. Raven 117 D2
Sandy La. Work 35 E2
Sandycliffe Cl. Mans 88 C1
Sandyford Cl. Nott 160 B2
Sandymount East. Har 9 D2
Sandymount West. Har 9 D3
Sandymount. Har 9 D3
Sanger Cl. Nott 195 E4
Sanger Gdns. Nott 195 E4
Sankey Dr. Nott 160 A4
Santon Cl. Mans 89 D1
Santon Rd. Mans 89 D1
Sapele Cl. Carl 163 D1
Sapphire Dr. K-in-A 115 E2
Saracen Cl. Gain 24 C3
Saracen's Head Yd. N-on-T 139 F4
Sargent Gdns. Nott 173 F3
Sartfield Rd. Mans 89 D1
Saskatoon Cl. R on T 175 F1
Saucers The. Scarr 178 C4
Saunby Cl. Arn 162 A4
Saundby Ave. Mans 87 E1
Saundby Rd. Saundby 23 E2
Savage's Rd. Rudd 196 B4
Savages Row. Rudd 196 B4
Saversick La. South 136 A4
Savile Rd. Bils 105 F3
Savile St. Ret 39 F3
Saville Cl. Staple 182 C4
Saville Rd. Arn 161 F3
Saville Rd. S in A 100 C3
Saville St. Blid 118 A3
Saville Way. Mar War 74 A2
Saw Pit La. Tibs 99 D3
Sawley Dr. Mans 103 D2
Sawyers Cl. N-on-T 140 A4
Saxby Dr. Mans 103 D2
Saxelby Gdns. Nott 160 A4
Saxilby Rd. Skel 71 F4
Saxon Green. Nott 172 C2
Saxon Way. Cotg 188 A1
Saxon Way. Har 8 C2
Saxondale Dr. Nott 160 C3
Saxton Cl. Bees 184 A3
Saxton Cl. Work 35 E1
Scafell Way. Nott 195 E4
Scalby Cl. East 143 E1
Scalford Dr. Nott 172 B2
Scampton Way. Gain 24 C4
Scarborough Rd. Bils 105 F3
Scarborough St. Nott 173 E3
Scarbrough Cl. Tick 8 A4
Scarcliffe Ct. S in A 100 C2
Scarcliffe La. Scarc 72 B4
Scarcliffe St. Mans 102 B4
Scarcliffe Terr. Scarc 59 D1
Scargill Ave. East 144 A1
Scargill Cl. East 144 A1
Scargill Wlk. East 143 F2
Scarle La. Eagle 84 B2
Scarrington Ct. Mans 103 D1
Scarrington Rd. W Brid 173 F1
Sceptre St. Nott 161 E1
School Ave. Huck 145 E2
School Cl. Nott 173 E1
School Green. E Lea 205 F1
School Hill. Ann Wo 130 A4
School House La. Walker 13 F3
School La. Beckin 142 B4
School La. Bees 183 E2
School La. Bing 177 F3
School La. Caun 109 D2
School La. Clayp 156 C4
School La. Co Ba 200 B4
School La. Cuck 60 A2
School La. E Sto 153 E4
School La. Farn 139 D2
School La. Halam 121 D2
School La. Harb 202 A2
School La. Knee 93 F3
School La. Lo Cl 211 E2
School La. Mans 88 B2
School La. N Sca 83 E1
School La. Norw 110 A4
School La. Oll 77 D2
School La. Remp 215 E3
School La. S Norm 113 D2
School La. What 179 D2
School Rd. Lan 16 C2
School Rd. Sels 129 D2
School Rd. Sels 129 D4
School St. K-in-A 115 D3
School St. Lough 220 A2
School Wlk. Baw 10 A4
School Wlk. Bes Vil 146 C2
Schrimshire's Rd. S Le S 32 A1
Science Rd. Nott 172 B1
Scot La. Baw 10 A4
Scotholme Ave. Nott 172 C4
Scotland Bank. Cotg 187 F2
Scotland Rd. Nott 160 C2
Scotsdale Wlk. Nott 161 F1
Scotswood Rd. Mans 88 A3
Scott Ave. Bees 184 A3
Scott Cl. Nott 159 F3
Scott Cl. Work 36 B2
Scott St. Gain 15 E1
Scott St. Scarc 59 D1
Scotton Sq. Ret 29 E1
Scotts Way. Ann Wo 115 D1
Scratta La. Whit 34 B1
Scrimshire La. Cotg 187 F2
Script Dr. Nott 160 C2
Scrivelsby Gdns. Bees 183 E2
Scrooby Rd. Bir 9 E2
Scrooby Rd. Har 8 C2
Seaburn Rd. Bees 182 C1
Seaford Ave. Nott 172 A3
Seaford Way. Ilk 157 F3
Seaforth Sq. Mans 101 E3
Seagrave Ave. Ann Wo 115 D1
Seagrave Rd. Nott 159 E1
Seamer Rd. Kim 158 C4
Searby Rd. S in A 101 E1
Searby Rd. S in A 101 E1
Searwood Ave. K-in-A 114 C4
Seatoller Cl. W Brid 186 B3
Seaton Cres. Nott 160 A1
Second Ave. Carl 162 C1
Second Ave. Carl 174 B4
Second Ave. Edwin 76 A1
Second Ave. Mans 89 D1
Second Ave. Mans 103 F1
Second Ave. N Clip 90 A2
Sedgebrook Cl. Nott 160 B2
Sedgebrook St. Mans 88 C2
Sedgeley Rd. Toll 186 B1
Sedgewood Gr. Nott 184 C2
Sedgley Ave. Nott 173 F3
Sedgwick St. La Mi 143 D2
Sedgwick St. Sels 128 A2
Sedley Ave. Nuth 159 E3
Seely Ave. Calv 148 C4
Seely Rd. Nott 173 D3
Sefton Ave. Staple 182 C4
Sefton Dr. Nott 161 E1
Selbourne Ct. Lough 220 B2
Selbourne St. Lough 220 B2
Selby Cl. Bees 182 C2
Selby La. Keyw 197 F1
Selby Rd. Styr 8 C1
Selby Rd. W Brid 185 F3
Selhurst Ct. Nott 172 C4
Selhurst St. Nott 172 C4
Selkirk Way. Nott 161 E1
Sellars Ave. Rudd 196 B3
Seller's Wood Dr W. Nott 159 F4
Seller's Wood Dr. Nott 160 A4
Selsey Ct. Ret 29 F1
Selside Ct. Bees 183 D2
Selston Dr. Nott 172 B2
Selston Rd. Sels 128 A3
Selwyn Cl. Nott 160 C3
Selwyn St. Mans 102 C3
Sennen Ct. Ret 29 F1
Serlby Rd. East 144 A2
Serlby Rise. Nott 173 F3
Seven Hills. N-on-T 125 D2
Seven Oaks Cres. Bees 171 E1
Seven Oaks Rd. S-by-D 170 A1
Seventh Ave. Mans 103 D4
Seventh Ave. N Clip 89 F1
Severals. Staple 182 C4
Severn St. Nott 160 A4
Seward St. Lough 220 A2
Seymour Rd. East 143 F1
Seymour Rd. Huck 145 F3
Seymour Rd. W Brid 186 A4
Seymour St. Nott 173 F3
Shackleton Cl. Nott 159 E1
Shacklock Cl. Bes Vil 147 D1
Shadwell Gr. R on T 175 F2
Shady La. Bees 183 E1
Shaftesbury Ave. Bu Jo 164 A3
Shaftesbury Ave. Lo Ea 193 D2
Shaftesbury Ave. Mans 87 F1
Shaftesbury Ave. Sand 182 A3
Shaftesbury St. Nott 161 D1
Shakespear St. Gain 24 B3
Shakespeare Ave. Mans 88 A2
Shakespeare Cl. Carl 174 C3
Shakespeare Rd. Awsw 158 B3
Shakespeare St. Bald 140 A3
Shakespeare St. Lo Ea 182 B1
Shakespeare St. Lough 220 A2
Shakespeare St. Nott 173 E3
Shakespeare St. Work 36 A2
Shakespeare Villas. Nott 173 E3
Shaldon Cl. Nott 146 C1
Shandwick Cl. Arn 148 A1
Shanklin Dr. Staple 182 B4
Shanwell Cl. Nott 159 E1
Shardlow Way. Mans 103 D2
Sharnford Way. Bees 171 D2
Sharp Cl. Lo Ea 193 E3
Sharphill Rd. W Brid 186 A2
Sharpley Dr. E Lea 205 F2
Sharrard Cl. Sels 129 D1
Sharrat Ct. Mans 103 D1
Shaw Cres. Huck 145 F2
Shaw Rd. G on H 12 C2
Shaw St E. Ilk 170 A3
Shaw St W. Ilk 170 A3
Shaw St. Mans 102 C4
Shaw St. Rudd 196 B3
Shaw St. Work 35 F2
Sheaf Pl. Work 35 F4
Shearing Cl. Carl 163 D1
Shearing Hill. Carl 163 D1
Sheepbridge La. Mans 101 F3
Sheepfold La. Rudd 196 B3
Sheepwalk La. Raven 116 C1
Sheepwash La. S in A 101 D1
Sheepwash La. Tick 8 C4
Sheffield Rd. Blyth 18 A2
Sheldon Cl. Lo Ea 182 A2
Sheldrake Rd. N-on-T 140 B4
Shelford Ave. K-in-A 114 B3
Shelford Cl. Bees 183 E2
Shelford Cl. R on T 176 A2
Shelford Cres. Bu Jo 164 A3
Shelford Dr. Bing 177 E2
Shelford Hill. Mans 101 F3
Shelford Hill. Shel 176 B4
Shelford Rd. Carl 162 B2
Shelford Rd. R on T 176 A3
Shelford Rise. Nott 174 A3
Shellburne Cl. Nott 160 C4
Shelley Ave. Mans 88 A2
Shelley Ave. Nott 184 C2
Shelley Cl. Bald 140 B2
Shelley Cl. Huck 145 E3
Shelley Cl. Kim 159 D3
Shelley Rd. Arn 161 E4
Shelley St. Work 36 A2
Shelthorpe Ave. Lough 220 A1
Shelthorpe Rd. Lough 220 A1
Shelton Ave. Huck 146 B2
Shelton Ave. N-on-T 139 F3
Shelton Cl. Mans 87 F1
Shelton Gdns. Rudd 196 A4
Shelton Rd. Mans 103 D1
Shelton St. Nott 173 E3
Shenfield Gdns. Nott 146 B1
Shepard Cl. Nott 159 F3
Shepherd Walk. Kegw 203 E1
Shepherd's Ave. Work 36 A3
Shepherd's Cl. Su Bo 213 E3
Shepherds Cl. Nott 172 A4
Shepherds Oak. S in A 100 C3
Shepherds Wood Dr. Nott 172 B4
Shepshed Rd. Hath 212 C1
Shepton Cl. Ship 157 E2
Shepton Cres. Nott 160 A1
Sheraton Dr. Nott 171 F2
Sherborne Rd. Nott 160 A1
Sherborne Rd. W Brid 185 F3
Sherbrook Ave. Arn 161 E3
Sherbrook Cl. Calv 148 C4
Sherbrook Rd. Arn 161 E3
Sherbrook Terr. Arn 161 E3
Sherbrooke Rd. Nott 161 D1
Sheridan Cl. Bald 140 B3
Sheridan Ct. Staple 170 C1
Sheriffs Way. Nott 173 E1
Sheringham Cl. Arn 161 F3
Sheringham Dr. Mans 102 B3
Sherriff's Lea. Bees 182 C1
Sherrington Cl. Nott 195 E4
Sherview Ave. Mans 103 D4
Sherwin Cl. Nott 173 E3
Sherwin Rd. Nott 172 C2
Sherwin Rd. Staple 170 C1
Sherwin Wlk. Nott 173 E3
Sherwood Ave. Blid 118 B3
Sherwood Ave. Calv 148 B4
Sherwood Ave. Edwin 76 A1
Sherwood Ave. N-on-T 140 A4
Sherwood Ave. Nott 161 E2
Sherwood Ave. Pinx 113 E2
Sherwood Ave. Shireb 72 C2
Sherwood Cl. Mans 102 C4
Sherwood Cres. Blyth 18 A1
Sherwood Dr. Oll 77 E2
Sherwood Dr. Shireb 72 C2
Sherwood Gr. Bing 177 E2
Sherwood Gr. Calv 148 C4
Sherwood Hall Gdns. Mans 102 C4
Sherwood Hall Rd. Mans 102 C4
Sherwood Lodge Dr. Arn 132 B1
Sherwood Pl. Ann Wo 115 D1
Sherwood Pl. N Clip 90 A2
Sherwood Rd. Har 8 C3
Sherwood Rd. Rain 104 A1
Sherwood Rd. Ret 39 F2
Sherwood Rd. S in A 100 C1
Sherwood Rd. Work 35 F2
Sherwood Rise. Ann Wo 115 D1
Sherwood Rise. East 144 A1
Sherwood Rise. Mans 88 C2
Sherwood Rise. Nott 173 D4
Sherwood St. Ann Wo 130 A4
Sherwood St. Huck 146 B3
Sherwood St. K-in-A 115 D3
Sherwood St. Mans 88 A1
Sherwood St. Mans 102 A3
Sherwood St. Mar War 74 A2
Sherwood St. Newt 99 D2
Sherwood St. S in A 99 F2
Sherwood Vale. Nott 161 F2
Sherwood Way. Sels 129 D4
Shetland Cl. Mans 88 C1
Shipley Ct. Ilk 157 E1
Shipley Rd. Nott 159 F1
Shipley Rise. Carl 174 C4
Shipstone St. Ilk 170 A3
Shipstone St. Nott 172 C4
Shipstones Yd. Nott 160 B4
Shirburn Ave. Mans 102 B4
Shire La. Clayp 156 A4
Shirebrooke Cl. Nott 160 B2
Shireoaks Ct. Mans 103 D1
Shireoaks Comm. Shire 34 C4
Shireoaks Comm. Work 35 D4
Shireoaks Rd. Rhod 35 D3
Shireoaks Rd. Shire 34 C3
Shireoaks Row. Shire 34 C4
Shires The. Mans 88 C1
Shirland Dr. Mans 103 D2
Shirley Dr. Arn 162 A4
Shirley Rd. Nott 173 E4
Shirley St. Lo Ea 193 D2
Shoreswood Cl. Nott 161 D4
Short Hill. Nott 173 E2
Short St. Mar War 74 A2
Short St. S in A 101 D2
Short Wheatley La. Coll 112 A3
Shortcross Ave. Arn 161 F2
Shortwood Ave. Huck 145 F3
Shortwood Cl. Nott 173 E2
Shortwood La. Omp 93 E4
Shorwell Rd. Nott 174 B4
Shoulder Of Mutton Hill. Ann Wo 115 D1
Shrewsbury Rd. Bir 9 D2
Shrewsbury Rd. Nott 174 A2
Shrewsbury Rd. Work 36 A1
Shrewsbury View. Ret 29 E1
Shrimpton Ct. Rudd 196 B3
Shropshire Ave. Sels 128 B2
Sibcy La. Bald 140 B2
Sibson Dr. Kegw 203 D1
Sibson Wlk. Nott 147 F1
Sibthorpe St. Mans 102 A3
Siddalls Dr. S in A 100 A2
Side La. Eakr 106 C4
Side Ley. Kegw 203 E2
Side Row. N-on-T 140 A4
Sidings Rd. K-in-A 115 E4
Sidings The. Sax 57 D2
Sidlaw Rise. Bes Vil 147 D1
Sidmouth Cl. Keyw 197 F2
Sidney Rd. Bees 183 F4
Sidney St. Kim 158 C3
Sidney St. Lo Ea 193 E3
Silbury Cl. Nott 195 E4
Silk St. S in A 100 C1
Silken Holme. S Norm 113 D2
Silver St. Gain 24 B4
Silver St. Grass 81 F2
Silver St. N Clift 68 C3
Silver St. Ret 39 E3
Silverdale Ave. Mans 88 A2
Silverdale Cl. Ret 29 E1
Silverdale Rd. Nott 160 C1
Silverdale. Staple 182 C3
Silverhill Cotts. S in A 100 A4
Silverhill La. S in A 99 F4
Silverwood Ave. Raven 117 D1
Silverwood Rd. Bees 183 F3
Silverwood Rd. Bott 181 D1
Silvey Ave. South 121 E1
Sime St. Work 35 F2
Simkin Ave. Carl 162 A1
Simon Cl. Wood 42 A1
Simone Gdns. Nott 184 C1
Simons Ct. Bees 171 E1
Simpson Cl. Bald 140 C2
Simpson Rd. Mans 101 E4
Singleton Ave. Mans 102 C4
Sisley Ave. Staple 182 C3
Sitwell Cl. Work 36 A2
Sitwell Rd. Work 36 B2
Six Hills La. Grim 219 D1
Sixth Ave. Edwin 76 A1
Sixth Ave. Mans 103 D4
Sixth Ave. N Clip 89 F2
Skeavington's La. Ilk 157 F3
Skegby La. Mans 101 E3
Skegby Mount. Mans 101 F3
Skegby Rd. Ann Wo 129 F4
Skegby Rd. S in A 100 A2
Skegby Rd. S in A 101 D2
Skegby Road. Nor on T 81 E4
Skerry Hill. Mans 102 C4
Skerry La. Bott 181 F1
Sketchley Ct. Nott 160 A4
Sketchley St. Nott 173 F3
Skipton Circus. Nott 174 A3
Skipton Cl. Ship 157 E2
Skirbeck Dr. Sax 57 D2
Skithorne Rise. Lowd 164 B4
Slack Wlk. Work 35 F1
Slack's La. Kneet 152 A1
Slade Cl. S Norm 113 D2
Slade Rd. Bees 183 D3
Slaidburn Ave. Nott 185 D3
Slake La. S Musk 124 C3
Slant La. Mans 88 A2
Slant The. Shireb 72 B2
Slater St. S in A 100 C2
Slaughter House La. N-on-T 124 C1
Sleaford Rd. B in W 126 B1
Sleaford Rd. Beckin 142 B4
Sleaford Rd. Codd 126 B1
Sleaford Rd. N-on-T 125 D1
Sleights La. Pinx 113 E1
Sloan Dr. Bees 171 D2
Sloane Ct. W Brid 185 E2
Slowthorne Gdns. Arn 161 E4
Small Gate. Mans 88 C3
Small's Croft. Woodb 149 E2
Smalley Cl. Sels 129 D1
Smeath La. Ret 30 B2
Smeath Rd. Ret 30 A2
Smeath Rd. Sels 129 D1
Smedley Ave. Ilk 170 A4
Smedley Cl. Nott 160 A1
Smedley's Ave. Sand 182 A3
Smeeton St. Hean 143 D1
Smite Cl. What 179 D2
Smite La. Orst 179 F4
Smite La. Thoro 179 F4
Smith Dr. La Mi 143 D2
Smith Sq. Har 8 C2
Smith St. Bald 140 B3
Smith St. Mans 102 C3
Smith St. N-on-T 140 A4
Smithfield Ave. Trow 170 B2
Smiths Cl. Cr Bi 189 D2
Smithson Cl. Bald 140 B2
Smithson Dr. Nott 171 F2
Smithurst Rd. Greas 158 A4
Smithy Cl. Nott 184 B1
Smithy Cres. Arn 161 F4
Smithy La. Lo Wh 212 A1
Smithy Row. Nott 173 E2

Smithy View. Calv 148 C4
Snaefell Ave. Mans 89 D1
Snape La. Styr 9 D1
Snape Nook Ct. Nott 159 F4
Snape Wood Rd. Nott 159 F4
Snead Ct. Nott 147 D1
Sneinton Bvd. Nott 173 F2
Sneinton Dale. Nott 174 A3
Sneinton Hermitage. Nott 173 F2
Sneinton Hollows. Nott 173 F2
Sneinton Rd. Nott 173 F2
Snell Cl. S on T 81 F1
Snipe Park Rd. Bir 9 D2
Snowdon Rd. Coll 112 A4
Soar La. N on S 213 E2
Soar La. Su Bo 212 C4
Soarbank Cl. Kim 158 C4
Sobers Gdns. Arn 162 A3
Softwood Cl. Nott 159 F4
Soloman Rd. Coss 158 A1
Solway Cl. Bees 183 F3
Somerby Ct. Bees 171 D2
Somerby Rd. Gain 15 F1
Somersall St. Mans 101 F4
Somersby Ct. Mans 103 D3
Somersby Rd. Arn 162 A3
Somerset Cl. Lo Ea 194 A4
Somerton Ave. Nott 185 D2
Sookholme Cl. Shireb 72 C2
Sookholme Dr. Mar War 74 A2
Sookholme La. Mar War 73 F3
Sookholme Rd. Mar War 73 F1
Sookholme Rd. Shireb 72 C2
Sophie Rd. Nott 172 C3
Soss La. Mist 7 D1
Sotheby Ave. S in A 101 E1
Soudan Dr. Nott 173 D1
Sough Rd. S Norm 113 D4
South Ave. Baw 10 A4
South Ave. R on T 176 A2
South Ave. Rain 104 A1
South Ave. Shireb 72 C2
South Ave. Work 36 A1
South Cres. Bott 181 D1
South Cres. N Clip 90 A2
South Croft. Ashkh 51 F1
South Devon Ave. Carl 162 A1
South Dr. Bald 140 C1
South Dr. Bils 105 F4
South End. Coll 111 F4
South La. Nor on T 81 F3
South Moor Rd. Walker 13 F3
South Par. Baw 10 A3
South Par. Gain 24 C4
South Par. Nott 173 E2
South Par. Work 36 A2
South Parade. Sax 57 D2
South Rd. Bees 184 A2
South Rd. Nott 173 D2
South Rd. W Brid 185 F3
South Ridge Dr. Mans 102 B2
South Scarle La. N Sca 83 E1
South Scarle Rd. Coll 98 A1
South Sherwood St. Nott 173 E3
South Snape Cl. Nott 159 F4
South St. Bole 23 F1
South St. East 143 F1
South St. Greas 158 B4
South St. Huck 146 A4
South St. Lo Ea 193 F4
South St. Lough 220 A2
South St. Mort 15 D2
South St. Nor on T 81 F3
South St. Ret 39 F3
South St. S Norm 113 D3
South View Dr. Clar 30 B2
South View Rd. Carl 162 B1
South View. Aust 3 E1
South View. Whit 45 D3
South View. Work 35 F3
Southampton St. Nott 173 F3
Southbreck Rise. Work 36 A1
Southchurch Dr. Nott 184 C1
Southcliffe Rd. Carl 174 B4
Southdale Dr. Carl 174 B4
Southdale Rd. Carl 174 B4
Southdene. Work 36 A3
Southend Ave. N-on-T 139 F4
Southern Wood. Work 46 C4
Southey St. Nott 173 D3
Southfall Cl. Ran 19 D3
Southfield Dr. S Norm 113 E3
Southfield La. Whit 45 D2
Southfield Rd. Nott 172 B3
Southfield. Bald 140 C2
Southfields Ave. Pinx 113 E2
Southfields Cl. Ann Wo 114 C1
Southfields Rise. N Le Ha 42 B4
Southfields. Lo Ea 193 F4
Southgate Rd. Mar War 74 B3
Southglade Rd. Nott 160 C3
Southgore La. N Le Ha 42 B4
Southgreen Cl. Mans 102 C1
Southgreen Hill. Mans 102 C1
Southlands Ave. Mort 15 D2
Southlands Dr. Mort 15 D2
Southlands Gdns. Mort 15 D2
Southlea Rd. Carl 174 B4
Southmoor La. Ne on T 69 D4
Southmoor Rd. Work 36 A1
Southolme. Gain 24 B4
Southpark Ave. Mans 102 C1
Southport Terr. Nott 172 C4
Southside. Arn 162 B4
Southview Gdns. Raven 117 D1
Southwark St. Nott 160 C2
Southwell Cl. E Lea 205 F1
Southwell Cl. K-in-A 115 D3
Southwell La. K-in-A 114 C3
Southwell Rd E. Mans 103 F1
Southwell Rd E. Rain 118 A4
Southwell Rd W. Mans 102 C3
Southwell Rd. Edin 120 A3
Southwell Rd. Farns 120 A3
Southwell Rd. Gona 150 C1
Southwell Rd. Kirk 120 C4
Southwell Rd. Lowd 150 C1
Southwell Rd. Nott 173 E2
Southwell Rd. Oxt 134 B2
Southwell Rd. Thur 151 E4
Southwold Dr. Nott 172 B3
Southwood Ave. S in A 100 B2
Sowter Ave. S in A 100 C2
Spa Cl. S in A 114 C4
Spa La. Orst 180 A4
Spa Rd. Ret 39 F3
Spafford Cl. Mart 44 B4
Spalding Rd. Nott 173 F3
Spalford La. N Sca 83 E2
Spalford Rd. N Sca 83 F3
Spang La. S in A 99 F2
Spaniel Row. Nott 173 E2
Sparken Cl. Work 46 C4
Sparken Dale. Work 46 C4
Sparrow Hill. Lough 220 A2
Sparrow La. H Marn 68 A1
Spean Ct. Nott 172 A3
Spean Dr. Nott 172 A4
Speedwell Pl. Work 35 F2
Spencer Ave. Carl 162 B3
Spencer Ave. Sand 182 A3
Spencer Cl. Rudd 196 A4
Spencer Cres. Staple 182 C4
Spencer Dr. Nuth 159 E3
Spencer St. Mans 102 A3
Sperry Cl. Sels 128 C3
Spey Cl. Huck 145 E2
Spindle Gdns. Nott 160 A4
Spindle View. Calv 148 C3
Spinney Cl. Cotg 187 F1
Spinney Cl. K-in-A 114 C3
Spinney Cl. Mans 88 C3
Spinney Cl. N-on-T 139 F3
Spinney Cl. W Brid 186 B2
Spinney Cres. Bees 182 C2
Spinney Dr. Lo Ea 182 B1
Spinney Rd. Bing 177 F2
Spinney Rd. Keyw 197 F2
Spinney Rd. Lo Ea 182 B1
Spinney Rise. Bees 182 C2
Spinney The. Arn 161 F2
Spinney The. Bes Vil 146 C3
Spinney The. Bulc 164 A3
Spinney The. Elst 153 E3
Spinney The. Shireb 72 B2
Spinney The. Wint 125 E3
Spinney Way. Nott 185 D2
Spinneymead. Ran 19 D3
Spinningdale. Arn 162 A4
Spital Hill. Gain 15 F1
Spital Hill. Ret 39 F4
Spital Rd. Blyth 18 A1
Spital Terr. Gain 15 E1
Spitalfields. Blyth 18 A1
Spondon St. Nott 161 E1
Sporton Cl. S Norm 113 D4
Sporton La. S Norm 113 D4
Spright Cl. Wint 125 E3
Spring Cl. Kim 159 D4
Spring Ct. Farns 119 F4
Spring Dale Gdns. Staple 170 B2
Spring Dr. Bald 140 C1
Spring Garden Terr. Ilk 157 F1
Spring Gdns. Baw 10 A4
Spring Gdns. Gain 24 B4
Spring Gdns. N-on-T 139 F4
Spring Green. Nott 195 F4
Spring Hill. Kim 158 C3
Spring Hill. Mans 88 A2
Spring Hill. South 136 C4
Spring Hill. Whit 45 D3
Spring La. Bald 140 C1
Spring La. Bald 140 C2
Spring La. Carl 162 C3
Spring La. Elmt 58 A4
Spring La. Farns 119 F4
Spring La. Flint 166 C4
Spring La. Lamb 163 D3
Spring La. Lo Wh 212 B1
Spring La. S Le S 32 B2
Spring La. Shire 34 C3
Spring Meadow. Cotg 188 A2
Spring Moor. Nott 174 B3
Spring Rd. Nott 160 B4
Spring Rd. S in A 100 C1
Spring St. Huck 146 A4
Spring St. Whit 45 D3
Spring Terr. Nuth 159 E3
Spring The. Lo Ea 193 E3
Spring Wlk. Work 35 F1
Springdale La. E Brid 165 F1
Springfield Ave. East 144 A1
Springfield Ave. Lo Ea 193 F4
Springfield Ave. Sand 182 A2
Springfield Ave. Shireb 72 C3
Springfield Cl. Cr Bi 189 D2
Springfield Cl. Gain 24 C4
Springfield Cl. Mans 103 D3
Springfield Ct. Staple 170 C1
Springfield Dr. Nott 159 F3
Springfield Gdn. Ilk 157 F1
Springfield Rd. Huck 145 E3
Springfield Rd. Nott 147 F1
Springfield Rd. Ret 39 F4
Springfield Rd. South 121 E1
Springfield St. Nott 160 C1
Springfield Way. K-in-A 115 E3
Springfield Way. K-in-A 115 E3
Springfield. Kegw 203 D1
Springfields. W Brid 185 E3
Springhead Ct. Nott 160 A3
Springhill Cl. Nott 146 A1
Springland Farm Cotts. Nuth 159 E3
Springs Rd. Miss 4 B3
Springthorpe Rd. Gain 24 C4
Springwood Gdns. Nott 161 F2
Springwood View Cl. S in A 100 B2
Spruce Ave. Sels 128 B3
Spruce Gdns. Nott 160 A4
Spruce Gr. Huck 146 A3
Spruce Gr. K-in-A 115 E3
Sprydon Walk. Nott 195 F4
Spur Cres. Work 47 D4
Square The. Bees 183 F3
Square The. Bes Vil 146 C2
Square The. Bott 181 D2
Square The. Cost 206 B1
Square The. Goth 195 D1
Square The. Keyw 197 F1
Square The. Nott 171 F2
Square The. Rain 104 A1
Square The. Ret 39 F4
Squires Ave. Nott 160 A4
Squires Cl. Cr Bi 189 D2
Squires Croft. N Clip 90 B3
Squires La. N Clip 90 A3
Squires Way. W Brid 185 E3
Stable Cl. Work 36 A4
Stacey Ave. Nott 160 C4
Stacey Rd. Mans 87 E1
Stafford Ave. Bald 140 B2
Stafford Ave. Nott 160 A3
Stafford Ct. Nott 159 F3
Stafford St. Lo Ea 193 F4
Stafford St. Mans 101 F4
Staffords Acre. Kegw 203 E1
Stagsden Cres. Nott 171 E3
Staindale Dr. Nott 160 B1
Stainforth St. Mans 88 B1
Stainmore Gr. Bing 177 E2
Stainsborough Rd. Huck 145 E3
Stainsby Dr. Mans 103 D4
Stamford Cl. Lo Ea 193 F2
Stamford Ct. Nott 161 D4
Stamford Rd. W Brid 186 A3
Stamford St. Awsw 158 B2
Stamford St. Greas 144 B1
Stamford St. Ilk 157 F1
Stamper Cres. S in A 100 C3
Stanage Ct. Mans 103 D3
Stancliffe Ave. Nott 160 B4
Standard Hill. Nott 173 D2
Standhill Ave. Carl 174 A4
Standhill Rd. Carl 174 A4
Stanesby Rise. Nott 184 C1
Stanford Gdns. R on T 175 F2
Stanford Hill. Lough 220 A3
Stanford La. Cotes 220 B4
Stanford Rd. N on S 213 F1
Stanford St. Nott 173 E2
Stanhome Dr. W Brid 185 E2
Stanhome Sq. W Brid 185 E2
Stanhope Ave. N-on-T 125 E2
Stanhope Cl. Wale 64 A1
Stanhope Cres. Arn 161 F4
Stanhope Cres. St Ba 175 F4
Stanhope Rd. Arn 161 F4
Stanhope Rd. Carl 162 B2
Stanhope St. Ilk 170 A3
Stanhope St. Lo Ea 193 E4
Stanhope St. Nott 173 E2
Stanhope Way. Bing 177 F2
Stanley Ave. Nott 173 D4
Stanley Cl. Raven 117 D2
Stanley Dr. Bees 171 D1
Stanley La. S in A 85 E1
Stanley Pl. Nott 173 D3
Stanley Rd. Carl 162 A1
Stanley Rd. Mans 89 D1
Stanley Rd. Mans 102 A2
Stanley Rd. Nott 173 D4
Stanley Rd. W Brid 185 F3
Stanley St. Gain 24 B3
Stanley St. Lo Ea 193 F4
Stanley St. Lough 220 A1
Stanley St. N-on-T 125 D1
Stanley St. Ret 40 A2
Stanley St. Work 35 F3
Stanley Terr. N-on-T 140 A4
Stanmore Cl. Nuth 159 F2
Stanmore Gdns. Arn 161 F3
Stansfield St. Nott 172 C3
Stanstead Ave. Nott 146 B1
Stanstead Ave. Toll 186 B1
Stanthorne Cl. Nott 185 D2
Stanton Cres. S in A 100 B2
Stanton Gate. S-by-D 170 B1
Stanton La. S-on-W 198 A1
Stanton Pl. Mans 102 A4
Stanton Pl. Plea 86 C4
Stanton Rd. Sand 182 A4
Stanton St. Plea 86 C4
Stanway Cl. Nott 174 B3
Stanwick Cl. Nott 171 F4
Staple La. Bald 140 B1
Stapleford La. Bees 182 C2
Stapleford La. Codd 126 B2
Stapleford La. Coll 112 B1
Stapleford Rd. Staple 170 B2
Stapleford Rd. Trow 170 B2
Staplehurst Dr. Nott 161 D2
Staples St. Nott 161 F1
Stapleton Rd. Ilk 157 F2
Starch Cl. E Lea 205 F1
Starch La. Sand 182 B4
Starr Ave. S in A 100 B2
Starth Wood Rd. Huck 145 E2
Statham Ct. Work 36 A3
Stathern La. Harb 202 A1
Stathern Rd. Harb 202 B2
Stathern Wlk. Nott 161 D4
Station Ave. Carl 163 D1
Station Ave. Ran 19 D3
Station Cl. Coll 112 A4
Station Ct. Ilk 157 F1
Station Hill. Mans 88 A2
Station La. Ald 128 A2
Station La. Edwin 76 A1
Station La. Farns 119 F4
Station La. Ol Da 218 C2
Station Rd. Awsw 158 B3
Station Rd. Ba Mo 28 C3
Station Rd. Baw 10 A4
Station Rd. Beck 23 E4
Station Rd. Bees 184 A3
Station Rd. Bleas 151 F4
Station Rd. Bott 181 E2
Station Rd. Bu Jo 163 F2
Station Rd. Carl 174 C4
Station Rd. Coll 112 A4
Station Rd. E Lea 205 E1
Station Rd. Edin 120 C3
Station Rd. Fisk 137 F2
Station Rd. Harby 70 C2
Station Rd. Hean 143 D1
Station Rd. Huck 146 A4
Station Rd. Ilk 157 F1
Station Rd. K on S 203 F1
Station Rd. K on S 204 A2
Station Rd. Kegw 203 F1
Station Rd. Keyw 197 F3
Station Rd. Kim 158 C3
Station Rd. La Mi 143 D1
Station Rd. Lo Ea 193 F4
Station Rd. Lowd 150 C1
Station Rd. Mans 102 A3
Station Rd. Miss 4 A2
Station Rd. Mist 7 D1
Station Rd. N Clip 89 F1
Station Rd. News 130 C3
Station Rd. Nott 160 B3
Station Rd. Oll 77 D2
Station Rd. Plum 197 F3
Station Rd. Rain 118 A4
Station Rd. Ran 19 D2
Station Rd. Ret 39 F3
Station Rd. Roll 138 A3
Station Rd. S in A 101 D1
Station Rd. S Le S 32 B3
Station Rd. S Lev 42 B4
Station Rd. S on T 96 C4
Station Rd. Sand 182 B3
Station Rd. Scro 10 A1
Station Rd. Sels 113 F1
Station Rd. Shireb 72 C3
Station Rd. South 121 F1
Station Rd. Sutt 28 C3
Station Rd. Thur 151 E3
Station Rd. Tork 44 A2
Station Rd. Up Br 218 B4
Station Rd. Walker 14 A3
Station Rd. Whit 45 D3
Station Rd. Widm 208 C3
Station St. Bing 177 F3
Station St. Coss 158 A1
Station St. K-in-A 115 D3
Station St. Lo Ea 193 F4
Station St. Mans 88 A2
Station St. Mans 102 A3
Station St. Mist 7 D1
Station St. Nott 173 E2
Station St. S in A 100 C1
Station Terr. Huck 146 A4
Station Terr. R on T 175 F2
Station View. Shireb 72 C2
Station Yd. S in A 100 C4
Staunton Dr. Nott 161 E2
Staunton Rd. N-on-T 139 F3
Staveley Ct. Lough 220 A3
Staverton Rd. Nott 171 F4
Staythorpe Rd. Aver 123 F1
Staythorpe Rd. Roll 138 B4
Staythorpe Rd. Stay 138 B4
Steadfold Cl. Nott 160 A3
Steads Cl. Carl 174 C4
Steedman Ave. Arn 162 A2
Steeles Way. Lamb 163 D4
Steeple Row. Lough 220 A2
Steetley La. Shire 35 D2
Steetley La. Whit 34 C2
Steetley La. Work 34 C2
Steinbeck Rd. Carl 174 B4
Stella Ave. Toll 197 E4
Stella Gr. Toll 197 E4
Stella St. Mans 102 A3
Stenton Cl. South 121 F1
Stepnall Hts. Boug 77 F3
Stepney Ct. Nott 159 F1
Sterndale Rd. Lo Ea 193 D3
Sternthorpe Cl. S on T 81 F1
Steven Cl. Bees 182 C2
Stevenholme Cres. Nott 161 D3
Stevens Rd. Sand 182 A3
Stevenson Cres. S in A 100 C1
Stevenson Gdns. Rudd 196 B3
Stewart Cl. C in L 25 F3
Stewart Rd. C in L 25 F3
Stewarton Cl. Arn 148 A1
Stiles Rd. Arn 162 B3
Stinsford Cl. Nott 161 E4
Stinting La. Mans 88 C1
Stinting La. Shireb 72 B1
Stirling Ave. Baw 10 A4
Stirling Ave. Mans 101 F3
Stirling Cl. Gain 15 F1
Stirling Dr. C in L 25 F3
Stirling Gr. Kim 158 C4
Stirling Grove. Nott 195 F4
Stirling Rd. Ret 39 E3
Stock Well. Nott 160 A3
Stockdale Cl. Bes Vil 147 D1
Stockhill Circus. Nott 160 B1
Stockhill La. Nott 160 B2
Stocking La. Ashkh 51 F2
Stocking La. E Lea 205 E2
Stocks Rd. Kim 158 C4
Stockton St. Nott 160 A4
Stockwell Gate. Mans 102 A3
Stockwell La. Cr Bi 189 D2
Stockwell The. Wyme 216 B2
Stockwith Rd. Haxey 7 E4
Stockwith Rd. Mist 7 E1
Stockwith Rd. Walk 14 B4
Stockwith Rd. Walker 14 A4
Stodman Mews. N-on-T 139 F4
Stodman St. N-on-T 139 F4
Stoke Ave. N-on-T 139 F2
Stoke Ferry La. Shel 164 A1
Stoke La. Bu Jo 163 F1
Stoke La. Carl 175 E4
Stoke La. St Ba 163 F1
Stoke La. St Ba 175 E4
Stolle Cl. Arn 162 B4
Stone Bridge Rd. Nott 173 F3
Stone Cres. Mans 101 E4
Stone Cross La. Mans 102 A4
Stone La. N Whea 31 E4
Stone Meadows. Lo Ea 193 F4
Stoneacre. Nott 161 D4
Stonebridge Ct Ind Est. Nott 173 F3
Stonebridge Dr. E Lea 205 F1
Stonebridge La. Mar War 74 A2
Stonebridge Rd. Mar War 74 A2
Stonechurch View. Ann Wo 130 A4
Stonehaven Cl. Arn 148 A1
Stonehill Cl. Ran 19 D3
Stonehills. Kegw 203 E1
Stoneleigh Cl. Bees 183 E3
Stoneleigh St. Nott 173 D3
Stonemasons Mews. K-in-A 115 D3
Stonepit Cl. Nott 161 F1
Stoney Bank. Lowd 150 B1
Stoney Houghton Gdns. Nott 159 F4
Stoney La. Brin 143 E3
Stoney La. Sels 128 C4
Stoney La. Trow 170 A3
Stoney St. Bees 183 F4
Stoney St. Nott 173 E2
Stoney St. S in A 101 D2
Stoneycroft Rd. Nott 160 C3
Stoneyford Rd. S in A 100 C2
Stonish Hill. Eakr 92 B1
Storcroft Rd. Ret 40 A3
Storey Ave. Carl 162 C1
Stormont Cl. S Norm 113 D2
Stornoway Cl. Bees 184 A3
Stort Sq. Mans 88 B1
Storth Ave. Huck 146 A3
Storth La. S Norm 113 D2
Storthfield Way. S Norm 113 D2

Story Gdns. Huck 146 B3
Stotfield Rd. Nott 171 D3
Stourdale Cl. Lo Ea 193 D3
Stow Ct. Mans 88 C2
Stow Park Rd. Mart 44 B4
Stowe Ave. W Brid 185 E3
Strafford St. Gain 24 B3
Straight Mile. Babw 38 B3
Strand The. Bees 183 F1
Stranraer Cl. Mans 88 B3
Stratford Cl. Carl 174 C3
Stratford Cres. Ret 39 E3
Stratford Rd. W Brid 185 F4
Stratford St. Ilk 157 F2
Strathavon Rd. C in L 25 F3
Strathglen Cl. Kim 158 C4
Strathmore Cl. Huck 145 F3
Strathmore Ct. Har 9 D3
Strathmore Dr. C in L 25 F3
Strathmore Rd. Arn 148 A1
Straw's La. E Brid 165 E2
Strawberry Bank. S in A 99 F2
Strawberry Hall La. N-on-T 125 D1
Strawberry Rd. Ret 40 A3
Street Lane Rd. N Le Ha 42 C4
Strelley La. Stre 171 D4
Strelley Rd. Nott 159 F1
Strelley St. Nott 160 A4
Stripe Rd. Tick 8 B4
Stripes View. Calv 148 C3
Strome Cl. Nott 173 E1
Strome Ct. Nott 173 E1
Stroud Ct. Bott 181 D2
Stroud's Cl. Hose 211 F4
Stuart Ave. Boug 77 E3
Stuart Ave. Mans 102 C4
Stuart Cl. Arn 162 A4
Stuart St. Mans 102 C4
Stuart St. S in A 100 C1
Stubbin's La. South 136 B3
Stubbing La. Work 35 E2
Stubbins Wood La. Shireb 72 C3
Stubbins Wood. Shireb 72 C3
Stubton Rd. Clayp 156 C3
Studland Way. W Brid 185 E3
Sturgate Wlk. Gain 24 C4
Sturgeon Ave. Nott 184 C2
Sturton Rd. N Le Ha 32 B1
Sturton Rd. S Whea 31 F4
Sturton Rd. Saundby 23 E2
Sturton Rd. Sax 57 D4
Sturton St. Nott 173 D4
Styring St. Bees 183 F3
Styrrup La. Malt 8 A1
Styrrup La. Styr 8 A1
Styrrup La. Styr 8 B1
Styrrup Rd. Har 8 C2
Styrrup Rd. Styr 8 C2
Sudbury Ave. Ilk 170 A4
Sudbury Ave. Sand 182 A3
Sudbury Ct. Mans 103 D3
Sudbury Mews. East 143 F1
Suez St. Nott 160 C1
Suff La. Pinx 113 E2
Suffolk Ave. Bees 184 B2
Suffolk Ave. Bir 9 E2
Suffolk Ave. Huck 145 E3
Suffolk Gr. Bir 9 E2
Suffolk Rd. Bir 9 E2
Sulby Cl. Mans 89 D1
Sullivan Cl. Nott 174 A3
Sumburgh Rd. Nott 185 D1
Summer Hill. Gain 15 F1
Summer Leys La. Nott 173 E2
Summer Way. R on T 175 F2
Summer's Rd. N-on-T 125 D1
Summercourt Dr. Raven 116 C2
Summerfield Rd. K-in-A 114 C4
Summerfields Way. Ship 157 E2
Summergangs La. Gain 24 B3
Summerwood La. Nott 195 F4
Summit Cl. K-in-A 115 D3
Summit Dr. Shireb 72 C2
Sunbeam St. What 179 D2
Sunbourne Ct. Nott 173 D3
Sunbury Gdns. Arn 148 A1
Sunderland Gr. Nott 159 E1
Sunderland Pl. Tick 8 A4
Sunderland St. Tick 8 A4
Sunfield Ave. Work 36 A2
Sunlea Cres. Staple 182 C3
Sunnindale Dr. Toll 186 C1
Sunningdale Av. Hean 157 D4
Sunningdale Cl. K-in-A 114 C4
Sunningdale Dr. Woodb 149 E3
Sunningdale Rd. Nott 160 C3
Sunningdale. Ret 39 E1
Sunninghill Dr. Nott 184 C2
Sunninghill Rise. Arn 148 A1
Sunny Bank. Mans 102 B2
Sunny Bank. Tibs 99 D3
Sunny Bank. Work 36 A2
Sunnydale Rd. Nott 174 A3
Sunnymede. Work 36 A3
Sunnyside Rd. Bees 183 E3
Sunnyside. Whit 45 D3
Sunnyside. Work 35 F3
Sunridge Ct. Nott 173 E4
Sunrise Ave. Nott 160 C3
Surbiton Sq. Nott 160 A2
Surfleet Cl. Nott 171 E2
Surgery La. Blid 118 A2
Surgey's La. Arn 148 A1
Surrey Dr. Mans 101 F4
Susan Cl. Huck 131 D1
Susan Dr. Nott 160 B2
Sussex Way. Sand 182 A3
Sutherland Cl. C in L 25 F4
Sutherland Dr. W Brid 186 A2
Sutherland Rd. Nott 174 A4
Suthers Rd. Kegw 203 E1
Sutton Ave. N-on-T 139 F3
Sutton Cl. S in A 101 D3
Sutton Cl. Su Bo 213 E3
Sutton Ct. East 143 F1
Sutton Gdns. Rudd 196 B3
Sutton La. Babw 29 D1
Sutton La. Gran 191 E3
Sutton Middle La. K-in-A 114 C3
Sutton Passeys Cres. Nott 172 A2
Sutton Rd. Beckin 142 C3
Sutton Rd. K-in-A 114 C3
Sutton Rd. Kegw 203 E1
Sutton Rd. Mans 101 F3
Sutton Rd. Nott 147 F1
Sutton Rd. S in A 100 C3
Swab's La. Co Ba 199 F4
Swab's La. Cr Bi 188 C1
Swain's Ave. Nott 174 A3
Swaledale Cl. Nott 160 B1
Swaledale. Work 36 A4
Swales Cl. Ret 39 E4
Swallow Ct. Mist 7 D1
Swallow Gdns. Carl 162 A1
Swallow Gr. Work 35 E4
Swallow Wlk. Hath 213 D1
Swallows Dr. Stat 202 C2
Swan Ct. Su Bo 213 D3
Swan Ct. Work 35 E4
Swan La. Mans 88 A2
Swan Meadow. Carl 174 C2
Swan St. Baw 10 A3
Swan St. Lough 220 A2
Swann Yd. S in A 99 F2
Swansdowne Dr. Nott 184 C1
Swanson Ave. S in A 99 F2
Swanwick Ave. Shireb 72 C2
Sweeney Ct. Nott 161 D4
Sweet Leys Dr. E Lea 205 F2
Sweet Leys Rd. Nott 173 E1
Swenson Ave. Nott 172 C2
Swift Ct. East 143 F1
Swift's Cl. Wyme 216 B2
Swigert Cl. Nott 159 F3
Swildon Wlk. Nott 160 C4
Swinburne Cl. Bald 140 B3
Swinburne St. Nott 173 F3
Swinburne Way. Arn 161 E4
Swinderby Rd. Coll 112 A4
Swinderby Rd. Eagle 83 F1
Swinderby Rd. Eagle 84 B1
Swinderby Rd. N Sca 83 F1
Swinderby Rd. S Sca 98 C3
Swindon Cl. Greas 158 B4
Swinecote Rd. Edwin 76 A2
Swiney La. Bees 183 D1
Swinfen Broun. Mans 102 B2
Swingate. Kim 159 D3
Swinnow Rd. Bir 9 E2
Swinscoe Gdns. Nott 160 C4
Swinstead Cl. Nott 171 F3
Swinton Copse. Boug 77 F3
Swinton Rise. Raven 117 D1
Swish La. Ruff 105 F4
Swithland Dr. W Brid 185 F2
Swynford Cl. Kettl 55 D2
Sycamore Ave. Glap 86 A4
Sycamore Ave. K-in-A 114 C3
Sycamore Cl. Bing 178 A2
Sycamore Cl. Hawt 139 E2
Sycamore Cl. Huck 145 F3
Sycamore Cl. Pinx 113 E2
Sycamore Cl. R on T 175 F1
Sycamore Cl. Rain 104 A1
Sycamore Cl. Sels 128 B4
Sycamore Cl. Work 35 F1
Sycamore Cres. Baw 9 F4
Sycamore Cres. Sand 182 A4
Sycamore Ct. Bees 184 A4
Sycamore Dr. Codd 125 F1
Sycamore Dr. Gain 15 F1
Sycamore Dr. Ilk 170 A4
Sycamore Gr. Mans 102 C3
Sycamore La. Bleas 152 A4
Sycamore Pl. Nott 173 E4
Sycamore Rd. Awsw 158 B3
Sycamore Rd. C in L 25 F4
Sycamore Rd. E Lea 214 B4
Sycamore Rd. Lo Ea 193 E3
Sycamore Rd. Mans 88 B3
Sycamore Rd. Oll 77 E2
Sycamore Rise. Nott 160 B1
Sycamore St. Mar War 74 A3
Sycamores The. East 143 F1
Sycamores The. S Norm 113 D3
Sydenham Ct. Nott 172 C1
Syderstone Wlk. Arn 161 F3
Sydney Cl. Mans 88 B3
Sydney Gr. R on T 175 F2
Sydney Rd. Nott 172 A3
Sydney St. N-on-T 125 D1
Sydney Terr. N-on-T 140 A4
Syerston Rd. Mans 103 D1
Syke Rd. Nott 160 C4
Sykes La. Bald 140 B2
Sykes La. Sax 56 C3
Sylvan Cres. S in A 101 D3
Sylvester St. Mans 101 F3
Synge Cl. Nott 195 E4
Sywell Cl. S in A 100 C3

Taft Ave. Sand 182 A3
Taft Leys Rd. E Lea 205 F1
Talbot Ct. R on T 175 F2
Talbot Dr. Staple 170 B1
Talbot Rd. Bir 9 D2
Talbot Rd. Work 36 A1
Talbot St. Mans 102 A2
Talbot St. Nott 173 D3
Talbot St. Pinx 113 E1
Tall Gables. D on T 54 B1
Tamarix Cl. Carl 163 D1
Tambling Cl. Arn 162 A3
Tame Cl. Nott 184 C2
Tamworth Gr. Nott 184 C1
Tamworth Rd. Lo Ea 193 E3
Tangmere Cres. Nott 159 F1
Tanner's La. Hath 213 D1
Tannery Wharf. N-on-T 139 F4
Tanyard. Egma 79 F3
Tarbert Cl. Nott 173 D1
Target St. Nott 172 C3
Tatham's La. Ilk 157 F1
Tattersall Wlk. Mans 88 C2
Tattershall Dr. Bees 184 A4
Tattershall Dr. Nott 173 D2
Taunton Rd. W Brid 185 F3
Taupo Dr. Huck 145 E3
Tavern Ave. Nott 160 B1
Tavistock Ave. Nott 161 E1
Tavistock Cl. Huck 145 E3
Tavistock Dr. Nott 161 E1
Tavistock Rd. W Brid 185 F3
Taylor Cl. Nott 174 A2
Taylor Cres. S in A 100 C1
Taylor Cres. Staple 182 C4
Taylor St. Ilk 157 F1
Taylor's Cl. Mans 102 C4
Teague Pl. Work 35 E2
Teak Cl. Nott 173 E4
Teal Cl. Shireb 72 B2
Teal Ct. Work 35 E4
Teal Wharf. Nott 173 D1
Tealby Cl. Nott 159 F4
Tealby Wlk. Mans 88 C2
Technology Dr. Bees 184 A3
Tedburn Dr. Mans 103 D1
Teesbrook Dr. Nott 171 D2
Teesdale Ct. Bees 183 D2
Teesdale Rd. Lo Ea 193 D3
Teesdale Rd. Nott 161 D1
Teignmouth Ave. Mans 102 C3
Telford Dr. Greas 144 A2
Telford Dr. N-on-T 125 E2
Temperance La. Coll 111 F4
Templar Rd. Bees 184 A3
Temple Cres. Nuth 159 E2
Temple Dr. Nuth 159 F2
Templemans Way. South 136 C4
Templemen Cl. Rudd 196 A4
Templeoak Dr. Nott 171 E2
Tenbury Cres. Nott 160 B1
Tenby Gr. Work 36 A1
Tene Cl. Nott 147 F1
Tenman La. Car Co 166 A1
Tennis Court Ind Est. Nott 174 A2
Tennis Dr. Nott 173 D2
Tennyson Ave. Carl 162 C1
Tennyson Ave. Mans 88 B1
Tennyson Ct. Huck 145 E3
Tennyson Dr. Bees 183 E1
Tennyson Dr. Work 36 B2
Tennyson Rd. Arn 161 F2
Tennyson Rd. Bald 140 B2
Tennyson Sq. Awsw 158 B2
Tennyson St. Gain 15 E1
Tennyson St. Ilk 157 F2
Tennyson St. K-in-A 115 D2
Tennyson St. Mans 102 A4
Tennyson St. Nott 173 D3
Tenter Cl. Lo Ea 193 E3
Tenter Cl. Nott 160 C4
Tenzing Wlk. Bald 140 C2
Terrace La. Plea 86 C3
Terrace Rd. Mans 102 B4
Terrace St. Nott 172 C4
Terrian Cres. W Brid 185 F4
Terry Ave. N-on-T 125 D2
Terton Rd. Nott 146 C1
Terton Rd. Nott 160 C4
Tetford Wlk. Mans 88 C2
Tetney Wlk. Nott 172 A3
Tettenbury Rd. Nott 160 C2
Teversal Ave. Mans 87 D2
Teversal Ave. Nott 172 C2
Tevery Cl. Staple 182 C4
Teviot Rd. Nott 160 C3
Tewkesbury Ave. Mans 88 B2
Tewkesbury Cl. W Brid 186 A3
Tewkesbury Dr. Kim 158 C4
Tewkesbury Dr. Nott 160 C2
Tewkesbury Rd. Lo Ea 193 F3
Thackeray Cl. Work 36 A3
Thackeray's La. Arn 161 F3
Thackerey St. Nott 172 C3
Thames St. Nott 160 A4
Thane Rd. Nott 184 C3
Thaxted Cl. Nott 171 E3
Theaker Ave. Gain 15 F1
Theaker La. Scaf 10 B3
Theatre Sq. Nott 173 E3
Thelda Ave. Keyw 197 F2
Theresa Ct. Bald 140 B2
Thetford Cl. Arn 162 A3
Thickley Cl. Shireb 72 C2
Thievesdale Ave. Work 35 F4
Thievesdale La. Work 36 A4
Third Ave. Carl 162 C1
Third Ave. Carl 174 A4
Third Ave. Edwin 76 A1
Third Ave. Mans 89 D1
Third Ave. Mans 103 F1
Third Ave. N Clip 89 F2
Thirlbeck. Cotg 188 A1
Thirlmere Cl. Lo Ea 182 A1
Thirlmere Cl. Nott 173 F4
Thirlmere Rd. Lo Ea 182 A1
Thirston Cl. Nott 159 F4
Thistle Cl. Greas 158 B4
Thistle Green Cl. Hean 143 D1
Thistledown Rd. Nott 195 F4
Thomas Ave. R on T 176 B2
Thomas Cl. Nott 173 E3
Thomas Parkyn Cl. Bunn 206 C4
Thomas Rd. Kegw 203 E1
Thomas St. Ret 39 F3
Thompson Ave. Har 8 C2
Thompson Cl. Bees 183 E2
Thompson Cres. S in A 100 C1
Thompson Gdns. Nott 147 D1
Thompson St. La Mi 143 D2
Thonock Dr. Sax 56 C2
Thonock Hill. Gain 15 E2
Thonock Rd. Thon 15 F3
Thor Gdns. Nott 146 C1
Thoresby Ave. Carl 162 B1
Thoresby Ave. Edwin 76 A1
Thoresby Ave. K-in-A 115 E2
Thoresby Ave. N-on-T 140 A3
Thoresby Ave. Nott 173 F2
Thoresby Ave. Shireb 72 C2
Thoresby Cl. Har 9 D3
Thoresby Cl. Mar War 74 B4
Thoresby Cl. R on T 176 A2
Thoresby Cres. S in A 100 B3
Thoresby Ct. Hello 173 A2
Thoresby Dale. Huck 146 A4
Thoresby Glade. Bils 106 A3
Thoresby Rd. Bees 171 E1
Thoresby Rd. Bing 177 E2
Thoresby Rd. Lo Ea 193 E3
Thoresby Rd. Mans 88 A2
Thoresby Rd. Rain 103 F1
Thoresby St. Mans 102 A4
Thoresby St. Nott 173 F2
Thoresby St. S in A 101 D2
Thorn Ave. Mans 87 F1
Thorn Bank. Haxey 2 B4
Thorn Bank. Wroot 2 B4
Thorn Dr. Greas 158 B4
Thorn Gr. Huck 146 A2
Thorn Tree Gdns. Greas 143 F2
Thornbury Dr. Mans 101 E4
Thornbury Hill La. Malt 16 B4
Thornbury Way. Nott 160 C4
Thorncliffe Rd. Nott 173 E4
Thorncliffe Rise. Nott 173 E4
Thorndale Rd. Nott 160 B1
Thorndike Cl. Bees 184 A2
Thorndike Way. Gain 24 C4
Thorne Rd. Baw 10 A4
Thorner Cl. Nott 160 C3
Thorney Abbey Rd. Blid 118 A3
Thorney Ct. Mans 103 D1
Thorney Hill. Nott 173 F4
Thorneywood Ave. Ann Wo 129 F4
Thorneywood Mount. Nott 173 F4
Thorneywood Rd. Lo Ea 193 F4
Thornham Cres. Ann Wo 129 F4
Thornhill Cl. Bees 171 D1
Thornhill Dr. Boug 77 F3
Thornhill La. N Le Ha 33 E1
Thornhill La. S Le S 33 E1
Thornhill Rd. Har 8 C2
Thornley St. Nott 172 C4
Thornton Ave. Nott 147 F1
Thornton Cl. Mans 103 D3
Thornton Cl. Nott 171 F2
Thornton Dale. Work 36 A4
Thornton Rd. Coll 112 A4
Thornton St. Gain 24 B4
Thornton St. S in A 100 C1
Thorntons Cl. Cotg 188 A1
Thorold Cl. Nott 184 C1
Thoroton Ave. Bald 140 B2
Thoroton St. Nott 173 D3
Thoroughfare La. Langf 125 E4
Thorpe Cl. Codd 126 A1
Thorpe Cl. N-on-T 139 F2
Thorpe Cl. Nott 161 D4
Thorpe Cl. Staple 182 B4
Thorpe Cres. Carl 162 A1
Thorpe La. Eagle 84 C1
Thorpe La. Shire 34 B3
Thorpe Lea. Gunt 165 D3
Thorpe Leys. Lo Ea 193 E3
Thorpe Rd. Greas 143 F2
Thorpe Rd. Mans 103 D1
Thorpe Rd. Matt 20 A4
Thorpe St. Head 52 B4
Thorpe St. Ilk 157 F2
Thorpelands Ave. Mans 88 C1
Thrapston Ave. Nott 147 F1
Three Leys La. S Le S 32 B2
Three Tuns Rd. East 144 A1
Thrumpton Ave. Lo Ea 194 A4
Thrumpton Cl. Ret 39 F2
Thrumpton Dr. Nott 173 D1
Thrumpton Lanes. Ret 39 F3
Thurgarton Ave. Nott 173 F2
Thurgarton La. Hover 151 F2
Thurgarton St. Nott 173 F2
Thurland St. Nott 173 E2
Thurlby Cl. Cr Bi 189 D2
Thurlby Ct. Mans 88 C2
Thurlby La. S-on-W 198 B1
Thurlby La. Widm 208 B4
Thurlby Rd. Gain 24 C4
Thurlestone Dr. Carl 162 B3
Thurley Wlk. Mans 103 D2
Thurloe Ct. W Brid 185 E2
Thurman Dr. Cotg 187 F2
Thurman St. Ilk 170 A3
Thurman St. Nott 172 C3
Thursby Rd. Nott 184 C2
Thymus Wlk. Nott 184 B1
Thyra Ct. Nott 161 F1
Thyra Gr. Bees 184 A3
Thyra Gr. Nott 161 F1
Tibshelf Rd. S in A 100 A4
Tickhill Rd. Baw 9 F4
Tickhill Rd. Har 8 C3
Tideswell Cl. Raven 117 D2
Tideswell Ct. Mans 102 B4
Tidworth Cl. Nott 172 A3
Tilbury Rise. Nott 160 A2
Tilbury Rise. Nott 160 A2
Till Bridge La. Mart 44 C4
Tiln Ct. Ret 29 F1
Tiln La. Ret 29 F1
Tilstock Ct. Greas 159 D4
Timothy Rd. Lax 79 E2
Tindale Bank Rd. Haxey 6 B4
Tinker La. Ba Mo 27 F3
Tinker's La. Best 97 F4
Tinsley Cl. Clayp 156 C3
Tinsley Rd. East 143 E1
Tintagel Green. Nott 184 C1
Tintern Dr. Nott 160 C1
Tip Tree Cl. Kim 158 C4
Tippett Ct. Nott 173 F3
Tippings La. Farns 119 F3
Tiree Cl. Staple 170 B1
Tishbite St. Nott 160 A4
Tissington Ave. Mar War 74 B4
Tissington Cl. Nott 173 D4
Tissington Rd. Nott 173 D4
Titchfield Ave. Mans 88 B2
Titchfield Ave. S in A 100 C1
Titchfield St. Huck 146 A4
Titchfield St. Mans 102 A4
Titchfield St. Mar War 74 A2
Titchfield Terr. Huck 146 A4
Tithby Ct. Mans 103 D1
Tithby Dr. Nott 161 E2
Tithby Rd. Bing 177 F1
Tithby Rd. Tith 189 E3
Tithe Barn Ct. N-on-T 125 D1
Tithe Gdns. Bes Vil 147 D1
Tithe La. Calv 148 C4
Tithes La. Tick 8 A4
Tiverton Cl. Huck 145 E3
Tiverton Cl. Nott 160 A1
Toad La. Elst 153 F2
Toad La. Epp 150 A3
Toad La. Lax 79 D1
Tobias Cl. Nott 160 C4
Todd Cl. Nott 195 E4
Todd Ct. Nott 195 E4
Toft Cl. Cotg 187 F1
Toft Rd. Bees 183 D2
Tokenhouse Yd. Nott 173 E2
Toll Bar Ave. Bott 181 D2
Tollerton Gn. Nott 160 B3
Tollerton Rd. Toll 186 C3
Tollhouse Hill. Nott 173 D3
Tolney La. N-on-T 139 F4
Tom Otter's La. Harby 70 C4
Tom Otter's La. Sax 70 C4
Tom Wass Rd. S in A 114 C4

Tomlinson Ave. Goth 195 D1
Ton La. Lowd 150 B1
Tonbridge Mount. Nott 171 E1
Tooley St. Gain 24 B4
Toothill La. Mans 102 B4
Toothill Rd. Lough 220 A3
Toothill Rd. Mans 102 A4
Top Green. Up Br 210 A1
Top La. Mans 87 D1
Top Pasture La. N Whea 31 F4
Top Rd. Blid 118 A1
Top Rd. Miss 4 B2
Top Rd. Rudd 196 B3
Top Rd. Thor 69 F3
Top Row. N-on-T 140 B4
Top Row. Sels 128 A3
Top Sandy La. Mar War 74 B2
Top St. Askh 51 F1
Top St. Baw 10 A4
Top St. E Dray 53 D2
Top St. Elst 153 E2
Top St. N Whea 31 E4
Top St. Rain 104 A1
Top Valley Dr. Nott 160 C4
Top Valley Way. Nott 160 C4
Topyard La. Hayt 30 B3
Tor La. Oll 77 D2
Torbay Cres. Nott 161 D3
Torkard Dr. Nott 160 C4
Torksey Ave. Sax 56 C2
Torksey Ferry Rd. Ramp 43 E1
Torksey Mews. Ret 39 E1
Torksey St. Ramp 43 D1
Torksey Wlk. Mans 88 C2
Torr St. Gain 24 B4
Torvill Dr. Nott 171 F3
Toston Dr. Nott 172 B2
Totland Dr. Nott 160 B1
Totland Rd. Bees 171 E2
Totley Cl. Nott 146 B1
Totnes Cl. Huck 145 E3
Totnes Rd. Nott 174 A3
Toton Cl. Nott 160 B3
Toton La. Bees 182 C3
Toton La. Staple 182 C3
Tottle Gdns. Nott 172 B3
Tow Ct. Farn 139 D2
Towe's Mount. Carl 174 C4
Tower Cres. Kim 159 D2
Tower St. Gain 15 E1
Towle St. Lo Ea 193 D2
Towlsons Croft. Nott 160 B2
Town Ct. Nott 161 D4
Town End La. Flint 167 D4
Town La. Newt 99 D2
Town St. Askh 52 A2
Town St. Bees 183 D4
Town St. Clay 21 E3
Town St. Clayp 156 B4
Town St. Cott 43 E3
Town St. Grass 81 F2
Town St. Hawk 167 E2
Town St. Lound 20 B1
Town St. Pinx 113 F2
Town St. S Lev 42 B4
Town St. Sand 182 A3
Town St. Sutt 28 C3
Town St. Tres 42 A2
Town View. Kim 158 C4
Townroe Dr. Mans 101 E4
Townsend Ct. Nott 147 D1
Townside Cl. Lo Ea 193 D2
Townside La. Tres 42 B2
Townside Rd. N Le Ha 32 B1
Towson Ave. La Mi 143 E1
Tracy Cl. Bees 171 F1
Trafalgar Cl. Nott 172 C3
Trafalgar Rd. Bees 184 A2
Trafalgar Rd. Lo Ea 193 E3
Trafalgar Sq. Lo Ea 193 F4
Traffic St. Nott 173 E2
Trafford Gdns. Nott 172 B4
Tranby Gdns. Nott 171 F2
Tranker La. Work 35 D3
Travell's Hill. N on S 214 A4
Travers Rd. Sand 182 A3
Treegarth Sq. Nott 147 D1
Trefan Gdns. Nott 161 D4
Trelawn Cl. Nott 161 E1
Tremayne Rd. Nott 171 E3
Trenchard Ave. Codd 125 F1
Trenchard Cl. New 177 E4
Trenchham Gdns. Bu Jo 163 E2
Trent Ave. Rudd 196 B4
Trent Bvd. W Brid 174 A1
Trent Cl. N Musk 110 C1
Trent Cl. Nott 173 F2
Trent Cres. Bees 183 F2
Trent Dr. Huck 145 E2
Trent Gdns. Bu Jo 164 A2
Trent La. Best 97 F3
Trent La. Bu Jo 164 B2
Trent La. E Brid 165 D2
Trent La. Girt 82 C1
Trent La. Kelh 124 A3
Trent La. Lo Ea 193 F3
Trent La. N Clift 68 C3
Trent La. N-on-T 125 D1
Trent La. Nott 174 A2
Trent La. S Clift 68 B1
Trent Port Rd. Mart 44 A4
Trent Rd. Bees 184 A2
Trent Rd. Mart 44 B4
Trent Rd. Nott 173 F2
Trent South Ind Park. Nott 174 A2
Trent St. Gain 24 B4
Trent St. Lo Ea 193 F4
Trent St. Nott 173 E2
Trent St. Ret 40 A3
Trent St. Work 35 F2
Trent Vale Rd. Bees 184 A2
Trent Valley View. Carl 162 A1
Trent View Gdns. R on T 176 A3
Trent Way. N-on-T 125 D1
Trent Wlk. Mans 88 C2
Trentdale Rd. Carl 174 B3
Trentham Dr. Nott 172 B4
Trentham Gdns. Nott 172 B4
Trenton Cl. Bees 171 D1
Trenton Dr. Lo Ea 194 A4
Trentside N. W Brid 173 F1
Trentside. Gunt 165 D2
Trentview Ct. Nott 173 F1
Tressall Cl. Ilk 170 A4
Treswell Ct. Mans 103 D1
Treswell Rd. Ramp 42 C1
Treswell Rd. S Lev 42 B3
Trevelyan Rd. W Brid 173 F1
Trevino Gdns. Nott 147 D1
Trevone Ave. Staple 182 C3
Trevor Rd. Bees 183 F3
Trevor Rd. W Brid 186 A3
Trevose Gdns. Nott 161 E2
Treyford Cl. Nott 185 D2
Triangle The. Ilk 170 A3
Tricornia Dr. Nott 160 A2
Tring Vale. Nott 161 D2
Trinity Cl. Ilk 157 F2
Trinity Cres. E Mark 66 A4
Trinity Cres. Lamb 163 E4
Trinity Cres. Wyme 216 A2
Trinity Rd. N-on-T 140 A2
Trinity Rd. Ret 29 E1
Trinity Rd. South 136 B4
Trinity Sq. Nott 173 E3
Trinity St. Gain 24 B4
Trinity St. Lough 220 B2
Trinity Wlk. Nott 173 E3
Trinstead Way. Nott 161 E4
Triumph Cl. Eakr 106 C4
Triumph Rd. Eakr 106 C4
Triumph Rd. Nott 172 B2
Trivett Sq. Nott 173 E2
Troon Cl. Kim 158 C4
Trough La. Greas 158 C4
Trough Rd. Greas 159 D4
Troutbeck Cres. Bees 183 E4
Troutbeck. Cotg 188 A2
Trowell Ave. Ilk 170 A3
Trowell Ave. Nott 171 D3
Trowell Ct. Mans 103 D1
Trowell Gr. Lo Ea 182 B1
Trowell Gr. Staple 170 C2
Trowell La. Su Bo 213 F4
Trowell Park Dr. Staple 170 B1
Trowell Rd. Nott 171 E3
Trowell Rd. Staple 170 B1
True Lovers Wlk. Lough 220 A2
Trueman Ct. Work 36 A3
Trueman Gdns. Arn 162 A3
Trueman St. Ilk 157 F2
Truman Cl. Nott 173 E3
Truman Dr. Huck 146 A3
Truman St. Coss 158 A1
Truman St. Kim 158 B4
Truman's Rd. Nott 173 E1
Truro Cl. E Lea 205 F1
Truro Cres. Nott 172 C4
Trusley Wlk. Mans 88 C2
Tryst The. N-on-T 125 D1
Tuckers Cl. Lough 220 B1
Tudor Ave. Mans 102 C4
Tudor Cl. Carl 174 C3
Tudor Cl. Lo Ea 182 C1
Tudor Cres. Rain 118 A4
Tudor Ct. Arn 162 A3
Tudor Ct. Huck 145 E3
Tudor Dr. Mans 102 B2
Tudor Dr. Mort 15 D2
Tudor Gr. Nott 173 D3
Tudor Rd. W Brid 185 F4
Tudor Sq. W Brid 185 F4
Tudor St. S in A 100 C1
Tudsbury Terr. S in A 101 D2
Tudwal Cl. Nott 161 D4
Tudwal Wlk. Nott 161 D4
Tulip Ave. Nott 173 E4
Tulip Rd. Awsw 158 A3
Tunnel Rd. Nott 173 D2
Tunnel Rd. Ret 39 F3
Tunstall Cres. Nott 160 A1
Tunstall Dr. Nott 160 C2
Tunstall Rd. Arn 161 F2
Turnberry Ave. K-in-A 114 C4
Turnberry Cl. Bees 183 E3
Turnberry Ct. W Brid 186 B2
Turnberry Rd. Nott 160 B3
Turnberry. Work 36 A3
Turner Ave. La Mi 143 D2
Turner Ave. Lough 220 A1
Turner Cl. Staple 182 C3
Turner Dr. Greas 158 B4
Turner Dr. Work 35 F2
Turner Rd. Lo Ea 193 E2
Turner Rd. Work 35 F2
Turner St. Huck 146 A4
Turners Croft. N Le Ha 42 B4
Turney St. Nott 173 E1
Turneys Ct. Nott 173 F1
Turnpike La. Nott 184 A4
Turnstone Wharf. Nott 172 C1
Turpin Ave. Carl 162 B2
Turpin Cl. Gain 15 F1
Turton Cl. La Mi 143 D2
Turvey La. Lo Wh 212 B1
Tuxford Ave. Mar War 74 C4
Tuxford Ct. Mans 103 D1
Tuxford Rd. Boug 77 F3
Tuxford Rd. E Mark 65 F3
Tuxford Rd. Egma 79 F4
Tuxford Rd. Nor on T 81 E3
Tuxford Rd. Wale 64 B1
Tuxford Rd. West 81 E3
Tuxford Wlk. Nott 173 F3
Twells Cl. Nott 173 F4
Twentylands Dr. E Lea 205 E1
Twin Oaks Dr. S in A 100 B1
Twitchell The. Bees 183 F2
Twitchell The. N-on-T 139 F3
Twitchell The. S in A 100 C1
Two Acres. Blyth 18 A1
Twycross Rd. Nott 161 D4
Twyford Gdns. Nott 184 C2
Twyford La. Elk 50 B2
Tyburn Cl. Bes Vil 147 D1
Tylden Rd. Rhod 35 D3
Tylden Way. Rhod 35 D3
Tyne Gdns. Huck 145 E2
Tynedale Cl. Lo Ea 193 D3
Tynedale Cl. Nott 160 B1

Ulldale Ct. Bees 183 D2
Ullswater Cl. Carl 162 C1
Ullswater Cres. Bees 183 E4
Ullswater Dr. Huck 145 F4
Ulster Rd. Gain 15 E1
Underwood Ave. Torw 19 D2
Underwood Gdns. Work 35 E2
Union Rd. Nott 173 E3
Union St. Bees 184 A3
Union St. Bing 177 F2
Union St. Lo Ea 193 F4
Union St. Lough 220 A2
Union St. Mans 102 A4
Union St. Ret 39 F4
Union St. S in A 100 C1
Union St. Sels 129 D4
Unity Cres. Carl 162 B1
Unity Rd. K-in-A 115 D4
University Bvd. Nott 184 B4
Unwin Rd. S in A 101 D2
Unwin St. S in A 100 A2
Uplands Ct. Nott 171 F3
Upminster Dr. Nott 147 F1
Upper Canaan. Rudd 196 B4
Upper College St. Nott 173 D3
Upper Dunstead Rd. Ald 143 D2
Upper Eldon St. Nott 173 F2
Upper Mexborough Rd. Sels 129 D4
Upper Orchard St. Staple 182 C4
Upper Parliament St. Nott 173 E3
Upper Row. D on T 54 A1
Upper Wellington St. Lo Ea 182 B1
Uppingham Cres. W Brid 185 E3
Uppingham Gdns. Nott 173 E1
Upton Dr. Nott 161 E3
Upton Hill. Askh 52 A2
Upton Mount. Mans 87 F1
Upton Rd. Askh 52 A2
Upton Rd. South 136 C4
Upton Rd. Upton 122 A1
Upton Wlk. Gain 24 C4
Urban Rd. K-in-A 115 D3
Utile Gdns. Nott 160 A4

Vale Ave. Mar War 74 A2
Vale Cl. Aslo 179 D2
Vale Cl. East 144 A1
Vale Cl. Mans 102 C2
Vale Cres N. Nott 172 B3
Vale Cres S. Nott 172 B3
Vale Dr. Shireb 72 C1
Vale Gdns. Carl 174 B3
Vale Rd. Carl 174 C3
Vale Rd. Mans 88 A2
Vale The. Ilk 157 F2
Valentine Ave. Sels 128 C4
Valeside Gdns. Carl 174 C3
Valetta Rd. Arn 162 A4
Valiant Rd. Codd 125 F1
Vallance St. Mans 88 A2
Valley App. Bils 105 F4
Valley Dr. East 144 A1
Valley Farm Ct. Nott 161 D4
Valley Gdns. W Brid 186 B3
Valley La. Dry Do 169 E4
Valley Prospect. N-on-T 139 E3
Valley Rd. Bees 183 D3
Valley Rd. Bils 105 F4
Valley Rd. Carl 162 A1
Valley Rd. Kim 158 B4
Valley Rd. Nott 161 D2
Valley Rd. R on T 176 A3
Valley Rd. Shireb 72 C3
Valley Rd. W Brid 186 A3
Valley Rd. Work 35 F3
Valley View. Codd 126 A1
Valmont Ave. Mans 103 D3
Valmont Rd. Bees 183 D4
Valmont Rd. Nott 161 D2
Vancouver Ave. R on T 175 F1
Vanessa Dr. Gain 15 E2
Vanguard Rd. Lo Ea 193 E3
Varden Ave. Nott 172 A1
Varney Rd. Nott 184 C2
Vaughan Ave. Bott 181 E1
Vaughan Ave. Huck 131 E1
Vaughan Pl. Shireb 72 C3
Vaughan Rd. Bees 183 D2
Vellus Ct. S in A 101 D1
Ventnor Rise. Nott 160 C2
Venus Cl. Nott 160 C3
Vera Cres. Rain 118 A4
Verbena Cl. Nott 173 E4
Verder Gr. Nott 160 C4
Vere Ave. S in A 100 C3
Vere St. Nott 160 A4
Verne Cl. Carl 174 B4
Verney St. Plea 86 C4
Verney Way. Plea 86 C4
Vernon Ave. Bees 183 F3
Vernon Ave. Carl 162 C1
Vernon Ave. N-on-T 140 A4
Vernon Ave. Nott 160 C2
Vernon Ave. Nott 185 D4
Vernon Ave. Raven 116 C1
Vernon Ave. Ret 40 A2
Vernon Cres. Raven 117 D1
Vernon Ct. Nuth 159 F2
Vernon Ct. Shireb 73 D2
Vernon Dr. Nuth 159 F2
Vernon Park Dr. Nott 160 C2
Vernon Rd. K-in-A 114 C3
Vernon Rd. Nott 160 C2
Vernon St. Ilk 157 F2
Vernon St. N-on-T 140 A4
Vernon St. Nott 173 D3
Vernon St. Shireb 73 D2
Vernon St. Work 36 A1
Verona Ct. Mans 103 D2
Veronica Dr. Carl 162 B1
Veronica Dr. Greas 158 B4
Veronica Wlk. Nott 184 B1
Veronne Dr. S in A 101 F4
Vesper Ct. Mans 102 C4
Vessey Cl. Bald 140 B2
Vessey Rd. Work 35 F4
Vexation La. Edwin 91 F4
Vicar La. Miss 4 B2
Vicar La. Tibs 99 D3
Vicar's La. Ramp 43 D1
Vicar's Wlk. Work 35 F1
Vicarage Cl. Nott 173 E3
Vicarage Ave. Ilk 157 E2
Vicarage Ave. N Le Ha 42 B4
Vicarage Cl. Coll 98 A1
Vicarage Cl. N Le Ha 42 B4
Vicarage Cl. Shireb 72 C2
Vicarage Ct. S in A 100 C4
Vicarage Dr. Bu Jo 163 F2
Vicarage Dr. Hayt 30 B3
Vicarage Green. W Brid 186 A2
Vicarage La. Beck 14 B1
Vicarage La. Farns 119 F3
Vicarage La. Kneet 151 F1
Vicarage La. N Musk 110 B2
Vicarage La. R on T 175 F2
Vicarage La. Rudd 196 B4
Vicarage Rd. Nott 160 C2
Vicarage Rd. South 136 B4
Vicarage St. Bees 183 F3
Vicarage St. Ilk 157 E2
Vicarage Way. Ann Wo 129 F4
Vicarage Wlk. N Le Ha 42 B4
Vickers St. Hello 173 A2
Vickers St. Mar War 74 A2
Victor Cres. Sand 182 B2
Victor Terr. Nott 161 E1
Victoria Ave. Lowd 150 C1
Victoria Ave. Lowd 164 C4
Victoria Ave. Nott 173 F2
Victoria Centre. Nott 173 E3
Victoria Cl. Boug 77 F3
Victoria Cl. Gain 24 C3
Victoria Cl. Nott 147 F1
Victoria Cres. Nott 161 E1
Victoria Ct. Ilk 157 F1
Victoria Ct. Mans 102 A3
Victoria Emb. Nott 185 E4
Victoria Gdns. Greas 145 D1
Victoria Gdns. N-on-T 140 A4
Victoria Park. Carl 175 D3
Victoria Rd. Bing 178 A3
Victoria Rd. Bunn 196 C1
Victoria Rd. Carl 175 D3
Victoria Rd. K-in-A 114 C3
Victoria Rd. Nott 161 D2
Victoria Rd. Pinx 113 E2
Victoria Rd. Ret 39 F3
Victoria Rd. Sand 182 A3
Victoria Rd. Sels 129 D4
Victoria Rd. W Brid 185 F4
Victoria Rd. Work 35 F1
Victoria Sq. Work 35 F2
Victoria St. Carl 162 C1
Victoria St. Huck 146 A4
Victoria St. Ilk 157 F2
Victoria St. Ilk 157 F2
Victoria St. Kim 159 D3
Victoria St. La Mi 143 E2
Victoria St. Lo Ea 193 D3
Victoria St. Lough 220 A2
Victoria St. Mar War 74 A3
Victoria St. N-on-T 139 F4
Victoria St. Nott 173 E2
Victoria St. R on T 175 F2
Victoria St. S in A 100 B3
Victoria St. S in A 100 C1
Victoria St. S Norm 113 D3
Victoria St. Sels 128 A2
Victoria St. Sels 129 D4
Victoria St. Shireb 72 C2
Victoria St. Staple 182 B4
Victoria Terr. Tibs 99 D4
Victory Cl. Lo Ea 193 E3
Victory Cl. Mans 89 D1
Victory Dr. Mans 88 C1
Victory Rd. Bees 184 A2
Villa Rd. Keyw 197 F2
Villa Rd. Nott 173 E4
Villa St. Bees 183 F4
Village Cl. Farn 139 D3
Village Cl. W Brid 186 A2
Village Farm Cl. W Lea 204 C1
Village Rd. N on S 213 E1
Village Rd. Nott 184 B1
Village St. Owth 199 F4
Village St. W Brid 186 A2
Village Way. Farn 139 D3
Villiers Rd. Arn 161 E2
Villiers Rd. Mans 102 C4
Villiers Rd. W Brid 186 A3
Vincent Ave. Bees 183 F3
Vincent Gdns. Nott 172 C4
Vine Cres. Sand 182 A3
Vine Rd. Tick 8 B4
Vine Terr. Huck 146 A4
Vine Tree Terr. Hoton 215 E1
Vine Way. N-on-T 140 A4
Vines Cross. Nott 171 F1
Violet Ave. East 144 A1
Violet Cl. Nott 160 B2
Violet Hill. Mans 103 D4
Violet Rd. Carl 162 B1
Violet Rd. W Brid 186 A4
Vista The. Staple 182 C3
Vivian Ave. Nott 173 D4
Voca Ct. Work 36 A3
Vulcan Cl. Nott 160 C2
Vulcan Pl. Work 35 F2
Vyse Dr. Lo Ea 193 E3

W End Cl. Bott 181 D2
W Furlong. Cotg 188 A1
W Leake La. K on S 204 B3
W Leake Rd. E Lea 205 E1
W Wlk. Nott 173 F2
Waddington Dr. W Brid 185 E2
Wade Ave. Ilk 170 A4
Wadham Rd. Arn 161 F3
Wadhurst Gdns. Nott 173 E3
Wadhurst Gr. Nott 171 E1
Wadnal La. West 80 C2
Wadsworth Rd. Staple 182 C4
Wagstaff La. Sels 128 B3
Wain Ct. Work 36 A4
Waingrove. Nott 185 D2
Wainwright Ave. Mans 101 E4
Wakefield Ave. R on T 176 A2
Wakeling Cl. South 136 C4
Walbrook Cl. Nott 160 A2
Walcot Green. Nott 184 B1
Walcote Dr. W Brid 185 E2
Waldeck Rd. Nott 161 D1
Waldemar Gr. Bees 184 A3
Waldron Cl. Nott 173 E1
Walesby Ct. Mans 103 D2
Walesby Dr. K-in-A 115 E3
Walesby La. Oll 77 E3
Walford Cl. Bott 181 D1
Walgrave Wlk. Nott 161 D4
Walk Mill Dr. Huck 131 D1
Walk The. Gain 24 C4
Walkden St. Mans 102 A4
Walker Cl. N-on-T 140 A4
Walker St. East 144 A2
Walker St. Nott 173 F2
Walkeringham Rd. Beck 14 A1
Walkeringham Rd. G on H 13 D2
Walkerith Rd. E Stock 14 B4

Walkerith Rd. Mort 15 D3
Walkerith Rd. Walk 14 C3
Walkers Ave. Brin 143 F3
Walkers Cl. Bing 177 F2
Walkers Cl. Mans 89 D1
Walkers Yd. R on T 175 F2
Wall St. Gain 24 B4
Wallace Ave. Carl 174 C4
Wallace Rd. Lough 220 A1
Wallace St. Goth 195 D1
Wallan St. Nott 172 C3
Wallet St. Carl 175 D4
Wallett Ave. Bees 183 F4
Wallingwells La. Wall 25 D3
Wallis Rd. Mans 102 B4
Wallis St. Nott 160 C2
Walnut Ave. Shire 34 C4
Walnut Ave. Tick 8 A4
Walnut Cl. Aslo 178 C3
Walnut Cl. Ilk 170 A4
Walnut Dr. Bees 183 D4
Walnut Dr. Calv 148 C4
Walnut Gr. E Brid 165 E1
Walnut Gr. R on T 175 F2
Walnut Paddock. Harb 202 A2
Walnut Rd. Bott 181 D1
Walnut Tree Gdns. Nott 159 F4
Walnut Tree Green. Mans 89 E1
Walnut Tree La. E Brid 165 E1
Walsham Cl. Bees 183 E1
Walsingham Rd. Arn 162 A3
Walter St. Nott 173 D3
Walters Cres. Sels 128 B3
Waltham Cl. Bald 140 B2
Waltham Cl. W Brid 186 A3
Waltham La. Harb 202 A1
Waltham La. Lo Cl 211 F1
Waltham Rd. Raven 117 D1
Walton Ave. Nott 173 F3
Walton Ave. Nott 173 F3
Walton Cl. Mans 103 D4
Walton Cres. Carl 174 C4
Walton Dr. Keyw 197 F2
Walton Dr. S in A 114 B4
Walton Rd. Arn 148 A1
Walton St. Lo Ea 182 B1
Walton St. S in A 101 D2
Walton's La. N Musk 110 C2
Wands Cl. South 136 B4
Wansbeck Cl. Nott 173 D3
Wanstead Way. Nott 146 C1
Wapping La. Mart 44 B4
Warburton St. N-on-T 125 D1
Ward Ave. Huck 130 C1
Ward Pl. Mans 101 F3
Ward St. Nott 172 C4
Ward's End. Lough 220 A2
Wardle Gr. Arn 162 A4
Wardlow Rd. Ilk 157 F2
Wareham Cl. Nott 160 A2
Wareham Cl. W Brid 185 E3
Warkton Cl. Bees 183 E3
Warnadene Rd. S in A 114 C4
Warner Pl. Lough 220 B2
Warner St. Nott 172 C3
Warrands Cl. South 136 B4
Warren Ave Ext. Staple 182 B4
Warren Ave. Ann Wo 130 B4
Warren Ave. Nott 161 D1
Warren Ave. Staple 182 B4
Warren Cl. Gain 15 D1
Warren Cl. S in A 100 A1
Warren Ct. Staple 182 B4
Warren La. Kegw 203 D4
Warren Rd. Ann Wo 115 D1
Warren Rd. Huck 145 E3
Warren The. Cotg 187 F1
Warrender Cl. Bees 171 E1
Warrener Gr. Nott 160 C4
Warrenhill Cl. Arn 161 E4
Warrington Rd. Nott 160 B4
Warser Gate. Nott 173 E2
Warsop La. Rain 117 F4
Warsop Rd. Mans 88 B2
Warton Ave. Nott 173 F4
Warwick Ave. Arn 161 F3
Warwick Ave. Bees 183 F4
Warwick Ave. C in L 25 F3
Warwick Cl. K-in-A 115 E3
Warwick Dr. Mans 102 C4
Warwick Dr. Ship 157 E2
Warwick Gdns. Cotg 187 F1
Warwick Rd. Bald 140 B2
Warwick Rd. Lo Ea 194 A4
Warwick Rd. Nott 161 E1
Wash Pit La. Co Ba 200 B4
Washdyke La. Huck 145 F4
Washington Dr. Staple 170 C1
Washington St. Gain 24 B3
Wasnidge Cl. Nott 173 E3
Wasnidge Wlk. Nott 173 E3
Watchwood Gr. Calv 148 C4
Watcombe Cir. Nott 161 E1
Watcombe Rd. Nott 161 E1
Watendlath Cl. W Brid 186 B3
Water La. C in L 26 A3
Water La. Lo Cl 211 F2
Water La. Mans 87 D2
Water La. N-on-T 124 C1
Water La. Oxt 134 A2
Water La. R on T 175 F2
Water La. Ret 39 F4
Water La. S Norm 113 D3
Water La. Shel 164 B1
Water La. Tick 8 A3
Water Meadows. Work 35 E1
Water Orton Cl. Bees 182 C2
Waterdown Rd. Nott 184 B1
Waterford St. Nott 160 C2
Waterfurrows La. Shel 164 B1
Waterhouse La. Carl 163 D1
Waterloo Cl. S Norm 113 E4
Waterloo Cres. Nott 173 D3
Waterloo La. Trow 170 C3
Waterloo Prom. Nott 173 D3
Waterloo Rd. Bees 184 A3
Waterloo Rd. Nott 173 D3
Watermeadow Cl. Mans 88 B3
Watermeadows The. Lo Ea 193 D4
Waterside Cl. Lough 220 A3
Waterside Cl. Sand 182 A2
Waterside Gdns. Nott 172 C1
Waterslack Rd. Bir 9 D2
Waterson Ave. Mans 102 C2
Waterson Cl. Mans 103 D2
Waterway St W. Nott 173 E1
Waterway St. Nott 173 E1
Waterway The. Sand 182 B2
Waterworks St. Gain 24 B3
Watford Rd. Nott 160 A1
Watkin St. Nott 173 E3
Watkins La. S Le S 32 B3
Watnall Cres. Mans 101 F4
Watnall Rd. Huck 145 F2
Watnall Rd. Kim 158 C4
Watnall Rd. Nuth 159 E3
Watson Ave. Mans 102 B4
Watson Ave. Nott 174 A3
Watson Rd. Work 35 F1
Watson St. Mar War 74 A2
Watson's La. Harb 202 A2
Wavell Cres. Matt 11 D1
Waveney Cl. Arn 162 A3
Waverley Ave. Bees 184 A3
Waverley Ave. Carl 163 D1
Waverley Pl. Work 47 D4
Waverley Rd. Mans 102 A2
Waverley St. Lo Ea 193 F4
Waverley St. Nott 173 D3
Waverley St. Tibs 99 D4
Waverley Way. Work 47 D4
Waverly Cl. K-in-A 115 E3
Wayford Wlk. Nott 160 A4
Wayne Cl. Nott 184 C1
Weardale Rd. Nott 161 D1
Wearmouth Gdns. Bes Vil 147 D1
Weaver La. Ann Wo 129 F2
Weavers Cl. E Lea 205 F2
Weavers The. N-on-T 139 E3
Weaverthorpe Rd. Arn 162 A3
Webb Rd. Nott 172 A4
Webster Ave. East 143 F1
Webster Cl. Rain 104 A1
Weedon Cl. Nott 174 A3
Weekday Cross. Nott 173 E2
Weetman Ave. Mar War 74 A3
Weetman Gdns. Nott 161 D4
Weighbridge Rd. Mans 102 B3
Weightman Dr. Greas 158 A4
Welbank Cl. Bees 183 D2
Welbeck Ave. Carl 162 B1
Welbeck Ave. N-on-T 125 D1
Welbeck Cl. Nott 173 E3
Welbeck Cl. S in A 100 C3
Welbeck Dr. Edwin 75 F1
Welbeck Gdns. Arn 162 A2
Welbeck Gdns. Bees 182 C2
Welbeck Gr. Bing 177 E2
Welbeck Pl. Tux 66 A2
Welbeck Rd. Har 9 D3
Welbeck Rd. Lo Ea 182 B2
Welbeck Rd. Mans 88 B2
Welbeck Rd. R on T 176 A2
Welbeck Rd. Ret 39 F2
Welbeck Rd. W Brid 185 F4
Welbeck Sq. S in A 100 B3
Welbeck St. Elmt 58 C4
Welbeck St. K-in-A 115 E3
Welbeck St. Mans 102 A4
Welbeck St. Mar War 74 A2
Welbeck St. S in A 100 C1
Welbeck St. Whit 45 D3
Welbeck St. Work 35 F2
Welbeck Wlk. Nott 173 E3
Welby Ave. Nott 172 C2
Welch Ave. Staple 182 C4
Welfare Cl. Shireb 72 C2
Welfitt Gr. Ne La 59 D1
Welham Cres. Arn 162 A4
Welham Gr. Ret 40 A4
Welham Rd. Clar 40 A4
Welham Rd. Ret 40 A4
Well Fen La. Clayp 156 B4
Well La. Up Br 210 A1
Welland Cl. N-on-T 125 D1
Welland Cl. Work 35 F4
Wellesley Cres. Nott 159 E1
Wellin Cl. W Brid 186 A2
Wellin Ct. W Brid 186 A2
Wellin La. W Brid 186 A2
Wellington Cir. Nott 173 D2
Wellington Cl. Mar War 74 A2
Wellington Cres. W Brid 185 F4
Wellington Gr. Baw 9 F4
Wellington Pl. East 143 F1
Wellington Rd. Bu Jo 164 A3
Wellington Rd. N-on-T 140 A4
Wellington Sq. Nott 173 D3
Wellington Sq. Ret 39 F4
Wellington St. East 143 F2
Wellington St. Gain 24 B4
Wellington St. Lo Ea 182 B1
Wellington St. Lough 220 B2
Wellington St. Nott 173 E3
Wellington St. Ret 39 F4
Wellington St. Staple 182 B3
Wellington Villas. Nott 173 D3
Wellow Cl. Mans 101 E4
Wellow Green. Oll 77 E1
Wellow Rd. Eakr 92 C1
Wellow Rd. Oll 77 E1
Wells Cl. Mans 88 B2
Wells Gdns. Nott 173 F4
Wells La. Cott 43 E3
Wells Road The. Nott 161 F1
Wellspring Dale. Staple 182 C3
Welshcroft Cl. K-in-A 115 D4
Welstead Ave. Nott 160 A1
Welton Gdns. Nott 160 A4
Welwyn Ave. Mans 88 C2
Welwyn Rd. Nott 171 F3
Wembley Gdns. Bees 171 D1
Wembley Rd. Arn 162 A3
Wembley Rd. Lan 16 C2
Wembley St. Gain 24 B4
Wemyss Gdns. Nott 172 B2
Wendling Gdns. Nott 161 D4
Wendover Dr. Nott 160 A1
Wenham La. S in A 99 F2
Wenlock Cl. Greas 158 B4
Wensley Rd. Arn 161 F3
Wensleydale Cl. Mans 88 C1
Wensleydale Cl. Nott 160 B1
Wensleydale Rd. Lo Ea 193 D3
Wensleydale. Work 36 A4
Wensor Ave. Nott 183 F4
Wentbridge Dr. Mans 103 D2
Wentworth Cnr. N-on-T 139 F3
Wentworth Croft. Hean 143 D2
Wentworth Ct. Kim 158 C3
Wentworth Green. Ret 39 E2
Wentworth Rd. Bees 183 E3
Wentworth Rd. K-in-A 114 C4
Wentworth Rd. Nott 161 D1
Wentworth St. Coss 158 A1
Wentworth Way. W Brid 186 B2
Wesley Cl. Bald 140 B2
Wesley Cl. Hath 213 D1
Wesley Gr. Nott 161 D1
Wesley Pl. Staple 182 C4
Wesley Rd. Ret 39 F4
Wesley St. Ann Wo 130 A4
Wesley St. Ilk 157 F2
Wesley St. La Mi 143 E2
Wesley St. Nott 161 D1
Wesley Way. Rudd 196 B3
Wesleyan Chpl Wlk. Staple 182 B4
Wessex Cl. Work 36 A3
Wessex Rd. Work 36 A3
West Ave. K-in-A 115 E2
West Ave. Sand 182 A3
West Ave. Staple 182 C4
West Ave. W Brid 185 F4
West Bank Ave. Mans 102 A4
West Bank Lea. Mans 88 A1
West Bank Link. Mans 88 A1
West Bank Mews. Kegw 203 E1
West Bank Wynd. Mans 102 A4
West Bank. Sax 56 C1
West Brook La. Coll 112 A3
West Carr Rd. Ret 39 E3
West Cl. Keyw 197 F1
West Cres. Bees 184 A2
West Cres. K-in-A 115 E2
West Ct. Ret 39 E4
West Dr. Edwin 76 A1
West Dr. Nott 184 A4
West End Arc. Nott 173 D3
West End St. Staple 182 B3
West End. Bees 183 F3
West End. Calv 148 B4
West End. Farn 138 C2
West End. Lo Cl 211 E2
West End. Lo Wh 212 A2
West End. Pinx 113 E2
West End. S in A 100 C1
West Furlong. Ret 39 E4
West Gate. Lo Ea 193 F4
West Gate. Mans 102 A4
West Gate. Tick 8 A3
West Grove Rd. Ret 39 F3
West Hill Ave. Mans 102 A4
West Hill Dr. Mans 102 A4
West Hill Park. Mans 88 A2
West Hill Rd. Ret 39 E2
West Hill Way. Mans 102 A4
West Hill. Mans 102 A4
West Hill. S in A 100 B3
West La. Edwin 76 A1
West La. Girt 82 C1
West Moor Rd. Walker 13 F3
West Moor. Nott 174 B2
West Park Pl. Ret 39 E3
West St. Arn 161 F4
West St. Har 9 D3
West St. Huck 146 A4
West St. Kim 159 D2
West St. La Mi 143 D2
West St. Mar War 73 E2
West St. Miss 4 A1
West St. Mort 15 D2
West St. Nott 173 F2
West St. Ret 39 F3
West St. Scarc 59 D2
West St. Work 35 F1
West Terr. Huck 146 A4
West Terr. Ilk 157 F1
West Thorpe. W-on-W 217 E4
West View Rd. Carl 174 C4
West View. C in L 25 F4
West View. W Brid 185 E3
West Wells La. G on H 12 C1
West Wlk. Ret 39 E4
West Wood Estate. Baw 9 F3
Westbourne Cl. Ret 40 A3
Westbourne Cl. S in A 100 B2
Westbourne Rd. S in A 100 B2
Westbourne Rd. Sels 129 D2
Westbourne View. S in A 100 B2
Westbrecks La. S Lev 43 D3
Westbrook Ave. Raven 116 C2
Westbury Cl. Bees 183 E2
Westbury Rd. Nott 161 D1
Westby La. Awsw 158 B2
Westby La. Kim 158 B2
Westcliffe Ave. Carl 162 B2
Westcliffe Ave. R on T 176 A2
Westcroft Dr. Sax 57 D3
Westcross Ave. Staple 182 C4
Westdale Ave. S in A 101 D3
Westdale Cl. Lo Ea 193 D3
Westdale Cres. Carl 162 C1
Westdale Ct. Carl 162 B1
Westdale La East. Carl 162 C1
Westdale La West. Carl 162 A2
Westdale Rd. Mans 88 A1
Westdale Rd. Sels 128 B2
Westerdale. Work 36 A4
Westerfield Way. Nott 185 D3
Westerham Cl. Nott 171 E4
Westerham Rd. Rudd 196 A3
Westerlands. Staple 182 C3
Western Ave. Bing 177 E3
Western Ave. K-in-A 115 D2
Western Ave. Mans 101 F3
Western Ave. Sax 56 C2
Western Bvd. Nott 172 B4
Western Dr. Bald 140 C1
Western Fields. Rudd 196 A3
Western Gdns. Nott 172 B4
Western St. Nott 173 E3
Western Terr. Nott 173 D2
Western Wlk. Baw 10 A4
Westfield Cl. Mans 101 F4
Westfield Dr. Mans 101 F4
Westfield Dr. Work 36 A3
Westfield La. Coll 111 F4
Westfield La. Mans 101 F4
Westfield La. Mans 102 A4
Westfield Rd. Ann Wo 115 D1
Westfield Rd. Bing 177 E2
Westfield Rd. Ret 39 E3
Westfield Way. Farn 139 D2
Westfields La. Woodb 149 D2
Westgate St. Nott 173 F3
Westgate View. Work 35 F1
Westgate. South 136 B4
Westgate. Work 35 F1
Westhay Ct. Nott 172 B3
Westholme Gdns. Nott 172 B3
Westhorpe Ave. Nott 173 F3
Westhorpe Dr. Lo Ea 193 E4
Westhorpe Market Pl. South 136 B4
Westland Ave. Huck 145 E2
Westland Dr. Pinx 113 E2
Westleigh Rd. Nott 159 F1
Westleigh. Mans 88 B3
Westminster Ave. K-in-A 115 E3
Westminster Ave. Staple 182 B3
Westminster Cl. Nott 173 F4
Westminster Cl. Work 36 A4
Westmoore Cl. Carl 162 A2
Westmoreland Ct. Nott 161 D1
Westmorland Ct. Bir 9 E2
Westmorland Dr. C in L 25 F4
Westmorland Way. Sels 128 A2
Weston Ave. Nott 173 D4
Weston Cl. Arn 161 F2
Weston Cl. S in A 115 E4
Weston La. Nor on T 81 E3
Weston Rd. Egma 80 A3
Weston St. Hean 157 D4
Westray Cl. Bees 171 D2
Westview Ct. Carl 174 C4
Westville Dr. Huck 145 F2
Westville Gdns. Nott 173 E4
Westward Ave. Bees 184 A3
Westway. Cotg 187 F1
Westway. Work 36 A4
Westwick Rd. Nott 171 E3
Westwick St. Ilk 170 A3
Westwood Rd. Nott 173 F2
Wetherby Cl. Kim 158 C4
Wetherby Cl. Nott 160 A1
Wetherlam Cl. Nott 173 E1
Wetsyke La. Bald 140 C2
Whaddon Ct. Lough 220 B1
Whaley Common. Scarc 58 B2
Whaley Rd. Scarc 58 C1
Wharf La. R on T 175 F2
Wharf Rd. Mist 6 C1
Wharf Rd. Nott 173 D2
Wharf Rd. Pinx 113 E1
Wharf Rd. Ret 39 F3
Wharf Rd. S in A 100 B3
Wharf St. Baw 10 A4
Wharfdale Rd. Lo Ea 193 D3
Wharfedale. Nott 171 D2
Wharfedale. Work 36 A4
Wharmby Ave. Mans 87 E2
Wharncliffe Rd. Ilk 157 F1
Wharncliffe Rd. Lough 220 B2
Wharncliffe Rd. Ret 39 F2
Wharton Ct. Mans 103 D2
Wharton St. Ret 40 A3
Whatton Rd. Hath 212 C1
Whatton Rd. Kegw 203 E1
Whatton Rd. Kegw 212 B4
Whatton Rise. Nott 161 E2
Wheat Cl. Nott 171 E3
Wheat Croft. Work 36 A4
Wheatacre Rd. Nott 184 C1
Wheatcroft View. W Brid 185 E2
Wheatfield Cres. Mans 88 C3
Wheatfield Dr. Tick 8 A4
Wheatfield Way. S in A 100 C4
Wheatfields Rd. Nott 174 A4
Wheatgrass Hill. Hock 122 B2
Wheatgrass Rd. Bees 183 D3
Wheatland Dr. Lough 220 B1
Wheatley Ave. K-in-A 114 C2
Wheatley Cl. Mans 88 C1
Wheatley Dr. Carl 174 B4
Wheatley Gr. Bees 183 F2
Wheatley La. Coll 112 A2
Wheatley Rd. Clay 21 F2
Wheatley Rd. S Le S 32 A3
Wheatsheaf Ct. Bu Jo 163 F2
Wheeldale Cl. Nott 171 D2
Wheeldon St. Gain 24 B4
Wheeler Ave. East 144 A1
Wheeler Gate. Nott 173 E2
Wheeler Gate. Sels 129 D1
Wheldon Ave. Carl 162 B1
Whernside Rd. Arn 161 F3
Whetstone Cl. Nuth 159 E2
Whickham Ct. Nott 173 E1
Whilton Cl. S in A 101 D3
Whimsey Park. Carl 174 C3
Whinbush La. Calv 133 F2
Whinfell Cl. Nott 184 C1
Whinleys Rd. Clar 31 D1
Whinney Bank. Mans 88 B2
Whinney Hill. Mans 88 B2
Whinney La. Boug 77 E3
Whinney Moor Cl. Ret 39 F3
Whinney Moor La. Ret 39 F3
Whinney Moor Way. Ret 39 F3
Whiston Cl. Nott 161 D3
Whitaker Cl. Ret 29 E1
Whitbread St. Nott 172 C4
Whitburn Rd. Bees 182 C2
Whitby Cl. Nott 171 D2
Whitby Cres. Arn 162 A3
Whitby Rd. East 144 A2
Whitby Rd. Har 9 D3
Whitchurch Cl. Nott 160 C4
Whitcombe Gdns. Nott 147 D1
White Ave. Lan 16 C2
White Furrows. Cotg 187 F1
White Hart La. Coll 112 A4
White Hart St. Mans 102 A4
White Hart Yd. Work 35 F1
White House Rd. Bir 9 E2
White Lodge Gdns. Nott 171 E4
White Rd. Nott 160 C2
White's Ave. Nott 174 A3
White's Wood La. Gain 24 C4
Whitebeam Gdns. Nott 159 F4
Whitechapel St. Nott 160 B1
Whitegate Vale. Nott 184 B1
Whitehall Ct. Ret 39 F3
Whitehall Gdns. Ret 39 F3
Whitehall Rd. Ret 39 F3
Whitehead Dr. Brin 143 E4
Whitehead La. S in A 100 C3
Whitehouse Ave. Lough 220 B1
Whitelands. Cotg 188 A1
Whitely Cl. Staple 182 C4
Whitemoor Ave. Nott 172 B4

Whitemoor Ct. Nott 172 B4
Whitemoor La. Coll 112 A2
Whitemoor Rd. Nott 160 B1
Whitemoss Cl. Nott 171 F2
Whitestone Cl. Mans 103 D2
Whitestub La. Kirk 106 C3
Whitewater La. Oll 63 D1
Whitewater Rd. Oll 77 E3
Whitewates La. Blyth 18 A3
Whitfield Cl. Nott 185 D3
Whitfield St. N-on-T 140 A4
Whiting Ave. Bees 182 C1
Whitney Cl. Mans 89 D1
Whitsun Dale. Work 36 A4
Whittaker Rd. Bees 183 D2
Whittaker Rd. Rain 118 A4
Whittier Rd. Nott 174 A2
Whittingham Ct. Carl 162 A2
Whittingham Rd. Carl 162 A2
Whittle Cl. N-on-T 125 D1
Whitton Cl. Nott 147 D1
Whitton Cl. Ran 19 D2
Whitwell Cl. Nott 159 F1
Whitwell Rd. Nott 159 F1
Whitwell Rd. Th Sa 34 A2
Whitworth Dr. Bu Jo 163 E1
Whitworth Dr. R on T 175 F1
Whitworth Rise. Nott 160 C4
Whomsley Cl. N-on-T 140 B4
Whyburn La. Huck 145 E4
Whyburn St. Huck 146 B3
Whyston Ct. Huck 145 E3
Wichnor Cl. Nott 184 C2
Wickens Wlk. Nott 173 F3
Wickerwood Dr. K-in-A 114 C3
Wickstead Cl. Nott 161 F2
Widdowson Cl. Nott 159 F4
Wide La. Hath 213 D1
Wide La. Wyme 217 E2
Wide St. Hath 213 D1
Widecombe La. Nott 195 E4
Widmerpool La. W-on-W 217 E4
Widmerpool Rd. Wys 207 F2
Widmerpool St. Pinx 113 E1
Wighay Rd. Huck 131 D1
Wighay Rd. Linby 131 D1
Wigley Cl. Nott 173 F3
Wigman Rd. Nott 171 F4
Wigsley Rd. Harby 70 B1
Wigsley Rd. N Sca 83 E3
Wigthorpe La. C in L 26 A2
Wigthorpe La. C in L 26 A3
Wigwam Gr. Huck 146 B4
Wigwam La. Huck 146 B4
Wilberforce Rd. Mans 87 E1
Wilcox Ave. Mans 88 A3
Wilcox Dr. Sels 129 D1
Wild Hill. S in A 99 F4
Wilde Cres. Sels 129 D3
Wilden Cres. Nott 184 C1
Wildman St. Nott 173 D3
Wildman Villas. Beck 14 A1
Wilford Cl. N-on-T 140 A4
Wilford Cres E. Nott 173 E1
Wilford Cres W. Nott 173 E1
Wilford Cres. Rudd 196 B4
Wilford Gr. Nott 173 E1
Wilford Gr. Nott 185 E4
Wilford La. Nott 185 E4
Wilford La. W Brid 185 E4
Wilford Rd. Mans 103 D2
Wilford Rd. Nott 173 D1
Wilford Rd. Nott 173 E2
Wilford Rd. Rudd 185 E1
Wilfred Ave. Bald 140 B2
Wilfrid Gr. W Brid 185 F2
Wilhallow La. Sels 128 C1
Wilkins Gdns. Nott 184 B1
Wilkinson Ave. Bees 183 F3
Wilkinson Cl. Plea 87 D3
Wilkinson St. Nott 172 C4
Willand Ct. Ret 29 F1
Willaston Cl. Nott 160 B2
Willbert Rd. Arn 148 A1
Willerby Rd. Arn 162 A3
Willersley Dr. Nott 173 E1
Willesden Green. Nuth 159 E2
Willetts Ct. S in A 100 C1
Willey La. Greas 144 A4
William Ave. East 143 F1
William Bradford Cl. Aust 3 E1
William Cl. Carl 175 D4
William Old Ct. Nott 172 A3
William Rd. Staple 182 B4
William Rd. W Brid 185 F4
William St. Huck 146 A4
William St. Lo Ea 182 B1
William St. Lough 220 A2
William St. N-on-T 140 A4
William St. Sax 57 D2
Williams Rd. Bees 183 D2
Williams St. Lan 16 C2
Williamson St. Mans 101 F4
Willingham Rd. Lea 24 C1
Willis Rd. N-on-T 139 F3
Willoughby Ave. Lo Ea 182 B2
Willoughby Ave. Nott 172 C2
Willoughby Cl. Nott 184 A4
Willoughby Ct. Mans 103 D1
Willoughby Ct. Nott 172 C2
Willoughby Rd. W Brid 185 F3
Willoughby Rd. Widm 208 B2
Willoughby St. Bees 184 A3
Willoughby St. Coss 158 A1
Willoughby St. Gain 24 B4
Willoughby St. Nott 172 C2
Willow Ave. C in L 25 F4
Willow Ave. Carl 175 D4
Willow Ave. Huck 145 E2
Willow Ave. K-in-A 114 C3
Willow Ave. Lo Ea 182 B1
Willow Ave. Mans 89 D1
Willow Ave. Mist 6 C1
Willow Ave. Shireb 72 B3
Willow Ave. Staple 182 B3
Willow Brook. Keyw 198 A1
Willow Cl. Bu Jo 163 F3
Willow Cl. E Lea 214 B4
Willow Cl. Gain 15 D2
Willow Cl. R on T 175 F1
Willow Cl. S Norm 113 D3
Willow Cl. Sax 57 D2
Willow Cl. Sels 129 D4
Willow Cl. Work 35 F1
Willow Cres. Carl 163 D1
Willow Cres. Lamb 163 E4
Willow Cres. S in A 100 B2
Willow Ct. Sels 129 D1
Willow Dr. N Musk 110 C1
Willow Hill Cl. Nott 160 A3
Willow Holt. Lowd 150 C1
Willow Holt. Ret 39 F2
Willow Ind Est. Nott 160 B4
Willow La. Carl 163 D1
Willow Pool La. Su Bo 213 E3
Willow Rd. Bald 140 B3
Willow Rd. Bing 178 A2
Willow Rd. Carl 175 D4
Willow Rd. Nott 172 C1
Willow Rd. W Brid 185 F2
Willow Rise. Sand 182 A3
Willow Tree Cl. Mans 89 E1
Willow Wong. Bu Jo 163 F3
Willowbridge La. S in A 100 B1
Willowbrook Ct. Nott 173 E1
Willows The. Farn 139 D2
Willows The. Nott 172 A4
Willwell Dr. W Brid 185 E2
Wilmington Ct. Lough 220 B1
Wilmington Gdns. Nott 161 E3
Wilmot La. Bees 183 F3
Wilmot St. Ilk 157 F1
Wilmot St. Lo Ea 193 D3
Wilne Ave. Lo Ea 193 D2
Wilne Rd. Lo Ea 193 D2
Wilsic Rd. Tick 8 A4
Wilson Ave. K-in-A 114 C3
Wilson Cl. Arn 162 A3
Wilson Cl. Matt 11 D1
Wilson Rd. East 143 F1
Wilson St. Gain 15 D1
Wilson St. Mans 87 E1
Wilson St. N-on-T 124 C1
Wilson St. Pinx 113 E2
Wilson's La. Morton 137 F2
Wilsthorpe Rd. Lo Ea 193 D3
Wilsthorpe Rd. Lo Ea 193 D4
Wilton Ave. Lough 220 B1
Wilton Pl. Ilk 157 F1
Wilton Rd. Nott 172 C3
Wilton St. Nott 160 C2
Wilton Terr. Nott 160 C2
Wiltshire Ave. Sels 128 A2
Wimbishthorpe Cl. Bott 181 D2
Wimbledon Rd. Nott 161 D2
Wimborne Cl. W Brid 185 E3
Wimpole Rd. Bees 171 E1
Winborne Cl. Mans 101 E3
Winchester Ave. Bees 183 F4
Winchester Cl. E Lea 205 F1
Winchester Cl. Mans 103 D2
Winchester Cl. Work 36 A4
Winchester Cres. Ilk 170 A4
Winchester Ct. Nott 161 F2
Winchester Dr. Mans 88 B2
Winchester St. Nott 161 E1
Winchester Terr. Nott 161 E2
Winchilsea Ave. N-on-T 140 A4
Windermere Ave. Har 8 C2
Windermere Cl. Carl 162 C1
Windermere Cl. Work 35 F4
Windermere Gdns. Lo Ea 182 A1
Windermere Rd. Bees 183 E4
Windermere Rd. Huck 145 F4
Windermere Rd. Lo Ea 182 A1
Windermere Rd. Nott 173 D4
Windley Dr. Ilk 157 E2
Windmill Ave. Huck 146 A3
Windmill Cl. Nott 173 F3
Windmill Ct. Keyw 197 F1
Windmill Gr. Huck 146 A3
Windmill Hill. Oxt 134 B3
Windmill La. Mans 102 B4
Windmill La. Nott 173 F3
Windmill La. Work 47 D4
Windmill Rd. Lough 220 B2
Windmill Way. Kegw 203 D1
Windrush Cl. Bees 171 E1
Windsmoor Rd. Brin 143 E4
Windsor Ave. N-on-T 139 F3
Windsor Ave. S in A 100 A2
Windsor Cl. Coll 112 A4
Windsor Cl. G on H 12 C1
Windsor Cl. Huck 146 A4
Windsor Cl. Trow 170 A3
Windsor Cres. Arn 162 A3
Windsor Cres. Staple 182 C4
Windsor Ct. Bing 177 E2
Windsor Ct. Har 9 D3
Windsor Ct. Sand 182 A2
Windsor Dr. Mar War 74 A2
Windsor Gdns. C in L 25 F3
Windsor Gdns. Mans 102 B3
Windsor Rd. C in L 25 F3
Windsor Rd. Mans 89 E2
Windsor Rd. Mans 102 B3
Windsor Rd. N-on-T 139 F3
Windsor Rd. Ret 29 E1
Windsor Rd. Sels 129 D4
Windsor Rd. Work 35 E4
Windsor St. Bees 184 A3
Windsor St. Staple 182 C4
Windy Ridge. Mar War 74 B2
Windyridge. Ever 11 E2
Wing Alley. Nott 173 E2
Wingate Cl. Nott 171 F3
Wingbourne Wlk. Nott 146 B1
Wingfield Ave. Work 36 A3
Wingfield Dr. Ilk 157 E2
Wingfield Dr. Nott 172 A1
Wingfield Rd. Mans 103 D2
Wings Dr. Huck 145 E2
Winifred Cres. Bu Jo 163 F2
Winifred St. Huck 146 A3
Winifred St. Rhod 35 D2
Winkburn La. Hock 121 F4
Winkburn Rd. Mans 101 F4
Winnery Cl. Tick 8 A4
Winrow Gdns. Nott 160 B2
Winscale Ave. Nott 161 D4
Winscale Gdns. Nott 161 D4
Winscombe Mount. Nott 195 F4
Winsford Cl. Nott 160 A1
Winster Ave. Carl 162 B1
Winster Ave. Raven 117 D2
Winster Cl. Nott 171 F1
Winston Cl. Carl 162 B3
Winston Ct. N-on-T 139 F3
Winston Dr. Elst 153 F2
Winston Gr. Ret 30 A1
Winston Green. Matt 19 F4
Winter Closes. Sels 128 C1
Winterbourne Dr. Staple 170 C1
Wintern Ct. Gain 24 B3
Winterton Cl. Arn 161 F3
Winterton Rise. Nott 161 D4
Winthorpe Rd. Arn 162 A4
Winthorpe Rd. N-on-T 125 D2
Winthorpe St. Mans 101 E3
Wintringham Cres. Arn 162 A3
Wire La. Newt 99 D2
Wisa Terr. Nott 161 E2
Wiseton Rd. Clay 21 E3
Wishford Ave. Nott 172 C2
Wisley Cl. W Brid 185 E2
Wistow Cl. Nott 172 C4
Witch La. S on T 96 C4
Witham Cl. N-on-T 125 D1
Withern Rd. Nott 159 F1
Witney Cl. Nott 160 C4
Wiverton Rd. Bing 177 F2
Wiverton Rd. Nott 173 D4
Woburn Ave. K-in-A 115 E3
Woburn Croft. Sand 182 A2
Woburn La. Mans 87 E2
Woburn Pl. Mans 87 E2
Woburn Rd. Mans 87 E2
Woburn Rise. Arn 162 A3
Wodehouse Ave. Goth 195 D1
Wolds Dr. Keyw 197 F2
Wolds La. Clip 187 E1
Wolds Rise. Keyw 197 F2
Wolfit Ave. Bald 140 C3
Wollacombe Cl. Carl 162 B3
Wollaton Ave. Carl 162 C1
Wollaton Cres. Bees 183 F4
Wollaton Ct. Nott 160 C3
Wollaton Hall Dr. Nott 172 B2
Wollaton Paddocks. Nott 171 E2
Wollaton Rd. Bees 183 F4
Wollaton Rd. K-in-A 115 E3
Wollaton Rd. Nott 172 B3
Wollaton Rise. Nott 171 F1
Wollaton St. Nott 173 D3
Wollaton Vale. Nott 171 F1
Wolseley Ct. S in A 100 C2
Wolsey Ave. Nott 172 C3
Wolsey Dr. K-in-A 115 D4
Wolsey Rd. N-on-T 125 D2
Wolsey Way. Lough 220 B2
Wong La. Tick 8 A4
Wood Ave. Elmt 58 B4
Wood Ave. Sand 182 A3
Wood Cl. Mans 102 C4
Wood End Dr. Raven 117 D1
Wood Gate. Lough 220 A2
Wood Gr. Calv 148 C4
Wood Hill. Ol Da 218 C2
Wood La. B-le-V 192 B1
Wood La. Beck 23 D4
Wood La. Carl 163 D1
Wood La. Egma 79 F3
Wood La. Elmt 58 B4
Wood La. Elmt 58 B4
Wood La. G on H 12 C2
Wood La. Goth 204 C4
Wood La. Huck 145 F4
Wood La. Kers 94 A1
Wood La. Mar War 73 F4
Wood La. N Whea 22 B1
Wood La. Plea 72 C1
Wood La. S Sca 98 C3
Wood La. Shireb 72 C1
Wood La. Tres 41 F2
Wood Link. Nott 159 F4
Wood Nook Cl. Sels 128 C3
Wood St. Arn 161 F4
Wood St. East 143 F2
Wood St. Ilk 157 F1
Wood St. Mans 102 A4
Wood St. Mar War 74 A3
Wood St. N-on-T 140 A4
Wood St. Nott 173 D3
Wood View Bsns Cntre. Nott 147 D1
Wood View. W Brid 186 A2
Wood's La. Flint 153 D1
Woodbank Dr. Nott 171 E1
Woodbeck Rise. Ret 39 E4
Woodborough La. Arn 148 B2
Woodborough Rd. Mans 87 F1
Woodborough Rd. Nott 161 F1
Woodbridge Ave. Nott 184 C2
Woodchurch Rd. Bes Vil 147 D1
Woodcoates Rd. Darl 67 D3
Wooden Beck Hill. Walker 13 E2
Woodfield Rd. Gain 15 F1
Woodfield Rd. Nott 159 F1
Woodfield Rd. Pinx 113 E2
Woodford Cl. Nott 146 C1
Woodford Rd. Arn 162 A3
Woodford Rd. Huck 146 A3
Woodgate Cl. Cotg 187 F2
Woodgate La. Beckin 142 C4
Woodgate La. Cotg 187 E2
Woodgate Rd. E Lea 214 B4
Woodhall Cl. K-in-A 114 C4
Woodhall Cl. Mans 102 C4
Woodhall Cres. Sax 56 C2
Woodhall Gdns. Mans 102 C4
Woodhall Green. Ret 39 E1
Woodhall Rd. Nott 172 A3
Woodhead Cl. Edwin 76 A1
Woodhedge Dr. Nott 174 A4
Woodhill Rd. Coll 98 A1
Woodhouse La. C in L 26 A4
Woodhouse La. Hod 17 D1
Woodhouse La. S in A 101 D4
Woodhouse Pl. Tux 66 A1
Woodhouse Rd. Mans 102 A4
Woodhouse St. Nott 173 F3
Woodhouse Way. Nott 159 E2
Woodhouse Way. Nuth 159 E2
Woodkirk Rd. Nott 184 C1
Woodlake Gdns. Nott 173 F4
Woodland Ave. Gain 15 D2
Woodland Ave. Ilk 157 E2
Woodland Ave. S in A 99 F2
Woodland Ave. Work 36 A1
Woodland Cl. Cotg 187 F1
Woodland Cl. Farns 120 A3
Woodland Cl. N Clip 90 A2
Woodland Cl. R on T 176 A2
Woodland Cres. Mans 102 C2
Woodland Dr. Mans 102 C2
Woodland Dr. Nott 161 E1
Woodland Dr. Nuth 159 F2
Woodland Dr. South 121 E1
Woodland Dr. Work 35 F3
Woodland Gr. Arn 161 E2
Woodland Gr. Bees 183 E3
Woodland Gr. Carl 174 C3
Woodland Gr. Mans 88 B2
Woodland Gr. Mar War 74 A2
Woodland Rd. Mans 102 C4
Woodland Rd. W Brid 173 F1
Woodland Rise. Raven 117 D1
Woodland View. Scarc 59 D2
Woodland View. South 136 B4
Woodland Walk. K-in-A 115 E3
Woodland Way. East 143 F1
Woodlands Cl. N-on-T 139 F3
Woodlands Cl. Wyme 216 B2
Woodlands Dr. Lough 220 A1
Woodlands Farm Cl. Huck 145 E2
Woodlands Gr. Huck 145 E2
Woodlands The. Blyth 18 A3
Woodlands The. Mans 88 A1
Woodlands The. Nott 160 B3
Woodlands The. Scarc 59 D2
Woodlands. Wint 125 E4
Woodley Sq. Nott 146 B1
Woodley St. Rudd 196 B4
Woodmill Ave. Gain 15 F1
Woods Hill. S in A 100 C1
Woods La. Calv 148 C4
Woods Terr. Gain 15 E1
Woodsend. Bu Jo 163 F2
Woodsetts La. Work 25 D1
Woodsford Gr. Nott 184 C1
Woodside Ave. Kim 159 D3
Woodside Ave. Mans 102 B2
Woodside Ave. R on T 176 A2
Woodside Cres. Ilk 157 E3
Woodside Cres. Lo Ea 193 D4
Woodside Dr. Arn 161 E4
Woodside Rd. Bees 183 D2
Woodside Rd. Bu Jo 163 E2
Woodside Rd. Nott 183 F4
Woodside Rd. R on T 176 A2
Woodside Rd. Raven 116 C2
Woodside Rd. Sand 182 A3
Woodside Rd. Shire 34 C4
Woodside Rd. Shireb 72 C3
Woodside View. Har 9 D2
Woodside. East 143 F2
Woodside. Farns 120 A3
Woodside. Ret 39 E4
Woodside. S in A 100 C4
Woodstock Ave. Nott 172 C3
Woodstock Cl. N-on-T 140 B4
Woodstock Rd. Bees 182 C2
Woodstock St. Huck 146 A3
Woodston Wlk. Arn 148 A1
Woodthorpe Ave. Arn 161 F2
Woodthorpe Ave. Lough 220 A1
Woodthorpe Ct. Nott 161 F2
Woodthorpe Dr. Arn 161 F2
Woodthorpe Gdns. Nott 161 F2
Woodthorpe Rd. Lough 220 A1
Woodthorpe Rd. Nott 161 F2
Woodview Ct. Nott 174 B3
Woodview Gdns. Mans 89 E1
Woodview. Cotg 188 A1
Woodville Cl. Bees 183 E3
Woodville Dr. Nott 161 E2
Woodville Rd. Nott 161 E1
Woodward St. Nott 173 E1
Woodyard La. Nott 172 A3
Woollaton St. Huck 146 A4
Woolmer Rd. Nott 173 E1
Woolpack La. Nott 173 E2
Woolpack St. Ret 39 F4
Woolsington Cl. Nott 159 E1
Woolsthorpe Cl. Nott 172 A3
Wootton Cl. Nott 171 E4
Worcester Ave. Mans 88 B3
Worcester Cl. Lowd 150 C1
Worcester Cl. Work 36 A4
Worcester Gdns. Arn 161 F3
Worcester Mews. Mans 88 B3
Worcester Rd. Arn 161 F3
Wordsworth Ave. Huck 145 E3
Wordsworth Ave. Mans 88 A2
Wordsworth Ave. S in A 100 A2
Wordsworth Dr. Bald 140 B3
Wordsworth Rd. Arn 161 E4
Wordsworth Rd. Awsw 158 B3
Wordsworth Rd. Nott 172 C3
Wordsworth Rd. W Brid 185 F3
Worksop Rd. Babw 49 E4
Worksop Rd. Blyth 18 A1
Worksop Rd. Budby 76 B3
Worksop Rd. Cuck 60 A2
Worksop Rd. Edwin 76 B3
Worksop Rd. Elk 49 E4
Worksop Rd. Nott 173 F3
Worksop Rd. Oll 76 B3
Worksop Rd. Whit 45 D4
Worksop Rd. Woods 25 D1
Worrall Ave. Arn 161 F4
Worrall Ave. Lo Ea 182 C1
Worth St. Carl 174 C4
Worthington Rd. Bald 140 C2
Wortley Cl. Ilk 170 A4
Wortley Ave. Staple 170 B2
Wortley Hall Cl. Nott 172 B1
Worwood Dr. W Brid 185 E2
Wossock La. W Lea 204 C2
Woulds Field. Cotg 187 F1
Wray Cl. Nott 173 F3
Wren Ct. Work 35 E4
Wrenthorpe Vale. Nott 184 C1
Wrenthorpe Vale. Nott 195 F4
Wright St. Carl 175 D4
Wright St. N-on-T 140 A4
Wright Wilson St. Ret 39 F3
Wrights Orch. Keyw 197 F1
Wrightson Cl. S in A 101 D2
Wroot Rd. Fin 1 A3
Wroughton Ct. East 144 A1
Wroxham Dr. Nott 171 E1
Wycar Rd. Bils 106 A2
Wychwood Dr. Staple 170 B1
Wychwood Rd. Bing 177 E2
Wycliffe Gr. Nott 161 F1
Wycliffe St. Nott 160 C1
Wycombe Cl. Nott 195 E4
Wye Gdns. Nott 172 B3
Wyggeston Rd. Bott 181 D2
Wyke La. Farn 138 C3

Wykeham Rd. Arn ............. 162 A3
Wykes Ave. Carl ............... 162 C1
Wymeswold Rd. Hoton ...... 215 F1
Wymeswold Rd. Remp ...... 215 F3
Wymeswold Rd. Wys ........ 207 E1
Wymondham Cl. Arn .......... 162 A3
Wynbreck Dr. Keyw .......... 197 F2
Wyndale Dr. Mans ............ 103 D3
Wyndham Ct. Bees ........... 183 D2
Wyndham Mews. Nott ........ 173 D4
Wyndings The. Arn ........... 161 F2
Wynhill Ct. Bing .................. 177 E3
Wynlea Dr. Old ..................... 16 C3
Wynndale Dr. Nott ............. 161 D2
Wynwood Cl. Bees ............ 183 D1
Wynwood Rd. Bees ........... 183 D1
Wyrale Dr. Nott .................. 159 F1
Wysall Cl. Mans .................. 87 F1
Wysall La. Keyw ................. 207 E4
Wysall La. Wyme ............... 216 B3
Wysall Rd. Bunn ................ 197 D1
Wysall Rd. Bunn ................ 207 D4
Wysall Rd. Cost ................. 206 C1
Wysall Rd. Remp ............... 215 F3
Wysall Rd. Widm ................ 208 A2
Wyton Cl. Nott .................... 161 D3
Wyvelle Cres. Kegw ........... 203 E2
Wyvern Ave. Lo Ea ............ 193 E3
Wyvern Cl. Greas ............... 158 A4
Wyville Cl. Nott ................... 172 C3

Yalding Dr. Nott .................. 171 E2
Yalding Gdns. Nott ............. 171 E2
Yarwell Cl. Nott .................. 174 B4
Yates Gdns. Nott ................ 161 D4
Yatesbury Cres. Nott .......... 171 F4
Yeoman Ave. Bes Vil ......... 146 C2
Yeomans Ct. Nott ............... 173 D2
Yeovil Ct. Mans .................. 103 D1
Yew Cl. E Lea .................... 214 B4
Yew Cl. Nott ....................... 161 E1
Yew Tree Ave. K-in-A ........ 114 C3
Yew Tree Ave. Nott ............ 161 E1
Yew Tree Cl. Oll ................... 77 E3
Yew Tree Cl. R on T .......... 175 E2
Yew Tree Dr. Baw .................. 9 F4
Yew Tree Dr. S in A ............. 99 F1
Yew Tree Dr. Shireb ............ 72 B3
Yew Tree La. Carl ............... 163 D1
Yew Tree La. Nott ............... 184 B1
Yew Tree Rd. Elk ................. 50 A2
Yew Tree Rd. Huck ............ 146 A2
Yew Tree Rd. Oll ................... 77 E3
Yewdale Cl. Nott ................ 195 E4
Yonge Cl. R on T ............... 175 F1
York Ave. Bees .................. 183 F2
York Ave. Sand .................. 182 A2
York Ave. Sels ................... 128 A2
York Cl. Carl ....................... 162 C1
York Cl. E Lea .................... 205 E1
York Dr. Nott ...................... 159 E1
York Pl. Shire ........................ 34 C4
York Rd. Har .......................... 9 D2
York Rd. Lo Ea ................... 182 B1
York Rd. Lough .................. 220 A2
York Rd. Shireb .................... 72 C2
York Rd. Tick .......................... 8 A4
York St. Carl ....................... 175 D4
York St. E Mark .................... 65 F4
York St. Mans ..................... 102 A3
York St. Nott ....................... 173 E3
York St. S in A .................... 100 C2
York Terr. Mar War .............. 74 A2
York Terr. Mist ........................ 7 D1
York Terr. Pinx ................... 113 E1
Yorke Dr. N-on-T ................ 125 D2
Yorke St. Huck ................... 146 A4
Yorke St. Mans ..................... 88 A1
Young Cl. Nott .................... 159 F3
Young Cres. S in A ............ 101 D2
Yvonne Cres. Carl ............. 174 C4

Zouch Rd. N on S ............. 213 D2
Zulla Rd. Nott ..................... 173 E4
Zulu Rd. Nott ...................... 160 C1

# STREET ATLASES

CSA94

| | Hardback | | Softback | | Pocket | | |
|---|---|---|---|---|---|---|---|
| | QUANTITY | TOTAL | QUANTITY | TOTAL | QUANTITY | TOTAL | |
| | £12.99 | | £8.99 | | £4.99 | | |
| **East Essex** | ISBN 0-540-05848-3 | £ . | ISBN 0-540-05866-1 | £ . | ISBN 0-540-05850-5 | £ . | £ . |
| **West Essex** | ISBN 0-540-05849-1 | £ . | ISBN 0-540-05867-X | £ . | ISBN 0-540-05851-3 | £ . | £ . |
| **North Hampshire** | ISBN 0-540-05852-1 | £ . | ISBN 0-540-05853-X | £ . | ISBN 0-540-05854-8 | £ . | £ . |
| **South Hampshire** | ISBN 0-540-05855-6 | £ . | ISBN 0-540-05856-4 | £ . | ISBN 0-540-05857-2 | £ . | £ . |
| **Nottinghamshire** | ISBN 0-540-05858-0 | £ . | ISBN 0-540-05859-9 | £ . | ISBN 0-540-05860-2 | £ . | £ . |
| **East Sussex** | ISBN 0-540-05875-0 | £ . | ISBN 0-540-05874-2 | £ . | ISBN 0-540-05873-4 | £ . | £ . |
| **West Sussex** | ISBN 0-540-05876-9 | £ . | ISBN 0-540-05877-7 | £ . | ISBN 0-540-05878-5 | £ . | £ . |
| | £10.99 | | | | £4.99 | | |
| **Berkshire** | ISBN 0-540-05738-X | £ . | | | ISBN 0-540-05835-1 | £ . | £ . |
| **Buckinghamshire** | ISBN 0-540-05660-X | £ . | | | ISBN 0-540-05711-8 | £ . | £ . |
| **Hertfordshire** | ISBN 0-540-05720-7 | £ . | | | ISBN 0-540-05840-8 | £ . | £ . |
| **East Kent** | ISBN 0-540-05661-8 | £ . | | | | | £ . |
| **West Kent** | ISBN 0-540-05662-6 | £ . | | | | | £ . |
| **Oxfordshire** | ISBN 0-540-05665-0 | £ . | | | | | £ . |
| **Warwickshire** | ISBN 0-540-05642-1 | £ . | | | | | £ . |
| | £10.99 | | | | £3.99 | | |
| **Surrey** | ISBN 0-540-05694-4 | £ . | | | ISBN 0-540-05708-8 | £ . | £ . |

*I enclose a cheque/postal order for* £ .
*made payable to* ***Reed Book Services*** *or please debit my* ◂ *Access* ◂ *American Express* ◂ *Visa account by* £ .

*Name*

*Address*

*Postcode*

*Account number*

*Expiry date*

*Signature*

*Please tick this box if you do not wish your name to be used by other carefully selected organisations that may wish to send you information about other products and services*

◆ ***Free postage and packing*** ◆ *All available titles will normally be dispatched within 5 working days of receipt of order, but please allow up to 28 days for delivery.*

Registered office: Michelin House, 81 Fulham Road, London SW3 6RB. Registered in England No 1974080